Probation and Parole

Theory and Practice

Probation and Parole

Theory and Practice

Ninth Edition

HOWARD ABADINSKY
St. John's University

PEARSON
Prentice
Hall

Upper Saddle River, New Jersey 07458

Library of Congress Cataloging-in-Publication Data

Abadinsky, Howard
  Probation and parole : theory and practice / Howard Abadinsky.—9th ed.
    p. cm.
  Includes bibliographical references (p.) and index.
  ISBN 0-13-118894-1
  1. Probation—United States.   2. Parole—United States.   I. Title.

HV9278.A2 2006
364.6'3'0973—dc22

2004027229

Executive Editor: Frank Mortimer, Jr.
Associate Editor: Sarah Holle
Production Liaison: Brian Hyland
Managing Editor: Mary Carnis
Director of Production and Manufacturing: Bruce Johnson
Manufacturing Buyer: Cathleen Petersen
Design Director: Cheryl Asherman
Production Coordination: *The GTS Companies*/York, PA Campus
Senior Design Coordinator: Mary Siener
Cover Design: Anthony Gemmellaro
Cover Photo: Getty Images, Photographer: Grant Faint

This book was set in Garamond by *The GTS Companies*/York, PA Campus. It was printed and bound by Courier Westford. The cover was printed by Coral Graphics.

Pearson Prentice Hall™ is a trademark of Pearson Education, Inc.
Pearson® is a registered trademark of Pearson plc
Prentice Hall® is a registered trademark of Pearson Education, Inc.

Pearson Education Ltd.
Pearson Education Singapore Pte. Ltd.
Pearson Education Canada, Ltd.
Pearson Education—Japan

Pearson Education Australia Pty. Limited
Pearson Education North Asia Ltd.
Pearson Educación de Mexico, S. A. de C.V.
Pearson Education Malaysia Pte. Ltd.

10 9 8 7 6
ISBN: 0-13-118894-1

**To dedicated probation and parole officers
and the American Probation and Parole Association**

For membership information: APPA, P.O. Box 11910, Lexington, KY 40578-1910; (606) 244-8207; fax (606) 244-8001

Contents

PART I
Probation

2
Juvenile Court and Juvenile Justice 20

3
Juvenile Probation, Institutions, and Aftercare 61

4
Probation and the Courts: History and Administration 91

5
Sentencing and the Presentence Investigation (PSI) 123

PART 2
Parole

6
American Prisons and Community-Based Corrections 174

PART 3
Rehabilitation and Supervision in Probation and Parole

9
Rehabilitation: Theory and Practice 276

10
Probation and Parole Officers 305

13
Intermediate Punishments 402

Preface

The first edition of this book was written while I was a senior parole officer for the New York State Division of Parole. Since that time, new concepts (or sometimes simply buzzwords) have affected both the theory and practice of probation and parole. Some, such as *community-based corrections*, had a brief life, while the *justice model* and *determinate sentencing* had long-lasting effects, creating the need for *graduated sanctions* and *intermediate punishments*. More recently, *restorative justice* and "*broken windows*" *supervision* have become popular expressions of the need to respond to political pressures for greater public safety without completely abandoning the rehabilitative ideal.

The further hardening of sentiments toward criminals generated "truth in sentencing" (no parole or early release) and "three-strikes-and-you're-out" (life imprisonment on third felony conviction) statutes. Political posturing produced such incongruities as *mandatory sentences* with *sanctioning flexibility* as the rush to punish encountered spending curbs and tax shortfalls. The results of "tough-on-crime" statutes and the "war on drugs" overburdened our correctional facilities, and soundbite polemics often replaced careful and thoughtful policy development. These swirling waters of criminal justice serve as a backdrop for the discussion of probation and parole in this book.

The ninth edition contains 14 chapters, with some reorganized to further enhance ease of classroom use. Juvenile justice is now found in chapter 2 (the juvenile court) and chapter 3 (juvenile probation, institutions, and aftercare). To remain at the cutting edge of the field, this edition continues to use materials from juvenile and adult probation and parole agencies throughout the country, providing a state-of-the-art examination of probation and parole practice. (Material whose source is not cited is from the appropriate agency.) As in previous editions, review questions appear at the end of each chapter. In addition, each chapter highlights key terms (which appear in a glossary) and ends with a list of key terms and relevant Internet sites. The instructor's resource guide available for this book provides a model curriculum and test questions.

The author would like to thank reviewers Jon Cella, Central Texas College, Killeen, TX; Terry Campbell, Western Illinois University, Macomb, IL; and Chandrika M. Kelso, National University, La Jolla, CA for their thoughtful reviews and suggestions.

Acknowledgments

Note: Names with an asterisk are new to the ninth edition.

Brian Anderson
(Connecticut Board of Parole)

Stacey Anderson
(Florida Department of Corrections)

Robert E. Bair
(Bucks County, PA, Adult Probation &
Parole)

Veronica S. Ballard
(Cook County Adult Probation
Department)

Stephen K. Benjamin
(South Carolina Department of Probation,
Parole and Pardon Services)

Robert L. Bingham
(Marion County, IN, Superior Court
Probation Department)

Peggy Carr*
(Denton County, TX, Adult Probation)

Mary Christensen*
(Washington State Department of
Corrections)

Martin Cirincione
(New York State Division of Parole)

Trudy A. Clark*
(Nebraska Board of Parole)

Elyse Clawson
(Multnomah County, OR, Department of
Community Justice)

Alan M. Crogan
(San Diego County Department
of Probation)

James E. Dare*
(Montgomery County, OH, Court of
Common Pleas, Criminal Justice Services)

Ben De Groot
(California Department of
Corrections/Parole)

Antonio B. Escamilla
(Wyoming Board of Parole)

William A. Fluck
(Dutchess County, NY, Office of Probation
& Community Corrections)

Kim Frentz*
(Volunteers in Prevention, Probation and
Prisons, Inc.)

Virginia M. Gibbons*
(Texas Department of Criminal Justice,
Parole Division)

Scott Hedlund*
(Lewis County, WA, Juvenile Court)

Jennifer Hitz
(Pennsylvania Board of Probation and
Parole)

Veter Howard
(Arkansas Department of Community
Punishment)

John M. Hughes
(Admin. Office of U.S. Courts, Federal
   Corrections and Supervision Division)

Sylvia J. Johnson*
(Alameda County, CA, Probation
   Department)

J. Scott Johnston*
(Missouri Board of Probation and Parole)

Robert E. Kelsey
(Bucks County, PA, Adult Probation and
   Parole Department)

Clarence Key, Jr.
(Iowa State Parole Board)

George Kostyrko*
(California Youth Authority)

Martin J. Krizay*
(Yuma County, AZ, Adult Probation
   Department)

Jean Kuehl
(Sixth District, IA, Department of
   Correctional Services)

Marlene Lichtenstadter
(Delaware Board of Parole)

Marvel J. Maddox*
(Community Supervision and Corrections
   Department, San Marcos, TX)

Michael Manguso*
(Florida Department of Correction)

Kenndall Y. Mayfield*
(Harris County, TX, Juvenile Probation
   Department)

Diane L. McGinnis
(Pima County, AZ, Adult Probation
   Department)

James McKenzie
(Nebraska Department of Correctional
   Services/Parole)

Mary Miller
(Marion County, IN, Superior Court
   Probation Department)

Brennan Mitchell
(Santa Barbara County, CA, Probation
   Department)

Linda Murken
(Iowa Department of Correctional Services)

Jennifer Nunez*
(Cook County, IL, Juvenile Court Probation
   Department)

Dennis E. Pankratz*
(Santa Barbara, CA, Probation Department)

Tabitha Perry
(Maricopa County, AZ, Superior Court
   Probation)

Walter M. Pulliam, Jr.*
(Virginia Community Corrections)

Nina H. Ramsey*
(Alameda County Probation Department)

Vicki L. Rascona-Saylor*
(Somerset County, PA, Probation
   Department)

David E. Sanders*
(Pima County, AZ, Adult Probation
   Department)

Linda Seidel*
(Pima County, AZ, Adult Probation
   Department)

John J. Sikora
(Lehigh County, PA, Probation)

Sara Simila*
(Ohio Adult Parole Authority)

John E. Thorstad*
(Lake County, IN, Probation Services)

Sue White
(Olympia, WA, Municipal Court Probation)

Fred Williamson
(Brazoria County, TX, Juvenile Probation
   Department)

Raymond B. Wingerd*
(San Bernardino County, CA, Probation
   Department)

Janice Young
(North Dakota Department of Corrections,
   Field Service)

Kathy Welch*
(Jefferson County, TX, Juvenile Probation
   Department)

Paul J. Werrell*
(Lehigh County, PA, Juvenile Probation)

Ron Whitmore*
(Tennessee Board of Probation and Parole)

Sheryl Zuna*
(Dutchess County, NY, Probation
   Department)

About the Author

Photo: Carolyn Feldman Bishop

Howard Abadinsky is professor of criminal justice at St. John's University. He was an inspector for the Cook County, Illinois, Sheriff's Office for 8 years and a New York State parole officer and senior parole officer for 15 years. The author holds a BA from Queens College of the City University of New York, an MSW from Fordham University, and a PhD from New York University. He is the author of several books, including *Organized Crime*, 7th ed., *Law and Justice*, 5th ed., and *Drug Abuse*, 5th ed.

Dr. Abadinsky encourages communication about his work and can be reached at St. John's University, 8000 Utopia Parkway, Jamaica, NY 11439; E-mail: abadinsh@stjohns.edu.

Probation and Parole

Theory and Practice

Probation and Parole in Criminal Justice

Probation and parole are part of a uniquely American system of criminal justice in which contradictory goals and competing expectations are reconciled in a swirling caldron of politics. Americans want greater protection from crime while insisting that efforts to afford this protection do not jeopardize treasured constitutional rights. We want a system that deters would-be miscreants and incapacitates those not deterred without imposing significant tax dollar costs (DiIulio, 1993). Probation and parole are often made scapegoats for the impossibility of achieving these competing expectations.

THE REALITY OF CRIMINAL JUSTICE

When a probationer or parolee commits a serious crime that generates publicity, questions are raised about why this person was not in prison. Even a single case can result in changes that typically make sound politics but poor practice. For reasons of *justice* (punishment fitting the crime) or *cost* (too expensive to incarcerate all offenders in prison indefinitely), most offenders are not imprisoned and more than 90 percent of all imprisoned offenders are eventually released. Convicted offenders can be placed on probation, released after completing their entire sentence, or paroled to supervision in the community. If laws are enacted that limit probation or increase the length of imprisonment, for example, by abolishing parole, there must be corresponding increases in prison space to accommodate the results. As any shopper or grocery clerk knows, you can't get 10 pounds into a 5-pound bag.

In the absence of costly prison building and staffing, the pressure of overcrowding leads to increased **front-door programs** (e.g., probation, intermediate punishments discussed in chapter 13), **back-door programs** (e.g., parole, early release for good behavior), or additional programs (e.g., "boot camps") that either

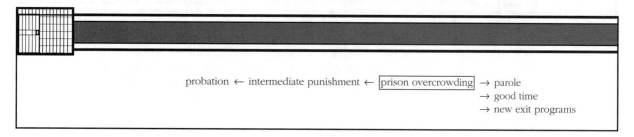

probation ← intermediate punishment ← prison overcrowding → parole
→ good time
→ new exit programs

Parole and Public Safety

The California parole board recognized that Richard Allen Davis posed a serious risk to the public safety and denied him release six times. When the state abolished parole, Davis was released on the basis of a computer computation of his sentence and time served. Less than 4 months later, in a case that generated national publicity, he murdered Polly Klass.

keep offenders from becoming inmates or let them out early. Thus, although there was a steady decline in the percentage of inmates released by parole boards between 1980 and 1995, the percentage of prisoners released from prison to the community remained virtually unchanged (*Correctional Populations in the United States, 1995*: 1997); this, despite building 213 prisons and hiring more than 100,000 additional prison employees between 1990 and 1995, while maintaining more than 3 million adults on probation. Virginia, for example, discontinued parole release, and probation increased more than 20 percent (Bureau of Justice Statistics data). Currently, the number of persons on probation is about 4 million; the current parole population is about 1 million. Interestingly, a study of inmates released in states that abolished parole revealed that they served 7 months less than inmates released in states with parole (Petersilia, 2000b).

If discretionary—parole—release is not an option (many states have abolished the parole board), then allowing inmates to earn good time at a rate of half or more of their sentences becomes the most viable option. However, so-called **truth-in-sentencing laws** have limited this approach, permitting only small grants of good time—10 or 15 percent. Many states have enacted **three strikes and you're out legislation,** meaning lifetime imprisonment on a third (or sometimes a second) felony conviction. In California, the third strike for one inmate serving a 25-year sentence without parole was theft of three golf clubs from a pro shop; another was sentenced to 50 years for his third strike—theft of children's videos from a department store (Greenhouse, 2003). As these unreleasable inmates age, they become increasingly expensive wards of the state. In 2003, the Supreme Court upheld the constitutionality of three strikes laws (*Ewing v. California*, No. 01-6978; *Lockyer v. Andrade*, No. 01-1127). In 2004, almost 10 percent of prison inmates were serving life sentences (Butterfield, 2004b).

In the absence of release by a parole board, when probationers or early releasees generate negative publicity, new legislation curtails the use of these schemes and, in an endless cycle, either new prison building and staffing must ensue, or additional schemes must be developed to reduce prison populations and achieve a semblance of equilibrium. Getting lost in this often simplistic approach to crime and criminals is any serious attention to the fate of persons released from prison: uneducated, unskilled, unemployed, and now hardened by the prison experience.

Two Strikes and You're ~~Out~~ In

Georgia's two strikes legislation, passed in 1995, mandates that persons convicted for the first time of murder, rape, armed robbery, kidnapping, aggravated sodomy, aggravated sexual battery, or aggravated child molestation serve all their prison sentence without possibility of parole. Persons convicted a second time of any of those seven crimes receive a life sentence.

Duh?

In New York in 1997, both the mayor of the city and the governor of the state called for the abolition of parole. The mayor cited the case of a man who had been paroled from a manslaughter conviction and charged with shooting a police officer. But the defendant's sentence was 4 years to 12 years, and the 12-year mark had already passed—he would have been free even without parole release. The governor cited the case of a man in Albany accused of killing a young woman. However, that man had been paroled after 5 years of serving 3½ to 7 years, so even if he had been kept in prison for 85 percent of his sentence, as the governor proposed, he would have been freed 1 year before the victim was killed (Peréz-Peña, 1998).

That such persons would resort to crime cannot be surprising, and the wheels of criminal justice continue to spin, generating heat but not light.

Then the reality: In *The New York Times*, Ken Butterfield noted: "After three decades of building ever more prisons and passing tougher sentencing laws, states are suddenly being forced to choose between keeping a lid on taxes or being tough on crime. Lower taxes are winning" (2003: 1, 20). Some states that passed three strikes laws, such as Texas and Kentucky, have discovered loopholes allowing them to release inmates early. Those that still have parole boards have asked them to increase releases, whereas those without are overhauling their sentencing laws.

AMERICAN CRIMINAL JUSTICE

American criminal justice is an outgrowth of a fundamental distrust of government. Authority is divided between central (federal) and state governments, and at each level, power is diffused further, shared by three branches—executive, legislative, judicial—in a system referred to as the "separation of powers." Furthermore, in each state authority is shared by governments at the municipal, county, and state levels. Thus, policing is primarily a function of municipal government, whereas jails are usually run by the county (often by the sheriff). Probation may be a county or state function, whereas prison and (usually) parole systems are the responsibility of state government, although in some states, Iowa and Oregon, for example, parole (and probation) supervision is a function of the county or judicial district. There is also a separate federal system of criminal justice (Figure 1.1).

As those who work in criminal justice recognize, a lack of joint planning and budgeting, or even systematic consultation, exists between the various agencies responsible for criminal justice. The result is **a system that is not systematic.**

Levels of Government	Branches of Government
Federal	Executive
State	Legislative
County	Judicial
	Municipal

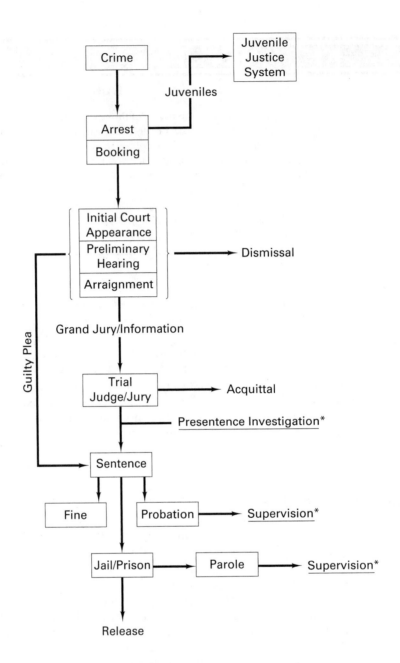

*Points at which probation and parole officers typically enter the system.
FIGURE 1.1 *Probation and Parole in a State Criminal Justice System.*

Although criminal justice agencies, whose members range from police to parole officers, are interdependent, they do not, *in toto,* constitute a system arranged with parts to form a unity. Although the operations of criminal justice agencies lack any significant level of coordination, each affects the others. A disproportionate share of the criminal justice budget (about 42 percent) goes to the agency that has the most public visibility, the police (plus 6 percent for federal law enforcement). The courts, prosecutors, and public defenders receive about 22 percent; corrections receives about 29 percent. An additional 1 percent is allocated for miscellaneous functions (U.S. Department of Justice statistics). As a result, more persons are brought into the system by the police than the rest of the system can handle adequately. Increasing the number of police officers and, thereby, the total number of arrests places further pressure on the rest of the system of criminal justice.

Rich Man, Poor Man, Criminal Man

The United States is the most economically stratified of industrial nations: "For 30 years the gap between the richest Americans and everyone else has been growing so much that the level of inequality is higher than in any other industrialized nation" (Stille, 2001: 15). "The wealthiest 1 percent of American households—with net worth of at least $2.3 million each—owns nearly 40 percent of the nation's wealth. Further down the scale, the top 20 percent of Americans—households worth $180,000 or more—have more than 80 percent of the country's worth, a figure higher than in other industrial nations" (Bradsher, 1995a: C4; Pérez-Peña, 1997). This inequality has continued to increase (Andrews, 2003).

A 1994 report for the Carnegie Foundation by a panel of prominent Americans revealed millions of children deprived of medical care, loving supervision, and intellectual stimulation, the result of parents overwhelmed by poverty. Many are subjected to child abuse and frequently witness random acts of violence (Chira, 1994). They become the pool from which the criminal justice system draws most of its clients.

Because of their large caseloads, judges and prosecutors tend to concentrate on the speedy processing of cases. This, in turn, encourages "bargain justice," which frequently is neither a bargain nor just. When a probation agency is understaffed, judges tend to send marginal cases to prison instead of using probation. Because prisons are underfunded and overcrowded, there is pressure on the parole board to accelerate the release of inmates, thereby overburdening parole supervision, which is also usually understaffed. In more recent years, many states have abolished their parole systems. Although this may have made political sense, it does not respond to the problem of prison overcrowding. As pressure builds on prisons, usually the result of judicial scrutiny and financial considerations, prison officials are forced to release inmates without benefit of the type of analyses a parole board usually provides. Prison overcrowding also places pressure on the judicial system, and more persons are placed on probation as the revolving door of criminal justice continues to spin.

Probation and parole are linked to particular segments of the criminal justice system, and criminal justice is tied to a system of laws most frequently invoked against a distinct type of offender. Law reflects the need to protect the person, the property, and the norms of those who have the power to enact laws—*the criminal law reflects power relations in society.* Thus, the harmful activities of those with power often are not even defined as criminal (e.g., certain antitrust violations), but may instead constitute only a civil wrong (e.g., the savings-and-loan debacle, which cost taxpayers an estimated $100 billion). When the criminal law is invoked, the results may represent distinctions in power; burglary prosecutions, for example, routinely invoke more significant penalties than do business crimes. For crimes committed by large corporations, the sole punishment often consists of warnings, consent decrees, or comparatively small fines. As the title of a book by Jeffrey Reiman (1998) notes, *The Rich Get Richer and the Poor Get Prison.*

WHAT IS A CRIME? WHO IS A CRIMINAL?

Quite simply, a *crime* is any violation of the criminal law, and a *criminal* is a person convicted of a crime. These definitions raise an important question: Is a person who violates the criminal law a "criminal" if he or she is not apprehended or convicted? Consider that most reported crimes do not result in an arrest and conviction. Furthermore,

National Crime Victimization Survey (NCVS) reports reveal that most crimes are simply not reported to the police. Thus, have probationers or parolees who are not arrested again been rehabilitated, or have they become more successful at avoiding detection? (Or have the police become either less adept or corrupt?)

Index Crimes

Crime statistics are regularly compiled by the Federal Bureau of Investigation (FBI) and divided into eight categories indicated in the *Uniform Crime Report*. The eight categories, or **index crimes,** are those most likely to be reported to the police by victims, that occur frequently, and that are serious by nature or as a result of their frequency of occurrence. They are divided into crimes against persons and crimes against property:

Crimes Against the Person

1. *Homicide:* causing the death of another person without legal justification or excuse
2. *Rape:* unlawful sexual intercourse by force or without legal or factual consent
3. *Robbery:* unlawful taking or attempted taking of property that is in the immediate possession of another, by force or threat of force
4. *Assault:* unlawful intentional inflicting or attempted inflicting of injury on the person of another

Crimes Against Property

5. *Burglary:* unlawful entry of any fixed structure, vehicle, or vessel used for regular residence, industry, or business with or without force with the intent to commit a felony or larceny
6. *Larceny-theft:* unlawful taking or attempted taking of property other than a motor vehicle from the possession of another, by stealth, without force and without deceit, with intent to deprive the owner of the property permanently
7. *Motor vehicle theft:* unlawful taking or attempted taking of a self-propelled road vehicle owned by another, with the intent of depriving him or her of it, permanently or temporarily
8. *Arson:* intentional damaging or destruction or attempted damaging or destruction by means of fire or explosion of property without the consent of the owner, or of one's own property with or without the intent to defraud

Other relatively frequent (nonindex) crimes include those that are *victimless*, referring to violations of the law unlikely to be reported by their victims, particularly drug offenses, prostitution, and gambling; *fraud*, using deceit or intentional misrepresentation of fact with the intent of unlawfully depriving a person of property; *driving under the influence*, operating any motor vehicle while drunk or under the influence of liquor or psychoactive substances; and *public order offenses*, violations of the peace or order of the community, or threats to public health through unacceptable public conduct; interfering with governmental authority; violating civil rights or liberties; weapons offenses; bribery; and tax law violations. There are also corporate crimes that include restraint of trade, securities violations, environmental pollution, and toxic waste-related offenses. (Crime statistics are also compiled by the NCVS based on information from a random survey of the population conducted by the Census Bureau. The NCVS has revealed a high level of nonreporting of crimes by victims.)

It is important for the study of probation and parole to consider who actually becomes identified as a criminal. Remember that there are corporate offenders who *do not* usually become identified as criminals. A composite sketch of the "average" offender convicted of a crime would reveal that he (more than 90 percent are male) is usually young (more than 40 percent are younger than age 20; more than 70 percent are younger than age 30), poor, and often from a minority group. Such persons tend to be clustered in particular sections of urban America—areas that are heavily policed, increasing the likelihood of arrest. Persons who have already been arrested become part of the official records of law enforcement agencies, increasing their susceptibility to further arrests, a fact of life with which all probation and parole personnel must deal. However, on average, only about one crime in four is cleared by an arrest. The result is prisons populated and repopulated by the least skillful criminals with multiple convictions.

As we see in later chapters, some offenders are given an opportunity to avoid being put through the criminal process; they are "diverted" out of the criminal justice system into some other method of being handled. Such programs can easily become another method for providing differential treatment whereby the middle class can avoid the stigma and severity of the criminal process, whereas the poor are made to face the full force and fury of criminal sanctions.

In response to the question of who is a criminal, some observers see the offender as a *victim* of poverty, discrimination, unequal and unjust laws, and law enforcement. In 1902, Clarence Darrow, the famed trial lawyer, noted that "the people who go to jail are almost always poor people" (1975: 29), and most persons on probation and parole come from an underclass. More than a century later, persons convicted of corporate crimes are still often able to avoid the stiff sanctions that typically befall the perpetrators of more conventional crime—those most likely to be committed by persons from deprived economic circumstances.

RESPONDING TO CRIME

Early responses to deviant behavior ranged from the payment of fines to trial by combat, banishment, and death by torture. *Lex talionis* (an eye for an eye), a primitive system of vengeance, emerged and was passed down from generation to generation as each family, tribe, or society sought to preserve its own existence without recourse to a written code of laws. About 4,000 years ago, Hammurabi, King of Babylon, authored a code inscribed on a block of diorite nearly 8 feet high and about 5 feet in circumference. Although in written form, his laws continued the harsh tradition of *lex talionis*—many crimes, including theft and harboring a runaway slave, were punishable by death (Harper, 1904).

Later, the Hebrews adopted the concept of an eye for an eye; however, under biblical law this meant financial compensation for the victim of crime or negligence (there was no compensation for murder, which carried the death penalty), except for the "false witness," in which case "ye shall do unto him, as he had purposed to do unto his brother" (Deuteronomy 19:19). A perpetrator who was unable to pay compensation was placed in involuntary servitude, a precursor to the concept of probation. The servitude could not last more than 6 years—release had to occur with the sabbatical year—and masters had rehabilitative obligations and responsibilities toward their charges. (Under the Code of Hammurabi, "If the thief has nothing wherewith to pay he shall be put to death" [Harper, 1904: 13].)

The Romans derided the use of restitution for criminal offenses and used the death penalty extensively in ways that have become etched in history. The fall of the Roman Empire resulted in there being little "rule of law" throughout Europe. When law was gradually restored, fines and restitution became an important form of punishment as those in power sought to increase their wealth. Offenders who were unable to pay, however, were often enslaved or subjected to mutilation or death. A parallel issue in contemporary criminal justice, the extensive use of restitution, is discussed in later chapters.

Trial by combat also flourished, in part because of the difficulty of proving criminal allegations. With the spread of Christianity, trial by combat was reserved for private accusations, whereas crimes prosecuted by the crown called for trial by ordeal, an appeal to divine power. A defendant who survived the ordeal—passing through fire, for example—was ruled innocent. The unsuccessful defendant often received verdict and punishment simultaneously. Trial by ordeal was eventually replaced with *compurgation* ("wager of law"): The accused was required to gather 12 reputable persons who would swear to the defendant's innocence. Reputable persons, it was believed, would not swear falsely for fear of divine retribution. Compurgation eventually evolved into testimony under oath and trial by jury (Vold and Bernard, 1986). Throughout the Middle Ages in Europe, there was a continuation of the extensive use of torture to gain confessions, and public executions were often accompanied by torture, flaying, or the rack.

Despite biblical admonitions—"You shall not respect persons in judgment; ye shall hear the small and the great alike" (Deuteronomy 1:17)—for many centuries disparity existed in the manner in which punishment was meted out, with the rich and influential receiving little or no punishment for offenses that resulted in torture and death for the less fortunate. This practice was challenged forcefully in the eighteenth century with the advent of *classicalism.*

CLASSICAL VIEW

Classicalism is an outgrowth of the European *Enlightenment* period of the eighteenth century (sometimes referred to as the "Age of Reason") whose adherents rejected spiritualism and religious explanations for criminal behavior. During this era, philosophers such Montesquieu (1689–1755) and Voltaire (1694–1778) spoke out against the French penal code and punishments that were both inhumane and inequitable. Jean Rousseau (1712–1778) and Cesare Beccaria (1738–1794) argued for a radical concept of justice based on *equality.* At a time when laws and law enforcement were unjust and disparate, and punishment often brutal, they demanded justice based on equality and punishment that was humane and proportionate to the offense. This revolutionary doctrine—*equality*—influenced the American Revolution with the declaration that "all men are created equal," and the French Revolution, whose National Assembly enacted a "Declaration of the Rights of Man and Citizen" (1789), which emphasized the equality of all citizens. The roots of this legal and political philosophy can be found in the concept of the social contract and natural rights.

The **social contract** is a mythical state of affairs wherein each person agrees to a pact, the basic stipulation of which is that all men being created equal, conditions of law are the same for all. "The social contract establishes among the citizens an equality of such character that each binds himself on the same terms as all the others, and is *thus* entitled to enjoy the same rights as all the others" (Rousseau [1762] 1954: 45). According to classical thought, by nature, man is free and endowed with natural rights, a philosophical basis for the first 10 amendments to the U.S. Constitution, the Bill of Rights. According to John Locke (1632–1704), all men are by nature free, equal, and independent, and no one can be subjected to the political power of another without his or her own consent. These sentiments were incorporated into the U.S. Declaration of Independence as "all men are created equal" whose "governments are instituted among men, deriving their just powers from the consent of the governed."

The classical notion of the social contract stipulates that all men being created equal, conditions of law are the same for all. Thus, Rousseau asserts, "One consents to die—if and when one becomes a murderer oneself—in order not to become a murderer's victim" (1954: 48). To be safe from crime, all people have consented to punishment if they resort to crime. This constitutes the greatest good for the greatest number; the social contract is rational and motivated by selfishness (Roshier, 1989).

Contrary to the manner in which law was being enforced, the classical school argued that law should respect neither rank nor station—all men are created equal—and punishment is to be meted out with a perfect uniformity. This premise was given impetus by Beccaria, who, in *An Essay on Crimes and Punishments* (1764; English edition, 1867), states that laws should be drawn precisely and matched to punishment intended to be applied equally to all classes of men. The law, he argued, should stipulate a particular penalty for each specific crime, and judges should mete out identical sentences for each occurrence of the same offense (Maestro, 1973). This makes the administration of justice rational, whereas law is taken, uncritically, as given. Punishment has as its purpose deterrence and must be "the minimum possible in the given circumstances, proportionate to the crime, dictated by the laws" (Maestro, 1973: 33). The prosecution of defendants must be accomplished without resort to torture, common during this period. Not only is torture inhumane but a highly unreliable method of determining guilt. Unlike the position of Rousseau stated earlier, Beccaria opposed capital punishment.

According to the classical position, punishment is justified because offenders who violate the social contract are rational and endowed with **free will.** This concept, which has biblical origins (Deuteronomy 30:15), holds that every person has the ability to distinguish and choose between right and wrong, and between being law abiding or criminal. In other words, behavior that violates the law is a *rational choice* made by a person with free will—in legal terms, **mens rea.** The classical school argues, however, that because humans tend toward *hedonism*—that is, they seek pleasure and avoid pain—they must be restrained, by fear of punishment, from pleasurable acts that are unlawful. Accordingly, the purpose of the criminal law is not simply *retribution* but also *deterrence*. In sum, the "individual is responsible for his actions and is equal, no matter what his rank, in the eyes of the law" (Taylor, Walton, and Young, 1973: 2). This approach has an economic perspective in **utilitarianism**—the cost–benefit analysis of behavior. According to Gary Becker (1968: 176): "A person commits an offense if the expected utility to him exceeds the utility he could get by using his time and resources at other activities." Becker argues that "a useful (utilitarian) theory of criminal behavior can dispense with special theories of anomie, psychological inadequacies, or inheritance of special traits [all discussed in chapter 9] and simply extend the economist's usual analysis of choice" (1968: 40). This approach parallels that of classical economics—capitalism—in which free persons motivated by rational self-interest, based on the principles of the free market, (purportedly) benefit the entire society.

Two additional requirements—*certainty* and *promptness*—round out the classical position. If law is to serve its deterrent purpose, the would-be violator must be in fear of the consequences. This element of fear requires certainty, whereas promptness, seemingly based on a primitive form of behaviorism (discussed in chapter 9), is necessary to make a more lasting impression—connecting the deed to the punishment.

The classical approach supported the interests of a rising eighteenth-century commercial class that was demanding legal equality with the privileged noble class, as well as protection from the economic-driven predations of the lower class. A contradiction remains between a defense of equality and the emphasis on maintaining an unequal distribution of wealth and property. Crime could, indeed, be a rational response to severe differentiations in wealth and opportunity. Free will is an oversimplification, because one's position in society determines the degree of choice with respect to committing crimes: "A system of classical justice of this order could only operate in a society where property was distributed equally," where each person has an equal stake in the system (Taylor, Walton, and Young, 1973: 6). It is irrational for a society, which in too many instances does not offer a feasible alternative to crime, to insist that criminal behavior is simply a matter of free will; the nature of our prison population for more than 200 years belies this claim. Nevertheless, as noted by Anatole France (1927: 91), "the law [based on classicalism], in its majestic equality, forbids both the poor man and the rich man to sleep under bridges, to beg in the streets, and to steal bread."

In sum, there are eight basic tenets of classicalism (Taylor, Walton, and Young, 1973):

1. Humans are rational.
2. All persons are created equal.
3. All persons have an equal stake in society, and thus, an equal stake in preventing crime.
4. Free will endows each person with the power to be law abiding or criminal.
5. People tend toward hedonism.
6. The purpose of punishment is deterrence.
7. Punishment must be meted out fairly, with absolute equality, and in proportion to the offense.
8. Punishment must be prompt and certain.

Classical theory is the basis of our legal system, and its pictorial representation appears on many courthouses and documents in the form of a woman—"Justice"—carrying scales and wearing a blindfold. The classical view provides the basis for *definite/determinate sentences*, which are discussed in chapter 7.

NEOCLASSICALISM

According to the classical position, punishment is justified because the offender who violates the social contract is rational, endowed with free will, and, therefore, responsible for his or her actions no matter what the person's rank. The focus is on laws and the legal system, not the nature of criminal motivation. In fact, under the U.S. system of justice, an explanation is not a justification unless it reaches the level of a (legal) compulsion, at which point the law does not blame the perpetrator—no *mens rea*. Classicalism provides the basis for a rational legal system that is relatively easy to administer, except for one annoying problem: Implementing a criminal code with perfect equality has proven elusive. This problem became apparent when the French Code of 1791 attempted to implement Beccaria's reforms. Equality and proportionality proved more difficult in practice than in theory, and the French increasingly added to the discretionary powers of judges in the form of neoclassicalism (Roshier, 1989).

Neoclassicalism maintains the basic belief in free will, while paving the way for the entry of mitigation (and subsequently aggravation) into criminal justice by considering:

- Past criminal record
- Insanity and retardation
- Infancy

Punishment can be justified only if crime is freely chosen, intentional, and rational—that is, reasoned behavior: The neoclassicist revisions created an entrée into the courts for the nonlegal expert, particularly psychiatrists and, later, social workers (Taylor, Walton, and Young, 1973). These experts determine the presence of mitigation, and the system is able to continue to maintain a belief in free will. Allowing for the possibility of differences between offenders raises the specter of **determinism**—that is, to varying degrees, the offender's choices are limited, which is the basic premise of positivism.

POSITIVE VIEW

Positivism, as formulated by Auguste Comte (1798–1857), refers to a method for examining and understanding social behavior. Comte argued that the methods and logical form of the natural sciences—the scientific method—are applicable to the study of man as a social being, producing the field of *social sciences*. Social phenomena, Comte stated, must be studied and understood by observation, hypothesis, and experimentation in a new discipline that he called *sociology*. Classical theory is based on philosophy and law, whereas positive view is based on *empiricism* in an effort to determine the *cause* of crime.

The positive approach to the study of crime became known as *criminology*, a discipline whose early efforts are identified with Cesare Lombroso (1835–1909), a Venetian physician. In his *L'uomo delinquente* (*The Criminal Man*), first published in 1876, Lombroso argued that the criminal is a "primitive throwback" to earlier developmental stages through which noncriminal man had already passed—the influence of **social Darwinism** is obvious (Degler, 1991). Lombroso's research centered on physiological characteristics believed indicative of criminality, although his later work (published in 1911) noted the importance of environmental factors in causing crime (Lombroso, 1968). Instead of the classical emphasis on criminal behavior as rational, positivists tend to see it as a symptom of some form of pathology—biological, psychological, or social. (Positive theories of crime are reviewed in chapter 9.)

While Charles Darwin and Herbert Spencer were concerned with a general construct of human evolution and its effect on society, the criminal anthropology initiated by the work of Lombroso employed evolution to explain criminal behavior. Lombroso contributed to the study of crime by using, albeit in a rather imperfect

Social Darwinism

The move toward using science to explain criminality received a major impetus from the work of Charles Darwin (1809–1882). Although his first book (*Origin of Species*, published in 1859) was concerned exclusively with nonhuman organisms, his second (*Descent of Man*, published in 1871) included the idea that humanity was shaped by the forces of natural selection. Darwin's thesis was advanced by the English philosopher Herbert Spencer (1820–1903), who coined the phrase "survival of the fittest," the credo for social Darwinism. Spencer (1961: 305) argued that "there can be no rational apprehension for the truths of Sociology until there has been reached a rational apprehension of the truths of Biology." According to Spencer (1961: 2), biology did not support help for the downtrodden: "As fast as they increase the provision for those who live without labor, so fast do they increase the number who live without labor; and that with an ever-increasing distribution of alms, there comes an ever-increasing outcry for more alms."

Darwin's theory of natural selection supplied the conceptual ammunition for an ideology (later labeled social Darwinism), which allayed the qualms of the rich about not helping the poor by telling them that the latter's sufferings were an inevitable price for societal advancement that could occur only through the struggle for existence ending in the survival of the fittest and the elimination of the unfit (Andreski, 1971). "If the unworthy are helped to increase, by shielding them from that mortality which their unworthiness would naturally entail, the effect is to produce, generation after generation, a greater unworthiness" (Spencer, 1961: 313). "Fostering the good-for-nothing at the expense of the good is an extreme cruelty. It is a deliberate storing-up of miseries for future generations. There is no greater curse to posterity than that of bequeathing them an increasing population of imbeciles and idlers and criminals" (314).

Are government policies based on such buzzwords as "self-sufficiency" and "individual responsibility" a twenty-first-century form of social Darwinism?

Classical View	Positive View
Free will	Determinism
Choice	Cause
Punishment/deterrence	Treatment/incarceration

If, as the classical view argues, a person has free will and is rational, he or she will weigh the costs of committing (or not committing) a crime. The threat of sanctions is seen as an effort to tilt the weighing process away from crime. The classical approach would view enhancing education and job skills as increasing choice away from crime. Positivists would view this response as a treatment dealing with the causes of crime.

way, the tools of science, and shifting the field of inquiry from law and philosophy to empiricism. Positive view places emphasis not on the crime but on the criminal. It contradicts the theory of free will for which positivists have substituted *a chain of interrelated causes* and, at its most extreme, a *deterministic* basis for criminal behavior: The criminal could not do otherwise. Because criminal behavior is the result of social and psychological, if not physiological, conditions over which the offender has little or no control, he or she is not culpable (in legal parlance, lacks *mens rea*) and thus punishment is inappropriate. However, because criminals do represent a threat to society, they must be "treated," "corrected," or "rehabilitated" (or according to early Lombrosians, separated from society, perhaps castrated or executed). In practice, the change in emphasis from punishment to correction did not necessarily result in a less severe response to criminal offenders. Some modern critics contend that rehabilitation opened the door to a host of questionable schemes for dealing with offenders under the guise of "treatment" and "for their own good." The American Friends Service Committee notes: "Retribution and revenge necessarily imply punishment, but it does not necessarily follow that punishment is eliminated under rehabilitative regimes" (1971: 20). The positive view provides a basis for the juvenile court discussed in chapter 4 and the *indeterminate sentence* discussed in chapter 7.

The views of the classical and positive schools are important because they transcend their own time and continue to influence contemporary issues in criminal justice. The question remains: *Do we judge the crime or the criminal?* This is a central question in the continuing debate over sentencing—definite versus indeterminate—discussed in chapter 7. Probation and parole, it is often argued, emanate from a positivistic response to criminal behavior, a view that is disputed in this book.

THE AMERICAN SYSTEM OF CRIMINAL JUSTICE

Probation and parole are part of the American system of criminal justice. The next section locates these two services within that system.

Entering the System

Most crime is not responded to by the criminal justice system because it has not been discovered or reported to the police; when reported, most crimes are never solved. For the police to arrest a suspect, they must have a level of evidence known as **probable cause.** The Ohio Adult Parole Authority offers the following definition: "Reasonable grounds for suspicion supported by facts and circumstances sufficiently strong in themselves to lead a reasonably cautious person to believe that a person

Levels of Evidence

Beyond a Reasonable Doubt

Guilt in a criminal trial

Finding of delinquency in juvenile court

Clear and Convincing Evidence

Used in extraordinary civil cases, such as commitment and child custody

Preponderance of the Evidence

Most civil cases

Status offense cases in juvenile court

Probation and parole revocation hearings

Probable Cause

Search warrants/arrest warrants

Warrantless arrests

Probation and parole preliminary violation hearings

is guilty of a particular crime." Probable cause is also the level of evidence required to initiate a probation or parole violation, and it is significantly less than that necessary to convict a defendant in a criminal trial.

When the police effect an arrest, the subject is transported to a holding facility, usually a police station equipped with cells—a "lockup." As opposed to a jail, a lockup is used on a temporary basis, for 24 to 48 hours. During this time, the suspect will be booked, photographed, and fingerprinted, and the police will request that formal charges be instituted by the prosecutor's office. A fingerprint check reveals whether the suspect has a previous arrest record, is wanted for other charges, or is on probation or parole.

Pretrial Court Appearances

Depending on what time of day the arrest occurred and whether it happened on a weekday, weekend, or court holiday, the suspect may have to spend 24 hours or longer in the lockup before being transported to court. At the first appearance, the primary question concerns bail, and the initial appearance may actually be a bond hearing at which bail is the only issue. If a defendant is under probation or parole supervision, the bail decision is affected; for example, in some jurisdictions, a probation or parole warrant will be filed to preclude release on bail. If the subject is unable to provide bail, or a probation/parole warrant is filed as a detainer, he or she will be kept in jail pending further court action. In many jurisdictions, probation or pretrial officers or other specialized court personnel will interview defendants with a view toward assisting the judge in making a bail decision. They may even provide supervision during the pretrial stage (see Pretrial Supervision in chapter 11).

Pretrial Hearings

At pretrial hearings (sometimes referred to as an initial appearance, preliminary hearing, or arraignment), the official charges are read, the need for counsel considered, and bail set or reviewed (if it has already been set at a bond hearing). Typically, these hearings last only a few minutes. If the case is a misdemeanor, it may be adjudicated at this time, often by a plea of guilty or dismissal of the charges on a motion by the prosecutor. If the charge(s) constitutes a felony, a *probable cause* hearing is held to determine if the arresting officer had sufficient evidence—probable cause—to justify an arrest. This hearing takes the form of a short minitrial during which the prosecutor calls witnesses and the defense may cross-examine and call its own witnesses.

If the judge finds probable cause—evidence sufficient to cause a reasonable person to believe that the suspect committed a crime—the prosecutor files an *information* (presents details of the charges), which has the effect of bringing the case to trial. In some states, the prosecutor may avoid a probable cause hearing by presenting evidence directly to a *grand jury*—generally, 23 citizens who hear charges in secret. If they vote a *true bill,* the defendant stands *indicted,* and the case proceeds to trial.

Trial or Guilty Plea

Few cases entering the criminal justice system actually result in a jury trial, an expensive and time-consuming luxury that most participants attempt to keep to a minimum. About 85 to 95 percent of all criminal convictions are the result of a guilty plea, and most guilty pleas are the result of **plea bargaining.** This widely condemned practice for disposing of cases involves an *exchange*: The defendant agrees to waive his or her constitutional right to a jury trial, providing the prosecutor with a "win," and saving the court a great deal of time and effort; the defendant is rewarded for this behavior by receiving some form of leniency (the impact of plea bargaining on probation services is discussed in chapter 5; on parole in chapter 7). If plea negotiations fail to result in an agreement, or if one or the other side refuses to bargain, the case is scheduled for trial. (For an extensive discussion of plea bargaining, see Abadinsky, 2003a.)

The trial is an adversary proceeding in which both sides are represented by legal counsel and whose rules are enforced by a judge. To sustain a criminal charge, the prosecutor must prove the *actus reus* and *mens rea.* **Actus reus** means a wrongful act or deed; it refers to the need to prove that a violation of the criminal law—a crime—actually occurred. The *actus reus* consists of a description of the criminal behavior and evidence that the accused acted accordingly. *Mens rea,* or "guilty mind," is a legal standard that refers to the question of *intent:* The prosecutor must be able to show that the defendant had a wrongful purpose—willfulness—in carrying out the *actus reus.* The defendant is presumed innocent; therefore, defense counsel need not prove anything but will typically attempt to raise doubts about the evidence or other aspects of the prosecution's case.

Each side can subpoena witnesses to present testimony and can cross-examine adverse witnesses. The defendant can take the stand on his or her own behalf or, if the defendant prefers not to testify, can maintain the Fifth Amendment privilege against self-incrimination. Defendants on probation or parole may be reluctant to testify because this would subject them to cross-examination and result in a disclosure of their criminal record to the jury. After lawyers for each side have introduced all their evidence, the judge instructs the jury on the principles of law applicable to the case. Every jury is told (charged by the judge) that the facts pointing to the guilt of the defendant must be established **beyond a reasonable doubt,** as opposed to the **preponderance** (greater weight) **of the evidence,** which is the standard in civil and some juvenile cases and probation and parole revocation hearings.

The jury now retires to deliberate in private; in most jurisdictions, the jury's decision for guilt or acquittal must be unanimous, or the result is a *hung jury.* If the jury cannot reach a unanimous verdict, the jurors are discharged; if the prosecutor decides, the case must be tried a second time before a different jury. Except in some relatively rare instances when there are violations of both federal and state law, the defendant who is acquitted cannot be tried again for the same charges because this would constitute *double jeopardy* (prohibited by the Fifth Amendment). If the jury finds the defendant guilty of one or more of the charges, the case moves to the sentencing stage, and the probation officer enters the case, usually for the first time. (In some jurisdictions, the probation officer is involved in gathering information—the *pre-plea investigation*—for the judge during the plea bargaining stage.)

Sentencing

After a verdict or plea of guilty, the judge decides on the sentence, although in some states the sentence is decided by the jury, particularly in cases of murder. The sentencing function reflects societal goals, which may be in conflict:

- *Retribution:* punishment dimension (*lex talionis,* an eye for an eye, or just deserts), which expresses society's disapproval of criminal behavior
- *Incapacitation:* reducing the opportunity for further criminal behavior by imprisonment
- *Deterrence:* a belief that punishment will reduce the likelihood of future criminal behavior by the particular offender (*individual/specific deterrence*), or by others in society who fear similar punishment (*general deterrence*)
- *Rehabilitation:* a belief that by providing services—social, psychological, educational, or vocational—an offender will be less likely to commit future crimes
- *Restitution:* having an offender repay the victim or society in money or service for the harm committed

Sentencing can be further complicated by concern for

- *Proportionality:* that punishment be commensurate with the seriousness of the crime
- *Equity:* that similar crimes receive similar punishment
- *Social debt:* that the severity of punishment should consider the offender's prior criminal record (Zawitz, 1988)

These issues are discussed in subsequent chapters.

The trial judge sets a date for a sentencing hearing and in many jurisdictions orders a presentence investigation to be conducted by the probation department. A probation officer will search court records; examine other reports (such as psychiatric and school records); and interview the defendant, spouse, employer, arresting officer, and the victim. Information from the presentence investigation will be presented in the form of a written presentence or probation report, which frequently contains the probation officer's sentencing recommendation. After reviewing the report, the judge conducts a sentencing hearing at which both defense and prosecution are allowed to make statements. The judge then imposes a sentence: fine, suspended sentence, probation, incarceration, or any combination thereof. A prison sentence may be definite (classical) or indeterminate (positive), depending on state law.

A sentence of probation places the defendant, now a "convict," under the supervision of a probation officer. A sentence of incarceration results in the defendant being sent to jail (if convicted of a misdemeanor), usually for not more than 1 year, or to a state (or federal) prison if convicted of a felony. In most jurisdictions, a parole board can release the defendant (now an "inmate") before the expiration of his or her sentence. In other states and the federal system, the inmate can be released early as the result of accumulating time off for "good behavior." Parolees and, in many states, persons released for good behavior, come under the supervision of a parole officer (the actual title varies from state to state).

Appeals

Although the prosecutor cannot appeal an acquittal (Fifth Amendment), the defendant is free to appeal a guilty verdict in hopes of obtaining a reversal. The defendant can ask an appellate court to review the proceedings that culminated in his or her conviction. In fact, American criminal justice is rather unique for the extensive postconviction review procedures to which a defendant is entitled. A prison inmate may petition the trial court for a new trial or take an appeal to the state's intermediate appellate court and, if unsuccessful there, can still appeal to the state court of last resort. If unsuccessful in state court, he or she can petition the Supreme Court. The prisoner can also attack the conviction *collaterally*, that is, using indirect means, by way of a writ of *habeas corpus*, claiming that his or her constitutional rights were violated in some way by the state court conviction. Having exhausted direct and indirect appeals in state courts, the inmate can move over to the federal courts, claiming again that the conviction was unconstitutional, usually on grounds of lack of due process.

The appellate court cannot act as a trial court, that is, receive new evidence concerning the facts already established at the original trial. It is limited to new theories or legal arguments regarding the law applicable to these facts or addressing procedural issues. The appellate court can uphold the verdict, overturn it, or order it reversed and remanded to the trial court for a new trial. The appellate court can also render decisions that affect other cases by setting a precedent or handing down a ruling that governs the actions of criminal justice officials; for example, in *Morrissey v. Brewer* the Supreme Court ruled that parolees are entitled to some basic forms of due process before they can be returned to prison for violation of parole.

PROBATION AND PAROLE: WHY BOTHER?

Why be concerned with probation or parole? Some simply say, "If you do the crime, do the time." Although later chapters elaborate on this issue, consider the following: There are about 5 million persons on probation and parole at an average yearly cost of about $1,500. The annual operating costs of housing a state prison inmate is about $30,000. In some states, such as Massachusetts, Minnesota, New York, and Oregon, the cost is closer to $40,000. The 50 states spend a total of about $30 billion in annual prison operating costs (Stephan, 2004). However, the cost of imprisonment is typically underestimated because it leaves out many actual expenses, such as fringe benefits for employees, which average more than 25 percent of salaries. The cost of building a maximum security prison averages more than $70,000 per cell. Although a state can float bonds to underwrite the cost of prison building, thereby amortizing the cost (which includes substantial interest) over a long period, operating costs such as staff salaries must be paid immediately out of the state's operating budget—it may be politically easier to build a prison than to staff and operate one.

Adding to these costs are the problems of acquired immunodeficiency syndrome (AIDS), tuberculosis, hepatitis C, and the increasing number of geriatric offenders, often the result of "get tough" and three strikes and you're out (actually *in* for life) legislation. The cost of housing an inmate older than the age of 50 with health problems is in excess of $60,000 per year.

There are about 1.5 million persons in America's prisons, and jails house about an additional 700,000 inmates. Factors of cost, mediated by overcrowded prisons, have led to a dramatic expansion in the use of probation and parole. In 1979, for example, there were 1,086,535 persons on probation; in 1987, there were 2,242,053, an increase of more than 100 percent. By 1990, the number had risen to 2,671,000, with the current figure at about 4 million. In 1979, 218,690 persons were on parole from American prisons; in 1987, there were 362,192, an increase of more than 65 percent.

Louisiana State Penitentiary, Angola, 2001

The inmate, "an old toothless man, Eugene Scott, whom the other inmates call Shippy because his head is as big as a boat, is dribbling in his wheelchair; a stroke has stripped him of his ability to speak. Another, fighting emphysema, is hooked to an oxygen tank; still another, blind from glaucoma, rolls about in bed" (Stolberg, 2001: 20).

By 1990, that number had risen to 531,000, with the current figure at more than 750,000 (U.S. Bureau of Justice Statistics). In 1994, Congress passed the Violent Crime Control and Law Enforcement Act, which provides prison construction grants. To qualify, however, states must have laws requiring persons convicted of a violent offense to serve at least 85 percent of their prison sentence—few states have the necessary resources to do so.

Now that this overview of criminal justice is complete, chapter 2 examines the U.S. court system and probation history and administration.

KEY TERMS

front-door programs	utilitarianism
back-door programs	neoclassicalism
truth-in-sentencing laws	determinism
three strikes and you're out legislation	positivism
a system that is not systematic	social Darwinism
index crimes	probable cause
classicalism	*actus reus*
social contract	plea bargaining
free will	beyond a reasonable doubt
mens rea	preponderance of evidence

INTERNET CONNECTIONS

General criminal justice links: www.lawguru.com/ilawlib/96.htm
National Institute of Justice: www.ojp.usdoj.gov/nij
National Criminal Justice Reference Service: ncjrs.org
Legal Resource Center: crimelynx.com/research.html
U.S. Department of Justice links: www.usdoj.gov/02organizations/02_1.html
Vera Institute of Justice: vera.org
Council of State Governments: www.csg.org

REVIEW QUESTIONS

1. What are the contradictory goals and competing expectations in American criminal justice?
2. What are the four levels and three branches of government?
3. How does this division affect criminal justice?

4. How does the criminal law reflect power relations in society?

5. How does classicalism differ from neoclassicalism?

6. How is free will an oversimplification?

7. How can changes in sentencing laws increase the need for front-door and back-door schemes for dealing with offenders?

8. Why can the use of probation be expected to increase when parole is abolished?

9. Why is the system of criminal justice in the United States not systematic?

10. What are the effects of providing the police with an inordinate percentage of the allocations for criminal justice?

11. How does the definition of crime determine who is subjected to probation and parole?

12. How is the enforcement of criminal law a factor in determining who is subjected to probation and parole?

13. What are the eight index crimes?

14. What factors increase the possibility of an offender being arrested?

15. What are the major elements of the classical view of law and justice?

16. What distinguishes positive view from classical view with respect to crime and criminal behavior?

17. Under a strictly positivistic view of criminal behavior, why is there an absence of culpability or *mens rea*?

18. What are the five societal goals of sentencing?

19. What concerns can complicate sentencing?

20. What is the importance of probation and parole in criminal justice?

21. Why has the abolition of parole in many states resulted in an increase in probation?

22. How has truth-in-sentencing legislation affected the prison population?

23. What is the effect of three strikes and you're out legislation on the prison population?

24. How do issues of cost explain the extensive use of probation and parole?

PART
I

Probation

CHAPTER 2

Juvenile Court and Juvenile Justice

A probation agency provides three basic services to the courts:

1. Juvenile services
2. Supervision of adult offenders
3. Presentence investigation

As opposed to the secondary role of the probation officer in the adult criminal court, the probation officer is at the center of juvenile court operations. In this chapter, we examine the history and unique qualities of the juvenile court and juvenile justice. We then consider youngsters in adult criminal court and the legal decisions that have affected juvenile justice.

THE HISTORY OF THE JUVENILE COURT

The system of justice used for juveniles in the United States is based on a philosophy radically different from the one on which the adult criminal justice system rests. Before we can examine the services provided by a probation agency to the juvenile court, it is necessary to understand the history and philosophy of this unique institution.

In Europe, from Roman times to the late eighteenth century, children were routinely abandoned by their parents; the classical philosopher Rousseau, for example, boasted of abandoning five of his children to foundling homes (Boswell, 1989). Abandoned children were subjected to extreme levels of deprivation and exploitation. English common law considered children as chattel, and a rather indifferent attitude toward children became characteristic of America, where they became creatures of exploitation. Indeed, the contemporary American concern with the problem of child abuse stands in marked contrast to our earlier history. Child labor remained an important part of economic life into the twentieth century. Children of the poor labored in mines (where their size was an advantage), mills, and factories with unsanitary and unsafe conditions. The Supreme Court reflected the prevailing belief in *laissez-faire* capitalism and would not intervene—statutes prohibiting children younger than 12 from employment and limiting the workday of youngsters older than 12 to 10 hours were ruled unconstitutional or routinely disobeyed. Increased immigration, industrialization, and urbanization drastically altered American society. The 10- and 12-hour workday left many children without parental supervision, and family disorganization became widespread. Many children lived in the streets, where they encountered the disorder and rampant vice of the urban environment.

In the early days of colonial America, the family remained the mainstay of social control, "although by 1700 the family's inability to accommodate and discipline its young was becoming more apparent" (Mennel, 1973: xxii). Numerous laws began to appear that threatened parents for failing to properly discipline their children. Furthermore, the British practice of transporting wayward young to America for indenture, which often involved neglect, cruelty, and immorality, left many youngsters without supervision as they fled from these onerous circumstances. By the end of the eighteenth century, society began to realize that a "system of social control would have to be developed apart from the family which would discipline homeless, vagrant, and destitute children—the offspring of the poor" (1973: xxvii). This need led to the rise of **houses of refuge**.

HOUSES OF REFUGE AND ORPHAN ASYLUMS

In 1817, the Society for the Prevention of Pauperism was established in response to the problem of troubled and troublesome children. In 1824, it was renamed the Society for the Reformation of Juvenile Delinquency. The society conducted campaigns against the "corrupting" influence of taverns and theaters, and opposed the use of jails to house children. Their efforts led to the establishment of houses of refuge, or houses of reformation, or reform schools (Krisberg, 1988).

The first house of refuge opened in New York in 1825 and was quickly followed by one in Boston (1826) and another in Philadelphia (1828). These institutions provided housing and care for troublesome children who might otherwise be left in the streets or, if their behavior brought them into serious conflict with the law, sent to jail or prison. The house of refuge was used "not only for the less serious juvenile criminal, but for runaways, disobedient children or vagrants" (Empey, 1979: 25–26). Orphan asylums were used for abandoned or orphaned children, for the children of women without husbands, or for children whose parents were deemed unfit. Both institutions "were established to inculcate children with the values of hard work, orderliness, and subordination and thereby ensure their future good behavior" (Mennel, 1973: 8). To achieve these ends, however, discipline and punishments were often brutal, and the house of refuge in New York experienced group escapes and inmate uprisings.

Although these institutions were operated by private charities, their public charters included the first statutory definitions of juvenile delinquency and provided the basis for state intervention into the lives of children who were neglected or in need of supervision, in addition to those youngsters who had committed crimes (Walker, 1980). In these charters was embodied a "medieval English doctrine of nebulous origin and meaning" (Schlossman, 1977: 8) known as ***parens patriae,*** originally referring to the feudal duties of the overlord to his vassals and later the legal duties of the monarch toward his or her subjects who were in need of care, particularly children and the mentally incompetent. In its original form, *parens patriae* provided the Crown with authority to administer the estates of landed orphans (Sutton, 1988).

"With the independence of the American colonies and the transplanting of the English common-law system, the state in this country has taken the place of the crown as the *parens patriae* of all minors" (Lou, 1972: 4). This concept gave almost complete authority over children to the state—the Bill of Rights simply did not apply to children (*Ex parte Crouse*, 4 Wharton 9, 1838)—and *parens patriae* became the legal basis for the juvenile court. Although this concept has become identified with the rehabilitation of juvenile delinquents, it originally applied only to dependent children.

THE CHILD SAVERS

As immigration, industrialization, and urbanization continued, the fearful image of masses of undisciplined and uneducated children gave rise to the **child-saving movement.** Led by upper-class women of earlier American ancestry, the child savers were influenced by the nativist prejudices of their day, as well as by *social Darwinism* (see chapter 1). Natural selection resulted in an inferior underclass in need of control but not of aid in the sense of the modern social welfare state. Something had to be done to save these children from an environment that would only lead them into vice and crime, and cause them to be the progenitors of the same. Reforming juvenile justice became the task of women who "were generally well-educated, widely-traveled, and had access to political and financial resources" (Platt, 1974: 77). The juvenile court was the result of their efforts, although controversy surrounds the interests and motivations of the child savers.

Anthony Platt argues that these women, although they "viewed themselves as altruists and humanitarians dedicated to rescuing those who were less fortunately placed in the social order," were actually motivated by boredom and middle- and upper-class social, economic, and political interests (1974: 3). "The child-savers were concerned not with championing the rights of the poor against exploitation by the ruling class but rather integrating the poor into the established social order and protecting 'respectable' citizens from the 'dangerous classes'" of people, who might otherwise be drawn into social revolution if not criminality (Platt quoted in Empey, 1979: 31). According to Platt, the juvenile court would serve to protect propertied and commercial interests from the predations of lower-class youngsters, while ensuring an adequate supply of disciplined and vocationally trained labor. In fact, however, many states had already separated juvenile cases from those of adults without establishing a distinct juvenile court. The movement to establish a juvenile court was part of a larger program of social reform advocated by the Progressives of the late nineteenth and early twentieth centuries. David Rothman (in Empey, 1979: 37) places the issue in perspective: The juvenile court movement "satisfied [both] the most humanitarian of impulses and the most crudely self-interested considerations."

THE JUVENILE COURT EMERGES

Although a juvenile might be sent to a house of refuge, an orphan asylum, or a reformatory—there was confusion over which children should be relegated to which institution—they could be arrested, detained, and tried as would any adult accused of a crime. Children older than 14, and sometimes younger, were routinely prosecuted as adults and punished as adults. Although some modifications of the trial process with respect to juveniles occurred as early as 1869, it was the Illinois Juvenile Court Act of 1899 that established the first law creating a special comprehensive court for juveniles. Consistent with the concept of *parens patriae,* in addition to children who were delinquent—persons younger than 16 years of age who had violated the law—the juvenile court was given jurisdiction over neglected and dependent children:

> For the purposes of this act the words dependent child and neglected child shall mean any child who for any reason is destitute or homeless or abandoned; or has not proper parental care or guardianship; or who habitually begs or receives alms; or who is found living in any house of ill fame or with any vicious or disreputable person; or whose home, by reason of neglect, cruelty or depravity on the part of its parents, guardian or other person in whose care it may be, is an unfit place for such a child.

Nondelinquents in whom the court was interested because of their behavior became known as **status offenders.**

Within 25 years of the Illinois Juvenile Court Act, every state but one had adopted legislation providing for one or all the features of a juvenile court organization (Lenroot and Lundberg, 1925). In Cuyahoga County (Cleveland), the first session of the juvenile court occurred on June 4, 1902, with 20 boys younger than 16 years of age appearing; the initial case involved a 14-year-old boy charged with delinquency for stealing a pair of shoes—he was placed in "care and custody" of one of the three dozen volunteers who served as probation officers. A juvenile court was established in the Territory of Arizona on March 21, 1907; later that year, a probation officer was appointed in Pima County "to make such investigation as may be required by the Court, to be present if practicable when juvenile cases are heard, to furnish such information and assistance as the judge may require, and to take charge of any child, before trial and after trial, as may be directed by the Court." Jefferson County, Texas, appointed its first paid probation officer in 1918, one of the earliest in Texas.

A book originally published in 1927 provides insight into the prevailing concepts of the juvenile court (Lou, 1972: 2):

> These principles upon which the juvenile court acts are radically different from those of the criminal courts. In place of judicial tribunals, restrained by antiquated procedure, saturated in an atmosphere of hostility, trying cases for determining guilt and inflicting punishment according to inflexible rules of law, we have now juvenile courts, in which the relations of the child to his parents or other adults and to the state or society are defined and are adjusted summarily according to the scientific findings about the child and his environments. In place of magistrates, limited by the outgrown custom and compelled to walk in the paths fixed by the law of the realm, we have now socially-minded judges, who hear and adjust cases according not to rigid rules of law but to what the interests of society and the interests of the child or good conscience demand. In the place of juries, prosecutors, and lawyers, trained in the old conception of law and staging dramatically, but often amusingly, legal battles, as the necessary paraphernalia of a criminal court, we have now probation officers, physicians, psychologists, and psychiatrists, who search for the social, physiological, psychological, and mental backgrounds of the child in order to arrive at reasonable and just solutions of individual cases.

Lou's statement clearly embodies the position of positive view—or, critics might say, positivism run amok, with the child being denied the most basic due process rights. The unstructured and informal system of juvenile justice used in Illinois quickly became the standard as juvenile courts were established throughout the United States. Differences between the adult criminal court and the juvenile court extended even to the terminology used.

Adult Criminal Court	Juvenile Court
Defendant	Respondent
Charges/indictment	Petition
Arraignment	Hearing
Prosecution/trial	Adjudication
Verdict	Finding
Sentence	Disposition
Imprisonment	Commitment
Inmate/prisoner	Resident
Parole	Aftercare

Adjudication: (1) hearing at which the minor enters a plea to one or more allegations of the petition and at which the judge pronounces the child a delinquent minor; (2) contested hearing (trial) at which witnesses testify and evidence is presented at the conclusion of which the judge determines whether or not the child has been found to be a delinquent minor

Adoptions: custody hearings, which grant custody to the prospective adoptive parents, and adoption hearings, which grant final adoption

Advisory: hearing for youth paper-referred to court at which the petition detailing the delinquent allegations is presented, a determination is made whether the minor qualifies for appointed counsel, and a trial review date is selected

Detention: hearing held within 24 hours of the filing of a petition for a detained youth at which counsel is appointed and the court considers whether the minor should be detained or released from custody

Disposition: hearing, analogous to the adult court sentencing, for which the probation officer prepares a comprehensive report of the adjudicated child's background and at which the judge determines what action(s) the court will take

Restitution: hearing at which the judge determines what restitution to a victim the child must pay to satisfy the conditions of probation

Review: review of the child's adherence to probation conditions to consider revising these conditions or terminating the minor from probation

Revocation: hearing to determine if the minor has violated probation by failure to adhere to the conditions of probation or by committing a delinquent act

Transfer: hearing to determine if the juvenile court should retain jurisdiction for the allegations set forth in the petition or whether the matter should be transferred for prosecution to the adult court

Trial review: hearing at which the child requests that the charges be set for a contested adjudication (trial) or at which he/she admits one or more allegations of the pending petition

FIGURE 2.1 *Guide to the Most Common Hearings Held at the Juvenile Court.*
(*Source:* Pima County, Arizona, Juvenile Court.)

Consistent with the concept of *parens patriae,* the terminology reflects a non-punitive approach to dealing with troubled and troublesome children (Figure 2.1). Critics often decry the lack of sufficient punishment inflicted in the juvenile court. Such comments indicate a complete misunderstanding of this court, which *should not punish.* Although the concept of *parens patriae* is paternalistic and not inconsistent with the concept of punishment (Weisheit and Alexander, 1988), the use of a punitive approach in juvenile court would make it simply a *criminal court for children* and, therefore, without grounding as a separate system of justice. Thus, although one could logically argue for abolishing the juvenile court, a juvenile court that imposes punishment has no basis in American history or in logic.

Because of the noncriminal approach, though, the usual safeguards of *due process* that were applicable in criminal courts were absent in juvenile court proceedings: rights to counsel, to confront and cross-examine adverse witnesses, and to avoid self-incrimination. Because the focus of the juvenile court was on providing help, procedures were often informal, if not vague, and the judge, with the assistance of the probation officer, was given broad powers over young persons. Platt argues that even if we assign benign motives to the child savers, "the programs they enthusiastically supported diminished the civil liberties and privacy of youth. Adolescents were treated as though they were naturally dependent, requiring constant and pervasive supervision. Although the child savers were rhetorically concerned with protecting children from the physical and moral dangers of an increasingly industrialized and urban society, their remedies seemed to aggravate the problem" (1974: 4).

The increasing concern about the extralegal operations of the juvenile court is reflected in the *Gault* decision (details later in this chapter), a 1967 case in which the U.S. Supreme Court ruled in favor of basic due process rights for persons adjudicated in juvenile court.

PROCEDURES IN THE JUVENILE COURT

The juvenile court system differs from state to state and even within states. Jurisdiction over juveniles may be located in a separate juvenile court, in a specialized branch of the superior court, or in various types of courts of limited jurisdiction. It is possible that within one state, jurisdiction may be located in two or more different types of courts. The legal age of a juvenile also varies from state to state from 14 to 18 years of age. Although juveniles are not routinely fingerprinted or photographed by the police, 47 states allow the police to fingerprint and 44 states allow them to photograph certain juveniles. In Texas, for example, all juveniles with alleged delinquent offenses that are crimes punishable by incarceration for adults are fingerprinted and entered into a statewide central repository. Their criminal history record may then be accessed by law enforcement and juvenile justice agencies throughout Texas. A juvenile's name is not usually printed in the newspapers, and the juvenile court has historically been closed to the public. However, 22 states now have open hearings in certain cases. In 1997, New York reversed its long-standing policy of keeping Family Court closed to the public. Although judges still have discretion to close cases, they must have compelling and specific reasons, such as ensuring the privacy of a victim of child sexual abuse (Finder, 1997). Florida also routinely opens its Family Court to the public (Sexton, 1997).

Although juvenile court records have traditionally been kept confidential, 39 states now permit the release of certain juveniles' names and/or photographs, and more and more juvenile records are becoming available to more agencies and the public. In many states, there are provisions for having a juvenile record sealed—not subject to examination except by special court order—and in some jurisdictions expunged (Figure 2.2). Eighteen states, however, prohibit the sealing or expunging of juvenile records (Sickmund, Snyder, and Poe-Yamagata, 1997). Until 1992, the FBI collected records only of juveniles tried as adults. In that year, however, new regulations gave the FBI's National Crime Information Center (NCIC) authority to receive juvenile court information. Although states do not have to submit juvenile court records to the FBI, the NCIC can instantly transmit to law enforcement agencies, and within days to some employers, juvenile court records formerly kept confidential. (For a review of this issue, see *Privacy and Juvenile Justice Records*, 1997.)

The juvenile court typically handles four types of cases:

1. *Delinquency:* behavior that, if engaged in by an adult, would constitute a crime
2. *Status offense:* behavior that, if engaged in by an adult, would not constitute a crime but (in accord with *parens patriae*) provides the basis for governmental intervention, for example, demonstrating chronic truancy, being beyond the control of parents or guardians, or running away
3. *Neglect or abuse:* children who are subjected to neglect or abuse by parents or guardians
4. *Dependency:* children who do not have parents or guardians available to provide proper care

As part of status offense, or separately under a special *addicted* category, juveniles may be subjected to juvenile court jurisdiction as a result of addiction to alcohol or other drugs.

```
STATE OF KANSAS
COURT SERVICES
INFORMATION PERTAINING TO
EXPUNGEMENT OF JUVENILE RECORDS
K. S. A. 38-1610
```

Any records or files specified in this code concerning a juvenile offender may be expunged upon application to a judge of the court of the county in which the records or files are maintained. The application for expungement may be made by the person who is the juvenile offender or, if a minor, by the person's parent or next friend.

There shall be no expungement of records or files concerning acts committed by a juvenile which, if committed by an adult would constitute: (1) indecent liberties with a child, (2) aggravated indecent liberties with a child, (3) aggravated criminal sodomy, (4) enticement of a child, (5) indecent solicitation of a child, (6) aggravated indecent solicitation of a child, (7) sexual exploitation of a child, (8) aggravated incest, (9) endangering a child, or (10) abuse of a child, or acts which would constitute an attempt to commit a violation of any of the offenses specified in this paragraph.

After a hearing, the court shall order the expungement of the records and files if the court finds that: (A) the person has reached 21 years of age or that two years have elapsed since the final discharge of the person; (B) since the final discharge of the person, the person has not been convicted of a felony or of a misdemeanor other than a traffic offense or adjudicated a delinquent or miscreant under the Kansas juvenile code or a juvenile offender under the Kansas juvenile offenders code and no proceedings are pending seeking such a conviction or adjudication; and (C) the circumstances and behavior of the petitioner warrant expungement.

Upon entry of an order expunging records or files, the offense shall be treated as if it never occurred, except that the offense may be considered if: (1) the petitioner is a person 16 years of age or over who is charged with a felony or with more than one offense of which one or more is a felony after having been adjudicated in two separate prior juvenile proceedings as having committed an act which would constitute a felony if committed by an adult and the adjudications occurred prior to the date of the commission of the new act charged, (2) upon conviction of a crime or adjudication in a subsequent action under this code the offense may be considered in determining the sentence to be imposed or disposition to be made.

The expungement of a felony adjudication does not relieve a person of complying with any state or federal law relating to the use or possession of firearms.

| I have been provided a copy of the above juvenile offenders code. | Consult your attorney for any questions regarding expungement of juvenile records. |

_____   _____
Offender   Court Services Officer

_____
Date

FIGURE 2.2 *Expungement of Juvenile Records.*
(*Source:* State of Kansas, Court Services.)

Instances of delinquency, status offense, neglect or abuse, or dependency that come to the attention of the authorities are often handled in a manner that does not involve the formal justice apparatus. School officials or the police, for example, may refer such cases directly to public or private social welfare or child protective agencies. Alternatively, the police may make a *station adjustment* so the child is allowed to return home with parents or guardians without further action. Those situations that come to the attention of the juvenile court enter by way of the intake section, which is usually staffed by juvenile probation officers. On the eastern end of New York's Long Island, the Suffolk County Probation Department—which supervises adult offenders—is responsible for juvenile intake services at the Family Court.

Intake

Children are referred to the juvenile court by the police, parents, school officials, or other public or private agency personnel, although law enforcement agencies are the source of more than 80 percent of delinquency referrals and a little less than half of the status offense referrals that reach the petition stage. In some jurisdictions, all cases

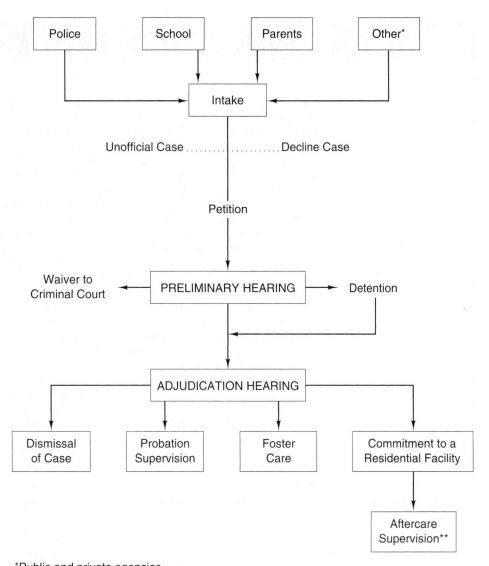

*Public and private agencies.
**Supervision provided by the probation department or a juvenile aftercare
(parole) agency.

FIGURE 2.3 *Juvenile Court Process.*

are received by a probation officer (PO) assigned to the **intake** or complaint unit. In others, cases that involve criminal complaints are first sent to the prosecutor's office. The first decision to be made at intake is the custodial status of the youngster: Does the respondent's behavior make him or her a danger to him- or herself or to the safety of others; will the youngster return to court voluntarily? (See Figure 2.3.)

Intake in the juvenile court is unique; it permits the court to screen cases not only on jurisdictional and legal grounds, but also on social dimensions. The PO interviews the presenting agent, the young person, and the child's parents or guardians. The officer then reviews court files for previous records concerning the child. If the case involves a serious crime or child abuse and has not already been screened by the prosecutor, the PO consults with that office. At this stage, the probation officer has a dual function: legal and social service.

The **legal function** requires that the PO determine if the juvenile court has jurisdiction, and also requires that the child and parents be advised of the right to counsel and the right to remain silent during the intake conference. H. Ted Rubin argues that "defense attorney participation at a[n intake] conference is rare, waivers

In Texas

It is 1:15 A.M. in Texarkana. James, 15 years of age, and an adult male have been arrested for aggravated robbery. Police are taking the juvenile to the detention center intake unit at the Bowie County Juvenile Probation Department. Harold Harlston, a probation officer on duty, has just been called to the intake office where he must decide if James will be detained or released. In checking the records, Harlston finds that James has a prior arrest for theft, but the initial police report suggests that this time James was influenced to participate in the robbery by the older man.

Harlston awakens James's parents with a phone call. They are quite upset and head for the center. While continuing to interview James, the PO is interrupted by a call alerting him that the police are bringing in a girl involved in a street fight. She is being charged with assault—again. Harlston anticipates a long, busy night.

The girl being brought in is 14 years of age and goes by her street name, "Decca." Streetwise, she has learned to cover her vulnerability with a defiant attitude and abusive vocabulary. She fidgets nervously as she waits for her intake interview. A file check reveals that Decca lives with her mother and several siblings. The father does not live in the home, and the family has a history of court referrals.

Harlston learns that James's parents have just arrived. He tells them their son will be held until his detention hearing, usually occurring within 48 hours. His parents express their disappointment; they want to take James home tonight. The PO explains the seriousness of the charges and the state law allowing juveniles to be tried in adult court for offenses as serious as aggravated robbery. If James is transferred to adult court, he could be sentenced to prison. The young man is lucky; his parents express their love and pledge to stand by him. Decca is not so fortunate. When her mother is contacted, she tells the probation officer: "Do whatever you want with her—I'm tired."

The night is young, and Harlston learns the police are bringing in two more youths. Detention center staff prepare for overcrowding by placing temporary cots in the dining area of the 10-bed facility.

of rights tend to be finessed, and the norm is for parents to encourage the child to discuss his or her participation in the alleged offense with the intake officer" (1980: 304; Feld, 1988). When defense attorneys are present in juvenile court, tension is inherent in their responsibilities to the client: "a choice between the traditional adversary role (or the procedural model that regulates professional behavior in the criminal court) and the historic treatment or rehabilitative concerns of the family [juvenile] court" (Fabricant, 1983: 41). Barry Feld reports that even when juveniles are represented by counsel, "attorneys may not be capable of or committed to representing their juvenile clients in an effective adversarial manner. Organizational pressures to cooperate, judicial hostility toward adversarial litigants, role ambiguity created by the dual goals of rehabilitation and punishment, reluctance to help juveniles 'beat a case,' or an internalization of a court's treatment philosophy may compromise the role of counsel in juvenile court" (1988: 395). Indeed, he notes that the presence of counsel may actually be disadvantageous to the juvenile—those represented by attorneys tending to receive more severe dispositions. Nevertheless, Feld, a law professor, advocates legislation that mandates counsel and does not permit a waiver of this important constitutional right.

The **social service function** involves an assessment of the child's situation—home, school, physical, and psychological—and can provide the basis for *adjusting* the case, handling it informally without the filing of a petition. This happens in about half of the cases reaching the juvenile court, when the situation is not serious, when the matter can best be handled by the family, and when neither the child nor the public is in any danger. When the child is in conflict with parents or school officials, the worker may serve as a mediator.

IN THE EIGHTH JUDICIAL DISTRICT COURT OF THE STATE OF NEVADA
IN AND FOR THE
COUNTY OF CLARK JUVENILE DIVISION

INFORMAL SUPERVISION AGREEMENT
In the matter of Michael Nelson
DATE OF BIRTH: July 12, 1987
COMPLAINT: School Vandalism

The minor admits the alleged offense as stated above.

The minor understands that an Informal Supervision period is an attempt by Clark County Juvenile Court Services, the minor, and his parents to resolve the alleged problems without formal judicial action.

The minor does hereby waive the right to a speedy trial and understands that he has the right to legal counsel and the right to remain silent throughout these proceedings and hereby waives these rights.

The minor understands that any information obtained during the supervision period will be admissible in evidence at any adjudicatory hearing and that the minor may withdraw from the Informal Supervision process at any time and demand an adjudicatory hearing.

The minor understands that the Clark County Juvenile Court Services or the District Attorney reserves the right to proceed on any petition heretofore filed against the undersigned and/or to proceed on other petitions for any new offense and may proceed to seek an adjudication on the pending matter in the event the minor fails to cooperate in the attempt at adjustment.

The minor and his parents further understand that the terms of this Informal Supervision Agreement are as follows:

1. That the minor will report in person to Probation Officer John Kerwin at the Clark County Juvenile Court Services, 3401 East Bonanza Road, Las Vegas, Nevada every Monday, on a weekly basis, until May 30, 2001.

2. That the minor will obey all laws of the city, county, state, and federal governments.

3. That the minor will attend school, unless legally excused, and make every effort to maintain good conduct and an acceptable scholastic record.

4. That the minor will obey the reasonable and proper orders of his parents.

5. That the parents agree to make restitution for the damage caused by the minor to school property.

We agree to the terms and conditions of this Informal Supervision Agreement and waive the rights as stated above.

Signed *Doris Nelson*   Date __2/27/02__
   (Parent)

Signed *Kevin Nelson*   Date __2/27/02__
   (Parent)

Signed **Michael Nelson**   Date __Feb. 27, 2002__
   (Minor)

ORDER
Good cause appearing, therefore, the minor is placed under Supervision for a period of 90 days, reviewable (if a petition was filed) on the 30th Day of May, 2002 at the hour of 10:00 A.M.
   Dated this February 28, 2002

Michael Harrison
   (Judge or Referee)

FIGURE 2.4 *Informal Probation Agreement.*

(*Source:* Clark County, Nevada, Juvenile Division.)

If the young person and parents agree to informal processing, the juvenile can be placed under supervision of a probation officer, usually for a period of 90 days (Figure 2.4). Although this may save the young person and his or her parents from the trauma of court action, unofficial handling has its critics. Informal processing requires an explicit or tacit admission of guilt. The substantial advantages that accrue from this admission (the avoidance of court action) also act as an incentive to confess. This approach casts doubt on the voluntariness and truthfulness of admissions of guilt. About 20 percent of delinquency cases brought to the juvenile court result in "unofficial probation."

The period of **informal probation** can be a crucial time in the life of a young person. If successful, the youngster may avoid further juvenile court processing; if unsuccessful, the child will face the labyrinth that is the juvenile court process and the serious consequences that can result. No one is more aware of this than the PO who, using all the skills and resources at the officer's command, attempts to assist the youngster and the youngster's parent(s) through the crisis. Counseling, group therapy, tutoring, vocational guidance, psychiatric and psychological treatment, and recreational services, if they are available, will be put to use to help the young person. If the intake worker is professionally trained, he or she may provide the counseling, thus avoiding the time-consuming referral process—a family is most effectively aided at the time of crisis. If informal efforts are unsuccessful, the PO can file a petition that will make the case an official one.

During the intake process, the PO must determine if the case is to be referred—*petitioned*—to the court for adjudication. Of the more than 1.5 million delinquency cases received annually by the juvenile court, a little more than half are petitioned; more than 125,000 status offense cases are petitioned annually. The filing of a petition is made through the prosecutor or directly via the clerk of the court who sets a date for the first of three types of juvenile court hearing.

Juvenile Intake in Grant County (Marion), Indiana.   Most cases received by the probation department are referred by school officials and law enforcement officers after receiving and investigating complaints from private citizens. Referring agents complete an intake information form, and on receipt, the probation department orders the child and his or her parent(s)/guardian(s) to report to the probation office for a preliminary inquiry.

The preliminary inquiry is conducted by the intake PO for the purpose of determining whether the child committed a delinquent act and the interests of society or the child require further action. The PO advises the child and parents of the nature of the inquiry, the alleged offense, and their constitutional rights. If the child and parents

Juvenile Intake in Texas

In Brazoria County, Texas, each juvenile referral to the department is evaluated by an intake officer, taking into consideration the nature of the offense and the juvenile's referral history. If additional contact with the juvenile is required, the intake officer schedules an interview with the family to assist in the evaluation of the juvenile's school performance, behavior, and family situation. Following the assessment, the intake officer makes a recommendation using state-mandated progressive sanction guidelines and pertinent departmental guidelines. In turn, the Assistant District Attorney considers the officer's recommendation and directs the course of action taken on any charge.

In Harris County (Houston), law enforcement officers may take a juvenile to one of two intake screening units at the Juvenile Probation Department. Intake screening is responsible for assessing immediate circumstances and deciding where the youth will stay prior to a court hearing. Two 24-hour intake units receive and review incoming cases.

Younger, nonviolent offenders may be offered the option of voluntary participation in the Deferred Prosecution Program. This program guides youth through 6 months of intensive counseling and supervision aimed at diverting them from further entry into the juvenile justice system. When a youth is believed to present a threat to the community or to him- or herself, the youth will be held in detention awaiting a court hearing.

choose to discuss the alleged offense, and if there is a determination of delinquency, the PO recommends to the court and to the prosecutor's office either that a formal petition alleging delinquency be filed or that the matter be adjusted informally.

If the PO decides during the preliminary inquiry that an informal adjustment should be entered into, parent(s) and child must complete a preliminary investigation form that provides information about the child and the child's family: offense, education, siblings, employment, hobbies, and recreation. An agreement is negotiated, and the child and parent(s) sign an informal agreement form describing the disposition agreed on and the terms of that disposition—for example, driver's license restriction, curfew, sessions with a PO, or referral to a community treatment—drug or alcohol—program or for psychological treatment. An informal adjustment agreement cannot extend beyond 6 months. If at the end of that time the terms have not been followed, or if the child commits another offense, the original charges can be filed with the court as a petition. If the PO recommends a petition instead of an informal adjustment, the prosecutor will file same with the court alleging delinquency.

Preliminary Hearing

Preliminary hearings consider those matters that must be dealt with before the case can proceed further. At the first hearing, the judge (or in some jurisdictions a referee) informs the parties involved of the charges in the petition and of their rights in the proceeding. If the case involves an abused, neglected, or dependent child, a **guardian ad litem** is usually appointed to act as an advocate for the child. Depending on the jurisdiction, this person may be an attorney or trained lay advocate, often a volunteer. If appropriate, the hearing may be used to determine whether an alleged delinquent should remain in detention or a shelter. If the judge determines, usually with the help of the probation officer, that the respondent's behavior makes him or her a danger to him- or herself or to the safety of others, or that he or she will probably not return to court voluntarily, the judge can order that the child remain in or be remanded to custody.

Detention facilities for juveniles have generally been inadequate. In some jurisdictions, they are merely separate sections of an adult jail. The 1974 Juvenile Justice and Delinquency Prevention Act requires "sight and sound" separation of juveniles held under juvenile court jurisdiction. The statute does not apply to youth in adult facilities prosecuted as adults in state court. California outlawed the practice of jailing of juveniles in 1986, and Utah makes the practice a misdemeanor.

Guardian Ad Litem

Dependent, neglected, or abused children and status offenders may be placed in foster care or a residential shelter. Under such circumstances, the judge will often appoint a temporary guardian for the child, a *guardian ad litem*, usually a representative of a child welfare agency, but sometimes a relative or friend of the family or lay volunteer. The judge may also issue an order of protection containing specific restrictions on a potential abuser or assailant, a violation of which allows the penalties for contempt of court—summary imprisonment. In Summit County, Ohio, the juvenile court *guardian ad litem's* role is to protect the interests of children who have been victimized by their caregivers in cases of abuse, neglect, and dependency throughout the court process. The guardian investigates, advocates, and monitors their cases and submits a written report at all court hearings recommending their findings as to what is in the best interest of the child. Volunteers must complete an intensive 40-hour training program and maintain 12 hours of continuing education annually.

Abusive Confinement

"Subjecting youth to abusive and unlawful conditions of confinement serves only to increase rates of violence and recidivism and to propel children into the adult criminal justice system" (Puritz and Scali, 1998: xi).

In New York City, the primary detention facility for juveniles, Spofford Juvenile Center in the Bronx, has been plagued with violence and other problems characteristic of adult jails. The facility was closed in 1998, but only briefly: Dramatic increases in young persons awaiting adjudication led the city—which has been holding up to 100 youngsters, some as young as 10 years of age, in a jail barge for adults—to reopen Spofford. The Cook County (Chicago) Juvenile Temporary Detention Center (Audy Home) has been beset with problems, including the assault and gang rape of residents, although there have been some improvements in more recent years (Marx, 1998). This facility houses youngsters 10 to 17 years of age, and although it was built to hold 498 children, it often houses as many as 200 more who sleep on cots in the common areas.

Kent County (Grand Rapids), Michigan, Juvenile Detention.   The facility, which was opened in 1963, provides secure custodial care for a maximum of 45 youngsters, 12 to 16 years of age, in three living units: two for boys and one coeducational. Forty-seven staff members are responsible for programmed activities in which the emphasis is on group living through a behavioral management program. A token economy (discussed in chapter 8) is used, permitting residents to earn points for engaging in positive behavior. These points are necessary for the youth to participate in various recreational activities and to purchase special snacks. Detention facility activities are designed to provide the staff with opportunities to understand the youngsters better and, at the same time, offer outlets for active, healthy adolescents who are living under controlled conditions.

Individualized instruction is provided at each resident's actual functioning level, and volunteer tutors are available for additional help in reading and math. Students earn credits toward a diploma, and these are transferred to an appropriate school program when the resident leaves the facility. Daily use is made of the gymnasium and outdoor athletic fields. In addition, teams from other local juvenile facilities are invited to compete at the facility in various athletic events. Many college, civic, and other community groups provide special activities and seasonal parties for the residents. A day room within each living unit provides an area for a variety of leisure-time activities, such as ping-pong and other table games, and television. A video cassette recorder is used for educational and entertaining movies. Adjoining the day rooms are quiet rooms that provide private space for letter writing and reading. A shop stocked with snacks, games, cards, and magazines provides an opportunity for youngsters to spend some of the points they have earned for good behavior. A separate game room with unique activities is also available on a privilege basis. Medical, dental, psychological, and religious services are available for each resident.

Jefferson County, Texas, Juvenile Detention.   The detention center can house 48 juveniles who are provided constant supervision by staff who through their interactions attempt to show concern and provide a positive role model. Highly structured programming centers around academics and recreation: The local school district provides teachers, and the center has indoor and outdoor recreational facilities.

A behavioral approach (discussed in chapter 9) attempts to maintain good behavior and provides consistent consequences for inappropriate actions. Every resident is assigned a probation officer who maintains regular contact with the juvenile's family and informs them of their child's progress.

In-Home Detention.   In Dauphin County (Harrisburg), Pennsylvania, the Juvenile Probation Department uses *in-home detention*, which provides supervision for juveniles who otherwise would be held in a detention facility. The program has two POs who share a caseload that does not exceed 14 youngsters. The clients are visited once or twice a day at home, school, or place of employment. A rigidly enforced curfew is set in cooperation with the youngster's parents. In-home detention is limited to 60 continuous days.

Candidates for the program are referred by the juvenile intake PO or juvenile "line" PO for juveniles who are awaiting a disposition based on allegations of delinquency. If the In-Home Detention Unit has already screened the case, admittance occurs immediately after the detention hearing. Otherwise, admission occurs at the earliest possible time after a determination to accept. The criteria for a referral to the program include

1. *Age.* The youngster must be between 10 and 17 years of age.
2. *Home.* The juvenile must have a home, real or surrogate, in which he or she may be placed, and its location must not offer a geographic impediment to daily supervision.
3. *Parents.* The youngster's parents, at the very least, must not be resistive to daily supervision of their child.
4. *Client.* The juvenile must not present a distinct, serious threat to the community and must exhibit a cooperative attitude concerning the basic elements of the program, including
    a. Daily contacts by a PO
    b. Daily school attendance/employment
    c. A curfew
    d. Compliance with other individualized guidelines as set forth by the PO

Youngsters who become involved in delinquent activity, who persistently evade supervision, or who exhibit persistent uncooperative and belligerent behavior may be removed from the program by probation administrators. A youngster is terminated from the program when the court makes a disposition of the case. The day before a juvenile in the program is scheduled to appear in court, a written report on his or her attitude and adjustment while in the program is given to the judge, district attorney, and defense counsel. This report can influence the court's disposition.

In Cuyahoga County (Cleveland), Ohio, the Home Detention Project has been in existence since 1981 and was established as an alternative to the "warehousing" of juveniles in the detention center. Youngsters referred to the juvenile court as delinquents or status offenders may be assigned to the program at intake, or at any time before disposition. To provide the program's staff with the legal authority to send a youth to the detention home if his or her behavior subsequently requires it, each juvenile is technically admitted to the detention center. Afterward, youngsters and their parents or guardians meet with the program supervisor to discuss and sign a contract delineating the rules of home arrest, a violation of which can cause a referral to the detention center.

In-home detention usually lasts 17 days, and each youth is assigned to a caseworker who ensures all court dates are met. The caseworker also works to keep the youngster out of any further trouble by counseling and spending time with him or her, having lunch together, attending sports events, and similar activities. Every day, unscheduled face-to-face contacts with the youth occur, and the caseworker also contacts the parents daily. The caseworker maintains a log that documents compliance (or lack of it) with the program requirements. Teachers are asked to complete a daily school report form that verifies attendance and behavior. Before the court hearing, the caseworker provides the judge/referee with a report summarizing the youngster's history in the program (Ball, Huff, and Lilly, 1988).

Home confinement can also include electronic monitoring (Figure 2.5) discussed in chapter 13.

In The Circuit Court of Cook County, Illinois

In the Interest of   )
)
_____ A Minor   )   Petition #_____

ORDER OF HOME CONFINEMENT WITH ELECTRONIC MONITORING

_____ Pre-Adjudication   _____ Pre-Dispositional   _____ Dispositional

This Cause now coming to be heard upon the petition filed herein and the appearance of the parent and the minor respondent being now in open court in his/her own proper person and the court having jurisdiction of all parties to this cause and the subject matter, finds that:

_____ There has been a finding of probable cause and urgent and immediate necessity and that the minor respondent is subject to confinement in the Juvenile Temporary Detention Center.

_____ The minor respondent has been adjudicated a delinquent minor and is pending a dispositional hearing and is subject to confinement in the Juvenile Temporary Detention Center.

_____ The minor respondent was placed on probation and a violation of probation hearing is pending and that there has been a finding of urgent and immediate necessity subjecting the minor to confinement in the Juvenile Temporary Detention Center.

Having considered the nature and circumstances of the pending offense(s), the history of delinquency charges and the propensity of the minor to abscond, the court finds that the unconditional release of said respondent, while pending either adjudication, disposition, or under an order of probation, would not provide the necessary protection of the respondent or the person or property of another. The court may place the respondent on home confinement in the home of his/her parent(s) in lieu of secure detention. Minor respondent is determined to be eligible for electronically monitored home confinement under the supervision of the probation department:

IT IS THEREFORE ORDERED THAT THE MITTIMUS OF THE MINOR RESPONDENT TO THE JUVENILE TEMPORARY DETENTION CENTER BE STAYED AND THE MINOR IS DIRECTED IMMEDIATELY TO THE HOME OF HIS/HER PARENT(S) OR GUARDIAN(S) SUBJECT TO THE FOLLOWING TERMS AND CONDITIONS:

1. MINOR must wear an electronic monitoring transmitter, 24 hours a day, during the term of this order;
2. MINOR must appear at all subsequent court hearings;
3. MINOR must reside and remain within the home of his/her parent(s) or guardian(s);
4. MINOR'S absences from home are limited to school attendance, emergency medical attention, and religious services as approved in advance by the probation officer;
5. MINOR must attend school and return home immediately after his/her last class;
6. MINOR must make himself/herself available to a probation officer's visits and telephone calls for the purpose of verifying compliance with this order;
7. MINOR must not consume or possess any alcohol or controlled substances;
8. MINOR must not violate any criminal statue of any jurisdiction, and shall not possess a firearm or any other dangerous weapons;
9. MINOR must maintain positive electronic connection at all times with a field monitoring device placed in the home;
10. MINOR and parent(s) or guardian(s) must permit the sheriff to enter the home to inspect, protect, or retrieve electronic monitoring equipment.

FIGURE 2.5 *Order of Home Confinement with Electronic Monitoring.*

(*Source:* Cook County, Illinois, Circuit Court.)

The minor applies to the Court for conditional release from detention under an Order of Home Confinement with Electronic Monitoring.

❏ MINOR understands that he/she will wear an Electronic Monitoring transmitter on his/her ankle 24 hours a day.
❏ MINOR understands that he/she will not be allowed to leave his/her home without Court permission.
❏ MINOR agrees not to damage or tamper with the Electronic Monitoring Equipment.
❏ MINOR understands the he/she will receive phone calls and will allow visits from the Probation Department and the Sheriff's Department to verify that he/she is home and to inspect, secure and retrieve the Electronic Monitoring equipment placed in his/her home and upon his/her person.
❏ MINOR understands that he/she will not violate any laws including use of alcohol or drugs and possession or use of weapons.
❏ MINOR understands that violating the Order of Home Confinement with Electronic Monitoring will constitute reasonable cause for his/her immediate detention in the Juvenile Temporary Detention Center.

THE COURT HEREBY RETAINS JURISDICTION OF THIS CAUSE FOR THE PURPOSE OF MAK-ING SUCH FURTHER ORDERS, AS THE COURT SHALL DEEM TO BE IN THE BEST INTEREST OF THE MINOR RESPONDENT AND THE PUBLIC.

THE MINOR RESPONDENT WILL IMMEDIATELY BE DETAINED WITHIN THE COOK COUNTY JUVENILE TEMPORARY DETENTION CENTER BY ANY LAW ENFORCEMENT OFFICER PRE-SENTING A VERIFIED AFFIDAVIT DECLARING A BONA FIDE BREACH OF THE ELECTRONIC MONITORING SYSTEM INSTALLED UPON THE PERSON OF THE MINOR RESPONDENT.

THE HOME CONFINEMENT OFFICERS SHALL IMMEDIATELY RETURN THE MINOR TO THE JUVENILE TEMPORARY DETENTION CENTER FOR SECURE DETENTION IN THE EVENT THAT THE ELECTRONIC MONITORING EQUIPMENT CANNOT BE PROPERLY INSTALLED IN THE MINOR'S HOME. THIS ORDER SHALL CONSTITUTE THE BASIS FOR AUTHORIZING THE MINOR'S DETENTION PENDING REVIEW BY THE COURT.

MINOR'S ADDRESS: _____ CHARGE: _____
MINOR'S PHONE: _____ D.O.B.: _____ SEX: _____ RACE: _____
NEXT COURT DATE: _____ CALENDAR: _____

I have read and agree to obey this court order:

_____
MINOR

I have read and agree to abide by this court order and report all violations of this Court Order to the probation officer:

_____
PARENT/GUARDIAN

_____   _____   _____
PROBATION OFFICER   DATE   JUDGE

FIGURE 2.5 *(continued)*

Adjudicatory Hearing

The **adjudicatory hearing**—"trial"—is for the purpose of deciding ("adjudge") whether the child should be made a ward of the juvenile court because he or she is delinquent, a status offender, abused, neglected, or dependent. If appropriate, the child (respondent) makes a plea, either an admission or denial of the allegations contained in the **petition**. The plea process has been the subject of criticism be-cause "much of the country either has not addressed it at all or has not fully devel-oped standards regarding the guilty plea process in juvenile court" (Sanborn, 1992: 142). Thus, pleas are being rendered by juveniles who are either incapable of fully understanding the process or to whom the process has not been adequately explained, bringing into question intelligence, voluntariness, and accuracy. This is particularly troubling in view of the move toward a more punitive response in juvenile court (discussed later in this chapter).

If a denial is made, evidence must be presented to prove "beyond a reasonable doubt" that a delinquent act occurred or, in the case of a status offender, with a simple "preponderance of evidence" that the child is in need of court supervision. If the allegations are sustained, the judge makes a *finding of fact* (that the child is delinquent, abused, neglected, or otherwise in need of supervision), sets a date for a dispositional hearing, and orders a social investigation or predisposition report.

Predisposition Report

The goal of the juvenile court is to provide services. To do so on the basis of the best available information, the judge orders a predisposition investigation. The PO who conducts the investigation will present his or her findings in a **predisposition report** that includes the sociocultural and psychodynamic factors that influenced the juvenile's behavior, providing a social history that is used by the judge to determine a disposition for the case. Because the judge's decision will often be influenced by the contents of the report, it must be factual and objective—a professional statement about the child's family, social and educational history, and any previous involvement with public or private agencies. It also indicates the physical and mental health of the child, as reported by a court psychologist or psychiatrist. The report will typically include the following:

- Review of court records
- Review of school records
- Review of police records
- Interviews with the respondent
- Interviews with family members
- Interviews with teachers and school officials
- Interviews with employers, youth workers, and clergy, whenever appropriate
- Interviews with complainant, police officer, or witnesses
- Results of any psychological or psychiatric examinations
- Recommendation, which should include the available treatment alternatives

POs must present their findings with supportive statements as to the actual situation found in the investigation. Other than a recommendation, suppositions or opinions are to be avoided. Sometimes the recommendation of the PO is not included in the report but is transmitted orally to the judge. The completed report should enable the judge to make the best disposition available based on the individual merits of the case and the service *needs* of the young person (Figure 2.6). One problem encountered at the disposition stage is the paucity of available alternatives for helping a youngster. This can be exacerbated by an inexperienced PO who recommends treatment that is simply not available. A youngster will often be placed on probation because of a lack of feasible alternatives.

Disposition Hearing

Traditionally, the disposition stage of the juvenile court process has been based on the concept of *parens patriae*. Distinctions between dispositions were based on the needs of children and not necessarily the behavior that brought a case to the attention of the juvenile court; dispositions were based not on *justice* but on *rehabilitation*. Although

(text continued on page 48)

PROBATION OFFICER'S REPORT OF PRELIMINARY INQUIRY AND/OR
PREDISPOSITIONAL REPORT

STATE OF INDIANA
Marshall County Superior Court

In the Matter of: ___John Smith___
A child alleged to be a Delinquent Child

Date Completed: ___9/25/04___
Assigned P. O.: ___Ernie Grabbits___   Report Prepared By: ___Ernie Grabbits___

JUVENILE INFORMATION

Case No.(s): ___86C01-9309-JD-665___
Legal Name: ___John Smith___
Alias(es)/Nickname(s): ___None___
Custodial Person(s) or Agency: ___Mike and Sue Smith, parents___
Street Address: ___1800 Wonder Valley South___
City: ___Bowling Green___   State: ___Indiana___   Zip: ___47186___
Telephone: ___(219)555-1234___   Social Security No.: ___305-77-7777___
DOB: ___5/22/87___   POB: ___Bowling Green, Indiana___
Age: _17_   Race: _W_   Gender: _M_   Ht.: _5' 7"_   Wt: _145_   Eyes: _Br_   Hair: _Br_
ID Marks: ___None___
Driver's Lic. No.: ___N/A___   State of Issue: _____   Status: _____

JUVENILE'S LEGAL INVOLVEMENT

__Chg(s) pending __Detainer(s) _X_ Inf. Adj. __Probation __Res. Plcmnts. __IDOC

__DFCS Ward   __Violations __Parole __Waived __Adult Status _X_ Other Contacts

DELINQUENT ACT(S) INFORMATION

Alleged Offense: ___Shoplifting___   Date Committed: ___8/22/04___
I.C.: ___35-43-4-3___   Class (if committed by an adult): _A_ Felony/(Misdemeanor)(Circle One)

Alleged Offense: ___Criminal Mischief___   Date Committed: ___9/4/04___
I.C.: ___35-43-1-2___   Class (if committed by an adult): _A_ Felony/(Misdemeanor)(Circle One)

Alleged Offense: ___Vehicle Theft: Poss. Stolen Property___   Date Committed: 9/18/04: 9/24/04
I.C.: _35-4-2.5: 35-43-4-2_ Class (if committed by an adult): _D_ (Felony)/Misdemeanor (Circle One)

Referring Agency: ___Marshall County Sheriff___
Custody Status: ___Electronic Home Detention___

Co-Offender(s)/Status: ___Alfred Doe - pending disposition___
Case No.(s): ___86C01-9309-JD-666___

PRIOR LEGAL HISTORY

Date of Referral	Charge(s)	Case No.	Disposition (Date/Type)
9/22/00	Curfew	N/A	9/29/03 - Warned and Released
4/2/01	Incorrigible	86C01-9304-JS-078	4/27/04 - Informal Adjustment

FIGURE 2.6 *Predisposition Report.*

(*Source:* Marshall County, Indiana, Superior Court.)

EDUCATION, EMPLOYMENT, HEALTH

School: ____Bowling Green High School_____ Grade/Status: ____11th/withdrew/compl.____
Special Educational Classification: __Yes _X_No   Special Educational Placement: __Yes _X_No

Mental Health Referrals: _X_Yes __No

Physical Problems: __Yes _X_No   If the answer is yes to any of the questions in this
                                           section, an explanation is required in the "additional
Alcohol/Drug Use: __Yes _X_No   information" section.

Gang Involvement: __Yes _X_No

Employer: ____Sam's Amoco Filling Station, 111 Elm Street, Bowling Green, IN_____
Position:____Attendant_____ Hours:_____16 hrs/week_____ $ _6.25_ /hr.

FAMILY INFORMATION

Father's Name: ____Mike Smith_____ SSN (if available): _____
Address: ____1800 North Wonder Valley, Bowling Green, Indiana 47112_____
Employment: ____Disabled_____ Hours: __N/A_____
Home Telephone: ____(812) 555-1203_____ Work Telephone: __N/A_____

Mother's Name: ____Sue Hemmingway Smith_____ SSN (if available): _____
Address: ____Same_____
Employment: ____Administrator for Nurses, Vernon Hospital____ Hours: _9am-4pm weekdays_
Home Telephone: ____(812) 555-1203_____ Work Telephone: _(812) 555-3340____

Guardian: _____
Address: _____
Employment: _____ Hours: _____
Home Telephone: _____ Work Telephone: _____

Significant Other(s): ____Alice Smith_____ Relationship: ____Grandmother____
Address: ____1955 North Wonder Valley, Bowling Green, Indiana 47112_____
Employment: ____Retired_____ Hours: _____
Home Telephone: ____(812) 555-6789_____ Work Telephone: _____

NAME	REL.	AGE	ADDRESS	LEGAL HISTORY
Melissa Ann Smith	S	12	Same as youth	None

FIGURE 2.6 (continued)

ADDITIONAL INFORMATION

Youth attended one appointment at the Marshall County Mental Health Center for a prior referral. Reports indicate that the parents were not willing to participate as needed. Youth indicates a desire to take the GED test and then enter the military. However, due to his age, he would need permission from the court to take the test.

EVALUATION/SUMMARY

John has two prior referrals to this court for status offenses. At this time, it appears that youth is remorseful about his actions. Parents appear to provide adequate supervision but, based on past behaviors, may not follow recommendations from the court without continued court involvement.

RECOMMENDATIONS

Preliminary Inquiry:

    __Dismissal   __Referral to Other Agency

    __Informal Adjustment   __Warning and Release

    _X_ File Petition   __Other _____

Reason for recommendation: ___Seriousness of offense_____

Custody Recommendation:

    _X_ Release to Parent   __Release to Guardian   __Informal Home Detention

    __ Formal Home Detention _X_ Electronic Surveillance __Shelter Care

    __Juvenile Center   __Not in Custody   __Other _____

Comments: ___Father is home at all times to provide supervision as he is disabled._____

Predispositional Report:

If juvenile admits to charge, recommendations for disposition (Complete if applicable): _____
Probation recommends the case be set for disposition in order to complete a predispositional report.

FIGURE 2.6 *(continued)*

JOHN SMITH
86C01-9309-JD-665

I. COURT INFORMATION

Marshall County Superior Court
Probation Officer: Ernie Grabbits
Address: 99 Public Square, Bowling Green, IN 47112
Telephone: (812) 555-1446
Defense Attorney: George D. Clar

Judge Bill Newark, Jr.
Prosecutor: Samuel Loven

C.A.S.A./G.A.L.: None

II. SOURCES OF INFORMATION

Mother—Sue Smith

Father—Mike Smith

School Records—Bowling Green High School

Bowling Green City Police Records

Marshall County Sheriff's Department Records

Marshall County Prosecutor's Records

Marshall County Probation Department Records

Indiana State Police Investigation Records

III. PRESENT OFFENSE

A. Official Version

See Bowling Green City Police case summary of events and the Petition for Delinquency, both attached herein.

B. Juvenile's Version

The juvenile made the following statement:

"We (Alfred Doe and I) got the Cadillac on Labor Day weekend. We had been talking about getting it and so I got the keys to it and Alfred drove it from the lot. We took it out into the county near where Alfred lived. We stored it out there in a barn and then Alfred lost the keys to it. We took the car to possibly sell it later. On Thursday, September 16, Alfred came down to the gas station where I worked and talked with me. I was real upset because my parents had just gotten on me about my grades and they were going to ground me, beginning the weekend. I discussed with Alfred about running away and starting a new life. On Friday morning, September 17, Alfred gave me his Subaru wagon. We had devised a plan in which he would tell the authorities that I had taken the vehicle after lending him the keys to get something out of the vehicle. I told him I would go to Muncie and spend time there with my friend, Josh Blanton."

"After driving up there, I learned that my friend was coming back to Bowling Green for the weekend so I drove back here too. I stayed in the wagon, near Alfred's house, that night. Alfred happened to see the wagon the next morning and came by to see if I was in it. He told me that he would pick me up that evening and take me to town. It was about 5:00 P.M. when he came by and got me. We left the wagon in the barn where the Cadillac was and went to town. During that evening we decided to get another vehicle since they would be looking for the wagon. We drove by the high school bus compound and I remembered that they usually left the keys in the vans

FIGURE 2.6 *(continued)*

in the compound. Alfred held up the fence while I crawled under it. The first van I checked did not have a key in it but the second van did. I turned the van around, hitting the white van in its side. I then gunned the van and ran through the gate of the compound. We drove the van out into the country and left it in the barn where the other two vehicles were parked."

"We then returned to town and went by the compound again. Alfred decided to take a vehicle this time so I let him out and he went and got another van. He drove that one out and he went and got another van. He drove that one out into the country and to the barn. We both slept that night in the vehicles and the next day I took one of the vans and went back to Muncie in it."

"During the week, I stayed in the van and Josh helped me out with food and clothing. He and I wrote to Alfred and told him to go to my house and get the key to the video store that Josh had made during the summer. We told him to sneak into my house, get the key and go to the video store and get money." (That letter was intercepted by Alfred's parents on the Friday John was arrested in Muncie.)

"Then on Friday, September 24th, I got picked up for shoplifting some clothes. I told the Muncie Police about the theft of the vans and the Cadillac and they called Marshall Police and reported the incident. Then that evening the Sheriff's Deputy and a State Policeman came to Muncie and got me and brought me back to Bowling Green. I was placed in detention at the Regional Detention Center and held until Tuesday morning when I was released to my parents under house arrest."

IV. PRIOR LEGAL HISTORY

A. Juvenile History

09/22/03 Marshall Co., IN	Curfew Warned & Released	09/29/03	Verified
04/02/04 86C01-9304-JS-078 Marshall Co., IN	Incorrigible Informal Adjustment	04/27/04	Verified
09/24/04 Muncie, IN	Shoplifting Released to Custody of Sheriff Dept in Marshall Co., IN	09/24/04	Verified
08/22/04 86C01-9309-JD-665 Marshall Co., IN	Possession of Stolen Property	Pending in this Disposition	Verified
09/04/04 86C01-9309-JD-665 Marshall Co., IN	Theft of Vehicle	Pending in this Disposition	Verified
09/18-19/04 86C01-9309-JD-665 Marshall Co., IN	Theft of 2 Vehicles	Pending in this Disposition	Verified

B. Previous Supervision and/or Placements

John had been warned and released by the Marshall County Probation Officer for his curfew violation in 2003. Then in the Spring of 2004, John was placed on three month Informal Adjustment for the crime of Incorrigible. During that period of time he was to report to the probation department on a regular basis (once per month), complete counseling and pay fees associated with such programs. He reported on four occasions, but did not complete the required counseling.

FIGURE 2.6 *(continued)*

Following his arrest in Muncie on this delinquency and upon his return to Bowling Green, he was placed in secure detention at the Clark County Regional Detention Center for a period of 3 days. He was released to the custody of his parents following the detention hearing. The court placed John on home detention with electronic monitoring. John has complied completely with the electronic monitoring program.

C. Adult History

None

D. Summary

This juvenile has been before the Probation Department in the past. He was picked up one night at the local Hardees' Restaurant at 2:30 A.M. The probation officer was contacted and his parents were notified. The parents indicated that they had a minor disagreement earlier in the evening and were not aware that he had left the home. His parents indicated that they were willing to deal with the problem and did not need probation's intervention. The juvenile was warned about this behavior and released to his parents.

Then in early Spring of 2004, the probation department was contacted because of his rebellious behavior at home. He was placed on Informal Adjustment for three months and required to attend counseling with his parents.

The juvenile is presently before the court on charges of Shoplifting in Muncie, IN and Possession of Stolen Property, three counts of Auto Theft and Criminal Mischief in Marshall County, IN.

When the juvenile was arrested in Muncie, IN and charged with shoplifting, he confessed to having with him a van that had been stolen from the Bowling Green High School Bus Compound the previous weekend. He also confessed to having assisted in the theft of two other vehicles and the damage to the bus compound.

The juvenile was held in detention pending full investigation of the incidents in Muncie and Marshall, IN.

C. Parental Response

Mrs. Smith stated that "Every time I hear this story, I just get mad. Me and Mr. Doe have volunteered to pay the fees and restitution for damages to the vehicles. I do have one hard feeling and that is if they had just leveled with us, some of it could have been prevented. I feel John has a chance to make something with his life if he gets in the service. But, if he sits around for half a year or so, he will get himself into something else. He took the GED, after the Judge signed an order allowing him to take it, and he has taken the test to get into the military. He also goes to New Albany on Saturday to take his SAT. According to his military test, there is indication he will be placed in the environmental section which is a good field if he applies himself. As far as the Court system, I thought it would move faster than it did. I'm trying to do what is best for the boy and that is what you would do if it was your boy. I don't condone what they have done. There is no reason for it. He has never been short of money, he had a good job, paying good money, and now he has thrown his life away."

V. VICTIM IMPACT INFORMATION

The Bowling Green Community School System, Mr. James Dobson, the owner of the Cadillac, and their respective insurance companies, wish to be reimbursed for their damages per claims filed with the probation department. Those claims are attached in this report. The total amount of restitution requested is $5,324.16.

FIGURE 2.6 *(continued)*

VI. FAMILY BACKGROUND

A. Maternal History

Name: Sue Hemmingway Smith   Phone#: (219) 555-1203
Address: 1800 North Wonder Valley, Bowling Green, IN 47112
Birth date: 9-18-55   Age: 49   SS#: 645-90-1234
Source of Information: Mr. Mike Smith and John Smith

Sue Hemmingway Smith was raised in Marshall County, having moved here with her parents at a very early age. She attended Bowling Green High School and Indiana University. She married Mike Smith and they adopted John when he was three years old, thinking they could not have children. Two years later she gave birth to a girl, Melissa Ann.

Sue was a Spanish teacher at Bowling Green High School for approximately 10 years. She also ran a day care center for about 4 to 5 years before becoming the Administrator for Nurses in North Vernon, IN, which she has done for the past 7 years. She is reported to be in good health, uses no drugs or alcohol, and has never been arrested for any criminal offense. She is a member of the Indiana University Alumni Association and is involved in the Indiana Nurses Organization.

John reports that the relationship between him and his mother is fine, but that they fight a lot. He states the reason they fight is because John does not do what his mother expects of him and she "gets on him." These are not physical fights, but are usually arguments that go on and on.

B. Paternal History

Name: Mike Smith   Phone#: (219) 555-1203
Address: 1800 North Wonder Valley S., Bowling Green, IN 47112
Birth date: 10-14-54   Age: 50   SS#: 671-48-1959
Source of Information: Mr. Mike Smith and John Smith.

Mike is a native of Marshall County. After graduation from Bowling Green High School he was married briefly to Beverly Johnson. This marriage ended in divorce after two years due to incompatibility. The relationship produced one child, a son, who is now married and lives in Louisville, KY. There is still contact between Mike and his son when they get the time.

Mike enlisted in the United States Army. He was involved in the Vietnam conflict, advancing to Sergeant, prior to being wounded in action. He lost one leg and severely hurt the other. He was in Walter Reed Army Hospital and Veteran's Hospital for about a year and then was discharged from the Army in 1972 with honors and full disability.

After returning from the Army, he married Sue Hemmingway. After trying to have children for two years, they adopted John when he was three years old. Two years after adopting him they had a daughter, Melissa Ann. According to Mr. Smith, ever since Melissa has been born there has been a strain between John and his mother. There has always been this resentment as to why she adopted a child when she learned she could have one herself.

Mike stated that John is the type of kid that will not listen, saying "He has to push you to the limit before he will do anything." Mike continued, "John goes ahead and does his thing and then he gets caught, he gets on your nerves." This has been his pattern over the years according to Mr. Smith. "I've been over protective of him. I tried to keep him from trouble and I believe I stood too tight to him, yet, I believe if I had not, he would have been in trouble long before now."

Mike enjoys restoring vehicles although he had farmed for a while after returning from Veteran's Hospital. He farmed approximately 70 acres, raising cattle and hay. The pain in his leg got to the point that he could not take the pressure any longer. They sold the farm and moved into town. Mike reports that his health is good, except for "what goes with age." He uses no drugs or alcohol, except an occasional social drink, and has never been arrested except for minor traffic offenses. He was active in the Veteran's Organization and Random Rider's Car Club, but has slowed down his involvement in these activities in the past few years.

FIGURE 2.6 (continued)

C. Step-Parent(s) History

None

D. Parental Finances

Both of John's parents receive a substantial income. His mother, Sue, is Administrator of Nurses, making $55,895.00 per year. She receives medical and dental care from the hospital and has very few bills outside the normal grocery and home cleaning supplies.

Mike Smith is receiving total disability compensation and benefits from the Army. He receives approximately $31,000 per year, including stipends for the children. His medical fees are covered by the Veteran's Hospital and he has privileges at Ft. Knox and other military facilities. They reinvested the money made from the sale of their farm into their new house. Their home is modestly decorated and they have no extraordinary bills or debts. He enjoys customizing vehicles and takes on the task of remodeling several during the year. This also gives him additional income.

E. Siblings

Mike Smith states that his daughter, Melissa Ann, was born on May 1, 1992, just two years after they had adopted John. They had thought that they could not have children at the time they adopted John. Melissa Ann is now twelve years old and is in the 8th grade at Bowling Green Junior High. She has had a difficult time with her brother's involvement with the court. Being from a small community, everyone knows about the incident John is involved in and Melissa Ann has received a great deal of teasing. She is an excellent student, but missed nearly a week of school, due to other children teasing her after her brother was returned home from detention.

Her relationship with her brother has been strained during this period of time. It is reported that they were quite close prior to his criminal involvement. It is also reported that John was jealous of her because of her relationship with her mother. John has sensed that he really wasn't wanted after Melissa Ann was born. This feeling has been unfounded by this writer, although Mrs. Smith seems to be quite strict with John.

F. Family Relationships

John was adopted when he was three years old. Two years later, a girl was born to Sue and Mike Smith. This addition has caused a great deal of strain on the family. They feel that the bonding of John never occurred and he has always been a problem child.

They state that they love him and feel very close to him, but there are indications these are just "surface feelings" and are not sincere. Both adopted grandparents live in the Bowling Green area and are involved in John's life. These relatives have supported John, although like John's parents, they, too, are not happy about what he did. For leisure time activities, the family typically watches TV or goes boating if the weather permits. John usually worked on Friday and Saturday nights, so there was little time to spend on other things. The parenting style of the family was having expectations of John; rules for him to follow and consistent discipline. As far as on a daily basis, John had worked most afternoons after school at a local gas station.

Mr. Smith states that John has been very manageable except for a few frustrating periods. There have never been any major upheavals, family violence or abuse. The family had talked to this officer in the past regarding the curfew violation, and was also brought before this officer on the Informal Adjustment. At no time did John indicate that his problems at home were getting to the point he would commit a crime to get out of the home. This writer feels that part of John's problem was seeking attention from his mother. He has felt that she was not as close to him as she has been with her daughter.

Since this delinquency involved an offense against the school, John was to be suspended for the remainder of the semester. However, rather than seeing him be suspended, the parents withdrew John and convinced the Court to give them special permission for John to take his GED. John and his family want him to enlist in the Army and leave the Bowling Green area. He has taken the military entrance exam, passing it with a high score.

FIGURE 2.6 (continued)

G. Home and Neighborhood

The Smith family live just on the edge of the Bowling Green city limits in a newly developed area. They have a very nice three bedroom brick ranch-style home. They have lived in this area for the past 6 years. Prior to this location they lived in a country setting approximately 3 miles outside of Bowling Green. Each of the children have their own room and the home is kept very neat and organized. The entire home is a very attractive, well-kept home.

The family has high expectations of John. He is required to comply with chores, curfew and appropriate peer relationships. It is reported that, although John has only a few chores, he has to be "ridden" by his parents to get them done. Generally, John's parents have shown an attitude of trust, support, acceptance and understanding. They have had their normal conflicts with John, but nothing "out of the ordinary."

It is reported by some community members that John's parents have been too strict on John, putting unnecessary pressure on him and grounding him over things that were not major or did not need such action.

There have been several occasions when his parents have caught him sneaking out of the home or doing some things they did not agree with. However, these problems have been generally handled at home, without requesting court intervention. The parents stated to this officer that they were embarrassed that they could not handle their child.

John has been described by Mr. James Dobson, his employer, as a trustworthy person. Mr. Dobson was in absolute shock when he learned that John had been involved in stealing the Cadillac from his gas station lot. John's parents feel that one of the good things John had in his favor was his job.

The parents' main method of discipline with John was "grounding" him. Although John feels that he was grounded unnecessarily at times, his parents feel their actions were justifiable and fair.

Mrs. Smith is perceived as the dominant parent with regard to discipline. John stated to this officer, "When she gets on your ass, she just doesn't get off. She just keeps at it until you either do what she says or you get grounded. She is persistent." John feels that, for the most part, his mother's discipline has been consistent and appropriate.

H. Other Agency Involvement

John's family has never needed or utilized public assistance of any kind. According to John, his parents have always been good providers. Although John and his family have been referred to the local community mental health center for personal and family counseling services, they have not attended.

VII. JUVENILE'S BACKGROUND

A. School History

John has been a student at Bowling Green Community Schools since beginning his school career. He had completed the 10th grade and was enrolled in the 11th grade at Bowling Green High School when the current delinquency occurred. He had a cumulative GPA of 2.929 his freshman year and a 2.696 with 29.5 credits by the end of his sophomore year. Attendance has been good and there were no recorded incidents of behavior problems or other disruptions at school.

B. Employment History

John has worked for the local Amoco filling station for the past year. John would usually work after school each day for a couple of hours and a few hours on weekends. He earned $6.25 an hour. During this time, his employer, Mr. James Dobson, came to know him as a person he could trust and have confidence in. To say the least, Mr. Dobson was shocked when he learned that John participated in stealing the Cadillac from his filling station lot.

FIGURE 2.6 (continued)

Mr. Dobson has agreed that, should the Court place John on probation, he would be willing to continue employing John. Mr. Dobson would also see that John uses his earnings to pay toward the restitution owed.

C. Juvenile's Financial Information

John worked at his gas station job approximately 16 hours per week, earning $6.25 per hour. John owns a small Sony stereo "rack" system, which he purchased last year for $500.00. John has no other income or valuable personal property.

D. Religious Orientation

The Smith family is a member of the Southside Christian Church. John and his family attend church once or twice per month. He feels that attending church gives him an opportunity to think and reflect on his actions.

E. Social Orientation

John did not have a large peer group with whom to associate. He primarily "hung out" with just a few individuals. Most of these were within his own age and grade level. One of John's few hobbies was playing golf, but he had ceased doing much of this in the last year or so. His statement was that he had to work all the time, so he had very little time for other things. John also stated that he was in the French Club last school year, but dropped out of it this year.

John has also been active in the local bowling league, where he has an average score of 198. He bowls each Saturday morning in a league at the local bowling center.

F. Physical Health

John is reported to be in excellent health. He has seldom missed school and has had no major illnesses.

G. Mental Health

Earlier this year, John was required to seek counseling with his family at the Marshall County Community Mental Health Center after he was placed on Informal Adjustment for Incorrigibility. The parents went to only one session, but felt that there was nothing the counselor could do for them or John. They did not return for further appointments. The parents believed that "it was just up to (the family) to get John going in the right path."

A preliminary evaluation and discharge summary are attached herein. The counselor, Don Straight, MSW, indicated that the parents appeared somewhat frustrated with John's behavior. However, they did not seem willing to engage in the necessary counseling to overcome their, or John's, problems.

John takes no medication and has never had any suicidal tendencies as far as his parents know.

H. Substance Use/Abuse

John stated that he had consumed alcohol (beer) on only one occasion at the age of 13, on an experimental basis, but has not made a practice of it. He stated that, to his knowledge, he has never taken any illegal drugs. He does not smoke and has never experimented with marijuana. (This officer gave him a urine screen when he was arrested and it was returned as negative in all areas of the test.)

VIII. EVALUATION/SUMMARY

The court has before it a 17-year-old, white male who has had two previous encounters with the probation department in the last year. Both of those encounters were status offenses. He is now

FIGURE 2.6 *(continued)*

before the court at this time on charges of Shoplifting, Theft of Vehicles (three counts), Criminal Mischief and Possession of Stolen Property.

John Smith reportedly has had a normal childhood after having been adopted at the age of three. He has made average grades in school during his formative years. According to various friends outside the family structure, his parents have seemingly provided appropriate discipline for him. At other times, however, they have grounded him for no apparent reason, other than that he did not do something exactly as they wished.

Currently at the age of seventeen, he has his learner's permit but not his driver's license. This is due to his parents "making deals" with him in response to his inappropriate behaviors. On one occasion, he was given the choice either to report to probation, or tear up his learner's permit. He chose to tear up his learner's permit.

John's recent school grades have been a big issue with the parents, and especially with his mother. Notably, John and his mother had a bad argument concerning his 6-week grades the evening prior to him leaving his home.

In looking at John's overall delinquent behavior, even though it has been brief, there are a number of facts and circumstances that should be chronologized and addressed.

1. Sometime in mid-August, John hid a key in his bedroom at home. This key was to the Video West Establishment, a key which his friend Josh Blanton had illegally duplicated while he was working there. This key would eventually be used to enter the business during the upcoming Christmas vacation. Josh had stated that the owner kept large sums of money there during the holidays.

2. John then participated in stealing a 1988 Cadillac Seville from the Sam's Amoco filling station on Saturday, September 4th or Sunday, September 5, 2004. John not only worked here, but had been entrusted with the business and was looked upon by the owner as a trusted employee. During the weeks following the theft, John worked at the station each afternoon and weekend, continuing to work side by side with the unsuspecting and trusting owner.

3. On Thursday, September 16, 2004, John and Alfred Doe discussed a plan in which John would run away from home. On Friday, September 17, 2004, John took Alfred's 1994 Red Subaru four door station wagon. He drove this vehicle to Muncie, IN, to see his friend, Josh Blanton. Learning that Josh would be coming home for the weekend, John returned to Bowling Green in the Subaru.

4. During the evening and early morning of September 18th and 19th, John and Alfred Doe stole two vans from the Bowling Green Community Schools Bus Compound. Extensive damage was done to the compound gate and fence, including damage to three vans. One of the vans, which was not taken, was damaged when it was hit by one of the two stolen vans. The two stolen vans were taken to the country and hidden. John took one of them to Muncie, IN, on Sunday, September 20, 2004.

5. John was soon arrested for shoplifting in Muncie on Friday, September 25, 2004. He confessed the theft of the vans and told the police about the Cadillac and Subaru which were stored in the barn near Alfred's house.

6. John was then placed in detention over the weekend. On Monday, September 28th, he was released to the custody of his parents, and placed on house arrest with electronic monitor pending his initial hearing.

7. An order was issued by the Court on September 27th allowing John to complete a course of study and all necessary testing so that he may complete his GED.

8. John took his GED exam and scored between the 86th and 99th percentile.

In consideration of the foregoing facts and events, this officer believes that John acted in an extremely irresponsible, careless, reckless and destructive manner. His consideration toward the feelings and property of others was, at a point, non-existent. However, in the past couple of months, John has shown a revived sense of responsibility and remorse for his actions. The parents, as well, have shown more of a willingness to do whatever is necessary to bring the family, and John, back

FIGURE 2.6 *(continued)*

"on track." With this in mind, this officer feels that John may now be able to overcome his more recent delinquent behaviors and begin acting like a young adult. John is honestly embarrassed by his actions; he has already asked for forgiveness from the victims, and he requests the Court's understanding and leniency.

It is this officer's impression, that with proper supervision, family intervention through counseling, and John's acceptance of responsibility through payment of restitution to the victims, John may indeed have an opportunity to become a productive and responsible adult.

IX. RECOMMENDATION

It is this officer's recommendation that the Court commit John Smith to the Indiana Boys' School until age 21. The Court should suspend this commitment and place John on formal probation until age 21, or until earlier release by the Court upon successful completion of the terms of probation. In addition to all of the regular rules of juvenile probation, the Court should order the following special conditions:

1. The juvenile shall complete 150 hours of community service as arranged by the Probation Department.

2. He shall write a letter of apology to each of the victims, as approved by the Probation Department.

3. The juvenile shall pay restitution to the victims in an amount to be determined by the Court. Should the juvenile's cohort in this matter, Alfred Doe, be placed on probation in the near future, John's responsibility for payment of the restitution may be reduced accordingly.

4. The juvenile shall not have regular contact with his cohort, Alfred Doe.

5. In accordance with the parental participation order, John and his parents should be required to attend and complete counseling through the Marshall County Community Mental Health Center. The parents would be responsible for all costs associated with this requirement.

6. The juvenile should also be ordered to pay the normal $15.00 monthly probation user fee.

Respectfully submitted,

Ernie Grabbits

Ernie Grabbits
Probation Officer
Marshall County Circuit/Superior Courts

FIGURE 2.6 *(continued)*

the Supreme Court ruled that the juvenile court must adhere to due process, its *raison d'être* as a separate court continued to be as a vehicle for providing social services to children in need. In many jurisdictions, however, the line between the adult criminal court and the juvenile court has become blurred as the latter moves toward a **justice model**—what the youngster *deserves*—rather than a **social service model**—what the youngster *needs*. (The *justice model* for adults is discussed in chapter 7.) The state of Washington provides an example of this trend.

In 1977, Washington State abrogated the doctrine of *parens patriae* and in its place adopted a new philosophy based on a justice model (Schram et al., 1981):

*   Make juvenile offenders accountable for their criminal behavior.
*   Provide for punishment commensurate with age, crime, and criminal history; nowhere is the rehabilitation of the juvenile offender mentioned as a purpose or intent in the law.

As part of this approach, the Washington Division of Juvenile Rehabilitation promulgated "Juvenile Disposition Sentencing Standards" to guide juvenile court judges in making uniform dispositions based not on the needs of the child but on the

The New Juvenile Court

"The concept of *parens patriae* has largely disappeared from the political and public agenda. The delinquency courtrooms now work more like the criminal system that the juvenile court was supposed to counter" (Kiernan, 1997: 12).

delinquent behavior—a classical approach. This, of course, reduces the role of the probation officer in juvenile court. Colorado, Idaho, and New York have mandatory minimum periods of incarceration for juveniles—a clear distortion of the purposes of the juvenile court. In Washington and other states that have adopted a "hard line" on juvenile offenders, statutes enable reconsideration of severe sentences for a variety of mitigating circumstances, including "manifest injustice." In fact, write Patricia Harris and Lisa Graff (1988), the "hard line against juveniles" is often less than meets the eye: Few of the harsher statutory provisions are mandatory. The state of Washington also relinquished juvenile court jurisdiction over status offenders. Barry Feld (1992: 59) refers to jurisdictional modifications that have narrowed "the scope of juvenile courts at the 'hard' end through the removal of serious juvenile offenders and at the 'soft' end through the removal of noncriminal status offenders."

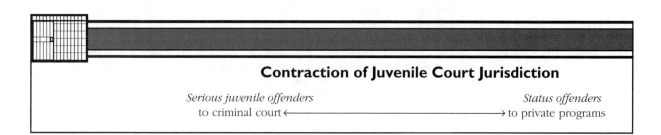

Contraction of Juvenile Court Jurisdiction

Serious juvenile offenders   *Status offenders*
to criminal court ⟵————————————————————⟶ to private programs

Disposition Hearing

William Price and his mother sat uneasily before the judge. The allegations of the amended petition had been sustained on the basis of a full admission. The judge was looking through the PO's report for information on which to base his disposition. His eye was drawn to the psychologist's report attached to the court report. The courtroom was silent, all eyes on the judge.

In the report, William was described as "fairly handsome" and "athletically built." The judge glanced up and looked directly at the boy. William turned his eyes away. The judge decided that the boy might be called handsome despite his "waterfall" haircut and a slight case of acne, but he was certainly not sufficiently robust to be dubbed "athletic."

The psychologist's report indicated that William might or might not be aggressive to girls in the future. "That's not much help," the judge thought, "it could apply to most young men. Chances are the boy feels worse about the situation than the girl. At least he *looks* remorseful."

"William, do you realize you could have seriously injured that girl?"

"I didn't mean to hurt her. I thought it was what she wanted."

"That was a dangerous supposition, young man. I hope you realize by now that any use of violence in any circumstances can have the most serious consequences. Society doesn't regard such things lightly."

"Yes, sir."

"Besides the offense with the girl, you also ran away from the officer who was trying to arrest you."

"I'm sorry about that. I guess I lost my head."

"Are you in the habit of losing your head?"

"No, sir. I just wasn't thinking."

"William," the judge said sternly, "I have serious doubts about allowing you to remain in the community. How do I know you won't lose your head again and really hurt someone the next time?"

"I promise, Judge. I won't do anything foolish again."

The judge turned to Mrs. Price and said sympathetically, "I know it has been very difficult for you to raise William by yourself. It would be a pity for all that effort to go to waste." Tears welled up in Mrs. Price's eyes. "Yes, Your Honor. Please let William come home. I know he'll be good. And I've changed my job now so I can be with him more," she said in a trembling voice. William's eyes were focused on his mother while she talked. The judge noted that concern for her was mirrored in his face.

"How has Bill been doing since he came home from Juvenile Hall, Mrs. Price?"

"Just like always, Judge. He's a good boy."

"William," the judge said, "what would you do with yourself if I allowed you to remain in your home?"

"Go to school."

"I see you are one year behind in your school grade. Do you plan to finish high school?"

"Yes, sir." William's face noticeably brightened.

"And then what do you plan to do?"

"I guess I'll go in the service."

The judge looked at the probation officer. "Mr. Clarke, I'm going to follow your recommendation and make William a ward of the court and place him on probation. If he stays out of trouble during the next year, I want him brought back to court so we can terminate his case. By my calculation he could be off probation about 9 or 10 months before he graduates. This should be long enough so that his record will not hinder him from entering the service."

The judge turned back to William. "I hope you've learned a lesson from this, son. You stay out of trouble and you should have a good opportunity to make something of yourself. The burden is on you. Don't spoil your chances for a career and for a decent life for yourself and your mother."

"Thank you, Judge," Mrs. Price said. "William is a good boy. I don't think he'll make any more trouble for anyone." She and her son left the room, the boy with his arm around her shoulders (based on Cohen, 1975).

Community Assessment Center Model

The Community Assessment Center (CAC), a "one-stop shop" approach for providing juvenile services, offers a 24-hour centralized point for intake and assessment. The CAC has a central booking and receiving facility for juvenile offenders and accommodations for dependent juveniles awaiting placement. It collects information about juveniles' needs, accelerates access to treatment, and coordinates resources from different public and private agencies. The CAC provides referrals to parents and children, expedites court proceedings by providing information to defense attorneys and prosecutors, and strives to streamline the fragmented service delivery system. Its resources are available for police officers, school officials, and other agency personnel. There are a number of communities that have established versions of the CAC model (Olivares et al., 2000).

In Florida

A youth younger than age 18 adjudicated for a crime is referred to the Florida Department of Juvenile Justice. The department has a Chief Probation Officer/Circuit Manager in each of the 20 judicial circuits throughout the state. The Chief Probation Officer/Circuit Manager supervises juvenile probation and community corrections efforts in that circuit. The department provides a recommendation to the state attorney (prosecutor) and the court regarding appropriate sanctions and services for the juvenile. The recommendation is based on interviews and information from the arresting law enforcement officer, the victim, the juvenile and his or her family, and other sources (e.g., school).

When making a recommendation, the department has several options that allow the juvenile to remain in his or her home community. One is diversion, which uses programs that are alternatives to the formal juvenile justice system. It is for juveniles who have just started offending and have been charged only with minor crimes. Another is court-ordered juvenile probation.

If a juvenile is placed on probation, he or she must complete court-ordered sanctions and services. For example, the juvenile may be ordered to work at a local community center. Or the juvenile may be ordered to pay money to the victim, if the victim was harmed or suffered losses as a result of the crime. The juvenile may also be ordered to abide by a curfew or attend substance abuse or mental health counseling. Each juvenile is assigned a Juvenile Probation Officer, who monitors compliance and helps the juvenile link up with services.

If the juvenile does not comply with probation, is charged with a serious crime, or has a significant history of offenses, the juvenile offender may be ordered to live in a Department of Juvenile Justice residential facility for a period of time. After the juvenile offender is discharged from the facility, he or she is placed on conditional release supervision (much like parole in the adult criminal justice system). Conditional release supervision is designed to provide monitoring and services to those juveniles who are transitioning back to the community after being in a residential juvenile justice facility. It is similar to probation supervision. Juveniles have court-ordered sanctions and services that they must complete.

Juveniles on probation, or conditional release, may be ordered by the court (or referred by the department) to attend a day treatment program while they are being supervised. Day treatment programs provide additional monitoring of juveniles and typically offer an alternative educational setting. They also provide additional services, such as anger management classes, social skills building, and substance abuse education.

STATUS OFFENDERS

As the juvenile court has moved closer to the adult criminal court in both application of legal principles and use of punishment, there has been a corresponding shift away from exercising jurisdiction over status offenders. Official intervention by the legal system into the lives of children who have not been accused of criminal behavior—status offenders—has long been a center of controversy. In 1976, this writer argued: "The juvenile court's continued use of coercion and the stigma it creates are grounds for serious concern. The 'bottom line' of juvenile court authority is the policeman, ready to use his revolver, club and handcuffs to carry out the court's orders. A society that considers preventive detention repulsive has, in some strange way, learned to tolerate the threat or the actual use of force against persons who have not been found guilty of a crime" (p. 458).

Those who support continued jurisdiction of the juvenile court over status offenders (sometimes referred to as "minors in need of supervision," MINS; "children in need of supervision," CHINS; or "persons in need of supervision," PINS) argue that status offenders are not essentially different from those youngsters committing delinquent acts—they are children in need of services; without the intervention of the juvenile court, these services would not be forthcoming.

Opponents argue that juvenile court intervention does not help youngsters because the services are often inadequate, and intervention intensifies existing problems by stigmatizing children. In other words, a juvenile may not be able to discern the subtle differences between the juvenile court and the criminal court—differences that are becoming vague (as in the *justice model*). Thus, the child, as well as the child's parents, friends, and community, may react to juvenile court intervention as if the child were facing charges in criminal court.

Edwin Schur warns that the "labeling" that results can set in motion "a complex process of response and counter-response with an initial act of rule-violation and developing into elaborated delinquent self-conceptions and a full-fledged delinquent career" (1973: 30). However, one research effort found that "the majority of those whose first referral was a status offense did not become more serious delinquents. If anything, they became something considerably less than serious delinquents" (Sheldon, Horvath, and Tracy, 1989: 214). Another study (Brown et al., 1991) also contradicted the labeling argument: Youngsters adjudicated in juvenile court on their first referral were less likely to have criminal records as adults than those whose referrals were delayed until further misbehavior.

Status offense (MINS, CHINS, PINS) petitions are most often filed on behalf of the children's parents, ostensibly because the youngsters are beyond their control. The child's behavior is often merely a symptom of a wider problem. Children frequently become status offenders by running away from pathological family situations or alcoholic and/or abusing parents. Girls are often subjected to juvenile court for sexual behavior that goes unnoticed when committed by boys (Chesney-Lind, 1997). Children who are found to be status offenders are usually warned or placed on probation in their initial encounter with the court. Probation can include placement in a shelter, group home, or foster care. If a youngster fails to cooperate with the treatment program, he or she can be returned to court for further disposition, which can lead to placement in a secure facility, such as a training school. The Juvenile Justice and Delinquency Prevention Act of 1974 requires the deinstitutionalization of status offenders, which sometimes required litigation to accomplish. "Slippage has occurred and researchers have documented wholesale replacement of juvenile court institutionalization of status offenders with 'voluntary' mental health commitments in some states" (Swanger, 1988: 211). In 1998, Georgia reached an agreement with the U.S. Department of Justice to stop incarcerating an estimated 8,000 status offenders annually (Butterfield, 1998c).

CHINS in Clark County (Las Vegas), Nevada.   The most common status offenses involve those youngsters who are unmanageable, runaways, or truants. Clark County responds by using community-based shelter care, counseling, and a network of community resources.

Crisis Intervention. Families in need of immediate assistance may come to the Admissions/Intake Division at Juvenile Court, which operates on a 24-hour basis, and meet with an intake officer who is experienced in crisis management. The officer will conduct an intake interview to

- Evaluate and assess the family situation and needs.
- Determine if alternative counseling or short-term emergency shelter care services are appropriate without further juvenile court intervention.
- Determine, if applicable, what services may be directly provided by the juvenile court—for example, information/referral, extended evaluation, psychological consultation, or 90-day probation supervision.

Diagnostic Interviews. The intake officer will consult with law enforcement and school officials and gather as much information as possible to thoroughly assess the family's situation. After completing the assessment, the officer develops a plan of action that requires continued parental involvement; the intent is to promote family unity. The officer will also explore parental rights and responsibilities regarding CHINS. Clark County Juvenile Services recognizes that CHINS' behaviors are difficult for everyone to deal with, and that at times parents become extremely frustrated with their children and look to the court for quick and easy solutions, which are not available. To help CHINS to grow up and behave better takes time, work, and patience. Court programs can be effective only if the parents and concerned others agree to address the problem.

Community Service Referrals. The community offers many excellent resources for families in need, and intake officers are aware of the various services of both public and private agencies. When a family's needs can best be met through a referral to one of them, such a plan of action is preferable. These agencies may divert CHINS from the court and into the most appropriate setting available within the community. Through such brokering, families may access the services they need.

Emergency Shelter Care. Some children are temporarily out of control. When the parent–child relationship has deteriorated to a point at which temporary separation is necessary, the intake officer can arrange for the child to be placed in an emergency shelter care facility and refer the family to the probation division for continued supervision under a Family Services Agreement. The county has contracts with five emergency shelter care homes, and CHINS are referred to these facilities rather than being confined in the court's secure detention center for delinquents.

Family Services Agreement. Some children continue to exhibit more severe and more chronic CHINS behavior despite previous service attempts. For these CHINS, the probation department has an ongoing supervision program. The Family Services Agreement is an informal voluntary contract between the family and the juvenile court that spells out mutual responsibilities and service expectations. Basically, it provides for 3 months of supervision by a probation officer and outlines what can be expected of the child, parents, and the court. Participation in individual or family counseling is usually indicated, and if the child is temporarily removed from the home and placed in shelter care, the agreement specifies the conditions for length of stay, reunification efforts, and financial obligations. Children are expected to obey reasonable and proper orders of their parents, attend school regularly, and participate in a treatment plan tailored to their individual needs. The PO monitors these expectations, coordinates interagency efforts, and participates in direct counseling with the child.

Mental Health Services. Psychological screenings and referrals for psychiatric services can be made in those instances in which a severely emotionally disturbed child comes to the court's attention as a CHINS referral.

JUVENILE COURT JUDGES

Central to implementing the helping philosophy of the juvenile court is the juvenile court judge. However, the position presents an anomaly—although most judicial posts require only a knowledge of law and legal procedure, the juvenile court judge, in addition, needs a working knowledge of several disciplines: sociology, psychology, and social work. If persons with such backgrounds were readily available, the relatively low prestige of the juvenile court would make their recruitment difficult. In most states the juvenile court is located at the bottom of the judicial organizational chart, and the position of juvenile court judge is often seen as the entry level for a future appointment to a more prestigious court. (Exceptions would include Illinois and Arizona, where the juvenile court is a division of the superior court.)

Cook County Juvenile Court

"It is a place where mostly white, middle-class lawyers and judges make decisions about the lives of families and children who are mostly black, Hispanic and poor" (Kiernan, 1997: 11).

In response to these difficulties, states provide training for juvenile court judges, often by, or in conjunction with, the National Council of Juvenile Court Judges. The council sponsors a national college located on the campus of the University of Nevada at Reno. The college trains judges and holds periodic sessions throughout the year on topics designed to help juvenile court judges keep abreast of the laws and behavior approaches related to the problems of delinquency, neglect, and child abuse. Other topics include drug and alcohol abuse, juvenile institutions and their alternatives, and waiver of cases to the criminal court. Some jurisdictions use *referees* or *masters,* specialized attorneys who represent the judge and who are empowered to hold certain juvenile court hearings.

JUVENILES IN CRIMINAL COURT

During the 1990s, legislation in nearly every state transformed the juvenile justice system. "Most notably, the jurisdiction of the juvenile courts over serious crimes, older juveniles, and repeat offenders has been cut back in State after State. The pool of cases eligible for criminal court handling has been vastly expanded" (Torbet et al., 2000: 1). About 20,000 juvenile cases a year are transferred to criminal court (Figures 2.7 and 2.8), with juvenile court judges accounting for about half of the transfers. Most, but not all,

---

WAIVER OF JURISDICTION, MARYLAND

(a) The Juvenile Court may waive the exclusive jurisdiction conferred by state law with respect to a petition alleging delinquency for:

1. A child who is fifteen years old or older, or
2. A child who has not reached his/her fifteenth birthday, but who is charged with committing an act which if committed by an adult, would be punishable by death or life imprisonment.

(b) The court may not waive its jurisdiction until after it has conducted a waiver hearing, held prior to an adjudicatory hearing and after notice has been given to all parties as prescribed by the Maryland Rules. The waiver hearing is solely to determine whether the court should waive its jurisdiction.

(c) The court may not waive its jurisdiction unless it determines, based on the preponderance of the evidence presented at the hearing, that the child is an unfit subject for juvenile rehabilitative measures. For the purpose of determining whether to waive its jurisdiction, the court shall assume that the child committed the delinquent act alleged.

(d) In making its determination the court shall consider the following criteria individually and in relation to each other on the record:

1. Age of the child
2. Mental and physical condition of the child
3. The child's amenability to treatment in any institution, facility, or program available to delinquents
4. The nature of the offense and the child's alleged participation in it
5. The public safety

FIGURE 2.7 *Juvenile Court Waiver to Adult Court.*

(*Source:* Maryland Juvenile Court.)

STATE OF INDIANA
COUNTY OF GRANT JUVENILE DIVISION

IN THE MATTER OF
Michael Silver; DOB: 8/14/82

A CHILD ALLEGED TO BE DELINQUENT
PROSECUTOR'S MOTION FOR WAIVER OF JUVENILE JURISDICTION

The State of Indiana, by the undersigned Deputy Prosecuting Attorney, hereby alleges and represents to the Court as follows:

1. That said child, Michael Silver, was born on the 14th day of August in the year 1982, and was fourteen (14) years of age or older, and under eighteen (18) years of age, at the time of the charged offense.

2. That said child is subject to the jurisdiction of the Juvenile Court herein by virtue of a Petition Alleging Delinquency having been filed on the 4th day of March in the year 1997.

3. That the act charged would be an offense if committed by an adult, to wit: ATTEMPTED MURDER.

4. That said offense charged is:

   (x) heinous or of an aggravated character;

   (x) an act against person;

   (x) part of a repetitive pattern of offenses (even though less serious in nature) in that the child has heretofore been arrested and/or adjudicated for: UNLAWFUL POSSESSION OF A FIREARM.

5. That there is probable cause to believe that said child committed the offense charged herein, and that said child is beyond rehabilitation under the juvenile justice system, and that it is in the best interest of the safety and welfare of the community that said child be required to stand trial as an adult, and that a waiver of juvenile jurisdiction is sought under the provisions of I.C. 31-6-2-4(b).

   WHEREFORE, your petitioner requests that a hearing be set by the Court to determine whether juvenile jurisdiction should be waived herein, and that after said hearing that the Court waive juvenile jurisdiction over the offense charged herein to the Criminal Court of Grant County, a Court that would have jurisdiction over the offense charged if that act were committed by an adult, and said waiver to be for the offense charged, and any lesser included offenses.

   Dated this 6th day of April, 1997.

   John L. Jamisen
   John L. Jamisen
   Deputy Prosecuting Attorney

FIGURE 2.8 *Waiver of Jurisdiction.*

(*Source:* Grant County, Indiana, Juvenile Division.)

states require transfer hearings before a waiver of jurisdiction to criminal court. "Although the term 'transfer' refers to three general mechanisms, only one (judicial waiver) actually involves the transfer of a juvenile from the juvenile court to the adult criminal court. Cases that follow the other two paths may never pass through the juvenile court system" (*OJJDP Research 2000*, 2001: 9). Every jurisdiction in the United States has one or more of these three basic mechanisms, and five states use them all.

1. *Statutory exclusion.* Statutory provisions exclude certain crimes from the jurisdiction of the juvenile court. Some states exclude only the most serious offenses against *persons*, such as murder, rape, or robbery with a firearm. In addition to the most serious crimes against persons, some states exclude traffic, boating, fish and game, and other minor violations, which typically do not involve incarceration. This approach is a purely classical one used in about 28 states (Puzzanchera, 2001).

2. *Judicial waiver.* Forty-six states permit juvenile court judges to "waive" (transfer) their jurisdiction over certain juvenile offenders, usually on a motion by the prosecutor (Puzzanchera, 2001). This discretion is limited by statutory criteria

regarding such factors as age, type of offense, prior record, amenability to treatment, and dangerousness: "[L]egislative exclusion uses the seriousness of the offense to control decisions about adult status, whereas judicial waiver relies upon clinical assessments of amenability to treatment or dangerousness to decide child versus adult status" (Feld, 1992: 66).

3. *Prosecutorial discretion.* In about 15 states, prosecutors can charge juveniles in either juvenile or adult courts. This discretionary power may be limited by statutory criteria regarding age and type of offense (Puzzanchera, 2001). "In most instances when a transfer request is denied, the case is then scheduled for an adjudicatory hearing in juvenile court" (Butts et al., 1996: 13).

The state of Florida, in a dramatic move toward a justice model, enacted legislation in 1981 that provides prosecutors with almost unlimited discretion—"when the public interest requires it"—to transfer 16- and 17-year-olds to criminal court. A study of transfer practices in Florida revealed that the direct transfer provisions have seldom been used for the serious and chronic offenders for whom transfer is arguably justified. In fact, the study found that relatively few cases are subjected to direct transfer provisions and that "many of those who are transferred seem inappropriate" (Bishop, Frazier, and Henretta, 1989: 195). In 1978, New York enacted the Juvenile Offender Law, considered at the time to be among the toughest in the country—children as young as 13 can be tried in criminal court. In practice, however, most juvenile cases sent to criminal court have resulted in dismissal or probation.

There is research indicating a lack of significant difference in sentence outcome for youngsters adjudicated in juvenile court and those tried in criminal court, controlling for the severity of the offense. The juvenile court is not as lenient as its critics would have it, and furthermore, minors are likely to be looked upon differently by prosecutors, probation officers, and judges in the criminal courts. They are younger than most defendants, and even jurors may view the young person in criminal court differently. In the cases examined, there were more findings of "not guilty" in the criminal court than in the juvenile court. "The labeling process may be different in the two courts. While a minor may be looked upon as a hardened criminal in the juvenile court, (s)he may be viewed as a mere innocent youngster in criminal court" (Sagatun, McCollum, and Edwards, 1985: 87).

In part, these outcomes may be the result of the types of cases being transferred to criminal court. A study in Cook County (Chicago), for example, revealed that 66 percent of the 393 youngsters transferred to adult court in 1999 had been charged with nonviolent drug offenses, and 61 percent had no previous prior juvenile convictions at all ("Youth Justice, Separate and Unequal," 2000). In another study, more than 90 percent of the judicial waiver or prosecutorial discretion cases tried in adult

Getting "Tough" Works—For Politicians

"'Commit an adult crime, do adult time.' It rhymes and it sounds good in a political speech. Unfortunately, just because something rhymes does not necessarily make it good policy" (Klein, 1998: 1). "If the rationale for enacting legislation to require youth to be prosecuted as adults because of specific offenses is to deter them from further criminal activity, the legislation is ineffective as demonstrated by the recent recidivism research in Florida. If, however, the intent of the legislation is to provide the illusion that politicians are concerned about juvenile crime and that they are taking action to deal with the problem, then the recent spate of legislation is a success" (Merlo, Benekos, and Cook, 1997: 163).

court resulted in guilty verdicts, with fines or probation imposed on half the convicted juveniles. In one jurisdiction, "property offenders with a long history of property offenses tend to receive a substantially lighter sentence in adult court than they would have received when moving up the ladder in juvenile court. Conversely, personal and aggravated personal offenders with few prior offenses received significantly more punitive treatment in adult court than did comparable offenders in juvenile court" (Barnes and Franz, 1989: 133). A study of juveniles sentenced in criminal court in Pennsylvania found that, as compared with other young adult offenders (ages 18 to 24), being a juvenile exerts "a significant influence on courtroom decision-making, resulting in a substantial juvenile penalty" (Kurlychek and Johnson, 2004; 506): juveniles received more severe sentences than their adult counterparts.

Blended Sentence

A more recent approach to juvenile dispositions is highlighted by legislation that took effect in Minnesota in 1995, creating a new category of serious juvenile offender: the **blended sentence.** These offenders are tried as juveniles but given full due process protections, including the right to a jury trial. If convicted, they are given an adult sentence, which is applied *only* in the event the juvenile does not satisfactorily complete the juvenile court disposition (Stevenson et al., 1996). In some states (e.g., California, Florida), the case is tried in criminal court, which has the authority to impose a juvenile or adult sanction. In other states, the case is adjudicated in either juvenile or criminal court, but the sentencing judge can impose a sanction involving the juvenile or adult correctional system (Torbet et al., 1996).

LEGAL DECISIONS

As noted in this chapter, the juvenile court operated for many decades without attention or adherence to due process requirements or scrutiny by the judicial branch of government. This era of juvenile court history ended during the latter half of the 1960s, an era marked by the judicial activism of the Supreme Court with respect to issues involving civil liberties. Because of the central role of the probation officer in the court, juvenile cases decided by the Supreme Court affected probation services.

In 1966, the Supreme Court reviewed the operations of the juvenile court in *Kent v. United States* (383 U.S. 541). While on probation, Morris Kent, 16 years of age, was convicted in criminal court of raping a woman in her Washington DC apartment and sentenced to a prison term of 30 to 90 years. In juvenile court, he would have faced a maximum term of incarceration until 21 years of age. In accord with existing federal statutes, the case had first been referred to the juvenile court, where over the objections of defense counsel, jurisdiction was waived to the criminal court. On appeal, in a 5–4 decision, the Supreme Court ruled that before a juvenile can be tried in criminal court, he or she is entitled to a waiver hearing with counsel, and if jurisdiction is waived, the judge must state the reasons.

Kent is significant for changing the Supreme Court's hands-off policy that had been in existence since the juvenile court was established in 1899. In its decision, the Court expressed concern over the lack of due process in the juvenile court:

> Although there can be no doubt of the original laudable purpose of juvenile courts, studies and critiques in more recent years raise serious questions as to whether actual performance measures well enough against theoretical purpose to make tolerable the immunity of the process from the reach of constitutional guarantees applicable to adults. There is much evidence that some juvenile courts, including that of the District of Columbia, lack the personnel, facilities, and techniques to perform adequately as representatives of the state in a *parens*

patriae capacity, at least with respect to children charged with law violation. There is evidence, in fact, that there may be grounds for concern that the child receives the worst of both worlds, that he gets neither the protections accorded to adults nor the solicitous care and regenerative treatment postulated for children.

The following year, the Supreme Court addressed the issue of due process in the juvenile court (*In re Gault*, 387 U.S. 1, 1967). Gerald Gault, age 15, had been arrested by the police on the complaint of a female neighbor that he and his friend had made lewd and indecent remarks over the telephone. Gerald's parents were not notified of their son's arrest and did not receive a copy of the juvenile court petition charging him with delinquency. Furthermore, Gerald was not advised of his right to remain silent or his right to counsel. The complainant was not present at the hearing, nor did the judge speak with her on any occasion. Instead, Gerald's mother and two POs appeared before the juvenile court judge in his chambers. No one was sworn, nor was a transcript made of the proceeding.

At a second hearing, a conflict occurred concerning what had transpired at the first hearing. For the second time, the complainant was not present; the judge ruled that her presence was not necessary. Gerald was declared to be a juvenile delinquent and committed to a state training school for a maximum of 6 years—until his 21st birthday. Had Gerald been an adult, older than 18 years of age, the maximum sentence would have been a fine of not more than $50 or imprisonment for not more than 60 days. Because no appeal in juvenile court cases was permitted under Arizona law, Gerald's parents filed a petition of *habeas corpus* (a legal challenge to custody), which, although it was dismissed by the state courts, was granted (*certiorari*) a hearing by the U.S. Supreme Court.

In its decision, the Supreme Court acknowledged the helping—*noncriminal*—philosophy on which the juvenile court is based, but the decision also revealed a sense of outrage over what had transpired in the case of Gerald Gault: "Under our Constitution, the condition of being a boy does not justify a kangaroo court." The justices stated that *even* a child cannot be denied reasonable standards of due process; he or she is entitled to

1. Written notice of the charges
2. Right to counsel
3. Protection against self-incrimination
4. Right to confront and cross-examine witnesses
5. Right to have written transcripts and appellate review

Because of the noncriminal nature of the juvenile court, instead of the *proof beyond a reasonable doubt* standard used in criminal trials, the level of evidence for a finding of delinquency was typically that used in a civil proceeding: *preponderance of the evidence*. In 1970, in the case of *In re Winship* (397 U.S. 358), the Supreme Court noted: "The reasonable-doubt standard plays a vital role in the American scheme of criminal procedure. It is a prime instrument for reducing the risk of conviction resting on factual error." Accordingly, the Court ruled that "the constitutional safeguard of proof beyond a reasonable doubt is as much required during the adjudicatory stage of a delinquency proceeding as are those constitutional safeguards applied in *Gault*."

The right to an impartial jury in criminal trials is guaranteed by the Sixth Amendment, but the Supreme Court decided against granting this right in juvenile proceedings. In the 1971 decision of *McKeiver v. Pennsylvania* (403 U.S. 528), the Court ruled that a juvenile court proceeding is not a criminal prosecution within the meaning of the Sixth Amendment. Accordingly, the Court held that "The imposition of the jury trial on the juvenile court system would not strengthen greatly, if at all, the factfinding function." Nevertheless, more than 15 states permit the use of juries in juvenile court.

In 1975, the Supreme Court was faced with the question of *double jeopardy*—which is prohibited by the Fifth Amendment—with respect to the juvenile court.

Breed v. Jones (421 U.S. 519) concerned a 17-year-old who was the subject of a juvenile court petition alleging armed robbery. After taking testimony from two prosecution witnesses and the respondent, the juvenile court judge sustained the petition. At a subsequent disposition hearing, the judge ruled that the respondent was not "amenable to the care, treatment and training program available through the facilities of the juvenile court" and ordered that Breed be prosecuted as an adult. The youngster was subsequently found guilty of armed robbery in criminal (superior) court, which led the Supreme Court to rule: "We hold that the prosecution of respondent in Superior Court, after an adjudicatory proceeding in Juvenile Court, violated that Double Jeopardy Clause of the Fifth Amendment, as applied to the States through the Fourteenth Amendment."

In 1984, the Supreme Court (*Schall v. Martin*, 467 U.S. 253), in a strong affirmation of the concept of *parens patriae,* upheld the constitutionality of the preventive detention of juveniles. *Schall* involved a New York statute that authorizes the detention of juveniles arrested for an offense when there is "serious risk" that before trial, the juvenile may commit an act that, if committed by an adult, would constitute a crime. In this case Gregory Martin, 14 years of age, with two others, was accused of hitting a youth with a loaded gun and stealing his jacket and sneakers; when arrested, he was in possession of the gun. The Court found that juveniles, unlike adults, "are always in some form of custody." That is, "by definition, [they] are not assumed to have the capacity to take care of themselves" but "are assumed to be subject to the control of their parents, and if parental control falters, the State must play its part as *parens patriae.*" The Court stipulated that the detention cannot be for purposes of punishment and must be strictly limited in time; the Court found that the maximum detention under the New York statute, 17 days for serious crimes and 6 days for less serious crimes, was proper.

Providing greater due process rights to juveniles has had unintended consequences—"legitimated the imposition of more punitive sentences." Barry Feld (2003) notes further that once juveniles are given adult-like protections, judges more readily depart from the pure rehabilitative model, which had formed the basis of the juvenile court.

In the next chapter, we examine the dispositions available for juvenile offenders.

KEY TERMS

houses of refuge	*guardian ad litem*
parens patriae	adjudicatory hearing
child-saving movement	petition
status offenders	predisposition report
intake	justice model
legal function	social service model
social service function	blended sentence
informal probation	

INTERNET CONNECTIONS

National Council of Juvenile and Family Court Judges: ncjcj.org

Office of Juvenile Justice and Delinquency Prevention: ojjdp.ncjrs.org

Council of Juvenile Correctional Administrators: http://cjca.net/sitecodxxcjca_home.html/

American Bar Association Juvenile Justice Center: www.abanet.org/crimjust/juvjus/home.html

REVIEW QUESTIONS

1. Into the twentieth century, what was the attitude toward children in America?
2. How does the juvenile court differ from the criminal court?
3. What is the traditional philosophy of the system of justice used for juveniles in the United States?
4. What were the houses of refuge?
5. Who were the child savers? Why are they controversial, and what did their efforts accomplish?
6. How does the terminology used in the juvenile court reflect its philosophy?
7. Why should the juvenile court not punish children?
8. What led to the establishment of the juvenile court?
9. What is the "justice model" in juvenile court?
10. Why does the juvenile court represent a manifestation of positive theory?
11. How does the concept of *parens patriae* conflict with due process?
12. What are the four different types of cases that may come under the jurisdiction of a juvenile court?
13. What is the purpose of a preliminary hearing in juvenile court?
14. What is informal probation in juvenile court?
15. What is the purpose of an adjudicatory hearing in juvenile court?
16. What is contained in a predisposition report, and what is its purpose?
17. What are the responsibilities of a juvenile court intake officer?
18. Why is it particularly difficult to be a judge in juvenile court?
19. What is a blended sentence?
20. What is a "waiver" of juvenile court jurisdiction?
21. What are the different ways of transferring a juvenile to criminal court?
22. What did the Supreme Court rule in the case of *Kent v. United States*?
23. What rights did the *Gault* decision provide respondents accused of delinquency in juvenile court?
24. According to the *Winship* decision, what is the standard of proof required in a delinquency proceeding?
25. What did the *McKeiver* decision rule with respect to jury trials in juvenile court?
26. What was the issue in *Breed v. Jones*, and what did the court rule?
27. What are the unintended consequences of providing youngsters greater due process rights in juvenile court?

CHAPTER 3

Juvenile Probation, Institutions, and Aftercare

After a juvenile has been adjudicated in juvenile court, a variety of dispositions are available:

- Reprimand with unsupervised probation
- Probation with supervision
- Foster care with or without probation
- Private school or residential treatment
- Training school
- Mental hospital
- Group home
- Community-based day treatment
- Community-based secure facility

We review these dispositions and the role of the probation officer in their accomplishment. This chapter then discusses juvenile offenders convicted in criminal court.

JUVENILE DISPOSITIONS AND THEIR ADMINISTRATION

Juveniles are sometimes released to the custody of their parents for placement in private boarding schools, military academies, and other private facilities. This disposition is most often limited to children from at least middle-income status, and Dale Mann notes: "One obvious effect is to guarantee that public institutions for juvenile offenders serve an underclass population" (1976: 12). Jerome Miller (1992: 5) states that a "two-tiered system of residential care has grown up across the country with a dramatic surge in short-term hospitalization in private psychiatric hospitals for recalcitrant, disobedient, or drug-abusing suburban adolescents." "The effect," he notes, "is to spare these youngsters the correctional diagnosis and the labels which undermine hope—'psychopath,' 'sociopath,' 'unsocialized aggressive.' Such terms apply only to the children of the poor and the racial minorities who populate our youth correctional institutions."

Female offenders often receive harsher treatment in juvenile court because of the lack of alternative programs for them: "Although a sentencing judge may be willing to consider a variety of dispositional alternatives, he or she is often faced with only one program possibility—the state training school or reformatory" (Female Offender Resource Center, 1979: 13). In addition, "once institutionalized, girls are afforded fewer services and program opportunities than boys. Boys, on the other hand, suffer from disadvantages which result from confinement in larger institutions which are filled to capacity. . . . Some people in the juvenile justice system justify the differences in programs and services available in girls' institutions by arguing that it is cost effective to spend the limited funds which do exist on boys who commit more serious crimes and who outnumber girls in the system nearly four to one" (13). There is no indication this situation is changing.

In many states, although a judge can order an adjudicated youth committed to the department having responsibility for institutional care, the judge cannot determine the type of institution to which he or she will be confined. In Idaho, for example, youth in the Department of Juvenile Corrections custody go through an observation and assessment process to determine the best placement; a judge may not specify secure confinement or make any recommendations for placement of adjudicated youth.

Basic to dispositions in the juvenile court is the concept of **least restrictive alternative,** meaning that a disposition should not be more restrictive than that which will adequately serve the needs of the child. The following review of dispositions generally follows this principle, progressing from the less to the more restrictive:

Level of Restrictions/Low to High

Probation supervision

Day treatment

Group home

Residential treatment center

Training school

PROBATION SUPERVISION

Probation supervision is used in about 20 percent of the adjudicated delinquency cases. This disposition is appropriate for children who are not seriously delinquent or in obvious need of intensive services available only in a residential setting. Youngsters with severe behavior problems may be placed on probation, however, not because it is necessarily the most appropriate response, but because probation is the only readily available response.

As a condition of probation, juveniles are usually required to obey their parents or guardians, attend school regularly, be home at an early hour in the evening, and avoid disreputable companions and places (Figure 3.1). The PO supervising the youngster works toward modifying some of the juvenile's attitudes to help the child relate to society in a law-abiding, prosocial manner (Figure 3.2). At the root of antisocial behavior in many juveniles is a difficulty in relating to authority and authority figures. Parents, school officials, and others who have represented authority to the young person have caused him or her to develop a negative, even hostile, attitude toward authority in general. This leads to rebellion at home and at school, or against society in general. The PO must help the young person revise his or her ideas about people in authority by providing a role model as a healthy authority figure or by helping the young person develop healthy attitudes toward others who can provide a desirable role model. These persons may be teachers, athletic coaches, or perhaps a recreation leader in the community.

The PO must be able to accept the young person, and to demonstrate an attitude of respect and concern. At the same time, the PO must be honest and firm with the youngster, setting realistic limits for him or her—something parents are often unable (or unwilling) to do. Misbehavior or antisocial activities cannot be accepted, but the client must be.

1. Attend all appointments as directed by a Probation Officer. Usually appointments will be made in advance, but circumstances may require little notice.
2. Attend School/Work regularly. You are expected to be enrolled in school full-time or work full-time. Both your conduct in school and your grades must show effort. Place of employment and hours must be approved by your Probation Officer.
3. Obey all laws. You are also not to be with any person who is violating the law. Any contact with the Police must be immediately reported to the Probation Department.
4. Obtain permission from a Probation Officer before applying for any license, or if you leave the County for longer than a day.
5. Notify the Probation Department immediately if you change your address, telephone number, school, or place of employment.
6. Obey your parents at all times. Have your parent's permission to be away from home. At all times, your parents are to know where you are, who you are with, what time you will return, and what you are doing.
7. Be in your home by _____ p.m. weeknights and _____ p.m. on weekends unless you are in the presence of a responsible person with the prior approval of parents and/or a Probation Officer.
8. No use or possession of any alcoholic beverages, or drugs, including marijuana. You are also not to be with any persons who are drinking or using drugs. Any tobacco products found in your possession will be confiscated.
9. At any time submit to a urinalysis. Any confirmed controlled or illegal substance or substance metabolites is a violation of probation and will result in further consequences which may include paying for that test.
10. At all times cooperate with your Probation Officer. Answer all reasonable inquiries by any Juvenile Court Representative.
11. Comply with all provisions of the Court Order placing you on probation.

We have had the above regulations given in writing, explained and understand all conditions. We know that breaking these rules could result in Court action, and/or placement in the Juvenile Detention Center. I agree to waive my Fourth Amendment right and allow reasonable search of my home, vehicle, and/or person by any Juvenile Court Representative and/or Law Enforcement Officer with a Juvenile Court Representative present.

_____

Juvenile/Probationer—Date

   As parent/guardian, it is my responsibility to:

1. Inform the Probation Department of any violation of these rules and to take reasonable steps to insure that my child is properly supervised.
2. Provide a proper role model for my child and to refrain from violating the law.
3. At all times cooperate with my child's Probation Officer. I shall answer all reasonable inquiries by any Juvenile Court Representative.
4. Understand that I share financial responsibility for all Court Costs and User Fees with my child and that I am responsible for all fees associated with all programs I and my child are ordered to participate in unless otherwise stated in the Court Order.

   We have had the above regulations given in writing, explained and understand all conditions. We know that breaking these rules could result in Court action, and/or placement of the Juvenile in the Juvenile Detention Center. I agree to waive my fourth amendment right and allow reasonable search of my child's room and vehicle operated by my child, by any Juvenile Court Representative and/or Law Enforcement Officer with a Juvenile Court Representative present to insure that my child's compliance with these rules.

_____

Parent/Guardian—Date

_____

Probation Officer—Date

FIGURE 3.1 *Rules of Probation.*

(*Source:* Porter County, Indiana.)

MONTHLY LOG

Name <u>Harold Bent</u>   Month <u>April 2003</u>

4-1-03 home visit	With youth and mother. Youth is home due to suspension from Jackson High School for fighting until next Thursday (4-9-03). PO counseled youth in alternate ways of handling conflict.
Later: School visit	With principal of Jackson High School, Mr. Jones. He advised youth was found with a small quantity of drugs as well. PO left a school report to be completed and mailed and telephoned youth officer to request copy of arrest report.
4-7-03 Report rec'd:	PO received arrest report on incident at school, which indicates he was station adjusted for battery and possession of a marijuana cigarette.
Later: TX	Called mother at home to advise of the problem as noted in police report and to notify that a VOP will be filed for 4-16-03 on Cal. #52.
4-16-03 Ct. Hrg.	Case on Cal. #52 for VOP for battery and possession of marijuana. Present were youth, mother and undersigned.
DISP:	Denial entered, cont. for trial to 5-26-03.
Later:	PO discussed possible drug problem with youth and mother. Both were urged to contact Treatment Alternatives to initiate an intake interview for drug abuse counseling.
4-19-03 TX	Call to Treatment Alternatives to complete referral. Intake wkr. Judy Watson verified Mrs. Jones called to set up appointment for intake on 4-26, and will obtain a release so the social inv. can be requested.
4-27-03 att. home visit	PO made unscheduled visit to home. No one responded to bell. Left card in door.

FIGURE 3.2 *Juvenile Probation Officer Monthly Log.*

(*Source:* Cook County, Juvenile Probation Department, Illinois.)

Lehigh County School-Based Probation Program

In the central Pennsylvania county of Lehigh, juvenile POs are stationed in the high schools where, in addition to monitoring probationers attending school, they visit classrooms to talk to students and faculty about the juvenile justice system. The program seeks to improve attendance and grades, avoid suspensions, and decrease the need for institutional placement. The POs are available to deal with clients involved in school violations. The officers also make home visits and involve family members in the student's program. The POs coordinate reentry conferences for students returning to school after suspension to help increase their chances of a positive reintegration.

Juvenile Probation Supervision, Amarillo, Texas

Barry Gilbert will visit schools this morning to check on eight youths on his intensive supervision caseload at the Randall County Juvenile Probation Department. He meets with Amarillo High School administrators to check out four probationers, and is glad to learn their attendance and behavior are good. The PO heads for Fannin Middle School and finds two other youths on his caseload are also doing well. As he is leaving, police officers checking a report of a gun on campus ask if he has time to help interview a suspect who is currently on probation. Gilbert values the cooperation his agency receives from the police department and is glad to assist.

Once he completes the investigative interview, the PO visits two other schools, grabs a quick lunch, and returns to his office where he prepares paperwork for residential placement of two children on intensive supervision. It takes time to complete the 30-page application required for out-of-home placement of children in Texas. Gilbert seeks drug treatment for one child and a suitable residential placement for the other.

The PO makes curfew checks on 24 of the 32 youngsters on his caseload. In the next few hours, he will make 18 face-to-face meetings with probationers who never know when he will drop by. Gilbert, a former youth pastor and police officer, makes sure they know that intensive supervision is serious business for youngsters in trouble.

In the course of the helping process, the PO will involve the family and meet with the young person on a regular basis. The PO will work with school officials, sometimes acting as an advocate for the child to secure a public school placement, which is often a difficult task. The youngster has often exhibited disruptive behavior at school and officials are, understandably, resistant to his or her return. If necessary, the officer will seek placement in a foster home for the client (and in some circumstances, adoption).

Orange County, California, Juvenile Court Work Program

The Juvenile Court Work Program was established about 30 years ago to provide a meaningful alternative to incarceration for certain juvenile offenders. The young men and women in the program are an average age of 15 to 16 years old, but they could be as young as 11 or as old as 21. In lieu of serving an institutional commitment in juvenile hall or a juvenile camp, these young men and women literally work off their debt to society on weekends. Typically, a juvenile will serve 20 eight-hour days (10 weekends) on a work crew of 10 to 12 young people. Accommodations are made for school sports events and weekend jobs. Juveniles who fail to complete the work program are returned to juvenile court for further sanctions—generally serving a commitment in a juvenile institution. Municipalities, school districts, and other government agencies pay to have these crews service their property. The money raised helps to offset program costs.

Rules are strict. Youth are not permitted to arrive to work under the influence of alcohol or illegal drugs. On any weekend day, 20 to 23 work program crews can be found spread throughout Orange County. The crews might be

- Weeding the Santiago Creek riverbed, as part of wetlands restoration
- Clearing brush from hillsides adjacent to public schools to remove hazards
- Clearing weeds and debris from street medians and alleys in cities
- Picking up debris and trash from city and county beaches
- Packing sandbags to fortify flood control channels
- Landscaping and collecting trash at county-run regional parks
- Painting over unsightly graffiti found on public property

Juvenile Court Services
BLACK HAWK COUNTY ± BUCHANAN COUNTY ± GRUNDY COUNTY
P.O. Box 1468
312 East 6th Street
WATERLOO, IOWA 50704
Phone (319) 291-2506

RE: Restitution

This letter is in regard to restitution for damages brought about in the

which occured on

If the offense is provable, our office will recommend reimbursement in your behalf. What we need is sufficient evidence of damages. Please fill out the enclosed restitution report. When the form has been completed, it should be signed and notarized on the back side. You may bring the form to Juvenile Court Services to get it notarized at no cost to you. Attach all supporting documentation to the report and return the information to Juvenile Court Services. If no restitution is involved, please write "none" on the form and return the form with any additional comments.

This information is needed immediatiely. If we do not receive it before

without an explanation of delay, our office cannot act in your behalf. You will have to take up the matter in Small Claims Court for reimbursement of your loss.

Please cooperate with us in this matter. We think it is important that juveniles be made responsible for their actions. Also, we feel victims should be reimbursed for their misfortunes.

Sincerely,

Kathy L. Thompson
Restitution Assistant

Enclosure

FIGURE 3.3 *Letter to a Victim, Waterloo, Iowa.*

(*Source:* Iowa Juvenile Court Services.)

Many orders of probation require restitution or community service (Figures 3.3 and 3.4). *Restitution* refers to the compensation provided by an offender to his or her victim; it can involve financial payments or a service alternative. An increasing interest in restitution as a condition of probation has been spurred by an increasing concern for the victims of crime. The *service* alternative is often imposed on youngsters who are unable to provide financial restitution, although it rarely means direct service to the victim. Instead, the juvenile is usually involved in unpaid work for a nonprofit community agency, such as the Salvation Army or the Red Cross. If the youngster violates any of the conditions of probation, the PO prepares a violation of probation report and the youngster can then be subjected to a motion to revoke probation in favor of a more restrictive setting, such as an institutional placement (Figure 3.5).

Dauphin County, Pennsylvania, Adolescent Foster Home Care Program.
Established in 1980, the Adolescent Foster Home Care (AFHC) program, in cooperation with County Social Services and Youth Agency, recruits, screens, and trains foster parents, and provides specialized services to both dependent and delinquent youth. The AFHC program provides carefully screened delinquent youth with

Superior Court of the District of Columbia

Social Services Division   Family Branch

Restitution Agreement
Juvenile Community Service Program

Superior Court of the District of Columbia
Social Services Division–Family Branch

I, _____ , agree to participate in the Juvenile Restitution Program. I agree to all the requirements listed below under the checked paragraphs:

DIRECT SERVICE TO VICTIM. _____ was a victim of this offense. I will work directly for   him   her   for a total of _____ hours in the following manner:

MONEY RESTITUTION. As a result of my offense _____ suffered monetary damages. I agree to repay   him   her   for the total sum of $ _____ , to be paid in the following manner:

COMMUNITY SERVICE. I agree to pay the community for my offense by performing _____ hours of community service. I will perform this service in the following manner:

_____

_____

_____

_____

_____

_____

_____

I agree that this agreement will become a condition of my probation and I further recognize that if I break this agreement, the Social Services Division may request that the Court revoke my probation and commit me to the Department of Human Services. I also recognize that I must fulfill other conditions in order to participate on probation in the Restitution Program. These conditon are:

_____

_____

_____

_____

PROBATIONER'S SIGNATURE: DATE:

ATTORNEY FOR DEFENDANT: DIVISION OF SOCIAL SERVICES:

COMMUNITY WORKER: VICTIM:

CORPORATION COUNSEL: MEDIATOR:

FIGURE 3.4 *Restitution Agreement, Washington DC.*

(*Source:* Washington DC, Superior Court.)

experiences in family living that are essential to positive and constructive growth and development.

The Referral Process. A delinquent youth is referred to the AFHC program by the active PO, either an intake officer or line officer. The foster home care specialist PO reviews all available information concerning the youth and the natural family. He or she interviews the youth and the natural family to explain the program and to determine the appropriateness of the referral. If the foster home care specialist deems the child to be amenable to treatment in foster home care (rather than in some other

Restitution in Utah

The statewide Utah Juvenile Court operates a structured juvenile restitution program. In most cases, youth make restitution directly in the form of financial payments. Others may be ordered to participate in community service programs to earn money to make restitution payments. Under state law, the Utah Juvenile Court may order youth to repair, replace, or make restitution for victims' property and other losses. Probation officers are authorized to develop restitution or community service plans, even in cases in which youth are not formally brought before the court by petition. In such cases, consent agreements are signed by youth and parents, and restitution is often paid directly to the victim.

The court may withhold a substantial portion of fines paid by juveniles to underwrite a work restitution fund. The fund allows juveniles otherwise unable to pay restitution to work in community service projects in the private or public sector to earn money to compensate their victims. The juvenile's earnings are paid directly from the fund to the victims.

modality of treatment), he or she schedules a placement planning conference with the child and youth agency to identify a prospective foster family.

A weekend preplacement visit for the prospective foster family and foster youth is arranged and implemented by the foster home care specialist. In this way, both the adolescent and the foster family have the opportunity to express any concerns they

---

IN THE CIRCUIT COURT OF
JACKSON COUNTY, MISSOURI
JUVENILE DIVISION

IN THE INTEREST OF
James Matthews
M/DOB: 7/12/86
PETITION NO. JV87-10010
LIFE NO. 11326

MOTION TO REVOKE PROBATION

COMES NOW the Juvenile Probation Officer and moves the Court to enter an order revoking the above-named juvenile's probation and, in support thereof, states to the Court:

1. On the 2nd day of November, 2001, the Court committed the above-named juvenile to the custody of the Juvenile Officer at McCune and suspended execution of said commitment and placed the juvenile in the custody of his mother, subject to rules of probation.

2. The juvenile has violated the following term of his probation: To obey all laws and ordinances.

3. The juvenile violated the aforesaid term of probation in that:
   On or about November 22, 2002, in Jackson County, Missouri, the juvenile knowingly altered and defaced a motor vehicle, a 2002 Nissan 300ZX automobile, without the consent of the owner thereof, in violation of Section 569.080 (Tampering, First Degree - Class C Felony), for which the juvenile would be criminally responsible if tried as an adult,

   WHEREFORE, the Juvenile Officer prays the Court revoke the juvenile's probation and enter a dispositional order in the best interests of the juvenile.

   Forestal Lawton
   Forestal Lawton
   Juvenile Officer

FIGURE 3.5 *Motion to Revoke Probation.*

(*Source:* Jackson County, Missouri, Juvenile Division.)

may have regarding the proposed placement. If foster family members do not believe they can meet the needs of a particular youth, they may disapprove the placement in their home. After a successful preplacement visit with the foster family, the youth is scheduled for a juvenile court dispositional hearing. The assigned PO recommends to the juvenile court judge that the youth be placed in the custody of the Dauphin County Social Services for Children and Youth Agency for placement in the AFHC program. The youngster is also placed on strict probation under the supervision of the Juvenile Probation Office. The foster home specialist supervises all delinquent youth in foster home care. In most cases, the youth is also placed on suspended commitment to an appropriate juvenile facility where the youth will go if he or she fails to comply with the terms of the AFHC program. Only the juvenile court judge can commit juveniles to the program.

Program Description. Each youth in the AFHC program is placed on strict probation supervision under the foster home care specialist, who serves as both a probation officer and a caseworker for the youth and foster family. Probation rules include a curfew and mandatory school attendance or employment. The foster parents serve as important members of the treatment team; along with the foster care specialist and any other professional involved with the youth, they participate in defining the needs of the youth and his or her family, and assist in implementing goals established for the youth during placement.

Within 30 days of a youth's placement, a plan is developed based on the individualized needs and interests of the foster youth. It includes goals and objectives to be accomplished by the youth and natural family, as well as specific actions to be taken by all parties to reach the stated objectives. The anticipated length of foster home care placement is also included in the plan. The plan is reviewed and updated every 6 months by means of a 6-month review hearing held at the Juvenile Probation Office. The review is conducted by a juvenile master who is appointed by the juvenile court judge. The youth, foster parents, natural parents, and foster home care specialist are present at each 6-month hearing. The juvenile court master ensures the objectives of the plan are being achieved and makes written recommendations to the court.

Initially, the foster home care specialist will have at least one personal contact each week with the youth and foster family to monitor the placement, to provide support services to foster parents, to assure the youth's compliance with the probation rules, and to assist the youth in the development and implementation of the placement objectives. As the needs of the client allow, supervision may be reduced to a minimum of two personal counseling contacts per month. The specialist will also meet with the natural family at least once per month for counseling and information sharing about the youth's progress and will supervise all home visits made by the youth. The specialist maintains regular contact with school personnel and/or the employer while the youth is in care.

When the goals of the Family and Placement Service Plan have been achieved and the foster home care specialist believes the child can be successfully reunited with the natural family (or alternative placement goal), he or she will recommend to the juvenile court judge that the youth be released from the program. If the youth returns to the natural or surrogate home, he or she remains under probation supervision for approximately 3 months to ensure continued successful community adjustment and to allow the foster home care specialist to provide continued support services to the reunited family unit.

DAY TREATMENT

Community-based day treatment programs are cost effective because they avoid the need to provide the total care environment of residential programs. Project RISE (Reentry into Successful Education) provides an example.

Located in Pima County, Arizona, which includes the city of Tucson, Project RISE is a community-based noncustodial response to troubled youth. Over the years, the Pima County Juvenile Court has found that there is a strong correlation between a child's school problems and delinquent behavior. All too often, school officials and the juvenile court would work in isolation. In 1982, a project at Howenstine School was begun to combine the treatments of the dual problems of delinquency and school failure. This program was a joint venture between the Tucson Unified School District and the Pima County Juvenile Court. Teachers, teacher aides, probation officers, and probation aides work side by side with a few juveniles to provide maximum supervision and a favorable environment for learning. The success of the Howenstine program was responsible for the Sunnyside School District inaugurating a similar program in 1983. Both programs are now known as Project RISE, a full-time day program for about 40 youngsters, combining the best of the educational and juvenile justice systems from which the project receives its clients. The goals of the program are to reduce serious delinquent activity, improve school attendance, decrease school behavioral problems, raise the child's reading level by 2 years, and inculcate positive social values and survival skills in the youth. To accomplish these goals, Project RISE is housed in facilities separate from the mainstream high schools. Students are either transported to school or issued city bus passes. The staff-to-child ratio is extremely low, ensuring intensive daily supervision in an innovative learning environment.

As children progress, their success is rewarded within the context of a behavior modification system (behavior modification is discussed in chapter 9). In this manner, undesirable activities and habits are eliminated, and healthy, socially acceptable behaviors are reinforced. The child's self-image is bolstered by repeated successes in interpersonal and academic tasks. Emphasis is placed on frequent organized outings to broaden the child's growing socialization.

THE GROUP HOME

Residential treatment can be classified according to the degree of custodial care provided. At the lower end of this scale is the group home. The group home may be privately operated under contract with the state (or other level of government), or it can be operated by the state. Generally, anywhere from 6 to 15 youngsters live in the home at any one time. The typical home has several bedrooms and baths, as well as a large living room, dining area, and basement recreation area. The interior of the home approximates that of a large single-family dwelling. Group homes are usually located in residential areas that are in proximity to public transportation, public schools, and recreation facilities.

The group home is for youngsters who

- Are in unresolvable conflict with their parents but are not seriously disturbed or psychotic
- Have inadequate homes and need to develop skills for independent living
- Need to deal with community social adjustment problems in a therapeutic family environment
- Need to deal with individual adjustment problems and to learn about themselves in relation to others
- Need to develop self-confidence through successful experiences

Each resident has daily chores, such as doing dishes, making the bed, or mowing the lawn. Houseparents, usually a married couple with graduate degrees in a therapeutic discipline such as social work or psychology, perform surrogate parent roles by preparing or overseeing the preparation of meals, enforcing a curfew, and helping with homework, as well as other tasks usually handled by parents in healthy families. Youngsters attend local schools on a full-time basis, or they have a schedule that incorporates both school and employment.

There are group counseling sessions conducted by group workers geared to help the residents understand and overcome problems that have led to the placement, and to define goals consistent with their individual ability. Individual counseling programs are provided for those youngsters who need help in preparing for independent living and improving their family relationships. Day-by-day counseling and conflict resolution are handled by the houseparents.

The most difficult aspects of the group home are relationships with the surrounding community—typically, vigorous neighborhood resistance exists to placing such a facility in most areas. Although both professionals and laypersons generally agree that the group home concept is an excellent one for many youngsters coming to the attention of the juvenile court, this has not translated into widespread acceptance of the reality. Group homes, not only for troubled youngsters, but also for persons with mental retardation and other disabilities, have been vigorously and all too often successfully resisted by local residents (Holloway, 1995).

This problem became so severe that in 1989 the U.S. Department of Justice brought suit against a Chicago suburb (Chicago Heights) because the municipality refused to permit the building of a group home for 15 adults with mental retardation (Johnson, 1989a). A similar suit was brought by United Cerebral Palsy against a group of Southeast Dade County (Florida) homeowners who were attempting to thwart the opening of group homes for persons with disabilities (Hartman, 1994). The 1988 Federal Fair Housing Act, which bars discrimination against persons with disabilities, has been interpreted by the courts as outlawing local zoning laws that deny housing to persons with mental retardation, the mentally ill, and drug addicts. In 1995, the Supreme Court ruled that this statute prohibits municipalities from using single-family zoning to bar group homes. In this case, the city of Edmonds, Washington, had attempted to prevent a national organization, Oxford House, from operating a group home for recovering substance abusers (*City of Edmonds v. Oxford House*, 514 U.S. 725). Although we may accept the moral imperative and recognize the value of helping the unfortunate, too often it is a concern for real estate values that prevails. *L'hypocrisie est un hommage que le vice rend à la vertu.*

RESIDENTIAL TREATMENT CENTER

The term **residential treatment center** (RTC) is being used to identify private and public institutions that provide residential care for youngsters, with or without intervention of the juvenile court and devoid of coercive elements associated with correctional facilities—locks, bars, and barbed/razor fences. Generally, the RTC provides a wide variety of enriched services, and the private RTC receives a great deal of public funding. Despite the fact that almost all receive tax-levy money, the private RTC retains the privilege of screening its residents, a luxury not afforded public institutions. One study found, however, that in southern California considerable competition exists for residents between private facilities, and juveniles admitted to private institutions do not significantly differ from those sent to public facilities (Shichor and Bartollas, 1990). Private centers can also mix adjudicated delinquents, status offenders, and voluntary clients in a manner that would not be permissible in a public institution, although the mixing of delinquent and nondelinquent children runs contrary to the prevailing wisdom in the field (Curran, 1988).

Log Cabin Ranch.   The San Francisco Juvenile Court operates a county rehabilitation facility offering residential care for boys ranging in age from 15 to 18 years. The Log Cabin Ranch has a total capacity of 86, and one-third of the overall school program is devoted to vocational instruction in auto mechanics, electronics, building maintenance, and culinary arts. After 4 weeks of orientation and testing, qualified students are assigned to one of the programs. Successful graduates are assigned to job developers who are responsible for the placement of these youths in apprenticeship programs or part- or full-time employment, depending on the age, skills, and needs of the particular youth.

Log Cabin provides a full range of individual and group counseling services to its students. Reports detailing each student's progress are submitted every 6 weeks. Case conferences involving the student, his probation officer, the head teacher, and the assistant director are held at regular intervals and provide each student with individualized attention and feedback. The Forensic Health Services of the Department of Mental Health provides psychological services, crisis intervention, individual counseling, and consultation.

The School Department offers the necessary individualized remedial instruction in basic skill areas, and a learning specialist from the Court School provides individual assessments of each youth's learning abilities. Computer-assisted instruction is available to the students on an individual basis. Log Cabin Ranch is an active member of the Central Coast Ranch League, fielding competitive teams in basketball, softball, volleyball, and cross-country.

Idaho Youth Ranch.   Opened in 1957, the Idaho Youth Ranch (IYR) campus is located on a 500-acre site. Over the years, the working farm and ranch has become a large campus with everything from a nondenominational chapel to an indoor riding arena. The ranch services boys from 8 to 18 and girls from 13 to 18 in five lodges housing up to 56 youngsters.

Referrals must be of "dull normal intelligence" or above, not committed for violent crime, and have failed or been ruled out for a less restrictive setting. The referrals come from private families, the juvenile justice system, and state training school. IYR also provides services for the 44 county juvenile probation and parole authorities.

In addition to the lodges, the ranch includes an activity center with a full-size gym, counseling center, a dining room, chapel, classrooms, carpentry and mechanic shops, an indoor riding arena, and staff housing. All residents of the ranch receive peer group treatment sessions, as well as individual sessions and specialized sessions for substance abuse, social skills, and cognitive skills building. They are also offered many opportunities to build responsible behavior through daily, weekly, and one-time responsibilities through chores, work projects, 4–H programs, and community service both on and off the ranch. As part of the restorative justice principle (discussed in chapter 11), youth who have harmed others in their community will have the opportunity to make amends through face-to-face meetings with the victim in the presence of a staff member trained in mediation.

The IYR Horse Breeding and Management Program began in 1974 as a project to keep a troubled boy occupied, and has grown into a stable of more than 20 broodmares and several racehorses. A regular part of the school day at the ranch, residents learn all aspects of life with horses from grooming and tack to animal psychology, biology, care, and, of course, riding.

A stable of 16 to 20 horses is maintained for resident use. Full-time, experienced instructors guide youth through a planned curriculum. A few years ago, a large riding arena was built through the generosity of a local foundation. In the cold winter months, the arena is a lively place allowing riding and the care and grooming of the animals in warmth and safety.

The ranch breeds and resells horses, constantly working to improve quality. Today, the ranch is home to 3 stallions and more than 15 high-quality broodmares. Each year, 10 to 15 foals are born and raised for sale privately and at auction. In the few years the ranch has been doing this, IYR has become the second largest breeder in Idaho.

Young people at the ranch are involved in all aspects of the horse program. They attend classes about breeding and caring. They get hands-on experience in foaling, imprinting, halter breaking, and preparing the young foals for sales. They attend the sales and show the horses to prospective buyers both in and out of the sale ring. The ranch accepts donations of horses that fit into either the riding program or breeding operation. IYR will find good homes elsewhere for horses that do not fit either program. Some of those horses have gone to dude ranches, become barrel racers, jumpers, and even polo ponies (Abruzzese, 1999).

Camp Wilmont Sweeney.   The Alameda County, California, Probation Department operates an unlocked facility for delinquent youth ranging in age from 15 to 18. Residents first enter the 60-bed transitional unit, and after an orientation period, move to one of four dormitories that house a total of 90 youth. During their last 3 months, residents who have demonstrated a high level of responsibility and positive change can return to the transitional unit to provide positive role models for new entrants.

Seven deputy POs who act as case managers, along with 25 group counselors and 3 psychologists, service the youth while in residence. The treatment approach uses a "normative model" emphasizing the importance of norms (social agreements) that bond people together. Residents are challenged to build a network of prosocial relationships, which will support them as they return to the community. Techniques used include "town hall meetings," guided group interaction (see the next section), and peer-led committees focused on specific tasks. Services available include drug and alcohol treatment, conflict mediation training, and gang violence prevention. Residents can earn their high school diploma and are offered classes in computer repair. Athletics, religious services, field trips, and cultural appreciation events round out the program.

By accomplishing individual case objectives that he developed with his treatment team—an on-site psychologist, his PO, a group counselor, a peer mentor, his parent(s) or guardians—and making positive contributions to the camp community, a resident can earn his graduation from the facility, usually within 6 months to 1 year.

Highfields.   On the former estate of Charles A. Lindbergh, near Hopewell, New Jersey, Highfields was established in 1950 under private auspices and was taken over by the state in 1952. Highfields provides a prototype for many private juvenile facilities throughout the United States. The treatment objective is to give delinquent boys an opportunity for self-rehabilitation by achieving a series of preliminary and prerequisite goals. Few formal rules exist because the purpose is to enable the youngster to develop a nondelinquent orientation through *guided group interaction* (GGI) that has four distinguishing characteristics (Grissom and Dubnov, 1989):

- GGI is a group process involving 5 to 12 group members and a trained adult group leader. Attendance is mandatory.
- The objective is the alteration of delinquent behavior. This is achieved by channeling group pressures toward prosocial goals. Behaviors and values are considered to reflect adaptations to the peer social group rather than immutable personality characteristics.
- The peer group wields genuine power in the treatment process. It may set its own agenda, place one of its members on the "hot seat" (i.e., subject his behavior to extensive scrutiny by the group), or prescribe negative sanctions (e.g., work detail or withdrawal of privileges) to alter a member's deviant behavior.
- Each member is required to explain how he got into trouble. On the basis of his response and the ensuing discussion, he is assigned problems or "roadblocks" that he must overcome. Acceptance by the group comes with evidence of the member's efforts to overcome these group-assigned problems. Status is accorded for assisting others and making the effort to understand the "why" of one's own and others' behavior.

The leader channels group pressures and molds norms so prosocial behavior and the expression of prosocial attitudes are reinforced, and delinquent norms or attitudes are challenged. He manages the formal process by seeing to it that every boy "tells his story." He reminds the group that negative sanctions must be applied constructively and not be strictly punitive.

Youngsters work or attend school during the day and in the evening meet in groups of about 10 for a daily therapy session lasting 90 minutes. The purpose is to help residents develop an understanding of their problems through unstructured interaction with others in similar circumstances:

> The subjects discussed in GGI revolve around the current problems of group members and the group itself. These problems emerge as a result of interaction with significant others, primarily peers, in a group setting. . . . The major emphasis in this technique is on the group and its development, rather than upon an exhaustive analysis of each individual group member. . . . Guided group interaction is considered to be most effective with adolescents because they seem to be more responsive to peer influences than any other age group. (Finckenauer, 1984: 198)

Highfields has no guards or locked doors, and authoritarian leadership is deliberately absent. The 20 residents, who have been adjudicated as delinquents and placed on probation, remain at Highfields for 4 months. Family and friends are encouraged to visit, and residents are given passes to visit nearby areas and sometimes go home on furlough. These privileges can be lost for misbehavior—the entire group is punished for the actions of any of its members. Several studies exist on the effectiveness of Highfields; claims and counterclaims abound.

Glen Mills. Located in Delaware County, Pennsylvania, Glen Mills covers 800 acres that include athletic fields—football, baseball, and track—a 100-year-old administration building, red-brick Victorian-era cottages, academic buildings, and a chapel. This facility is an open institution—always referred to as a school and residents as students—devoid of any coercive elements once part of Glen Mills (e.g., locks, bars, gates, fences). The population of about 600, many of whom have committed serious felonies, resides in cottage houses of 40 to 50 students, subdivided into four living areas of 10 to 15 students. Each cottage has a staff that includes a senior counselor, two counselor-teachers, and a counselor-specialist.

Glen Mills is essentially a school, and the program centers on vocational and academic education. Classes typically have between 10 to 16 students and provide individualized instruction; teacher-counselors conduct classes in the cottage. Like Highfields, Glen Mills is based on GGI; there is an absence of formal rules:

> Reliance upon rules to maintain control in institutions for delinquents suffers from several weaknesses. . . . [T]he delinquent has been socialized in a subculture which places high value on the ability to manipulate or "con" others, especially authority figures. Since many have little respect for authority and a strong incentive (i.e., peer group status) to disobey them, the imposition of rules confirms the delinquents' view of authority as oppressive and provides them with an opportunity to earn their stripes by "getting over on" (subverting) those in authority. Rules are rarely presented (never convincingly) as in the best interests of the boy. They are seen as instruments of control established by and for the convenience of institutional authorities; staff spend an inordinate amount of time enforcing them. They represent a challenge which the boys readily accept as part of a game that the institution finds difficult to win without abandoning all pretense at rehabilitation. (Grissom and Dubnov, 1989: 15)

Instead, unwritten group norms (e.g., respect each other, take care of property, confront norm violations) are closely monitored, with transgressors being confronted in a nonthreatening manner to avoid humiliation; positive behavior is rewarded.

Oregon Juvenile Corrections Assessment Center

The Juvenile Corrections Assessment Center (JCAC) is the central receiving point for juveniles committed to the training schools by the courts. The JCAC is a time-limited program designed to produce consistent assessments and appropriate placements for committed youth in the community and close custody treatment programs.

Male youth who are committed to the training schools are transported to the JCAC located at MacLaren School in Woodburn. Female youth are transported to Hillcrest School in Salem. Within a 2-week period, the youth undergo educational testing, drug/alcohol self-assessments, and sex offender screening. Private agencies interview and assess youth who may be diverted to their community programs. The Close Custody Review Board examines each case, and places the youth in a program that addresses community protection issues and meets the youth's treatment needs. Youth who are not diverted to the community are placed within the close custody system, comprising four camps and two training schools, Hillcrest and MacLaren.

Escapes are not an issue because all a student has to do is request to leave, and transportation is provided—he will be sent back to juvenile court. Disagreements about confrontations and other matters are the subject for cottage group meetings. Chronic misbehavior results in expulsion and a return to juvenile court. The school screens out youngsters who like to intimidate others or who are quick to respond aggressively when challenged.

TRAINING SCHOOL

The **training school** is a public institution that accepts all youngsters committed by the courts. Each training school is usually set up to handle particular categories of juveniles who may be assigned on the basis of age, aggressiveness, or delinquent history. This is done to avoid mixing older children with younger ones, adjudicated delinquents with status offenders, or more disturbed youngsters with those having less serious problems. The training school usually provides a level of security not available in other types of juvenile institutions (although less than that offered in a correctional facility). Juveniles are committed to training schools based on four criteria:

1. A *finding of fact* occurs indicating that the child has committed an offense that would be punishable by imprisonment if committed by an adult.
2. The parents are unable to control their child or provide for his or her social, emotional, and educational needs.
3. No other child welfare service is sufficient.
4. The child needs the services available at the training school.

The establishment of the Lyman School for Boys in Massachusetts, which opened in 1847 for 400 boys, began an era of providing separate facilities for juvenile offenders. These prejuvenile court facilities—training or reform schools—were patterned after adult prisons. They were regimented with large impersonal dormitories. Each provided some basic medical and dental treatment and limited educational and vocational training. Although the juvenile court "forced a breach in the wall of the criminal justice system," notes Jerome Miller (1992: 8), it did not fully resolve the question of whether to treat or punish, and this dilemma "was complicated by the existence of reform schools, which had been around for most of the century

Juveniles in Massachusetts

Under the leadership of Jerome Miller, Massachusetts closed most of its training/reform schools in favor of contracting with private providers—Lyman, under this program, was the last to close in 1972 (Miller, 1992). By 1975, however, the Department of Youth Services (DYS) was coming under increasing criticism because, it was alleged, deinstitutionalization did not provide enough public accountability or security—fewer than 50 secure beds were available in the state. This number has increased dramatically as has the commitment of youngsters deemed dangerous. Although the typical juvenile delinquent sent to the DYS is discharged after his or her eighteenth birthday, particularly dangerous youngsters may, with permission of the court, be held until 21 years of age. Those younger than 17 years of age who are convicted of murder in adult court are committed to DYS and subsequently transferred to prison as adults.

before the juvenile court was invented. Their presence ensured that juvenile offenders would receive the worst the system could offer—punishment labeled as treatment."

Over the years, there has been an increased emphasis on vocational training, remedial education, and rehabilitation through the use of social workers, teachers, psychiatrists, psychologists, and recreation workers. Like a prison or hospital, a training school operates 168 hours per week; this fact, combined with the level of security and services provided, makes the training school an expensive institution in which annual costs can easily run in excess of $30,000 per resident. In Idaho, for example, the estimated per resident annual cost in a Department of Juvenile Corrections facility ranges from $36,000 to $48,000.

One training school, the Warwick School for Boys, is located 55 miles from New York City. It is one of the training schools operated by the New York State Office of Children and Family Services. The school is a pleasant-looking institution with 700 acres of lawns and trees; it houses about 170 residents in several dormitories. Some individual rooms are also assigned on a "merit" basis. The residents are adjudicated delinquents who have committed offenses ranging from petty larceny to serious felonies, all before their sixteenth birthday. The school has about 180 staff members, and there are no walls or gates around the school—security is maintained through the use of supervised activities and a high staff-to-resident ratio. The daily schedule calls for 2 hours of compulsory academic instruction and 2 hours of physical education, with additional services for those who require more help. Both individual and group counseling are provided, as is vocational training in such areas as mechanical drawing, woodworking, electricity, and painting.

The Giddings State School of the Texas Youth Commission is a maximum security facility for more than 300 juveniles, mostly boys (96 percent); more than 25 percent have committed murder. Located in a rural community about 50 miles northeast of Austin, a high fence surrounds the campus of one-story buildings. Only the lockup rooms—for rule violators—provide a prison-like aura. An accredited high school and extensive vocational training—for automobile repair, welding, and building trades—a gym, indoor pool, game room, and television rooms in the dorms are available. Sports teams and arts and crafts instruction are some of the other extracurricular activities. Residents sleep in large open rooms arranged barracks style. The training school provides specialized treatment for violent sex offenders, those chemically dependent, and "capital offender treatment." Treatment includes guided group interaction: members live, eat, and attend class together; problems are dealt with in a group process. Medical, psychiatric, and psychological services are all provided at the facility.

The juvenile facility at St. Charles, Illinois, is operated by the state Department of Corrections. Designed for no more than 318 inmates, it typically houses more than 500 who are supervised by a staff of more than 300. Located on 125 acres of rolling hills in Chicago's far western suburbs, the facility is surrounded by two tall fences topped with razor wire; inmates are housed in cells—those designed for one youngster hold two; those designed for two, hold four.

Los Angeles County Residential Treatment Program.   The Los Angeles County Probation Department Residential Treatment Program is divided into two age groupings: senior, 16 to 18 years of age, and junior, 13 to 15 years of age. One junior camp and two senior camps are secure (fenced); the remainder are open (not fenced) camps. The security camps are used to maintain minors who represent a significant escape risk—essentially impulsive youngsters with a low degree of self-control. In these camps, emphasis is placed on developing self-control.

The system is composed of 15 institutions; 14 are located in mountain settings. An intake facility with 60 beds is maintained at San Fernando Valley Juvenile Hall. Almost all boys ordered to camp are screened here for medical or psychiatric problems, and academic levels are established before the minor is assigned to a camp. Girls are processed directly from the juvenile hall in which they are detained. Deputy probation officers in all camps provide ongoing individual and group counseling to all camp wards. Treatment programs are individual, and the length of stay for each minor is dependent on individual progress in the camp setting.

The principal objective of junior camps is to evaluate academic skills and achievement. These youngsters spend the bulk of the program day in school and work is limited to in-camp maintenance and culinary assistance. The focus in senior camps is oriented more toward instilling work ethic disciplines. Senior youngsters ordinarily spend half of each day in school and half in parks and recreation work crews. A juvenile alternative work services program has been implemented whereby work crews are provided to public agencies on a contract basis. Extensive vocational training in such areas as welding, foundry work, and automobile repair is available at one of the camps.

Hennepin County (Minnesota) County Home School.   The distinction between a residential treatment center and a training school is often blurred, as the County Home School reveals: It houses youngsters in both open units and a secure unit. With an annual budget in excess of $10 million, the 167-acre facility houses boys and girls between the ages of 12 and 18 who have been committed by the juvenile court. The campus includes seven 24-bed cottages, a school with a full gymnasium, and an administrative building that also contains a secure residential unit. This 16-bed unit is for the custody and control of youngsters who have exhibited serious disciplinary problems in the cottages.

Four cottages house boys with commitments of 7 to 24 months who have committed major property offenses and crimes against persons. They are staffed by juvenile correctional officers who provide custody, behavioral supervision, recreation, and social activities to meet the needs of adolescent boys in a residential setting. Three social workers are assigned to each cottage, and treatment is based on cognitive behavioral theory (discussed in chapter 9). Each resident begins his or her commitment with a thorough orientation and assessment prior to assignment to one of the four cottages. Assignment is based on chronological and developmental age, combined with a consideration of risk factors and an assessment of criminal sophistication.

A fifth cottage houses boys who have committed sex offenses. In addition to juvenile correctional officers, the sex offender cottage has staff specially trained to deal with this population. Treatment stresses residents' sexuality, their specific offense behavior, the impact on their victim, and family and community work. Their commitment length is indeterminate with a furlough option at 12 months. The sixth cottage is reserved for less serious property offenders or those who have violated their probation, and residents have commitments of 3 or 6 weeks. The cottage has no social workers assigned; the focus is on deterrence through highly structured physical work which can take place at the facility or an off-campus site, such as parks in the community. A seventh cottage serves girls with 8- to 14-month commitments and provides a twofold program: a core treatment that addresses all residents, and three components specific to each resident's needs and strengths. Individual and group counseling are provided by staff specifically trained to work with this young female population. Coeducational activities are restricted, and carefully planned and supervised.

The County Home has two consulting psychiatrists who also provide diagnostic services and direct medical treatment. A nurse is on duty 12 hours per day and on call the remainder of the time, and a pediatrician from the county medical services provides medical care. The education program consists of small classes with teachers certified in special education assisted by specially trained classroom aides. Chaplains and recreation therapists round out the program personnel. Aftercare is provided by probation officers who have their offices at the County Home School.

THE YOUTH AUTHORITY

Some states, for example, California, Ohio, and New York, have a state agency responsible for receiving cases from both juvenile and criminal courts. Typically, youngsters adjudicated delinquent in juvenile court, persons prosecuted and convicted under youthful or young offender statutes in criminal court, and juveniles prosecuted in criminal court under mandatory or optional waiver provisions are remanded to the **youth authority** for a period of confinement and aftercare (parole) supervision.

California Youth Authority. The California Youth Authority (CYA) was created in 1941, and in 1943, began providing institutional care and parole supervision for juvenile and young adult offenders. It is the largest youthful offender agency in the United States, with more than 10,000 young men and women in institutions and camps, and approximately 6,000 more on parole.

After a youngster is committed by the court and accepted by the authority, he or she is transferred to a reception center and clinic for about 4 weeks for evaluation and testing, before making an appearance before the seven-member Youthful Offender Parole Board. Community assessment reports are generated by CYA parole agents after visiting the ward's family and contacting appropriate local agencies. These reports add information about the ward's family and community relationships to information gathered by the clinic staff from the ward, probation reports, and any psychological or educational testing done at the clinic. All this information is compiled into a document called a clinic study and presented to the Youthful Offender Parole Board. The board uses this report in making decisions about the youngster. Once the ward appears before the board and decisions about length of stay and program are made, the youngster is transferred to his or her institution.

The Youth Authority's offender population is housed in 11 institutions, 4 rural youth conservation camps, and 2 institution-based camps. Two institutions are used primarily as reception. Female offenders are housed at Ventura Youth Correctional Facility, where there also is an intake center for them. A youth is assigned to a facility based on age, maturity, delinquent sophistication, educational/vocational needs, security needs, and behavior. Although in most cases wards are placed in an institution or conservation camp for a period of time and then released on parole, a few are placed on parole immediately after diagnostic studies. Under certain circumstances, a youngster committed from a criminal court may be assigned to an institution of the Department of Corrections. Commitments from both criminal and juvenile courts may also be assigned to an institution of the Department of Mental Health.

While in a CYA institution, younger residents attend school all day, while older ones might be in school part-time and in vocational training part-time. Many are assigned jobs within the institution, for example, working on the grounds or in food preparation. All wards are assigned a counselor, and some are placed in psychiatric or psychological treatment. The CYA has special programs for drug and alcohol abusers, sex offenders, and the seriously mentally ill. Because of limited resources, not everyone needing specialized treatment can be assigned to these programs.

When the ward is considered ready for parole by the Youthful Offender Parole Board, the parole agent makes all the necessary arrangements for his or her return to the community. The agent contacts family members, law enforcement, and other agencies, and assesses the need for special conditions of parole that the youngster must follow. The agent then completes the reentry report, which includes a preliminary parole plan describing employment, training, and education, and establishes goals to be achieved during the first 30 to 90 days. For the first 90 days on parole, intensive reentry services are provided. The parole agent has frequent contact with the youngster and his or her family, and provides needed brokerage with community agencies. The level and intensity of supervision gradually diminish as the ward becomes increasingly self-sufficient. The decision to reduce the level of supervision uses a classification system that determines the level of control necessary based on the youngster's potential risk score and his or her need for supportive services.

Parole staff work out of 16 parole offices. There also are two residential, intensive drug treatment programs for parolees who have evidenced drug and alcohol problems but who have committed no new criminal act. The department is also using electronic monitoring as an enhancement to parole supervision. In selected cases, this occurs at the time of release on parole. In other cases, it may be applied as a control or sanction when a technical parole violation occurs.

Like many states, California has significant problems with institutional care for young offenders. A study commissioned by the state found deplorable conditions in CYA institutions, with poorly maintained and antiquated facilities producing more than 4,000 serious assaults annually and dozens of attempted, and some successful, suicides (Broder, 2004).

Ohio Department of Youth Services.   The Ohio Department of Youth Services (DYS) provides a secure environment, education, vocational guidance, and other developmental programs for young people 12 to 18 years of age who have been charged with felony-level offenses and committed to the department by one of the state's 88 county juvenile courts. Serious felonies require a minimum commitment of 1 to 3 years; less serious felonies, 6 months. A judge may order early release at any time during the minimum commitment period, and in all commitments, a youth may be held until his or her twenty-first birthday.

The department's philosophy emphasizes care that is aimed at ultimate reintegration of troubled youth into the community. Planning for this reintegration begins at the time of commitment to DYS, when he or she is first assigned to the diagnostic reception center for 3 weeks of testing and planning. There are also special classes to prepare the youth for effective group living in an institutional setting and to heighten awareness of the harm done to victims. A team consisting of DYS staff and the ward, as well as his or her family, establishes a plan of development when the youth is committed to DYS. Obtainable goals, including educational goals, are established to help the youth develop self-control and discipline. The DYS Youth Recovery Program focuses on helping youth become free from chemical dependency, developing skills to avoid further contact with the juvenile justice system, and eliminating vocational handicaps as a result of being chemically dependent.

A reception center, eight institutions with capacities ranging from 120 to 200, three residential treatment centers whose capacities do not exceed 42, three private facilities with a capacity of 20 to 30 residents, a central medical facility, and eight regional offices are within the jurisdiction of the DYS. Youth assignments to DYS institutions are made on the basis of age, felony level of offense committed, and the proximity of the DYS institution to the youth's home. Some youngsters are placed in private facilities under contract with the DYS. The average daily institutional population is about 2,000—at a per diem cost of more than $120—with another 2,700 in the aftercare program where they are supervised by DYS parole officers operating out of regional offices located in every major metropolitan center in the state.

Included in the array of institutions is the Indian River School, located near Akron, which houses about 200 of the most serious felony offenders and residents from other institutions who are security risks and/or have exhibited assaultive behavior. Indian River has 8 units with 24 rooms, a school, a library, a modern gymnasium, and a 6-acre athletic field, all surrounded by a 14-foot chain link fence; windows are barred, and there are electronic metal doors on all dormitories and exits, as well as closed circuit televisions for continuous surveillance.

Each DYS institution has a fully accredited school that all youth are required to attend. Educational opportunities are available for all residents, including those with learning disabilities and special needs. Some institutions offer college-level courses in conjunction with local universities. Vocational programs in several of the DYS institutional high schools offer youth a variety of possible career paths to choose from once they are reintegrated into their communities. These programs include automobile mechanics, graphic arts, building maintenance, small engine repair, cosmetology, and barbering. A variety of recreational activities and extracurricular activities are available at each institution. At one location, youth have a chance to be on the award-winning DYS drill team or in the break-dancing group, which gives public performances throughout the year at schools and community events. Youth at DYS make positive contributions to the community through the volunteer work they do in litter control programs and by working with elderly citizens.

New York Office of Children and Family Services. Established in 1945, the New York Office of Children and Family Services (OCFS; formerly New York State Division for Youth), is the oldest comprehensive agency serving youth in the United States. The agency operates state training schools and secure facilities for juveniles tried as adults, and regulates juvenile detention facilities. Youngsters are classified according to the level of security they require and are assigned to the most appropriate OCFS facility or program.

It should come as no surprise that students typically enter the juvenile justice system with significant educational deficits. Prior to placement, many of these youth were having difficulties passing courses, completing grades, or attending school. They are typically several years behind in reading and math—it is common for a 16-year-old OCFS student to have a third-grade reading level. Approximately 40 percent of OCFS students are classified as educationally disabled to such a degree that learning is adversely affected. Moreover, most of the 2,500 youngsters placed annually with OCFS are from single-parent families with an income below the poverty level. As a result, New York expends between $6,000 and $7,000 per resident on academic and vocational services.

Secure Centers. Ranging in size from 10 to 100 beds, these facilities are characterized by physically restricting construction, hardware, and procedures, including security fencing and screens. The facility is either a single building or a small cluster of buildings in close proximity, surrounded by a security fence. Most centers have single rooms that are locked at night. They are located in nonurban areas, and virtually all services are provided on the grounds—a "total institution." The secure center admits juvenile offenders tried in adult courts and serious delinquents adjudicated in family (juvenile) court. They typically have an extensive history of delinquent behavior and involvement with the juvenile justice system, including prior institutional commitments; many exhibit serious psychological and emotional problems. Certain residents may be given the privilege of temporary release from facility grounds for carefully regulated periods for special reasons—for example, a death in the family, medical or dental treatment, community services program, industrial training, education, or work release.

One of these centers is located at Goshen, about 75 miles north of New York City, and houses 60 residents who are serving criminal sentences for felonies committed before 16 years of age, several for murder. Residents 18 to 20 years old can be transferred to an adult facility, and at 21 years of age, all unexpired terms must be completed at an adult institution. At Goshen, residents receive vocational education, academic tutoring, counseling, and recreational services, all under strict discipline—the superintendent is a former marine sergeant with a master's degree in social work. This facility costs in excess of $75,000 per year for each resident.

Limited Secure Centers. Ranging in size from 36-bed centers to 120-bed training schools, limited secure centers are located in rural areas and characterized by highly structured programs with virtually all services provided on the grounds. Residents are frequently transferred to less secure settings before returning to their home community. These facilities are also used for certain youth previously placed in secure centers as a first step in their transition back to the community.

Nonsecure Facilities. Moderately structured and varied noncommunity-based facilities are for youth who need to be removed from the community but are not high security risks. Limited trips for community activities, under close staff supervision, are an integral component of their programs. Some of the residents have previously been placed in secure and limited secure facilities and are transferred as part of the transition back to their own communities. In other cases, youth who have been initially placed in community-based programs and have been unable to function there are transferred to these residential centers—they are in the middle of the OCFS's continuum of residential services. These centers may admit all categories of delinquents, and youths placed as a condition of probation, as well as cases placed through a bureau of child welfare (i.e., without court intervention).

Youth Development Centers. Specialized community-based youth development centers are configured and staffed to provide an entire array of services to youths within their community-based structure. These centers may admit delinquents, status offenders, youth placed as a condition of probation, and adolescents placed through a bureau of child welfare.

Group Homes/Centers. Group homes are small residential units with 7 to 10 beds located in residential neighborhoods that use community resources to provide many of the needs of the residents: education, medical/dental services, recreation, and so on. Residents are allowed frequent and unescorted access to the community. These centers may admit delinquents, status offenders, youths placed as a condition of probation, or those placed through a bureau of child welfare.

Foster Homes/Alternative Programs. Foster home and alternative programs serve youths who have been placed with the OCFS but who can function in an alternative home situation rather than in an institutional setting: delinquents, status offenders, and those placed as a condition of probation or through a bureau of child welfare. Many of the (nonsecure) facilities used by the OCFS are the result of contracts with private residential child care agencies.

Aftercare. Once a youth is in placement at either an OCFS or private child care agency, a Youth Service Team counselor monitors his or her progress, and serves as a liaison between the facility, the family, and the community. The counselor assists facility staff efforts to meet a youth's service needs as defined in the service plans and to modify such plans to meet developing needs. Aftercare services include a variety of counseling and brokering services for youth who have been released from facilities and are living at home. Individual advocacy is provided by aftercare staff to help youth obtain services for which they are eligible, such as schooling or medical help, and to help them take advantage of opportunities for which they must apply, such as jobs or scholarships. This frequently involves intervening directly on a youth's behalf to try to reduce the reluctance of some agencies to accept or serve youth with delinquent backgrounds.

AFTERCARE AND PAROLE

Aftercare is the planned release of a juvenile from a residential placement (group home, residential treatment center, training school, correctional institution) to supportive services in the community. The juvenile may be supervised by a juvenile probation officer (as is the case with Glen Mills in Pennsylvania), youth agency parole officer/agent (as in California and Ohio), or other aftercare worker. Aftercare services are usually provided by the same state agency that administers the juvenile training schools (Hurst and Torbet, 1993). For example, I worked for the New York State Department of Social Welfare, which used to operate the state training schools. My job title was "youth parole worker," and I was responsible for supervising juveniles released from the boys' training schools. In 1978, New York enacted the Juvenile Offender Law, which mandates that youngsters 13 to 19 years of age who commit certain felonies be prosecuted in adult criminal court. If convicted, the youngster can serve a term in a secure facility of the DFY (now the OCFS). During that term, the juvenile becomes subject to the jurisdiction of the New York State Board of Parole for a release decision—parole—and eventual community supervision by a parole officer. Thus, the same agency that supervises adult felons in New York, the Division of Parole, also supervises juveniles convicted of certain violent felonies. In the state of Washington, parole counselors from the Juvenile Rehabilitation Administration (JRA) supervise those released from JRA institutions for a period of no more than 24 weeks (except for certain sex offenders).

Similarly, in Minnesota, parole agents of the Department of Corrections supervise juveniles who have been sentenced to a correctional facility. The release of juveniles from a correctional institution in Minnesota is the responsibility of a juvenile hearing officer, who uses a scale that incorporates the severity of the offense and the delinquent history (Figure 3.6). For example, a juvenile who committed burglary second degree would have a *severity level* of II; if his or her *delinquent history factors* equaled 2, the inmate would normally be paroled sometime between the fifth and eighth month. The scale makes no reference to rehabilitation or prognosis—it is a "justice"/classical model.

In Michigan, youngsters 12 to 19 years of age who have been adjudicated delinquent or found to be in need of supervision (status offenders) by the juvenile division of a probate court can be committed to the Department of Social Services for placement in their own home, a foster home, group home, youth camp, diagnostic center, halfway house, residential treatment center, or state training school. In Michigan, status offenders are often committed to the Department of Social Services when the particular juvenile court has insufficient resources available for the youngster.

The department offers secure juvenile residential treatment facilities, which may be used as the "last resort" for the most seriously delinquent youth. Delinquent wards remain under state authority until they are discharged by the Youth Parole and Review Board (YPRB) or reach 19 years of age. The YPRB is a three-member board within the Department of Social Services that conducts parole release, violation of parole, and discharge hearings for state delinquency wards. The Colorado Juvenile Parole Board is responsible for release decisions concerning juvenile delinquents who have been committed to the Department of Institutions. It grants, denies, revokes, suspends, or modifies conditions of parole to youth offenders who

Juvenile Commitment to the Minnesota Department of Corrections

Projected Institution Length of Stay in Months					
Severity Level	Most Serious Current Offense	Delinquent History Factors			
		0	1	2	3
I	Violation of Probation Contempt of Court Prostitution Assault – 4th & 5th Degree Drivers Under Influence of Alcohol Negligent Fires Burglary – 3rd & 4th Degree Damage to Property – $2,500 or less Forgery – $2,500 or less Possession of Controlled Substance Receiving Stolen Goods – $2,500 or less Theft – $2,500 or less Unauthorized Use of Motor Vehicle Dangerous Weapons (not including firearms) Trespass All Other Misdemeanors and Gross Misdemeanors	4 – 3	5 – 3	6 – 4	7 – 5
II	Assault – 2nd & 3rd Degree Burglary – 2nd Degree Damage to Property – Over $2,500 Forgery – Over $2,500 False Imprisonment Receiving Stolen Goods – $2,500 Felony Possession/Sale of Controlled Substance Theft From Person Theft – Over $2,500 Arson – 3rd Degree Criminal Sexual Conduct – 3rd & 4th Degree Simple Robbery Terroristic Threats Criminal Vehicular Homicide Dangerous Weapons – Firearms	6 – 3	7 – 4	8 – 5	9 – 6
III	Burglary – 1st Degree Criminal Negligence Resulting in Death Aggravated Robbery Arson – 1st and 2nd Degree Criminal Sexual Conduct – 1st & 2nd Degree Kidnapping Manslaughter Assault – 1st Degree	10 – 6	11 – 7	12 – 8	13 – 9
IV	Murder (all degrees)	**	**	**	**

 * Commitment offenses not specifically listed shall be placed on the grid at the discretion of the hearing officer at the time of the initial institution review.
** Murder shall be dealt with on an individual basis.

FIGURE 3.6 *Projected Institution Length of Stay, in Months.*

(*Source:* Minnesota Department of Corrections.)

have been adjudicated as delinquent. The board is comprised of seven members: four from various state executive departments, two citizen members, and a local elected official, appointed by the governor and confirmed by the senate. Most hearings are conducted by panels comprised of two board members; in cases of offenders committed as violent juveniles, the entire board must consider release. When considering a youngster for aftercare, a parole/release board will consider the case record, which includes a report and recommendation from an institutional social worker (Figure 3.7).

Utah Youth Parole Authority

Youngsters committed to any secure facility in the state come under the jurisdiction of the Youth Parole Authority, whose 10 members are appointed by the governor for terms of 4 years; they serve part-time. The authority initially establishes a length of stay guideline for each committed youth, and reviews his or her progress to determine when parole to the community is appropriate. The authority also conducts violation of parole hearings.

JACKSON COUNTY JUVENILE COURT SERVICES
McCUNE SCHOOL FOR BOYS

REQUEST FOR CONDITIONAL RELEASE/AFTERCARE
NAME: Michael DeWitt
BIRTH DATE: July 12, 1989
ADDRESS: 1900 West Briar Place
ENROLLMENT: June 6, 2005
DATE OF REPORT: November 28, 2005

I. REASON FOR PLACEMENT

Michael was committed to the McCune School for Boys on June 6, 2005, by Judge Harrison for Sexual Abuse.

II. ADDITIONAL REFERRALS

There have been no additional referrals.

III. ADJUSTMENT DURING PRESENT PERIOD OF SUPERVISION

While at McCune, Michael has made substantial advancement. Upon entrance into the program he was unable to work with his peers. Michael was often the target of harassment from other residents. He had told a story about his being offered chili to eat from resident Timothy Mordell working in the cafeteria. Michael asked if the meat in it was human flesh, and the incident became the source of ridicule during the remainder of his stay at McCune.

Over the past six months, Michael learned how to deal more appropriately with the harassment. He was also able to overcome racial problems that he had experienced since entering McCune. He has learned to deal with his prejudice in a fashion that permitted friendships to be established interracially.

He did so well in the McCune School that he was selected for Resident of the Week on three occasions. His grades reflect this:

English	B+
Science	A
Physical Ed	A
Vocational Preparation	A
Math	A
Social Studies	A
Citizenship	A

There were no problems in the community, and Michael spent almost all of his furlough time with his parents. On one occasion, his mother brought Michael back to McCune early because they saw and spoke with an individual who was associated with the victim. The resident and his mother were fearful that this individual would accuse Michael of some indiscretion, so he wanted to check back in at McCune. No complaints were received.

The only medical problem was the result of Michael striking a glass hallway window and putting his hand through it on the weekend of June 26, 2005, following a verbal altercation with another resident. Michael was taken to the hospital where he received both stitches and a medical furlough.

FIGURE 3.7 *Request for Conditional Release/Aftercare.*

(*Source:* Jackson County, Missouri, Court Services.)

IV. FAMILY SITUATION AND RELATIONSHIPS

Michael is an only child and lives at the above address with his parents, Charles and Barbara DeWitt; his relationship with his parents has improved significantly while being at McCune. Barbara DeWitt has attended virtually every Family Group Therapy session. As a result, mother and child have moderated their interactions; previously, they were characterized by emotional exaggeration. Michael earned all but two possible home visits.

V. DIAGNOSIS AND PLAN OF TREATMENT

Michael has completed all four of the four phases of the program. He has made great strides in the areas of authority, peer interaction, school and family relationships. Possible problems in the future will involve his reputation for sexual acting out, although this has not yet been the case. He has been on furlough and attended Newtown High School.

VI. SPECIFIC RECOMMENDATION

Michael has successfully completed his three-week furlough period. McCune staff, as well as his family, feel Michael is ready to return home. It is, therefore, recommended that Michael DeWitt be placed on Conditional Release and receive the services of an Aftercare Worker.

Carol Spalding
Carol Spalding
Social Worker

FIGURE 3.7 *(continued)*

Aftercare supervision is similar, if not identical, to probation supervision and, as noted earlier, is sometimes provided by a juvenile probation agency. The first responsibility of the aftercare worker is to plan for the release and placement of the young person. Placement plans include where the juvenile will live, whether he or she is to work or attend school or a training program, or both, and arrangements for any supportive services that may be needed by the client that are available in the community. The young person released/paroled from a training school may be returned to his or her own home, if this is desirable, or be placed in an alternative setting such as foster care, a group home, or halfway house. (Halfway houses are discussed in chapter 12.) The aftercare worker usually investigates placement alternatives and finalizes a program plan that is submitted to training school officials and those responsible for the release decision.

Once back in the community, the young person will be supervised by an aftercare worker, probation officer, or parole officer. The youngster will be required to abide by a set of rules and regulations (Figure 3.8), the violation of which can cause a return to a "secure setting" (Figure 3.9). The worker will make regular visits to the youngster's residence, school, or place of employment. He or she will involve family and school officials in an effort to facilitate the young person's reintegration and rehabilitation. However, juvenile aftercare has typically been underfunded, despite its obvious importance (Altschuler and Armstrong, 1994).

Aftercare in Dauphin County, Pennsylvania.   Aftercare is the responsibility of juvenile aftercare workers who have caseloads of not more than 25 youngsters who are in placement or are receiving postplacement services. All delinquent and most dependent youths placed in a group home or institutional care by the juvenile court become clients of the program. The goals of aftercare are to reduce the amount of time that a youth spends in placement and to reduce the rate of recidivism experienced by youths returning from institutional care. Aftercare workers serve as case managers, bridging the gap between the community and the placement resource, and as counselors, helping the youth to improve decision-making ability. Each aftercare worker is assigned to specific placement resources so all county youth at a particular placement have the same aftercare worker.

OHIO DEPARTMENT OF YOUTH SERVICES

RULES OF PAROLE

I have reviewed the attached Community Case Plan and the parole rules listed below and I agree to follow all of it. I understand that violation of these rules may result in my return to an institution or other appropriate sanctions.

I.   Parole Rules:

   I will obey all federal, state and local laws.
   Before leaving Ohio, even for a visit, I must get written permission from my Parole Officer.
   I will follow the instructions of my Parole Officer.
   I will follow through with what I have agreed to do in my case plan.
   I will not purchase, possess, or have under my control any weapon such as firearms, knives, etc.
   I will follow the rules of my parents/guardians or placement facility and remain in my placement
     residence until my Parole Officer tells me otherwise.
   I will keep a _____ curfew and will be at my residence between _____ and _____ on weekdays.
   On Saturday and Sunday I will be at my residence between _____ and _____.
   The only time I may be away from my residence after curfew is

   _____ .

   Special Rules Set by the Court:

II.   Placement:

      Name:_____ Relationship: _____

      Address: _____

      Phone: _____ Date of Placement: _____ Transportation: _____

III. Discharge Conditions:

My tentative discharge date is _____. I am expected to follow the rules of parole and complete the objectives in my case plan by that date. If I complete all of them before that time, I may be considered for early discharge. If I do not complete my conditions, my parole may be revoked by the Court and/or my parole period may be extended by the Department of Youth Services. I will be discharged from parole upon my 21st birthday.

SIGNATURES

_____	_____	_____	_____
Youth	Date	Parent/Guardian/Provider	Date
_____	_____	_____	_____
Parole Officer	Date	Casework Supervisor	Date
_____	_____	_____	
Judge	Date		

Revised 5-1-97

FIGURE 3.8 *Ohio Rules of Juvenile Parole.*

(*Source:* Ohio Department of Youth Services.)

   The aftercare worker begins involvement with the case during placement discussions before the dispositional hearing. The worker acts as an advisor during the placement planning process and, when possible, accompanies the intake worker and the client to the preplacement interview at the placement resource. Whenever possible, the worker attends the court hearings for a client who is being recommended for a placement resource to which he or she is assigned.

   The worker assists in the transportation of the client to the placement resource and ensures the child, parents, and institutional staff understand the role that the aftercare worker will play during and after placement. Within 30 days of the youth's placement, the worker prepares a written family service plan stating the short- and long-term service objectives, the services to be provided, and the anticipated length of the placement. At least once each month, the aftercare

COLORADO DIVISION OF YOUTH SERVICES
Central Region

Name: Willis, Carol
DOB: 2-22-88
Comm. Date: 4-10-2003
Hrg. Panel Date: 4-7-2004
Com. County: Jefferson
Current Placement: Pine Street

Risk Score: 2
Region/Client Manager: Central/Sims
Parole Counselor: Sims
Date of Report: 3–19–04
Sentence: Minimum months 0
        Maximum months 24

Parole Adjustment Report

Original Placement and Plan:
Carol was paroled on April 7, 2004 to live with her parents Jill and Tim Willis at 440 Hampton Place, Arvada. Carol had no other authorized placements. She left her parents' home on June 23, 2004 without the permission of her parents or parole officer.

Level of Supervision:
Carol was on maximum supervision. That included weekly contacts with her parole officer and twice weekly contacts with her tracker.

Employment/Vocational/Education:
Upon parole, Carol was placed in the Excelsior Youth Center Day Treatment Program. She was transported to and picked up from Excelsior five days per week from April 7, 2004 through June 5, 2004. This was done to enable Carol to finish her school semester and for her and her parents to continue in therapy.
Carol was enrolled in the Jefferson County Youth Summer Employment Program and began working on June 15, 2004. This was to last until July 31, 2004. Carol was registered to begin school at Arvada West High School on August 17, 2004.

Arrests and Dispositions:
Carol had no arrests prior to her runaway on June 23, 2004. When she was contacted by the Arvada Police on July 17, 2004 she was charged with Giving False Information. There is a hearing set for September 14, 2004 at 9:30 am in the Arvada Municipal Court.

Restitution:
There was no court-ordered restitution.

Parole Violation:
Carol went to work on June 23, 2004. She left work without permission that same day and did not return. The parole officer received a call from Mr. Willis on June 23, 2004 stating that Carol had left. I asked Mr. Willis to call me on June 24, 2004 if Carol did not show up. Mr. Willis called on June 24, 2004 to tell me that Carol had not shown up. At that time the parole officer placed a warrant for Carol's arrest.

At this time, both Carol and Mr. and Mrs. Willis feel that returning home is not an alternative, The parole officer feels that emancipating Carol at 16 years of age is unrealistic. The parole officer has been unable to find an appropriate placement for Carol in order to continue her parole.

Therefore, I am recommending Carol's parole be violated.

FIGURE 3.9 *Violation of Parole.*

(*Source:* Colorado Division of Youth Services.)

worker visits the youth and the staff at the placement resource, attends institutional meetings, and assists in the development of the treatment plan and monitors its implementation.

During placement, the aftercare worker meets at least once a month with the youth's family for counseling and information sharing about the youth's progress, and supervises all home visits made by the youth. In the fifth month of the youth's continuous placement, the worker prepares a written review of the placement and family services plan in preparation for the 6-month review-of-placement hearing before the juvenile court master. Before the youth's release, the aftercare worker coordinates the development of an aftercare plan that will be followed during postplacement supervision. To implement these aftercare plans effectively, the worker must develop cooperative relationships with schools, employers, and local social service agencies.

After release from the placement resource, the aftercare worker supervises the client for 3 to 6 months. Initially, at least one personal contact is made each week to provide counseling and monitor the aftercare plan goals. As the needs of the client allow, supervision may subsequently be reduced to a minimum of two personal counseling contacts per month. Cases are reviewed with the aftercare supervisor at least once each month. On completion of the aftercare plan goals, the aftercare worker recommends to the juvenile court judge that supervision be terminated and the case closed.

ADMINISTRATION OF JUVENILE SERVICES

The administration of juvenile services is complex, with different levels and branches of government sharing responsibility. Juvenile probation is administered by the juvenile court in most states, although a few have a statewide executive branch agency administering juvenile probation. State institutions for delinquent juveniles are always in the executive branch. However, states vary in the type of executive department they choose to place the responsibility for juvenile corrections: the social service department (e.g., Michigan), the corrections department (e.g., Illinois), or separate departments for either family and children's services or youth services (e.g., Idaho Department of Juvenile Corrections). The 168 juvenile probation agencies in Texas are monitored by the Texas Juvenile Probation Commission (TJPC), which sets standards and provides technical assistance to guarantee uniformity of services. The TJPC also monitors juvenile facilities through audits and unannounced visits to ensure health and safety are in compliance. States without a specialized youth authority/commission typically have their juvenile facilities under the auspices of the same department responsible for incarcerating adults. In Illinois, for example, the Juvenile Division of the Department of Corrections receives delinquents adjudicated in juvenile court and those youngsters tried as adults in criminal court. (From 1954 to 1970, these were responsibilities of the Illinois Youth Commission, which was subsequently abolished.) The Juvenile Division provides secure custody and rehabilitation programs to about 1,500 youths 13 to 21 years of age in six centers statewide that range from minimum to maximum security. Per resident annual cost is between $25,000 and $40,000. (By way of comparison, average annual costs in the state of Washington are more than $45,000.)

Getting Tough

"Forty-seven of the 50 states and the District of Columbia have substantially changed their juvenile justice laws in recent years to include more transfers of youth to adult court, more mandatory minimum sentences, and more incarceration, all of which have exacerbated the unlawful conditions found in many facilities where youth are held. These increasingly overcrowded and significantly deficient facilities hold disproportionate numbers of nonwhite youth for nonviolent property and drug crimes" (Puritz and Scali, 1998: xi).

IN THE CRIMINAL COURT

A youth tried in adult criminal court, depending on the state, may be sent to an institution operated by the same agency with responsibility for adults—a department of correction—or to a specialized agency that provides institutionalization for juveniles and young adults. For example, the Illinois Department of Corrections has a juvenile division that receives delinquents and juvenile offenders who have not reached their twenty-first birthday—at which time they may be transferred to an adult facility. In California, a judge has the option to sentence offenders 16 to 20 years of age to state prison but order them housed in a California Youth Authority (discussed earlier) facility until their twenty-fifth birthday or expiration of their sentence, whichever occurs first. Offenders younger than 16 years of age in New York are sent to a facility operated by the Office of Children and Family Services (discussed previously), whereas those who have reached their sixteenth birthday are sent to a reformatory operated by the Department of Correctional Services.

Both conventional wisdom and research have revealed that juvenile offenders in adult facilities present a significant management problem for institutional officials. One study, for example, found that compared with other young inmates, "imprisoned juvenile offenders exhibited significant adjustment problems in the institutional environment" (McShane and Williams, 1989: 266). Juvenile correctional facilities are often quite inadequate. In 1998, in an agreement with the U.S. Department of Justice, the state of Georgia promised to reform "egregious," "abusive," and "grossly substandard" conditions in its juvenile prisons. Similar agreements or court orders have impacted juvenile prisons in Kentucky and Louisiana (Butterfield, 1998c, 1998e). Relatively few facilities exist for the most violent adolescents, and as a result, youths are often released after less than 1 year of confinement (Treaster, 1994). Tens of thousands of offenders younger than the age of 18 are now confined in adult correctional facilities. In response to the problem of mixing adolescents with adult offenders, prison officials in many states are attempting to segregate this population: "At the core of their response is the realization that teenagers in adult prisons are vulnerable to sexual assault and physical assault and that being around older inmates can turn youthful offenders into hardened criminals" (Rimer, 2001: 13). At the other end of the problem, youthful offenders can be hard to control and a threat to older inmates.

Now that we have completed our examination of juvenile justice, chapter 4 examines prisons and parole.

Imprisoning Juveniles

The juvenile offender, "when he is released back into the community in his twenties—undereducated, unsocialized, unemployable, and at the peak of his physical power—he will be the very model of the very person we wished most to avoid" (Dighton, 1997: 12). In 1994, voters in Oregon passed "Measure 11," which requires youngsters 15 to 17 charged with certain serious crimes to be tried in adult court. If convicted, they must be imprisoned—they cannot receive probation—and are not eligible for early release for good behavior or parole.

KEY TERMS

least restrictive alternative   youth authority
residential treatment center   aftercare
training school

INTERNET CONNECTIONS

National Institute of Corrections: nicic.org

Office of Juvenile Justice and Delinquency Prevention: ojjdp.ncjrs.org

Council of Juvenile Correctional Administrators: cjca

American Bar Association Juvenile Justice Center: www.abanet.org/crimjust/
juvjus/home.html

REVIEW QUESTIONS

1. Why are the juvenile services provided to girls usually inferior to those provided to boys?
2. What is meant by "the least restrictive alternative"?
3. What is a group home?
4. What are the advantages of community-based day treatment?
5. What is the difference between a training school and a residential treatment center?
6. What are the purposes of juvenile aftercare?
7. What is the Youth Authority?
8. What agencies provide juvenile aftercare services?
9. What are the sentencing options for youth convicted in criminal court?
10. What are the problems associated with placing youngsters in correctional institutions as if they were adults?

Probation and the Courts: History and Administration

Probation is the most common sentence in the United States (Petersilia, 1998a). The administration of probation services may be under the auspices of the judiciary or an agency in the executive branch of government; in either event, a probation agency provides services to the judicial branch of government. Before examining these services and their administration, it is necessary to look first at federal and state court systems.

COURT SYSTEMS: FEDERAL AND STATE

In only one case is the jurisdiction of a court established by the U.S. Constitution: Article III, Section 2, states that "the judicial power of the United States shall be vested in one supreme Court, and in such inferior Courts as the Congress may from time to time ordain and establish." Similarly, state courts derive their authority from state constitutions and legislative enactments.

Jurisdiction

Jurisdiction is basic to understanding the organization of a court system; it is the geographic area, subject matter, or persons over which a court can exercise authority. The area of geographic jurisdiction is referred to as **venue,** and it can be limited to a particular district, city, or county. Venue in criminal cases is relatively simple—it is where the crime is alleged to have occurred. The criminal jurisdiction of a state court never extends beyond that state's borders. Although there are systems of trial and appellate courts in each state, most are not at all systematic. The history that shaped our judicial systems has mitigated against uniformity (see Abadinsky, 2003b, for a discussion).

In both federal and state justice systems, there are four levels of courts stratified by their jurisdiction, but the 50 state court systems present a complex array of structures—no two state court systems are alike. There are two basic types of courts: those that try cases (trial courts) and those that consider cases only on appeal (appellate courts) from a trial court or a lower appellate court. These courts are known by a confusing variety of names in different states, so we use generic titles (Figure 4.1).

Supreme Court

(appellate jurisdiction of last resort)

|

Intermediate Court of Appeals

(appellate jurisdiction; not used in all states)

|

Superior Court

(trial court of general jurisdiction; there are more than 2,600)

|

Lower Court

(limited jurisdiction; there are more than 13,500)

FIGURE 4.1 *Organization of State Courts for Criminal Cases.*

THE STATE COURTS

State court systems are characterized by decentralization based on territorial jurisdiction or on the nature of the case, and sometimes both. This system resulted from the need to bring the courts closer to litigants in an expanding nation where transportation was primitive. Each court played an important political and social role in the life of its community. When court convened in the county seat, often only once per month, it was a major event. Many people came to town, conducted business, discussed politics, and socialized with one another (Walker, 1980). Those were the days before radio, motion pictures, and television, and people flocked to the courtrooms to hear the oratory of noted attorneys. Courtroom oratory and successful advocacy gained an attorney a following and clients (Friedman, 1973). Following the Revolutionary War, there was a trend throughout the states toward establishment of a separate appellate branch. The lower courts were neglected and became unwieldy, inefficient, and in many areas tied to corrupt political machines—a link that would remain a problem in many urban areas well into the twentieth century.

Although there is one unitary federal court system, each state has a distinct history, and no two court systems are exactly alike. In states with a *unified court system*, such as Illinois, there is no "lower court." Thus, all preliminary hearings and misdemeanors will be heard in superior court (called the circuit court in Illinois and the supreme court in New York). In most states, however, there is a lower court that has limited jurisdiction. Sometimes referred to as magistrate's court, city or county court, police court, criminal court, and, in some rural areas, justice of the peace court, a lower court has authority to try misdemeanors (crimes for which, in most states, the maximum penalty is 1 year of imprisonment), traffic offenses, and sometimes juvenile cases; it is also the entry level for felony cases. This court will receive a defendant shortly (usually within 24 hours) after an arrest for an initial appearance that involves the formal reading of charges and setting of bail. In felony cases, the lower court may arrange for counsel and conduct a preliminary (probable cause) hearing. Because this is a court of limited jurisdiction, if the charge(s) constitutes a felony, the case will be moved to the grand jury (in states that use this body for charging offenders) or directly to superior court (on the basis of a prosecutor's information).

The lower courts typically dispense what many observers refer to as **rough justice** (Feeley, 1979; Robertson, 1974). That is, they are characterized by heavy caseloads—about 90 percent of all criminal cases are disposed of at this level—and speed: justice dispensed rapidly, often in a minute or less. Anything that tends to delay case processing is avoided. Under such circumstances, little attention may be paid to the niceties of individualized justice and due process, which serve to slow

Grand Jury

In 14 states, the grand jury is required for all felony crimes; in others, it is required in cases of capital and/or life imprisonment cases (Rottman et al., 2000). Many states follow the federal practice of requiring that indictments be used to charge serious crimes but allowing informations (or complaints) to be used to bring charges for lesser felonies and misdemeanors. In 25 states, the use of indictments is a prosecutor's option. In the federal system, a **grand jury** is a body of 23 citizens empowered to operate with a quorum of 16; 12 votes are required for an indictment. In the 50 states the minimum varies considerably, but nowhere does the maximum number of grand jurors exceed 23. Although some states adhere to the federal rule of 12 for an indictment, in others the range is anywhere from 4 to 9. Like those serving on a petit, or trial, jury, grand jurors are generally selected from the voting roles.

The members of a grand jury meet in secret sessions in a court building to consider evidence presented by the prosecutor in the absence of a judge, defendant, or defense attorney. Secrecy prevents subjects from escaping before arrest or tampering with witnesses and encourages witnesses to speak freely without fear of retaliation. Testimony is recorded by a court stenographer, and the transcript can be used at trial if the witness dies or cannot be called to testify for some other reason. If the witness testifies at trial, but says something different than what he or she said before the grand jury, the prosecutor or defense attorney can use the transcript to impeach trial testimony.

A presiding judge convenes the grand jury, usually at the request of the prosecutor, selects the jurors, and rules on any motions that are brought by witnesses who do not want to testify. The judge will also rule on any other legal matters and, at the request of the prosecutor, will provide immunity from prosecution in order to compel testimony that would otherwise be barred by the Fifth Amendment. Although a witness can refuse to reply to any questions if the answers may be incriminating, he or she can be granted immunity and, under the threat of being jailed for contempt, be required to answer all questions.

---

down the pace of case processing. The defendant who insists on his or her "rights" may be viewed as disruptive, and this can entail costs. The defendant is likely to receive higher bail or a more severe sentence than is the norm. Conversely, the typical case adjudicated in a lower court receives rather lenient treatment, a force for gaining the acquiescence of defendants. Persons on probation or parole are in a particularly disadvantageous position during this stage of criminal justice. A plea of guilty, although it may result in leniency from the lower court, can cause the defendant's probation or parole to be revoked.

A **superior court** has **general jurisdiction,** meaning that it can try any type of case—violations (e.g., traffic offenses), misdemeanors, and felonies—although this court usually handles only felony cases. Most cases entering superior court have been transferred from a lower court (directly via a prosecutor's information or by way of the grand jury). Because the superior court receives only a small percentage of the cases that enter the criminal justice system, the hectic pace encountered in the lower court is absent. Because of the seriousness of felony charges, there is usually scrupulous concern for due process. There is also a lack of jury trials, most cases being adjudicated by a judge (in a "bench trial") or negotiations that end in a plea of guilty.

An *intermediate court of appeals* exists in about half the states; the courts are called "intermediate" because on the judicial organization chart they are situated between the superior court and the state's highest court. As is the case with all appellate courts, the intermediate court of appeals does not try cases; it receives cases on appeal from the superior court. An appeal from the decision of an intermediate court of appeals goes to the court of appeals or supreme court. In states without an intermediate court of appeals, an appeal from superior court goes directly to the supreme court, the state *court of last resort.*

Decisions of the supreme court are binding on all of the courts in the state, unless overturned by the U.S. Supreme Court. The supreme court generally sits in the state capital, but may hear cases in other cities. The court hears cases *en banc;* that is, all the justices—none has more than nine—of the court sit in judgment. The decisions of a supreme court are often elaborate legal treatises that provide material for the case method and the rule of precedent (Abadinsky, 2003b).

From the American Revolution until 1832, most states provided for both elected and appointed (by the legislature or governor) judges. In that year, Mississippi initiated the popular election of all judges; in 1846, New York did the same. Within 10 years, 15 of the 29 states that then made up the Union had followed suit, and every state that entered the Union after 1846 stipulated the popular election of all or most of its judges (Hurst, 1950). Several other states experimented with both electoral and appointment systems—sometimes, as Texas did, going back and forth (Friedman, 1973).

Currently, most state court judges and justices (appeals court judges) are elected on a partisan (identified by political party—Republican or Democrat) or nonpartisan basis. In a single state, some judges may be elected (on a partisan or nonpartisan basis), whereas others are appointed, usually by the governor. In some states, there is a so-called merit system for filling judicial vacancies: A gubernatorial commission nominates several persons for each judicial vacancy, and the governor must pick one of them. The judge serves for 1 year, and his or her name is submitted to the voters for confirmation—or removal. (For the advantages and disadvantages of each system, see Abadinsky, 2003b.)

FEDERAL COURTS

There is a *U.S. District Court* in each of the 94 federal judicial districts (89 within the 50 states, and 5 for the U.S. territories and the District of Columbia [Figure 4.2]). Each state has at least one (only one district crosses a state line), and heavily populated states, such as California, New York, and Texas, have as many as 4. There are about 630 district court judges and several (semi-) retired—or senior—judges who assist as trial judges. The number of judges assigned to each district varies with the size of the population, the largest being the Southern District of New York, located in Manhattan, which has 28. Each judicial district has a U.S. attorney (federal prosecutor), a U.S. marshal, and a chief probation officer; they are assisted by hundreds of employees: assistant U.S. attorneys, deputy U.S. marshals, and U.S. probation officers.

Supreme Court
(appellate jurisdiction; *the* court of last resort)

|

Courts of Appeals
(appellate jurisdiction)

|

District Court
(trial court of general jurisdiction)

|

Magistrate's Court
(limited jurisdiction)

FIGURE 4.2 *Organization of Federal Courts for Criminal Cases.*

Unlike most state judges, all federal judges are appointed to lifetime terms by the president (with the "advice and consent" of the Senate); lifetime tenure helps to insulate judges from both political pressures and popular sentiment.

In dealing with criminal cases, district courts employ *U.S. magistrate judges*, attorneys who are appointed by the district court judges for terms of 8 years (or 4 years in the case of those who serve only part-time). The approximately 500 magistrates are authorized to issue warrants and conduct preliminary hearings and nonfelony trials held without a jury. A magistrate is usually the first judicial officer before whom a federal criminal defendant appears. Decisions of a magistrate can be appealed to a district court judge. District courts have general jurisdiction involving the violation of federal statutes. However, they actually have *exclusive jurisdiction* in only a relatively few types of criminal cases—most crimes involve violations of state law—and often their jurisdiction is shared with state courts. For example, drug trafficking and bank robbery are both federal *and* state crimes. As a result of efforts to deal with organized crime, many state crimes, if committed in a certain pattern, also violate the (federal) Racketeer Influenced and Corrupt Organizations (RICO) statute; for example, bribing a *state* judge would fall within this category (see Abadinsky, 2003b, for more information).

The *U.S. Court of Appeals* (sometimes referred to as *circuit court*) has jurisdiction over cases already decided in a federal district court—it does not act as a trial court. The country is divided into 11 circuits, each of which embraces several states, and a twelfth circuit, which serves the District of Columbia. The Second Circuit, for example, serves New York, New Jersey, and Connecticut. Each circuit court has at least four judges, and a circuit with a great deal of litigation, such as the Second Circuit, will have more than 20 appellate judges. The chief judge (the most senior judge in terms of service in the circuit who has not reached 70 years of age) has supervisory responsibilities for the circuit. Court of appeals cases are usually considered in panels of three judges, although, occasionally, important cases will be heard by the full court of the circuit (referred to as *en banc*). Judges of a court of appeals (appellate courts have no juries) review issues of law that have been applied by the district courts in their circuit, and the rulings of a court of appeals are binding on only the district courts in their circuit, although they may influence other circuits and even the Supreme Court. Each circuit has a Supreme Court justice assigned to it who is empowered to act in emergencies when the Supreme Court is not in session; this most often involves cases of capital punishment, and the justice can order a stay until the High Court convenes.

The *U.S. Supreme Court*, the only court established by the Constitution, is unique—it is the least democratic U.S. governmental institution. The president (executive branch) and the Congress (legislative branch) must, more or less, be responsive to the concerns of the voting public, whereas the judicial branch remains aloof. Although the other branches of government reflect popular sentiment, the Supreme Court can render the decisions of elected executives and legislators null and void—that is, *unconstitutional*. The Supreme Court can protect the rights and interests of persons who, in a democratic society, are weak, who do not represent a significant block of votes or source of funds, and who may be unpopular, such as accused criminal offenders. The Supreme Court decisions that this book examines, for example, have provided important rights to juvenile delinquents, prison inmates, probationers, and parolees—persons whose rights are not likely to be championed by elected officials.

As the highest court in the federal system, the Supreme Court is *the* court of last resort. The eight associate justices and the chief justice, who presides over the deliberations of the Supreme Court, are appointed for life by the president. Unlike the court of appeals, since 1914 (except in certain rather rare circumstances), the Supreme Court has had the power to decide which cases it will consider. Before the Court will consider an appeal, a *writ of certiorari* is required—a minimum of four justices must agree to place the case on the Court's calendar—and *certiorari* is granted in less than 4 percent of the cases appealed to the Supreme Court. The decisions of a state court of last resort are appealed directly to the Supreme Court. In the federal system, there are also specialized courts, such as the court of claims, but only the court of military appeals handles criminal matters.

PROBATION HISTORY

Although probation has antecedents that reach back to biblical times, its American history dates back to the nineteenth century.

Early Probation and John Augustus

The concept of probation, from the Latin *probatio*—period of proving—evolved out of the practice of *judicial reprieve*, used in English courts to serve as a temporary suspension of sentence to allow a defendant to appeal to the crown for a pardon. Although originally intended to be only a temporary postponement of punishment, it eventually developed into a *suspended sentence* whereby punishment was never actually imposed. In the United States, the suspended sentence was used as early as 1830 in Boston and became widespread in U.S. courts, although there was no statutory authorization for such practice. At first, judges used "release on recognizance" or bail and simply failed to take further action. By the mid-nineteenth century, however, many courts were using a judicial reprieve to suspend sentences, and this posed a legal question.

"A judge had always had the power to suspend a sentence, if he felt for some reason that the trial had miscarried. But could judges suspend sentences wholesale, after trials that were scrupulously fair, simply to give the defendant a second chance?" (Friedman, 1973: 518). In 1894, this question was litigated in New York, and the court determined that the power to suspend sentence was inherent in criminal courts only when this right had been granted by the legislature. In 1916, the U.S. Supreme Court, in a case (*Ex Parte United States*, 242 U.S. 27) that affected only federal courts, ruled that judges did not have the discretionary authority to suspend a sentence. In its decision, however, the Court stated that Congress could authorize the temporary or indefinite suspension of sentence—a predecessor to probation statutes.

The term *probation* was applied by John Augustus to the practice of bailing offenders out of court followed by a period of supervised living in the community. This pioneer of modern probation was born in Woburn, Massachusetts, and became a successful shoemaker in Boston. In 1852, a "Report of the Labors of John Augustus" was published at the request of his friends, and in it Augustus wrote: "I was in court one morning . . . in which the man was charged with being a common drunkard. He told me that if he could be saved from the House of Correction, he never again would taste intoxicating liquors: I bailed him, by permission of the Court" (1972: 4–5). Thus began the work of the nation's first probation officer, a volunteer who worked without pay.

Augustus's first experience with a drunkard led to an interest in helping others charged with the same offense. He would appear in court and offer to bail a defendant. If the judge agreed, which usually happened, the defendant would become Augustus's charge. The shoemaker would assist the offender in finding work or a residence; Augustus's own house was filled with people he had bailed. When the defendant returned to court, Augustus would report on his progress toward rehabilitation and recommend a disposition of the case. These recommendations were usually accepted. During the first year of his efforts, Augustus assisted 10 drunkards who, because of his work, received small fines instead of imprisonment. He later helped other types of offenders, young and old, men and women, and reported only 10 **absconders** (persons who jumped bail or probation) out of 2,000 cases.

Augustus continued his work for 18 years and generally received support from judges and newspapers that reported on his efforts. Prosecutors, however, viewed him as an interloper who kept court calendars crowded by preventing cases from being disposed of quickly. Policemen and court clerks opposed his work because they received a fee for each case disposed of by a commitment to the House of

Correction. As a result of his probation work, Augustus neglected his business and eventually experienced financial ruin; he required the help of friends for his support.

Several aspects of the system Augustus used remain a basic part of modern probation. Augustus thoroughly investigated each person he considered helping, considering "the previous character of the person, his age and the influences by which in the future he would likely be surrounded" (1972: 34). Augustus not only supervised each defendant, but he kept a careful case record for each that he submitted to the court. Augustus died in 1859, and until 1878, probation in Massachusetts continued to be the work of volunteers.

Early Probation Statutes

After his death in 1859, supporters of John Augustus successfully lobbied the legislature, which in 1878 enacted the first probation statute, authorizing the mayor of Boston to hire a PO, who would be supervised by the superintendent of police. For the first time, the position of PO was given official recognition as an arm of the court. The law authorized a PO to investigate cases and recommend probation for "such persons as may reasonably be expected to be reformed without punishment." Probation was made available in Boston to young and old, men and women, and felons and misdemeanants. In 1880, the legislature granted to all municipalities the authority to employ POs, but few towns and villages did so. In 1891, the power to appoint POs was transferred to the lower courts, and each was required to employ a PO. In 1898, this requirement was also extended to the superior courts. The second state to adopt a probation statute was Vermont, which in 1898 authorized the appointment of a PO by the courts in each county, each officer serving all the courts in a particular county.

Another New England state, Rhode Island, soon followed Vermont with a probation law that was novel—it placed restrictions on who could be granted probation, excluding persons convicted of treason, murder, robbery, arson, rape, and burglary. This practice violated a basic tenet of positivism: Judge the offender, not just the offense. The restrictive aspects of Rhode Island's probation law, however, were copied by many other states. The Rhode Island probation law, which applied to children and adults, also introduced the concept of a state-administered probation system. A state agency, the Board of Charities and Correction, appointed a state PO and deputies, "at least one of whom should be a woman" (Glueck, 1933: 231).

In 1894, Maryland authorized its courts to suspend a sentence generally or for a specific time, and judges could "make such order to enforce terms as to costs, recognizance for appearance, or matters relating to the residence or conduct of the convicts as may be deemed proper." The courts of Baltimore began using agents of the Prisoner's Aid Society and later appointed salaried POs. In 1897, Missouri enacted a "bench parole law," which authorized courts to suspend sentence under certain conditions. The courts also appointed POs (mis)named "parole officers," to carry out this probation ("bench parole") work (Glueck, 1933). In 1931, the Alabama legislature passed a law giving the judges power to suspend execution of sentences and place offenders on probation. This act was declared unconstitutional in 1935. If it had been constitutional, it would have done little more than authorize suspended sentences because, in most cases, there was no provision for investigation and supervision.

Probation at the Turn of the Twentieth Century

The spread of probation was accelerated by the juvenile court movement, which started in the Midwest and developed rapidly (discussed in chapter 2). In 1899, Illinois enacted the historic Juvenile Court Act, which authorized the world's first juvenile court. The law also provided for the hiring of POs to investigate cases referred by the courts, but made no provision for payment of the POs. It was not until 1919 that the Illinois legislature enacted a law providing that counties pay the salaries and expenses of POs. At the end of the first year, there were six POs, supported by the Juvenile Court Committee of the Chicago Women's Club. In addition, in each police district a police officer spent part of his time out of uniform performing the duties of a PO (Schultz, 1973: 465).

In 1899, Minnesota enacted a law that authorized the appointment of county POs, but the granting of probation was limited to those younger than 18 years of age. Four years later, this was changed to 21 years of age. In 1901, New York State enacted a probation law that was initially limited to those younger than 16 years of age, limited to certain cities, and provided for volunteer POs. In 1903, legislation authorized probation throughout the entire state and included both children and adults.

In 1899, Colorado enacted a compulsory education law that enabled the development of a juvenile court using truant officers as POs. By 1925, probation was available for juveniles in every state (Glueck, 1933). In 1873, Michigan instituted a statewide system of juvenile POs they named county agents. Volunteers at first, in 1875, county agents were paid $3 per case for their part-time work—an American-born Detroit manufacturing worker at the time earned $457 a year (Hurl and Tucker, 1997). In New York, it was not until 1901 that legislation authorizing the appointment of salaried POs was enacted—until that year they were volunteers (Lindner and Savarese, 1984). In 1908, Suffolk County on Long Island appointed its first PO: "At the time, there was little appreciation of the value of probation, and the appointment was more in the nature of an experiment. As a part-time position, the PO had no office, and the probationers reported to him at his home, or by mail." The county appointed a full-time PO in 1919, and he was given a small office. Probation for juveniles was authorized in Pennsylvania in 1903 and extended to adults in 1909: Except for the offenses of murder, administering poison, kidnapping, incest, sodomy, rape, assault with intent to rape, and arson or burglary of an inhabited dwelling, a judge could suspend the sentence and place the offender on probation.

In the early 1900s, federal POs were volunteers. In 1916, the Supreme Court (*Ex Parte United States*, 242 U.S. 27) ruled that federal judges did not have the authority to place offenders are probation. In 1925, Congress enacted legislation establishing the Federal Probation System, and in 1929, the first paid U.S. probation officer was appointed under the Department of Justice. In 1939, probation administration was shifted to the newly created Administrative Office of the United States Courts.

Although Texas enacted the Suspended Sentence Act in 1913 to provide an alternative to incarceration, probation supervision of the convicted offender was not required until 1947. Probation for adults in Alabama did not begin until 1939, when the governor approved an enabling act giving the legislature power to authorize adult probation. Before that, it had been held that courts did not have the inherent power to suspend sentences because it was deemed to be an encroachment on the executive power to pardon, commute, and reprieve. By 1956, probation was available for adults in every state (Task Force on Corrections, 1966).

The first directory of POs in the United States, published in 1907, identified 795 probation officers working mainly in the juvenile courts. Like the first PO in Illinois, many were volunteers, and some who were paid worked only part time. Training for POs was either limited or nonexistent; appointments were often based on considerations of political patronage; and salaries were typically low even when compared with those of unskilled laborers.

ADMINISTRATION OF PROBATION

Probation in the United States is administered by more than 2,000 separate agencies supervising in excess of 3 million adult offenders on probation for felonies and misdemeanors. In about three-fourths of the states, adult probation is located in the executive branch of state government (where it is typically combined with parole). For example, adult probation in Georgia is a division of the Department of Offender Rehabilitation, which also includes the state prison system and parole board (Board of Offender Rehabilitation). In Pennsylvania, the Board of Probation and Parole, an independent state agency, in addition to its parole responsibilities, supervises probationers sentenced to less than 2 years when directed to do so by the courts. The board also oversees county probation agencies. In Michigan, adult felony probation is the responsibility of the Department of Corrections, which also administers parole, whereas adult misdemeanor probation is the responsibility of district court (limited jurisdiction) probation departments. In Illinois, probation is a county-level responsibility that is part of the judicial branch. In Iowa, probation (and parole supervision) is the responsibility of the state's judicial districts, each of which encompasses several counties. In New York, each county and New York City has a probation department that is part of the executive branch of county/municipal government. In Massachusetts, probation is a state agency employing more than 1,200 probation officers.

More than one-half of the agencies providing juvenile probation services are administered on the local level. Juvenile probation may be provided by a separate juvenile agency or a (juvenile or family) division of the same agency that administers adult probation as in Nassau County, New York. Fortunately, the administration of parole, which is discussed in chapter 8, is much less complex: one agency per state and always in the executive branch. Even with parole, however, there is a slight variation: In some states (e.g., Pennsylvania), persons paroled from a local jail come under the supervision of a *county* probation and parole department. In Oregon and Iowa, probation *and* parole supervision are at the county and judicial district levels.

The administration of probation systems can be separated into six categories, and a state may have more than one system in operation:

- *Juvenile*. Separate probation services for juveniles are administered on a county or municipal level, or on a statewide basis.
- *Municipal*. Independent probation units are administered by the lower courts or the municipality under state laws and guidelines.
- *County*. Under laws and guidelines established by the state, a county operates its own probation agency.
- *State*. One agency administers a central probation system providing services throughout the state.
- *State combined*. Probation and parole services are administered on a statewide basis by one agency.
- *Federal*. Probation is administered nationally as an arm of the courts. Federal probation officers also supervise parolees.

Most states (about 60 percent) combine probation and parole in one statewide agency. However, in the largest states, California, Illinois, New York, and Texas, only parole is a state function, whereas probation is administered by the judiciary or executive branch on a county or municipal level.

Probation services in the executive branch can be part of state government under the office of the governor, county government under a chief executive officer, or municipal government under a mayor. For example, in 1974, probation services in New York City were removed from the jurisdiction of the Judicial Conference of the State of New York and became part of the executive branch of city government with a director appointed by the mayor. Probation services may be part of a larger department of corrections, as in Georgia, or as part of an independent probation and parole agency, as in Alabama and South Carolina. Probation services as part of the judicial branch of government usually places these services under the judges of the county. For example, in New Jersey,

> The judges of the County Court in each county, or a majority of them, acting jointly may appoint a *chief probation officer, [and] such men and women probation officers* as may be necessary. Probation officers and *volunteers in probation* shall be appointed with standards fixed by the Supreme Court. All

probation officers and *volunteers in probation* shall be responsible to and under the supervision of the *Chief Probation Officer* of the county who shall be responsible to and under the supervision of the judge of the county court or, in counties having more than one judge of the county court, the county court judge designated by the Assistant Judge to be responsible for the administration of the *probation department* in the county in accordance with the applicable statutes, rules of the Supreme Court, and directives of the Chief Justice, the Administrative Director of the Courts, and the Assignment Judge of the county.

In the state of New York, since 1974, all local probation directors have been accountable to their respective chief county officials (executive branch) or, in the case of New York City, the mayor. Although administered locally, supervisory oversight of the administration of probation statewide is the responsibility of the New York State Division of Probation and Correctional Alternatives.

There are also some variations. For example, Iowa is divided into eight judicial districts, each with a multicounty correctional department operating under a board of directors. The board appoints a director who administers probation, parole, and related services that are funded and monitored by the Iowa Department of Corrections. In Texas, probation services are located in 120 Community Supervision and Corrections Departments, organized by the judges of each judicial district and funded by supervision fees and state aid. The Ohio Adult Parole Authority, in addition to parole services, provides probation services to 45 (of the state's 88) counties. Although the 31 counties participating in the Minnesota Community Corrections Act (CCA) provide services to persons on probation, supervised release or parole, the state provides these services to adult offenders in the remaining 56 counties. Juvenile probation and parole services in non-CCA counties are provided by county probation agents or by state agents under contract to the counties. In either case, the state pays up to 50 percent of the agent's salary.

Two basic issues arise in the administration of probation services:

1. *Should probation be part of the judicial or executive branch of government?*
2. *Should probation be under municipal/county or state jurisdiction?*

Those who support placement of probation services into the judicial branch (Nelson, Ohmart, and Harlow, 1978) contend that

- Probation is more responsive to the courts, to whom it provides services, when administered by the judiciary.
- The relationship of probation staff to the courts creates an automatic feedback mechanism on the effectiveness of various dispositions.
- Courts will have greater awareness of the resources needed by the probation agency.
- Judges will have greater confidence in an agency for which they are responsible, allowing probation staff more discretion than they would allow members of an outside agency.
- If probation is administered on a statewide basis, it is usually incorporated into a department of corrections. Under such circumstances, probation services might be assigned a lower priority than they would have as part of the judicial branch.

Those who oppose the placement of probation in the judiciary note the following disadvantages:

- Judges, trained in law, not administration, are not equipped to administer probation services.
- Under judicial control, services to persons on probation may receive a lower priority than services to the judge, for example, presentence investigations.

- Probation staff may be assigned duties unrelated to probation.
- The courts are adjudicatory and regulative; they are not service-oriented bodies.

Placement in the *executive branch* has these features to recommend it:

1. All other human service agencies are within the executive branch.
2. All other corrections subsystems are located in the executive branch.
3. With executive branch placement, program budgeting can be better coordinated, and an increased ability to negotiate fully in the resource allocation process becomes possible.
4. A coordinated continuum of services to offenders and better use of probation personnel are facilitated.

E. Kim Nelson and her colleagues (1978) conclude:

When compared, these arguments tend to support placing probation in the executive branch. The potential for increased coordination in planning, better utilization of manpower and improved services to offenders cannot be dismissed. A state administered probation system has decided advantages over local administration. A total system planning approach to probation as a subsystem of corrections is needed. Such planning requires state leadership. Furthermore, implementation of planning strategies requires uniformity of standards, reporting, and evaluation as well as resource allocation. (92)

Mitchell Silverman (1994) points out, however, that state control typically means probation agencies administered by the state executive branch with centralized administrators who are frequently far removed, both physically and intellectually, from the PO in the field. Often the central administrators have little knowledge and understanding of the important factors that are operating in the local community where the individual PO works. The distance has the potential of creating conflicts of interest when the state-level policy makers demand from the field worker one approach to clients, whereas the local community, in which the PO and client live, demands another. Local administration enhances creativity by providing the capacity to adopt county-specific programs with shorter lines of decision making.

Probation administered by the judiciary (usually) on a *county level* promotes diversity. Innovative programming can be implemented more easily in a county agency because it has a shorter line of bureaucratic control than a statewide agency. A county agency can more easily adapt to change, and the successful programs of one agency can be more easily adopted and unsuccessful programs avoided by probation departments in other counties. Those most familiar with the local community—its resources, attitudes, and politics—will be responsible for providing probation services; this can increase public confidence in the services provided by the agency. Although the judiciary is nominally responsible for the administration of probation, the day-to-day operations are in the hands of a professional administrator—the chief probation officer.

Conversely, county-level administration results in a great deal of undesirable variance between agencies. For example, the ratio of POs to clients may differ dramatically from one county to the other—this would not happen with a statewide agency. Because each county sets its own budget, probation staff cannot be shifted from a low-ratio county to a high-ratio county to equalize the services provided. In New Jersey, for example, the State Advisory Board for Probation, in its 1985 report, noted that whereas juvenile supervision caseloads statewide averaged about 80 per officer, in individual counties the range was between 35 and 145. For adult probation caseloads, the state average of 160 ranged from 71 to 284, amounting to a fourfold difference between the extremes.

The New Jersey board found variance with respect to the amount each county expended on probation services and "a great deal of variation in the way work is processed. Thus, the sequence of probation work from county to county is far from uniform" and the board noted that,

> There is no accepted definition of what comprises quality probation services. Probation supervision, for example, suffers from a lack of definition and structure, making it difficult to determine what is high quality supervision. Finally, there is great variance from county to county in the environment which produces the need for probation services, creating large differences among counties in the work probation services must perform. The extent and seriousness of criminal, social, and economic problems has important implications for staffing, procedures, and resource requirements from county to county.

This finding, of course, can serve as an argument for county control of probation services. The board, however, raises a question: Does the lack of uniformity in administering probation make justice less equitable statewide?

This issue has led states with county-based probation systems to create statewide oversight agencies for better coordination and uniformity of probation services—only Indiana and California operate probation locally without a state oversight agency (Parent et al., 1994). In Illinois, for example, the Probation Division of the Administrative Office of the Illinois Courts works to "improve the quality and quantity of probation and related court services throughout Illinois, provide more uniformity of organization, structure, and services, and increase the use of probation as a meaningful alternative punishment for nonviolent offenders. As part of these efforts, for example, the division promulgates regulations for the hiring and promotion of all probation personnel throughout the state."

The Texas Community Justice Assistance Division (formerly the Texas Adult Probation Commission) is responsible for establishing statewide standards and providing

New York State Division of Probation and Correctional Alternatives

The New York State Division of Probation and Correctional Alternatives (DPCA) was established in 1985 to exercise general supervision over the operation of local probation agencies and the use of correctional alternative programs throughout the state. DPCA also administers a program of state aid funding for approved local probation services and for municipalities and private nonprofit agencies that have approved alternative to incarceration service plans. These plans allow localities to maintain inmates in local correctional facilities more efficiently. The agency also funds designated demonstration and other specialized programs.

DPCA's mission is to promote and facilitate probation services and other community corrections programs through funding and oversight. These programs are generally designed to provide a continuum of sanctions, methods of supervision, and approaches to treatment that, when used individually or in combination, provide options to the judiciary and to the state's criminal justice system for the effective handling of offenders and juveniles in the community.

The director adopts and promulgates rules and regulations concerning methods and procedure used in the administration of local probation services, and develops standards for the operation of alternative-to-incarceration programs. The director also serves as the Chairman of the New York State Probation Commission. The commission members, appointed by the governor, provide advice and consultation to the director on all matters relating to probation in the state.

state aid to those local adult probation departments that choose to participate and are in compliance with the standards. As part of these efforts, the division has supported research and experimental probation programs throughout Texas. The agency has promulgated a "Code of Ethics for Texas Adult Probation Officers" and published standards for all phases of adult probation in Texas. For example, caseload size: "A caseload average within a department should be calculated by dividing the number of cases under direct supervision by the number of officers within the department devoting 80 percent or more of their time to direct case supervision. The average caseload of a probation officer in a department should not exceed 100 cases." Although the standards are not mandatory, the failure of a probation department to maintain them can result in a loss of the considerable funding provided by the state.

The trend in adult probation services has been toward moving from the judicial to the executive branch—in about 75 percent of the states probation is in the executive branch—and toward centralization under a state agency (Petersilia, 1998a).

GRANTING PROBATION

Most states have statutory restrictions on who may be granted probation in felony cases. Crimes such as murder, kidnapping, and rape usually preclude a sentence of probation, as do second or third felony convictions. In Texas, a defendant may elect to be sentenced by a jury but can thereby receive probation only if it is proved that he or she "has never before been convicted of a felony in this or any other State." In any event, no person in the Lone Star state is eligible to receive probation for a felony unless assessed a sentence of 10 years or fewer by a judge or jury. In Georgia, a defendant who pleads guilty (or *nolo contendere*—"no contest") and who has never before been convicted of a felony can be placed on probation without the court entering a judgment of guilty. If the person successfully completes the terms of probation, he or she "shall not be considered to have a criminal conviction." In Michigan, those convicted of any crime except treason, criminal sexual conduct in the first degree, robbery while armed, and major controlled substance offenses can be granted probation.

When probation is a statutory alternative, judges differ in their approach to granting it. Although the recommendation of the probation department would be important—it is difficult to envision too many cases in which judges would grant probation against the recommendation of a probation officer—judges may also seek advice from the police and prosecutor. The geographic area where the court is situated may also affect the granting of probation. Social and political attitudes in rural and urban jurisdictions can differ and thus affect the process. When court calendars are crowded, as they are in many urban areas, plea bargaining is more likely to result in probation being granted. The pressing problem of jail and prison overcrowding also exerts influence. One research effort found that in the rural districts studied, many felons are placed on probation as the result of a plea bargain. One study found that in Tennessee this appears to be directly related to the severe prison overcrowding experienced by that state (Champion, 1988a). The judge's feelings toward the particular offense or the offender may also enter into the sentencing decision. The many factors that determine if a defendant is granted probation contribute to the continuing controversy over "differential punishment," a challenge to the classical approach to criminal justice.

However, some factors, to a greater or lesser extent, are considered in all cases relative to the granting of probation: the age and rehabilitation potential of the defendant; the defendant's criminal record, including indications of professional criminality, organized crime, and crimes of violence; the defendant's relationship with his or her family; evidence of any deviant behavior, such as drug abuse or sex offenses; and the attitude of the community toward the particular offense and the particular offender. Other questions may also be considered: Does the defendant's

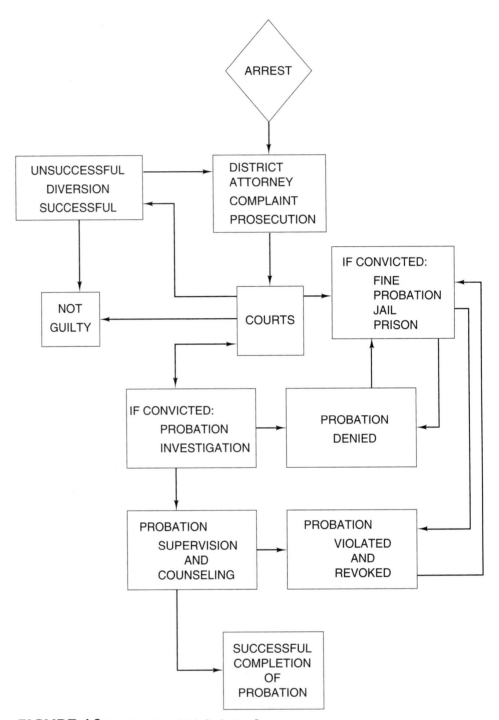

FIGURE 4.3 *San Francisco Adult Probation Process.*

attitude toward the offense indicate genuine remorse? Was probation promised to the defendant to induce him or her to plead guilty? Will being placed on probation enable the defendant to provide the victim with restitution? Will being placed on probation enable the defendant to provide support and care for his or her family?

The sentencing judge must also consider the quality of service provided by a probation agency. Unfortunately, in too many jurisdictions, probation is nothing more than a suspending of sentence because little or no supervision is actually provided. Under such circumstances, a judge who might otherwise be inclined to place an offender on probation may, instead, impose a sentence of imprisonment. The

cost to both the offender and the taxpayer is high—according to most es
prisonment costs from 10 to 13 times as much as probation. In many juris
built-in incentive actually exists for sentences of imprisonment, even whe
tion is a feasible alternative. If probation services are funded by the county,
cost of prisons is always borne by the state, each defendant sent to prison ı
of being placed on probation represents a savings to county government. A Florida
study revealed a pattern of inappropriate sentencing in some counties apparently
because they can save money by sending more offenders to state-funded prisons
(Sever, 2000). This result can be, at least in part, overcome with a **probation sub-sidy** through which the state reimburses the county for offenders placed on probation instead of being sentenced to a state prison.

The American Bar Association (ABA) presents the advantages of probation
rather than imprisonment (1970: 3–4):

1. The liberty of the individual is maximized by such a sentence; at the same
   time, the authority of the law is vindicated and the public effectively protected
   from further violations of the law.
2. The rehabilitation of the offender is promoted affirmatively by continuing normal community contacts.
3. The negative and frequently stultifying effects of confinement are avoided,
   thus removing a factor that often complicates the reintegration of the offender
   into the community.
4. The financial costs of crime control to the public treasury are greatly reduced
   by reliance on probation as an important part of the correctional system.
5. Probation minimizes the impact on innocent dependents of the offender.

The ABA sets forth these conditions for a sentence of imprisonment rather than probation (1970: 3–4):

- When confinement is necessary to protect the public from further criminal activity by the defendant
- When the offender is in need of correctional treatment that can effectively be
  provided if he or she is confined
- When the seriousness of the offense would be unduly depreciated if a sentence of probation were imposed

Figure 4.3 shows the flow of criminal cases from arrest through successful
completion of probation.

CONDITIONS OF PROBATION

Although the Task Force on Corrections (1966: 34) observed 4 decades ago that "differential treatment requires that the rules [of probation] be tailored to the needs of the
case and of the individual offender," this suggestion is often not put into practice.
Probation agencies require a defendant to sign a standard form usually containing a
variety of regulations that may or may not reflect the client's individual needs. There
are also special conditions that can be imposed by the judge or the probation department, such as ordering a child molester to avoid places frequented by children.

When conditions of probation are too restrictive, or perhaps appear unreasonable or unrealistic, the PO is inclined to overlook their violation. This can result in
the PO losing the respect of the probationer, making the supervision process difficult. The ABA (1970: 9) recommends that the conditions of probation be spelled out
by the court at the time of sentencing and emphasizes that they should be appropriate for the offender.

It is the order of the Bucks County Court of Common Pleas that you shall comply with the following rules and conditions of supervision:

1. I will report to my Officer as directed and permit this officer to visit me at my home or place of employment.
2. I will respond promptly to any summons to appear at Court or the Office of the Probation Department. My travel is limited to adjoining Counties within PA. Any travel beyond those Counties, out of State, or overnight travel must be approved by my Probation Officer.
3. I will comply with all Federal, State, and local laws. If I am arrested or have contact with law enforcement authorities during supervision, I will notify my officer by the next working day. I will comply with all terms and conditions included in a Protection From Abuse Order.
4. I will report any change of address immediately to my Officer.
5. I will make every effort to obtain and hold a legitimate job and support my dependents. I will report promptly to my officer any change in my employment status.
6. I am forbidden to use, possess, or distribute Controlled Substances and/or dangerous drugs. I will abstain from the excessive use of alcohol.
7. I will voluntarily submit urine, blood, or breath tests as requested.
8. I will not own, use, or possess any type of lethal weapons.
9. I will pay all fines, costs, supervision fees, and restitution in monthly installments as directed by the Probation Officer.
10. I understand that the Adult Probation Department has the authority to search my person, place of residence, or vehicle without a warrant, if there is reasonable cause.
11. I will not enter into any agreement to act as an informant or a special agent of a law enforcement agency without the permission of the Probation Department.
12. I will not physically or verbally threaten, nor engage in religious, ethnic, or racial intimidation toward any Probation Officer.
13. I will abide by the Case Plan, which will be developed by my Probation Officer. I am aware that I will be given the opportunity for input into the plan.
14. I will also comply with the following special conditions imposed by the Court:

_____.

I will keep in mind that I am conditionally released and the Court may at any time revoke my probation or county parole for cause. I am aware that should I violate probation or parole, the Bucks County Adult Probation Department has the authority to incarcerate me pending a Violation Hearing. I am further aware that if I am convicted of a new offense during my probation or parole period I will be brought back before the Court for a Violation Hearing.

FIGURE 4.4 *Bucks County Rules and Conditions of Supervision.*

(*Source:* Bucks County, Pennsylvania, Adult Probation Department.)

The American Probation and Parole Association (APPA) recommends that the only condition that should be imposed on every person sentenced to probation is that the probationer lead a law-abiding life during the period of probation: "No other conditions should be required by statute, but the probation officer in making recommendations [in the PSI report discussed in chapter 5] should recommend additional conditions to fit the circumstances of each case." In a draft of a position statement, the APPA recommends that conditions "be reasonably related to the avoidance of further criminal behavior and not unduly restrictive of the probationer's liberty or incompatible with his freedom of religion. They should not be so vague or ambiguous as to give no real guidance."

The APPA draft states that conditions may appropriately include, but not be necessarily limited to, matters such as the following:

1. Cooperating with the program of supervision
2. Meeting family responsibilities
3. Maintaining steady employment or engaging or refraining from engaging in a specific employment or occupation (e.g., a drug abuser prohibited from employment in a medical setting)

4. Pursuing prescribed educational or vocational training
5. Undergoing medical or psychiatric treatment
6. Maintaining residence in a prescribed area or in a prescribed facility established for, or available to, persons on probation
7. Refraining from consorting with certain types of people or frequenting certain types of places
8. Making restitution for the fruits of the crime, or reparation for losses or damages caused thereby
9. Paying fines, restitution, reparation, or family support
10. Requiring the probationer to submit to search and seizure[1]
11. Requiring the probationer to submit to drug tests (e.g., urine tests) for analysis as directed by the probation officer

Probation regulations in different probation agencies tend to be similar (Figures 4.4 and 4.5). They typically exhort the probationer to live a law-abiding life, work, and support dependents. They require that the offender inform the PO

SOMERSET COUNTY
ADULT PROBATION OFFICE
Court of Common Pleas, 16ᵗʰ Judicial District

DATE: _____

DEFENDANT: _____   CASE NUMBER: _____

CONDITIONS OF PROBATION/PAROLE

In accordance with authority conferred by the Commonwealth of Pennsylvania Probation Laws, you have been placed on probation/parole until _____ by the Honorable _____.

This probation/parole is granted with the full understanding that you have been placed under the supervision of Somerset County Adult Probation Department. Upon parole you must report to the Probation Department immediately. Everyone on probation/parole must comply with the general rules of supervision. You must comply with any special Court Order or conditions imposed by the Court at the time of your sentencing, or subsequently added during the course of supervision. The Probation Office also has the authority to impose special conditions during the course of your supervision, as the need for such may become evident. A probation/parole officer will be assigned to your case, whose responsibility it is to assure your compliance with the terms of your probation/parole. Should problems arise, or questions occur, concerning the conditions of your probation/parole, consult with your probation officer.

Field visits may be conducted by the supervising officer. By law, you must permit search of your person, vehicle, and/or residence. Drug paraphernalia, controlled substances, intoxicants, firearms, and other dangerous weapons and/or contraband are subject to seizure by a probation/parole officer.

Your probation/parole is granted on the following terms:

1. You must notify your probation/parole officer prior to any change of address or employment. You will make every effort to obtain and maintain employment, and meet your financial and family responsibilities.
2. You must not have any type of firearm or other dangerous weapon in your possession for any reason, including hunting, unless authorized by the Court.
3. You shall make regular monthly payments as agreed upon in the Installment Payment Agreement. A fee of $20.00 will be assessed for any check returned due to insufficient funds.
    You will secure written permission of your probation/parole officer prior to entering into a contractual agreement.

FIGURE 4.5 *County Adult Probation Conditions.*

(*Source:* Somerset County, Pennsylvania, Adult Probation Office.)

[1]Probation (and parole) officers have extraordinary authority to conduct warrantless searches of clients and items, as well as places under their control (*Griffin v. Wisconsin*, 483 U.S. 868, 1987).

4. You shall not leave Somerset County without prior permission of your probation/parole officer. If traveling out of Pennsylvania, you must obtain a travel permit from your probation officer.
5. You will follow your probation officer's instruction, advice, and report as directed to the Court or your probation officer and permit your probation officer to visit your home.
6. You will refrain from any violation of criminal laws (Federal, State, and Local) as well as the provisions of the Vehicle Code (75 PA C.S.S. 101 35 seq.) and Liquor Code (47 P.S. 1-101-et seq.). You shall contact your probation officer within 48 hours if arrested or questioned by a law enforcement officer.
7. You shall refrain from the unlawful possession, use, or sale of illicit drugs as defined by the Controlled Substance, Drug, Device, and Cosmetic Act without a valid prescription and submit to urinalysis drug screening when directed to do so by your probation officer. You shall be responsible for payments of any costs for urinalysis testing if the test result obtained is positive or confirms the use of illicit drugs.
8. You shall refrain from the excessive consumption of alcohol and submit to a breathalyzer test when directed to do so by your probation officer. If involved in drug and/or alcohol treatment or on the intensive supervision program, you shall refrain from the consumption or possession of any alcohol.
9. You will refrain from behavior, which threatens or presents a clear and present danger to yourself or others.
10. Special conditions ordered by the Court are as follows:

It is your obligation to acquaint yourself with the terms and conditions as reported above. If you commit an offense while under supervision, or violate any of the conditions of your case, the Probation Officer will review the circumstances and nature of the violation. As a result, the Court may be informed of the violation, for a formal or informal decision. The Probation Office is also authorized by the Court to detain you, which will in effect keep you confined until resolution of the violation. The specifics of any detainer will be brought to the Court's attention.

A violation of any of the above conditions could result in the revocation of your parole and/or probation periods, or the termination of your A.R.D. A revocation may result in incarceration.

If you believe any of your civil rights have been violated as a result of your probation/parole supervision, you may submit a timely complaint in writing to the supervisor of your probation officer. If your complaint is not resolved to your satisfaction, you may then submit your complaint in writing to the Deputy Chief Probation Officer.

I have read or have had read to me the foregoing conditions of my probation/parole. I fully understand them and agree to abide by them.

_____	_____	_____	_____
Probationer/Parolee	DATE	Probation Officer	DATE

FIGURE 4.5 *(continued)*

of his or her residence and that permission be secured before leaving the jurisdiction of the court. Some require that the probationer obtain permission before getting married, applying for a motor vehicle license, or contracting any indebtedness. Many probation departments require that the offender pay a supervision fee, restitution, or community service as a condition of probation. In Pennsylvania, for example, probation and parole clients must pay $25 per month unless the fee is waived. In Virginia, clients who are unable to pay the supervision fee may apply for an exemption; they need to prove unreasonable hardship based on insufficient monthly net income. The issue of fees is discussed in chapter 11. (See Figure 4.6.)

MONTHLY REPORT FORM–ADULT

SEND OR DELIVER TO: **FILE #:** _____ **DPO:** _____
Siskiyou County Probation Department
805 Juvenile Lane   **DATE:** _____
Yreka, CA 96097
Phone: (530) 841-4180   FAX: (530) 841-4188

NOTE: This form is due on the *FIRST* day of each month. All lines *MUST* be filled in
            completely. Just writing "same" is not acceptable.

            ☐ Check this box if this is a new address.
            ☐ Check this box if requesting additional Monthly Report Forms mailed.

Name: _____
Address:
_____
            Street Number   City   State   Zip Code
Mailing Address:

_____
            Street Number   City   State   Zip Code
I live with: _____ Phone No. _____

Employer: _____
            Street Number   City   State   Zip Code
Job Title _____ Work Location _____ Take Home Pay/Monthy $ _____
Unemployed Since _____ Unemployment/Monthly $ _____
Other Family Income: AFDC   SSI   SSP   Other   Amount $ _____
Family Vehicle(s):   Year _____   Model _____   Color _____   License No. _____
                        Year _____   Model _____   Color _____   License No. _____
Purchases Over $200.00 this Month _____

- -

NOTE: **Fill Out the Following Items If They Are a Term of Your Probation:**
            Have you been arrested, cited, or contacted by law enforcement since the
                last report?   Yes   No
                If yes, please explain _____
            I have paid $ _____ on my fine/restitution on _____ (date)
            I have paid $ _____ supervision fee on _____ (date)
            I have completed _____ hours of community service this month.
            I have attended NA/AA _____ times this month on _____ (dates)
            My counselor is _____

- -

NOTE: **Please List Any Changes of Your Probation Status from Last Month:**
            _____
            _____

I have obeyed all the terms of my Probation   Yes   No
I declare that the above information is true to the best of my knowledge.

                                            _____
                                                       Signature

---

FIGURE 4.6 *Monthly Report Form.*

(*Source:* Siskiyou County, California, Probation Department.)

LENGTH OF SUPERVISION

The length of probation terms varies from state to state. The ABA recommends that
the term should be 2 years for a misdemeanor conviction and 5 years for a felony.
In Illinois, it is 4 years for the more serious felonies and 30 months for other felonies;
for a misdemeanor, it is 1 year. In Texas, "the court may fix the period of probation
without regard to the term of punishment assessed, but in no event may the period

Objectives of Probation Supervision

- To provide public protection in keeping with the special duties of a probation officer
- To prepare the probationer for independent, law-abiding living
- To provide an opportunity for full participation of the probationer in planning his or her activities in the community
- To identify, use, and create resources in the community to fulfill program needs of probationers
- To provide a system of differential supervision based on the classification and program needs of all probationers
- To conduct a cost-effective supervision program
- To provide restitution or reparation to victims of criminal acts whenever applicable

Source: New York State Code of Criminal Procedure.

of probation be greater than 10 years or less than the minimum prescribed for the offense for which the defendant was convicted." In the federal system, termination for a misdemeanor may occur at any time and for a felony after 1 year.

Some states authorize early termination of probation without actually having statutory guidelines as to when it is to be exercised. In most states, however, statutes provide for the termination of probation and the discharge of the offender from supervision before the end of the term. This allows the judge some needed flexibility because it is difficult to determine, at the time of sentencing, how long the term should actually be. In Texas, for example, "at any time, after the defendant has satisfactorily completed one-third of the original probationary period or 2 years of probation, whichever is the lesser, the period of probation may be reduced or terminated by the court." In Illinois, "the court may at any time terminate probation . . . if warranted by the conduct of the offender and the ends of justice." In Oklahoma, probation supervision "shall not normally exceed two years unless it is determined [that] the interests of the public and the probationer would best be served by an extended period of supervision not to exceed the length of the original sentence." In Virginia, probation may be terminated for cases placed on supervision for 2 years or more after serving one-half of the term or 3 years, whichever comes first.

The decision to terminate probation early and discharge the offender from supervision should be based on exemplary conduct. Unfortunately, the termination decision may not have any direct relationship to the merits of the case, but it is often a reflection of the need to keep caseloads down to a manageable size. This means that probationers may be discharged even though they are in need of further supervision. (For a discussion of using early termination as a casework tool, see Torres, 1999.)

Probation Supervision in Philadelphia.   Once a person has been sentenced to probation, a PO is assigned to conduct an orientation to the rules of supervision, and assess the needs and risks of the offender. The PO then works with the offender to ensure special conditions that have been stipulated by the judge are met. This department has placed a high priority on the collection of restitution, which is a frequent stipulation imposed by judges. A probation plan is then developed that will aid the offender in completing his or her term successfully.

When necessary, referrals are made to community-based agencies to help clients who require intensive and special treatment for severe drug, alcohol, and mental health problems. These clients may have the option of remaining in a treatment facility, if necessary, even when their probation has expired. Offenders who are polydrug abusers or who have obvious psychiatric problems are evaluated by the department's assessment team, composed of psychologists and a psychiatric social worker. A supervision plan is then developed to assist the PO in supervising the case.

If it is found to be appropriate, some clients are referred to a residential drug treatment program at the Philadelphia State Hospital, which provides group and individual counseling to drug abusers and is administered by a staff person from this department. The department also has a special unit that provides group counseling to clients who cannot or will not take advantage of community mental health services. This unit operates under the supervision of a trained psychologist and serves primarily psychiatric and sex offenders. Offenders charged with driving under the influence are supervised within a special unit called the Alcohol Highway Safety Unit. This unit handles cases that are both within pretrial and posttrial status. The unit monitors the offender's attendance in safe-driving school and in the specified treatment facility.

The Victim Services Unit provides appropriate direct and referral services to victims, helps coordinate victim services among providers so resources can be provided efficiently and effectively, and increases victim input at sentencing and before an inmate's release on parole.

VIOLATION OF PROBATION

The *New York State Code of Criminal Procedure* states:

> Probation as a sentence or disposition is a means of offering the offender the opportunity for law-abiding adjustment in the community. Although the probationer is not deprived of his liberty, his life situation is circumscribed by the conditions which are intended to ensure protection of the community and adjustment of the probationer through effective supervision. It is the Probation Department's responsibility to see that the conditions of probation are properly enforced and to inform the court of any significant deviation.

There are two types of probation violation:

- *Technical.* When any of the conditions of probation has been violated, a technical violation of probation exists.
- *New offense.* When a violation involves a new crime, it is a nontechnical or new offense violation.

The probation response to a violation is a matter of considerable discretion. For example, in Philadelphia, the Adult Probation Department advises its probation officers: "Minor violations of probation/[county] parole do not necessarily need to be brought to the attention of the sentencing Judge, but may be handled between the P.O. and the P/P (probationer/parolee) if such violations are not repeated and do not develop into a pattern." Several probation (and parole) agencies provide for a structured measured response to violations. In Utah, this includes a point system based on the offender's history and the present violation that determines the level of the violation—minimum, medium, maximum—and each level provides a choice of responses such as reprimand or more restrictive conditions (e.g., curfew, residential drug treatment, incarceration).

In many jurisdictions, Allen County, Pennsylvania, and New York, for example, the PO has the authority to "discuss the alleged violation(s) with the probationer and inform him that repeated or more serious violation(s) will be dealt with by the court." If the behavior continues, but a formal violation of probation in not necessary, in New York, "the court shall be informed of the alleged violation(s) and the department's action to date . . . [and] a recommendation may be made to the court requesting that the court require that the probationer appear before it . . . for a judicial reprimand."

To minimize the number of violations filed with the court, POs in Marion County, Indiana, are encouraged to use administrative hearings to address instances

FIGURE 4.7 *Notice of Administrative Hearing.*
(*Source:* Marion County, Indiana, Probation Department.)

where a formal violation of probation is not yet warranted but the probationer is exhibiting some behavior that could lead to a future, more serious, violation. The PO notifies the probationer in writing of the date, time, and reasons for the hearing, which is attended by the probationer, the PO, and the PO's supervisor. A failure to appear results in the filing of a violation of probation request for a warrant. At the conclusion, a hearing report, which can include a modification of the conditions of probation, is signed by the three participants (Figure 4.7).

Some observers are critical of the discretionary powers exercised by probation departments; they maintain that **technical violations,** for example, changing residence without immediately notifying the PO, are often ignored until it is believed that the probationer has committed a new crime. "Invoking the technical violation thus becomes the result of the probation officer making the adjudication that a crime has been committed. The probationer has a hearing on the technical violation, but is denied a trial on the suspected crime which triggered the technical violation" (Czajkoski, 1973: 13). As we will see, it is easier to find a person "guilty" of a violation of probation than it is to prove criminal charges.

The revocation process originates with POs who exercise a "quasi-judicial role" in that they decide whether to seek revocation (Czajkoski, 1973). The PO's attitude toward the probationer and the violation will influence whether revocation action is initiated. Although the actual procedures differ from jurisdiction to jurisdiction, typically the PO confers with his or her superiors; if a violation is considered serious enough, a notice will be filed with the court (Figure 4.8).

The case will then be placed on the court calendar, and the probationer will be given a copy of the alleged violations and directed to appear for a preliminary or **probable cause hearing.** In some jurisdictions, the preliminary hearing is conducted

STATE OF ILLINOIS
SEVENTEENTH JUDICIAL CIRCUIT
WINNEBAGO COUNTY

NOTIFICATION OF ALLEGED PROBATION VIOLATIONS

NAME: Mario B. Benti   CHARGE: Theft over $300.00
ADDRESS: 3642 Renthrow Street   DATE GRANTED: 4/30/02
              Rockford, IL 61103   TERMINATION DATE: 10/30/04

CASE #:   93-CF-507

The above-named probationer has violated the following conditions of his probation in that

1. Defendant failed to pay restitution in the amount of $2285 as ordered.

2. Defendant failed to pay statutory fine and costs as ordered.

3. Defendant failed to pay probation fees of $25 per month as ordered.

4. Defendant failed to report to his probation officer "when and how directed."

5. Defendant was arrested for Violation of an Order of Protection and Criminal Damage to Property on or about 2/1/03.

RECOMMENDED OPTIONS

( ) Extension of probation for payment of costs, fees, restitution, or for completion of counseling.

( ) Recommend petition be filed—probation modified.

(x) Recommend petition be filed—probation vacated.

( ) No petition at this time.

PROBATION OFFICER'S COMMENTS

1. Defendant has been working full time through Corporate Services since 11/30/02, earning $8 per hour.

2. Defendant was on parole for forgery when he was arrested and convicted for theft over $300, for which he is on probation. Parole has since been revoked.

3. Defendant claims he was evaluated by Treatment Alternatives to Street Crime (TASC) for probation back in 1996 but was not accepted for drug treatment. He claims he has never been to treatment before. During this term, this PO has attempted to assist the subject in getting into treatment. He was placed on the waiting list at Sojourn House, Freeport, but was taken off said list for failure to call in weekly as directed. (See attached letters.) Therefore, he has had the opportunity to get help for drug problems but failed to comply with what was required. He carries a diagnosis of cocaine and cannabis dependency.

4. Defendant said he has a record for Theft of Firearm in Beloit, WI. He has two (2) prior residential burglary convictions. (Refer to the pretrial services reports in file.)

Gary M. Meyers
Gary M. Meyers
Probation Officer   February 2, 2003

FIGURE 4.8 *New Arrest Violation of Probation.*
(*Source:* Winnebago County, Illinois, Judicial Court.)

by an official other than a judge, and in some jurisdictions, for example, Texas: "A probationer is not entitled to a preliminary hearing or examining trial to determine whether there is probable cause to proceed to a revocation hearing." In Texas, in cases of violation, the case goes directly before a judge for a revocation hearing. (A probable cause hearing is necessary only if the probationer is to be held in custody pending the revocation hearing.) In any event, if a probationer fails to respond to

COMMONWEALTH OF PENNSYLVANIA :   IN THE COURT OF COMMON PLEAS
                     :   DAUPHIN COUNTY, PENNSYLVANIA

V.

                     :   NO(S):
                     :   CHARGE(S):   CD 20 _____

Waiver of Prerevocation Preliminary Hearing

I hereby waive (give up) my right to have a prerevocation preliminary hearing in the above captioned case. I understand that I have been accused of committing certain violations of my probation/parole as set forth on the notice of alleged violations dated _____.

    I understand and it has been explained to me that:

____ 1. I am not required to waive (give up) my right to have a prerevocation preliminary hearing.

____ 2. The prerevocation preliminary hearing (sometimes called a "Gagnon 1 hearing") is held for the purpose of having a neutral (impartial) hearing officer determine whether there is probable (reasonable) cause to believe that I have committed acts which would constitute a violation of my probation/parole conditions.

____ 3. At such prerevocation preliminary hearing I would have an opportunity to speak in person, present witnesses and documentary evidence and confront and cross-examine adverse witnesses (unless the hearing officer specifically finds good cause for not allowing confrontation.)

____ 4. At such prerevocation hearing, the hearing officer may also make a determination as to probable cause to detain me pending a revocation hearing to be scheduled before the Dauphin County Court of Common Pleas.

____ 5. At such prerevocation hearing, I would be able to have the evidence against me disclosed and obtain a written summary of the hearing from the hearing officer.

____ 6. After having all of the above explained to me, and being given a chance to read this document and ask questions, I was further advised that I could have a lawyer represent me at such prerevocation hearing and that if I could not afford to pay for a lawyer for this hearing that the Court would appoint a lawyer free of cost to me.

Understanding all of the above, I still give up my right to have a prerevocation preliminary hearing.

DATE: _____   _____
                                             PROBATIONER/PAROLEE

_____   _____
WITNESS   PROBATION/PAROLE OFFICER

FIGURE 4.9 *Waiver of Prerevocation Preliminary Hearing.*

(*Source:* Dauphin County, Pennsylvania, Court of Common Pleas.)

a notice or summons to appear for a hearing, the judge will usually issue a warrant. A probationer may also waive the right to a preliminary hearing (Figure 4.9).

Preliminary/Probable Cause Hearing

The accompanying flowchart (Figure 4.10) indicates the possibilities presented at each stage of the probation revocation process. At the preliminary hearing, the probationer can deny the charges of probation violation or plead guilty to them. If the plea is "guilty," the judge may deal with the case at once. If the probationer denies the charges, the judge will decide if there is sufficient (probable) cause to believe that probation was violated (in order to remand the probationer to custody), and a revocation hearing is scheduled. The judge may remand the probationer to custody

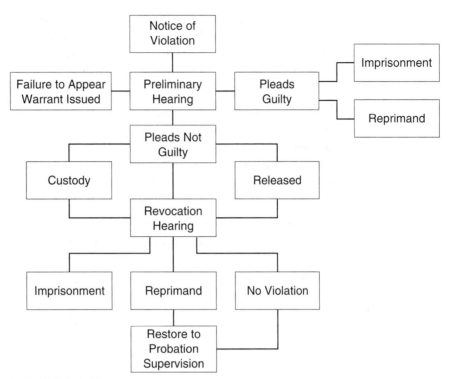

FIGURE 4.10 *Probation Violation Flowchart.*

pending the hearing or can release him or her on bail or on his or her own recognizance. The probation department will subsequently prepare a violation of probation report (Figure 4.11): "The report shall contain a summary of the probationer's supervision activities to date, and the alleged facts which would be sufficient, if proven, to establish any violation(s) of probation occurred" (*New York State Code of Criminal Procedure*).

As opposed to a narrow legal document, the violation of probation report contains information about the probationer's behavior under supervision—for example, employment record—and is presented to the judge prior to the revocation hearing.

Revocation Hearing

At the **revocation hearing,** the probationer will have an opportunity to testify and present witnesses. An attorney may be present to represent the probationer (according to the provisions outlined in the *Mempa* and *Gagnon* decisions discussed later in this chapter), and in some jurisdictions it is common for the defense attorney and the prosecutor to plea bargain in probation revocation proceedings as they do when new criminal charges are filed. If the judge finds no violations, the probationer is restored to supervision. If the judge sustains any of the charges brought by the probation department, the probationer can be reprimanded and restored to supervision, or probation can be revoked and imprisonment ordered. In most cases, the defendant is actually sentenced at the time of conviction, but the imposition of sentence is suspended in favor of probation. Less frequently, the defendant is placed directly on probation without being sentenced. In the latter case, if the violation charge(s) is sustained, the judge can revoke probation and sentence the probationer to a term of imprisonment. The sentence, however, must be in accord with the penalty provided by law for the crime for which the probationer was originally convicted.

Proof of guilt in a criminal trial must be **beyond a reasonable doubt**, but at a probation revocation hearing need not be greater than by a **preponderance of the evidence**, a lower standard used in civil cases. In a criminal trial, the testimony of an accomplice usually requires **corroboration**—supportive evidence—but no such requirement exists for revocation hearings. Evidence that would not ordinarily be admitted in a criminal trial, such as hearsay testimony, can be entered into evidence at a revocation hearing. When the judge renders a decision on the charges, he or she can consider only the evidence presented at the hearing. When making a decision as to the disposition of a probationer found in violation, the judge can consider many items, such as employment record, relationship to spouse and children, and efforts at drug treatment. The range of options after a finding of "guilty" has been increasing as states seek to avoid the traditional two-dimensional outcomes—

THE COMMON PLEAS COURT OF MONTGOMERY COUNTY, OHIO
April 30, 2003

THE STATE OF OHIO
     Plaintiff

-vs-

Mary Wright
     Defendant

The Honorable Michael T. Hall, Judge:

Case No.:   2001-CR-2777
Offense: Possession of Cocaine (Crack) (F-5)
Community Control: 11-13-2001
Maximum Expiration Date: 5-10-2007
     (Adjusted)
Attorney: Countess Taylor/ Public Defender

**REQUEST FOR COMMUNITY CONTROL
SANCTIONS VIOLATION HEARING
(SB-2 Case)**

Information

Home Address: 4045 Ithaca Street
              Dayton, OH 45418

Employment: Unemployed

Means of Support: Family

		Court Costs	Restitution
Financial Obligation:	Original Balance:	$ 145.00	None
Payment Schedule: $25/Monthly	Paid to Date:	$ 145.00	
	Present Balance:	$ -0-	
		Supv. Fee	Fine
	Original Balance:	$ 50.00	N/A
	Paid to Date:	$ 50.00	
	Present Balance:	$ -0-	

Agency Involvement: Grace House

Sanctions: 1) A term of five years basic supervision (not complied); 2) A requirement that the offender obtain full-time verifiable employment (not complied); 3) A requirement that the offender complete a drug alcohol assessment and recommended treatment by agency, Court, or Adult Probation Department (complied); 4) A requirement that the offender abide by a curfew term from 7:00 p.m. to 7:00 a.m. (not complied).

Narrative and Recommendation

On November 13, 2001, Wright was sentenced to five (5) years community control based upon her conviction of Possession of Cocaine (Less than one gram, crack) (F-5) in C#2001-CR-2777. Wright is a medium supervision offender and her sanctions are outlined above.

FIGURE 4.11 *Probation Violation Report.*

(*Source:* Montgomery County, Ohio, Common Pleas Court.)

REQUEST FOR COMMUNITY CONTROL SANCTIONS VIOLATION HEARING
April 30, 2003
Page 2

On April 28, 2003, I received a call from Pretrial Services informing me that Ms. Wright had been arrested. They sent me the Dayton Police Department's police report which indicates on April 27, 2003, the Dayton Police Department was called to a robbery scene at 300 Edison Street. Upon arrival, they made contact with Sue Smith who advised the police officers she was robbed by Wright and an unknown black male. The police found Ms. Wright approximately one block away from the scene. She was immediately taken into custody and later identified by Ms. Smith. Ms. Smith indicated that Ms. Wright started asking her for money which Ms. Smith refused to give, at which time Ms. Wright called a black male. She states that the black male pulled out a black automatic handgun and pointed it at her. She also stated that Ms. Wright began to beat her in the back with a closed fist. Ms. Wright then took $32 out of Ms. Smith's left hand as well as a cellular telephone. Ms. Smith indicates that Ms. Wright then fled the area but was later picked up. Ms. Wright was arrested for Aggravated Robbery (received a detective release), a capias for Soliciting and Loitering to Engage (C#2002-CRB-07992), and Robbery (C#2003-CRA-3914). On July 5, 2002, Ms. Wright pled guilty in C#2002-CRB-07992, was sentenced to 30 days (suspended), and granted one year probation. On October 25, 2002, a warrant was issued for Ms. Wright's arrest for failure to report to the Dayton Municipal Probation Department. Ms. Wright has a preliminary hearing on May 7, 2003, for C#2003-CRA-3914. On April 29, 2003, Ms. Wright was listed on the Pre-Indictment list for the offense of Robbery (Use of Force) F-3 in C#2003-CR-1448. This case is scheduled to go before Grand Jury on May 15, 2003. Subsequently, she was charged with Robbery and is currently being held in the Montgomery County Jail on a $15,000 bond.

Since Ms. Wright has been on community control, she had been declared an absconder on March 15, 2002. She was reinstated onto community control sanctions on July 23, 2002. She has attended and completed a Crisis Care assessment and the Diversified Community Service Program on December 28, 2002, paid off all court costs in full, complied with her curfew, and her last urinalysis conducted on May 1, 2003, tested positive for the illicit drug cocaine. Ms. Wright has not reported to this office since February 4, 2003. On April 25, 2003, a home visit was conducted but Ms. Wright was not home.

Your Honor, based upon the above information, it is respectfully recommended that Ms. Wright appear for a violation hearing in C#2001-CR-2777 and that bond be set at $10,000.

Respectfully submitted,

Lynn A. Mirovsky
Community Control Officer II
Extension 6168

Terri L. Hawk
Supervisor
Extension 4296

LAM/tkm 4-30-2003

FIGURE 4.11 (continued)

prison or continue supervision—that can affect prison overcrowding or, at the other extreme, undermine the supervision process. Responses now include short terms in a local jail or halfway house, electronic monitoring, intensive supervision, or some combination thereof (all discussed in chapters 11, 12, and 13).

Street Time

A defendant is convicted of burglary and sentenced to 3½ years' imprisonment (written 3-6-0: 3 years, 6 months, 0 days). His sentence is suspended in favor of probation. The probationer spends 1 year (1-0-0) under supervision and then violates the conditions of probation in an important respect. After a revocation hearing, the judge revokes probation and orders the probationer to begin serving the 3-6-0 sentence in prison. Must the offender serve a maximum of 3-6-0 in prison, or is the 1-0-0 year of probation supervision ("street") time to be subtracted from the 3-6-0 sentence?

The answer to this question varies from state to state. Some states do not recognize the time spent under supervision as time served against the sentence unless the full probationary term is successfully completed. A minority of states provide **street time** credit for probation violations not involving the commission of a new crime; others leave it to the discretion of the judge.

LEGAL DECISIONS

As the least democratic of our three branches of government, the judiciary—particularly the federal courts and, especially, the U.S. Supreme Court—can decide cases in a manner that may be politically unpopular. It can champion the legal rights of persons who (1) do not represent a significant block of votes or a source of campaign funding, or (2) cannot generate a great deal of media attention, sympathy, or public support. Thus, in 1966, the Supreme Court rendered the famous *Miranda* decision (*Miranda v. Arizona*, 384 U.S. 436), which mandated that police suspects be informed of certain rights (to remain silent, to have counsel) before any questioning. The following year, in another Arizona case, the Supreme Court rendered the *Gault* decision, which gave important rights to juveniles (discussed in chapter 2). That same year, the *Mempa* decision gave probationers the right to counsel in certain instances of probation violation. The Court continued to show an interest in persons with a "disadvantaged status"—juveniles, probationers, welfare recipients, prison inmates, the mentally ill, and parolees—in the many cases that are discussed in this section and in chapters 2 and 8.

Legal decisions that affect probation usually affect parole and vice versa. For example, the *Gagnon* decision to be discussed in this section used the *Morrissey* decision (discussed in chapter 8), which concerned parole violation, as a precedent. However, for purposes of study, the significant decisions in probation and parole have been divided according to the primary thrust of the case. The basis for these decisions has been the constitutional concern for **due process** contained in Amendments Four through Eight. The Fourteenth Amendment, which was adopted in 1868 to protect newly freed slaves, applied these amendments to the states: "No state shall make or enforce any law which shall abridge the privileges or immunities of citizens of the United States; nor shall any State deprive any person of life, liberty, or property, without due process of law." However, the courts did not uniformly apply the Fourteenth Amendment to all constitutional guarantees. In 1961, the Supreme Court decided the case of *Mapp v. Ohio* (367 U.S. 643): Evidence (pornographic materials) seized by the police in violation of the Fourth Amendment could not be admitted to evidence in a *state* trial (such evidence was already inadmissible in federal trials since 1914). This decision provided a basis for the so-called **exclusionary rule,** which *does not* apply to probation (or parole) violation proceedings—evidence seized in violation of the Fourth Amendment can generally be used in a probation (or parole) violation hearing (*Pennsylvania Board of Probation and Parole v. Scott*, No. 97-581, 1998; for a discussion of this issue, see Hemmens and del Carmen, 1997).

Conditions of Probation

In general, the courts can impose any conditions of probation that are reasonably related to the rehabilitation of the offender (e.g., to undergo treatment for drug addiction) or the protection of community (e.g., to avoid the possession of any weapons). The state has a compelling interest in setting limits on the behavior of probationers, and therefore, the Fourth Amendment notwithstanding, probationers enjoy a **diminished expectation of privacy.** Thus, an offender with a history of drug addiction can be required to submit to periodic urinalysis, as a condition of probation, and a warrantless search by a PO is permitted, although the same search by a police officer would constitute a violation of the Fourth Amendment. Probationers can be required to report in person and to answer all reasonable inquiries by the PO, the Fifth Amendment right to remain silent notwithstanding, although the probationer need not incriminate him- or herself (*Minnesota v. Murphy*, 104 S. Ct. 1136, 1984). Probationers can be required to avoid bars or "notorious" parts of a city (e.g., areas where a great deal of drug trafficking is known to occur).

In 1982, the U.S. Court of Appeals for the Fifth Circuit reviewed a case involving the First Amendment (*Owens v. Kelley*, 681 F.2d 1362). The plaintiff (probationer) claimed that a probation condition requiring him to participate in a program called "Emotional Maturity Instruction" violated his First Amendment freedom of religion because of the religious content of the course. The court stated that a "condition of probation which requires the probationer to adopt religion or to adopt any particular religion would be unconstitutional. . . . It follows that a condition of probation which requires the probationer to submit himself to a course advocating the adoption of religion or a particular religion also transgresses the First Amendment."

Owens also challenged a probation condition that required him to "submit to and cooperate with a lie detector test . . . whenever so directed by the Probation Supervisor [title of probation officers in Georgia] or any other law enforcement officer." The probationer claimed that this condition violated his Fifth Amendment privilege against compelled self-incrimination. The court of appeals rejected this claim: "The condition on its face does not impinge upon Owens' Fifth Amendment rights. The condition does not stipulate that Owens must answer incriminating questions. If any question is asked during [the lie detector] examination which Owens believes requires an incriminating answer he is free to assert his Fifth Amendment privilege, and nothing in the probation condition suggests otherwise."

Probation Violation and the Three Theories of Probation

Traditionally, a person on probation has not been considered a free person, despite the fact that the probationer is not incarcerated. The basis for imposing restrictions (conditions) on a probationer's liberty—and for punishing violations—is contained in these theories:

- *Conditional privilege.* Probation is an act of mercy by the judge that has not been earned by the defendant. As such, probation can simply be withdrawn if any condition of the privilege is violated.
- *Contract theory.* Each probationer is required to sign a *contract*—a stipulation agreeing to certain terms in return for conditional liberty. As in any contractual situation, a breach of contract can result in penalties—in this case, revocation of probation.
- *Custody theory.* According to **custody theory,** persons placed on probation in lieu of imprisonment are in the legal custody of the court and, therefore, quasi-prisoners, with their constitutional rights being abridged accordingly. Under such conditions, the court has the authority to move the convict from a community setting to a prison setting in the event of a violation of the conditions of supervision.

Legal decisions discussed in this chapter have challenged these theories.

Probation Revocation.   In 1967, the Supreme Court ruled (*Mempa v. Rhay*, 389 U.S. 128) that under certain conditions a probationer is entitled to be represented by counsel at a revocation hearing. In 1959, Jerry Mempa entered a plea of guilty to the charge of "joyriding" in a stolen car in the state of Washington. Imposition of sentence was deferred, and Mempa was placed on probation for 2 years on the condition that he spend 30 days in the county jail. About 4 months later, the Spokane

County prosecutor moved to have Mempa's probation revoked on the ground that he had been involved in a burglary while on probation. Mempa, who was 17 years old at the time, was not represented by counsel at his revocation hearing, nor was he asked whether he wanted to have counsel appointed for him.

At the hearing, Mempa was asked if it was true that he had been involved in the alleged burglary, and he answered in the affirmative. A PO testified without cross-examination that according to his information Mempa had been involved in the burglary and had previously denied participation in it. Without asking the probationer if he had any evidence to present or any statement to make, Mempa's probation was revoked, and he was sentenced to 10 years' imprisonment. The judge added that he would recommend to the parole board that Mempa be required to serve only 1 year.

In a companion case considered by the Court, William Earl Walkling was placed on probation (for burglary) with imposition of sentence deferred. At a subsequent revocation hearing, Walkling informed the court that he had retained an attorney. When the attorney did not arrive on time, the court proceeded with the hearing, at which a PO presented hearsay testimony to the effect that the probationer had committed 14 separate acts of forgery and grand larceny. The court revoked probation and imposed a sentence of 15 years. No record was kept of the proceeding. The *Walkling* case was consolidated with the *Mempa* case by the Supreme Court.

The Supreme Court noted that previously it had held that the right to counsel is not confined merely to representation during a trial. The Court stated that counsel is required at *every* stage of a criminal proceeding when substantial rights of an accused criminal may be affected, and sentencing is one of these critical stages. In *Mempa*, the Court stated that counsel could aid in marshaling facts; introducing evidence of mitigating circumstances; and, in general, assisting the defendant in presenting his or her case with respect to sentence. The Court ruled that some rights could be lost if counsel were not present at a sentencing hearing, and "we decide here that a lawyer must be afforded at this proceeding whether it is labeled a revocation of probation or a deferred sentencing." The importance of the *Mempa* case goes beyond the limited finding made by the Court—it was the first time that the Supreme Court had ruled in favor of the rights of a person on probation.

In the next important probation/parole case (*Morrissey v. Brewer,* 1972), the Supreme Court stipulated that the amount of due process rights to which a person is constitutionally entitled is directly related to the potential loss that can result. The greatest amount of potential loss is clearly in a criminal case—total liberty and, at times, life itself—may be forfeited. Thus, the criminal process represents the extreme end of the due process continuum: rights to counsel, to remain silent, to a jury trial, and to cross-examine adverse witnesses. Located somewhere at the other extreme would be the due process rights of a student to challenge a course grade. Where are probation and parole located along this due process continuum?

In *Morrissey v. Brewer* (discussed in chapter 8), the Court ruled that parolees accused of violating the conditions of parole are entitled to certain due process rights, including a preliminary and revocation hearing. In 1973, the Court rendered a similar decision in the case of a probation violation, *Gagnon v. Scarpelli* (411 U.S. 778). In 1965, Gerald Scarpelli pled guilty to a charge of armed robbery and was sentenced to 15 years' imprisonment, but the sentence was suspended and he was placed on probation for 7 years. The probationer was given permission to reside in Illinois (under the Interstate Compact discussed in chapter 12), where he was placed under the supervision of the Cook County Adult Probation Department. Shortly afterward, Scarpelli was arrested in a Chicago suburb with a codefendant and charged with burglary. The following month, his probation was revoked, and Scarpelli was incarcerated in the Wisconsin Reformatory to begin serving the 15 years to which he had originally been sentenced. At no time was he afforded a hearing; Scarpelli appealed.

Scarpelli was released on parole in Wisconsin, at which time his appeal reached the U.S. Supreme Court. He claimed that revocation of probation without a hearing and counsel was a denial of due process. The Court ruled that, in legal jargon, Scarpelli had a **liberty interest:** "Probation revocation, like parole revocation, is not a stage of a criminal prosecution, but does result in a loss of liberty. Accordingly, we hold that a probationer, like a parolee, is entitled to a preliminary and a final revocation hearing under the conditions specified in *Morrissey v. Brewer*, supra." In other words, as noted in a 1982 state of Texas decision (*Rogers v. State*, 640 S.W. 2d 248), liberty on probation, although indeterminate, "includes many of the core values of unqualified liberty, such as freedom to be with family and friends, freedom to form other enduring attachments of normal life, freedom to be gainfully employed, and freedom to function as a responsible and self-reliant person."

In *Gagnon*, the Supreme Court held that a probationer is entitled to

- A notice of the alleged violations
- A preliminary hearing to decide if there is sufficient (probable) cause to believe that probation was violated (to remand the probationer to custody)
- A revocation hearing, which is "a somewhat more comprehensive hearing prior to the making of the final revocation decision"

At these hearings, the Court ruled, the probationer will have the opportunity to appear and present witnesses and evidence on his or her own behalf, and a conditional right to confront adverse witnesses. With respect to the right to counsel, the Court was ambiguous: "We . . . find no justification for a new inflexible constitutional rule with respect to the requirement of counsel. We think, rather, that the decision as to the need for counsel must be made on a case-by-case basis." In practice, however, probationers have been afforded the right to privately engaged or appointed counsel at probation revocation hearings.

Now that we have completed our look at the history, administration, and legal issues surrounding probation supervision, in chapter 5, we examine the presentence investigation report.

KEY TERMS

jurisdiction	revocation hearing
venue	beyond a reasonable doubt
grand jury	preponderance of the evidence
rough justice	corroboration
superior court	street time
general jurisdiction	due process
absconders	exclusionary rule
probation subsidy	diminished expectation of privacy
technical violations	custody theory
probable cause hearing	liberty interest

INTERNET CONNECTIONS

Federal Judicial Center: www.fjc.gov

The Nation's Court Directory: courts.net

State Department of Corrections links: www.doc.state.co.us/links.htm

State Justice Institute: statejustice.org

National Center for State Courts: www.ncsconline.org

Probation department links: cppca.org/10_links.shtml

American Probation and Parole Association: www.appa-net.org

Federal Probation & Pretrial Officers Association: fppoa.org

REVIEW QUESTIONS

1. What are the responsibilities of a U.S. magistrate?
2. Why do the federal courts have exclusive jurisdiction in relatively few criminal cases?
3. What is meant by a "court of limited jurisdiction"?
4. What category of courts do not try cases?
5. What is meant by a "court of general jurisdiction"?
6. What is the jurisdiction of a U.S. district court?
7. Why is the U.S. Supreme Court the least democratic part of the U.S. tripartite form of government?
8. Why do the lower courts often dispense what has been referred to as "rough justice"?
9. What is a "court of last resort"?
10. What is the difference between a suspended sentence and probation?
11. What activities of John Augustus are part of the services of a modern probation agency?
12. How does placing restrictions on who can be granted probation violate a basic tenet of positivism?
13. What led to the dramatic increase in the use of probation officers in the United States?
14. What are the six categories into which the administration of probation services can be placed?
15. What are the advantages and disadvantages of placing probation services in the judicial branch of government?
16. What are the advantages of placing probation services in the executive branch of government?
17. How can uniformity be encouraged in states where probation services are administered on a county level?
18. What are the variables that can affect the granting of probation?
19. Why, in some jurisdictions, is there a built-in incentive to sentence a defendant to prison instead of probation?
20. How can the geographic area where the court is situated affect the granting of probation?
21. What is the probation subsidy?
22. Under what conditions is a sentence of imprisonment to be preferred over a sentence of probation?
23. Why would offenders be discharged from probation when their behavior did not justify early termination of supervision?
24. Why is the judiciary in a better position than the other branches of government to guarantee the rights of probationers and parolees (and others)?
25. What are the options available when a PO discovers a violation of probation?
26. What three theories have formed the basis for imposing restrictions on a probationer's liberty?
27. What is "street time"?
28. What have the courts ruled with respect to conditions of probation?
29. What was the issue decided in the case of *Mempa v. Rhay*? What was the real significance of the *Mempa* case?
30. What rights were provided to persons accused of violating probation in the case of *Gagnon v. Scarpelli*?

Sentencing and the Presentence Investigation (PSI)

The presentence investigation is the basis for a **presentence investigation report,** sometimes referred to as a "probation" report, or simply a PSI. After the conviction of a defendant and before the sentencing hearing, a judge may (depending on the circumstances and the statutes of the jurisdiction) order a PSI, which traditionally has reflected positive view interest in the offender (not just the offense). The report may be short form, usually used in misdemeanor or less serious felony cases, or long form, used in most felony cases. In more recent years, changes in sentencing laws have led to a new type of PSI, one that is grounded in the classical view: The focus is on offense history, not the social history, of the offender. This chapter provides examples of all three types of PSI.

REQUIRING A PSI REPORT

In some states, the law requires a PSI report for crimes punishable by more than 1 year of imprisonment; in others, the judge retains the discretion to order a report. In New York and Michigan, for example, a long-form report is required in all felony cases; in misdemeanor cases, the report is discretionary and, when done, is usually in the short form. In Utah, a PSI report is required for all felony and serious misdemeanors. In Missouri and Nevada, a PSI is mandatory in all felony cases unless the defendant waives the requirement—in which case, at the judge's discretion, a PSI may still be compiled. In Texas, no legal requirement exists that a PSI be prepared in each felony case; the trial judge has discretion to order a report or to sentence without one. In Illinois, "a defendant shall not be sentenced for a felony before a written presentence report of investigation is presented to and considered by the court," although this right is frequently waived by the defense counsel because a plea agreement has already been arranged (discussed later).

PURPOSES OF A PSI REPORT

The PSI has four basic purposes:

1. The primary purpose is to help the court make an appropriate disposition of the case. The report should help in deciding for or against probation and determining the conditions of probation, or in deciding among available institutions and determining the appropriate length of sentence.

2. The PSI serves as the basis for a plan of probation or parole supervision and treatment. The report indicates problem areas in the defendant's life, his or her capacity for using help, and the opportunities available in the environment and community. During the investigation, the defendant usually begins to relate to the probation department, learning how POs work and gaining some understanding of the nature of the agency.

3. The PSI assists jail and prison personnel in their classification and treatment programs. Institutions are often dependent on the report when the inmate is first received, a time when little is known other than what is contained in commitment documents: conviction and sentence data. The PSI helps institutional staff to understand and classify the offender; it can provide valuable information that will help in planning for the care, custody, and rehabilitation of the inmate. This includes everything from the type of custody required and the care of physical needs to the planning of the various phases of the institutional program.

     Many institutions will have little, if any, background or social, medical, and psychological information other than that provided by the PSI report. This means that the report will have an effect on the way in which an inmate is viewed and approached by institutional personnel because they will take the word of the PO over that of the offender. The ideal report can give focus and initial direction to institutional authorities for treatment and training, as well as care and management.

4. If the defendant is sentenced to a correctional institution, the report will eventually serve to furnish parole authorities with information pertinent to release planning and consideration for parole, as well as determination of any special conditions of supervision.

In more recent years, an additional dimension—determining the financial condition of defendants—has become important in preparing a presentence report. In the 1984 Criminal Fine Enforcement Act and the 1987 Criminal Fines Improvement Act, Congress cited the need to determine a defendant's ability to pay fines. Financial information is also necessary to assess the defendant's ability to make restitution and to pay any probation supervision fees, which have become rather common. In the federal system, offenders must disclose to POs their assets and liabilities, and the sources and amounts of their incomes and expenses. POs must then confirm these amounts by reviewing documentation provided by the offender. "Probation officers carefully review statements from savings and checking accounts including canceled checks, statements from stockbrokers, closing statements and appraisals from real estate transactions, sales and loan agreements on automobiles and other assets, credit card statements, and documentation on other consumer debt. The probation officer examines the supporting documentation to determine if it is consistent with the offender's financial statement" (Berg, 1997: 29).

Some states include a separate **victim impact statement** (VIS) that is attached to the PSI and usually includes a "description of the harm in terms of financial, social, psychological, and physical consequences of the crime" (Figure 5.1). The VIS may also include a statement concerning the victim's feelings about the crime, the offender, and the proposed sentence (Figure 5.2).

---

1. Identify the victim of the offense. (Should the victim be deceased, information will be gathered from the surviving spouse, adult children, or closest blood relative.)
2. Itemize economic losses suffered by the victim as a result of the offense.
3. Identify any physical injury suffered by the victim as a result of the offense along with its seriousness and permanence.
4. Describe any change in the victim's personal welfare or familial relationships as a result of the offense.
5. Identify any request for psychological services initiated by the victim or the victim's family as a result of the offense.

FIGURE 5.1 *Victim Impact Statement Maryland.*

Court of Common Pleas
GENERAL DIVISION
MONTGOMERY COUNTY
ADULT PROBATION DEPARTMENT

COURTS BUILDING
ROOM 107
41 NORTH PERRY STREET
P.O. BOX 972
DAYTON, OHIO 45422-2001
(937) 225-4264
Fax (937) 225-4360

TO: _____
_____
_____
_____

Date: _____
Offender: _____
Case No.: _____
Offense: _____
Date of Offense: _____

As part of our department's Presentence Investigation, we would like to have your input in the report. This report will be submitted to the Court prior to sentencing of the defendant. Please complete the following information as thoroughly as possible so that the Court will have a good idea of any loss or injuries that you may have incurred. Please return this form by _____.

A. ECONOMIC LOSS
   Was there economic loss?   Yes ( ) No ( )
   Please itemize your loss, including loss of income due to lost time at work because of any injury, any property loss, damage to property, medical costs, or funeral expenses incurred as a result of the criminally injurious conduct. Please attach verification of your losses. Please indicate what property, if any, was recovered. Use a separate sheet of paper if necessary.

   _____
   _____
   _____
   _____

   Have you received any reimbursement for losses?   Yes ( ) No ( )

   How much? $_____   From whom? _____
   Was amount covered by insurance?   Yes ( ) No ( )
   If yes, provide name and address of insurance company.

   _____
   _____

   Amount paid _____   Deductible paid by you _____
   Any monies collected will be sent to your address as shown below. If you move, we must be contacted so that payments will be mailed to the correct address. If a forwarding address is not given, payments will cease. The address to be used for future mailing is:
   Address: _____
   _____
   Telephone: Business: _____ Home: _____

   PLEASE FORWARD THIS FORM AND FUTURE ADDRESS CHANGES TO:
   Montgomery County Adult Probation Department
   41 North Perry Street
   Dayton, Ohio 45422-2001
   ATTN: _____, Probation Officer

B. INJURY
   1. Did you suffer any physical injuries as a result of this offense?
      Yes ( ) No ( ) If yes, describe injury(ies) _____
      _____
      _____
      Were you hospitalized? Yes ( ) No ( ) If yes, how long? _____
      _____
      Are you still under doctor's care? Yes ( ) No ( )
   2. Did you suffer any psychological injury as a result of this offense?
      Yes ( ) No ( ) If yes, please describe _____
      Were you hospitalized Yes ( ) No ( ) If yes, how long? _____

FIGURE 5.2 *County Victim Impact Statement Form.*

(*Source:* Montgomery County, Ohio, Adult Probation Department.)

Are you presently under the care of one of the following:
Psychiatrist   Yes (   ) No (   )   Name _____
Psychologist   Yes (   ) No (   )   Name _____
Counselor   Yes (   ) No (   )   Name _____

C. <u>CHANGE IN YOUR HOME, WORK, OR FAMILY CAUSED BY THIS OFFENSE</u>
Please state in your own words any change that this offense has caused in these areas of your life.

_____
_____
_____
_____

D. <u>WHAT WOULD YOU LIKE TO SEE HAPPEN TO THE OFFENDER?</u>
Check one and state your reason
(   ) Sentence/Incarceration (Will serve time in prison)
(   ) Community Control (Subject to Court requirements, conditions, and rules)

_____
_____

E. <u>DO YOU HAVE ANY OTHER COMMENTS WHICH YOU WOULD LIKE THE COURT TO BE AWARE OF?</u>

_____
_____
_____
_____

F. <u>WOULD YOU LIKE TO PARTICIPATE IN VICTIM OFFENDER MEDIATION?</u>   YES (   ) NO (   )
"Victim-Offender Mediation means a reconciliation or mediation program that includes a meeting between the offender, victim, and mediator to discuss the offense, any restitution and consider other sanctions for the offense."

G. I _____, the undersigned allege that all information regarding restitution is true. I understand that I may be subject to criminal prosecution for falsifying information, in accordance with the Ohio Revised Code, Section 2921.13.

_____   _____
              Signed   Date

victim/impact/statement (Revised 7-1-96)

FIGURE 5.2 *(continued)*

The investigating officer may also be required to provide offender information to a victim. In Indiana:

> The Probation Officer who interviewed victim(s) and witnesses of a felony, as part of the presentence investigation, shall inform them of their right to receive from the Indiana Department of Corrections (IDOC), information regarding when the offender is to be discharged from prison; to be released on parole; is to have a parole release or violation hearing; has escaped; or is going into a temporary release program. The Probation Department shall provide the IDOC with the most recent list of addresses and/or phone numbers of victims no later than five days of receipt of the information from the victim(s). Victims may give the IDOC written notification that they do not wish to receive notification.

In the PSI, the PO attempts in the report to "focus light on the character and personality of the defendant, and to offer insight into his problems and needs, to help understand the world in which he lives, to learn about his relationships with people, and to discover salient factors that underlie the specific offense and conduct in general" and to "suggest alternatives in the rehabilitation process" (Division of Probation, 1974: 48). The report is not expected to show guilt or innocence, only to relate the facts that the PO has been able to gather during the course of the presentence investigation.

CONTENT OF A PSI REPORT

PSI reports should be flexible in format, reflecting a difference in the background of different offenders and making the best use of available resources and probation department capabilities. A full report should normally contain the following items (American Probation and Parole Association and the Administrative Office of the Illinois Courts):

1. *Legal Data.* Arresting officer, victim, original charges filed, and a summary of court action. A complete description of the offense and circumstances surrounding it, not limited to aspects developed for the record as part of the determination of guilt.
2. *Defendant Statement.* Defendant's version of the offense and attitude.
3. *Codefendant(s).* Information about any codefendant(s), including age and court status.
4. *Victim Statement.* A statement from the victim and a description of the victim's status, the impact on the victim, losses suffered by the victim, and restitution due the victim.
5. *Prior Record.* A full description of any prior juvenile and/or criminal record.
6. *Probation/Parole.* Prior adjustment and performance on probation, parole, or any other supervised sentence.
7. *Education and Employment.* A description of the educational background of the offender, present employment status, financial status, and capabilities.
8. *Military Service.* A description of any military record.
9. *Social History.* This includes family relationships, marital status, dependents, interests and activities, residence history, and religious affiliations; and reports from clinics, institutions, and other social agencies with which the offender has been involved.
10. *Medical and Mental Status.* The offender's medical history and, if desirable, a psychological or psychiatric report.
11. *Environments.* Information about environments to which the offender might return or to which the defendant could be sent should probation be granted.
12. *Community Resources.* Information about special resources that might be available to assist the offender, such as treatment centers, residential facilities, vocational training services, special educational facilities, rehabilitation programs of various institutions to which the offender might be committed, special programs in the probation department, and other similar programs that are particularly relevant to the offender's situation.
13. *Summary and Analysis.* Summary and analysis of the most significant aspects of the report, including specific recommendations as to the sentence. A special effort should be made in the preparation of PSI reports not to burden the court with irrelevant and unconnected details.

Some jurisdictions have been including **prediction scales** in their PSI reports. These instruments rate the defendant according to criminal history, education and employment record, family and marital history, companions, alcohol and drug problems, emotional and personal attributes, and attitude or orientation—supportive of crime and unfavorable toward convention. A total score recommends for or against probation and level of supervision.

GATHERING INFORMATION FOR THE PSI

Information in the PSI is derived from persons and documents. Obviously, interview skills and the ability to locate and interpret written material are crucial in preparing a PSI.

Interviews

In probation and parole, much of the necessary information is received directly from people. Thus, report quality is often dependent on the interview skills of probation and parole personnel. In the PSI, a great deal of information is gained by interviewing the defendant: "Interviews shall be directed toward obtaining and clarifying relevant information and making observations of the defendant's/respondent's behavior, attitudes and character" (*New York State Code of Criminal Procedure*, 350.6–3ii). These interviews are conducted in all types of surroundings: from hot and noisy detention pens, where dozens of people may be awaiting a court hearing, to the relative quiet of the probation office.

A quiet, comfortable setting with a maximum of privacy is obviously the best environment for an interview. A place that lacks privacy or has numerous distractions will adversely affect the productivity of the interview. Sometimes interviews are conducted in the defendant's home, which provides an opportunity to observe the offender's home situation and adds an additional and sometimes vital dimension to the report. New York statutes advise: "Whenever possible, interviews with the defendant/respondent shall be at the probation office; however, visits to the defendant's/respondent's residence may be made when there is an indication that additional information will be obtained that is likely to influence the recommendation or court disposition."

The interview is an anxiety-producing situation for the defendant. Previous experiences in similar situations, such as questioning by the police, may have been unpleasant. The PO tries to lower anxiety by cordially introducing him- or herself and clearly explaining the purpose of the interview and the PSI report. This approach is especially important for the defendant who is not familiar with the criminal justice system in general and the court process in particular.

The PO may try to deal with matters of concern to the defendant. A male defendant may be engaged in a discussion of how his wife and dependents can secure public assistance in the event he is imprisoned. The PO might offer to write a letter of referral for his wife to take with her to the welfare department or other social agency that can provide assistance. Female offenders with children will need help in planning for their care in the event of a sentence of imprisonment. In some way, the officer must show genuine concern and interest in the defendant, while being realistic enough to expect many answers and statements that will be self-serving. Because the probation officer's contact with the defendant is limited, the officer cannot expect to probe deeply into the defendant's personality.

Some defendants will be overtly hostile; others will mask their hostility or anxiety with "wisecrack" answers. The PO must control both temper and temperament. He or she is the professional and must never lose sight of that fact during an interview. In questioning, generalized queries (e.g., "What have you been doing?") should be avoided (lest the interviewer be told, "Nothin' much"). Questions should be specific but require an explanation rather than a simple yes or no answer. The PO must avoid putting answers into the defendant's mouth—for example, by asking, "Did you quit that job because it was too difficult?"

When the PSI is complete, the defendant should be reinterviewed to give him or her an opportunity to refute certain information or clarify any aspect of the report that may be in conflict with other parts of the report. In addition to the defendant, the PO may interview the arresting officer, the victim, employers, and significant others in the defendant's environment, such as spouse, parents, siblings, teachers, and clergy. Some recommend interviewing defense counsel and prosecutor (Storm, 1997).

Review of Records and Reports

The PO will be reviewing records and reports in the course of the PSI. The first is the arrest record of the defendant, referred to as a "rap sheet." This record will take the form of an arrest sheet(s) of a law enforcement agency, such as the state police. Each rap sheet entry is usually the result of the subject being fingerprinted. The sheet typically contains numerous abbreviations that the PO must decipher if the record is to be useful—for example, *Att Burg* (attempted burglary) or *DUI* (driving under the influence). The arrest sheet does not describe the offense and may not even indicate if it is a felony or misdemeanor; it simply contains the official charge, for example, *Burg 2.* There is usually no mention of the premises that were burgled or what, if anything, was taken. In addition, the sheet often omits the disposition of the arrest. The officer may not be able to determine from the arrest report what happened to a particular case. Therefore, it is often necessary to check court records or to contact out-of-state agencies to determine the disposition of a case.

The nature of the defendant's prior record is important. The law usually provides for a harsher sentence if the defendant has a prior felony conviction(s). In addition, the defendant's eligibility for probation and a variety of treatment programs, such as drug rehabilitation, may be affected by a prior criminal record. Also, there are the "three strikes and you're out" laws. The PO is especially interested in any information that may influence the sentence that was omitted during the trial, particularly any mitigating or aggravating circumstances, and information that can provide a different perspective on the case. The officer will review any previous PSI reports, as well as reports of other correctional agencies that have had contact with the defendant. These might include training schools or residential treatment centers, as well as prison and parole agencies. The PO may also be interested in reviewing the educational records of the defendant. With the increasing number of substance-abusing defendants coming into the criminal justice system, POs must review this dimension of each defendant and explore the appropriateness of a recommendation for chemical abuse treatment.

If there are any medical, psychiatric, or psychological reports available, the PO will review and analyze them. To do this review, he or she must understand the nomenclature and the meaning of any tests used by medical and mental health professionals who often refer to the *Diagnostic and Statistical Manual of Mental Disorders* (often referred to simply as *DSM*), and probation (and parole) agencies should have copies available for their officers. The PO should make a judgment as to whether a psychiatric or psychological referral should be made during the PSI. Indiscriminate referrals to mental health or court-based clinics waste resources—a crime may be rational, and criminal behavior is not generally symptomatic of an internalized conflict. In cases in which symptoms of mental disorder are apparent, and in those situations in which the offender may benefit from an exploration of his or her problems, a referral should be made. If no referral is made, and a lack of psychiatric and psychological information exists, the PO should present his or her own observations concerning the defendant's intellectual capacity and personality—for example, level of social functioning and contact with reality.

If the PO has received conflicting information about the defendant and is unable to reconcile the discrepancies, this difficulty should be pointed out in the report and not left up to the reader to discover (or, more likely, not discover). "The probation officer must also distinguish between facts and the inferences, or opinions, or conclusions based upon those facts" (Storm, 1997: 13).

Of crucial importance in any PSI report are the sections entitled "Evaluative Summary and Recommendation" (although in some jurisdictions a recommendation is not provided). In Nevada, statutes require the PSI to contain "a recommendation of a definite term of confinement or an amount of fine or both." Nothing should appear in either of these sections that is not supported by the rest of the report. The summary contains the highlights of the total report and should serve as a reminder to the reader of the information that has already been presented. The recommendation is a carefully thought-out statement, based on the officer's best professional judgment. It contains the alternatives that are available in the case and reflects the individualized attention that each case received (Carter, 1966). The PO is in a unique position with respect to making a recommendation to the judge: "The officer has had an opportunity to observe the defendant in the community, not only from a legal-judicial, investigative perspective, but also from the viewpoint of a general life style" (41). To present a meaningful recommendation, the PO must have knowledge of the resources and programs that are available. An inexperienced PO may submit a recommendation for a treatment program that is not available either in the community or at a correctional institution.

One issue that the PO must decide is the recommendation for or against a sentence of probation. In many jurisdictions, a conviction for certain crimes, or a previous felony conviction, precludes a sentence of probation—the PO must know the statutes of the jurisdiction. The officer must also weigh the potential danger the defendant poses to the community, must evaluate the defendant's rehabilitative potential and ability to conform to probation regulations, and must consider whether probation will be construed by the community as too lenient in view of the offense, or by the defendant as "getting away with it."

PSI Process in Nevada.   When a defendant pleads guilty, *nolo contendere* (no contest), or is found guilty after trial, a date is scheduled for sentencing, usually 30 days away. The district attorney refers the case file to the Division of Parole and Probation, at which time an officer is assigned to the case, and he or she begins to research the offender's criminal history and records. Eventually, the defendant completes a preliminary questionnaire and is interviewed by the investigating officer.

During the interview and from the questionnaire, the officer obtains information regarding the offender's social and environmental background, employment history, education, mental health and substance abuse problems, residential stability, support systems, finances, military experience, future goals, and his or her feelings regarding the offense. The investigator must strive to be a perceptive listener and skilled interviewer who lends a keen ear toward attitudes, remorse, candor, and a cooperative spirit. It is important to remember that officers interview all types of people, including juveniles, first-time offenders, career criminals, members of organized crime, the mentally disturbed, substance abusers, and white-collar criminals. As one might assume, these people can be hostile, manipulative, and con-wise, or they may be pleasant—their crime(s) notwithstanding.

The investigator must then begin to verify as much information as possible by contacting the victim, the police, and any other relevant persons/agencies. He or she then begins to formulate the report. Using sentencing guidelines that mix classical and positive elements, the PO determines the probation success probability (positive) and length of sentence (classical). The report is dictated, typed, proofread, approved, and distributed. The PO's recommendation addresses the risk and needs of the offender, the community, and the victim. The report may recommend special conditions of probation appropriate for the offender and his or her criminal activity. POs attend sentencing hearings and are called upon to answer questions by the judge, district attorney, and defense counsel. Recommendations, however, are disclosed only to the judge.

SHORT- AND LONG-FORM PSI REPORTS

There are three basic types of PSI reports: *short form, long form,* and *classical.* The **short-form PSI** is usually less exhaustive and less time consuming, and is typically done in misdemeanor or less serious felony cases. The *New York State Code of Criminal Procedure* states:

The abbreviated investigation for short-form reports shall consist of the defendant's legal history and primarily current information with respect to: the circumstances attending the commission of the offense, family and social situation, employment and economic status, education and, when available, physical and mental conditions. Such investigation may also include any other matter which the probation department conducting the investigation deems relevant to the recommendation or court disposition and must include any matter directed by the court.

Figure 5.3 is an example of the short form.

(text continued on page 135)

THE MONTGOMERY COUNTY COMMON PLEAS COURT, ADULT PROBATION DEPARTMENT
PRESENTENCE REPORT
THE HONORABLE DAVID A. GOWDOWN

PROSECUTOR: Julie Bruns   **DEFENSE ATTORNEY: Harold Rhine**
                                                                                     Retained

-------------------- I.   CASE INFORMATION --------------------

A. DEFENDANT: Ralph Byrne   **C. JAIL STATUS:**
  ALIAS (ES): None   AMOUNT OF BOND: EHDP (Posted)
  ADDRESS: 110 Hampton Street   DAYS IN CUSTODY: 49
          Dayton, OH 45431
  PHONE: **D. FINGERPRINTED: X** YES   NO
  DATE OF BIRTH: 2/13/77 (Age 25)
  SOCIAL SECURITY NO: 4032175192   **PTS   APD**
  PERSON ID#: 17702   **E. URINALYSIS ORDERED: YES NO X YES X NO**
  DRIVER LICENSE #: 35121460   URINE (S) COLLECTED: N/A   1
     STATE: OH EXP. DATE: 2/19/06   RESULT (S) POSITIVE: N/A   0
     STATUS: Suspended/Expired   RESULT (S) NEGATIVE: N/A   1

B. CASE NO.: <u>2001-CR-3334</u>   **F. PROBATION OFFICER:** David K. Taylor/ISP
     REFERRED: 2-11-2002   **G. CODEFENDANT STATUS:** None
     DISPOSITION: 3-11-2002   **H. RESTITUTION:** $915.72
                                                  I. COURT COSTS: $234.40
                                                  J. SUPERVISION FEE: $50.00

------------------ II.   CHARGE INFORMATION ------------------

A. CURRENT ADJUDICATED CHARGE (S)/   **B. INDICTED CHARGE:**
O.R.C./PENALTY: (Post SB-2)   Failure to Comply With Order or Signal of a
Guilty Plea—As Charged   Police Officer
<u>FELONIOUS ASSAULT (DEADLY WEAPON)</u>   2921.331 (B) /2921.371 (C) (5) (a) (ii) F-3
<u>(PEACE OFFICER) (COUNT 3)</u>   Assault (Peace Officer)
2903.12 (A) (2) F-1   2903.13 (C) (3) F-4
3 to 10 Years CRC   Felonious Assault (Deadly Weapon) (Peace
Presumption for Prison Term   Officer)
$10,000 Maximum Fine   2903.12 (A) (2) F-1
Mandatory Driver License Suspension
for Thirty (30) Days to Three (3)
Years   **C. ORIGINAL JURISDICTION:**
NOLLED: Counts 1 & 2   Kettering Municipal Court (C#2001-CRA-1851)

                                             D. OTHER PENDING CASES/DETAINERS:
                                               Resisting Arrest, Disorderly Conduct, Public
                                               Intoxication (C#2000-CRB-0586) (Kettering
                                               Municipal Court)—unsupervised probation;
                                               Resisting Arrest (C#2001-CRB-1852A); No
                                               Operator's License (C#2001-TRD-12014)—
                                               sentencing 3-18-2001 (Kettering Municipal Court)

FIGURE 5.3 *Adult Probation Department Presentence Report.*

(Source: Montgomery County, Ohio, Adult Probation Department.)

E. PRIOR FELONIES:

None

— — — — — — — — — — — — — **III.   CLIENT INFORMATION** — — — — — — — — — — — — — —

A. PHYSICAL

   SEX _Male_   **RACE** _White_   **HEIGHT** _72″_

   WEIGHT _195_   **EYES** _Blue_   **HAIR** _Red_

   PRESENT HEALTH _Good_

B. SOCIAL

   MARITAL STATUS _Single_

   NO. OF DEPENDENTS _0_

   CUSTODY OF DEPENDENTS IF SENTENCED _N/A_

   EMPLOYMENT STATUS _Unemployed_

   LAST GRADE COMPLETED _12th_

   SOCIAL SERVICE INVOLVEMENT

   PAST _None_

   PRESENT _Eastway; Nova House_

   LIMITATIONS: Chemically Dependent

PART I.   THE OFFENSE

On October 2, 2001 at approximately 7:00 p.m., Montgomery County Sheriff's Deputies were dispatched to 17 Tripp St. on a report that Ralph Byrne had just left the area in a blue Ford pickup truck and was supposedly driving under the influence of alcohol and driving under suspension. As deputies were responding to the area, they observed the pickup truck traveling southbound on McEwen Road. Deputies followed Mr. Byrne and activated their overhead lights. Mr. Byrne turned onto McEwen Road then stopped in the middle of the lane. Deputy McGlaughlin approached the driver's side window and asked Mr. Byrne to roll the window down. Mr. Byrne rolled the window down approximately four inches. Deputy McGlaughlin asked Mr. Byrne for his driver license and could tell that Mr. Byrne had a strong odor of alcoholic beverage on or about his person. Additionally, his eyes were bloodshot and glassy and he had very slurred speech. Mr. Byrne advised the deputy that he did not have his license. During this time additional deputies had arrived to assist Deputy McGlaughlin. Mr. Byrne was asked to turn the truck off and step from the vehicle, but he refused. Both Deputy McGlaughlin and Sergeant Worley ordered Mr. Byrne out of the vehicle numerous times, but he refused. Mr. Byrne told Deputy McGlaughlin that he was "being a dick" and refused to talk to him further. Mr. Byrne demanded to talk to the officer in charge and Sgt. Worley stepped around to the driver's side door. Sgt. Worley tried several times to get Mr. Byrne to come out of the truck, but Mr. Byrne stated that he did not trust anyone in uniform and would only talk to someone without a gun and not in uniform. After repeated attempts to get Mr. Byrne out of the vehicle had failed, Sgt. Worley and Captain Hobbs, who had also arrived on the scene, requested a SWAT Team callout. While the deputies awaited arrival of the SWAT Team, they maintained various positions around the truck. A perimeter was established around the truck and Lyons and McEwen Roads were closed. Numerous pedestrians were evacuated from the area. Sgt. Glaser then began a conversation with Mr. Byrne who was becoming visibly upset with the growing number of police personnel on the scene. Mr. Byrne started screaming loudly at Sgt. Glaser then put his truck in reverse and started gunning the engine. Mr. Byrne rocked the truck forward and backward several times until he accelerated over an island and headed southeast through a parking lot. Deputies decided not to pursue the vehicle but then learned that a Centerville Police Officer was almost struck by Mr. Byrne when he turned onto McEwen Road. At that point, a pursuit began. The pursuit by Sheriff deputies and Centerville Police officers continued to Waterloo Road where Mr. Byrne locked his brakes and came to a stop. Deputy Jack Shaw stopped immediately behind Mr. Byrne and exited his vehicle. Mr. Byrne then put his truck in reverse and rammed into Deputy Shaw's cruiser. Mr. Byrne then continued on Waterloo Road and traveled on numerous city streets until he came to 110 Hampton Street (his home) and turned into the driveway.

   Mr. Byrne exited the vehicle and ran into the garage with Deputy Shaw in pursuit. Mr. Byrne turned and grabbed Deputy Shaw by the throat with both hands and started to strangle him. At this point, Sgt. Wilson shot Mr. Byrne with a less than lethal (beanbag) shotgun, striking Mr. Byrne and causing him to release Deputy Shaw. Deputy Shaw and Sgt. Wilson then tackled Mr. Byrne inside the house. Mr. Byrne struggled with several deputies in the residence, and he was eventually handcuffed and a hobble restraint was applied. Mr. Byrne was transported to the Montgomery County Jail where he was booked on numerous charges including Felonious Assault on a Peace Officer.

FIGURE 5.3 *(continued)*

During the Presentence Investigation interview, Mr. Byrne stated that on the night of the instant offense, "stuff was not going my way." Mr. Byrne stated that he had been drinking to forget his problems and decided he wasn't drunk enough so he got in his truck and left for the store to get some more alcohol. Mr. Byrne's mother and neighbor saw him driving off and someone called the police. Mr. Byrne's stated that the police pulled him over and the officer ordered him out of the truck, but he took off instead. Mr. Byrne admitted that he backed into the cruiser and headed for home. He also admitted that he grabbed Deputy Shaw by the throat. Mr. Byrne admits that his actions were "stupid" and that he should not have done the things that he did. However, Mr. Byrne also stated significant contempt for local law enforcement and stated that he had been beaten up by them on numerous occasions. He described the offense as "just another night's work" for the deputies involved. Mr. Byrne does not believe that he caused any physical injury or harm in any way to the deputies involved in his arrest.

PART II.   CRIMINAL RECORD SECTION

A. Juvenile

Mr. Byrne had no criminal arrests as a juvenile. He admitted that he was involved in a Criminal Damaging at age 15 when he shot car windows out with a BB gun, but this complaint does not appear on his juvenile record. Most likely he was referred to a diversion program.

B. Adult

   Misdemeanor

5-23-96	RESISTING ARREST, PUBLIC INTOXICATION (C#96-CR-0276) (Kettering Municipal Court)	Sentenced 90 days, suspended
5-16-98	IN PARK AFTER HOURS (C#98-CRB-1004) (Kettering Municipal Court)	Fine and costs
10-25-98	SALE OF LIQUOR TO UNDERAGE PERSON (C#98-CRB-2089) (Kettering Municipal Court)	Sentenced 180 days, suspended, two years unsupervised probation
7-27-99	DRIVING UNDER THE INFLUENCE (DUI) (KENTUCKY)	License Suspension
4-7-2001	RESISTING ARREST, DISORDERLY CONDUCT, PUBLIC INTOXICATION (C#2000-CRB-0586) (Kettering Municipal Court)	Sentenced 90 days, suspended, two years unsupervised probation
12-3-2001	RESISTING ARREST (C#2001-CRB-18524), NO OPERATOR'S LICENSE (C#2001-TRD-12014) (Incurred with Instant Offense)	Sentencing 3-18-2001

   Felony

2-11-2002	FELONIOUS ASSAULT (DEADLY WEAPON) (PEACE OFFICER) (C#2001-CR-3334)	Instant Offense

PART III.   EMPLOYMENT/OTHER PERTINENT DATA

Ralph Byrne was born and raised in Centerville, Ohio. He lived with both parents while growing up and has one sister, age 26. Mr. Byrne's father, Harold Byrne, was employed through the Department of Veterans Affairs. Harold Byrne died approximately five years ago of heart failure. Mr. Byrne presently resides with his mother, Rose Byrne, who is employed at United Health Care. Mr. Byrne reports that he has never been married and has no children. During his leisure time, Mr. Byrne reports that he hangs out with his friends, works on cars, and he enjoys martial arts.

   Mr. Byrne attended Centerville High School and graduated in 1995. He states that he was suspended twice, once when he had an altercation with another student, and again when he

FIGURE 5.3 *(continued)*

"flipped off" a teacher. Mr. Byrne indicated that he participated on the football and wrestling teams in high school. Mr. Byrne has recently attended Sinclair Community College through the Internet and wants to attend school to learn automotive maintenance.

Mr. Byrne is presently unemployed. He last worked for a cleaning company from 1999 to 2000, where he was paid under the table. Mr. Byrne advised that he quit because he got tired of the travel. Prior to that he worked in merchandise stocking at Best Buy for several months during 1999. Mr. Byrne served in the United States Army from 1996 to 1998. He stated that he got a General Conduct Discharge because he did not want to stay and he had one year left on his enlistment.

According to Mr. Byrne he is in good physical health without any medical treatment or current problems. Mr. Byrne reports that he suffered a kidney injury in 1997 and 1998 after getting into a fight when he was drunk. He reports a significant chemical abuse history, particularly with alcohol. He advised that he first drank alcohol at age 8 and has been drinking on a regular basis since that time. He admits that the instant offense was alcohol related, as were most of his criminal offenses. Mr. Byrne advised that he is a binge drinker who at times drinks significant amounts of hard liquor. When questioned about his consumption of alcohol and his desire to quit, he stated that he should not drink under most circumstances, and probably should not drink hard liquor. He advised that he is not going to quit drinking completely, and sees nothing wrong with drinking beer and wine. Mr. Byrne reported that he has not consumed any alcohol or other drugs in the past month. However, on February 15, 2002, a Montgomery County Sheriff's Deputy was dispatched to the Byrne residence on the report of loud music. Deputy Combs made contact with Mr. Byrne and detected a moderate odor of alcoholic beverage on his person. Deputy Combs also noted that his eyes were glassy and Mr. Byrne stated, "I'm working on a beer." It is apparent that he is not being truthful about his consumption of alcohol. In addition to alcohol, Mr. Byrne states that he has been smoking marijuana since age 15, and has also not used that drug in the past month. He is presently in treatment at Nova House (outpatient) for substance abuse and at Eastway to deal with "general problems and anger." His last summary report from Nova House, dated February 27, 2002, states, "client minimally takes treatment seriously, often using his time here to grandstand about his ideas. Client needs to take this intervention more seriously or be closed unsuccessfully." Mr. Byrne readily admitted that he was using drugs while in the Montgomery County Jail to help pass the time.

Mr. Byrne's mother, Rose Byrne, was also interviewed for this report. Mrs. Byrne stated that her son is suffering from depression. She stated that during the summer of 2001, Ralph broke up with his girlfriend, started drinking more, and was suicidal. Mrs. Byrne and police reports have confirmed several incidents where he attempted suicide, once by hanging, and at least once when Mrs. Byrne had to take a gun away from him. In December 2001, Mr. Byrne was "pink slipped" to Kettering Medical Center where he was diagnosed with Bi-Polar Disorder. His psychiatrist recommended medication, but he has refused to take them. Mrs. Byrne stated that Ralph and his father were extremely close, and his father's death had a significant impact on him. At the time of Mr. Byrne's death, he was on duty in Saudi Arabia and had to find out by telephone. Mrs. Byrne stated that he pretends to be a "tough guy" but has a soft spot for people he cares about. She related that Ralph had problems in the military due to alcohol abuse and not getting along with COs. She also stated that he had significant problems in school and was in counseling, beginning in kindergarten. He was believed to have ADHD, and was placed on Ritalin without benefit. Mrs. Byrne stated that her son went several places for counseling as a juvenile and the family was involved in family counseling. When his school guidance counselor suggested that he drop out, the family arranged through the school for him to have an in-home tutor. He in fact finished his education at home, not in the school. Mrs. Byrne stated that since he has been home on Electronic Home Detention Program (EHDP), he has improved, and is pleasant to be around and cooperative.

One urinalysis sample taken during this investigation was negative.

VICTIM IMPACT STATEMENT

Judge:	The Honorable David A. Groton
Case No.:	2001-CR-3334
Name of Victim:	Deputy Jack Shaw Montgomery County Sheriff's Office 330 W. Second Street Dayton, Ohio 45422

FIGURE 5.3 (continued)

Name of Defendant:	Ralph Byrne
Disposition Date:	March 11, 2002

A. Economic Loss

   $915.72 is due for damages to the Montgomery County Sheriff's Office cruiser. Restitution is to the Montgomery County Sheriff's Office, OCA Code 236323, Attention Tom Mundey.

B. Physical Injury

   None

C. Change in Personal Welfare or Familial Relationships

   None

D. Psychological Impact

   None

E. Comments

   Deputy Shaw was faxed a Victim Impact Statement, which has yet to be returned.

FIGURE 5.3 *(continued)*

In cases of all, or only the more serious felonies, judges will order a **long-form PSI** report. Figure 5.4 is an example.

SENTENCING GUIDELINES, MANDATORY SENTENCES, AND THE CLASSICAL PSI

By 1994, every state had **mandatory sentencing laws,** the latest being three (and sometimes two) strikes and you're out (actually in for life—the baseball metaphor accounting for at least some of its popularity). In California, for example, the law requires that persons convicted of a violent crime, who have two prior convictions (which need not be violent), must serve a minimum of 25 years. Some states require that the instant offense and the prior felonies be for violent crimes, whereas others permit consideration of juvenile adjudications for violent offenses.[1]

A violent crime does not necessarily mean violent behavior on the part of an offender. For example, in New York, residential burglary during the day is a "violent" offense even in the absence of the possession of a weapon or encounter with an occupant. The same applies to the lookout during a street robbery or a battered woman who severely injures or kills her abuser. Offenders who are convicted of a violent crime in their youth become the subject of mandatory sentencing as adults even when the offense is nonviolent. Ironically, research reveals that violent offenders who are released from prison are much less likely to be convicted of a new offense than nonviolent inmates, particularly drug offenders. This raises questions about the strategy for reducing prison overcrowding by incarcerating only violent offenders.

About 20 states and the federal government use sentencing guidelines primarily in an attempt to limit judicial discretion and reduce sentence disparity—a turn toward classicalism. In Minnesota, for example, sentencing guidelines were instituted in 1980

(text continued on page 148)

[1]These laws could make potential three-strikers desperate, more likely to kill witnesses, and/or more likely to violently resist law enforcement officers.

STATE OF INDIANA   Date Ordered 6-24-03
PRESENTENCE INVESTIGATION REPORT   Date Completed 10-30-03

FACE SHEET

COURT INFORMATION
MARION SUPERIOR COURT CRIMINAL DIVISION, ROOM 3

Judge: The Honorable John R. Barney
Prosecutor: Brian Poindexter
Defense Attorney: Carolyn Radar
Probation Officer: Cindy Humerickhouse
Marion County Superior Court, Criminal Division, Probation Department   Tel. 317-327-3060
200 East Washington Street, Suite 322T, Indianapolis, IN 46204

OFFENDER INFORMATION

Case No.(s): 703216
Name: Carl Mintz
Alias(es): None
Address: 6425 Atlanta Drive
City: Indianapolis   State: IN   Zip: 46241
Telephone: 317-856-4668   SSN: 317-70-1515
DOB: 1-19-65   POB: Indianapolis, IN
Age: 38 Race: White Sex: Male Ht: 5'8" Wt.: 160 Eyes: Brown Hair: Brown
ID Marks: None
U.S. Citizen: ☒Yes ☐No   Alien Status: N/A
Driver's License No.: Unknown   State of Issue: IN   Status: Susp.
Criminal Involvement (Check all that apply)
Charges(s) ☒Pending ☒Jail ☒Felony ☒Probation ☐Comm. Corr. ☐Juvenile ☐Res. Placement
Detainer(s) ☐Prison ☒Misdemeanor ☐Parole ☐Violation(s) ☐Juv. Detention ☐IBS/IGS

OFFENSE INFORMATION

Present Offense(s): Ct. I, Murder, Ct. II, Murder, Ct. III, Kidnapping (A), Ct. IV, Kidnapping (A), Ct. V & VI, Burglary (A), Ct. VII, Carrying a Handgun w/o a License (A/m), Request for the Death Sentence (III);

B.A.C. N/A

Arrest Date: 8-5-00   Type of Release: None

Sentencing Date: 11-1-03   Jail Credit: 1185
Co-Defendant(s): None

ADDITIONAL INFORMATION

Found Guilty by Jury Trial to: GAC to Ct. I, Murder, Ct. II, Murder, Ct. III, Kidnapping (A), Ct. IV, Lesser Included Confinement (B), Ct. V, Burglary (A), Ct. VI, Burglary (A), Ct. VII, Carrying a Handgun w/o a License (A/m), Request for the Death Sentence (III);

PRESENTENCE INVESTIGATION

I. SOURCES OF INFORMATION

IPD Juvenile and Adult records
Marion County Prosecutor Files
Marion Superior Court III, files
Indiana State Police, records
Ben Davis High School transcript
Hoosier Neurology, P.C., Adult & Child Neurology Report
completed by Dr. Norman Martinson, M.D.

FIGURE 5.4 *Presentence Investigation Report.*

(*Source:* State of Indiana.)

Indianapolis Neurosurgical Group Inc., Neuropsychology Report Adult Tests
St. Francis Hospital & Health Centers, records
Letters submitted by Doris Knight, Cathy Knight, and Randy Knight
Marion County Probation files

II. PRIOR LEGAL HISTORY

A. Juvenile Record

The defendant has no known juvenile record in Marion County, IN.

B. Adult Record

Date	Agency	Offense	Disposition
11-8-84		Disorderly Conduct (B/m) Docket #97711195	11-9-77, indigent, 6 mos. Prob.

The defendant was discharged from probation on 5-9-85.

The above offense was not listed on the defendant's IPD criminal history and was obtained through the defendant's probation records.

Date	Agency	Offense	Disposition
4-4-85		Criminal Mischief	Disposition Unknown
1-27-86		Drunk (1479-909)	3-26-86, GAC, F/C, 180 days Prob.

The defendant was discharged from probation on 8-13-87.

The above offense was not listed on the defendant's IPD criminal history and was obtained through the defendant's probation records.

Date	Agency	Offense	Disposition
5-29-86	MCSD	Theft reduced to Conversion (A/m) (5-79-4578)	8-13-86, F/C, 90 days w/ 74 days Susp., 4 Jail wkds., $600 Restitution, 1 yr. Prob.

The defendant took four tires and wheels, two mirrors and one set of taillights from Delanty Ford, Inc.

The defendant was discharged from probation on 8-13-87.

Date	Agency	Offense	Disposition
4-22-87	MCSD	Public Intoxication (B/m) (580-03202)	Disposition Unknown
9-28-87		Criminal Mischief (1380-90064)	11-13-87, F/C, 28 days Susp., 6 mos. Prob. Restitution paid, 8 jail wkds.

The defendant threw a rock and hit Joyce Gault's residence and broke her picture window. Damages totaled $275.00.

A probation violation was filed on 2-11-88 for failure to report to the Marion County Jail for three of his jail weekends. The status of this violation is unknown, but it appears the defendant was discharged from probation on 6-4-88.

The above offense was not listed on the defendant's IPD criminal history and was obtained through the defendant's probation records.

Date	Agency	Offense	Disposition
6-23-88	IPD	Drunk (1081-05469)	6-23-88, F/C, 90 days Susp., 6 mos. Prob., Alcohol Rehab.

FIGURE 5.4 (continued)

The defendant was discharged from probation on 12-24-88.

9-22-88	IPD	Battery (M108107337)	1-20-89, F/C, 180 days Susp., 6 mos. Prob., Stay away & refrain from contacting witnesses, May need treatment/alcohol couns.

The defendant struck Terry Gault, his girlfriend at the time, in the head and face with his fists.

The defendant was discharged from probation on 7-20-89.

2-4-89	IPD	Theft reduced to Conversion (1083-01342)	3-31-00, F/C, 180 days Susp., 1 yr. Prob.

The defendant took a twelve pack of beer from the Patton's Drug Store at 147 Pinecrest Avenue.

The defendant was discharged from probation on 3-31-91.

1-1-92	MCSD	Public Intox., (B/m)	2-22-92, Nolle
2-2-92	MCSD	Resisting (B485-0004)	2-22-92, Nolle
4-24-92	MCSD	Public Intox., (B/m) (A485-01756)	4-25-92, Nolle
4-24-92	MCSD	Battery w/ Injury (A0485-00504)	7-23-92, Nolle

A narrative was unavailable.

10-24-92	IPD	Battery on a Police Officer (A058506007)	4-17-93, Nolle
		Disorderly Conduct (B/m) (B058506007)	4-17-93, F/C, 60 days Susp., 1 yr. Prob., Alcohol Treatment
		Resisting Law Enforcement (C058506007)	4-17-93, Nolle

The defendant had a dispute with Deanna Best and shattered the passenger side window of her vehicle. He then refused to give Deanna Best her purse. When a responding Unit arrived, the defendant became hostile, began using profanities, spit and attacked the Unit.

The defendant was discharged from probation on 4-17-94.

11-17-92	MCSD	Criminal Recklessness (A985-6499)	4-23-93, 10 days Exec., 170 days Susp., 6 mos. Prob., F/C, Stay away from Denise Mae Best

The defendant was hiding in a bedroom closet at 1024 Seventh Street, a residence belonging to the defendant's girlfriend at the time, Deanna Best, and her sister, Denise Best. The affidavit for probable cause indicates the defendant pointed a gun at Denise Best. He said "I'm gonna kill you Bitch" and she ran to her bedroom and leaned against the door. He put his fist through the door. When he got halfway in he stuck the gun to Denise's nose and said he was going to shoot her and Deanna "execution style."

The defendant was discharged from probation on 10-23-93.

The above offense was not listed on the defendant's IPD criminal history and was obtained through the defendant's probation records.

FIGURE 5.4 (continued)

5-21-93	ISP	Resisting Law Enforcement (A/m) (A1486-02128)	6-2-93, No Affidavit
1-25-93	MCSD	Battery (A048605773)	4-10-94, Nolle
3-19-93	IPD	Failure to Stop After Accident (A586-1140)	5-20-93, 180 days Susp., 6 mos. Prob., F/C, Restitution in the amount of $200.00.

The defendant's probation was discharged on 11-20-93.

12-15-95	IPD	Ct. I, Operating a Vehicle While Intoxicated (A/m) Ct. II, Operating a Vehicle w/ .10% BAC (C/m) (49F108812CM151899)	2-16-96, GAC to Ct. I, 363 days Susp., credit for 1 day served, F/C, 180 days restricted license in lieu of suspension, 1 yr. Prob., Alcohol Eval.

The defendant was stopped by officers in his vehicle and appeared to be intoxicated. He was given several field sobriety tests which he failed. He was taken to headquarters, where tests were run on Intoxilyzer 5000 with a result of .18 % BAC.

Marion County Municipal Court Probation records indicate the defendant was discharged from probation on 2-16-97.

2-7-96	MCSD	Ct. I, Battery (A/m) Ct. II, Battery (B/m) (49F048809CM104291)	9-27-96, GAC to Ct. II, F/C, 1 yr. Susp., 1 yr. Prob., Restitution to Barbara Slattery in the amount $269.80, A.E.T.

Barbara Slattery arrived at her residence at 3550 Kent St. Apt. 3C and observed Mintz and his girlfriend, Deanna Best, in her living room. Carl Mintz allegedly followed Barbara into the bedroom. Mintz allegedly accused her of stealing her boyfriend's things. As Barbara was putting things in her bag, Mintz grabbed her bag and threw the bag on her dresser.

She then attempted to call the police and Mintz allegedly came in and grabbed the telephone away and threw it to the floor. Mintz allegedly pushed Barbara and told her to leave, and she pushed him back at which time he fell into the bathroom and hit his ribs on the toilet. Barbara states she went into the bathroom when Mintz grabbed her bag and threw it. He then allegedly shoved her backwards into the bathtub. She tried to get up and the defendant allegedly pushed her several times back into the tub. Ms. Slattery was treated for a hairline fracture of the left side of the jaw.

On 8-30-97 restitution was paid in full and the defendant was successfully discharged from probation on 9-27-97

5-20-98	MCSD	Battery (A/m) (49F189104CM054479)	9-12-98, GAC, 1 day Exec., 364 days Susp., 1 yr. Prob.

On 4-7-98 Harry Troy was driving his vehicle and came to a stop sign when another car slammed on his brakes. The driver of that vehicle, Mintz followed Troy's vehicle so close he could not see his headlights. As Troy came to the stop sign, the defendant illegally passed Troy. The defendant then exited his vehicle and ran back to Troy's vehicle. He then struck Troy three times in the face with a closed fist, causing his glasses to break and fall off. Injuries included a bloody nose, swollen jaw, and bruised jaw and face.

A probation violation was filed on 1-27-99 alleging a new arrest. On 3-18-99 the violation was found untrue and the defendant's probation was continued to 5-27-99. The defendant's probation was continued several times. A probation violation was filed a second time on 2-4-00 for a new arrest. The violation was found untrue and the defendant's probation was terminated on 5-13-00.

FIGURE 5.4 *(continued)*

| 10-8-98 | MCSD | Battery (A/m) (49F189107CM095870) | 1-2-99, GAC, 3 days Exec., 27 days Susp. |

The defendant struck Carol Knight (victim in the instant offense) with a closed fist causing bruising to her chest and arm.

The defendant was also ordered to serve one (3 day) weekend at the Marion County Jail.

| 10-8-98 | MCSD | Criminal Mischief (B/m) (49F189107CM095929) | 1-2-99, GAC, 15 days Exec., 165 days Susp., 180 days Prob. |

The defendant struck Doris Knight's 1987 Ford with his fist. Damages to the car hood were approximately $100.00.

As conditions of probation the defendant was ordered to pay fines and costs, restitution to Doris Knight in the amount of $200, and the defendant was ordered to serve commitment as five (3 days) weekends at the Marion County Jail.

A probation violation was filed on 1-27-99 alleging a new arrest. On 3-18-99 the violation was found untrue and the defendant's probation was continued to 5-27-99. The defendant's probation was continued several times. A probation violation was filed a second time on 2-4-00 for a new arrest. The violation was found untrue and the defendant's probation was terminated on 5-13-00.

| 1-3-99 | MCSD | Ct. I, Criminal Recklessness (B/m) Ct. II, Battery (D) Ct. III, Criminal Recklessness (A/m) Ct. IV, Battery (A/m) (49F099201CF001858) | 8-26-99, GAC to Ct. Ct. II, 365 days. Exec., 360 days Susp., 360 days Prob. |

According to the Affidavit for Probable Cause, on 1-3-99 the MCSD was dispatched to the 5000 block of West Minnesota Street to investigate the report of a fight. The Deputy discovered that an altercation involving several people had occurred earlier at that location. During the incident, Carol Knight (victim in the instant offense) jumped on the hood of a vehicle operated by Mintz. He drove forward and by doing so, threw Mrs. Knight off of the vehicle. She was subsequently transported to Wishard Hospital for treatment of head, neck, and back injuries.

Per a Court of Appeals Decision, on 8-17-00 the defendant was resentenced and convicted only of Count IV, Battery, as a Class A Misdemeanor. He was found indigent and sentenced to one year executed. The Court having heard evidence on a violation of probation found no violation and the defendant's probation was terminated, per his new sentence and no longer on probation.

| 4-4-99 | MCSD | Ct. I, Criminal Recklessness (D) Ct. II, Battery (A/m) (49F169204CF048640) | 6-25-99, Dismissed |

According to the police report obtained through Justis, the defendant allegedly became involved in an argument with his girlfriend at the time, Cathy Knight. The argument allegedly escalated into the defendant striking Ms. Knight several times in the face, causing severe swelling and bleeding to her face. The defendant also allegedly took a small kitchen knife and cut her legs and hands causing minor cuts and bleeding.

| 1-3-00 | MCSD | Disorderly Conduct (B/m) Public Intoxication (B/m) (93-000580) | 1-4-00, Not Filed |

| 1-13-00 | MCSD | Ct. I, Battery (A/m) (49F169301CM000982) | 5-11-00, Dismissed |

FIGURE 5.4 *(continued)*

According to the police report obtained through Justis, on 12-24-92 the defendant allegedly went to 465 Morris Rd. (his parents' home) and started a disturbance during which he cornered Janet Shepard and refused to let her out of the bathroom. When she tried to get out of the bathroom the defendant allegedly hit her in the face causing pain and swelling to her lip and nose. While Marion County Sheriff's Deputies were at the residence the defendant allegedly called and threatened to burn down the house and harm them. He also allegedly threatened the police officers.

6-17-00	MCSD	Cts. I & II, Criminal Deviate Conduct (B) Ct. III, Battery (C) Ct. IV, Criminal Confinement (D) (49G039306CF074403)	Pending Jury Trial set for 2-24-04

The defendant allegedly forced Cathy Knight to perform fellatio on him after he placed his finger in her vagina against her will. He also allegedly cut Ms. Knight in the arm and face with a knife; and allegedly confined Ms. Knight by holding her under the water in the bathtub. According to the affidavit for probable cause, Ms. Knight indicated to police she had broken up with the defendant and he became angry because she ended the relationship. Ms. Knight stated she had continued her relationship and contact over the past few weeks prior to this with Mintz only because he told her he would kill her and her daughter. She said she knew he had been stalking her even after she moved in with her grandmother (victim in the instant offense) and was afraid he would get angry and come after her and harm her grandmother.

8-5-00	MCSD	Cts. I & II, Murder Cts. III & IV, Kidnapping (A) Ct. V & VI Burglary (A) Ct. VII, Carrying a Handgun w/o a License (A/m) (49G039308CF095544)	Instant Offense

See attached IPD Criminal History.

C. CRIMINAL ORIENTATION

The defendant has no known juvenile record. His adult criminal history began in 1984. The defendant has prior convictions for Disorderly Conduct (twice), Drunk (twice), Criminal Mischief (twice), Criminal Recklessness, Failure to Stop After Accident, and OVWI. In addition, the defendant has been arrested for Battery related charges ten times. He has been convicted of Battery six times and has charges of Criminal Deviate Conduct, Confinement, and Battery pending. Cathy Knight is the alleged victim in this offense.

It is evident that many of the defendant's arrests and convictions have been violent in nature. The defendant was convicted of battering Carol Knight, victim in the instant offense on 1-2-99 and a separate time on 8-26-00. Doris Knight and Cathy Knight, also a victim in the instant offense have been victimized by the defendant in the past. Mr. Mintz has been placed on probation fifteen times since 1984. There is no evidence that any of those terms of probation were ever revoked. However, it appears the defendant was technically on probation at the time he committed the instant offense, as his probation term began on 8-26-99 and was not terminated until 8-17-00.

D. SUMMARY OF LEGAL HISTORY

See above.

III. PRESENT OFFENSE

A. Official Version

Carl Mintz was convicted by jury of Count I, Murder for on or about August 3, 2000, knowingly kill another human being, namely: Randy Knight, by shooting a deadly weapon, namely: a

FIGURE 5.4 *(continued)*

handgun, at and against the person of Randy Knight, thereby inflicting mortal injuries upon Randy Knight, causing him to die.

Mintz was convicted by jury of Count II, Murder for on or about August 3, 2000, knowingly kill another human being, namely: Carol Knight, by shooting a deadly weapon, namely: a handgun, at and against Carol Knight, thereby inflicting mortal injuries upon Carol Knight, causing her to die.

Mintz was convicted by jury of Count III, Kidnapping, a Class A Felony for on or about August 3, 2000 did, while armed with a deadly weapon, that is: a handgun, knowingly remove Cathy Knight by force, fraud, enticement, threat of force, that is: at gunpoint from one place to another place, that is: from a residence located at 4817 West Plainfield Avenue to an unknown location, with intent to use Cathy Knight as a shield or hostage.

He was convicted by jury of Count IV, Lesser Included Confinement, as a Class B Felony for on August 3, 2000, did knowingly or intentionally confine Ann Knight without consent and removed her from the residence located at 4005 Ithaca St. to an unknown location at gunpoint.

Mintz was convicted by jury of Count V & VI, Burglary, as Class A Felonies for on or about August 3, 2000, did, while armed with a deadly weapon, that is: a handgun, break and enter the building or structure and dwelling of Randy Knight, situated at 4005 Ithaca St., with intent to commit the felony of Murder therein; that is: with intent to knowingly kill another person namely: Randy Knight and Carol Knight, by shooting a deadly weapon, causing them to die; and said offense resulted in serious bodily injury to Randy and Carol Knight, that is: mortal gunshot wounds.

Subject was convicted by jury of Count VII, Carrying a Handgun Without a License, as a Class A Misdemeanor for on or about August 3, 2000, did, in a place, not his dwelling, property, or fixed place of business, unlawfully carry a handgun on or about his person without a license.

Request for the Death Penalty (III) under I.C. 35-50-2-9 was recommended by the jury in this cause which states that Carl Mintz on or about the 3rd of August A.D., 2000, at and in the County of Marion in the State of Indiana, did commit the crime of Murder of Carol Knight as heretofore alleged in this cause; and in the commission of said Murder, the following aggravating circumstances did exist: subject committed said Murder by intentionally killing Helen Benefiel, while committing or attempting to commit Kidnapping, which is to knowingly or intentionally remove Ann Knight by force, fraud, enticement, threat of force, that is: at gunpoint from one place to another place, from a residence located at 4005 Ithaca St. in Marion County, Indiana to the State of Tennessee, with intent to use Cathy Knight as a shield or hostage.

According to the affidavit for probable cause, on or about 8-3-00, at approximately 11:50 p.m. David Knight and David Knight II were watching television in a bedroom at the residence located at 4005 Ithaca St., Indianapolis, Indiana, when David Knight II aroused his father, David Knight and stated that he heard several gun shots in the residence. At the same time David Knight heard the voice of the subject yelling where is Davey, where is Davey.

David Knight shoved his son David Knight II out of the bedroom and fled out of a side door of the residence and into a garage and fled across the street to a neighbor's home to summon Sheriff's Deputies. As both Knights' reached the door of the neighbor's residence they heard a commotion at the residence of 4005 Ithaca St., and saw Mintz forcing Cathy Knight and her one year old daughter, Ann out of the rear door of the house and into the 1984 Isuzu white pick-up truck and flee westbound on Ithaca St.

David Knight then awoke the neighbor and called 911 for emergency assistance and then returned to the residence and observed his father lying on the living room floor and the kitchen area in shambles. David Knight then left the residence as deputies and paramedics arrived.

Paramedics from the Wayne Township Fire Department examined the bodies of Randy Knight W/M/66 and Carol Knight W/F/65 and advised that neither of the victims had any life signs and notified deputies on the scene that both victims were deceased. The male victim appeared to have suffered two gunshot wounds to the upper torso. The female victim had what appeared a single gunshot wound to the top of the head.

During the investigation a description of the white Isuzu pick-up was broadcast and the vehicle was located at a Bigfoot Gas Station on Kentucky Ave. just east of High School Rd. A K-9 ran a

FIGURE 5.4 (continued)

track from the vehicle to a trailer park just north and west of where the vehicle was located. The track ended at a trailer located at 1623 Otis Avenue. The address of Deanna Mintz, the ex-wife of the suspect, Carl Mintz W/M/35 DOB 2/12/65.

An attempt was made to contact the occupants of the trailer located at 1623 Otis Avenue with negative results. With the knowledge that the suspect had threatened the life of the ex-wife a SWAT Team was called to check the trailer. The SWAT Team made entry to the trailer and found it to be empty, but did find a blue T-shirt that was wet and covered with grass and a 9 mm bullet located on a table in the trailer. The 9 mm bullet was believed to be the same type used in the double homicide and the blue T-shirt was worn by the suspect, Carl Mintz as he fled the homicide scene.

Missing from the trailer of Deanna Mintz was a 1987 blue Dodge with t-top and a gray stripe on the sides with Z-28 in the stripe. The license plate on the vehicle was Indiana License 752 2650.

B. Defendant's Version

The defendant indicated he understood his current legal situation and the possible legal penalties he faces at sentencing. The defendant indicates he has reviewed the probable cause affidavit several times with his attorneys. He did not wish to make a statement to this officer regarding the instant offense. However, this officer has been told a statement is being prepared and that statement will be forwarded to the Court upon receipt.

IV. VICTIM'S IMPACT STATEMENT

Notification of Victim's Rights Information and the sentencing date was sent to David Knight, son of victims Randy and Carol Knight on 7-19-03. This officer has received letters regarding the instant offense and sentencing of the defendant from Doris Knight, Cathy Knight, and Randy Knight. Those letters have been attached.

V. FAMILY/PERSONAL BACKGROUND

A. Family

Carl Mintz, age 38 is the older of two children born to Charlie Mintz, age 61, and Nancy, age 59, in Indianapolis, IN. The defendant reports his parents remain married and his father is employed for a paving company. Mr. Mintz indicates his mother is disabled and bed-ridden. She suffers from multiple sclerosis and was diagnosed with the disease in 1991. She also suffers from arthritis and has been diagnosed with Charcot-Marie-Tooth, a disease also shared by the defendant. The defendant has one sibling, Janet Henry, age 31. Janet is married and has three children. She and her family reside with the defendant's parents at this time.

Mr. Mintz reports having a close relationship with his mother, but states the relationship he shared with his father was much more distant. The defendant reported no actual physical abuse as a child, but stated the treatment he experienced as a child greatly affected his adult behavior. He did not wish to expand on this.

Mr. Mintz states several family members on his mother's side suffer from alcoholism including his maternal grandfather and uncle. The defendant reports he is unaware of any family member having been arrested in the past and none are currently incarcerated.

Mr. Mintz indicates he has resided in Indianapolis, IN, all of his life and reports no arrests outside Marion County.

B. Marital/Dependent Status

The defendant reports he married Deanna Best in 1996 and the couple divorced in 6/03. The defendant states his relationship with Deanna actually began in 1983 and they remain friends. The defendant has no children from this relationship. The defendant was residing with Deanna at the time the instant offense took place and reported her current address as his own, being 6425 Atlanta Dr. According to the defendant, Deanna may be attending the sentencing hearing along with other family members.

FIGURE 5.4 (continued)

Subject believes he may have fathered one child, Ann Knight, age 4, from a relationship with Cathy Knight. According to the defendant, paternity was never established and he has some doubts as to whether he is the father. The defendant reports the relationship between he and Cathy was "often stormy" and lasted approximately a year and a half between 1998 and 1999. The defendant indicates when he and Cathy remained together he saw Ann regularly, but when they were apart he rarely saw his daughter. Mr. Mintz states he is not court ordered to pay child-support for Ann, but considers her to be his daughter. The defendant has fathered no additional children.

C. Education

Carl Mintz attended Mars Hill Elementary and South Wayne Middle School before enrolling in Ben Davis High School. It appears the defendant attended South Wayne Middle School from the 1978-79 school year through the 1980-81 school year and earned 15 credits his seventh grade year, ranking 321 out of 369 students with a GPA of 1.69 on a 4 point scale. During the defendant's eighth grade year it appears he earned a class ranking of 308 out of 361 students and his GPA dropped to 1.5. The defendant's grades began to drop further his ninth grade year and on 8-29-81 the defendant enrolled in Ben Davis High School.

The defendant attended two full years at Ben Davis High School, but failed or withdrew from most of the courses he was taking. He earned only 3 credits the 1981-82 school year and ranked 894 out of 989 students. He earned zero credits the 1982-83 school year and quit school on 4-27-03. The defendant states he quit school following a disagreement with a teacher who accused him of smoking. The defendant states he was not smoking and was going to be suspended and so opted to quit.

The defendant's high school transcript further reflects the defendant began the Adult Education Program offered through Ben Davis High School on 8-30-04. It appears he completed only one course in the Fall of the 1904-05 school year having withdrawn from the additional three classes he had begun taking. The defendant has yet to earn his GED or high school diploma.

For six weeks in the 1991-92 school year the defendant states he attended Ivy Tech where he completed a course in Heating/Air-conditioning.

According to a Neuropsychology Report dated 11-16-95 from the Indianapolis Neurosurgical Group Inc., which has been attached, the defendant obtained a Verbal Scale IQ of 75, a Performance Scale IQ of 82, and a Full Scale IQ of 78 (7th percentile). On the Wechsler Adult Intelligence Scale-Revised (WAIS-R), the defendant's intellectual functioning rated into the Borderline Range (5th percentile) for abilities related to language comprehension and usage, and into the Low Average Range (11th percentile) for abilities related to visual-spatial analysis and reasoning, organization, and speed of manual manipulation. Several additional tests were administered to the defendant and are outlined in the Neuropsychology Report.

Mr. Mintz indicates he would like to further his education while incarcerated.

D. Employment

The defendant indicates the following positions of employment:

Dates of Employment	Employer	Position	Wages
1-00 to 8-00 (8 mos.)	European Tanning Salon	Labor	$5.50/hr. (Full-time)
1998 to 1900 (1½ yrs.)	Culbertson Automotive 1815 S. Lynhurst Dr.	Mechanic	Varied (Full-time)
1990 to 1995	Harvey Freeman Co.	Maintenance Supervisor	$7.50/hr. Free Apt.
1983 to 1989	McCormick's Food Service	Service Person	$7.15/hr. (Full-time)

FIGURE 5.4 *(continued)*

The defendant reports he has also been self-employed as a handyman and has worked in heating/air-conditioning and as a mechanic.

E. Military

N/A

F. Financial

The defendant is presently unemployed as he is incarcerated and has no income. He reports no assets and no liabilities.

G. Religion

N/A

H. Interests and Leisure Activities

The defendant enjoys building Street Rods and enjoys Stock Car racing. He also enjoys reading racing material and attended the Indianapolis 500 every year with his family prior to his arrest for the instant offense.

VI. HEALTH

A. Physical

Subject rates his physical health to be poor and reports the following difficulties. As a child the defendant states he was diagnosed with hystoplasmosis, a lung disease which caused him to miss a year of school. At the age of 20, the defendant states he was diagnosed with Type II Charcot-Marie-Tooth disease which is defined as a hereditary disease affecting the peripheral nerves. The disorder most commonly affects the muscles of the feet, lower legs, and hands resulting in weakness and atrophy, as well as mild loss of sensation.

A report completed on 6/13/03 by Dr. Norman Martinson, M.D. of the Hoosier Neurology P.C. Adult & Child Neurology indicates the following. "The defendant's disease is advanced and progressing. The manifestations of this in his early life were those of shaking and tremor and poor motor performance and endurance. Currently, he has advanced peripheral nerve disease. Dr. Norman Martinson, M.D. was unable to detect any specific muscles left in his feet. He has very slow nerve conduction times and is developing severe numbness in his hands. This is a generalized disease and will lead to progressive disability with the loss of the ability to walk and use his hands and loss of dexterity. Charles had nerve conduction times in his legs, reported by him, to be 17 to 18 M/SEC in his twenties. He now has the very slow nerve conduction times of his arms with dramatically prolonged latencies."

"The patient (defendant) will become disabled and eventually bedfast from this disease. There is no way to predict with medical certainty how rapidly it will progress, but with the apparent progression in the last 15 years, one would predict that he will be bedfast and totally disabled in the next five to ten years."

Although not self-reported by the defendant, the above report indicates the defendant may have had multiple severe head injuries. "Temporal lobe injuries of this type, with damage to the brain, can produce rage and explosive behaviors." The report also states the concept of pathological intoxication (patients who drink small amounts of alcohol and develop severe problems with behavior and impulse control) appears to be present in the defendant. Dr. Oestrike concludes that it is his opinion that the defendant does in fact have organic dysfunction in his temporal lobe with the inability to control his behavior and rages. (See attached report completed on 6/13/03 by the Hoosier Neurology P.C. Adult & Child Neurology.)

The defendant currently is taking no prescribed medication. He states he has been prescribed Inderal in the past for tremors associated with Charcot-Marie-Tooth. The defendant reports the Inderal also had a calming effect on him when he was taking it.

The defendant reports in 2002 blood was found in his stool and he began losing weight. The defendant states he has been told his condition may be attributed to colon problems, but he

FIGURE 5.4 *(continued)*

refuses to be treated. According to the defendant, the bleeding has since stopped. However, the defendant does report he is on a special diet in which he is given extra meals because of his severe weight loss.

In addition, the defendant states he is farsighted and in need of glasses.

B. Mental

The defendant states he has never been treated for an emotional disorder with the exception of Anger Control Counseling he was ordered to complete as a condition of probation. The defendant indicates he attended 46th Street Counseling, but this counseling does not appear to have been extensive. Mr. Mintz reports he has always been a nervous person and suffers from low self-esteem. The defendant related he believes counseling would have been helpful prior to the instant offense and could have possibly altered his behavior. Since his arrest for this offense, the defendant indicates he has been under great amounts of stress.

C. Substance Abuse

Carl Mintz reports to having used or ingested marijuana, LSD, cocaine, speed, barbiturates, Darvocets, methampehtamines, and quaaludes in the past. The defendant relates he also abused Mini Thins and took them as a solution to a hangover after he had been drinking. Prior to the instant offense, the defendant indicates he was taking several Mini Thins. For many years the defendant reports his drug of choice was quaaludes because they relieved his feelings of nervousness. However, the defendant states he stopped using them when he met his ex-wife, Deanna. The defendant states beginning in 1992 he would also consume alcohol daily, mostly beer and Schnapps. However, the defendant considers his alcohol usage to have been more of a "crutch." Mr. Mintz indicates he first used alcohol at the age of 15. The defendant reports he was ordered to complete alcohol classes as a condition of various terms of probation, but received no long term treatment.

On 7-30-00 the defendant admitted himself into St. Francis Hospital & Health Centers in an attempt to quit drinking as he believed Cathy Knight would let him see his daughter. He remained until 8-1-00 at which time he requested to be discharged. He was discharged at that time against medical advice. During his stay he was prescribed Librium and placed on Detox Protocol. St. Francis Hospital records indicate the defendant was often quite agitated during his stay. The instant offense occurred two days following his discharge from St. Francis Hospital.

VII. EVALUATION/SUMMARY

Carl Mintz is before the Court having been convicted of two counts of Murder, and one count of Kidnapping (A), Confinement (B), Burglary (A), and Carrying a Handgun Without a License (A/m). The jury has recommended the defendant receive the Death Penalty.

Carl Mintz, age 38 is the older of two children born to Charlie Mintz, age 61 and Nancy Mintz, age 59 in Indianapolis, IN. The defendant reports his parents remain married. Mr. Mintz indicates his mother suffers from multiple sclerosis, is disabled and bed-ridden. She has been diagnosed with Charcot-Marie-Tooth, a disease also shared by the defendant. The defendant has one sibling, Janet Henry, age 31. Janet is married and has three children. She and her family reside with the defendant's parents at this time. Mr. Mintz reports having a close relationship with his mother, but states the relationship he shared with his father was much more distant. The defendant reported no actual physical abuse as a child, but stated the treatment he experienced as a child greatly affected his adult behavior.

He married Deanna Best in 1996 and the couple divorced in 6/03, but remain friends. The defendant shared a relationship with Cathy Knight from 1998 to 1999. The defendant believes he may have fathered one child from this relationship, Ann, age 4. However, paternity was never established and the defendant has some doubts as to whether he is the father.

Mr. Mintz has yet to earn his high school diploma or GED. According to a Neuropsychology Report dated 11-16-02 from the Indianapolis Neurosurgical Group Inc., which had been attached

FIGURE 5.4 *(continued)*

the defendant obtained a Verbal Scale IQ of 75, a Performance Scale IQ of 82, and a Full Scale IQ of 78 (7th percentile). He would like to continue his education while incarcerated.

Mr. Mintz suffers from Type II Charcot-Marie-Tooth disease and according to a report completed on 6/13/03 by Dr. Norman Martinson, M.D. of the Hoosier Neurology P.C. Adult & Child Neurology, the defendant's disease is advanced and progressing. Dr. Martinson, M.D. indicated the defendant will become disabled and eventually bedfast from this disease. There is no way to predict with medical certainty how rapidly it will progress, but with the apparent progression in the last 15 years, it has been predicted that he will be bedfast and totally disabled in the next five to ten years.

Although not self-reported by the defendant, Dr. Martinson, M.D. also indicated the defendant may have had multiple severe head injuries which can produce rage and explosive behaviors. He stated the concept of pathological intoxication appeared to also be present in the defendant. Dr. Martinson concluded that in his opinion the defendant has organic dysfunction in his temporal lobe with the inability to control his behavior and rages. (See attached report completed on 6/13/03 by the Hoosier Neurology P.C. Adult & Child Neurology.)

In addition, the defendant reports in 2002 blood was found in his stool and he began losing weight. The defendant states he has been told his condition may be attributed to colon problems, but he refuses to be treated. According to the defendant, the bleeding has since stopped. However, the defendant does report he is on a special diet in which he is given extra meals because of his severe weight loss.

The defendant states he has never been treated for an emotional disorder with the exception of Anger Control Counseling he was ordered to complete as a condition of probation. Mr. Mintz reports he has always been a nervous person and suffers from low self-esteem. Since his arrest for this offense, the defendant indicates he has been under great amounts of stress.

Subject reports to having used or ingested a number of illicit drugs. He admits daily use of alcohol and abuse of Mini Thins prior to the instant offense. On 7-30-00 the defendant admitted himself into St. Francis Hospital & Health Centers in an attempt to quit drinking as he believed Cathy Knight would let him see his daughter. He remained until 8-1-00 at which time he requested to be discharged. He was discharged at that time against medical advice.

The defendant has no known juvenile record. His adult criminal history began in 1984. The defendant has prior convictions for Disorderly Conduct (twice), Drunk (twice), Criminal Mischief (twice), Criminal Recklessness, Failure to Stop After Accident, and OVWI. In addition, the defendant has been arrested for Battery related charges ten times. He has been convicted of Battery six times and has charges of Criminal Deviate Conduct, Confinement and Battery pending. Cathy Knight is the alleged victim in this offense.

It is evident that many of the defendant's arrests and convictions have been violent in nature. The defendant was convicted of battering Carol Knight, victim in the instant offense on 1-2-99 and a separate time on 8-26-00. Doris Knight and Cathy Knight, victim in the instant offense have also been victimized by the defendant in the past. Mr. Mintz has been placed on probation fifteen times since 1984. There is no evidence that any of those terms of probation were ever revoked. However, it appears the defendant was technically on probation at the time he committed the instant offense, as his probation term began on 8-26-99 and was not terminated until 8-17-00.

By statute, the instant offense is nonsuspendable and the Court may wish to consider the following statutory factors.

Aggravating:

1. The person has a history of criminal or delinquent activity.

a) The seriousness of prior crimes.
b) The number of prior crimes.
c) The pattern of prior crimes.
d) The criminal cases pending against the persons.

FIGURE 5.4 *(continued)*

2. The person is in need of correctional or rehabilitative treatment that can best be provided by commitment of the person to a penal facility.

      a) There were prior attempts at rehabilitation; the defendant was placed on probation fifteen times as an adult.

3. Imposition of a reduced sentence or suspension of the sentence and imposition of probation would depreciate the seriousness of the crime.

      a) The facts of the crime are particularly heinous.
      b) The person or property of the victim was injured by the crime.
      c) The crime required the defendant to confront the victims.

4. The advanced ages of the victims.

This officer could find no statutory mitigating factors.

The defendant's criminal history is extensive and his prior arrests and convictions have been violent in nature. He has had the benefit of probation supervision fifteen times. His criminal history includes ten arrests for Battery related charges and he has pending charges of Criminal Deviate Conduct, Confinement and Battery. (Cathy Knight is the alleged victim in the pending cause.) The defendant's crimes have gained in severity and continue to become more violent then the last. The defendant had been convicted of victimizing both Carol and Cathy Knight in the past.

The instant offense is particularly heinous in that the defendant went to the Knight's home, burglarized their residence and shot to death Randy Knight, age 66, and Carol Knight, age 65. He then kidnapped Cathy Knight, confined their daughter Ann Knight and fled the State to avoid apprehension. The defendant's violent tendencies show him to be a threat to society.

VIII. RECOMMENDATION

N/A

Respectfully submitted;

Cindy Humerickhouse
Probation Officer

FIGURE 5.4 (continued)

and are changed periodically (Figure 5.5). A judge is provided with a sentencing grid that considers only the severity of the instant offense and the offender's prior criminal history. Departures from mandatory sentences derived from the grid are permitted only under limited circumstances. Probation officers (actually, state parole and probation agents) are responsible for completing the sentencing guidelines worksheet and calculating the presumed sentence; they no longer write PSI reports.

The Federal Sentencing Reform Act of 1984, which became effective in 1987, was designed to reduce sentence disparity and phase out parole release by 1992. The statute also generated a great deal of confusion and litigation—many judges opposed the legislation's sentencing guidelines that removed much judicial discretion. On January 18, 1989, however, the Supreme Court ruled that the 1987 sentencing rules, established by a commission created under the 1984 statute, were constitutional (*Mistretta v. United States*, 488 U.S. 361). This ruling did not end the controversy: Appeals over guidelines interpretation have burdened appellate courts, and judges have been concerned about the lack of consideration given to such factors as age, education, and family ties for rendering sentencing decisions.

The commission established 43 offense levels and assigned each federal offense to one of the levels: murder, for example, scores 43; blackmail, 9. Judges

MINNESOTA SENTENCING GUIDELINES GRID
Presumptive Prison Sentence Lengths in Months

LESS SERIOUS ◀──────────────────────────▶ MORE SERIOUS

SEVERITY OF OFFENSE (Illustrative Offenses)	CRIMINAL HISTORY SCORE						
	0	1	2	3	4	5	6 or more
Sale of simulated controlled substance	12*	12*	12*	13	15	17	19 *18–20*
Theft Related Crimes ($2500 or less) Check Forgery ($200–$2500)	12*	12*	13	15	17	19	21 *20–22*
Theft Crimes ($2500 or less)	12*	13	15	17	19 *18–20*	22 *21–23*	25 *24–26*
Nonresidential Burglary Theft Crimes (over $2500)	12*	15	18	21	25 *24–26*	32 *30–34*	41 *37–45*
Residential Burglary Simple Robbery	18	23	27	30 *29–31*	38 *36–40*	46 *43–49*	54 *50–58*
Criminal Sexual Conduct 2nd Degree	21	26	30	34 *33–35*	44 *42–46*	54 *50–58*	65 *60–70*
Aggravated Robbery	48 *44–52*	58 *54–62*	68 *64–72*	78 *74–82*	88 *84–92*	98 *94–102*	108 *104–112*
Criminal Sexual Conduct, 1st Degree Assault, 1st Degree	86 *81–91*	98 *93–103*	110 *105–115*	122 *117–127*	134 *129–139*	146 *141–151*	158 *153–163*
Murder, 3rd Degree Murder, 2nd Degree (felony murder)	150 *144–156*	165 *159–171*	180 *174–186*	195 *189–201*	210 *204–216*	225 *219–231*	240 *234–246*
Murder, 2nd Degree (with intent)	306 *299–313*	326 *319–333*	346 *339–353*	366 *359–373*	386 *379–393*	406 *399–413*	426 *419–433*

▪ At the discretion of the judge, up to a year in jail and/or other non-jail sanctions can be imposed instead of prison sentences as conditions of probation for most of these offenses. If prison is imposed, the presumptive sentence is the number of months shown.

☐ Presumptive commitment to state prison for all offenses.

Notes: 1. Criminal history score is based on offender's prior record and seriousness of prior offenses. 2. Numbers in italics represent the range of months within which a judge may sentence without the sentence being deemed a departure from the guidelines. 3. First degree murder is excluded from the guidelines by law and carries a mandatory life sentence.

*One year and one day

FIGURE 5.5 *Minnesota Sentencing Guidelines.*

(*Source:* Minnesota Sentencing Guidelines Commission, Effective August 1, 1994.)

must impose sentences according to these levels, adding to or subtracting from them based on factors such as the offender's age, prior record, use of a firearm, or cooperation with the prosecution. "Ordinarily, the judge must choose a sentence from within the guideline range unless the court identifies a factor that the Sentencing Commission failed to consider that should result in a different sentence. However, the judge must in all cases provide the reasons for the sentence. Sentences outside the guideline range are subject to review by the courts of appeals for an abuse of discretion, and all sentences can be reviewed for incorrect application of the relevant guidelines or law" (U.S. Sentencing Commission flier). The guidelines manual is thicker than this book, and hundreds of amendments have been added. Inmates can earn a maximum of 54 days off their sentence per year for good behavior, instead of the more typical 1 day for each day served in determinate sentencing jurisdictions. In 2004, the Supreme Court declared unconstitutional a Washington State guidelines scheme based on the federal one, dooming that and other similar sentencing systems. The Court found that any factors that increase a criminal sentence, except prior convictions, must be proved beyond a reasonable doubt (Liptak, 2004).

The 1984 law resulted in radical changes in the content and format of the PSI and significantly changed the role of federal POs. Instead of preparing PSIs based on a positivistic approach to the offender, the PO must now focus on the details of the offense and prior criminal history (Figure 5.4). A federal PO in Philadelphia pointed out that it is imperative "that every detail about offense and offenders be included when these reports are prepared. Otherwise, minor point fluctuations on either offense level or criminal history can make a significant difference of several years in time to be served by convicted offenders" (Marshall, 1989: 10).

In preparing the PSI report, "the probation officer sets out the details of the offense and the defendant's criminal history. The probation officer then applies the sentencing guidelines to those facts" (Adair and Slawsky, 1991: 60). To make a relevant sentencing recommendation, the PO must be familiar with any applicable sentencing guidelines and mandatory sentences in his or her jurisdiction. The PO must study the case to determine whether there are valid grounds for a departure from the guidelines. "The presentence report has become more a legal document than a diagnostic tool, citing facts, statutes, and guidelines, justifying and supporting positions the guidelines treat as relevant in arriving at a sentencing range. The format and presentation of information is dominated by facts related to the offender's offense behavior and criminal history, the two primary factors establishing a defendant's sentencing range. Social and personal history information is reported, however, primarily to aid the court in choosing a point within the range, imposing conditions of release, and/or departures" (Denzlinger and Miller, 1991: 51).

In those jurisdictions where sentencing guidelines and mandatory sentencing significantly restrict a judge's sentencing discretion, the positive view-focused PSI has become obsolete. In its place a new form of PSI, one that centers on present offense and past criminal history—*classical*—is the norm. Figure 5.6 provides an example of the **classical PSI** from the federal system.

(text continued on page 162)

IN UNITED STATES DISTRICT COURT
FOR THE WESTERN DISTRICT OF OREGON

UNITED STATES OF AMERICA	)	
	)	
vs.	)	**PRESENTENCE INVESTIGATION REPORT**
	)	
Michael Mali	)	**Docket No.** CR 94-010-01-KGG

Prepared for: The Honorable Kelly G. O'Grady
U.S. District Judge

Prepared by: Craig T. Finkle
U.S. Probation Officer
Breaker Bay, OR 97010
(503) 111-4281

Assistant U.S. Attorney   **Defense Counsel**
Mr. Robert Nelson   Mr. Arthur Birg
United States Courthouse   737 North 7th Street
Breaker Bay, OR 97010   Breaker Bay, OR 97045
(503) 111-1219   (503) 112-2763

Sentence Date: June 9, 2004

Offense: Count one: Conspiracy to Violate Federal Narcotics Laws
(21 U.S.C. § 846)—10 years to Life/$4,000,000 fine

FIGURE 5.6 *Presentence Investigation Report Focusing on Details of Offense and Prior Criminal History.*

(*Source:* Western District of Oregon.)

Release Status:	Detained without bail since 6/19/02
Detainers:	None

Codefendants:	Sammy Maples—CR 94-011-02	Authur Kent—CR 94-011-04
	John Smith—CR 94-011-03	Leon Williams—CR 94-011-05

Related Cases:	None

Date Report Prepared: 5/15/04   **Date Report Revised:**   5/26/04

Identifying Data:

Date of Birth:	3/19/71
Age:	33
Race:	White
Sex:	Male
S.S. #:	292-09-3156
FBI #:	422-22-67B
USM#:	73621-679
Other ID #:	Not Applicable
Education:	11th grade
Dependents:	Two
Citizenship:	U.S.
Legal Address:	1430 Bird Avenue
	Breaker Bay, OR 97001
Aliases:	None

Optional Photograph

PART A. THE OFFENSE

Charges and Convictions

1. Michael Mali, Sammy Maples, Arthur Kent, John Smith, and Leon Williams were named in a two-count indictment returned by a Western District of Oregon grand jury on November 1, 2001. Count one charges that from December 1994 until June 19, 2001, the defendants

FIGURE 5.6 *(continued)*

conspired to violate the federal narcotics laws, in violation of 21 U.S.C.§ 846. Count two charges that on June 19, 2003, the defendants possessed with intent to distribute 500 grams or more of heroin, in violation of 21 U.S.C. §§ 812, 841(a)(1), 841(b)(1)(B) and 18 U.S.C. § 2.

2. On December 1, 2003, Michael Mali and Sammy Maples both pled guilty to count one and are scheduled to be sentenced on June 9, 2004. On December 12, 2003, Leon Williams pled guilty to count one, and he is scheduled to be sentenced on June 13, 2004. On December 13, 2003, Arthur Kent pled guilty to count one and is scheduled to be sentenced on June 15, 2004. All of the above defendants have pled guilty in accordance with the terms of written plea agreements which require a plea of guilty to count one in return for the dismissal of count two in the original indictment. On December 14, 2003, John Smith was found guilty on count two after a jury trial, and he is scheduled to be sentenced on June 15, 2004.

3. The assistant U.S. attorney has filed a motion pursuant to 18 U.S.C. § 3553(e) and U.S.S.G. § 5K1.1, advising that the defendant has provided substantial assistance to the government. Accordingly, the government will recommend a sentence below the mandatory minimum sentence and applicable guideline range.

The Offense Conduct

4. This case was initiated by the Drug Enforcement Administration in December 2001, upon the receipt of information from a confidential informant that Michael Mali and Sammy Maples were involved in the distribution of multiple-ounce quantities of heroin from an apartment located in the Breaker Bay housing project. Subsequent investigation revealed that Mali and Maples were regularly distributing heroin to Arthur Kent. After several months of investigation and surveillance, drug enforcement agents learned that Kent regularly purchased heroin from Mali and Maples, and sold the heroin to Leon Williams, who would travel to the Breaker Bay area each month from Bodega Bay, Oregon, a small community approximately 200 miles south of Breaker Bay. Williams gave Kent the money to purchase the heroin, but generally waited in a parked car near the housing project while Kent conducted the heroin transaction inside apartment 4J in the housing project. Mali and Maples relied on a number of heroin sources, including two unidentified Asian males, and on at least two occasions, John Smith.

5. According to information provided by a confidential informant and testimony presented at John Smith's trial, sometime in August 2001, Mali met Smith while they were being held by local police authorities on unrelated drug charges. While in custody, Mali told Smith that he sold small quantities of heroin in Breaker Bay and relied on various suppliers. Mali complained that his suppliers were unreliable and frequently provided him with heroin of poor quality. Smith, although cautious and somewhat suspicious of Mali, revealed that he might be aware of other suppliers whom Mali might use once he was released from custody and ready to resume his drug distribution operation. The two exchanged telephone numbers and agreed to discuss the use of Smith's suppliers in the future. Several days later, Mali was released from custody and shortly thereafter resumed his heroin distribution operation with his partner Maples.

6. In late December 2001, Mali contacted Smith by telephone and discussed the possibility of obtaining 10 ounces of heroin. After several weeks of negotiations, Smith agreed to meet with Mali at Mali's apartment in the housing project. On February 14, 2002, Smith was observed by federal agents outside the housing project near Mali's apartment, accompanied by an unidentified Hispanic male. Prior to entering the apartment building, Smith was observed handing a package, which investigators later learned contained 300 grams of heroin, to the Hispanic male. Once inside the apartment, Mali tested a small sample of the heroin, and agreed to purchase the package of heroin for $80,000. Mali gave Smith the $80,000 in cash, and, in turn, Smith directed the Hispanic male to give Mali the package of heroin. A short time later, Smith and his companion were observed leaving Mali's apartment.

7. Later that afternoon, federal agents observed Arthur Kent and Leon Williams driving a 2000 Porsche in the vicinity of the housing project. Williams parked the vehicle nearby and Kent was observed carrying a brown duffle bag as he entered the housing project where he proceeded to Mali's apartment. According to the confidential informant, once

FIGURE 5.6 (continued)

inside the apartment, Kent briefiy spoke to Mali and the two proceeded to a back bedroom where Mali was known to weigh and package drugs. A few moments later, Kent and Mali returned to the living room of the apartment and Mali was carrying the brown duffle bag that Kent brought to the apartment. Mali then emptied the duffle bag that contained a large sum of U.S. currency, bound in $50, $20, and $10 denominations. Mali assured Kent that he would find the heroin to be of high quality and agreed to provide additional quantities of heroin to Kent whenever his out-of-town buyer needed them. A short time later, Kent left the apartment and returned to the vehicle in which Williams was waiting.

8. For several months, agents maintained surveillance on Mali's apartment, and on several occasions, the agents monitored Smith's arrival at Mali's apartment, followed by the arrival of Kent and Williams. On each occasion, Williams would remain outside, sitting in the 2000 Porsche, while Kent entered Mali's apartment. Kent would deliver a large duffle bag to the apartment and return a short time later carrying a small package under his arm. On June 14, 2002, an undercover agent of the Drug Enforcement Administration, posing as a drug purchaser, met with Mali in the vicinity of the housing project to negotiate the purchase of 10 grams of heroin. Mali told the undercover agent that he expected to receive a shipment of heroin the following day and that, while he anticipated transacting a large heroin deal with another out-of-town customer, he would be able to sell the undercover agent 10 grams of heroin from the shipment for $7,500.

9. For the next two days, federal agents maintained 24-hour surveillance of the housing project, and on June 19, 2002, the agents observed Smith when he arrived at Mali's residence carrying a shopping bag. Smith arrived at the apartment with the shopping bag and had a gun, which was visible in his waist band. Smith remained in Mali's apartment and a short time later, Williams and Kent arrived. As on previous occasions, Williams remained in the car parked nearby while Kent went to Mali's apartment, carrying a blue gym bag. Shortly thereafter, the agents entered the apartment, and the defendants scattered. The agents observed Maples, Kent, and Smith seated in the back bedroom of the apartment, and they were all placed under arrest without incident. Other federal agents, who were positioned outside of the apartment building, observed Mali as he jumped out of the apartment's kitchen window and landed in a patch of bushes on the ground below, where he was placed under arrest. At the time of his arrest, a loaded .38-caliber revolver was found in the bushes near the spot where Mali landed. In addition, other agents proceeded to the parked Porsche where Williams was waiting. At the time of Williams's arrest, agents recovered a .357 magnum from his waist band. Williams told the agents that he had driven to Breaker Bay from Bodega Bay and had driven Kent to the vicinity to visit some friends.

10. The agents searched Mali's apartment and recovered a large quantity of suspected heroin from the toilet that the defendants had attempted to destroy. The agents safeguarded the seized narcotics using plastic bags. The following day, the bags were reopened and the water/heroin solution was drained into plastic bottles for laboratory submission. According to the results of a later laboratory report, the agents recovered a total of 725.12 grams of 20 percent pure heroin. In addition, the agents recovered an additional 55.4 grams of 20 percent heroin from the top of the refrigerator in the kitchen, and heroin residue from a table in the bedroom, along with an Ohaus triple beam scale, a strainer, and other drug-related paraphernalia. Moreover, the agents seized $103,160 in cash bundles of U.S. currency from the blue gym bag that the agents had previously observed being carried by Kent, and $16,870 from Kent's jacket pocket.

11. The agents then proceeded to apartment 6J, where, according to confidential informant information, Mali was believed to store narcotics proceeds and other property. The apartment was occupied by Michael Mali's mother, Carol Mali, who consented to a search of the apartment. Agents recovered an additional $13,000 in cash and jewelry, later appraised to be valued at $5,500.

12. All of the participants in this offense shared equally important functions in this loosely organized heroin distribution operation. Defendant John Smith was the supplier of the heroin for the February 14, 2002 and June 19, 2002 transactions. Michael Mali and Sammy Maples were the brokers, while Arthur Kent was the middleman (and Williams's courier). Williams was a buyer, who authorities believe operated a street-level heroin distribution

FIGURE 5.6 (continued)

operation in Bodega Bay, Oregon, and he frequently traveled to Breaker Bay to purchase heroin. A total of 1090.52 grams (or slightly more than one kilogram) of heroin were distributed during the course of this offense, with an estimated wholesale value of $400,000.

Victim Impact

13. There are no victims in this offense.

Adjustment for Obstruction of Justice

14. Although the defendant attempted to flee prior to his arrest, he was apprehended almost immediately. The probation officer has no other information to suggest that the defendant impeded or obstructed justice.

Adjustment for Acceptance of Responsibility

15. During an interview with drug enforcement officials shortly after his arrest, and later during an interview with the probation officer, Mali readily admitted his involvement in this offense. In substance, Mali acknowledged that he participated in this conspiracy to distribute heroin and takes full responsibility for his conduct.

Offense Level Computation

16. The 2001 edition of the *Guidelines Manual* has been used in this case.

17. **Base Offense Level:** The guideline for a 21 U.S.C. § 846 offense is found in U.S.S.G. § 2D1.4. That section provides that the base offense level for a narcotics conspiracy shall be the same as if the object of the conspiracy or attempt had been completed. In this case, the defendant conspired to distribute 1090.52 grams of heroin. In accordance with the provisions found in U.S.S.G. § 2D1.1(a)(3)(c)(6), the base offense level is 32.   <u>32</u>

18. **Specific Offense Characteristic:** Pursuant to the provision found in U.S.S.G. § 2D1.1(b)(1) because the agents retrieved a loaded .38-caliber revolver in the bushes where the defendant was arrested, the offense level is increased by two levels.   <u>+2</u>

19. **Victim Related Adjustments:** None   <u>0</u>

20. **Adjustment for Role in the Offense:** None   <u>0</u>

21. **Adjustment for Obstruction of Justice:** None   <u>0</u>

22. **Adjustment for Acceptance of Responsibility:** The defendant has shown recognition of responsibility for the offense and a reduction of two levels for Acceptance of Responsibility is applicable under U.S.S.G. § 3E1.1.   <u>−2</u>

23. **Total Offense Level:**   <u>32</u>

Chapter Four Enhancements

24. **Career Criminal Provision:** In accordance with the provisions found in U.S.S.G. § 4B1.1, because the defendant was at least 18 years old at the time of the instant offense, the instant offense is a felony controlled substance offense, and the defendant has at least two prior felony controlled substance convictions as detailed below. Mali is a career criminal and the adjusted offense level is 37.   37

25. **Adjustment for Acceptance of Responsibility:** The defendant has shown recognition of responsibility for the offense and a reduction of two levels for Acceptance of Responsibility is applicable under U.S.S.G. § 3E1.1.   <u>−2</u>

26. **Total Offense Level:**   <u>35</u>

FIGURE 5.6 (continued)

PART B. THE DEFENDANT'S CRIMINAL HISTORY

Juvenile Adjudication(s)

27. None

Adult Criminal Conviction(s)

Date of Arrest	Conviction/ Court	Date Sentence Imposed/Dispo.	Guideline/ Points	
28. 3/2/93	Criminal Sale of Controlled Substance, Class D Felony, Breaker Bay Superior Court, Breaker Bay, Oregon Dkt. #86541	9/23/94, 5 years probation	4A1.1(c)	1

The defendant was represented by counsel. Mali was arrested, along with Sidney Reynolds, after Breaker Bay police officers observed them selling a quantity of heroin to a third individual not arrested. At the time of arrest, the police recovered 20 glassine envelopes of heroin, which, according to a later laboratory report, had a total net weight of 3 grams. Mali was represented by counsel and subsequently pled guilty as noted above, although during his interview with the Breaker Bay county probation officer, he denied his guilt in the offense, stating that he pled guilty in return for the assurance that he would be placed on probation supervision. According to local county probation records, Mali successfully completed probation supervision and was given an early discharge from that supervision on September 27, 1995.

Date of Arrest	Conviction/ Court	Date Sentence Imposed/Dispo.	Guideline/ Points	
29. 4/4/97	Criminal Sale of Controlled Substance, Class C Felony, Breaker Bay Superior Court, Breaker Bay, Oregon Dkt. # 86926	10/24/97, 2 to 4 years imprisonment, paroled 8/4/97 parole revoked 2/27/98, returned to custody.	4A1.1(a)	3

The defendant was represented by counsel. Police officers observed the defendant passing glassine envelopes to others in exchange for money. At the time of his arrest, police officers recovered 55 glassine envelopes containing 2.5 grams of heroin and 16 glassine envelopes containing 26 grains of cocaine, marked "Freeze," wrapped to Mali's arm. Mali failed to return to court as scheduled, and on July 26, 1997, a bench warrant was issued for his arrest. The defendant was subsequently returned to court when he was arrested on a new unrelated charge. During his interview with the probation officer, Mali freely acknowledged possession of the narcotics, although he explained that the drugs were for his own personal use. Mali was arrested on the below-listed charges shortly after his release on parole. According to state parole officials, the defendant's parole was violated, and he was returned to state custody. His sentence ran to expiration.

Date of Arrest	Conviction/ Court	Date Sentence Imposed/Dispo.	Guideline/ Points	
30. 4/14/97	Criminal Possession of Marijuana, 5th degree, Class B Misd., Breaker Bay Criminal Court, Breaker Bay, Oregon Dkt. #89541	4/19/97, 7 days imprisonment	4A1.1(c)	1

FIGURE 5.6 (continued)

The defendant was represented by counsel. Mali was arrested and originally charged with assault, resisting arrest and criminal possession of marijuana, while at liberty on bail in connection with the above-mentioned offense.

31.	8/19/99	Robbery 3rd degree, Class E Felony, Breaker Bay Superior Court, Breaker Bay, Oregon	2/27/00 18 months to 3 years imprisonment, paroled 8/4/01 discharged maximum expiration on 8/4/02	4A1.1(a)	3

The defendant was represented by counsel. Mali was arrested by Breaker Bay Transit police officers after he snatched a gold chain from a victim's neck. According to the victim, who sustained minor injuries, the defendant approached him at gun point and demanded that he remove the gold chain. When the victim resisted, Mali snatched the chain and fled, but was apprehended when he ran into two transit officers who were standing nearby. The term of imprisonment ran concurrently with his parole revocation of February 27, 2000.

According to information provided by the Oregon State Department of Corrections and a review of his parole supervision file, while incarcerated, Mali received five disciplinary reports, which specifically included threats and disturbing the order of the facility, failure to abide by posted rules, and refusing direct orders. The defendant lost his privileges, and on two occasions he was placed in solitary confinement for short periods of time.

The defendant was released to parole supervision on August 4, 2001 to reside with his grandmother, Claudia Mali in Breaker Bay, and worked as a messenger and a waiter while under supervision. While the defendant's overall adjustment to parole supervision was satisfactory, he was arrested in the instant offense prior to his maximum expiration of parole supervision of August 4, 2002. The Oregon State parole officials have declined to file parole violation charges and have advised that Mali's parole supervision was allowed to expire.

Criminal History Computation

32. The criminal convictions above result in a subtotal criminal history score of 8.

33. At the time that the instant offense was committed, Mali was on parole supervision for his August 19, 1999, offense. In accordance with the provisions of U.S.S.G. § 4A1.1(d), two points are added.

34. The instant offense was committed less than two years following Mali's release from custody on August 4, 2001, for the sentence imposed regarding the offense of August 19, 1999. As such, pursuant to U.S.S.G. § 4A1.1(d), one point is added.

35. The total criminal history score is 11, and according to the sentencing table found in chapter 5, part A, 10 to 12 criminal history points establish a criminal history category of V; however, the defendant's criminal history category is enhanced to VI because he is considered a career criminal.

36. As detailed above, the defendant has three prior felony convictions involving controlled substances and a crime of violence, and as such pursuant to the provisions found in U.S.S.G. § 4B1.1, Mali is a career criminal and his criminal history category must be VI.

PART C.   OFFENDER CHARACTERISTICS

Personal and Family Data

37. Michael Mali was born on March 19, 1971, in Breaker Bay, Oregon, to the union of Carl and Carol Mali, nee Hewson. His parents were never married and seldom lived together, making it necessary for his mother to obtain public assistance for financial support. According to the

FIGURE 5.6 (continued)

defendant, his father died in 1999 following a massive heart attack. Prior to his death, the father collected public assistance for financial support and had difficulty maintaining employment. Michael has one brother, David Mali, age 34, who was reared by his maternal grandmother in Washington, D.C. David was previously convicted of narcotics charges in the District of Columbia in May 2000 and sentenced to 30 months' imprisonment. At the present time, David is serving a three-year term of supervised release in this district and is living with his mother, age 67, at the Breaker Bay public housing development in the apartment where the defendant was arrested in the instant offense.

38. The defendant was reared by his paternal grandmother, Claudia Mali, now age 75, who has resided at the Breaker Bay housing project at 1430 Bird Avenue, for the past 30 years. According to the defendant, he has a good relationship with his mother and brother David, although he acknowledged that he has not seen them in several months primarily because his mother abuses alcohol and is difficult to talk to when she is intoxicated.

39. According to the defendant's grandmother, she assumed responsibility for Michael when he was approximately 12 years old because of the frequent fights and discord in the mother's residence, which is located in a nearby building within the same housing project. Michael was a quiet child and was frequently neglected by his mother, who never provided a positive living environment for Michael and frequently allowed him to miss school. The defendant's mother has a reported history of narcotics abuse and was frequently hospitalized and treated for alcohol and narcotics abuse. The grandmother explained that she was employed as a laundry worker prior to her retirement eight years ago and now collects social security insurance and retirement benefits for financial support. She explained that she has always felt that Michael had the potential for positive contributions to the community but was frequently "sidetracked" by his friends.

40. The defendant has never been married, but from 1995 until 1999 maintained a long-term relationship with his former girlfriend Jackie Smith, now age 27. This union produced one child, Chanel Mali, now age five, who currently resides with Smith's mother in an apartment at the Breaker Bay housing project. Several attempts to contact Ms. Smith have been unsuccessful.

41. Simultaneously, from 1989 until the present, Mali has maintained an ongoing relationship with Sandra Dee, now age 26. This union has produced one child, Cynthia Mali, who was born on October 1, 2001. Mali states that for approximately four months prior to his arrest, he was residing in a third-floor apartment in a three-family house in Bodega Bay, Oregon, which he shared with Ms. Dee that rented for $700 per month. Mali states that after his arrest, Ms. Dee lost the apartment because she was unable to pay the rent and now resides with her mother in an apartment on the lower west side of Breaker Bay. Attempts to contact Ms. Dee have proven negative in that she has failed to appear at the probation office for several scheduled interviews. Although the defendant describes his relationship with Ms. Dee in positive terms, he has elected to reside with his grandmother upon his release from custody.

Physical Condition

42. Michael Mali is 5'7" tall and weighs 170 pounds. He has brown eyes and brown hair and, at the time of our interview, he wore a mustache and goatee. The defendant states that he is in good general health but noted that he was hospitalized in April 2001 and treated for a gunshot wound to the arm, which he states he received from a stray 9-mm hollow point round fired by his codefendant, Leon Williams, at someone else in a dispute. The defendant states that the bullet broke his arm, and he still has bullet fragments in his arm. Medical records have been requested and are awaited. In addition, Mali noted that he was hospitalized in 1997 after he received a stab wound on his left arm during an argument with his then girlfriend, Jackie Smith.

Mental and Emotional Health

43. The defendant states that he has never been seen by a psychiatrist and describes his overall mental and emotional health as good. We have no documented evidence to suggest otherwise. During our interview, the defendant communicated effectively, but his demeanor is streetwise and tough.

FIGURE 5.6 (continued)

Substance Abuse

44. The defendant states that prior to his arrest he drank alcohol almost every day; however, he does not believe that he is in need of alcohol treatment. The defendant revealed that he has smoked marijuana regularly since 1994 and from 1996 until 1997, he inhaled cocaine and smoked crack cocaine. According to Mali, prior to his state incarceration, he spent approximately $250 a day to support his cocaine addiction but has been relatively drug-free since his release from state custody, although he will occasionally inhale small quantities of cocaine at parties. While in state custody, Mali completed the Network Substance Abuse Program. He attended an outpatient drug treatment program for a brief period after he tested positive for cocaine in January 2002 while under parole supervision. At the time of his arrest in this offense, a urine specimen collected from the defendant by a pretrial services officer tested positive for marijuana and opiates.

Educational and Vocational Skills

45. Mali attended Breaker Bay High School from September 1989 until October 6, 1990, when he was discharged in the first semester of the 12th grade at age 19. According to school officials, the defendant had a poor scholastic record but had an average attendance record and attitude. According to state corrections records, the defendant was administered the BETA IQ test in November 1997 and scored 93. The defendant was enrolled in adult education programming and a pre-GED course in July 1998 until December 1998, while in custody but was removed from the program due to disciplinary action. While in the program he was characterized as an average student, according to available academic reports. Prior to his removal, Mali was characterized as an average student. While incarcerated, the defendant participated in a vocational training building-maintenance program from December 1998 until May 5, 1999 and took office machine repair courses from September 23, 1998 until May 5, 1997. Mali received average to excellent evaluations and was awarded a certificate in plumbing and basic electronics.

Employment Record

46. Mali states that he was briefly employed by messenger services prior to his state prison sentences. While under parole supervision, Mali was gainfully employed for a messenger service, was a waiter, and later a cook until approximately February 2002. Mali was also employed as a porter and dishwasher, earning $8.00 per hour, with Caroline's at the Breaker Bay Sea Port from October 2, 2001 until he resigned in February 2002. According to a representative from Caroline's, Mali was reliable and a good worker and would be considered for rehire.

47. Mali candidly admitted that during significant periods of employment, he sold marijuana, cocaine, and heroin to support himself. Mali asserts that he has earned as much as $20,000 a day from his narcotics activities. Such claims cannot be directly verified, but the government seized approximately $13,000 in cash and $5,500 in jewelry from the apartment of the defendant's mother on the day of the defendant's arrest. Mali states that he used the money to enjoy the "fast life," which included the purchase of a 1995 Audi 5000, also recently seized by the government.

Financial Condition: Ability to Pay

48. The defendant prepared a signed financial statement, wherein he reported no assets or liabilities. His counsel has been appointed by the court, and a recent credit bureau inquiry reveals that the defendant has never established credit. Mali has no known sources of income and upon his release he will be financially dependent on others.

PART D. SENTENCING OPTIONS

Custody

49. **Statutory Provisions:** The minimum term of imprisonment for this offense, a Class A felony, is ten years, and the maximum term of imprisonment is life, pursuant to 21 U.S.C. § 846 and 841(b)(1)(A).

50. **Guideline Provisions**: Based on an offense level of 35 and a criminal history category of VI, the guideline range of imprisonment is 292 to 365 months.

FIGURE 5.6 (continued)

Impact of Plea Agreement

51. Under the plea agreement, Mali has entered a guilty plea to count one, the conspiracy count, in return for the dismissal of all other counts. Pursuant to U.S.S.G. § 3D1.2(d), counts involving the same transaction are grouped together into a single group. All of the substantive counts in this offense pertain to the same transactions. Accordingly, a conviction on the additional counts would not affect the offense level or any other guideline calculation.

Supervised Release

52. **Statutory Provisions:** If a term of imprisonment is imposed, a term of supervised release of five years must also be imposed, pursuant to 21 U.S.C. § 846 and 841(b)(1)(A).

53. **Guideline Provisions:** The guideline range for a term of supervised release is at least five years, pursuant to U.S.S.G. § 5D1.2(a).

Probation

54. **Statutory Provisions:** The defendant is ineligible for probation pursuant to 21 U.S.C. § 846 and 841(b)(1)(A).

55. **Guideline Provisions:** The defendant is ineligible for probation, pursuant to U.S.S.G. § 5B1.1(b)(1).

Fines

56. **Statutory Provisions:** The maximum fine for this offense is $4,000,000, pursuant to 21 U.S.C. § 846 and 841(b)(1)(A).

57. A special assessment of $50 is mandatory, pursuant to 18 U.S.C. § 3013.

58. **Guideline Provisions:** Pursuant to U.S.S.G. § 5E1.2(c)(3) the minimum fine for this offense is $20,000, and the maximum fine is $4,000,000.

59. Subject to the defendant's ability to pay, the court shall impose an additional fine amount that is at least sufficient to pay the costs to the government of any imprisonment, probation, or supervised release, pursuant to U.S.S.G. § 5E1.2(i). The most recent advisory from the Administrative Office of the U.S. Court suggests that a monthly cost of $1,210.05 be used for imprisonment, a monthly cost of $91.66 for supervision, and a monthly cost of $938.44 for community confinement.

Restitution

60. Restitution is not an issue in this case.

Denial of Federal Benefits

61. **Statutory Provisions:** Pursuant to 21 U.S.C. § 862, upon a second conviction for possession of a controlled substance a defendant may be declared ineligible for any or all federal benefits for up to five years as determined by the court.

62. **Guideline Provisions:** Pursuant to U.S.S.G. § 5F1.6, the court may deny eligibility for certain federal benefits of any individual convicted of distribution or possession of a controlled substance.

FIGURE 5.6 (continued)

PART E. FACTORS THAT MAY WARRANT DEPARTURE

63. The assistant U.S. attorney has filed a motion pursuant to 18 U.S.C. § 3553(e) and U.S.S.G. § 5K1.1, advising that the defendant has provided substantial assistance to the Government. Accordingly, the Government will recommend a sentence below the mandatory minimum sentence and applicable guideline range.

Respectfully submitted,

Chief U.S. Probation Officer

by _____
Craig T. Finkel
U.S. Probation Officer

Approved:

_____
Mark T. Clark   Date 5/30/2004
Supervising U.S. Probation Officer

SENTENCING RECOMMENDATION

UNITED STATES DISTRICT COURT FOR THE WESTERN DISTRICT OF OREGON
UNITED STATES V. MICHAEL MALI DKT. # CR 91-010-01-KGG

TOTAL OFFENSE LEVEL: 35
CRIMINAL HISTORY CATEGORY: VI

	Statutory Provisions	Guideline Provisions	Recommended Sentence
CUSTODY:	10 years to life	292 to 365 months	180 months
PROBATION:	Ineligible	Ineligible	Not applicable
SUPERVISED RELEASE:	5 years	At least 5 years	5 years
FINE:	$4,000,000	$20,000 to $4,000,000	$0
RESTITUTION:	Not applicable	Not applicable	Not applicable
SPECIAL ASSESSMENT:	$50	$50	$50

FIGURE 5.6 *(continued)*

Justification

We have been advised by the assistant U.S. attorney, who has filed a motion for downward departure in this case, that Mali entered into a cooperation agreement shortly after his arrest. In addition to his testimony at the trial of his codefendant, John Smith, Mali has reportedly provided substantial and extraordinary cooperation relative to organized crime figures, over and beyond the scope of this offense. Although the government has filed a motion for downward departure, the conduct in this offense, coupled with the defendant's prior criminal record, would have otherwise supported a sentence near the higher end of the guideline range. Mali has an extensive criminal record, which includes two prior drug-related convictions. At the age of 33, Mali has a limited employment record and, by his own admission, has primarily supported himself through lucrative narcotics trafficking. He has a history of violence and appears to be extremely streetwise and tough. As such, his overall prognosis for rehabilitation is extremely poor, he poses a risk for recidivism, and a sentence of 15 years imprisonment appears appropriate for the protection of the community.

The mandatory five-year statutory term of supervised release is recommended in this case with a special condition requiring drug testing and treatment in view of the defendant's history of drug and alcohol abuse. Although the defendant is subject to the provision of federal benefit denial, in view of his expected jail sentence, these provisions will expire prior to his release from custody. The defendant does not have the ability to pay a fine at this time. No fine is recommended, and, therefore, the fine payment should be waived by the court. Although the court may deny federal benefits to the defendant for up to five years, denial of such benefits is not recommended. Unless the defendant were to receive less than a five-year sentence in this case, the period of ineligibility would expire while he is incarcerated.

Voluntary Surrender

The defendant has been detained without bail since his arrest. In light of his conviction and expected lengthy jail sentence, Mali is not eligible for voluntary surrender in accordance with the provisions found in 18 U.S.C. § 3143(a)(2).

Recommendation

It is respectfully recommended that sentence in this case be imposed as follows:

Pursuant to the Sentencing Reform Act of 1988, it is the judgment of the court that the defendant, Michael Mali, is hereby committed to the custody of the Bureau of Prisons to be imprisoned for a term of 180 months.

Upon release from imprisonment, the defendant shall be placed on supervised release for a term of five years. Within 72 hours of release from the custody of the Bureau of Prisons, the defendant shall report in person to the probation office in the district to which the defendant is released.

While on supervised release, the defendant shall not commit another federal, state, or local crime. The defendant shall be prohibited from possessing a firearm or other dangerous device, and he shall not possess a controlled substance. In addition, the defendant shall comply with the standard conditions of supervised release as recommended by the United States Sentencing Commission. The defendant shall also comply with the following special conditions of supervised release: The defendant shall participate in a program of testing and treatment for drug and alcohol abuse, as directed by the probation officer, until such time as the defendant is released from the program by the probation officer.

FIGURE 5.6 *(continued)*

THE COURT FINDS that the defendant does not have the ability to pay a fine.

IT IS ORDERED that the defendant pay a special assessment in the amount of $50 for count one which shall be due immediately.

Respectfully submitted,

Chief U.S. Probation Officer

by _____
Craig T. Finkel
U.S. Probation Officer

Aproved:

_____
Mark T. Clark   Date 6/2/2004
Supervising U.S. Probation Officer

FIGURE 5.6 *(continued)*

U.S. Pretrial Services Officer. U.S. pretrial services provide to the court two important services—investigation and supervision—and are often the first court representatives defendants encounter after their arrest. In general, the officer's mission is to investigate defendants charged with a federal crime, recommend in a report to the court whether to release or detain the defendants, and supervise the defendants who are released to the community while they await their day in court. At the core of the day-to-day work of officers is the hallowed principle of criminal law that the defendant is presumed innocent until proven guilty. Officers must balance this presumption with the reality that some persons—if not detained before their trial—are likely to flee or to threaten others. Defendants may pose danger to a person, such as a victim or a witness, or to the community—that is, a threat that the defendant may engage in criminal activity. The officer's job is to identify persons who are likely to fail to appear or be arrested if released, to recommend restrictive conditions that would reasonably assure the defendant's appearance in court and the safety of the community, and to recommend detention when no such conditions exist. If the person does not pose such risk, the officer's mandate is to recommend to the court the least restrictive conditions that will reasonably assure the person appears in court and poses no danger.

The officer conducts a pretrial services investigation, gathering and verifying important information about the defendant and the defendant's suitability for pretrial release. In the pretrial services investigation—which forms the basis of the officer's report to the court—the officer interviews the defendant and confirms information the defendant conveys through other sources. The investigation begins when the officer is first informed that a defendant has been arrested. The arresting or case agent calls the pretrial services office and, ideally, provides information about the defendant (e.g., the defendant's name, date of birth, social security number, the charges, the circumstances surrounding the arrest, where the defendant can be interviewed).

Before interviewing the defendant, the officer runs a criminal history check and also, if possible, speaks to the assistant U.S. attorney about the defendant, the charges, and the government's position as to whether to release or detain the defendant. The purpose of the interview is to find out what the defendant has been doing, where the defendant has been living, and where the defendant has been working (or what the defendant's source of support is). What the officer learns from collateral sources—other persons, documents, and online research—may verify what the defendant said, contradict it, or provide something more. The officer's research, for instance, may include contacting the defendant's family and associates to confirm background information, employers to verify employment, law enforcement agencies to obtain a criminal history, financial institutions to obtain bank or credit card statements, and the motor vehicle administration to check the defendant's license and registration.

Conducting the investigation in time for the defendant's initial appearance in court can be quite a challenge. Sometimes the officer must wait for the arresting agents to make the defendant available or for the U.S. marshals to finish processing the defendant. Sometimes the defense counsel is interviewing the defendant or tells the defendant not to answer the officer's questions. Sometimes the officer must wait for an interpreter or for an interview room. Sometimes verifying information is hard because the defendant gives false information or a false identity or because persons able to verify information are not available. The interview may take place in the U.S. marshal's holding cell, the arresting law enforcement agency's office, the local jail, or the pretrial services office. During the interview, the officer talks to the defendant in private if possible, remains objective while interacting with the defendant, and explains that the information will be used to decide whether the defendant will be released or detained. The officer does not discuss the alleged offense or the defendant's guilt or innocence. The officer also does not give legal advice to the defendant or recommend an attorney.

When the investigation is complete, the officer prepares a report that helps the court make an informed release or detention decision. In preparing the pretrial services report, the officer addresses two basic questions: Is the defendant likely to come back to court and stay out of trouble? If not, what conditions should the court impose to increase the likelihood? The officer considers both danger and nonappearance factors before making a recommendation to the court to release or detain the defendant. For example, the offense with which the defendant is charged and the defendant's substance abuse history may present both danger and nonappearance considerations. Factors such as prior arrests and convictions or a history of violent behavior raise danger concerns. Factors such as the defendant's immigration status and ties to family and community may influence nonappearance. If no risk factors are evident, the officer recommends release on personal recognizance. If risk factors exist, the officer recommends either release with conditions or detention. Release conditions are tailored to the individual defendant, but always include the universal condition that the defendant not commit a federal, state, or local crime during the period of release. The officer may recommend, and the court may set, conditions to accomplish any number of goals, including prohibiting possession of weapons, contact with victims, or use of alcohol or drugs; restricting the defendant's freedom of movement or with whom the defendant associates; and requiring the defendant to seek or maintain employment, obtain education or training, or surrender a passport. If the defendant is likely to fail to appear, the officer may recommend a financial bond, which the defendant (or the defendant's family) forfeits if the defendant fails to appear in court as directed.

The officer supervises offenders in the community to make sure they comply with court-ordered conditions of release. Officers supervise defendants released to the community until they begin to serve their sentence, the charges are dismissed, or they are acquitted. They monitor defendants' compliance with their release conditions; manage risk; provide necessary services as ordered by the court, such as drug treatment; and inform the court and the U.S. attorney if the defendant violates the conditions.

When a case is received for supervision, the officer reviews the information about the defendant, assessing any potential risk the defendant presents and any supervision issues that may affect the defendant's ability to comply with the release conditions. The officer selects appropriate supervision strategies and develops a supervision plan, which the officer modifies if the defendant's circumstances change. The officer carries out risk management activities to help ensure the defendant complies with the release conditions: monitoring the defendant through personal contacts and phone calls with the defendant and others, including family members, employers, and treatment providers; meeting with the defendant in the pretrial services office and at the defendant's home and job; helping the defendant find employment; and helping the defendant find medical, legal, or social services.

At the request of the U.S. attorney, the officer investigates whether the defendant is suitable for placement in a pretrial diversion program. Pretrial diversion is an alternative to prosecution that diverts the defendant from prosecution to a program of supervision administered by the pretrial services officer. The U.S. attorney identifies candidates for diversion—persons who have not adopted a criminal lifestyle and who are likely to complete the program successfully. The pretrial services officer investigates the individual, recommends for or against placement, and recommends length of supervision and special conditions. Diversion is voluntary; the person may opt to stand trial instead. If the individual is placed in the program, he or she is supervised by a pretrial services officer. If the person successfully completes supervision, the government declines prosecution and makes no record of the arrest.

PLEA BARGAINING AND THE PRE-PLEA INVESTIGATION

Most court cases in the United States, criminal and civil, are settled not by trial but by negotiation (or dropping of the action). In the criminal justice system, negotiated settlements are referred to as **plea bargaining**—an ad hoc exchange between a defendant who agrees to plead guilty to a criminal charge and a prosecutor who, explicitly or implicitly, offers leniency in return. Plea bargaining is criticized for providing criminals with excessive leniency and coercing defendants to waive their constitutional rights to a trial. Its extensive use can be explained by the time it saves the prosecutor and defense, and the certainty of outcome it offers to both. (For a more detailed discussion of plea bargaining, see Abadinsky, 2003b.)

The extensive use of plea bargaining has reduced the need for a PSI because the plea agreement may actually specify the sentence a defendant will receive. This is particularly true in determinate sentencing (discussed in chapter 7) jurisdictions that limit judicial discretion. Under such conditions, a presentence report would not serve any useful purpose at a sentencing hearing. Plea bargaining, however, has resulted in the use of a pretrial/plea investigation report (Figure 5.7). If prosecutor and defense counsel negotiate a plea agreement and the judge retains a great deal of discretion over the sentence to be imposed (which is the case in many states—see chapter 7), the judge may request a pretrial investigation before agreeing to the negotiated plea. In Illinois, for example, for a simple burglary as a first offense, the judge has the discretion to sentence an offender to a term of 3, 4, or 5 years, all the way up to 14 years. In Cook County, which includes the city of Chicago, judges often require a pretrial/plea investigation report before confirming a plea agreement; in fact, short-form pretrial reports are more frequent than PSI reports.

The practice of using a pre-plea investigation (PPI) report requires the defendant to agree to the investigation *(New York Code of Criminal Procedure)*:

> The probation department shall conduct a pre-plea investigation only upon a court order and written authorization by the defendant, his attorney, the prosecuting attorney and the judge ordering the investigation. Such written authorization shall include statements that no probation department personnel will be called to testify regarding information acquired by the probation department, that information obtained by the probation department may not be

used in a subsequent trial, and that this exemption does not apply to defense or prosecution material which may be included in the plea report.

Probation officers in Georgia are instructed: "If the defendant or his/her attorney refuses to sign the authorization, discontinue the investigation and report this fact to the court." In Ohio, a PSI cannot be conducted prior to a finding of guilty unless the defendant, on advice of counsel, has consented to allow the

---

STATE OF FLORIDA
DEPARTMENT OF CORRECTIONS
PROBATION AND PAROLE SERVICES
PRE-PLEA RELEASE FORM

Defendant _____Circuit _____County _____

Docket No. _____

DEFENDANT'S APPROVAL TO CONDUCT A PRESENTENCE
INVESTIGATION BEFORE CONVICTION OR PLEA

I, _____ defendant, hereby consent to a Presentence investigation by the Department of Corrections, Probation and Parole Serivces Office, for the purpose of obtaining information useful to the Court in the event I should hereafter plead guilty, or *nolo contendere*, or be found guilty.

By this consent, I do not admit any guilt or waive any rights and I understand that any report prepared can be shown to the Court before I have been found guilty only if I so agree in writing. Otherwise, I understand that any report prepared will not be shown to anyone unless and until I have been found guilty or entered a plea of guilty or *nolo contendere*.

I have read, or had read to me, the aforegoing consent and fully understand it. No promise has been made to me as to what final disposition will be made of my case.

_____   _____
(Date)   (Signature of Defendant)

_____   _____
(Date)   (Defense Attorney)

- -

DEFENDANT'S CONSENT TO THE COURT'S INSPECTION OF THE PRESENTENCE INVESTIGATION PRIOR TO PLEA OR FINDING OF GUILT

I, _____ defendant, hereby consent to review of my presentence investigation report by a Circuit Judge at any time, including the time prior to entry of a plea of guilty or *nolo contendere* or a finding of guilt.

I have read, or had read to me, the aforegoing consent and fully understand it. No promise has been made to me as to what final disposition of my case will be.

_____   _____
(Date)   (Signature of Defendant)

_____   _____
(Date)   (Defense Attorney)

_____   _____
(Date)   (Prosecuting Attorney)

FIGURE 5.7 *Florida Pre-Plea Release Form.*

(*Source:* State of Florida, Department of Corrections, Probation and Parole Services.)

investigation to proceed before adjudication, and adequate precautions are taken to ensure information disclosed during the PSI does not come to the attention of the prosecution, the court, or the jury prior to adjudication. As in Georgia, refusal of the defendant, his attorney, or both to sign the waiver constitutes an end to the investigation.

CONFIDENTIALITY OF THE PSI REPORT

Some controversy exists concerning whether any or all the contents of a PSI report should be disclosed to the defendant or his or her attorney. The basic argument against disclosure is that sources of information must be protected or they will hesitate to provide information. Family members or employers may fear retribution from the defendant if they provide negative information. In addition, law enforcement agencies may be reluctant to provide confidential information if the defendant or the defendant's attorney will be privy to it.

The basic argument in favor of disclosure is to enable the defendant to contest information that he or she considers unfair and to be protected from the effects of unfounded information. Disclosure of the contents of the PSI is more likely to ensure the information presented is more objective and accurate. The ABA recommends that all information that adversely affects the defendant be discussed with the defendant or his or her attorney. The President's Commission on Law Enforcement and Administration of Justice stated that "in the absence of compelling reasons for nondisclosure of specific information, the defendant and his counsel should be permitted to examine the entire presentence report" (1972: 356). The National Advisory Commission on Criminal Justice Standards and Goals recommended that the PSI be made available to the defense and the prosecution; the commission rejected the argument that sources of information will dry up: "(1) those jurisdictions which have required disclosure have not experienced this phenomenon; and (2) more importantly, if the same evidence were given as testimony at trial, there would be no protection or confidentiality" (1973: 189).

The U.S. Supreme Court has consistently upheld the confidentiality of the PSI report. This has been based on the (presumed) neutrality/objectivity of the probation officer—he or she has no interest in punishment; by disposition and training the PO is a helping, not a prosecutorial, agent. Thus, in the 1949 case of *Williams v. New York* (337 U.S. 241), the judge imposed a sentence of death based on information contained in the PSI report. The defendant had been convicted of murder, but the jury recommended life imprisonment. The PSI—to which the jury was not privy—revealed that Williams was a suspect in 30 burglaries. Although he had not been convicted of these crimes, the report indicated that he had confessed to some and had been identified as the perpetrator of others. The judge had referred to parts of the report indicating that the defendant was a "menace to society."

Williams appealed the death sentence, arguing that the procedure violated due process of law "in that the sentence of death was based upon information supplied by witnesses with whom the accused had not been confronted and as to whom he had no opportunity for cross examination or rebuttal." The Supreme Court rejected this argument, stating:

> Under the practice of individualizing punishments, investigational techniques have been given an important role. Probation workers making reports of their investigations have not been trained to prosecute but to aid offenders. Their reports have been given high value by conscientious judges who want to sentence persons on the best available information rather than on guesswork and inadequate information. To deprive sentencing judges of this kind of information would undermine modern procedural policies that have been cautiously adopted throughout the nation after careful consideration and experimentation. We must recognize that most of the information now relied

upon by judges to guide them in the intelligent imposition of sentences would be unavailable if information were restricted to that given in open court by witnesses subject to cross-examination. And the modern probation report draws on information concerning every aspect of a defendant's life. The types and extent of this information make totally impractical if not impossible open court testimony with cross-examination. Such procedure could endlessly delay criminal administration in a retrial of collateral issues.

Williams was executed.

In the federal system, since 1983 the contents of the PSI have been disclosed to the defendant, his or her counsel, and the attorney for the government, and the 1984 Sentencing Reform Act "largely rejected the sentencing philosophy expressed in *Williams*" (Adair and Slawsky, 1991: 58). Under the federal system of sentencing guidelines, the contents of the report determine the parameters for imposing a sentence. As a result, the sentencing hearing has become increasingly hostile. In response to defense attorney objections, the PO "is obligated to review the objections, reinvestigate if necessary, reevaluate decisions made, and discuss the findings with counsel. Any unresolved objections must be summarized for the court in an addendum to the report. On occasion this process consumes more time than the preparation of the presentence report" (Denzlinger and Miller, 1991: 51).

In some jurisdictions, law or custom allows the defendant access to the report, whereas some states give the judge the option of disclosing the contents of the report. In Texas, the statutes require that the entire contents of the report be revealed to the defendant. However, a trend exists toward adopting the position previously used in the federal system. The PSI can be revealed to the defendant or counsel, but the *Rules of Criminal Procedure* exclude the probation officer's recommendation and any "diagnostic opinion [such as a psychiatric report] which might seriously disrupt a program of rehabilitation, sources of information obtained upon a promise of confidentiality, or any other information which, if disclosed, might result in harm, physical or otherwise, to the defendant or other persons."

In Michigan, although the court must permit the prosecutor, the defendant's attorney, and the defendant an opportunity to review the report prior to sentencing, "the court may exempt from disclosure information or a diagnostic opinion which might seriously disrupt a program of rehabilitation or sources of information obtained on a promise of confidentiality. . . . Any information exempted from disclosure by the court must be specifically noted in the PSI and is subject to appellate review." In Ohio, "the Probation Department shall have the report completed no later than ten days prior to sentencing. When the report is completed, it shall be sent to the assigned judge and made available, at the probation department, for review by the defendant's attorney (or by the defendant if he is not represented by an attorney) and the prosecutor. . . . The report made available for review by the attorneys or the defendant shall reflect the fact that information, if any, has been deleted pursuant to [Ohio statutes] and the general categories of the deleted information shall also be noted."

CRITICISM OF THE PSI REPORT

Some critics maintain that many judges do not even read the PSI report, whereas others carefully select passages critical of the defendant to justify their sentences. Judges may discount the report because of the hearsay nature of the information (Blumberg, 1970). One report (Dickey, 1979: 33–34) notes the types of inaccurate or misleading information found in the PSI reports of one state:

(1) rumors and suspicions that are reported without any factual explanations; (2) incomplete explanations of events that leave a misleading impression; (3) factual errors relating, usually, to the criminal record of the offender

Rumors and suspicions are often reported in presentence reports and identified as such. The report that the rumor exists may be accurate. What is objectionable is the fact that the subject of the rumor may cause the reader to give more weight to the rumor than it deserves, if any. If the rumor is without foundation, reference to it is particularly troubling.

It is difficult to assess the impact of rumors, although they sometimes seem to directly affect correctional decisions. For example, one sex offender's presentence report contained the statement that the offender "was rumored to have killed his mother." This was referred to in several parole decisions before it was investigated. Upon inquiry, it was determined to the satisfaction of the parole board that the offender had been confined in another state at the time of his mother's death and had no connection to it.

Some reports do not contain complete information and are therefore misleading. One inmate's PSI contained the statement that he "had been arrested for attempted first degree murder after a barfight. The charges were later dropped." Investigation showed that the reason the charges were dropped was that the inmate was actually the victim of an attack and not the aggressor. The other person involved was later charged with a crime for the attack.

The most frequently recurring factual problem with the reports is related to past offenses. The so-called "FBI Rap Sheet" or "Yellow Sheet" is part of the report. It contains a confounding listing of past offenses that is frequently repetitious (i.e., it reports the same offense more than once). The repetitions are not so identified. Past charges do not always contain their disposition, so the reader is never sure how many offenses there actually were which were dropped and why, what the facts underlying the charges and offenses are, and what the outcome was.

One observer is concerned with the enormous dependence on the PSI that he argues tends to make the PO, rather than the judge, the sentencer (Gaylin, 1974). Numerous studies have indicated a high correlation between the recommendation of the PO and the judge's sentence. Research by the American Justice Institute (1981), for example, using samples from representative probation departments throughout the United States, found that recommendations for probation were adopted by the sentencing judge between 66 and 95 percent of the time. A study in Utah revealed that judges followed the recommendation 92 percent of the time (Norman and Wadman, 2000). A study of 1994 sentencing recommendations in Nevada revealed a concurrence rate of 97 percent when probation was recommended and 88 percent when the recommendation was imprisonment. A study in one Iowa judicial district (Campbell, McCoy, and Osigweh, 1990) revealed much less congruity and in a surprising direction. In many cases, those recommended for incarceration (44 percent) were, instead, sentenced to probation or some lesser sanction, such as diversion or a fine. The researchers concluded that these decisions were probably the result of a plea bargain and prosecutor's recommendation for a nonincarceration sentence.

One study examined the relationship between plea bargaining, the PO's recommendation, and the final disposition of the case in a large western county. In this county, after the defendant has accepted a "bargain" in exchange for a plea of guilty, the case is sent to the probation department for a PSI report. The researchers found a high correlation (93 percent) between the recommendation and the sentence (Kingsnorth and Rizzo, 1979). However, the PO may write into the PSI the recommendation that the PO believes will be well received by the judge. One observer suggests that the prosecutor often finds a way of communicating the plea bargain agreement to the probation department, and the latter responds with a conforming recommendation (Czajkoski, 1973). Conversely, in Wisconsin, "the prosecutor is often influenced by the recommendation in the report and the information underlying it. Some prosecutors frequently adopt the report's recommendations as their own recommendation to the court or use it as a benchmark in deciding on their recommendation. Sometimes a plea agreement will include the condition that the prosecutor will adopt the report's recommendation as his own" (Dickey, 1979: 30). In one county the minutes of the plea bargaining session, including the details of the negotiated agreement, are sent to the probation department before the submission of the PSI report. "Probation officer concurrence with previously negotiated sentence agreements is a consequence, not of case characteristics, but of pressures emanating from the organizational structure of which the probation department is a part, namely the court system itself" (Kingsnorth and Rizzo, 1979: 9). These and other studies serve to remind us that the probation officer is simply one actor in a rather complex setting. How much influence the PO can exert may often depend on procedural or structural variables, or perhaps the officer's force of personality.

In many jurisdictions, the PO is overburdened with PSIs and does not have the time to do an adequate investigation and prepare a (potentially) useful report. In courts in which the judge usually pays little or no attention to the contents of the report, the PO will not be inclined to pursue the necessary information and prepare well-written reports. Jonas Robitscher (1980: 35), an attorney and psychiatrist, states that although psychiatric reports and evaluations contained in the PSI often make the difference between probation, a short sentence, or a long sentence, "Many of these reports and evaluations contain dynamic formulations about the cause of behavior based on as little as twenty minutes spent with the subject of the report."

Walter Dickey found a most distressing problem related to the issue of erroneous information in the report: "Even when an alleged error is challenged at sentencing and a contrary finding made, it does not necessarily follow that the report will be corrected. When a judge makes a finding of fact that is inconsistent with the presentence report, he usually states the finding in the record of the sentencing hearing" (1979: 35). However, Dickey points out, "Without more, this leaves the report itself uncorrected. The sentencing transcript is not made a part of the report; it is not attached to it. The oral finding does not signal anyone to amend the report or any of the copies of it. Subsequent users of the report, correctional and parole authorities, rely on the uncorrected report. Rarely is the report amended to reflect additional information or findings of fact inconsistent with it at sentencing" (1979: 35).

In Michigan, however, state law requires that "if the court finds that challenged information is inaccurate or irrelevant, that finding will be made part of the court record, and the inaccurate or irrelevant information must be stricken from the report prior to distribution." To improve the reliability of the report, the Massachusetts commissioner of probation provides the following standards:

- The PO should identify the sources of information in the report.
- The PO should make personal contact with informants or sources of information, when practicable, who can substantiate information. The PO should clearly state in the report those instances in which information has not been substantiated.
- The PO should obtain pertinent documentation, such as letters, clinical reports, school reports, and certified statements, when practicable. The PO should indicate when information in the report is supported by such documentation.
- Sources of information should be identified in most instances; however, this does not exclude from a report relevant information from unnamed sources or informants with whom the PO has had personal contact. If a PO includes such information in an investigative report, the PO shall clearly indicate in the report that the information was obtained from sources or informants not being identified in this report.

Defendants are often dissatisfied with the role of their attorneys in the sentencing process (Dickey, 1979), and Federal District Court Judge Irving Cooper (1977: 101) states: "It is particularly distressing that many attorneys for the defense, who have proven themselves competent as to the facts and law in the case at trial . . . display on sentence hardly more than a faint glimmer as to who their clients really are as human beings."

> Another source of the sense of injustice is the belief that lawyers do not provide the court with positive information about the offender to supplement the presentence report which, it is frequently asserted, is incomplete. Sophisticated defendants realize that even the most forceful statements, if they are general, are of little value to their case. They recognize the importance of presenting the court with alternatives to confinement (i.e., job or school plan, place to live) if probation is sought or a specific statement of plans after release if a short period of confinement is the goal. These defendants are usually dissatisfied because they feel the court is forced to rely on an incomplete report because their lawyers did not provide the additional information. (Dickey, 1979: 36)

In response to this problem, the Legal Aid Society in New York City has used social workers to prepare sentencing memoranda for use by defense counsel at the sentencing hearing. In Buncombe County, North Carolina, I set up a similar effort using senior undergraduate students from Western Carolina University. The students worked for the public defender, providing PSI reports for use by defense counsel. Other profit and nonprofit agencies prepare PSI reports, and privately—for-profit—commissioned PSI reports have proliferated. This trend raises a serious question of equal justice because only those with the necessary financial resources can commission such a report.

In chapter 6, we turn to the system of juvenile justice and the central role of the juvenile court.

KEY TERMS

presentence investigation report

victim impact statement

prediction scales

short-form PSI

long-form PSI

mandatory sentencing laws

classical PSI

sentencing guidelines

plea bargaining

INTERNET CONNECTIONS

Probation department links: cppca.org/10_links.shtml

National Criminal Justice Reference Service: ncjrs.org

American Probation and Parole Association: www.appa-net.org

National Association of Pretrial Services Agencies: napsa.org

REVIEW QUESTIONS

1. Why is the PSI report a manifestation of positive view?
2. Why does a judge order a PSI?
3. What are the other purposes to which the PSI report can be put?

4. What are the differences between a positive (short- or long-form) PSI report and a classical PSI?
5. What are the categories of information contained in a PSI report?
6. What are the sources of information for a PSI?
7. What type of questions should the PO avoid during PSI interviews? Why?
8. What are the difficulties encountered by the PO when trying to decipher/understand the arrest record/"rap sheet"?
9. Why is the nature of a defendant's prior criminal record important for a PO to determine?
10. What variables are considered in making a recommendation for or against a sentence of probation?
11. What is the law and practice with respect to requiring a PSI report?
12. How can plea bargaining influence the PSI?
15. Why can the federal PSI be considered a classical approach?
14. What are the arguments for and against the contents of a PSI report being disclosed to a defendant or defense counsel?
15. What is the basis of the Supreme Court's determination that a PSI report is confidential?
16. What are the various criticisms of the PSI report?
17. What has led to the use of the privately commissioned PSI report?
18. Why does the privately commissioned PSI report raise a question of equal justice?

PART 2

Parole

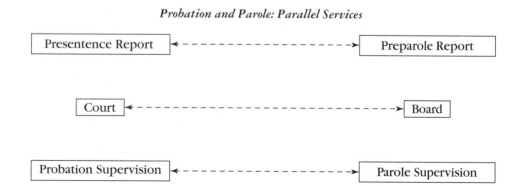

Probation and Parole: Parallel Services

CHAPTER 6

American Prisons and Community-Based Corrections

"The degree of civilization in a society is revealed by entering its prisons."

—*Dostoyevsky,* The House of the Dead

Compared with other industrialized nations, Americans tend to be more religious and entrepreneurial. We have more millionaires, we are the world leader in Nobel Prizes, and we send more people to university—and prison—than any other Western nation (Murphy, 2001). To understand the development of parole and its current state, we need to appreciate the crisis in American prisons and the history of the American prison system.

AMERICA'S PRISON CRISIS

Whom will we find upon entering America's prisons? About 1.5 million persons[1]— 93 percent are male; almost half are black and about 20 percent are Hispanic; more than 60 percent are younger than 30 years of age; about 70 percent have not completed high school, and about 40 percent are unable to read; more than 20 percent are incarcerated for a drug offense, and most inmates have a history of substance abuse. About one-half grew up primarily in one-parent households, and many have been victims of neglect and/or child abuse. A federal study (Widom and Maxfield, 2001: 1) revealed that "being abused or neglected as a child increased the likelihood of arrest as a juvenile by 59 percent, as an adult by 28 percent, and for a violent crime by nearly 30 percent." About one-half of prison inmates were unemployed or employed only part-time at the time of their arrest. A majority are parents of a child younger than the age of 18. *In America's prisons are persons who are poorer, darker, younger, and less educated than the rest of the population.*

It should come as no surprise that America leads the industrial world in the percentage of its citizens that are incarcerated, while having the widest gap between rich and poor (Bradsher, 1995b; Myers, 1995). The rate of incarceration for the United States is about 700 per 100,000 adults, compared with less than 100 per 100,000 for most Western European countries, and less than 40 per 100,000 for Japan (U.S. Department of Justice figures).

What will we find upon entering America's correctional institutions? A system not capable of managing such a large population in a manner that meets constitutional

[1]In 1985, the number was less than a half-million persons.

standards. In 2003, state prisons were operating at between 1 percent and 17 percent above capacity, while federal prisons were operating at 33 percent above capacity (Harrison and Beck, 2003). Despite a significant decline in the crime rate since 1992, by 2000 the incarceration rate was 702 per 100,000 persons, more than double the 1985 rate of 313 (Beck, 2000a, 2000b; Beck and Karberg, 2001). Although there were 592 state and federal prisons in 1974, that number grew to 1,023 by 2000. In 1923, there were only 61 (Butterfield, 2004a).

In Oklahoma, whenever the prison population exceeds 95 percent of capacity, inmates who have served at least 15 percent of their sentence and are within 1 year of their parole consideration date can be released. Legislation to accomplish this release was necessary because of the severity of overcrowding—previously the state was simply releasing inmates without benefit of parole supervision. In Florida, if the prison population reaches 98 percent for a period of 7 consecutive days, the Department of Corrections has authority to release certain inmates that meet established criteria. In Connecticut, the prison population went from 3,600 in 1980, to more than 18,000 in 2000; a state law mandates the immediate release of 10 percent of the prison population if the number of male prisoners exceeds 110 percent of capacity for 30 consecutive days. In Texas, in 2000, the legislature balked at a $500 million bond proposal for building 3 new maximum security units to deal with chronic overcrowding. Instead, lawmakers pushed the parole board to liberalize its guidelines and release more inmates—and it worked. The Texas inmate population in July 2001 was 146,855, down from a peak of 153,500 in July 2000 (Moritz, 2001). In 2004, Arkansas officials released almost 700 inmates to ease overcrowding and adhere to a court-ordered maximum—another 800 were being housed local and county jails awaiting transfer to state prisons ("Arkansas: Early Release for 630 Inmates," 2004).

Security problems generated by overcrowding are exacerbated by America's antiquated prisons. In Illinois, for example, the "newest" maximum security prison was opened in 1920. Along with a number of other states, Illinois recently opened a "supermax" prison—built at a cost of $73 million, with operating expenses for each of the 500 inmates averaging about $35,000 per year—because the overcrowded state prisons "had become so violent and so overrun by gangs . . . that prison staff were no longer safe" (Eig, 1998: 62). Supermax inmates spend 23 hours per day in solitary confinement—a return to the Pennsylvania system (discussed later).

A tremendous increase in the number of prison facilities and expansion of existing facilities during the last few years—in excess of 30,000 beds—has not had a significant impact. At any one time, 35,000 inmates are being housed in local jails because of a lack of state prison space, and many jails are also under court order to reduce overcrowding. For a decade, spending on prisons has been the fastest- or second fastest-growing part of state budgets (competing with education). The bills have arrived for those tough crime laws.

The economic realities of imprisonment began to loom large as declining state revenues intertwined with a critical shortage of correction officers. In response, many systems are hiring officers as young as 18—the only viable alternative to substantially increasing salaries and thus the cost of imprisonment. In some states, the problem of a shortage of corrections officers is so serious that it has contributed to prison breaks or attacks on staff (Belluck, 2001). With the largest prison system in the country, 137 prisons in operation, Texas has been unable to hire and retain experienced correction officers sufficient to provide an adequate level of protection for staff, inmates, and the public—a shortage of about 2,600 officers with a 25 percent annual turnover rate. Many have not received the required in-service training. This was highlighted in 2001, when seven inmates escaped from a maximum security prison and subsequently killed a police officer during a robbery (Graham, 2001b). How did we reach this crisis? The historical review in this chapter and chapter 7 is designed to help answer this question.

ORIGINS OF THE AMERICAN SYSTEM OF PRISONS

The American colonies inherited an English approach to crime and punishment, and the English system of laws into the eighteenth century impresses one with the extent to which the death penalty was used, often for seemingly minor offenses: "Thus it is believed that Henry VIII [1491–1547] executed 72,000 thieves and vagabonds during his reign"; under George III (1738–1820), as many as 220 offenses were punishable by death (Hall, 1952: 116). By 1780, 350 capital crimes existed, most of which were for property offenses (Lilly and Ball, 1987).[2] At the same time, England established institutional approaches to the elderly and the infirm, vagrants, beggars, homeless children, and certain criminals: gaols, bridewells, and houses of correction (Hirsch, 1992).

Local jails emerged throughout the American colonies, usually under management of a sheriff. These poorly constructed institutions, David Rothman (1971: 56) notes, "were not only unlikely places for intimidating the criminal, but even ill-suited for confining him"—escapes were frequent. In Massachusetts, under Puritan rule, fines and corporal punishment—stocks, pillory, lashes, and dunking—prevailed, while capital punishment was relatively rare (Hirsch, 1992).

Dramatically different conditions in England and the colonies resulted in differing needs, and this affected the response to criminals. In England, land was scarce and an excess labor supply had the potential for political and social unrest. "As a matter of policy," notes Bradley Chapin, "it must have seemed that no great harm was done if the hangman thinned the horde of vagrant Englishmen. In the colonies, the need for labor urged the use of penalties that might bring redemption" (1983: 9). Consequently, beginning with William Penn in 1682, the use of capital punishment in the American colonies was severely restricted and virtually banned for property crimes (Melossi and Pavarini, 1981).

In Pennsylvania, however, Quakers were in an economic quandary: British law was so severe that colonial juries would often find defendants not guilty rather than subject them to the extreme punishments in place for property offenses. "In this way, criminals had escaped all discipline, and the community had allowed, even encouraged, them to persist in their ways" (Rothman, 1971: 60). It was Quaker property that was often at risk in Philadelphia, where their Calvinist urgings—honesty, thrift, and hard work—resulted in economic success as a rising commercial class. (For the relationship between Calvinism and economic success, see Weber, 1958.) The use of imprisonment provided a way to mete out punishment in a manner that was proportionate to the severity of the offense, a classical concept. This appealed to both the humanitarian and economic concerns of the Quakers, who rejected the Calvinist belief in the immutability of human character in favor of redemption (Hirsch, 1992).

Three intertwined developments led to the establishment of the American system of prisons: religious doctrine, the American Revolution, and classicalism. Thorsten Sellin states, "credit for the gradual substitution of imprisonment for corporal and capital punishments must go to the [classical] philosophers of the 18th century" (1967: 19). After the Revolution, repugnance for things British inspired Americans to discard corporal punishment in favor of imprisonment, a process that was complete at about the time of the Civil War. The type of imprisonment that resulted had its origins in quasi-Calvinist socioreligious doctrine, which can be seen in the life of John Howard (1726–1790), who coined the term **penitentiary** as a place to do penance, and the work of Quaker reformers in Philadelphia and New York (Teeters, 1970).

Prison history in the United States can be conceived of in terms of five overlapping eras:

1. Pennsylvania
2. Auburn

---

[2]In practice, however, there was extensive use of pardons and the dismissal of indictments for technical reasons (Kelman, 1987).

3. Big House
4. Corrections
5. Just Deserts

PENNSYLVANIA: WALNUT STREET AND OTHER EARLY PRISONS

The first prison in the United States was authorized by the Connecticut legislature in 1773, and that same year the colony converted an abandoned copper mine into a prison for serious offenders (Durham, 1989c). Newgate (not to be confused with a New York prison by the same name) consisted of a wooden lodging house for communal habitation built about 20 feet below the surface. The first keeper, a retired military officer, lived across the road, and a lack of security personnel presented a problem. Within 3 weeks of receiving its first prisoner, the prisoner managed to escape, and escapes continued to plague Newgate. As opposed to early prisons established elsewhere, no reformative or rehabilitative agenda existed, and it was expected that the prison would be self-supporting. In the early days of the prison, miners were hired to provide inmate instruction, but mining failed to achieve a profit. Other trades were initiated, but they also failed to achieve any level of economic success. The Revolutionary War and a rash of violent incidents led to the closing of Newgate in 1782; it reopened in 1790 as a Connecticut state prison (Durham, 1989c).

By 1762, Quaker reformers in Philadelphia were successful in having the list of capital offenses limited, and in substituting fines and imprisonment for torture and execution for many offenses; in 1786, the Pennsylvania legislature enacted penal reform to replace capital punishment for certain crimes. The law called for convicted felons who were lodged in the Walnut Street Jail to be subjected to hard labor "publicly and disgracefully imposed . . . in streets of cities and towns, and upon the highways of the open country and other public works" (Atherton, 1987: 1). With shaved heads, bizarre dress, and wearing heavy metal balls and chains riveted to their ankles, the convicts working in the streets drew the ridicule and abuse of passing crowds—the work was both onerous and humiliating. However, Paul Takagi (1975) states that convicts working in the city streets drew large crowds of sympathetic people, including friends and relatives of the prisoners. They made contact, and, at times, received liquor and other goods. At the urging of Benjamin Rush, the Philadelphia Society for Alleviating the Miseries of the Public Prisons (later renamed the Philadelphia Prison Society and then the Pennsylvania Prison Society) was formed at the home of Benjamin Franklin in 1787. In 1789, the society succeeded in having the 1786 law repealed.

John Howard, the son of a Calvinist merchant, was born in England in 1726. His interest in penal reform led him to publish *The State of the Prisons* a year after the American Declaration of Independence. Working out of a strong religious commitment, Howard influenced other religiously endowed reformers, Quakers of the Philadelphia Society for Alleviating the Miseries of the Public Prisons, with whom he was in contact. As a result, in 1790, a law was enacted creating a *penitentiary* in a portion of the Walnut Street Jail, and the jail became a state prison based on a Calvinist model of hard labor, isolation, and religious study (Atherton, 1987).[3]

At Walnut Street, most inmates were confined in separate cells and released to work in a courtyard during the day at a variety of tasks: handicrafts, such as weaving and shoemaking, and routine labor, such as beating hemp and sawing logwood, all in total silence. The "hardened and atrocious offenders," persons who formerly would have been whipped, mutilated, or executed, were confined in isolation and almost total darkness with nothing but a Bible: "The old Quakers, sensitive as they were to the inflicting of bodily pain, seem to have been unable to form in their

---

[3]Takagi (1975) states that it was the Episcopalians of the Philadelphia Society who argued for hard labor, while the Quakers stressed solitary confinement.

minds an image of the fearful mental torture of solitude in idleness" (Wines, 1975: 152). These convicts were blindfolded on arrival and remained in their cells until released; they never saw another inmate. Inspectors from the Prison Society provided oversight at Walnut Street and had the authority to hire and fire penitentiary officials.

Solitary confinement was seen as a way of preventing fraternization between prisoners, behavior that would only lead to the spread of evil inclinations among inmates. In 1833, two European observers reported that "If it is true that in establishments of this nature, all evil originates from the intercourse of the prisoners among themselves, we are obliged to acknowledge that nowhere is this vice avoided with greater safety than at Philadelphia, where the prisoners find themselves utterly unable to communicate with each other; and it is incontestable that this perfect isolation secures the prison from all fatal contamination" (Beaumont and de Tocqueville, 1964: 57).

John Howard and the Quakers shared a common religious lifestyle that led them to favor imprisonment as a form of purgatory, "a forced withdrawal from the distractions of the senses into silent and solitary confrontation with the self." It was out of solitude and silence that the convict "would begin to hear the inner voice of conscience and feel the transforming of God's love" (Ignatieff, 1978: 58).[4] News of the "success" of Walnut Street attracted many persons from other states and countries. One of these visitors was a Quaker from New York, Thomas Eddy (1758–1827), who had been imprisoned briefly as a Tory during the Revolutionary War. A successful businessman, he was able to devote himself to philanthropy.

Eddy was influenced by what he saw in Philadelphia—orderly and humane management, and claims of success in making the streets of Philadelphia safer—and as a result of his efforts, New York constructed its first penitentiary in Greenwich Village, a then rural part of what is now lower Manhattan. Newgate was named after the famous British prison, and Eddy became its first agent. Consistent with the prevailing belief of prison reformers, Eddy maintained that the goal of deterrence required inflicting pain on criminal offenders (Lewis, 1965). However, he discarded the idea that it was necessary to keep inmates in solitary all day; instead, convicts slept in congregate rooms measuring 12 feet by 18 feet and housing eight inmates. Fourteen cells for solitary confinement were used as punishment for violating prison rules. Eddy encouraged religious worship, established a night school, and approved of provisions in the law that prohibited corporal punishment at Newgate. Despite improvements in treatment at the prison, in 1802, a bloody riot and mass-escape attempt required calling in the military. In response to these developments, Eddy recommended that future penitentiaries use single cells for all inmates at night and shops where they could work in strict silence during the day. His suggestions were incorporated into a new prison that was built in Auburn, New York.

Eddy was either removed because of political considerations (Lewis, 1965) or resigned in protest when, in 1803, the state turned the prison industries over to a private contractor (McKelvey, 1972). In either event, difficulties increased at Newgate, and a return to flogging was legislated in 1819 (Lewis, 1965). Although it was built to house less than 450 prisoners, by 1821, the population reached 817 and was kept in check only by a liberal use of "good time" laws and pardons ("Newgate," 1998). In 1828, the penitentiary was abandoned in favor of a newly completed prison at Ossining: Sing Sing.

In Philadelphia, overcrowding caused the demise of Walnut Street. Industry and isolation became unworkable in the congested prison, and discipline lapsed and riots ensued (McKelvey, 1972): "While the original inspectors were still active in the oversight of the prison, thus preventing rampant corruption of guards and overseers," there was little they could do to prevent the decline of conditions at the institution. "The funds needed to create a system of solitary confinement were simply greater than had been anticipated" (Dumm, 1987: 105).

---

[4]The traditional form of Quaker worship is based on silent meditation, a turning inward to hear one's inner voice.

Pennsylvania After Walnut Street

The Pennsylvania Prison Society succeeded in having prisons built in Pittsburgh (Western State Penitentiary opened in 1826) and in the Cherry Hill section of Philadelphia (Eastern State Penitentiary opened in 1829). These institutions featured massive stone walls, 30 feet high and 12 feet thick, around a building that branched out from a central rotunda like the spokes of a wheel—architecture influenced by the *panopticon* penitentiary, a circular design advanced by the British classical philosopher Jeremy Bentham (1748–1832). The design has a guardhouse at the center and prevented prisoner contact; inmates remained in their (12- by 7-feet, 16-feet-high) cells and work area, except for 1 hour of exercise in a yard also designed to prevent inmate contact. Prisoners could not see one another, even at Sunday religious services, because pews were designed as individual cubicles.

The **Pennsylvania system** "isolated each prisoner for the entire period of his confinement. According to its blueprint, convicts were to eat, work, and sleep in individual cells, seeing and talking with only a handful of responsible guards and selected visitors. They were to leave the institution as ignorant of the identity of other convicts as on the day they entered" (Rothman, 1971: 82). In addition,

> The guiding principles were punishment and reformation through penitence: The convicted prisoner was to be kept totally separated from other prisoners, but not from human contact. The avenue to reform was through repentance—the true and deep recognition of one's "sins" and acceptance of God's leadership in one's life. It was obvious that prisoners left totally alone would be unable to follow this path; for this, guidance was needed, good examples, people who could help the convict accept responsibility for his/her crimes and embark on the difficult path of repentance and redemption. (Atherton, 1987: 7)

Guidance and role models were provided by four groups of people: prison staff, chaplains, officials of the Prison Society, and the Board of Inspectors.

The penitentiary reached its apex during the 1830s; facilities proliferated, and "visitors traveled great distances to view American prisons in action" (Hirsch, 1992: 112). It was during this period that the French philosopher/politician Alexis de Tocqueville (1805–1859), most noted for his *Democracy in America* (1835), traveled to the United States to study its penitentiary system. Although he came away with a generally favorable view, economics would soon lead to the demise of the penitentiary, which had been adopted by only two other states, New Jersey and Rhode Island.[5] Stateville, in Illinois, which opened in 1925, has one unit based on the panopticon design—it is the only one currently in operation in the United States.

The Pennsylvania system proved expensive—the cost of constructing an institution for solitary confinement was staggering, and little profitable exploitation of inmate labor under such conditions could occur (McKelvey, 1972). Eastern Penitentiary was built to house 250 inmates at a cost of $780,000, an enormous sum in those days (Dobrzynski, 1997). At the beginning of the nineteenth century, an increasing need for labor existed: New legislation made slave trading more difficult, new territories were settled, and rapid industrialization with a corresponding increase in wages occurred. Prisons with solitary confinement deprived the market of needed labor (Melossi and Pavarini, 1981). As a result, most states patterned their prisons after the next great milestone in American prison history, an institution suggested by Thomas Eddy, which became the world's most frequently copied prison. Even New Jersey and Rhode Island abandoned the Pennsylvania model. Beginning in the 1850s, the isolation of prisoners at Eastern State Penitentiary was breaking down,

[5]Outside the United States, however, the Pennsylvania system proved popular, and hundreds of prisons were built on this model.

and inmates began sharing cells: "In 1913 the system, which had become so diluted as to be unrecognizable, was officially abolished and from then on, it became just another Auburn-type prison" (Teeters, 1970: 11).[6]

AUBURN SYSTEM

Auburn Prison opened in 1819, and as designed by its first agent, featured a center that comprised tiers of cell blocks surrounded by a vacant area—the yard—with a high wall encircling the entire institution. In Auburn, each cell measured 7 by $3\frac{1}{2}$ feet and was 7 feet high:

> It was designed for separation by night only; the convicts were employed during the day in large workshops, in which, under the superintendency of Elam Lynds (1784–1855), formerly a captain in the army, the rule of absolute silence was enforced with unflinching sternness. Captain Lynds said that he regarded flogging as the most effective, and at the same time the most humane, of all punishments, since it did no injury to the prisoner's health and in no wise impaired his physical strength; he did not believe that a large prison could be governed without it. (Wines, 1975: 154)

Instead of replacing corporal punishment with imprisonment, as was advocated by the religious reformers, the practice of flogging became widespread in the penitentiary system—criminals were punished with imprisonment, and prisoners were punished with flogging and other forms of corporal punishment. No written regulations governed the use of the whip; guards were simply authorized to impose flogging—up to 39 lashes (the number has biblical roots)—when "absolutely necessary."

Auburn divided its inmates into three classes. The most difficult inmates were placed in solitary, a less dangerous group spent part of the day in solitude and worked the rest of the time in groups, and the "least guilty" worked together throughout the day and were separated only at night when they returned to their individual cells. As in Walnut Street, solitary confinement played havoc on the psyche—inmates jumped off tiers, cut their veins, and smashed their heads against walls. Solitary confinement in Auburn was discontinued, except as punishment for violations of prison rules (Lewis, 1965).

New Yorkers believed that the complete isolation of prisoners from arrival to release was inhumane, unnatural, and cruel. Far from reforming men, they believed such absolute solitude resulted in insanity and despair. In addition, there was the issue, perhaps more pressing, of expense to the state. Inmates restricted to their cells 24 hours per day contributed nothing to the cost of their own confinement. The state had to provide all food, clothing, supplies, and materials to its prisoners. "If the prisoners were to learn the advantages and satisfactions of hard work and thrift, New York authorities believed, there could be no better way than to be compelled to work together in harmony. If such a system also offered the potential for inmates to grow and harvest their own vegetables, raise and butcher their own meat, make their own clothes, and manufacture other items for use or sale by the state, such a boon to the state's budget could not be reasonably ignored" (New York State Special Commission on Attica [Attica Commission], 1972: 8).

Under the system developed by Lynds, an army captain in the War of 1812 who became warden when William Brittin died in 1822, prisoners worked in small, strictly supervised units in workshops, outdoors during the daytime, and returned to individual cells at night. They dressed in grotesque and ridiculous-looking black-and-white–striped uniforms and caps; they marched in complete silence, worked in

---

[6]Eastern Penitentiary's last 28 prisoners were moved to modern quarters in 1970. It is now a national historic site and tourist attraction (Dobrzynski, 1997).

complete silence, and ate in complete silence: "A breach of this rule was punished by flogging. Discipline was extremely strict in all other respects. Inmates were required to keep their eyes downcast when walking" (Erikkson, 1976: 50).

Auburn developed the infamous lockstep shuffle. Inmates stood in line with the right foot slightly behind the left and the right arm outstretched with the hand on the right shoulder of the man in front of him; they moved together in a shuffle, sliding the left foot forward, then bringing the right foot to its position just behind the left, then the left again, and then the right. Heads had to be turned toward the "keeper" so lip movements could be detected; keepers tiptoed shoeless up and down cellblocks to detect whispers. Citizens were encouraged to visit the prison, where for a small fee they could view the inmates, an act that was designed to cause further degradation. Prisoners were known only by number and, as in Pennsylvania, their reading matter was limited to a Bible ("Auburn Correctional Facility," 1998). Beaumont and de Tocqueville report on their visit to Auburn: "Nothing is heard in the whole prison but the steps of those who march, or the sounds proceeding from the workshops. But when the day is finished, and the prisoners have retired to their cells, the silence within these vast walls, which contain so many prisoners, is like that of death. We have often trod during night those monotonous and dumb galleries, where a lamp is always burning: we felt as if we traversed catacombs; there were a thousand living beings, and yet it was a desert solitude" (1964: 65).

The administrators of Auburn believed their most important task was the breaking of an inmate's spirit to drive him into a state of submission. Some had differences of opinion about what to do after the "breaking" process. One school of thought stressed deterrence as its goal and was determined to derive as much economic benefit from inmate labor as possible. In fact, in the early years, Auburn actually made a net profit for the state. Another school of thought held that rehabilitation was the ultimate goal, and that, after breaking, inmates should be helped through education and religion so they could return to society as better persons (Lewis, 1965).

The **Auburn system** consisted of an unrelenting routine of silence, hard labor, moderate meals, and solitary evenings in individual cells 6 days per week: "Their labor is not interrupted until the hour of taking food. There is not a single instant given to recreation" (Beaumont and de Tocqueville, 1964: 65). On Sundays, when there was no work, inmates attended church—in silence—where they were addressed by the prison chaplain who stressed the American virtues of simple faith and hard work (Attica Commission, 1972). A Sunday school was established, and those not participating were locked in their cells and forced to stand until lights out ("Auburn Correctional Facility," 1998).

The Auburn-style prison became the prototype for American prisons; it was cheaper to construct than those of Pennsylvania and allowed for a factory system that could make profitable use of inmate labor. The concept of reformation gradually declined; by the end of the nineteenth century, rehabilitation had virtually disappeared—prisons were viewed simply as places to keep criminals incarcerated as cheaply as possible. This view was reflected even in the name of the warden's first assistant, the "principal keeper" (Attica Commission, 1972). Prisons became bleak and silent factories with labor pools of broken people disciplined with summary floggings.[7]

Convict Labor

Imprisonment has its roots in penal servitude: "The prisons operated on the Auburn plan, in particular, were, most of them, notorious for the maltreatment of prisoners and for the excessive labor required of them in an attempt to meet the demand of legislators that prisons be self-supporting and even show a profit if possible"

---

[7]Although flogging was outlawed at Auburn in 1847, it was replaced by other gruesome punishments ("Auburn Correctional Facility," 1998).

(Sellin, 1967: 21). The use of convict labor often made American prisons not only self-supporting institutions, but also profit-making enterprises throughout the nineteenth century and well into the twentieth century. Auburn Penitentiary balanced its books in 1829 and produced a profit of $1,800 in 1831, and Sing Sing netted $29,000 in 1835 (Melossi and Pavarini, 1981). In Alabama, prison labor netted the state profits of almost $1 million annually, and just one prison industry manufacturing shirts in Florida netted that state almost $150,000 annually (Gillin, 1931). Minnesota's Stillwater Prison netted $25,000 annually as late as 1930 and served as a model for other northern prisons (Hagerty, 1934). In 1964, the Arkansas state penitentiary showed a net profit of nearly $500,000; it also gave rise to the scandalous conditions uncovered at the Tucker Prison Farm, which were portrayed in the motion picture *Brubaker*. However, prison industries also prevented the forced idleness that plagues many contemporary correctional institutions and helped maintain discipline.

Three systems were used to exploit convict labor:

1. **Contract system.** Under the **contract system,** convict labor was sold to private entrepreneurs who provided the necessary machinery, tools, raw materials, and, in some cases, the supervisory staff. In many cases, the prison was built as a factory with walls around it: "As late as 1919 a committee of the American Prison Association reported, after a national survey, that most prisons worked their prisoners in a manner reminiscent of the early forms of penal servitude and that reformation was an empty word" (Sellin, 1967: 21).

2. **Lease system.** Under the **lease system,** prisoners were leased out to private business interests for a fixed fee. This system was used extensively in agriculture and mining, particularly in the South. In Florida, for example, in 1877, the state "transferred the control and custody of prisoners to private contractors who could now employ them anywhere in the State. Prisoners were leased to individuals and corporations and set to work in phosphate mines and in turpentine camps in forests" (Sellin, 1967: 22). In North Carolina, as early as 1875, private employers could lease inmates as laborers. Under the lease, businesses had complete responsibility for the inmates. Many worked in rock quarries and built railways. In 1901, the system was changed to provide for contract inmate labor. Inmates worked for private employers, but prison officials retained responsibility for the inmates' custody. A system of mobile camps developed that moved from worksite to worksite. In the post–Civil War South, this system exploited emancipated blacks, providing a readily available source of cheap labor (Hallet, 2004).

3. **State-use system.** Under the **state-use system,** prison inmates produce goods for use or sale by state agencies, for example, office furniture and license plates. Other than that necessary for prison maintenance, this work is the most frequent form of prison labor in use today. In Texas, the agricultural division grows or raises most of the food consumed by staff and inmates, and the sale of its surpluses raise several million dollars annually (Silverman, 2001).

By 1874, the contract system was used in 20 state prisons, the lease system in 6, and a mixed system in 7 (Mohler, 1925). For wardens of the convict labor era, the ability to turn a profit was the determining factor in whether he kept his job: "The nineteenth century's most famous wardens first gained recognition because of their fiscal success" (Durham, 1989a: 127). Wardens unable to run self-sufficient institutions were replaced by legislators forced to appropriate funds to maintain the prison.

During the latter part of the nineteenth century and into the twentieth century, numerous scandals involved the use of inmate labor. The growing labor union movement in the United States saw inmate labor undermining employee leverage for increased wages and improvements in working conditions. At times, inmate labor was leased out to break strikes. The National Anti-Contract Association, a manufacturers' group whose members—small businessmen—suffered from having to compete with goods produced by cheap convict labor, campaigned against the contract system. These activities resulted in laws curbing convict labor in several industrial states: Massachusetts, New York, and Pennsylvania. The federal government enacted legislation in 1887 that forbid the contracting of any federal prisoners (McKelvey, 1977).

In the states of the Confederacy, the lease system continued to be widespread into the twentieth century, when southern states slowly began to abolish the practice, the last to do so being Alabama in 1928 (Sellin, 1967). In its place, states turned to the chain gang and prison farms. Shackled together, inmates toiled on roads, and built levees and railroads. Penal farms increased profits by diversifying into light industry and further reduced costs by employing inmate guards, trusties who were armed and received early release for their service. Texas continued to use (unarmed) inmate guards until the Supreme Court decision (*Ruiz v. Estelle*, 503 F. Supp. 1265, 1980) put an end to the practice.

The contract system remained widespread until the Great Depression, and the passage of the Hawes-Cooper Act in 1929 and the Ashurst-Sumners Act in 1935. These federal statutes eventually curtailed the interstate commerce in goods produced with convict labor, and their constitutionality was upheld by the Supreme Court in 1936 (*Whitfield v. Ohio*, 297 U.S. 439).

The curtailing of convict labor had two long-ranging effects:

1. It increased the cost of imprisonment and thus encouraged the development of parole (whose history is reviewed in chapter 7).
2. It forced prison officials to find other ways to deal with prison idleness. As a result, many prisons initiated programs to train and educate their inmates.

Modern Prison Industries

In 1979, Congress enacted the Prison Industry Enhancement Act, which removed the blanket federal restrictions on the sale of prisoner-made goods in interstate commerce. Instead, the amendment sets forth minimum conditions under which such sales can occur, including consultation with labor unions, the need to avoid any impact on local industries, and a requirement that inmates be paid the prevailing local wage for work of a similar nature. The law also permits the establishment of pilot projects using prison labor by private enterprise. The Comprehensive Crime Control Act of 1984 further expanded the scope of prison industries, and by 1987, 38 such projects employed more than 1,000 inmates (Auerbach et al., 1988). In 1997, when more than 18,000 inmates were employed, criticism from manufacturers began to increase. The American Furniture Manufacturers Association, for example, endorsed legislation that would curtail the advantages enjoyed by Federal Prison Industries, a division of the Federal Bureau of Prisons, which, among other products, produces furniture ("Manufacturers Complain of Prison Work Programs," 1997). For years, small businesses have lobbied in Congress against a policy that requires federal agencies to purchase goods from Federal Prison Industries (Hoover, 2001). Nevertheless, by 2000, there were 80,000 inmates employed by government or private companies. Private sector employment programs are operating in 36 states employing 3,500 inmates, while the federal government employs more than 20,000 in a program that has become a $546 million business (Hoover, 2001; Leonhardt, 2000).

In response to prison overcrowding and prison construction costs, some states now use inmate labor to help build correctional facilities. These states are typically those in which organized labor is relatively weak, such as South Carolina where inmates have been constructing new correctional facilities and expanding and renovating existing facilities. Inmates are volunteers from medium- and minimum-security institutions who are paid $0.35 an hour and become eligible for salary increases and bonuses. They also

(continued)

receive additional days off their sentences depending on their level of skill, which serves as an incentive to improve their skills through available training programs. Unsatisfactory performance or rule violations result in being dropped from the program. In other states, inmates are not paid but receive time off their sentences while learning employment skills. Inmate-worker turnover and the need to take counts of inmates several times a day reduce the efficiency of these construction projects. An audit of inmate construction projects revealed that they took twice as long to build, but labor costs were 50 percent less than private contracting.

California uses more than 3,000 inmates in its Conservation Camp Program. In 38 conservation camps run by the Department of Corrections in cooperation with the Department of Forestry and Fire Protection, inmates fight fires that periodically threaten the state's forests. They also clear streams, plant trees, and do flood control work and other community service projects. The inmates are carefully screened volunteers; those with histories of violent crimes, sex offenses, arson, or escape are excluded. In North Carolina and about a dozen other states, inmate volunteers staff tourist information services. From behind prison walls and barbed wire, female inmates answer telephone inquiries from people who call the toll-free tourist information number.

THE BIG HOUSE

"The move from 'hard labor' to 'hard time,' begun in the Depression and completed by war's end, forced prison administrators to overhaul their management practices. Always authoritarian, prison wardens had to rely much more on pure regimentation, epitomized by the **Big House** of the 1930s and 1940s" (Weiss, 2001: 262). Architecturally, the Big House is an Auburn-style prison: one- or two-inmate cells clustered in cell blocks on tiers surrounded by a high stone wall with guard towers, often holding in excess of 2,000 inmates. Unlike Auburn, however, silence, hard labor, the lockstep shuffle, and official use of corporal punishment were absent. The cells had toilets and sinks, were ventilated and heated, and had more space than the typical Auburn cell. In the Big House, inmates were frequently permitted to furnish and decorate their own cells. The better-equipped institutions had recreational facilities, baseball diamonds, and basketball and handball courts. Many prisoners were black, but in most Big Houses outside the South, the inmates were mostly white. A great deal of idleness and an absence of rehabilitative programming were problems (Irwin, 1980).

Scholarly studies of the prison environment, such as the one by Donald Clemmer (1958) during the 1930s, reported a phenomenon that became known as **prisonization** and the existence of an **inmate subculture.** Prisonization refers to the process by which an inmate is socialized into the prison environment. Although they may arrive with varied backgrounds, prisoners share a common suspicion and fear of other inmates and guards. In response, they tend to align themselves into cliques that serve to counter, if not subvert, the power of prison officials. These cliques form the basis of the prison subculture that emerged in the less rigid environment of the Big House. This subculture developed and enforced its own rules. Several contemporary scholars argue, however, that the subculture found in the Big House by earlier researchers did not develop in prison but was actually brought into the prison by inmates who shared a common subcultural orientation. In either event, the guards faced a terrifying problem.

Big House guards were vastly outnumbered by often idle inmates who were organized into cliques and formed a distinct subculture in opposition to the prison administration. Although prison officials could rely on help from outside forces, such as the state police and National Guard, sufficient coercive force was not immediately available for them to be routinely in effective control of the institution. Corporal punishment was no longer (officially) permitted, and loss of "good time" (time off for "good behavior") or solitary confinement often proved ineffective in controlling behavior in the volatile atmosphere of a prison. As a result, guards developed effective informal control strategies involving personal agreements and corrupt favoritism (Irwin, 1980). *Personal agreements* between guards and inmates were implicit or tacit exchange relationships in which an inmate would refrain from rule-violative behavior in return for some favor or special consideration from a guard. *Corrupt favoritism* involved guards who granted special privileges to key prisoners who served as inmate leaders, in return for their support in maintaining order:

- By keeping their own violations within acceptable limits and supporting the prevailing prison norm, which required inmates to "do your own time"—that is, mind your own business and "don't make no waves" (which encouraged conformity)
- By threatening or actually using violence against prisoners who disrupted the prison routine and thereby endangered the privileged inmates' special arrangements with the guards

Prison officials tolerated and sometimes encouraged these activities and the convict organization because they promoted a high degree of order within the prison. In effect, the inmates ran the prison and officials rarely needed to intervene. There was little emphasis on rehabilitation (Austin and Irwin, 2001).

We have moved from Walnut Street and the Pennsylvania system to Auburn and the Big House; the next stop is in California, where a new model of penology, based on positivism, emerged.

CORRECTIONS

Toward the end of World War II, a penological revolution occurred in California, where former prosecutor Earl Warren (1891–1974) had been elected governor in the wake of a prison scandal. Under Warren's leadership, California reorganized its prison system according to the positive ideal of individual reformation. The system was organized not for punishment, but around rehabilitation. California would apply the methods of the behavioral sciences to *correct* criminal behavior.

To operationalize the new approach to penology, California implemented an extreme version of the *indeterminate sentence:* Judges would remand a criminal with an indefinite sentence to the California Adult (or Youth) Authority, which would determine his or her *treatment* needs through a process of classification and assign the *convict-client* to an appropriate facility—not a prison but a *correctional institution.* A convict would remain "under treatment"—incarcerated—until the Adult Authority determined that the client had been rehabilitated, at which time he or she would be paroled to a community-based treatment program—that is, supervision by a parole agent.

Prisons no longer existed in California; they became "correctional institutions." Guards were no longer present; they became "correction officers." Wardens no longer existed; they became "superintendents." New institutions—medium- and minimum-security correctional facilities—were built. Adult Authority clients could be moved from maximum- to medium- to minimum-security facilities, and to parole. Or, if their behavior requires, they could be moved from parole supervision back into the institution for further "treatment in a secure setting."

Correctional Institutions: Divisions, Rebellions, and Riots

Into these correctional institutions came the *treaters;* new superintendents often had extensive education in the behavioral sciences, and their institutions employed teachers, social workers, psychologists, and psychiatrists to implement a rehabilitative

Prison Security Levels

There are four types of prisons for adults, and within each there are different custodial levels, depending on perceived risk presented by the inmate:

• *Supermaximum-security* prisons are comprised of cells with sliding cell doors that are remotely operated from a secure control station. Inmates remain in their 6- by 12-feet cells for 23 hours per day. During the other hour, they may be allowed to shower and exercise in the cell block or in an exterior cage. All inmate movement is strictly controlled with the use of physical restraints and correctional officer escort. The perimeter barrier is designed with a double fence with armed watch towers and/or armed roving patrols.

• *Maximum-/close-security* prisons are comprised of single cells and divided into cell-blocks, which may be in one building or multiple buildings. Cell doors are usually controlled remotely from a secure control station. Each cell is equipped with its own combination plumbing fixture, which includes a sink and toilet. The perimeter barrier is designed with a double fence, armed watch towers, and/or armed roving patrols. Inmate movement is restricted and supervised by correctional staff. Inmates are allowed out of their cells to work or attend various programs and recreation inside the facility. About 30 percent of all prisons are supermaximum or maximum. More than one-third of inmates are confined in maximum-security facilities.

• *Medium-security* prisons are comprised of single cells—as in maximum-security institutions—housing two inmates each, or secure dormitories that provide housing for up to 50 inmates each. Each dormitory contains a group toilet and shower area as well as sinks. Dormitory inmates sleep in a military-style double bunk and have an adjacent metal locker for storage of uniforms, undergarments, shoes, and so on. Each dormitory is locked at night with a correctional officer providing direct supervision of the inmates and sleeping area. There is less supervision and control over the internal movement of inmates than in a maximum-security prison, although the facility usually has a double-perimeter fence with armed watch towers or armed roving patrols. Most inmate work and self-improvement programs are within the prison, although selected medium-custody inmates work outside the prison under supervision of armed correction officers. Each medium-security prison typically has a single cell unit for the punishment of inmates who violate prison rules. A little more than 40 percent of all prisons are medium security.

• *Minimum-security* inmates live in nonsecure dormitory-style rooms divided into cubicles and routinely patrolled by correction officers. Like the medium-security dorm, it has its own group toilet and shower area adjacent to the sleeping quarters that contain double bunks and lockers.

Some facilities may be surrounded by a fence and guard tower; others have a single-perimeter fence that is inspected on a regular basis, but has no armed watch towers or roving patrol. There is less supervision and control over inmates in the dormitories and less supervision of inmate movement within the prison than at a medium facility. Minimum-custody inmates at minimum-security prisons usually participate in community-based work, and all inmates may participate in prerelease transition programs. About 30 percent of all prisons are low or minimum security.

regimen. Slowly, but steadily, the California system was copied, at least in part, by all the other states and the federal system—prisons virtually disappeared from the United States. Parole and the indeterminate sentence became intertwined with the idea of corrections and a medical model approach to dealing with criminal behavior, subjects discussed in chapter 7.

Despite the corrections revolution, prison officials remained preoccupied with management and security issues; most of the allocations for correctional institutions

Offender Employment

"For some inmates, institutionalization is a traumatic hell for which suicide or attempts to escape are strong considerations. For others, prison is a welcome relief from the stresses of using drugs and living on the streets. But for all, prison creates a deep hunger for everything that cannot be had and a thirst for self-respect and dignity. If upon release from prison, a person is not prepared to secure work and be self-supporting, his or her return to prison is almost inevitable. For without viable work, self-respect cannot be restored and life is without dignity" (Krienert and Fleisher, 2004: ix).

were for administration and security, leaving about 5 percent for items that could reasonably be labeled "rehabilitative." Providing such services has always been problematic. Correctional salaries are relatively low, and most prisons are located in rural areas—where land is relatively cheap and the prison provides important economic benefits to local residents[8]—areas not particularly attractive to urban graduates trained in therapeutic disciplines.[9] Inadequate funding results in vocational training that is out-of-date and often of little use to inmates seeking employment based on skills developed in the correctional institution.

The problems encountered by the corrections approach were compounded by differences between correction officers and the treaters. Older members of staff, particularly those responsible for prison security, were often resistant to the changes brought in by the treaters. This resistance could be expected from an examination of their differing backgrounds. Correction officers were typically rural, white Protestants, socially and politically conservative with, at best, a high school education; they tended to be poorly trained. The treaters tended to be reform-minded urban college graduates, many of whom were Catholics and Jews—and women.

Furthermore, the rhetoric did not match the reality, and prisoners soured on rehabilitative programs that raised unrealistic expectations (Irwin, 1980: 63): "After prisoners were convinced that treatment programs did not work (by the appearance

The Benefits of Imprisonment

Prisons in impoverished rural areas have become a cornerstone of economic development (Kilborn, 2001; Schlosser, 1998). In Connecticut and New York, for example, "Republican lawmakers representing rural constituencies that benefit economically from new prisons have opposed relaxing the tough mandatory minimum sentences for drug offenses" ("Full-Employment Prisons," 2001; Wren, 1998: 23). Despite the fact that they cannot vote, inmates count as county residents, thus increasing the electoral clout of prison communities. Federal benefits to counties are based on population, and the census counts inmates where they are incarcerated, not where their homes are located (Butterfield, 2004).

[8]A 1,200-bed prison requires about 200 construction workers and about 500 permanent positions.

[9]There is research indicating that prisons do not actually provide significant economic benefits to rural communities (King, Mauer, and Huling, 2004).

of persons who had participated fully in treatment programs streaming back to prison with new crimes or violations of parole), hope shaded to cynicism and then turned to bitterness."

During the 1950s, prisoners were usually divided to the point of impotence: "The prisonization process, which had aligned the great majority of inmates against their keepers, had also divided them from one another, making effective collaboration extremely difficult. Only a rumor of an excessively brutal incident or a report of revolts elsewhere could arouse a sense of community sufficient to support a riotous outbreak" (McKelvey, 1977: 323). There were such outbreaks during the 1950s in California, Louisiana, Massachusetts, Michigan, Missouri, New Jersey, Ohio, Pennsylvania, and Washington.

Into this environment came thousands of new African American and Latino inmates. During the 1950s, the number of blacks and Latinos committed annually to adult federal and state prisons increased from 17,200 to 28,500 (McKelvey, 1977), and this figure continued to grow during the 1960s and 1970s. Although the predominantly white inmates of the Big House could relate to their keepers, the young urban black and Hispanic found no such comfort. In 1954, the Supreme Court handed down its decision in *Brown v. Board of Education of Topeka, Kansas* (347 U.S. 483), which helped set off the civil rights revolution in the United States.

Rising black consciousness occurring in the wider community took on more radical dimensions inside the prison. The Black Muslims emerged as a major separatist organization and confronted prison officials with demands based on religious freedom. The antiwar movement and activities of radical groups, such as the Black Panthers and Students for a Democratic Society, stirred and politicized inmates, black and white. These inmates confronted correctional officials with demands often couched in Marxist terminology.

The traditional relationship between inmates and correction officers, *rapprochement* based on private agreements or corrupt favoritism, started to come apart. Inmates became increasingly militant in their refusal to cooperate with their keepers. Correction officials responded in the best tradition of the Big House—with repression that touched off violence in institutions throughout the United States, including riots at California's San Quentin in 1967 and Holmesburg Prison in Philadelphia in 1970. In 1968, correction officers and police killed 6 inmates and wounded 68 others in quelling a riot at North Carolina's Central Prison. Correctional institutions simmered throughout the 1960s into 1971, when in September the focus of attention shifted to a small upstate New York town where the last of the Auburn-style prisons was built. The events at Attica would prove to be a turning point in corrections and the history of parole.

Attica

The state prison at Attica, a town 30 miles east of Buffalo that in 1971 had a population of fewer than 3,000, was completed in 1931. It boasted of being the most secure, escape-proof prison ever built; at the time, it was also the most expensive prison ever built. Attica was a response to an outbreak of prison riots throughout the United States in the late 1920s. In 1929, Clinton Prison in Dannemora, New York, experienced a riot protesting overcrowded conditions; three inmates were killed. In that year, the prison at Auburn experienced a riot in July during which four inmates escaped and two others were killed; several guards were seriously injured and two were shot. In December, another riot ensued. Inmates with firearms took the warden, six guards, and a foreman hostage, and the principal keeper was shot and killed. The prison was retaken after eight prisoners were killed and seven employees injured. Three inmates were later executed for their role in the riot ("Auburn Correctional Facility," 1998).

Typical of prisons in New York and elsewhere, Attica was placed in a rural area where residents would accept the institution as a basis for employment and other economic benefits. On July 8, 1970, Attica, as well as the other state maximum-security prisons in New York, received a name change. There were no more prisons in New York; in their places, instead, stood six maximum-security "correctional facilities." The prison wardens became "institutional superintendents," the former principal keepers became "deputy superintendents," and the old-line prison guards/keepers awakened that morning to find themselves suddenly "correction officers." "No one's job or essential duties changed, only his title" (Attica Commission, 1972: 18).

Fourteen months later, Attica Correctional Facility had more than 2,000 inmates who were locked in their cells for 12 to 16 hours per day being "rehabilitated," and who spent the remainder of the day with little to occupy their time. No gymnasium was available, and recreational opportunities were limited. Meaningful rehabilitation programs were almost totally absent. Showers were available for most inmates—once a week.

Most inmates were African Americans and Hispanics from the downstate New York area or upstate cities, such as Buffalo, Syracuse, and Rochester. All but one (he was Puerto Rican) of the fewer than 400 correction officers were non-Hispanic whites drawn primarily from the communities surrounding Attica. Although the superintendent had a master's degree in correctional administration, correction officers who began their jobs between World War II and the late 1950s received no formal training. Those who started after that were given 2 weeks of training. They were expected to enforce the dozens of petty rules typical of correctional institutions and to relate in a meaningful way to inmates with whom they had little in common.

Attica had a large number of Black Muslims (members of the Nation of Islam) who had difficulty with a prison diet that was heavy with pork. Muslims also objected to the lack of ministers. Correctional officials would not allow the ministers, many of whom had prison records, into Attica. Black Muslims spent their recreation time in the yard engaging in worship and highly disciplined physical exercise. The correctional staff, which never understood the Black Muslims, was quite fearful of this group, who exhibited military-type discipline and remained aloof from both staff and other inmates.

Typical of large correctional institutions, in Attica "popular conceptions of homosexual advances and assaults in prison were not exaggerated" (Attica Commission, 1972: 78). Correction officers were unable to protect inmates who were forced to resort to forms of self-protection, such as carrying a "shiv" (homemade knife), in violation of prison rules: "The irony was not lost on the inmates. They perceived themselves surrounded by high walls and gates, and tightly regimented by a myriad of written and unwritten rules; but when they needed protection, they often had to resort to the same skills that had brought many of them to Attica in the first place" (79).

During the summer of 1971, a number of peaceful protests by inmates over conditions at Attica occurred. Leaders of previously antagonistic inmate groups, such as the Young Lords, a Puerto Rican group, and the Black Panthers and Black Muslims, gained greater political awareness, submerged their differences, and joined with white inmates in a peaceful effort to effect changes at Attica. "Inmates had petitioned state correction officials to ease chronic overcrowding and censorship rules, and to improve conditions that limited them to one shower a week and one roll of toilet paper a month" (Haberman, 2000: 23). The new solidarity among inmates frightened officials. The superintendent responded by attempting to transfer the leaders as "troublemakers." He was prevented from doing so by the new Commissioner of the Department of Correctional Services, Russell G. Oswald, who had been chairman of the New York State Board of Parole. Oswald met with inmate representatives at the prison but was called away on a personal emergency—his wife was seriously ill—before any agreement could be arranged.

On September 8, 1971, when a correction officer attempted to discipline two inmates who appeared to be sparring, a confrontation ensued. The incident passed without any action on the part of the outnumbered staff. That evening officers appeared and took the inmates from their cells. A noisy protest ensued during the evening, and it was renewed when inmates gathered for breakfast on the morning of September 9. A melee broke out, correction officers were taken hostage, and a riot quickly developed. Prison officials had no plan, nor had they been trained to deal with such an emergency. As a result, within 20 minutes inmates secured control of the four main cell blocks and seized 40 hostages. Correction officers were beaten, and one died later as a result of his wounds. The Black Muslims, who had not taken part in the initial uprising, moved to protect the hostages who were used as a basis for negotiations. An inmate committee for that purpose was formed.

When he arrived at Attica, Commissioner Oswald found the police were not prepared to retake the prison immediately. By the time sufficient forces had gathered, negotiations were already under way and Oswald chose to continue them in an effort to avoid more bloodshed. At the request of the inmate committee, several outside observers were permitted to enter Attica, including reporters, lawyers, and politicians. Although the negotiations were quite disorganized, Oswald agreed to most of the inmate demands for improved conditions at Attica. The negotiations broke down, however, over the issue of complete amnesty because one of the injured officers had died after the negotiations began. Governor Rockefeller ordered that the prison be retaken.

On the morning of September 13, in a poorly planned and uncoordinated 9-minute assault, heavily armed state police and correction officers retook the prison—more than 2,000 rounds of ammunition were fired. Two hostages were seriously injured by the inmates, and 10 hostages and 29 inmates were killed by state troopers and correction officers (Wicker, 1975). In 1989, the New York State Court of Claims awarded $1.3 million to seven inmates who, although they had not participated in the uprising, had been injured at Attica by state police gunfire (Kolbert, 1989). In 1997, the first of 1,281 plaintiffs in the Attica litigation was awarded $4 million. Paroled in 1973, the former inmate, who has worked as a paralegal investigator for more than 20 years, had been tortured by correction officers in the aftermath of the uprising (McFadden, 1997). In 1999, his $4 million award was overturned by a federal appeals court. In 2000, New York agreed to pay $8 million to 1,280 inmates or their survivors who claimed they were tortured, beaten, and denied medical treatment in the aftermath of the Attica rebellion—$6,500 to $125,000 each. The state also agreed to pay the inmates' lawyers up to $4 million in legal fees and costs. In the agreement, the state admitted no wrongdoing (Chen, 2000).

A number of official investigations occurred in the aftermath of the rebellion at Attica. In particular, rehabilitation, the parole board, and indeterminate sentencing received severe criticism. As Cullen and Gilbert point out, "Americans in the first half of the 1970s were faced with the prospect of an intractable crime rate and confronted with the reality—powerfully symbolized by Attica—that their prisons were both inhumane and grossly ineffective. In this context, a culprit was needed to take the blame, and a candidate was readily found. Rehabilitation would take the rap" (1982: 6), and a new prison era would emerge—**just deserts.**

JUST DESERTS: CONTEMPORARY CORRECTIONAL INSTITUTIONS

Did the events at Attica result in any lasting changes? At Attica, Islam is now a recognized religion, inmates are allowed to stay in the exercise yard into the evening, and prisoners who can afford them are allowed television sets in their cells (Cohen, 1992). Observers of the current state of our prisons, however, would be hard-pressed to document any positive changes of substance. A distinct political turn to the right has increased the number of prison commitments and lengthened the terms of imprisonment in many states that now have no parole system with which to deal with overcrowding. This has been exacerbated by politicians scrambling on board the "tough on crime" bandwagon with policies that, although they fail to deal with public protection, pander to constituent emotions. Some have focused on making prison life more difficult by prohibiting television, exercise equipment, and other recreational material that aid prison officials in maintaining discipline and control. In some states, legislation bars certain amenities—air conditioning, for example—that inmates do not have. In 1998, Congress enacted laws prohibiting federal prisons from showing movies rated R, NC-17, or X. The legislation also prohibits instruction in boxing, wrestling, weightlifting, judo, karate, or kickboxing.

John Irwin and James Austin (1994: 82, 111) point out that

> Now prison administrators and other policy makers have completely abandoned the goal of reducing prisoners' isolation from outside society. They build prisons in the remotest regions of the state with only security in mind and further reduce contact with outside organizations and individuals through their custody-oriented policies. These practices, along with greatly diminished rehabilitative resources, are producing prisoners who have deteriorated in prison and return to the outside much less equipped to live a conventional life than they were when they entered. . . . We should be concerned by the fact that the prison systems are spewing out such damaged human material, most of whom will disappear into our social trash heap, politely labeled the "homeless" or the underclass, or, worse, will violently lash out, perhaps murdering or raping someone, and then be taken back to the dungeon.

During an era when crime has been declining, the prison population has increased dramatically, and across the United States there has been a trend toward returning to the old Pennsylvania system, now referred to as the **super- (or maxi-) max prison.** These modern institutions are characterized by solitary confinement and minimal human contact. Cells, which inmates rarely leave, are self-contained units with showers; food and other services, such as law books from the library, are brought to the cells, and religious services are via closed-circuit television. The cost of imprisonment is roughly double that of a typical maximum-security prison (Anderson, 1998). In California, more than 1,200 inmates every year go from isolation to the street: Locked in their cells for 23 hours at a time and fed all their meals through a slot in the door—the next day they are on a bus heading home (Schlosser, 1998).

Twenty-Four Hours in Prison—North Carolina Department of Correction

In *close-security prisons*, inmate movement from one area of the prison to another is restricted. Armed correctional officers man security towers to stop escape attempts. At 3:30 AM, the first inmates are awakened—kitchen workers who get up to prepare the morning meal. These inmates live and work together. Correctional officers escort them to the kitchen as a group.

All inmates are awakened at 6 AM for the formal inmate count. Correctional staff count and recount inmates repeatedly throughout the day. Around 7 AM, breakfast begins. All inmate workers report to their jobs at 7:30 AM. Second-shift inmate workers may use the gyms, recreation yard, and canteens. Inmates work in the kitchen, license tag plant or laundry, or perform maintenance or janitorial tasks during the day. Around 3 PM, the inmate usually checks his mail and spends some time in the recreation yard prior to returning to the dining hall for the evening meal at 4 PM. After the evening meal, the

(continued)

inmate will have access to the gym, auditorium, or recreation yard. Depending on the day of the week, he may be involved in some organized recreational activities. On Wednesdays, Fridays, Saturdays, and Sundays, there is noncontact visitation with individuals who are on the inmate's approved visitors list. The visits are usually from 1 hour to $1\frac{1}{2}$ hours in duration. At approximately 6:30 PM, inmates may attend classes in the school or take part in other activities such as Alcoholics or Narcotics Anonymous. At 8:30 PM, another formal count is conducted. At 9 PM, inmates return to their housing area and are allowed to watch television; play checkers, chess, or cards; or write letters. At 11 PM, the inmate is locked into his cell and the lights are dimmed for the night.

The routine in *medium-security prisons* is similar, except inmates are housed in dormitories and some inmates leave the prison under armed guard to work on road squads cutting brush or working the fields at the state prison farm. *Minimum-security prisons* prepare inmates for return to the community. Although those entering minimum custody are assigned to jobs and remain at the prison, inmates in later phases leave the prison for work assignments. In the final stage of minimum custody, inmates may take part in work-release jobs and family visits.

Infectious Diseases

Adding to the numerous safety and health problems endemic to prisons is that presented by several infectious diseases, in particular, HIV/AIDS, tuberculosis (TB), and hepatitis C. About one in six AIDS patients has spent time in an American prison or jail. AIDS and its precursor immunodeficiency virus (HIV) were first identified in the United States in 1981. Intravenous drug users and male homosexuals have been identified as primary groups at risk from the disease, and prisons house many intravenous drug users and inmates who resort to homosexual practices in the absence of available female partners. AIDS also spreads in prison through rape, a rather widespread problem officials appear unwilling or unable to curtail (Lewin, 2001a). Inmates frequently sport prison tattoos, and the sharing of primitive tattoo needles is also a source of infection. The infection rate of prisoners is nearly six times the rate of the rest of the population, and "corrections budgets have been overwhelmed by the cost of the new treatments" (Purdy, 1997: 1). The number of HIV-positive cases in correctional institutions increased 66 percent from 1990 to 1993, reaching almost 12,000, 94 percent of whom were male—roughly in proportion with the gender distribution in prisons and jails (Hammett, Harrold, and Epstein, 1994). By the end of 1999, the HIV figure had increased to more than 26,000, with an additional 7,000 having AIDS (Maruschak, 2001). In response, Florida built a special needs facility that houses HIV/AIDS inmates: Through economies of scale, reduced hospitalization and security costs, Florida expects to improve the quality, while reducing the cost, of care for inmates with HIV/AIDS.

Additional dangers arrived at the prison gate with increases in TB, a bigger killer worldwide than AIDS. "TB is not usually a highly contagious disease but, given the right conditions . . . the probability of transmission increases significantly"

Death Sentence for Auto Theft

In 1993, Michael B. began serving a 7-year sentence for auto theft in the Menard Correctional Center, a maximum-security prison in Illinois. After the first few times he was raped, he got an HIV test—the married 24-year-old tested negative. However, the assaults did not stop. Michael B. was turned into a sex slave, traded by gang members for cigarettes and drugs. According to a lawsuit he filed later, he was raped by 10 men in the showers, by his cellmate while in "protective custody," and on dozens of other occasions. In March 1994, he was again tested for HIV; this time, he was positive (Weed, 2001).

(Wilcock, Hammett, and Parent, 1995: 2). "Prisons and jails, like other congregate facilities, are high-risk settings for the spread of tuberculosis infection. Living conditions are invariably crowded, and many buildings have antiquated systems with poor ventilation and air circulation. Inmates are already more susceptible to TB infection and TB disease because of factors associated with their high-risk lifestyles and inadequate access to health care services, as well as increased prevalence of HIV/AIDS among them. Finally, the appearance of multidrug resistant tuberculosis raises the threat of an often untreatable disease spreading in a closely confined population" (Hammett et al., 1994: xi). Approximately 12,000 inmates with TB are released each year (Butterfield, 2003b).

TB infection is spread through the air in tiny droplets containing the bacterium exhaled by persons with active TB disease, primarily when they cough or sneeze. TB commonly affects the lungs but may attack other parts of the body (Hammett et al., 1994). Inmates weakened by AIDS are at particular risk for new drug-resistant strains of TB, but all inmates and prison personnel are at risk from this contagious disease. TB can be contracted by an otherwise healthy individual because the disease is spread by coughing in an environment without adequate ventilation: "Not only do inmate populations contain concentrations of persons at risk for both TB and HIV, but the facilities themselves are high-risk settings for TB transmission because of crowded conditions and poor ventilation" (Crawford, 1994: 31). The Centers for Disease Control have guidelines for isolating persons with active TB; however, in a prison setting, these are expensive to implement, and most prisons are inadequate for dealing with TB.

Hepatitis C, an often fatal liver disease, is spread primarily through contact with human blood and sexual contact, and is prevalent among intravenous drug users. An estimated 4 million Americans have the disease. About 1.5 million inmates with the disease are released each year (Butterfield, 2003b). Carriers often have no symptoms, and the disease can progress undetected for years, silently destroying the liver. Although most state prisons do not require hepatitis C testing for inmates—it is expensive—the number of those with the disease has been estimated by health officials to be about 20 percent of the prison population. Treatment requires the use of drugs at a per-patient cost of about $10,000 to $20,000 per year; advanced cases can only be cured with a liver transplant. In 2001, New York was treating 95 infected inmates at a cost of $6 million per year. There is great concern in the medical community that hepatitis C will spread as infected inmates are released into the community. There is also concern about the safety of prison workers (Rhode, 2001).

Drug-abusing and Mentally Ill Inmates

Prison officials are also acknowledging the difficulties created by widespread use of drugs in their institutions: "Drug use has become a major problem with a variety of ramifications, including threats to prison order, violence among inmates, and

"Dark Side of America"

"Drug-resistant strains of tuberculosis, easily transmitted in tight spaces, have become a common problem. Illegal drugs ferried in by prison employees—and used by inmates who share needles—have made prison a high-risk setting for HIV infection and most recently liver-destroying hepatitis C. . . . By failing to confront public health problems in prison, the country could be setting itself up for new epidemics down the line" (*New York Times* **Editorial, May 17, 2004, p. 20**).

corruption of guards and other employees" (Malcolm, 1989c: 1), and this problem is apparently widespread (Purdy, 1995). In Pennsylvania, for example, in a 6-year period, 11 inmates died of drug overdoses (Associated Press, 1995). The dramatic increase in convicted drug offenders has been a driving force behind prison over-crowding and the smuggling of drugs into correctional institutions. In Illinois, drug offenders have been the fastest-growing segment of the prison population for sev-eral years. In New York, the number of inmates serving time for drug-related of-fenses has surpassed those imprisoned for any other type of crime.

Beginning in the 1960s, states began closing their institutions for treating the mentally ill. According to the plan, instead of expensive residential care, patients would be treated more economically with antipsychotic drugs at mental clinics in their communities. However, the clinics failed to materialize, and the mentally ill often live in the streets or are incarcerated. Because the authorities—police and judges—have nowhere else to send them, mentally ill persons are being sent to in-stitutions of last resort: jails and prisons. Thus, in addition to all the other problems facing our correctional institutions, they are also being used to make up for the in-adequacies of our mental health system (Butterfield, 1998b).

Prison Violence

Prison violence is widespread: Assaults on employees increased from fewer than 1,700 per year in 1988 to more than 13,000 in 1994 (Porter, 1995). In 1985, dozens of inmates were murdered by other inmates in Texas prisons. A particularly grisly prison outbreak occurred at the New Mexico State Penitentiary, which was built in 1957 to house 850 inmates. On February 1, 1980, the prison had nearly 1,000 in-mates and was badly understaffed; only 18 correction officers were on duty when prisoners took over the institution. Although the prison was quickly retaken by po-lice and National Guard, inmates had systematically slaughtered 33 of their fellow prisoners—many of whom were tortured to death.

Overcrowding was seen as a major reason for the 1989 2-day prison riot at the Correctional Institution at Camp Hill, Pennsylvania, a facility built to house 1,826 that had 2,607 inmates; more than 118 persons were injured, and half the facility's 31 build-ings were destroyed. At the Southern Ohio Correctional Facility at Lucasville, over-crowding was a modest 120 percent of capacity—the lowest for all the state's prisons. Nevertheless, in 1993, led by a Muslim faction aligned with members of the white Aryan Brotherhood, inmates rioted, seized 18 staff members as hostages, killed 1 correction officer and 9 inmates, and injured 48 inmates and several correction officers—one lost an eye—before surrendering. Prison overcrowding has been exacerbated by the peren-

Sexual Violence

He was forced to have oral sex with one inmate. A second demanded anal inter-course. When he refused, the inmate tore off his pants, shoved a pillow over his head so he could not scream, and raped him. It was quite painful. For the next 4 hours, several dozen inmates dragged him from cell to cell, raping him. The next night, he was gang raped again (Marx, 1994).

In Texas, a 23-year-old inmate was attacked by a group of some 20 inmates within a week of entering prison. The inmates demanded sex and money, but the victim refused. He was beaten for almost 2 hours and died of head injuries a few days later ("Rape Crisis in U.S. Prisons," 2001).

nial problem of prison discipline, and violence has been exacerbated by court orders limiting the authority of correctional officials and the phenomenon of prison gangs.

Prison Gangs. Some gangs developed in prison, often as mutual-protection groups; others were brought into the institution by convicted gang members. In either case, the contemporary prison has provided fertile soil for the proliferation and growth of these often dangerous entities. In most instances, gangs are organized along racial or ethnic lines. Instead of the politicized groups of the 1960s, an array of gangs with exotic-sounding names has appeared. So extensive is gang membership that a U.S. court of appeals in Illinois concluded that 90 percent of Pontiac Correctional Center's inmates are gang members and that they were running much of prison life (Crawford, 1988). The gangs have increased the potential for violence with members using the power of their gang affiliations for various extortionate practices. Inmates without the protection of the gang are vulnerable and often easy prey for the violence-prone gang members. Attempts by correctional officials to dissipate the power of the gangs by transferring their leadership to other institutions have often served only to spread the phenomenon. The gangs often transcend the prison, with members active inside and outside the institution, which has obvious implications for parole officers.

Gang members engage in extortion and drug and weapons trafficking: "Many prison gangs have a 'blood-in-blood-out' policy, meaning that an inmate may become a member only after killing or assaulting another prisoner or staffer and that his blood will be spilled before he is allowed to quit the gang. Members released from prison remain in the gang, often providing support and enforcement for the organization outside" (President's Commission on Organized Crime [PCOC], 1986: 75). The U.S. Department of Justice has identified more than 100 different prison gangs with greatly varying structures, the largest being the Aryan Brotherhood, Black Guerrilla Family, Texas Syndicate, La Nuestra Familia, and the Mexican Mafia.

Mexican Mafia

Found in at least nine state prison systems and reputed to be the most powerful of the prison-organized groups (also known as "la M"—pronounced emee), the Mexican Mafia is comprised primarily of Mexican American convicts and ex-convicts from the barrios of East Los Angeles. Like many other prison gangs, as well as their street counterparts, the Mexican Mafia has a blood-in-blood-out credo: Murder or the drawing of blood is a prerequisite for membership, and those seeking to resign will be killed.

Its origins are traced to the Deuel Vocational Institute in Tracy, California, where in 1957, 20 young Mexican Americans from the Maravilla area of East Los Angeles formed the Mexican Mafia as a self-protection group. They soon began to control such illicit activities as homosexual prostitution, gambling, and narcotics. Attempts by the Department of Corrections to diminish gang power by transferring members to other institutions only helped to spread their influence. Vigorous recruiting occurs among the most violent Mexican American inmates, particularly those housed in adjustment centers for the most dangerous and incorrigible. In 1967, Mexican Mafia reliance on wholesale violence increased, and in that year members attacked the first Mexican American outside their group. This attack on an inmate from rural northern California led to the formation of a second Mexican American gang, La Nuestra Familia, with whom the Mexican Mafia has been feuding since 1968.

By the mid-1960s, the Mexican Mafia had assumed control over prison heroin trafficking and numerous other inmate activities. In 1966, it started to move its operations

(continued)

outside the prison and is reputedly attempting to organize Hispanic gangs into a confederation to confront black Los Angeles gangs for control of the drug trade (Mydans, 1995). The gang asserts control over drug trafficking by Hispanic street gangs and collects "street taxes" in exchange for the privilege of staying in business and protection against encroachment by other gangs. In 1998, 12 members of la M were convicted in a federal court in California for directing a terror campaign from their prison cells to control drug trafficking by street gangs (Associated Press, 1998).

Aryan Brotherhood

Founded in 1964 by white inmates at San Quentin, primarily members of outlaw motorcycle clubs, in opposition to the Black Guerilla Family, they soon became infamous for their level of violence, extraordinary even by prison standards. By 1975, the gang had spread into most of California's prisons, with members sporting a green shamrock on their hands. Once dismissed as a fringe white supremacist gang, the gang has taken control of large parts of America's maximum-security prisons in California, Illinois, Texas, and Kansas. Also known as A.B. and the Brand, the Aryan Brotherhood established a hierarchical structure and asserted control over various prison rackets, including gambling—debtors pay up by having a relative or friend send an untraceable money order to a designated member on the outside. In an effort to thwart their power, prison officials have transferred many identifiable members to supermax prisons. Although the leadership is serving life sentences, released members maintain gang ties and represent a community threat (Grann, 2004).

PRISONS AND THE COURTS

Throughout most of our history, the courts have been unwilling to intervene in matters pertaining to prisons "out of concern for federalism and separation of powers and a fear that judicial review of administrative decisions would undermine prison security and discipline" (Jacobs, 1980: 433). Once the requirements of due process had been met, leading to conviction and sentencing, the judiciary had taken a "hands-off" policy. Prisons are difficult to manage, and this difficulty made judges reluctant to impose their legal standards in place of the expertise of prison administrators. In 1961, however, the Black Muslims began to litigate their First Amendment claims in New York, California, and the District of Columbia. These cases served to "open the floodgates" of prison litigation (Cripe, 1997). Once the courts became involved in prisons, they had no easy way to withdraw.

In 1968, 14 years after segregation in public schools was declared unconstitutional, the U.S. Supreme Court ruled that the racial segregation of prisoners violated the Fourth Amendment (*Lee v. Washington*, 390 U.S. 333). The following year, the Court ruled that prison officials must permit prisoners ("jailhouse lawyers") to assist their fellow inmates with legal questions (*Johnson v. Avery*, 393 U.S. 483). In 1971, the Court expanded this right by requiring prison officials to provide legal materials, law books, legal forms, and so on, for inmates (*Younger v. Gilmore*, 404 U.S. 15). In 1974, the Court extended its previous decisions by requiring correctional officials to provide either adequate law libraries or adequate legal assistance (*Bounds v. Smith*, 430 U.S. 817). That same year, the Court limited the power of prison officials to censor inmate letters (*Procunier v. Martinez*, 417 U.S. 817). In 1989, however, the Court (*Thornburgh v. Abbott*, 104 L.Ed.2d 459) limited the *Procunier* decision to *outgoing* mail and held that incoming items can quickly circulate throughout the institution and be a source of disorder. Accordingly, the Court gave prison officials greater flexibility in censoring publications that inmates may receive: "In the volatile prison environment, it is essential that prison officials be given discretion to prevent such disorder."

In 1974, the Supreme Court ruled that prisoners are entitled to minimal due process protections whenever disciplinary action threatens their "liberty" by imposing solitary confinement and loss of privileges of good time (*Wolff v. McDonnell*, 418

U.S. 817): "[T]hough his rights may be diminished by the needs and exigencies of the institutional environment, a prisoner is not wholly stripped of constitutional protections when he is imprisoned for a crime. There is no iron curtain drawn between the Constitution and the prisons of this country." In 1977, however, the Court apparently decided to draw a line between the prison and the Constitution: It rejected the notion that prisoners had the right under the First Amendment to organize an inmate union (*Jones v. North Carolina Prisoners' Union*, 433 U.S. 119). In 1978, the Court ruled that solitary confinement in a harsh setting for more than 30 days constitutes cruel and unusual punishment (*Hutto v. Finney*, 437 U.S. 678).

A great deal of litigation has arisen over prison conditions, particularly with respect to overcrowding. Federal and state courts in many jurisdictions have ordered prison officials to reduce inmate populations and to take other corrective steps to bring their institutions into line with constitutional requirements. In 1979 (*Bell v. Wolfish*, 441 U.S. 520) and 1981 (*Rhodes v. Chapman*, 452 U.S. 337), however, the Supreme Court overturned lower court decisions that found overcrowding per se to be unconstitutional. The Court ruled that the Constitution does not require inmates to be housed in single cells; double-bunking is permitted even for those prisoners in jail awaiting trial, who are legally still innocent. In *Chapman*, the Court ruled that prison conditions were constitutional as long as the totality of the conditions does not "involve the wanton and unnecessary infliction of pain." The 1994 federal "Crime Bill" prohibits federal judges from finding that prison or jail overcrowding is unconstitutional "in general terms." Instead, the statute requires a plaintiff to prove that the overcrowding causes the infliction of cruel and unusual punishment—a violation of the Eighth Amendment—*on that particular inmate*.

In 1983 (*Hudson v. Palmer*, 468 U.S. 517), the Supreme Court ruled that the Fourth Amendment's protection against unreasonable search and seizure does not apply to prison cells. In a 5–4 decision, the Court held: "The recognition of privacy rights for prisoners in their individual cells simply cannot be reconciled with the concept of incarceration and the needs and objectives of penal institutions." In *Hudson*, the Court overturned a U.S. court of appeals decision that had upheld the right of a convicted bank robber in Virginia to sue prison officials for the destruction of his property resulting from a search of his cell by correction officers. In 1994, the Court ruled unanimously that prison officials can be found liable for failing to protect inmates from the violence of other inmates. The successful litigant, an inmate at the federal prison at Terre Haute, Indiana, alleged that the beatings and rapes he suffered were the result of official indifference (*Farmer v. Brennan*, 62 L.W. 4446). In a 1995 decision (*Sandin v. Conner*, 115 S.Ct. 2293), a 5–4 majority made it substantially more difficult for prisoners to challenge prison officials: only when their actions impose "atypical and significant hardship on the inmate." Prison officials should have, the Court ruled, the flexibility "in fine-tuning of the ordinary incidents of prison life." The case involved an inmate in Hawaii who had not been allowed to call witnesses at a disciplinary hearing that imposed solitary confinement for 30 days—he lacked a "liberty interest" (an issue that was discussed in chapter 4 and is examined again in chapter 8). The federal Prison Litigation Reform Act of 1996 "has, for all practical purposes, removed the federal courts from involvement in correctional issues except in the most flagrant violations of the Constitution" (Breed, 1998: 15): Before an inmate can file a civil rights action in federal court the inmate must exhaust all available administrative remedies and show physical injury to receive damages for mental or emotional injury suffered while in custody.

COMMUNITY-BASED CORRECTIONS

By the 1960s, the "correctional" expectations of prisons were not being fulfilled: "The spending of years in confined quarters, perhaps as small as eight by ten feet, in a setting dominated by a toilet and a possibly criminally-aggressive cellmate, can hardly be considered conducive to encourage socially acceptable behavior upon release" (Hahn, 1976: 6). The prison is what Erving Goffman (1961: xiii) refers to as a **total institution**: "a place of residence and work where a large number of like-situated individuals, cut off from the wider society for an appreciable period of time, together lead an enclosed, formally administered round of life." As such, these institutions have a tendency to mold persons into compliant and often shapeless forms to maintain discipline and a sound working order, or for less utilitarian reasons. The prison provides a dreary uniformity that leaves little room for self-assertion and decision making—the requisites for living in the free community.

"Even the most well-developed treatment program," Paul Cromwell points out, "if totally contained within the institution, will lack one ingredient essential to an inmate's success after release. The missing factor is contact with the community and family" (1978: 68). In place of these "rehabilitative" factors, the inmate is to counter the negative influence of the inmate subculture. Instead of abandoning the rehabilitative ideal, supporters of the corrections approach in the late 1960s and early 1970s argued for a new approach they referred to as **community-based corrections.**

Belinda and Bernard McCarthy trace the concept of community-based corrections "back to the years following World War II, when returning veterans encountered adjustment problems as they attempted to reenter civilian life" (1984: 9). The successful integration of many servicemen was accomplished with assistance ranging from informal outpatient counseling to education; job preparation; and, in some cases, intensive therapy in residential settings. In 1967, the President's Commission on Law Enforcement and Administration of Justice stated: "Institutions tend to isolate offenders from society, both physically and psychologically, cutting them off from schools, jobs, families, and other supportive influences and increasing the probability that the label of criminal will be indelibly impressed upon them. The goal of reintegration is likely to be furthered much more readily by working with offenders in the community than by incarceration" (1972: 398). The commission added that the high cost of incarceration also served to make community-based corrections attractive.

In 1965, the Federal Rehabilitative Act authorized programs designed to aid in the rehabilitation of offenders while holding down the number of persons in prison. In 1968, Congress enacted the Omnibus Crime Control and Safe Streets Act, which led to the establishment of the Law Enforcement Assistance Administration (LEAA). With encouragement and funding from LEAA, state correctional officials began to look outside the prison for ways to rehabilitate offenders. The approach they adopted centered on reintegrating the offender back into the community, and it became known as "community-based corrections." Vernon Fox (1977: 1) states that community-based corrections refers to that part of corrections, other than traditional probation, prison, and parole, which makes use of community resources to assist the more traditional functions.

Several programs are generally offered as part of community-based corrections, including diversion, pretrial release, deferred sentencing, halfway houses, and work release:

1. **Diversion.** The President's Commission on Law Enforcement and Administration of Justice (1972) noted that for many persons who come to the attention of the criminal justice system, criminal sanctions would be excessive; however, these persons are often in need of treatment or supervision. Because the courts are overburdened with cases, programs that provide needed services for nonserious offenders, while easing court congestion, proved attractive. **Diversion** programs were operated by or in conjunction with police and prosecutor's offices; they dealt with adults and juveniles. Instead of being arrested and/or prosecuted, these offenders were sent for "treatment." Criticism of diversion centered on research indicating that persons who are diverted would often not have been arrested or prosecuted in the first place—diversion programs frequently *increased* ("net widening") the number of persons involved in criminal justice.

The most recent attempt at diversion has been an effort to respond to the problem of drug abuse. When the "war on drugs" policy of the 1980s (see Abadinsky, 2004) exacerbated already overcrowded prisons and court dockets, new methods were devised to divert drug abusers from the criminal justice process and into treatment (Gebelein, 2000). Judges increasingly made participation in drug treatment a condition of probation, as did parole boards. In 1989, treatment and punishment were melded in the form of a specialized **drug court** in Miami, Florida (Boldt, 1998). This high-volume court expands on traditional drug-defendant diversion programs by offering 1 year or more of court-run treatment; defendants who complete this option have their criminal cases dismissed. Between 1991 and 1993, Miami influenced officials in more than 20 other jurisdictions to establish drug courts (*Drug Court Movement*, 1995). The 1994 Crime Act provides federal funding to establish or expand drug courts, and by the end of 1999 they were available in almost every state. In 1994, the National Association of Drug Court Professionals was formed by about a half-dozen judges; 5 years later, its annual training meeting drew 3,000 participants (Gebelein, 2000).

Drug courts typically target nonviolent drug-abusing offenders, and in a "slow track process," retain jurisdiction over the case until the defendant satisfactorily completes the treatment or, if he or she fails, is returned to court for further processing—prosecution and possible incarceration. In addition, "Drug courts funded by the 1994 Crime Act may process only nonviolent offenders, but many drug courts that are wholly State funded or locally funded accept some violent offenders" (Gebelein, 2000: 4).

2. **Pretrial release.** Persons who lack the funds necessary to be released on bail and are detained pending trial suffer from significant disadvantages. The jail experience itself is punishing, but the person is also separated from the community, including family and friends, and places of employment. This experience handicaps the defendant and also burdens the criminal justice system, which must provide for the pretrial detention. **Pretrial release** programs use investigators—sometimes probation officers—to screen persons after they have entered the criminal justice system and before bail has been set. This approach enables the judge to make an informed bail decision, particularly in cases in which the investigator indicates that the defendant is a good candidate for release on his or her own recognizance (ROR). Some programs expanded to include supervision and a variety of services to persons on ROR (discussed in chapter 5).

3. **Deferred sentencing.** A program of **deferred sentencing** usually involves a plea of guilty followed by either restitution or some form of community service instead of a sentence. Satisfactory completion of the conditions of the deferred sentence

Drug Court

The Madison County, Illinois, drug court was fueled by a 437 percent increase in drug arrests between 1988 and 1992. The program targets persons arrested on felony drug charges who are diagnosed with alcohol or drug dependence that could be treated on an outpatient basis. Those who successfully complete the program have their charges dismissed. The program provides job assistance, which includes vocational training and high school equivalency education. Initially, clients are scheduled for three to five intensive 3- to 4-hour counseling sessions per week. As they progress, the number and length of sessions is reduced. Depending on a client's progress, the program can be completed in about 1 year or less. Random drug tests are given, and failure to comply with program requirements results in prosecution for the original felony offense (Illinois Criminal Justice Authority, 1999).

results in the charges being dropped; conversely, a failure can result in incarceration. Some programs use probation officers to supervise deferred offenders.

4. **Halfway houses.** This type of facility may be operated by a public or private agency. Some provide room and board and help with employment; others provide, in addition, a whole range of social services. **Halfway houses** may be used to place probationers in lieu of prison (halfway in) or for parolees in need of supportive services when they are released from prison (halfway out).

5. **Work release.** Like the halfway house, **work release** is designed to prepare inmates for the freedom of community living. Typically, an inmate leaves the institution or work-release center during the day for employment and returns at the end of the work day. Work release may also be granted to secure employment or to attend job training or educational programs.

David Greenberg questions some of the basic assumptions of community-based corrections: "One might ask why, if the community is so therapeutic, the offender got into trouble there in the first place? Indeed, an offender's home community, where he is already known as a delinquent or criminal, might pose more obstacles to the abandonment of criminal activity than some new residential location" (1975: 4). Furthermore, Greenberg argues, to the extent that criminal behavior is a rational response to the lack of lawful employment opportunity, it is beyond the ability of community-based corrections to correct.

The impetus for the expansion of community-based corrections was the availability of federal funding; Andrew Scull notes that "since the creation of the Law Enforcement Assistance Administration, efforts have been under way to manipulate federal funding and support for state and local law enforcement so as to provide sizable financial incentives for the development of community corrections' programs" (1977: 45). During the early 1980s, however, funding through LEAA dried up, and the agency was dismantled. State and local governments, already severely pressed for services while trying to hold the line on taxes, slowly abandoned the often costly programming that adequate community-based corrections required. The focus on the rehabilitative potential of the prison changed dramatically, *incapacitation* becoming the "principal justification for imprisonment in American criminal justice: offenders are imprisoned in the United States to restrain them from offending again while they are confined" (Zimring and Hawkins, 1995: 3). However, how much incapacitation can we afford? In part, the answer to this question has led to the development of privately built and operated prisons.

PRISONS FOR PROFIT

Although prisons have proved to be a costly liability for state governments since the Great Depression, some localities and private entrepreneurs view them as a source of potential income. For example, the farming community of Appleton, Minnesota, population about 1,500, built a 472-bed medium-security prison at a cost of $28.5 million. The town issued prison bonds in anticipation of the economics of imprisonment. Although the state has an overcrowded prison system, Minnesota does not have money available to make use of the Appleton facility (Terry, 1993). In 1993, however, after a national search, an agreement was reached with Puerto Rico to house 170 of the commonwealth's inmates at Appleton. Colorado's Fremont County, population 40,000, according to local souvenir T-shirts is the "Corrections Capital of the World." The claim is not an exaggeration: Its 13 prisons are the economic lifeblood of the county (Brooke, 1997).

One of the more recent responses to the problem of an increasing prison population has been the "privatization" of corrections: "Confinement service or facility management contracts are another way of expanding corrections capacity—without imposing any burden for facility construction on the government" (Mullen, 1985: 4).

Private firms have been able to establish and operationalize facilities more quickly than public agencies, which are constrained by a variety of political and bureaucratic requirements—private prisons can be built without the need for public approval. By the end of 2000, there were more than 184 privately operated prisons (Austin and Coventry, 2001).

According to Charles Logan (1990: 75), competition between public and **private prisons** will provide long-needed improvements in incarceration:

> Competition does not just contain costs; it advances other goals as well. When it is possible for a commercial company to take business away from a competitor (including the state) by showing that it can do a better job, then that company becomes a self-motivated watchdog over other companies (and over the state). Such a company will have an interest in critically evaluating the quality of its competitors' services and an interest in improving its own.
>
> In the case of prisons, the existence of competition, even potential competition, will make the public less tolerant of facilities that are crowded, costly, dirty, dangerous, inhumane, ineffective, and prone to lawsuits. Indeed, the fact that these conditions have existed for so long in monopolistic state prisons is a big part of what makes private prisons seem attractive.

The private facility has long been accepted in the area of juvenile care, whereas with adults this facility is more controversial. Several dozen of these facilities exist; most, but not all, are equipped to handle only minimum-security inmates and are thus more closely related to halfway houses (discussed in chapter 12) than traditional prisons. The largest customer of the private facility has been the U.S. Immigration and Naturalization Service (INS), which has contracted out the detention of illegal aliens to the Corrections Corporation of America, Inc. (CCA) based in Nashville. In 1985, the CCA proposed a takeover of the entire correctional system in Tennessee, but that bid was rejected by the state legislature. CCA has been criticized for making profits by understaffing its institutions and employing guards with little or no experience to handle high-security prisoners. This has led to an extraordinary number of escapes and violence (Yeoman, 2000). Another INS prison contractor, Esmor Correctional Services, was the subject of a scathing report that found poorly trained guards preying on immigrant detainees, a situation that resulted in a violent uprising (Dunn, 1995). The firm has successfully bid on numerous corrections projects by submitting low bids and cutting costs (Sullivan and Purdy, 1995).

Entry of the private sector into what has traditionally been thought of as a public responsibility is controversial; for example, it has been opposed by the National Sheriffs' Association, although state correction commissioners have tended to be more supportive. Supporters of the idea contend that private operators can maintain or exceed the level of services provided by public agencies at less cost. They are not bound by the bureaucracy or mandated salaries and retirement benefits of government agencies whose employees are often unionized—about 70 percent of prison operating costs are related to employees' salaries and benefits (Austin and Irwin, 2001).

Opponents question the propriety of handing over to private entrepreneurs so basic a public responsibility as punishment. Opposition has been vigorous on the part of organized labor, particularly by the American Federation of State, County, and Municipal Employees, which represents many prison workers.

Although minimum-security facilities have generated less concern, the question of turning over medium- and maximum-security prisoners to a private firm has troubled observers who point out that in such institutions the constant threat of the use of force, including deadly physical force, exists. The privately employed security officers are typically trained at the same state academies that train public correction officers and enjoy the same peace officer powers. Whether private employees should be entrusted by government with such authority is an unanswered legal question. In at least one case, a guard for a private prison operating under contract with the INS accidentally discharged a shotgun, killing one inmate and wounding another (*Medina v. O'Neil*, 589 F. Supp. 1028 S.D. Tex. 1984). At the other end of the spectrum of possibilities, in 1990, the leader of a multimillion-dollar drug ring used a .25-caliber handgun to overpower his guards and escape with two other inmates from a jail being run by the Wackenhut Corporation under contract with Bexar County, Texas. In 1997, the Supreme Court ruled (*Richardson et al. v. McKnight*, No. 96-318) that "employees of companies that run prisons under contract with a state or local government are not entitled to the [qualified] immunity from prisoner lawsuits that shields prison guards who are on the public payroll" (Greenhouse, 1997: 12). Qualified immunity (as opposed to the absolute immunity enjoyed by judicial officials) is a powerful shield, making it extremely difficult to successfully sue a public official.

Some opponents contend that to keep jail and prison space at a maximum level, private corrections corporations would seek to make Americans even more fearful of crime, through advertising and political campaigns. Other issues include the following: What will happen in the event of a strike by the private employees of a private prison? What if the firm decides to go out of business or enters into bankruptcy? One of the most basic of many legal issues involves the power of government to delegate its authority to private entrepreneurs to provide as basic a service as imprisonment. "A private entity," notes Ira Robbins, "exercises governmental power when it deprives a person of life, liberty, or property at the behest of government" (1988: 36–37). Because a private prison might have an economic interest in imposing a punishment that denies privileges (thereby decreasing prison costs) or denying good-time credits (which keeps the inmate incarcerated, from which the firm may benefit financially), the prison would not typically be permitted control over such actions. Arguments for contracting out prison services would also appear to justify similar contracting for police services—or, perhaps, probation and parole. In any event, James Austin and Gary Coventry (2001: ix) found that private prisons "offer only a modest cost savings, which are basically a result of moderate reductions in staffing patterns, fringe benefits, and other labor-related costs." They typically perform at the same level as public institutions (Austin and Irwin, 2001).

In more recent years, some of the worst conditions in juvenile facilities have been found among the growing number of privately operated prisons (Butterfield, 1998d). At one such facility in Florida, guards staged gladiator matches in which 13- and 14-year-olds beat each other before fellow inmates. Some juveniles were held beyond their release dates to increase company income (Jackson and Grumman, 1999). In 2000, Louisiana agreed to end its use of private facilities for juvenile offenders, in the wake of lawsuits that disclosed numerous abuses, including the denial of food, clothing, and medical care to inmates, who were also routinely beaten (Butterfield, 2000a). "Gone are the heady days of the mid-1990s, when private prisons were portrayed as an inexpensive panacea that would provide economical beds for state governments and deliver fat profits to investors." Stock prices have plummeted as criticism and problems have mounted. James Austin and Garry Coventry (2003) report that although private prisons have dramatically increased over the past two decades, inroads were limited to certain geographic areas, in particular the South and to a lesser extent the West, and is tapering off. Absence of such facilities in the Midwest and Northeast, they argue, is related to the power of labor unions, which have successfully resisted attempts to privatize. Nevertheless, in 2003, privately operated facilities housed about 94,000 inmates (Harrison and Beck, 2003).

Although there are policy issues—should the power to deprive people of their liberty be delegated to private firms; should power to use coercive force, including deadly force, be delegated to private firms—that are unresolved, issues of cost and efficiency have largely been determined. There is little, if any, evidence that private prisons are cheaper to operate. "There is nothing that is much different between the public and private prison. . . . Private prisons have no unique management system, innovative architectural design, or high tech innovations. The same people that were wardens in public prisons are now governing the private system" (Austin and Coventry, 2003: 6).

Chapter 7 examines the development of parole and the indeterminate sentence, and the impact of the "just deserts" model on both.

KEY TERMS

penitentiary	super- (or maxi-) max prison
Pennsylvania system	total institution
Auburn system	community-based corrections
contract system	diversion
lease system	drug court
state-use system	pretrial release
Big House	deferred sentencing
prisonization	halfway houses
inmate subculture	work release
just deserts	private prisons

INTERNET CONNECTIONS

The Official Home of Corrections: corrections.com

National Institute of Corrections: nicic.org

American Correctional Association: aca.org

Corrections industries links: corrections.com/industries

American Jail Association (AJA): corrections.com/aja/index.shtml

REVIEW QUESTIONS

1. How does the prison population differ from the rest of the population in the United States?
2. How did different conditions in England and the colonies result in different responses to criminals?
3. What are the five eras of prison history?
4. Why were colonial juries often unwilling to find defendants guilty?
5. What were the three intertwined developments that led to the establishment of the American system of prisons?
6. What was the Quaker approach to punishment?
7. What led to the demise of the Walnut Street Jail?
8. What are the characteristics of the Pennsylvania system?
9. Why did most states pattern themselves after the Auburn system rather than the Pennsylvania system?
10. What are the characteristics of the Auburn system?
11. What are the three categories of convict labor?
12. What factors led to the demise of most forms of convict labor?
13. What were the long-range effects of the curtailing of convict labor?
14. What is meant by a Big House prison?
15. What are prisonization and inmate subcultures?

16. How did guards maintain control of a Big House despite being vastly out-numbered by inmates?

17. What are the types of jobs that currently use inmate labor?

18. What led to the reemergence of positivism in penology after World War II?

19. What were the factors that led to the prison disturbances of the 1960s and early 1970s?

20. What has made the problem of prison discipline more difficult today than in the period of the Big House?

21. Why was the riot at Attica a turning point in American prison history? What model emerged out of Attica?

22. What is "community-based corrections"?

23. What led to the popularity of community-based corrections?

24. What are the programs traditionally included in community-based corrections?

25. What is the purpose of drug court?

26. What led to the demise of community-based corrections?

27. Why was the corrections approach difficult, if not impossible, to implement in prisons?

28. Why are TB, hepatitis C, and AIDS particularly problematic in prisons?

29. Why were the courts reluctant to consider inmate lawsuits against prison conditions?

30. What are the rights to which the Supreme Court has ruled inmates are entitled?

31. What are the pros and cons of using private prisons?

Parole and the Indeterminate Sentence

Parole, from the French *parol*, referring to "word of honor," was a means of releasing prisoners of war who promised not to resume arms in a current conflict. Modern parole, "a period of conditional supervised release following a prison term," has several antecedents (Glaze, 2003: 5).

TRANSPORTATION TO AMERICA

In colonial America early in the seventeenth century, a shortage of labor led to the transporting of children—the indentured poor and delinquents—as well as pardoned criminals from England. In the beginning, no specific conditions were imposed on those who received these pardons. However, after several of those pardoned evaded transportation or returned to England before the expiration of their term, certain restrictions had to be imposed. Around 1655, the form of pardons was amended to include specific conditions and provide for the nullification of the pardon if the recipient failed to abide by the conditions imposed.

During the early days of transportation, the government paid a fee to contractors for each prisoner transported. Subsequently, this arrangement was changed, and the contractor was given "property in service"—custody of the prisoner until the expiration of his or her full term. Once prisoners were delivered to the contractor, the government took no further interest in their welfare or behavior unless they violated the conditions of the pardon by returning to England prior to the expiration of their sentences.

When the pardoned felons arrived in the colonies, their services were sold to the highest bidder. The contractor then transferred the "property in service" agreement to the new master, and the felon was no longer referred to as a criminal but became an **indentured servant.** These indentures bear a similarity to the procedure now followed by parole boards. Like the criminal *qua* indentured servant, a prisoner released on parole agrees in writing to accept certain conditions. A release form is signed by the prisoner and the parole board, and some of the conditions imposed today on parolees are similar to those included on the indenture agreement (New York State Division of Parole, 1953). The termination of the Revolutionary War ended transportation to America, and England then sent her convicts to Australia, until 1879 (Hughes, 1987).

MACONOCHIE AND NORFOLK ISLAND

Torsten Erikkson refers to 1840 as the year in which "one of the most remarkable experiments in the history of penology was initiated" (1976: 81). In that year, Alexander Maconochie (1787–1860), a former naval officer, became superintendent of the remote British penal colony on Norfolk Island, about 930 miles northeast of Sidney, Australia. The island was reserved for convicts who had committed crimes while in Australian or Tasmanian prisons. Maconochie set out a philosophy of punishment based on reforming the individual criminal: The convict was to be punished for the past and trained for the future. Because the amount of time needed to instill self-discipline and train a criminal could not be estimated in advance of sentencing, Maconochie advocated sentences that were open ended, what is known today as an *indeterminate sentence*. He set up a system of *marks* to be earned by each inmate based on good behavior; a sentence could not be terminated until a certain number of marks had been achieved.

Norfolk housed the most dangerous felons, and riots occurred both before Maconochie's arrival and after he left the island. His system, however, brought tranquility to the colony. Convicts passed through three stages on the way to release, each with an increasing amount of personal liberty; misbehavior moved an offender back to an earlier stage. Although Maconochie's experiment at Norfolk was successful from the standpoint of penology, he was opposed by authorities back in Australia who viewed him as "coddling criminals" while incurring extra costs on the government. Maconochie was relieved of his position in 1844 and returned to England, where, in 1849, he became governor of a new prison. Two years later, criticism of his approach as too lenient again led to his dismissal and Maconochie embarked on a campaign for penal reform as a writer and speaker. One of those he influenced was Walter Crofton.

CROFTON AND THE IRISH SYSTEM

In 1853, Parliament enacted the Penal Servitude Act, which enabled prisoners to be released—paroled—on a **ticket of leave** and supervised by the police. That same year, Sir Walter Crofton (1815–1897) was commissioned to investigate conditions in Irish prisons, and in 1854, he became director of the Irish prison system. Crofton was familiar with the work of Alexander Maconochie, and their views on the reformation of criminals were similar. The **Irish system** that Crofton established was based on Maconochie's work at Norfolk Island and consisted of four stages:

1. The *first stage* involved solitary confinement for 9 months; during the first 3 months, the inmate was on reduced rations and was allowed no labor whatsoever. It was reasoned that after 3 months of forced idleness, even the laziest prisoner would long for something to do. He would then be given full rations, instructed in useful skills, and exposed to religious influences.
2. In the *second stage*, the convict was placed in a special prison to work with other inmates, during which time he could earn marks to qualify for a transfer to the third stage.
3. *Stage three* involved transportation to an open institution where the convict, by evidencing signs of reformation, could earn release on a ticket of leave.
4. In the *fourth stage*, ticket-of-leave men were conditionally released and, in rural districts, supervised by the police; those residing in Dublin, however, were supervised by a civilian employee who had the title of inspector of released prisoners. He worked cooperatively with the police, but his responsibility was to secure employment for ticket-of-leave men. He required them to report at stated intervals, visited their homes every 2 weeks, and verified their employment—he was the forerunner of a modern parole officer.

DEVELOPMENTS IN THE UNITED STATES

A modified version of the Irish system was adopted in England, and Crofton's work was widely publicized in the United States. American supporters of the Irish system, however, did not believe that adoption of the ticket of leave would ever be accepted in the United States. Their attitude was apparently based on the belief that it would be un-American to place any person under the supervision of the police, and they did not believe that any other form of supervision would be effective. A letter written by Crofton in 1874, in reply to an inquiry sent to him by the secretary of the New York Prison Association, stressed that the police of Ireland were permitted to delegate competent persons in the community to act as custodians for ticket-of-leave men, and he suggested a similar system for the United States (New York State Division of Parole, 1953). These principles were first implemented in the Elmira Reformatory.

Elmira Reformatory

In 1869, a **reformatory** was authorized for Elmira, New York, to receive male offenders between the ages of 16 and 30. The following year, the first convention of the American Prison Association met in Cincinnati. A paper based on the Irish system, dealing with the idea of an indeterminate sentence and the possibilities of a system of parole, was presented by the noted Michigan penologist Zebulon R. Brockway. The prison reformers meeting in Cincinnati urged New York to adopt Brockway's proposal at Elmira. When the Elmira Reformatory opened in 1876, Brockway was appointed superintendent. Instead of the nineteenth-century penology of silence, obedience, and labor, Elmira's goal would be reform of the convict ("Elmira," 1998).

Brockway drafted a statute directing the sending of young first offenders to Elmira under an indeterminate sentence not to exceed the maximum term that was already in place for nonreformatory offenders. The actual release date was set by the board of managers based on institutional behavior: "After the inmate accumulated a certain number of marks based on institutional conduct and progress in academic or vocational training, and if the investigation of his assurance of employment was positive, he could be released" (New York State Division of Parole, 1984: 6). An entire building was set up as a trades school and, by 1894, there was instruction in 34 trades ("Elmira," 1998). Also, "the Elmira system was designed to instill youthful offenders with the habits of order, discipline, and self-control and to mold obedient citizen-workers" (Pisciotta, 1994: 7–8). According to Brockway (1926: 111), this was a difficult task because the inmates "constitute a living antisocial human mass not easily resolved and brought into accord with the orderly life of a good community."

The Reverend Frederick Wines, a colleague of Brockway, described the principles on which the Elmira system was based, a clear manifestation of positivism:

> Criminals can be reformed; that reformation is the right of the convict and the duty of the State; that every prisoner must be individualized and given special treatment adapted to develop him to the point in which he is weak—physical, intellectual, or moral culture, in combination, but in varying proportions, according to the diagnosis of each case; that time must be given for the reformatory process to take effect, before allowing him to be sent away, uncured; that his cure is always facilitated by his cooperation, and often impossible without it. (1975: 230)

Cooperation was fostered by corporal punishment and the use of inmate classifications, according to which privileges were dispensed. Behavior judged to be "reformative" was rewarded by reclassification, which meant increased privileges, eventually leading to release on parole.

Brockway, reflecting the popularity of social Darwinism in his day, believed that his charges "belong to the grade of humanity that is inferior. The whole inmate population may be divided in this connection into two grades of inferiority—those whose defectiveness is apparent and others whose mental and moral defects are concealed under good (and sometimes quite brilliant) capabilities in given directions" (1926: 110). Despite its reform pretensions, Elmira "was overcrowded, understaffed, and grossly mismanaged. Key treatment programs did not fulfill their stated goals and objectives. Violence, escapes, smuggling, theft, homosexuality, revolts, arson, and other forms of inmate resistance were serious problems. Inmates suffered extraordinarily harsh punishments—including severe whippings and months of solitary confinement in dark, cold dungeons—and deliberate psychological torture. Elmira was, quite simply, a brutal prison" (Pisciotta, 1994: 33–34). Investigations led to charges against Brockway, but he succeeded in remaining superintendent until his retirement in 1900 ("Elmira," 1998).

On being admitted to Elmira, each inmate was placed in the second grade (of classification). Six months of good conduct meant promotion to the first grade—misbehavior could result in being placed in the third grade, from which the inmate would have to work his way back up. Continued good behavior in the first grade resulted in release—America's first parole system. Paroled inmates remained under the jurisdiction of reformatory authorities for an additional 6 months, during which the parolee was required to report on the first day of every month to his appointed guardian (from which parole officers evolved), as well as provide an account of his situation and conduct. Some believed that a longer period under supervision would be discouraging to the average parolee: "Inmates were released conditionally, subject to return if the Board believed there was actual or potential reversion to criminal behavior" (New York State Division of Parole, 1984: 6). However, no real attention was given to the training of prisoners toward their future adjustment in the community, and both prison administrators and inmates soon accepted the idea that reformed or unreformed, allowance of time for good behavior was automatic, and release at the earliest possible date was a right rather than a privilege. After release, supervision was either nonexistent or totally inadequate. This deficiency was also the case in other states using parole release, such as Minnesota and Illinois (Pisciotta, 1992).

INDETERMINATE SENTENCE AND PAROLE

The Elmira system—which included military-style uniforms, marching, and discipline—was copied by reformatories in other states, such as the Massachusetts Reformatory at Concord, the Minnesota State Reformatory at St. Cloud, and the Illinois State Reformatory at Pontiac, and made applicable to all or part of the prison population in Pennsylvania and Michigan (Pisciotta, 1992; Wines, 1975). In 1893, Nebraska granted the governor the power to parole any inmate who had served the minimum time for the crime for which they were convicted. In 1911, Nebraska established a three-member parole board. Alabama enacted a parole law in 1897, while Ohio and California had parole release statutes in place before the turn of the twentieth century (Zevitz and Takata, 1988). In 1907, New York extended indeterminate sentencing and parole release to all first offenders, except those convicted of murder. On the heels of prison riots in 1930, New York established a three-member full-time parole board, transferring release decisions from the Department of Corrections, and created the Division of Parole to supervise parolees (Dressler, 1951). Georgia enacted legislation in 1908 that gave the Prison Commission authority to implement a system of "parole or conditional pardons." However, there were no parole officers to provide supervision—offenders were placed under supervision of an employer or sponsor. By 1940, the state employed six parole officers.

In 1911, Minnesota enacted indeterminate sentencing for all felony offenders who could be kept under the jurisdiction of the Board of Control until they reached their maximum. In 1913, Massachusetts established the Commonwealth Board of Parole; before that, the commissioner of prisons and many correctional institutions conducted independent discharge or conditional release programs. In 1907, Montana authorized parole release by the Board of Prison Commissioners. By 1939, only four states (Florida, Mississippi, South Carolina, and Virginia) did not have provisions for parole. Instead, Florida used the governor's authority to pardon inmates in an effort to keep down the cost of imprisonment—the governor and his cabinet often presided over 200 pardon applications in a day. In 1941, the Florida Parole Commission was established. South Carolina began to use parole that same year, and Virginia established a parole system in 1942. By 1944, all 48 states had enacted parole legislation. Although most states had a mechanism in place for parole release prior to 1929, the impetus for the expansion of the use of parole was the Great Depression, as these statistics for parole release indicate (Cahalan, 1986):

$$1923 = 21{,}632$$
$$1926 = 19{,}917$$
$$1930 = 29{,}509$$
$$1936 = 37{,}794$$

The Great Depression, which began in 1929 and ended with the onset of World War II, resulted in many unemployed workers and, as noted in chapter 6, led to legislation that effectively abolished the economic exploitation of convict labor. This abolishment was accompanied by the prohibitive cost of constructing prisons, prison overcrowding, and an outbreak of prison riots. A 1931 report by the National Commission on Law Observance and Law Enforcement described the overcrowding of America's prisons as "incredible"; Michigan, for example, had 78.6 percent more inmates than its original capacity; California, 62.2 percent; Ohio, 54.1 percent; and Oklahoma, 56.7 percent. In 1923, 81,959 inmates were in prison (74 per 100,000 population); in 1930, 120,496 (98 per 100,000 population); and in 1940, the eve of World War II, 165,585 (125 per 100,000 population) (Cahalan, 1986). *Pressing economic conditions, not the press of prison reform, led to the popularity of parole release.*

By 1935, more than 60,000 persons were on parole in the United States, although only six states had what was described as "suitable" parole systems (Prison Association of New York, 1936). For example, although Texas had a system of parole release—actually conditional pardons—as early as 1905, there were no parole officers until 1937 when volunteer parole supervisors were authorized; they were the only form of supervision until well past World War II.

Before the depression, parole systems stressed employment—"criminals were idlers who needed to be disciplined"—and depended on employers to monitor parolees. This was weakened by widespread unemployment during the depression and, at the same time, pressure to release more persons on parole (Simon, 1993: 70). With World War II, industrial production increased, unemployment decreased, and parolees became eligible (for the first time since 1833) for military service. Before the war ended, every state had a parole system in place.

POSITIVISM REEMERGES AS THE MEDICAL MODEL

Despite its ravaging consequences, war can provide the impetus for many long-lasting social and scientific advances: With total mobilization, widespread unemployment ends, and improvements in manufacturing, communication, transportation, and medicine occur. During World War II, the United States experienced such important developments as the jet plane and the rocket, streptomycin, radar, sonar, and atomic energy. The war also provided psychologists with funds and an environment for extensive research and experimentation (Herman, 1995). By the end of the war, the horizons of science appeared to be unlimited, and the influence of the positive view reemerged in penology.

The great faith in science was occurring during a period of concern over the apparent rise in crime as measured by the *Uniform Crime Report*. The war had kept the wheels of industry spinning; unemployment did not exist. Suddenly, wartime production had ceased, and millions of young men who had been trained to kill and destroy, and who had done little else for several years, were returning from overseas. The vast allocation of societal resources in wartime had proved successful in the area of science. Perhaps a corresponding commitment of resources could prove successful in dealing with the problem of crime: a (scientific) "war on crime," introducing the **medical model.**

The positive approach to crime and criminals seeks to explain and respond to criminal behavior in a manner not dependent on (classical) issues of law, philosophy, or theology. Instead, criminal behavior is to be examined using the principles and methods of science, much as physical illness is subjected to examination by the physician (Robitscher, 1980: 44): "This new approach to criminal behavior stressed deviance as pathology. The criminal was not seen as 'bad' but as 'mad,' and he was to be given the benefit of the medical approach to madness. He should be helped to understand his unconscious motivation and to go through a process of psychoanalytic change."

"In its simplest (perhaps oversimplified) terms, the medical model as applied to corrections assumed the offender to be 'sick' (physically, mentally, and/or socially); his offense to be a manifestation or symptom of his illness, a cry for help" (MacNamara, 1977: 439). The medical metaphor extended to the postconviction process:

- *Examination* = presentence investigation report
- *Diagnosis* = classification
- *Treatment* = correctional program

According to the medical model, as applied to corrections, the effects of a treatment program are subjected to review by the parole board, which determines if the offender is sufficiently rehabilitated to be discharged from the correctional institution. A positive response means that treatment will continue on an outpatient basis in the form of parole supervision. The American Friends Service Committee (AFSC) sums up the rationale for this approach: "It rejects inherited concepts of criminal punishment as the payment of a debt owed to society, a debt proportioned to the magnitude of the offender's wrong. Instead it would save the offender through constructive measures of reformation, [and] protect society by keeping the offender locked up until the reformation is accomplished" (1971: 37).

The medical model is based on two questionable assumptions:

1. Criminals are "sick" and can thus benefit from treatment/therapy.
2. The behavioral sciences can provide the necessary treatment/therapeutic methods.

Although a paucity of systematic research supported this approach to criminal behavior, the medical/corrections model was adopted in most states, in theory, if not practice. William Parker argues that the theory never actually matched the practice: "The theory of rehabilitation has made some changes in the prison: terminology has changed, there are more programs, sweeping floors is now work therapy. The theory of rehabilitation has merely been imposed upon the theories of punishment and control" (1975: 26).

From its inception in California in 1944 under Governor Earl Warren, the corrections approach continued without serious opposition into the 1970s. Any opposition came primarily from the right of the political spectrum, as exemplified by the attacks of FBI director John Edgar Hoover who saw parole as "coddling" criminals, releasing them before they completed their sentence. During the 1970s, however, the attack on the corrections approach shifted to the political left.

In 1971, the Quaker-sponsored AFSC published the first comprehensive attack on the indeterminate sentence and parole. The committee noted that the indeterminate sentence and parole rested on a view of crime as a result of individual pathology that can best be "cured" by treating *individual* criminals. Such an approach, the AFSC noted, downgrades environmental factors, such as poverty, discrimination, and lack of employment opportunities. Furthermore, the committee argued, even if the medical model approach is valid, the achievement level of the behavioral sciences does not offer a scientific basis for treatment.

The work of the AFSC had only limited impact and no practical effect until 1974. In that year, sociologist Robert Martinson published a review of correctional treatment efforts—"What Works?"—to which he answered: Virtually nothing! "What Works?" (1974) was actually a synopsis of the research findings of Martinson, Douglas Lipton, and Judith Wilks; the complete work was published the following year. The three researchers surveyed 231 studies of correctional programs up until 1968 about which Martinson (1974: 25) concluded: "With few and isolated exceptions, the rehabilitative efforts that have been reported so far have had no appreciable effect on recidivism." Although the Martinson summary is more critical than the larger report, both lent credence to the arguments of the AFSC. In a review of the Lipton, Martinson, and Wilks (1975) research, a panel of the National Research Council concluded that it was "reasonably accurate and fair in the appraisal of the rehabilitation literature." In fact, the panel concluded, Lipton et al. "were, if anything, more likely to accept evidence in favor of rehabilitation than was justified" (Sechrest, White, and Brown, 1979: 31).

According to Paul Gendreau and Robert Ross, the research examined by Martinson was dated; furthermore, substantial literature since 1968 (Martinson's cutoff date) demonstrated that "successful rehabilitation of offenders had been accomplished, and continued to be accomplished quite well" (1987: 350). In fact, "between 1973 and 1980 reductions in recidivism, sometimes as substantial as 80 percent, had been achieved in a considerable number of well-controlled studies. Effective programs were conducted in a variety of community and (to a lesser degree) institutional settings, involving predelinquents, hardcore adolescent offenders, and recidivistic adult offenders, including heroin addicts" (1987: 350–351). These results were not short lived: "Follow-up periods of at least two years were not uncommon, and several studies reported longer follow-ups" (1987: 351). The debate over correctional treatment effectiveness continued (e.g., Andrews et al., 1990; Lab and Cullen, 1990), with rigorous analysis indicating positive outcomes in a variety of studies.

Whatever the merits, criticism of the indeterminate sentence, corrections, and parole increased. David Fogel presented a **justice model** in which he criticized the unbridled discretion exercised by correctional officials, particularly parole boards, under the guise of "treatment":

> It is evident that correctional administrators have for too long operated with practical immunity in the backwashes of administrative law. They have been unmindful that the process of justice more strictly observed by the visible police and courts in relation to rights due the accused before and through adjudication must not stop when the convicted person is sentenced. The justice perspective demands accountability from all processors, even the "pure of heart." (1975: 192)

Instead of the often hidden discretion exercised by parole boards, Fogel recommended a return to flat time/determinate sentences, with procedural rules in law limiting sentencing discretion, and the elimination of parole boards and parole agencies.

Furthermore, Fogel argued, whatever "treatment" is offered in a prison should be voluntary and should in no way affect the release date of an inmate.

Andrew von Hirsch (1976) offered the concept of **just deserts,** according to which the punishment is to be commensurate with the seriousness of the crime—a return to the classical approach: "A specific penalty level must apply in all instances of lawbreaking which involves a given degree of harmfulness and culpability" (von Hirsch and Hanrahan, 1978: 4). Indeterminacy and parole are to be replaced with a specific penalty for a specific offense.

The Twentieth Century Fund Task Force on Sentencing offered **presumptive sentencing**: Each category of crime would have a presumptive sentence "that should generally be imposed on typical first offenders who have committed the crime in the typical fashion" (1976: 20, italics deleted). For succeeding convictions or other aggravating circumstances, the judge could increase the presumptive sentence by a specific, albeit limited percentage. Mitigating circumstances could, similarly, reduce the presumptive sentence.

In sum, the basic thrust of these criticisms and proposals was to limit judicial discretion, eliminate the indeterminate sentence, and abolish the parole board. Here was an issue on which both the political left and right could agree—but for different reasons. Alfred Blumenstein notes:

> In the mid-1970s a striking consensus of the political left and the political right emerged in opposition to the indeterminate sentence. The political left was concerned over the excess of discretion in decisions about individual's liberty and the excessive disparity that appeared in sentences in presumably similar cases. The political right appeared to be far more concerned about "leniency" than about disparity. They viewed the parole boards as excessively ready to release prisoners early, and expressed shock that prisoners were back on the street on parole well before the maximum sentence. (1984: 130, edited)

Franklin Zimring and Gordon Hawkins (1995: 9) point out that this coalescing of otherwise divergent views "is a pretty reliable indication that some of the participants in the policy debate do not have a clear understanding of the practical implications of their stance."

As sentiments toward crime and criminals hardened, political changes generated by (often pandering) politicians led to "tough on crime" statutes that have further clogged our correctional facilities. "Sound-bite policy" replaced careful and thoughtful policy development. In Michigan, for example, the governor proposed abolishing parole and establishing a determinate sentencing system. He called this system **truth in sentencing,** which has now become a popular metaphor for eliminating release discretion, but which offers no method for controlling the prison population. He also proposed eliminating good time credit for violent criminals and

Good Politics Can Generate Bad Policy

The parole board is always vulnerable to criticism, and parole release often proves a tempting target for demagogic attack. After all, no one supports the release of a prison inmate who subsequently commits a heinous crime—the value of predictive hindsight. The issue, of course, is not *if* an inmate should be released, but what mechanism will be used to make the release decision. Prisons are overcrowded, and virtually all inmates will eventually be released, facts usually overlooked in the focus on a particular crime or parolee. Nevertheless, governors in many states would rather advocate abolishing parole than have to defend such a politically vulnerable system.

And Almost All Will Be Released

"Because states sharply curtailed education, job training and other rehabilitation programs inside prisons, the newly released inmates are far less likely than their counterparts two decades ago to find jobs, maintain stable family lives or stay out of trouble that leads to more prison. Many states have unintentionally contributed to these problems by abolishing early release for good behavior, removing the incentive for inmates to improve their conduct" (Butterfield, 2000b: 1).

making "the threat of additional punishment [sic] the best incentive for inmates to behave in prison." These proposals must be viewed against the realities of Michigan's prison population, which increased 220 percent since 1985, a year when the state was automatically releasing inmates as new commitments were received. Michigan parole supervises about 13,000 offenders per year (probation supervises another 55,000).

In at least nine states, prosecutors were active in leading the fight to abolish the indeterminate sentence and parole. "Clearly, parole was an easy target for those looking for political opportunities," notes Barbara Krauth, and "the emotional appeal of an attack on the system that released criminals to the streets may have benefited some political careers more than it actually addressed any of the complex problems of criminal justice" (1987: 52). By 1980, eight states had already adopted some form of determinate sentencing, including (in 1977) the pioneering state of California; the federal government and several other states have abolished the indeterminate sentence and parole release since that time, although a few—for example Colorado and Connecticut—have reintroduced the indeterminate sentence and parole supervision.[1] Even the terminology changed. Arkansas, for example, retained indeterminate sentencing but created a new agency to administer probation and parole—the Department of Community Punishment. Most states that have retained discretionary parole release restrict eligibility. In Georgia, for example, persons convicted of such serious crimes as rape and armed robbery must serve their entire sentence.

The federal Sentencing Reform Act of 1984, which abolished the indeterminate sentence, was designed to reduce sentence disparity and phase out parole release by 1992. However, the discretion lost by judges has been assumed by prosecutors. The result has been longer prison terms and an increasingly overcrowded federal prison system. As the next section indicates, this scenario has often been repeated in state systems. Federal judges have been vociferous in their criticism of their lack of discretion in rendering sentencing decisions (Urbina, 2003).

INDETERMINATE AND DETERMINATE SENTENCING

Under **indeterminate sentencing,** originally established as part of the Elmira system, a judge imposes a prison term that has both a minimum and a maximum length.[2] For example, a defendant convicted of a class 3 felony could receive a sentence with a minimum of 3 years (written 3–0–0) and a maximum of 9 years (written 9–0–0); the actual release of the inmate (between 3–0–0/9–0–0) is determined by a parole board. A provision is usually made for **good time,** which is deducted from the

[1]Actually, Connecticut uses a determinate sentence, but persons convicted of nonviolent offenses are eligible for parole release after serving half their sentence.

[2]In 1995, New York enacted legislation permitting judges to sentence select second felony offenders convicted of nonviolent crimes directly to parole supervision.

maximum sentence because of good institutional behavior, typically one-third, although in Iowa it is 50 percent. For example, an inmate with a maximum sentence of 9–0–0 could accumulate up to 3–0–0 years of good time, thus being released after 6–0–0 years without the intervention of the parole board. In some states, so-called truth-in-sentencing legislation has abolished parole and reduced or eliminated the use of good time, leaving prison officials without an effective mechanism to discipline inmates.

Under a system of indeterminate sentencing, persons convicted for the same class of offense could receive different sentences. For example, a first-degree robbery may carry a minimum sentence that ranges from 2–0–0 to 6–0–0 and a maximum sentence range of 8–4–0 to 25–0–0. Even those who receive the same sentence, for example, 3–0–0/9–0–0, can be released (paroled) at different times: 3–0–0, or 4–0–0, or 5–0–0, or . . . all the way up to 9–0–0 (minus good time). Criticism of the indeterminate sentence has involved this differential treatment of persons convicted of similar crimes, which is contrary to the classical approach to criminal behavior: "Critics of the indeterminate sentence argued that the treatment model has never realized its lofty objectives in practice and that, given the nature of the correctional system, these goals never will be realized. Furthermore, they maintained that the indeterminate sentence has created a situation of gross sentencing disparity that no longer can be justified by referring to treatment goals" (Goodstein and Hepburn, 1985: 17).

In response to criticism of indeterminate sentencing and parole boards, a variety of so-called flat, definite, or **determinate sentence** schemes have been adopted. Although each requires the setting of a *specific* sentence—no minimum and maximum—they differ according to the amount of discretion left to the judge:

1. *Definite sentence/no discretion.* The legislature provides for a specific sentence for each level of offense. For example, all crimes that constitute a class 2 felony would require the judge to impose a specific sentence—no deviations permitted. If a class 2 felony was punishable by imprisonment for 7 years, all judges would be required to sentence all defendants convicted of a class 2 felony to 7–0–0.

2. *Definite sentence/wide discretion.* The legislature provides for a range of sentences for each level of offense. For example, a class 2 felony would be punishable with a sentence between 3–0–0 and 7–0–0. Under this system the judge retains discretion to sentence a class 2 offender to 3–0–0, or 4–0–0, all the way up to 7–0–0. The sentence imposed is definite—for a specific number of years—but the judge's discretion is wide.

3. *Presumptive/narrow discretion.* The legislature limits discretion to a narrow range of sentences for each level of offense; for each level, a presumed sentence exists from which the judge cannot deviate, except if aggravating or mitigating circumstances apply, and then in only a limited manner. In other words, if a defendant is convicted of a class 2 felony, the judge would be required to set a sentence of (for example) 5–0–0. On a showing of *aggravation* by the prosecutor, however, the judge could increase the presumptive sentence to (for example) 6–0–0; on a showing of mitigation by the defense, the judge could decrease the presumptive sentence to (for example) 4–0–0. In some states, such as Minnesota, the presumed sentence is increased by a fixed amount based on the severity of any prior convictions (see Figure 5.5 in chapter 5).

4. *Presumptive/wide discretion.* As in the presumptive sentence with narrow discretion, the legislature provides three possible terms for each class of felony. However, although each class has a presumptive sentence, the judge may decrease (for mitigation) or increase (for aggravation) by significant amounts (Figure 7.1). For example, in Indiana, for a class "B" felony, the sentencing judge can add 10 years to or subtract 4 years from the presumptive sentence of 10 years.

Determinate sentencing systems usually include a provision for good time to promote prison discipline, ranging from 15 to 50 percent off the sentence. A

OFFENSE	RANGE	PRESUMPTIVE SENTENCE (YR)	AGGRAVATING FACTORS, ADD UP TO	MITIGATING FACTORS SUBTRACT UP TO (YR)	MAXIMUM FINE ($)
Murder	30–60 yr	50	10 yr	10	10,000
Class A felony	20–50 yr	25	20 yr	10	10,000
Class B felony	6–20 yr	10	10 yr	4	10,000
Class C felony	2–8 yr	4	4 yr	2	10,000
Class D felony	6 mos.–3 yr	1.5	1.5 yr	1	10,000
Class A misdemeanor	0–1 yr	None	NA	NA	5,000
Class B misdemeanor	0–180 days	None	NA	NA	1,000
Class C misdemeanor	0–60 days	None	NA	NA	500

FELONY SENTENCING ENHANCEMENTS

ENHANCEMENT DESCRIPTION	MINIMUM	MAXIMUM
Violent habitual criminal	Life without parole	
Habitual criminal	1x presumptive	3x presumptive; 30-yr maximum
Use of assault weapon	1x presumptive	2x presumptive; 10-yr maximum
Habitual controlled substance offender	3 yr (1 yr if more than 3 yr since last prior)	8 yr

FIGURE 7.1 *Presumptive Sentencing, Indiana.*

defendant sentenced to a determinate sentence of 5–0–0 in a system using 50 percent good time would be released (presuming good behavior) after 2–6–0. In practice, good time is deducted in advance, when the offender is first received at the institution; misbehavior results in time being added. In some states, an inmate may be entitled to additional time off the sentence for exemplary performance: "meritorious good time" or "industrial good time." These grants of additional time off (which can be used to circumvent truth-in-sentencing laws) are usually the result of prison overcrowding in states without parole release. They may also be used to reduce sentence minimums so inmates can more quickly qualify for parole release. More than half of inmate releases are the result of good-time provisions (Glaze, 2003).

In Florida, which abolished the indeterminate sentence and parole release in 1983, one-third was taken off the sentence when the inmate is received at a correctional institution, called Basic Gaintime. On the first day of each month, an inmate received an additional 20 days off, Incentive Good time, as a reward for attending classes, satisfactory work performance, and general good behavior. One-shot Meritorious Gaintime gave up to 60 days for exemplary performance. As a result of critical overcrowding, in 1987, the legislature provided for Provisional Release Credit, an additional 60 days per month whenever the prison system is more than 97.5 percent of capacity. As a result of these schemes, the average Florida inmate served a little more than one-third of his or her sentence (Malcolm, 1989a). In response, the legislature put its "get tough" mode in full gear and—ignoring the pressing problem of prison overcrowding—enacted mandatory minimum sentences for a host of offenses (Bales and Dees, 1992), which, of course, exacerbated overcrowding and required new schemes for early release. The wheels of Florida justice continued to spin: In 1993, Florida became one of the first states to repeal mandatory sentences for several crimes, particularly possession of small amounts of drugs. The following year, as a result of increased prison construction and a reduction in the number of felony cases receiving prison sentences—expanded use of probation—Florida achieved compliance with court-ordered reductions in prison population, and the governor ordered a cutback in the amount of good time granted to inmates who had been serving about 45 percent of their sentence. Florida's experience reveals the often poor fit between theory and practice when it comes to "getting tough on criminals."

Abolishing Parole

- "When a board has no ability to *select* those who will be granted release, they are forced to supervise a population not of their own choosing. . . . It is impossible to assure cooperation of offenders when they know they must be released regardless of their willingness to agree to certain conditions. And we have seen, in states such as Illinois, that when the parole board loses its discretion over release, it tends to lose its visibility and power in the system. Field supervision tends to be underdeveloped and, eventually, underfunded and understaffed" (American Probation and Parole Association, 1995: 14).

- Although nearly 600 of the 1,700 inmates housed at the Big Muddy River Correctional Center in Illinois are sex offenders, empty beds remain in the sex offender unit, which houses up to 200 inmates. The program administrator notes why—a simple lack of motivation. Illinois does not have parole, and in the absence of discretionary release, sex offenders apparently have no incentive to enter treatment (Monti, 1997).[3]

In many states without parole, an inmate released under good time ("mandatory release") provisions is placed under the supervision of a parole officer. In the absence of discretionary release, however, the incentive for adequate funding of offender supervision is often absent—no one (governor or parole board) can be held accountable for the serious misconduct of mandatory releases. In Illinois, for example, a budget crisis in 1987 led to the layoff of 98 of the state's 159 parole agents. Most were reinstated at the beginning of 1989, and 29 new agents added, because of a substantial increase in parole violations and new arrests among releasees against whom no delinquency action was taken because parole agents were not available— violations had dropped from 35 to 20 percent. By 1995, however, the number of agents was down to 69, and they were "supervising" about 30,000 offenders. The governor responded to criticism by recommending that offenders be released without any supervision. In the state of Washington, parole release and supervision were abolished in 1984. Subsequently, the public reacted adversely to serious offenders being released without community supervision, and in 1988, supervision was restored.

In place of parole, any number of states have substituted "spit sentencing," reversing the normal sequence of probation, prison, and parole. The offender is sentenced to a term of imprisonment and upon completion is released to probation supervision. In Virginia, for example, which abolished parole release in 1995, about 80 percent of inmates have supervised probation following incarceration: "the name of the game has changed, but the game continues."

DETERMINATE SENTENCING, PROSECUTORIAL DISCRETION, AND DISPARATE JUSTICE

Although in theory the determinate or definite sentence was supposed to reduce unwarranted variation in sentencing and amount of time served in prison, the practice has been otherwise. No state, for example, has adopted a determinate sentence with

---

[3]Research into the Sex Offender Treatment Program of the Alaska Department of Corrections revealed that inmates "who were in treatment longer tended to last longer in the community without a re-offense. Those who completed all stages of treatment through the advanced stage had a zero re-offense rate for sexual re-offenses. This included Sexual Assault offenders (rapists) who generally tend to re-offend more quickly and at a higher rate" (Mander et al., 1996: 2).

Determinate Sentencing

"Legislatively mandated determinate sentencing has not proved to be a workable alternative to the traditional indeterminate system. Because uniform punishments assigned to each crime lead to unjust results in many cases, prosecutors and judges find ways to adjust the charges accordingly" (Wright, 1998: 4).

no discretion, whereas several have adopted schemes with wide discretion. Thus, in Illinois, a defendant convicted of selling drugs as a first offense can receive a *determinate* sentence of anywhere from 4–0–0 all the way up to 30–0–0.

The issue of prosecutorial discretion presents the most obvious deficiency in the proposals set out by Fogel, von Hirsch, and others. This discretion is typically exercised privately, outside the scrutiny of official review and affects sentencing more often and more significantly than does judicial discretion. Although a judge, acting under a definite system with narrow discretion or a presumptive system with narrow discretion, must apply a specific sentence for a particular class of crime (in the absence of mitigation or aggravation), the prosecutor, using charging powers, determines the particular class of crime and whether to move for aggravation or oppose a motion for mitigation.

In return for cooperation—a plea of guilty—the prosecutor can reduce the class of crime for which the offender will be charged; he or she may also agree not to move for *aggravation* or to accept *mitigation* offered by defense counsel. By manipulating the charging decision, the prosecutor, not the judge, can often determine the actual sentence. Thus, determinate sentencing can increase the ability of a prosecutor to engage in **plea bargaining.** In many instances, determinate sentencing merely shifts discretion away from judges and parole boards and toward the prosecution end of criminal justice. In other words, release decisions are being made at the front end rather than the back end of the system. Because the defendant's primary interest is in how much time he or she must actually serve, new laws limiting good time (under so-called truth in sentencing provisions) are now added to the plea bargaining equation.

Furthermore, the abolition of parole boards, a practical accomplishment of determinate sentencing schemes, ignores the role of the board in reducing the sentence disparity that the classicalists decry. Because the parole board reviews the sentences of all state prisoners, it is in a position to act as a panel for mediating disparate sentences for similar criminal behavior. In Nebraska, for example, the board of parole "serves as an 'equalizer.' Within the framework of the law, it attempts to produce equity and uniformity in the sentencing structure caused by the inherent disparity which understandably results from having ninety-three prosecuting offices and multiple judicial districts." The Georgia Board of Pardons and Paroles states that "the board's unique central position and authority allow it to reduce sentencing disparity. Excessive harshness is more readily reduced, but excessive leniency in the form of a too-light confinement sentence may be corrected partially by parole denial." Figure 7.2 provides a hypothetical example of the parole board as a sentencing review panel. "All parole boards, either implicitly or explicitly, serve the vital function of equalizing justice between judges, courts, and counties. Board members removed from the heat of trial are familiar with case practices in all jurisdictions, and are able to apply a common statewide standard of justice. Left to their own devices, the differences in judges, district attorneys, defense counsel, juries, community temperament and the sophistication of defendants produces some very strange and disparate results" (Holt, 1995: 20).

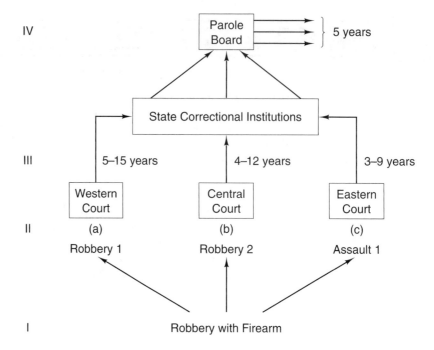

I   Three offenders, (a) (b) (c), each enter stores in different counties within the same state.
They each brandish loaded revolvers and rob several hundred dollars.

II   Defendant (a) is processed in Western Court. Attempts at plea bargaining fail, he stands
trial and is convicted of First Degree Robbery.
Defendant (b) is processed in Central Court. He is alowed to plead guilty to Second
Degree Robbery.
Defendant (c) is processed in Eastern Court. He is allowed to plead
guilty to First Degree Assault.

III   Defendant (a) is sentenced to a minimum of 5 years and a maximum of 15 years in state
prison.
Defendant (b) is sentenced to a minimum of 4 years and a maximum of 12 years in state
prison.
Defendant (c) is sentenced to a minimum of 3 years and a maximum of 9 years in state
prison.

IV   The parole board, recognizing that the three defendants have committed the same
criminal acts and despite variations in the legal category of conviction (Robbery 1,
Robbery 2, Assault 1), requires that each serve 5 years before being paroled.

Under a determinate sentencing scheme devoid of a parole board, the sentences for
this hypothetical example would be:

defendant (a) would serve 8 years;
defendant (b) would serve 6 years;
defendant (c) would serve 4 years.

FIGURE 7.2 *The Parole Board as Sentencing Review Panel.*

THE "WHY?" OF PAROLE

Some presume (AFSC, 1971; Fogel, 1975; MacNamara, 1977) that parole is based on
a medical model or some humanitarian effort gone astray. However, the history of
prisons and parole in the United States underscores the fact that parole release has
been used, possibly abused, as a mechanism for maintaining prison discipline and reducing prison overcrowding. The parole board evolved out of the power of governors to issue pardons to selected convicts. Before the creation of parole boards,
governors often used their pardoning powers to relieve prison overcrowding. In the

middle of the nineteenth century, pardons accounted for more than 40 percent of the releases from U.S. prisons (Hibbert, 1968). In Ohio, for example, whenever the state prison exceeded a certain number of inmates, the governor granted pardons to make room for new prisoners. In 1867, Nevada created a pardon board with the power to release inmates through commutation. In 1909, the board's authority was expanded to include the parole of prisoners who were required to report to the governor's private secretary at least once per month. In 1898, Virginia passed an act permitting prisoners who had served half their sentence to file a petition with the governor, who on the recommendation of the board of penitentiary directors, could grant a conditional pardon. The act was later amended—the word "parole" was substituted for pardon and release authority transferred from the governor to the penitentiary directors. As late as 1938, "parole" was simply a conditional pardon in many states.

In Florida, the pardon board often presided over as many as 200 pardon applications per day until the Parole and Probation Commission was established in 1941. In Utah, the Board of Pardons continues to have parole responsibilities, and the Alabama Board of Pardons and Paroles, established in 1939, has final authority on all pardons. The Vermont Parole Board was created in 1968; until that time, release from prison was by conditional pardon granted by the governor.

Blumenstein (1984: 131) points out that "one of the functions the parole agencies carried out during the period of indeterminate sentencing was serving as a 'safety valve' for crowded prisons. As prison populations began to approach or exceed the prison capacity, the parole board could simply lower the threshold of the degree of rehabilitation that warranted release." The clear use of parole as a safety valve for prison population control is highlighted by the Texas experience. Faced with overcrowding during the 1980s, Texas simply increased parole releases: "In 1983, about 40 percent of inmates were released on parole after their first hearing. By the end of the decade, this had increased to nearly 80 percent" (Kelly and Ekland-Olson, 1991: 604). In 1980, with 15,257 prison admissions, the parole board released 5,660 inmates. In 1991, when prison admissions reached more than 37,000, the parole board released more than 31,000 inmates—an increase of more than 400 percent (Bodapati, Marquardt, and Cuvelier, 1993). A similar situation occurred in Georgia where, in 1980, 14,000 inmates were in prison; a decade later there were 44,000 prisoners, and county jails were backing up with prisoners sentenced to state prison. A class-action lawsuit—which state officials believed they would lose—was initiated. In response, the parole board accelerated the parole release of thousands of inmates (for which the board was labeled "soft on crime"). Nationally, increases in the prison population result in even greater increases in the parolee population. In 1983, there were 437,248 prisoners and 251,708 parolees, a ratio of 58 percent; in 1988, there were 627,402 prisoners and 407,977 parolees, a ratio of 65 percent (National Institute of Justice data).

In many states using determinate sentencing, the same release function is being carried out by prison officials using good-time or "special release" provisions. However, prison officials lack the information, time, or expertise to make rational release decisions—a reason why parole boards developed. In Delaware, which abolished parole release (but not the parole board) in 1989, the Department of

Parole is the Answer. The Question Is . . .

At the end of 2001, faced with severe prison overcrowding, the Arkansas parole board (Board of Correction and Community Punishment) agreed to increase the parole of eligible inmates (Associated Press, 2001).

Correction may apply to the parole board for a modification of the inmate's sentence. The board then holds a hearing for the purpose of providing a recommendation to the sentencing judge. Those who see parole as simply a rehabilitative device have bought the *rhetoric* but not the *reality*—parole is more realistically understood as *risk management*. Corrections officials in several states that have abolished the indeterminate sentence have, by necessity caused by overcrowding, become de facto parole boards. Indeed, in Florida, as the result of overcrowding (and a federal lawsuit) the parole board was reconstituted as the Control Release Authority to act under the state's determinate sentencing laws in essentially the same capacity as it had under indeterminate sentencing—"a change in name but not the game."

As schemes for relieving overcrowding in the absence of parole increased, in 1990, Connecticut dumped the determinate sentence, reintroducing indeterminate sentencing and parole release. In Maine, the first state to abandon parole release, along with parole supervision, a clemency board assists the governor in making commutation decisions whose purpose is to relieve prison overcrowding (Burke, 1988). Postrelease supervision was reestablished by Maine's judges in the form of split sentences—"judicial parole"—whereby offenders are sentenced to imprisonment followed by a period of probation supervision (Anspach and Monsen, 1989).

David Greenberg and Drew Humphries (1980) argue that the forces of the political right co-opted the issue of sentencing reform and abolition of parole and were successful in implementing changes that are increasing the length of time served by offenders, now without the possibility of parole release, in a prison atmosphere devoid of any rehabilitative component. Illinois provides an example: The state went from indeterminate to determinate sentencing in 1978, and since that time tough on crime legislation has significantly increased the penalties for criminal behavior without any available modification via the parole board. In a strong defense of the correctional/rehabilitative model, Francis Cullen and Karen Gilbert (1982: xxix) state: "Whatever its failings, criminal justice rehabilitation has thus persisted as a rationale for caring for offender needs and not for making the wayward suffer. Without its humanizing influence," they argue, "the history of American corrections would be even bleaker than is now the case."

The relevant question is now at issue: Do we entrust the decrease of prison populations, reduction of sentencing disparity, and risk management of criminal offenders, to judges, prison officials, or parole boards? A review of the history that led to the establishment of parole in the first instance argues for this discretion to be the responsibility of a professional parole board.

Figure 7.3 below summarizes chapter 7. Now that the review of the history of prisons and parole is complete, chapter 8 examines the services provided by a parole agency.

	Corrections model (positivism)	**Justice model** (classicalism)
Cause of crime	Psychological/sociological factors over which the offender has little or no control	A rational choice made by the offender operating with free will
Sentence	Indeterminate/parole	Determinate/definite
Sentencing goals	Rehabilitation	Punishment/deterrence
Discretion	High	Low; stress on equality of punishment commensurate with the offense

FIGURE 7.3 Corrections *Model vs. Justice Model.*

KEY TERMS

indentured servant	presumptive sentencing
ticket of leave	truth in sentencing
Irish system	indeterminate sentencing
reformatory	good time
medical model	determinate sentence
justice model	plea bargaining
just deserts	

INTERNET CONNECTIONS

Corrections news/topics: corrections.com

American Probation and Parole Association: www.appa-net.org

Parole boards and departments of correction: www.crime-guide4all.com

Probation and parole links: www.talkjustice.com/links.asp?453053932

Probation and parole links: www.co.pinellas.fl.us/bcc/juscoord/eprobation.htm

REVIEW QUESTIONS

1. What are the similarities between the "property in service"/indentured servant agreement and the procedure followed by parole boards?
2. What is the connection between the system employed by Alexander Maconochie at Norfolk Island and the indeterminate sentence?
3. What was the Irish System established by Walter Crofton?
4. What is meant by the "Elmira system"?
5. Why did events in 1929 lead to the expansion of parole in the United States?
6. What are the characteristics of the penological revolution that occurred at the end of World War II?
7. What is meant by the medical model approach to criminal behavior?
8. What are the questionable assumptions on which the medical model approach to corrections is based? Why are they questionable?
9. What is the difference between an *indeterminate* and a *determinate* or definite sentence?
10. What did Robert Martinson's 1974 review of correctional treatment efforts in his article "What Works?" conclude?
11. What were the criticisms that led some states to abandon the indeterminate sentence and parole?
12. What is the basis of criticism of the indeterminate sentence by those on the right of the political spectrum?
13. What is the basis of criticism of the indeterminate sentence by those on the left of the political spectrum?
14. How do the four types of determinate, or definite, sentences differ?
15. What is meant by good time, and how does it affect inmates?
16. What is meant by truth-in-sentencing laws?
17. What is the relationship between determinate sentencing and plea bargaining?
18. What has developed in light of prison overcrowding and the absence of parole release in some states?
19. Why is parole an easy political target?
20. What are the arguments in favor of maintaining parole release?

CHAPTER 8

Parole Administration and Services

A parole agency can provide three basic services: parole release, parole supervision, and executive clemency. For administrative purposes, these can be classified into three categories:

1. Parole services—institutional
2. Parole services—field
3. Parole services—executive clemency

In several states that have abolished parole release—California, for example—parole officers/agents continue to supervise offenders released from prison (not by a parole board but) on "good time." The administration of parole is less complex than that of probation because parole services are usually administered centrally on a statewide basis. Some local jurisdictions, for example, Los Angeles County, have their own city/county parole from jails with supervision provided by *probation* officers. In Iowa, probation and parole supervision is the responsibility of a judicial district. In 1998, Oregon moved probation and parole supervision from being a function of the state to a function of individual counties. Oregon counties hired most of the state's former probation and parole officers.

ADMINISTRATION OF PAROLE SERVICES

There are two basic models for administering parole:

- **Independent model.** A parole board is responsible for making release and revocation determinations *and* for the supervision of persons released on parole (and good time). It is independent of any other state agency. This model is used in Connecticut.
- **Consolidated model.** The parole board is an autonomous panel within a department that also administers correctional institutions. The board makes release and revocation decisions, but supervision of persons released on parole (and good time) is under the direction of the commissioner of corrections. This model is used in Colorado, Rhode Island, and most other states that have parole boards.

In both models, probation services are sometimes combined with parole services in a single statewide agency. For example, Alabama, North Dakota, Vermont, and Wyoming use a consolidated model in which probation services are part of the

Department of Corrections. In Pennsylvania, the courts have the statutory alternative of referring presentence investigations and the supervision of probationers and (county jail) parolees to the Board of Probation and Parole rather than the county probation department. In Nevada, probation and parole supervision are the responsibility of the Division of Parole and Probation headed by a chief appointed by the governor and located within the Division of Motor Vehicles and Public Safety. In Alabama, while the Board of Pardons and Parole determines which prisoners serving in the jails and prisons of the state will be paroled, the Jefferson County Parole Board exercises jurisdiction over jailed inmates in that county. The Task Force on Corrections (1966) summarized the arguments for the independent model:

- The parole board is in the best position to promote the idea of parole and to generate public support and acceptance. Because the board is often held accountable (by the public, news media, public officials) for parole failures, it should be responsible for supervising parolees.
- The parole board in direct control of administering parole services can more effectively evaluate and adjust the system.
- Supervision by the parole board and its officers properly divorces parole release and parolees from the correctional institution.
- An independent parole board in charge of its own services is in the best position to present its own budget request to the legislature.

The Task Force (1966) also summarized the arguments for including both parole services and institutions in a single department of corrections:

- The correctional process is a continuum; all staff (institutional and parole) should be under a single administration rather than be divided, with resultant competition for public funds and friction in policies.
- A consolidated correctional department has the advantage of consistent administration, including staff selection and supervision.
- Parole boards are ineffective in performing administrative functions. Their major focus should be on case decisions, not on day-to-day field operations.
- Community-based programs partway between institutions and parole, such as work release, can best be handled by a single centralized administration.

Critics contend that the independent model tends to be indifferent or insensitive to institutional programs, and that the parole board, in this model, places undue stress on variables outside the institution. Conversely, critics of the consolidated model argue that the parole board will be under pressure to stress institutional factors in making parole decisions, although these are of dubious value in making a parole prognosis.

CONDITIONAL RELEASE

Conditional (sometimes called "mandatory") **release** is the term used to describe inmates released on good time. In such cases, either the parole board denied them parole release, or the state does not have a parole board. Inmates in most states are eligible for good time; that is, they can accumulate days, months, and years off their maximum sentence by avoiding institutional infractions and/or participating in prison programs. Georgia is an exception to the near unanimous use of "good time."

In addition, some states have meritorious good time for exemplary behavior and emergency good-time provisions to reduce the prison population in cases of severe overcrowding. In states using the indeterminate sentence and parole board, good time can usually be accumulated at the rate of 10 days per month—one-third off the maximum sentence. In some of these states, good time may also be subtracted from the minimum sentence, making the inmate eligible for parole before the minimum sentence has actually been served. In Texas, inmates classified as "Trusties" earn 30 days for each 30 days served and may earn up to an additional 15 days of good conduct time per month for completing vocational or educational programs while in prison. The Texas parole board may block good-time releases "when it determines that an offender's good conduct does not accurately reflect the potential for rehabilitation and that the offender's release would endanger the public." In Maryland, good time is granted at the monthly rate of 5 days for good behavior; 5 days for performing industrial, agricultural, and administrative tasks; and an additional 5 days for making satisfactory progress in vocational and educational training. In Wyoming, in addition to being eligible for 10 days per month good time, inmates can receive an additional 15 days of "special good time" for exemplary behavior.

In states using determinate sentencing, good time usually amounts to 1 day off for every day served. Those with truth-in-sentencing laws have reduced this to 15 percent of the sentence (although in cases of severe prison overcrowding it can be increased by any number of schemes). In New York, where determinate sentencing is now the rule for most offenders, they must serve at least 6/7 of the sentence (*unless* prison overcrowding demands otherwise).

Most states in which parole release has been abolished have retained supervision requirements for offenders released on good time. In California, for example, all persons serving nonlife terms are released to community supervision that cannot exceed 3 years. In some of these states, decisions regarding good time and revocation of conditional release are the responsibility of a variety of boards: in California, it is the Board of Prison Terms; in Illinois, it is the Prisoner Review Board. In Missouri, the Board of Probation and Parole was placed in the Department of Corrections and Human Services, where it deals with questions of good time and supervision revocation. In Minnesota, where the parole board has been abolished, supervision of conditional releasees is the responsibility of the commissioner of corrections, who delegates this authority to the executive director of adult release.

These (nonparole) boards are also responsible for making parole decisions for persons imprisoned under indeterminate sentencing statutes that have since been repealed and for persons serving "life sentences." Some also serve as a "pardons board," considering requests for the granting of executive clemency. In California, as in most states, the Department of Corrections is responsible "for deducting good time credit from the sentence and for establishing procedures to deny good time credit." If good time is denied to an inmate, the person can appeal through department appeals procedures. A final department appeal can be submitted for review to the Board of Prison Terms, which conducts a hearing on the matter. In Illinois, the Prisoner Review Board has broader responsibilities:

> Through panels of at least 3 members [the board has 10 members] hear and decide cases brought by the Department of Corrections against prisoners in custody of the Department for alleged violation of Department rules with respect to good conduct credits . . . in which the Department seeks to revoke good conduct credits, if the amount of time at issue exceeds 30 days or when, during any 12-month period, the cumulative amount of credit revoked exceeds 30 days. However, the Board is not empowered to review the Department's decision with respect to the loss of 30 days of good conduct credit for any prisoner or to increase any penalty beyond the length requested by the Department. . . . Upon recommendation of the Department the Board restores good conduct credit previously revoked.

THE PAROLE BOARD

In most states, parole board members are appointed by the governor and usually serve 6-year terms. In Georgia, the 5 members of the Board of Pardons and Paroles are appointed by the governor and serve 7-year terms; in Utah, the

3 members of the Board of Pardons are appointed by the Board of Corrections for 6-year terms; in South Dakota, the Board of Pardons and Paroles has 9 members who serve terms of 4 years: 3 appointed by the governor, 3 by the attorney general, and 3 by the state supreme court. The Texas Board of Pardons and Paroles has 18 members appointed by the governor for 6-year terms; Missouri has a board of 7 who serve 6-year terms. The 5 members of the Alaska Board of Parole are appointed by the governor for 5-year terms. In Connecticut, the chairperson and 2 vice-chairpersons serve full-time 4-year terms; the other 12 members serve part-time 4-year terms. The Iowa Board of Parole consists of 5 members; the chairperson and vice-chairperson serve full time, while the 3 other members are on a per diem basis. The New York State Board of Parole has 19 members whose chairman serves as director of the Division of Parole whose officers supervise released offenders.

Parole boards have been criticized because members may lack relevant background or education. Specific professional qualifications are required for board members in only a few states. Maryland requires "at least a B.A. or B.S. degree in one of the social or behavioral sciences or related fields . . . [and] at least three (3) years experience in a responsible criminal justice or juvenile justice position, or equivalent experience in a relevant profession such as law or clinical practice." In Vermont, the governor "shall appoint as members persons who have knowledge of and experience in correctional treatment, crime prevention or related fields, and shall give consideration, as far as practicable, to geographic representation to reduce necessary travel to the various parole interview centers of the state." In Iowa, the board must contain one minority group member, one attorney knowledgeable in correctional procedures and issues, and one person with a master's degree in social work or a counseling-related discipline who is knowledgeable in corrections.

The role of patronage politics in the selection of parole board members is similar to that of many other responsible government positions, although the relatively low salary and extensive travel requirements tend to make parole board membership less attractive to those with other opportunities for political appointments.

Parole in Texas

Several months before an offender's parole eligibility review date, he or she is interviewed by an institutional parole officer. The parole officer prepares a case summary that includes the facts of the offender's offense; other relevant information such as assaultive behavior or the use of narcotics; personal history; assignments, adjustment, and disciplinary record while in prison; physical and mental condition; and a summary of positive and negative factors.

As the offender's parole eligibility review date approaches, the offender's case is reviewed by a board parole panel. The offender may be interviewed by one of the members of this panel before the panel votes. For most offenders, the panel will consist of three members of the board, and two of the three panelists must vote for parole before it can be granted. A few categories of offenders may be paroled only upon a two-thirds majority vote of the entire 18-member board.

Parole panel members look at the circumstances and seriousness of the offense; prior prison commitments; relevant input from victims, family members, and trial officials; adjustment and attitude in prison; the offender's release plan; and factors such as alcohol or drug use, violent or assaultive behavior, deviant sexual behavior, use of a weapon in an offense, institutional adjustment, and emotional stability. Based on the entirety of the available information, the parole panel then determines whether the offender deserves the privilege of parole (Figure 8.1).

Parole Board Procedures

Typically, from one to three members briefly interview an inmate who is eligible for parole. Parole board members usually hold release hearings in the state's prisons. In Maryland, these hearings are open to the media as well as victims or their designees. In Iowa, the board uses a two-way fiber optic system for interviews that are conducted from the board's conference room. The members of the board panel will have available a case folder prepared by an institutional parole officer (or correctional staff person) containing information about each inmate: the presentence investigation report; institutional reports relative to education, training, treatment, physical and psychological examinations, and misconduct; and a release plan in the event that parole is granted (Figure 8.2).

In some states, this aspect of parole release is handled by hearing examiners who interview the inmate and report back to the board with a recommendation; some states do not conduct hearings or interviews—decisions are made on the basis of written reports. In New Jersey, a hearing officer considers each inmate for release at an interview session held between 4 and 6 months before parole eligibility. If parole is recommended by the hearing officer, the case is reviewed by a panel of parole board members. If they accept the recommendation, a parole release date is set. If the hearing officer recommends against parole, or if the parole panel denies parole, a panel hearing at which the inmate appears is arranged (Figure 8.3). In Colorado, the manner in which the parole hearing is conducted depends on the seriousness of the inmate's offense. For violent crimes or for inmates with a history of violence, two board members may conduct an initial hearing and submit their recommendation to the seven-member board—four affirmative votes are required for parole release. A single board member may hear nonviolent cases, which can be face-to-face or by telephone. If the decision is to grant parole, an additional board member must agree (West-Smith, Pogrebin, and Poole, 2000).

According to David Stanley, the parole hearing is of dubious value. "It is a traumatic experience for the inmate, and parole board members are subjected to the rigors of holding hearings far away from home, with hours spent in travel and in prisons" (1976: 42). Furthermore, Stanley reports, hearings "are of little use in finding out whether the inmate is likely to succeed on parole," and he argues that a strong case can be made for abolishing parole hearings because "in cases where the information in the file and the board's own precedents plainly show that parole must surely be granted or denied, the hearing is a charade. And in those cases where the outcome is not so obvious it is a proceeding in which the inmate is at a great disadvantage and in which he has reason to say anything that will help his chances for parole. The atmosphere at such a hearing is full of tension and latent hostility. Under these circumstances the hearing is an ineffective way to elicit information, evaluate character traits, and give advice, all of which parole boards try to do" (1976: 43).

One way to deal with some of these issues is to permit the inmate to have representation at the hearing. The National Advisory Commission on Criminal Justice Standards and Goals believes representation helps promote a feeling of fairness and can enable an inmate to communicate better and thus participate more fully in the hearing; they state that "representation can also contribute to opening the correctional system, particularly the parole process, to public scrutiny" (1973: 403). The commission makes note of the fact that representation at parole hearings may be considered "annoying" to parole officials—there is fear that the hearing may take the form of an adversary proceeding—but adds that "these inconveniences seem a small price for the prospective gains" (1973: 403). The Hawaii Paroling Authority not only permits representation at its release hearings, but offers inmates the right to appointed counsel if they cannot afford to hire an attorney. However, this is unusual—most jurisdictions do not permit representation at parole hearings.

- Maryland: "Relatives or other interested and responsible individuals may request a conference with the Commission, submit letters, or other pertinent data

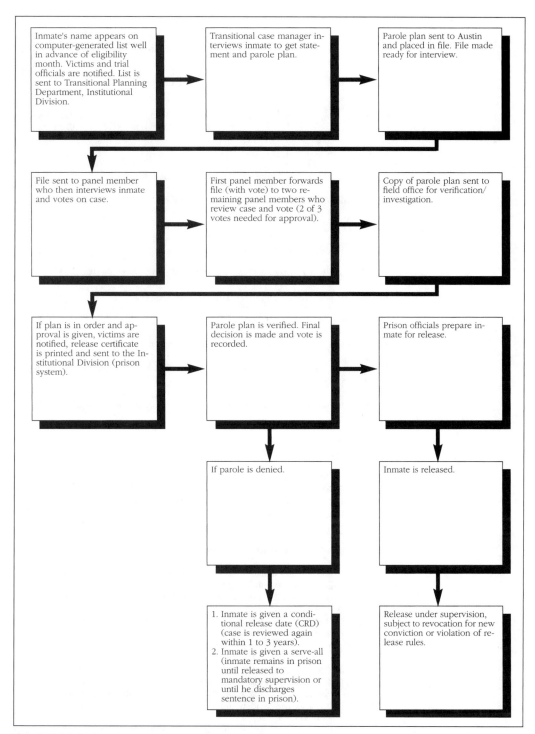

FIGURE 8.1 *Texas Parole Procedures.*

(Source: Texas Pardons and Paroles Division.)

relative to an inmate's parole consideration at any time prior to the hearing. They may not appear at parole hearings."

- Missouri: Offenders may have one person of their choice at the hearing who may offer a statement on behalf of his or her release and respond to parole board questions.

(text continued on page 230)

STATE OF NEW YORK —EXECUTIVE DEPARTMENT-—DIVISION OF PAROLE
INMATE STATUS REPORT FOR PAROLE BOARD APPEARANCE

<u>10/03</u> BD. INITIAL

Name: Hughes, Sam   *DOB:* 12/23/73   *NYSID:* 4172822M
                             CR: 12/27/06   *ME:* 12/27/09

Rec'd Date: 7/13/01;

Crime, (felony class), sentence & date p(lea) or v(erdict)

1.) Att. Robbery, 1(c)   2.) Att. Robbery, 1 (c)
    1-6-0/4-6-0   1-6-0/4-6-0 cs.
    7/8/01-p.   7/8/01-p.

Guideline Range: 20-38 months

Mand. SPP: No ; *Citizen:* Yes ; *INS Warrant:* No ; *Other Warrants:* No

Official Statements: Judge: No ; DA: No; Def. Atty.: No ;

Certificate of Relief: E I Y.O.

Codefendants: William, Ruby - no information in computer

Special Conditions Recommended: SOME/Academic program or vocational program; periodic urinalysis; outpatient drug treatment program.

Parole Residence: Sylvia Butler Hughes, wife; 3140 Atlantic Avenue, Brooklyn, NY 718-485-4104, Apt.
3B.

Parole Employment: None submitted. Inmate interested in youth counseling.
Comments: None

Present Offense Offense #1:
On 8/5/00 at 9:15 A.M., Hughes and Williams followed a 10-year-old male complainant and his 10-
year-old cousin from a store into the lobby of 668 Howard Avenue. Once inside the building, the subject displayed a knife, twisted the complainant's arm and demanded money from him. The subject
cut the complainant's left finger and then took $18.00 from him. Both subjects then fled.

The complainant reported this incident to the police.

On 8/5/00, the complainant identified the defendants in the street at 9:32 A.M. Both defendants were
placed under arrest by police officers of the 73rd Precinct.
    The arresting officer recovered a gravity knife from the defendant's pants pocket as well as
$18.00.
    After being placed under arrest and advised of his rights, the subject made no statement, but his
codefendant, Williams, stated, "I don't know what happened; he grabbed the little boy and the next
thing I knew he was running so I ran."

Present Offense #2:
On 12/18/00, a 16-year-old girl who was six months pregnant entered the elevator at 2770 86th
Street at about 6:25 P.M. The subject followed her into the elevator, placed his hand inside his jacket
as if he had a weapon and announced a holdup. The subject took $105.00 worth of clothing from
this complainant and fled.
    On 1/3/01, at 8:45 P.M., the complainant, a 10-year-old boy, entered the elevator at 2770 86th
Street where he was confronted by the subject. The subject pointed a knife with a long blade at the
complainant and demanded money from him. The subject took $5.00 from the complainant's pock-
ets and a bag of groceries that the complainant was holding. The complainant then fled.

FIGURE 8.2 *Inmate Status Report for Parole Board Appearance.*

(*Source:* State of New York, Executive Department, Division of Parole.)

The incident was reported to the police. On 1/3/01, police officers of the 60th Precinct spotted the subject who fit the description provided over the radio. In the meantime, a housing police officer transported the complainant and his sister, the 16-year-old girl who was robbed on 12/18/00, and both positively identified the subject.

The subject was then placed under arrest at this time stating, "I was coming from my girlfriend's house." At arrest the subject had about $3.00 and change in his possession.

Prior Record

Arrest Date	Arrest Charges	Place	Disposition
7/31/01	Public Lewdness	Queens Crim.	11/29/01 —pled guilty to Disorderly Conduct Sent.: 10 days
11/22/01	Robbery Assault	Kings Supreme	8/22/02—Adjudicated Y.O. for Att. Robbery 1 (C) Sent.: 3 years Paroled 9/9/91 Revoked 5/8/92 Held to M.E. 9/1/92
3/19/02	Public Lewdness	Kings Crim.	9/9/94—dismissed
3/20/02	Public Lewdness	Kings Crim.	7/5/92—dismissed
3/29/02	Public Lewdness	Kings Crim.	7/5/92—dismissed
6/20/02	Crim. Trespass 3 Public Lewdness	Kings Crim.	9/9/94—dismissed
7/11/02	Intent to Fraudulently Obtain Transportation without Pay.	Kings Crim.	9/9/94—dismissed
11/7/94	Public Lewdness	Kings Crim.	5/23/95—Conditional Discharge
5/22/98	Harassment	Kings Crim.	8/27/98—pled guilty to Public Lewdness (B Misd.) Sent.: 1 year
3/31/00	Disorderly Conduct	Kings Crim.	4/1/00—Conditional Discharge

Pending Legal Actions
None.

Parole Interview:
The inmate was interviewed on 9/20/03 at Woodbourne C. F. in regard to the instant offenses. Hughes reluctantly admitted his guilt in all three of the robberies and expressed remorse for his behavior. He attributes his participation to the fact that he was unemployed due to long-term medical problems, and that his unemployment benefits had run out. Hughes felt pressured and needed to feed his children. He also admits to being high on crack at the time.

Institutional Adjustment:
Although Hughes initially did not address his drug abuse, he enrolled in drug treatment in 8/02. He has received several certificates for participating in substance abuse programs (Project Aware and Compadre Helper). He received his GED in 2002 and has worked as a teacher's aide at Woodbourne for 8 months, receiving positive evaluations. He also worked in the Barber Shop for 7 months and received satisfactory reports.

FIGURE 8.2 *(continued)*

Disciplinary:
Inmate's discipline is marginal. The inmate has received disciplinary reports for fighting; however, most disciplinary reports are for being out of place, refusing a direct order, and out of place. The most recent report is dated 7/2/03 for count procedure.

Proposed Residence:
The subject's proposed residence is with his wife, Sylvia Butler Hughes, who resides at 3140 Atlantic Avenue, Apt. 3B, Brooklyn, NY 11212; (718-485-4104). Mrs. Hughes is available after 4:00 P.M.

Proposed Employment:
Needs to be developed. Inmate claims interest in counseling youths. He has no reasonable assurance offers.

Inmate's Plans:
The inmate hopes to pursue a job in the field of youth counseling since he feels that his life experiences qualify him for such a position. He holds a GED and is considering furthering his education. Hughes reports that his wife and three children are extremely supportive, and he plans to reside with them.

Supervision Needs:
Issues of substance abuse and employment are key considerations. Urinalysis is recommended regularly, and outpatient drug treatment is most appropriate. Community based supervision should also be sensitive to Hughes' medical condition, his prior history of public lewdness arrests, and his proclivity for armed robberies of vulnerable victims.

Special Conditions Recommended:
S.O.M.E./Academic Program; periodic urinalysis; outpatient drug counseling.

CONFIDENTIAL INFORMATION

Psychiatric/Psychological Reports:
Hughes was hospitalized at Woodhull Hospital for psychiatric treatment on one occasion prior to his incarceration.
　　At this facility, he was interviewed in August of 1989 by a Dr. Goldman who diagnosed: "Unspecified personality disorder with a history of exhibitionism." The inmate's reading level is 9.6; math level is 7.9; Beta I.Q. is 118.

Medical Reports:
A health discharge summary has been requested in this case. Hughes reports that he is on daily medication for hypertension.

Confidential Written Reports:
None.

Evaluation:
The subject has performed fairly well during this period of incarceration by participation in academic programs and substance abuse treatment. This would seem to indicate that Hughes is making efforts to reconcile his lengthy criminal history and significant history of substance abuse. He also has a supportive environment to return to. However, the inmate has demonstrated a long term disregard for the laws of NYS and is currently incarcerated for three robberies of young victims. He expresses some remorse, but seems to feel that he had no other alternative to provide food for his family. Yet, he simultaneously was abusing drugs, a costly habit. Hughes impresses during interview as having a low frustration tolerance. He also has a poor work record in the community and has minimal job skills.

Approved by:	*J. Burke*	Prepared by:	*N. Harrison*
	S.P.O.		P.O.

Date: 9/28/03　　Facility: Woodbourne C. F.

FIGURE 8.2 *(continued)*

- Nebraska: Parole hearings are open to the public and anyone wanting to appear on behalf of, or in opposition to, an offender's release on parole may attend. Those attending are invited to come forth to be sworn and present testimony.
- Pennsylvania: "As the interview is not an adversarial process, the Board does not permit counsel representation at these interviews."
- Vermont: "[T]he Board in its discretion may hear oral statements or arguments by attorneys or other persons with a valid interest in the case before the Board." Furthermore, "it is the Board's policy to grant the inmate's legal

INVESTIGATION REPORT

COMMUNITY PREPARATION _____ R&E _____ OTHER _____

NAME: Hughes, Sam   NYSID: 4172822M

SENTENCE;   1-6-0/4-6-0   DIN: #87-A-5840
             1-6-0/4-6-0 cs.

DATE OF SENTENCE: 7/8/01   INSTITUTION: Woodbourne C. F.

OFFENSE: Att. Robbery, 1st   LAST BOARD APPEARANCE: 10/03
            Att. Robbery, 1st

MAXIMUM EXPIRATION: 12/27/09   DECISION: Open date 12/27/03

CR DATE: 12/27/2006   AREA OFFICE: Brooklyn IV—73rd Precinct

PROSPECTIVE RESIDENCE

ADDRESS: 3140 Atlantic Avenue, Brooklyn   3B   718-485-4104
           NUMBER   STREET   CITY   APT. #   TELEPHONE #

RENT: 230/mo___ PVT. HOUSE _____ APT. X   FURNISHED ROOM _____ OTHER _____

ACCOMMODATIONS AVAILABLE TO RELEASE: The subject will share a bedroom with his wife,
Sylvia Butler Hughes.

PERSONS IN HOUSEHOLD:

Sylvia Butler Hughes	wife	Turquoise Hughes, Age 6	daughter
NAME	RELATIONSHIP	NAME	RELATIONSHIP
Ronnie Hughes, age 11	son	Saphire Hughes, Age 3	daughter
NAME	RELATIONSHIP	NAME	RELATIONSHIP

| Sylvia Butler Hughes | 11/30/03 | 5:00 P.M. | home visit |
| PERSON CONTACTED | DATE | TIME | METHOD |

PROSPECTIVE EMPLOYER/PROGRAM

NAME: Drayton Grocery Store   TYPE OF BUSINESS: Grocery Store

ADDRESS: 395 Livington Street   Brooklyn   718-452-0383
         NUMBER   STREET   CITY   TELEPHONE #

POSITION OFFERED: Grocery Clerk   SALARY: 180   HOURS: 5 days Tu-Sat. 12-8 P.M.

SUPERVISOR: George Clark   DUTY DESCRIPTION: Check out

PERSON CONTACTED: George Clark   DATE: 12/1/03   TIME: 6 P.M. METHOD: visit

COMMENTS

Residence: Subject has a satisfactory residence program in the home of his wife, Sylvia Butler
Hughes, at 3140 Atlantic Avenue, Apt. 3B, Brooklyn, NY 11212 (718-485-4104).

On 11/30/03, at 5:00 P.M., the writer visited the proposed residence. The residence is located
in a high crime area of the 73rd precinct in Brooklyn. The apartment itself is located on the 3rd
floor. The building entrance is in disrepair, and access is no problem.

The apartment is at the end of the hallway and is clearly labelled #3B. It contains four rooms (2
bedrooms, kitchen, living room and bathroom). There is only one entrance which opens into the living room and no fire escape. The subject will share the large bedroom with his wife while the three
children share the smaller bedroom. The home was neat, clean and well furnished. No pets were
reported or seen.

The writer interviewed the subject's wife at the residence. Also present were the subject's three
children: Ronnie, Turquoise and Saphire. Mrs. Hughes and the children appear eager for the subject's

FIGURE 8.2 *(continued)*

representative access to the inmate's parole packet at a reasonable time in advance of the parole hearing."

- Wisconsin: "Representation by legal counsel during the interview is not allowed. [However,] a spokesperson for the inmate will be allowed . . . in cases
  of severe speech impediment or where the inmate suffers a severe physical
  disability which impedes verbal communication, or in cases where the inmate's primary language is not English and the individual lacks adequate
  fluency to represent himself or herself."

homecoming. Mrs. Hughes advised that she has had a relationship with the subject since the early 1990s with occasional periods of living together. She attributes Hughes's previous criminal activities to his history of drug abuse. The two were legally married at Woodbourne C. F. in 8/03, and Mrs. Hughes does not anticipate any problems upon her husband's return. She and the children visit Hughes at Woodbourne once a month and letters are exchanged regularly.

During the interview, Mrs. Hughes advised that she maintains the home with her income of approximately $28,000 per year. She has been employed at J & B Retailers at 1433 De Kalb Ave., Brooklyn as a computer entry clerk from 7:30 A.M. to 3:30 P.M. Monday to Friday for the past 3.5 years. The home rents for $550. month plus utilities. The two older children attend P.S. 101 while the youngest receives day care with Mrs. Hughes's sister, Mildred Butler Fuller, at her home at 732 Livonia Avenue, Brooklyn (718-462-9133). Mrs. Hughes has resided at this residence for the past year. Mrs. Hughes suffers from sickle cell anemia, which requires occasional hospitalization.

According to Mrs. Hughes, she and her husband have relatives in the NYC area, but none maintains contact with the subject other than his brother, Frank Hughes of 732 Lenox Ave., NY, NY (apt. unknown).

The writer advised Mrs. Hughes that our parole population is at high risk for HIV infection and encouraged her to discuss this with her husband. The Division's educational package, "Healthy New Start" was provided and discussed at this time. The Rules and Regulations of Parole were also discussed during the interview; Mrs. Hughes advised that she understood the conditions.

A check of the parolee residence cross references indicate that parolee Joe Brown NYSID 1473650B, resides at 3140 Atlantic Ave., Apt. 11B, Brooklyn, NY 11212 (P.O. Gilbert).

Employment: Subject has a satisfactory employment offer with Drayton Grocery Store at 395 Livingston Ave., Brooklyn, NY (718-452-0383).

During the home visit, Mrs. Hughes provided the prospective employment program for the subject. On 12/1/03, at 6:00 P.M. the writer interviewed George Clark, the owner of Drayton Grocery at 395 Livingston Avenue, Brooklyn. He advised that he has known the subject for over ten years and is willing to employ him as a grocery clerk upon release. He will provide 40 hours of work per week at $6.50 to start per hour.

Mr. Clark presently employs 24 workers and has been in business over 20 years. The store is well known in the area and is suitable considering the subject's limited job skills.

Special Conditions	curfew
	support dependents
	Mental Hygiene referral at discretion
	of P.O.—P.O. to monitor

The subject should make his arrival report within 24 hours of release to the Parole Office at 340 Livingston Street, Brooklyn, NY (5th floor).

FIGURE 8.2 *(continued)*

In 1979, the U.S. Supreme Court (*Greenholtz v. Inmates*, 442 U.S. 1) ruled that the Constitution does not require that an inmate be given the opportunity to participate in parole board hearings (or to be informed of the reasons for denial of parole). However, Stanley (1976) concludes that given the present parole system, hearings are necessary as an expression of our national tradition and culture. "A man has his day in court before he is convicted and sentenced. In all sorts of situations we feel outraged if a person is not even confronted with the evidence before something adverse is done to him. In the hearing the prisoner is at least given a chance to state his case, correct erroneous statements, and impress the board with his determination (real or alleged) to reform" (43).

Victim Participation

More than 30 states permit victims or their next of kin to appear before the parole board, and about a dozen others permit written statements to be considered at the parole hearing. In Nevada, for example, state law "provides that victims of crimes may attend meetings of the Nevada Board of Parole Commissioners. The Parole Board will provide notice of pending parole hearings if the victim of crime provides the board with a current address and requests such notice." In Alabama, "Victims

---

EXAMINATION BY NELSON HARRIS,
MEMBER OF THE BOARD OF PAROLE

Re: Smith, Louis, No. 092340136

Q: Louis Smith?

A: Yes.

Q: Smith, I am wondering if you got a chance on parole, what do you think would happen? Do you think the time is right?

A: I would go and pick up my life where I left it before.

Q: Do you think there was anything about the way you were living when you came in that needs changing?

A: A little could be altered so I am quite sure I would change them around now.

Q: Can you pinpoint, tell us some of the areas where you think you will change?

A: There is quite a few areas I can see where I am making mistakes. I am making a mistake by coming here, that is one right there.

Q: Anything that you could do to stay out of places like this would definitely be something that would be of good intentions?

A: Yes.

Q: Do you have any plans? How are you going to try and go about making it when you get out of here?

A: First of all, I am starting back to work, which I am doing now and take it on from there.

Q: Staying in the big city area?

A: Yes.

Q: Can you cope with it?

A: I don't understand.

Q: Can you cope with the city, the bigness and all that?

A: Yes, I can.

Q: What is this job that you have?

A: It's the closest thing that they can give me to the job I have in the joint, that was all I have.

Q: Anybody that can get a foothold in that field really has something going for him and can make good money.

A: Yes.

Q: What can you do? How are your skills? What is the most you ever earned from it?

A: Well, the most I earned, brought in in one week was close to $1,000.

Q: You made that kind of money?

A: Yes.

Q: You noticed I have not referred to the crime?

A: Yes.

Q: You probably talked about it time and again.

A: Not very much, but some.

Q: This is thoroughly reported here. You did not have anything in your past like it and from what I read, it was certainly something you did not intend.

A: You are right, it wasn't intended. It was done through an accident. Mostly I was drinking and that is one problem I think I can handle now.

Q: Do you think you need anything outside yourself with reference to any drinking you did before?

A: I wasn't a regular drinker, I just drank sometimes. Now one thing I learned that if I get a problem, stay away from a bottle, that's what I learned.

Q: As a result of this, you also know that even though you don't drink all the time, it can still be a problem?

A: I found that out.

Q: Okay, your recommendations here are reasonably good and folks that have worked with you say they believe that there is no reason why you can't make it.

A: I hope I can.

Q: In the event you get the opportunity—

A: I hope I can make it.

Q: You feel that way?

A: Yes.

Q: Maybe there is something that you want to call to our attention?

A: No.

Q: Thanks for coming in. We will make a decision and let you know what it is.

FIGURE 8.3 *Parole Examination.*

of violent crimes and families of children who have been abused are notified prior to an inmate's being considered for parole by the Board. The Victim's right to be present at the Parole Hearing and to express their concerns in person and in writing to the Board is provided by law." In New Jersey, at the time of sentencing, the prosecutor notifies any victim injured as a result of a crime in the first or second degree, or the nearest relative of a murder victim, of the opportunity to present a

Massachusetts Victims Services Unit

Established in 1987, the Victims Services Unit provides a wide array of support services to victims who have been certified to receive information regarding offenders by the Criminal History Systems Board. The unit's staff acts as the parole board's representative in addressing and advancing victim/witness issues by collecting victim/witness input for board consideration, providing timely notifications of parole hearing dates and hearing results, providing information about parole and criminal offender record information, assisting citizens in completing impact statements, directing referrals to other criminal justice or social service agencies for collateral assistance, and heightening the community's level of awareness regarding victim/witness issues through both the media and direct contact.

statement to be considered during a parole hearing, or to give in-person testimony before the board concerning the victim's harm. The board notifies victims or relatives who have contacted the board requesting an opportunity to submit a statement or to provide testimony. In Connecticut, victims are notified of pending hearings and advised of their right to appear and testify. In Iowa, victims can use the state's two-way fiber optics communication system to address the board from a site near their residence. Many states include a VIS as part of the documentation considered by the parole board.

PAROLE BOARD PROCEDURES

Parole boards usually consider the crime, the length of time served, the inmate's age, prior criminal history, use of alcohol or drugs, and institutional record. Some parole boards may request a recommendation from the prosecutor. All will certainly consider opposition to an inmate's parole from the police and the news media. A study of parole decisions in Massachusetts (Luther, 1995) found that the election of a "law and order" governor caused the board (whose membership remained almost unchanged) to decrease parole release rates, particularly for high-security inmates for whom they were virtually eliminated. The widespread use of parole guidelines has reduced the importance of general criteria.

Parole Board Countervailing Pressures

Prison overcrowding—————→/←—————Political (public-media) reaction

Parole Board Guidelines

As criticism of parole and parole boards began to mount in the 1970s, the U.S. Board of Parole engaged a group of researchers to develop a model for improved decision making. In particular, the board was interested in a means of reducing disparity and making the decision-making process intelligible (and defensible) to both inmates and the public. The researchers derived a set of variables that they saw as fairly representative of those used by board members in making decisions— the most salient being the seriousness of the offense and parole prognosis. They also conducted a 2-year study of 2,500 federal parolees and uncovered a variety of "success factors," which they reduced to seven variables. The combined variables for *severity of offense* and *parole prognosis* were arranged in the form of a grid

(Figure 8.4) to determine the actual length of imprisonment. For example, an adult offender convicted of forgery under $1,000, "Category Two," whose parole prognosis is "good," would normally be released on parole after serving between 8 and 12 months; an offender convicted of multiple robbery, "Category Six," with a parole prognosis of "poor," would normally serve between 78 and 100 months before being paroled.

Parole board guidelines typically go well beyond the *rehabilitative/medical model*, on which the indeterminate sentence is often presumed to be based. Indeed, satisfactory progress in those institutional programs that are "rehabilitative" may not even affect the parole decision. Good institutional behavior is *expected*, not rewarded, although poor behavior can be punished with denial of parole (Krajick, 1978). In fact, the institutional adjustment of an offender has never been an accurate guide for predicting postinstitutional behavior (Dolan, Lunden, and Barberet, 1987); some evidence exists that certain offenders (e.g., substance abusers and professional criminals) most often perform well in prison but tend to recidivate.

In effect, the use of guidelines whose primary focus is *just deserts* is a form of deferred sentencing. Some critics claim that no justification exists for deferring sentence (the term of imprisonment) and that it creates problems by adding to the offender's uncertainty. Others argue that the parole board is relatively free of the "heat" that certain crimes and criminals can generate. The board does not typically operate with the same high visibility of a court; unlike a sentencing judge, the parole board is not normally under the gaze of the community and news media. These observers stress that the parole board, using guidelines, is better equipped to make a rational decision commensurate with just deserts than is a sentencing judge. The possibility of parole release also serves as an incentive for inmates to control their behavior and take advantage of rehabilitative programming.

Guidelines used by state parole boards consider the seriousness of the present offense and prior criminal history; most also consider rehabilitative items and parole prognosis. For example, the Georgia Board of Pardons and Paroles, in a mix of the classical and positive views, states: "Justice demands that punishment should be tailored to fit both the offense and the offender." A board hearing examiner identifies an inmate's crime severity level from a table of offenses ranked in seven levels from lowest to highest in severity. The higher the severity, the longer the inmate will be recommended to serve. Then the hearing examiner calculates the inmate's parole success likelihood by adding weighted factors with proven predictive value from the inmate's criminal and social history. A history of factors such as prior imprisonment, parole or probation failure, heroin use or possession, and joblessness would increase the risk of paroling the inmate and cause him or her to be recommended for longer confinement (Figures 8.5 and 8.6).

The parole board may go beyond the guideline range in the event of mitigating or aggravating circumstances, but the detailed reason for such decisions must be provided to the inmate in writing.

PAROLE SERVICES—INSTITUTIONAL

The primary responsibility of institutional parole staff is to prepare reports on inmates for the parole board. The staff also helps inmates secure furloughs, work release, or halfway house placement, and it may assist with personal problems ranging from matters relating to spouse and children to questions of a technical or legal nature.

Under ideal conditions, when an offender is first received at the institution, he or she is interviewed by a member of the parole staff. The results of the interview, psychiatric and psychological tests, and the information in the presentence report are then used to help plan an institutional program for the inmate. The parole staff periodically

Offense Characteristics:
Offense Severity (Some Crimes Eliminated or Summarized)

OFFENDER CHARACTERISTICS: PAROLE PROGNOSIS

Offense Characteristics	Very Good	Good	Fair	Poor
Category One *Low*: possession of a small amount of marijuana; simple theft under $1,000	*Adult Range* ≤ 6 months *(Youth Range)* (≤) 6 months	6–9 months (6–9) months	9–12 months (9–12) months	12–16 months (12–16) months
Category Two *Low/Moderate*: income tax evasion less than $10,000; immigration law violations; embezzlement, fraud, forgery under $1,000	*Adult Range* ≤ 8 months *(Youth Range)* (≤) 8 months	8–12 months (8–12) months	12–16 months (12–16) months	16–22 months (16–20) months
Category Three *Moderate*: bribery; possession of 50 lb. or less of marijuana, with intent to sell; illegal firearms; income tax evasion $10,000 to $50,000; nonviolent propery offenses $1,000 to $19,999; auto theft, not for resale	*Adult Range* 10–14 months *(Youth Range)* (8–12) months	14–18 months (12–16) months	18–24 months (16–20) months	24–32 months (20–26) months
Category Four *High*: counterfeiting; marijuana possession with intent to sell, 50 to 1,999 lb. auto theft, for resale; nonviolent property offenses, $20,000 to $100,000	*Adult Range* 14–20 months *(Youth Range)* (12–16) months	20–26 months (16–20) months	26–34 months (20–26) months	34–44 months (26–32) months
Category Five *Very High*: robbery; breaking and entering bank or post office; extortion; marijuana possession with intent to sell, over 2,000 lb. hard drugs possession with intent to sell, not more than $100,000; nonviolent property offenses over $100,00 but not exceeding $500,000	*Adult Range* 24–36 months *(Youth Range)* (20–26) months	36–48 months (26–32) months	48–60 months (32–40) months	60–72 months (40–48) months

	Adult Range			
Category Six *Greatest I*: explosive detonation; multiple robbery; aggravated felony (weapon fired—no serious injury); hard drugs, over $100,000; forcible rape	40–52 months	52–64 months	64–78 months	78–100 months
	(Youth Range)			
	(30–40) months	(40–50) months	(50–60) months	(60–76) months
Category Seven *Greatest II*: aircraft hijacking; espionage; kidnapping; homicide	*Adult Range*			
	52–80 months	64–92 months	78–110 months	100–148 months
	(Youth Range)			
	(40–64) months	(50–74) months	(70–86) months	(76–110) months
Category Eight[a]	*Adult Range*			
	100+ months	120+ months	150+ months	180+ months
	(Youth Range)			
	(80+) months	(100+) months	(120+) months	(150+) months

[a]*Note:* For Category Eight, no upper limits are specified because of the extreme variability of the cases within this category. For decisions exceeding the lower limit of the applicable guideline *by more than 48 months*, the pertinent aggravation case factors considered are to be specified in the reasons given (for example, that a homicide was premeditated or committed during the course of another felony; or that extreme cruelty or brutality was demonstrated).

FIGURE 8.4 *Guidelines for Decision Making, Customary Total Time to Be Served Before Release (Including Jail Time).*

updates the material with additional information. Staff members discuss release plans with inmates and request the field staff to visit and interview family members and prospective employers. When an inmate is ready to meet the parole board, the staff provides a report on the inmate that includes an evaluation of changes made since the offender was first received at the prison (Figure 8.7). The report may also contain a completed "parole guidelines" form and a recommendation if requested by the board.

Institutional parole staff may also hold group meetings with new inmates to orient them about parole. These group sessions are then followed up with individual interviews. At preparole group sessions, parole staff attempt to lower anxiety about meeting the board or hearing examiners. When an inmate has been granted

---

PAROLE SUCCESS LIKELIHOOD FACTORS

| NAME | NUMBER | INSTITUTION | DATE |

These guidelines indicate the customary range of time to be served for various combinations of offense and offender characteristics. It is emphasized that mitigating or aggravating factors may warrant decision outside the guidelines and, in appropriate circumstances, the Board will exercise its discretion as provided by law. The basic guideline presupposes good institutional adjustment and program progress. Deviation from the normal conduct expected of all inmates could result in decisions outside the guidelines.

If the convicted person is servicing sentences for multiple offenses, the most serious offense will determine the crime severity level. "Attempted" offenses will be rated one grade below the principal offense.

Convicted persons will appear for parole consideration when they have met the requirements of Nevada law.

As stated in NRS 213. 10989, the establishment of these standards is not intended to create any right or interest in liberty, nor to create any reasonable expectation of parole, nor to establish any basis for a course of action against the State, its political subdivisions, agencies, boards, commissions, departments, officers or employees. The release or continuation on parole is an act of grace of the State.

Further, the Board's actions are also goverened by NRS 213. 1099, which delineates State policy on the granting of parole.

1. Age at first commitment:
   18 or older . . . . = 2
   17 or younger . . . . = 0 . . . .

2. Prior convictions (F & M):
   None . . . . = 3
   One . . . . = 2
   Two/three . . . . = 1
   Four or more . . . . = 0 . . . .

3. Incarcerations since age 17
   prior to instant offense:
   None . . . . = 2
   One . . . . = 1
   Two or more . . . . = 0 . . . .

4. Parole/probation failure:
   No failure . . . . = 1
   Otherwise . . . . = 0 . . . .

5. No use, possession or attempt
   to obtain heroin, cocaine, opiates,
   amphetamines . . . . = 2
   History of drug abuse . . . . = 0 . . . .

6. Current offense did not involve
   burglary or forgery, credit card or
   bad checks . . . . = 1
   Otherwise . . . . = 0 . . . .

7. Fully-employed or full-time
   school for 6 months in year
   preceding offense . . . . = 1
   Otherwise . . . . = 0 . . . .

8. Injury to /death of victim:
   Yes . . . . = 0
   Otherwise . . . . = 2 . . . .

9. Use of weapon:
   Yes . . . . = 0
   Otherwise . . . . = 2 . . . .

10. Not previously convicted of
    similar offense . . . . = 1
    Otherwise . . . . = 0 . . . .

11. Prison programming:
    Has addressed educational/voca-
    tional deficiencies . . . . = 1 . . . .
    Has sought and participated in
    counseling on substance abuse,
    alcohol or psychological programs . = 1
    No history of prison problems . . . . = 1
    All . . . . = 3 . . . .

Parole Success Likelihood Score . . .   .

FIGURE 8.5 *Parole Success Likelihood Factors.*

(*Source:* State of Nevada.)

GUIDELINES—RECOMMENDED MONTHS TO SERVE

Read across from your Crime Severity Level and down from your Parole Success Likelihood Score to find your guidelines-recommended months to serve. For Crime Severity Level I through V, the grid reflects a shift in months to serve based on the court-imposed sentence length. If your sentence is less than 25 percent of the statutory maximum penalty, the lesser figure is used. If your sentence exceeds 75 percent of the statutory maximum penalty, the greater figure is used. For all other sentence lengths, the median figure is used. For Crime Severity Levels VI or VII, the guidelines recommendation will be one-third of the court imposed sentence length or the grid recommendation, whichever is greater. The Board, using its descretion in your case, may depart from guidelines recommendation.

PAROLE SUCCESS LIKELIHOOD SCORE

Crime Severity Level	Excellent 15–20	Good 10–14	Average 6–9	Poor 0–5
I	4	6	8	14-16-18
II	12	14	16-18-20	18-20-22
III	20-22-24	22-24-26	24-26-28	26-28-30
IV	28-30-32	30-32-34	32-34-36	34-36-38
V	36-38-40	38-40-42	40-42-44	42-44-46
VI	48	54	60	66
VII	60	66	72	78
VIII	90	102	114	126
IX	138	150	162	174

Crime Severity Level: ....

Parole Success Liklihood Score: ....

Guideline-Recommended Months ....

FIGURE 8.5 *(continued)*

parole or becomes eligible for conditional release, he or she will meet with a parole staff member for a final discussion of the release program and rules of supervision before leaving the prison.

In some jurisdictions, institutional parole staff are responsible for notifying victims and local law enforcement agencies of the impending release of certain offenders. (Some states require that when an offender is released, the police in the

Institutional Parole Officer, Connecticut

In correctional institutions, the parole officer performs case management and counseling activities for an assigned group of inmates; meets with and interviews inmates who are eligible for parole consideration; reviews Department of Correction files and retrieves data relevant to offense and sentencing information; verifies parole eligibility and discharge dates; obtains information and verifies inmates involvement in rehabilitative programs; provides inmates with information regarding parole process; conducts administrative reviews of cases and makes disposition recommendations to Board of Parole in accordance with agency criteria; coordinates attendance of victim and inmate families at Board of Parole hearings; ensures completeness of inmate files; attends Board of Parole hearings and serves as administrative hearing officer; presents case documentation to board members; answers questions from Board members regarding case files; takes notes at Board hearings, records official minutes, and processes disposition of Board hearings; and processes violation of parole cases.

area where the parolee is to reside, or where the crime occurred, be notified. In some instances, the parolee must register in person with the local law enforcement agency.) The institutional parole staff must determine the probable disposition of any warrants that have been lodged against an inmate. When appropriate, the staff arranges for an out-of-state program under the Interstate Compact (discussed in chapter 12). In some states, the nonparole institutional staff perform the same, or similar, functions as institutional parole officers; these persons sometimes have the title of *correctional counselor*.

Georgia State Board of Pardons and Paroles
Parole Decision Guidelines - Notice of Tentative Action

NAME: _____   DATE: _____

NOTICE:
    THE BOARD SPECIFICALLY RESERVES THE RIGHT TO EXERCISE ITS DISCRETION UNDER GEORGIA LAW TO DENY PAROLE EVEN THOUGH GUIDELINES CRITERIA ARE MET BY AN INMATE. IT IS NOT THE INTENTION OF THE BOARD TO CREATE A "LIBERTY INTEREST" OF THE TYPE DESCRIBED IN GREENHOLTZ VS. NEBRASKA PENAL INMATES 442 US 1 (1979).

Parole Decision Guidelines help the Board make a more consistent, soundly based, prompt, and explainable parole decision. Guidelines help the Board decide on a Tentative Parole Month for the inmate or decide that the inmate will complete his sentence without parole. When making decisions, the Board may depart from the Guidelines Recommendation and make an independent decision using the full discretion given it under Georgia Law. The length of the prison sentence imposed by the court will be considered in establishing a Tentative Parole Month.

CRIME SEVERITY LEVEL: Your Crime Severity Level is selected from the table of offenses on the back of this sheet.

PAROLE SUCCESS FACTORS: Your Parole Success Likelihood Score is found by adding the points which apply to you.

A. AGE AT FIRST COMMITMENT
    (26 or over = 5)
    (22–25   = 3)   ____
    (18–21   = 2)
    (17 or less = 0)

B. PRIOR CONVICTIONS (JUVENILE AND ADULT)
    (none   = 3)
    (1   = 2)   ____
    (2–3   = 1)
    (4 or more = 0)

C. PRIOR INCARCERATIONS SINCE AGE 17
    (none   = 2)
    (1   = 1)   ____
    (2 or more = 0)

D. PAROLE OR PROBATION FAILURE
    (No failure   = 4)
    (Probation only = 2)
    (Parole only   = 1)   ____
    (Both   = 0)

E. NO USE, POSSESSION OR ATTEMPT TO OBTAIN HEROIN OR OPIATE
    DRUGS   = 1   ____
    OTHERWISE = 0

FIGURE 8.6 *Parole Decision Guidelines.*

(*Source:* Georgia State Board of Pardons and Paroles.)

F. COMMITMENT OFFENSE(S) DID NOT
    INVOLVE BURGLARY OR FORGERY = 2
    OTHERWISE   = 0   ——

G. FULLY EMPLOYED DURING 6 MONTHS PRECEDING ARREST ON CURRENT
    OFFENSE   = 1
    OTHERWISE   = 0   ——

H. HAD WRAT SCORE OF 8 OR HIGHER
    AT TIME OF INITIAL TESTING = 2
    OTHERWISE   = 0   ——

PAROLE SUCCESS LIKELIHOOD SCORE ——

GUIDELINES RECOMMENDED MONTHS TO SERVE

Read across from your Crime Severity Level and down from your Parole Succeli-
hood Score to find your Guidelines Recommended Months to Serve. For Crime Severity
Levels I through V the grid reflects a shift in months to serve based on the court imposed
sentence length. If your sentence is less than 25% of the statutory maximum penalty,
the lesser figure is used. If your sentence exceeds 75% of the statutory maximum penalty, the greater figure is used. For all other sentence lengths, the median figure is used.
For Crime Severity Levels VI or VII, the Guidelines Recommendation will be one-third of
the court imposed sentence length or the grid recommendation, whichever is greater.
The Board, using its discretion in your case, may depart from the Guidelines Recommendation.

PAROLE SUCCESS LIKELIHOOD SCORE

		EXCELLENT 13–20	GOOD 11–12	AVERAGE 9–10	FAIR 6–8	POOR 0–5
	I	4 4 5	5 6 7	6 8 10	10 12 14	14 18 22
	II	5 6 7	6 8 10	7 9 11	11 14 17	17 21 25
CRIME	III	6 8 10	7 9 11	10 12 14	12 15 18	19 24 29
SEVERITY	IV	8 10 12	10 12 14	12 15 18	14 18 22	22 27 32
LEVEL	V	16 20 24	20 25 30	24 30 36	32 40 48	42 52 62
	VI	36	48	54	60	78
	VII	60	72	78	90	102

Crime Severity Level   _____

Parole Success Likelihood Score   _____

Recommended Months to Serve from the Grid, or   _____
    One-third of Court Imposed Sentence

Guidelines Recommended Tentative Parole Month   _____

TENTATIVE BOARD DECISION

All decisions made by the Board herein are considered tentative and may be changed at
the discretion of the Board at any time. Only the paragraph with the "X" applies to you.

( ) The Board has tentatively decided to parole you during the above Tentative Parole
     Month.
( ) Because your Tentative Parole Month is later than your discharge date, you should
     expect to be discharged from your sentence without parole.

FIGURE 8.6 *(continued)*

PAROLE SERVICES—FIELD

Field services staff usually operate out of district offices located throughout the state.
The New York State Division of Parole, for example, has field staff assigned to the
supervision of parolees and conditional releasees in 20 field area offices throughout
the state. They conduct field investigations requested by institutional staff relative to
parole release programs, as well as supervise parolees and conditional releasees.
Parole field staff may also be involved in a variety of special programs, such as work
release and furloughs. In New York, "some Field Officers are assigned to

(   ) The Board has determined that the Crime Severity Level and/or the Parole Success Factors do not adequately reflect the true nature of your case. Therefore, they have departed from the Guidelines Recommendation and have taken the following action:

_____ The specific reasons for departing are listed below:

If you believe your Crime Severity Level or any Parole Success Factor has been scored incorrectly, you may ask the Board, within 30 days, to recompute your scores. The Board will consider any verifiable information submitted to substantiate your request. Such requests may be submitted in any written form and should be directed to the Parole Guidelines Director, State Board of Pardons and Paroles, Floyd Veterans Building, Fifth Floor East, 2 Martin Luther King, Jr., Drive, S.E., Atlanta, GA 30334.

If the Board's tentative decision is to depart from the Guidelines Recommendation, and the number of months to serve is more than three years beyond the Guidelines Recommendation, your case will be reviewed at the Guidelines Recommendation and each three years thereafter.

Your institutional conduct has not been evaluated at this time. The Board expects you to use your time in confinement in a constructive manner. Exemplary conduct may result in a parole release prior to your scheduled release month. Institutional misconduct will result in a delay in your parole release or a decision to deny parole.

FIGURE 8.6   *(continued)*

Institutional Parole Services in New Jersey

Members of the institutional parole staff are housed in 14 major institutions, providing services to all state penal and correctional facilities and training schools. They conduct personal interviews with inmates, provide counseling on specific matters to resolve problems, and help develop suitable preparole plans. Staff members afford every inmate prerelease classes. They also assist inmates in obtaining necessary clothing and transportation from institutions to residences. Parole staff members also provide institutional services to county correctional institutions and to various community release/residential centers. The increase in the use of home visits and furloughs, as well as the number of state prisoners in county correctional facilities, have added considerably to the workloads of institutional parole office staff.

Street Readiness Program in Nevada

The Street Readiness Program of the Department of Probation and Parole works with inmates about to be released into the community on parole and those committed for 120-day evaluations who are returning to court for sentencing. These inmates become students 3 hours per day for a period of 3 weeks, normally just before their release. The curriculum consists of classroom lecture, discussions, activities, and homework. Subjects include parole orientation, goals, decision-making skills, substance abuse, domestic relations, financial responsibility, citizenship, employment skills, sex education, law, insurance, human relations, and driver training. Established in 1981, the program is almost totally dependent on community volunteers.

correctional facilities to supervise Temporary Release participants—inmates permitted by the Department of Correctional Services to work, attend school, provide community service, and reestablish family ties (furloughs)."

Field Services in California. The California legislature has found and declared that the period immediately following incarceration is critical to successful reintegration of the offender into society and to positive citizenship. In the interest of public safety, the state should provide for the supervision and surveillance of parolees,

---

BOARD OF PAROLE

PREPAROLE INVESTIGATION
DATE: January 11, 2003

TO: Carolyn Koslowski, Executive Director

FROM: Karel E. Yedlicka, Jr., Parole Examiner

RE: Robert L. Smith, SP #172362

I. OFFENSE

The subject was involved in a burglary of a home in which merchandise valued at over $1800 was stolen, and damage to the house itself occurred. The presentence report indicates that the victim was in the house at the time of the burglary but thought it was her son and, therefore, did not investigate the subject coming into the home by the back door. The subject also received an enhanced penalty on numerous prior felony convictions with a current parole release date of September 1, 2003.

II. PERSONAL BACKGROUND

Robert Smith will be temporarily staying with his sister who has legal custody of the subject's daughter, Judith Smith, age 14. Judith is currently enrolled in Joseph Mittner Junior High School and has been cared for by the subject's sister, Margaret Smith, since the subject's incarceration in 1990. Currently, she is receiving $325 per month in Aid to Dependent Children toward the care of Judith. This sum will be reduced when the subject is able to provide support for his daughter. Ms. Smith indicated that the subject has every intention of living with his daughter, securing his own residence, and raising her. He has not had the benefit of being with her very much during the past 12 years. This examiner recommends that as a special condition of parole, the subject be required to provide adequate support for his daughter, whose mother's whereabouts are unknown at this time.

III. RESIDENCE

The subject will be residing with his sister Margaret Smith, who, along with her brother Raymond Smith, owns a brick and wood frame home with four bedrooms and one bath located at 1526 Cincinnati Street, Madisonville. In 2001, the subject's father moved to Charleston, South Carolina, and turned the house over to Margaret and Raymond. Margaret stated that the subject will probably stay with her without a need to pay for room and board until he can get on his feet.

IV. EMPLOYMENT

The subject is employed on work release at Briarcliff Manor, a 24-hour nursing home at 1001 Briarcliff Boulevard, Madisonville. His employment was verified by Mona Mitchell, the bookkeeper. The day supervisor, Melanie Harris, stated that the subject is an excellent worker and has experienced no problems. He is employed as a dietitian's assistant who helps with meals and other minor duties in the nursing home, earning $7.10 per hour, 30 to 40 hours per week. The subject receives Worker's Compensation but no other benefits at this time. The nursing home also employs more than 30 other individuals on a 24-hour basis.

The subject has been employed at this job, obtained through the work-release center, since 10/13/02. No driver's license is required in that the subject works exclusively in the facility. However, the subject's sister stated that their father left an old car that the subject can use when paroled for transportation back and forth from northside to southside.

FIGURE 8.7 *Preparole Investigation Report.*

V. SPECIAL PROGRAMS OR TREATMENT FEATURES

As previously verified, restitution is owed, and the subject should make restitution accordingly; a recommended rate is $25 per month for a period of four years. In addition to supporting his daughter, a drug-testing clause should reflect his problem with heroin as indicated in the PSI. In view of the seriousness of his criminal history, the subject will need close supervision.

VI. RECOMMENDATIONS

This examiner recommends that the subject be paroled on 3/7/03 for a minimum supervision period of four years because of the severity of the instant offense and the need to pay restitution. The proposed residence appears to be valid, and the subject's employment appears to be an excellent opportunity at this time for him to reintegrate into society. The subject has been out only briefly in the latter part of 1993 before being rearrested in 1994 with the rest of the time spent incarcerated back to 1990. The subject is now 35 years of age, and if he cannot make parole at this time, it is unlikely that he will make one in the future.

Carole Simmons

Parole Examiner

FIGURE 8.7 *(continued)*

as well as educational, vocational, family, and personal counseling necessary to assist parolees in the transition between imprisonment and discharge.

The overall objective of the Parole and Community Services Division is to reduce the frequency and severity of criminal behavior and to facilitate the community adjustment of adult offenders, fully recognizing their individual and changing circumstances and actions, through a program structure of appropriate prerelease, supervision, and support management functions. Supervision, surveillance, and services delivery are the responsibilities of parole field staff throughout the state. The primary means by which a parole agent fulfills these responsibilities is through contacts with parolees and persons involved with the parolee. Parole staff will cooperate and collaborate with criminal justice and human service agencies that may be involved with the parolee. It is the duty and obligation of the parole agent to:

- Obtain information about parolee activities and needs.
- Intervene in parolee behavior that violates the conditions of parole or may jeopardize the safety of the public or the parolee.
- Provide supportive services to assist the parolee in the transition between imprisonment and discharge.
- Share information about the parolee with law enforcement personnel and the personnel of other agencies who have a demonstrated a compelling need to know.

Field Services in Pennsylvania.   Once the board has made a decision to release an inmate on parole, the board's Bureau of Supervision staff plays a significant role in assisting the parolee in adjusting to life in the community. The parole period is a time of transition from the structured, confined environment of the institution to life as a free citizen. Parole is also a time to test the readiness of the parolee to handle the responsibilities of community life.

The immediate goal of parole supervision is the protection of society, which can best be accomplished by reintegrating the offender into the community as a responsible and productive citizen. Specifically, this goal means helping the parolee obtain and hold a meaningful job; resolving any adjustment problems within the family and the community; meeting education, mental health, or other normative needs, when relevant; and becoming part of the community through participation in activities and organizations that reflect the person's interests and capability. This involves not only working with the person under supervision, but also with the various community agencies and resources that have the capability of assisting in solution of problems of parolees.

One of the tools of the supervision staff is "Conditions Governing Parole/ Reparole" established by the board to be used as a structuring force in the life of the parolee. These conditions define what course of behavior is acceptable if the client wants to complete the period of parole supervision successfully. Although several common conditions are to be adhered to, the board recognizes the needs of the individual offender and has provided for one or more special conditions to be imposed as needed.

CONDITIONS OF PAROLE

Every conditionally released or paroled prisoner is required to sign an agreement to abide by certain regulations. This aspect of parole has its origins in the ticket of leave, and as noted in chapter 7, modern parole conditions resemble ticket-of-leave regulations. Parole conditions are similar throughout most jurisdictions, and they are also similar or identical to probation regulations. Conditions of parole can generally be grouped into *standard conditions* applicable to all parolees/conditional releasees, which typically involve restrictions on travel, associating with other offenders, drug and alcohol use, employment, and residence, and *special conditions* that are tailored to the individual requirement of a particular offender (Figures 8.8 and 8.9). For example, persons with a history of sex offenses against children will be prohibited from areas where children typically congregate, such as playgrounds; persons with a history of alcohol abuse may be prohibited from using alcohol or being in facilities, such as bars, where alcohol is consumed. In more recent years, some parole agencies have been requiring parolees to pay supervision fees. In Texas, parolees are required to pay a standard monthly fee of $10 plus $5 for the victim's fund; those convicted of certain offenses must pay an additional $8 to the fund. In New York, parolees are required by law to pay a supervision fee of $30 per month.

LENGTH OF SUPERVISION

The length of time an offender must spend on parole/conditional release supervision is governed by the length of the sentence and the laws of the state where convicted. In Oregon, a conditional releasee "is subject to a period of supervision similar to parole, not to exceed six months or the maximum date, whichever comes first." In Indiana, persons are to be discharged no later than 1 year after conditional release. In Illinois, the length of supervision for conditional releasees varies from 1 to 3 years, depending on the class of crime for which the offender was convicted. In California, for persons sentenced under a life sentence, the maximum period, including time under parole supervision and time under revocation status, cannot exceed 7 years. For persons sentenced under a nonlife sentence, the maximum period, including time under supervision and time under revocation status, cannot exceed 4 years. In Ohio, those convicted of serious felonies must be under supervision for 3 to 5 years. For less serious felonies, supervision up to 3 years is discretionary with the parole board, which may reduce the term. In Missouri, after 3 years of successful supervision, the parole board may discharge an offender from parole or conditional release.

In most states, a parolee/releasee can be discharged before the expiration of sentence or mandated period of supervision. In California, based on satisfactory

(text continued on page 249)

RULES AND CONDITIONS OF PAROLE

1. I will report to my parole officer and my employer immediately upon arrival at my destination.
2. I will obey all city, state and federal laws. I agree to immediately report any new arrests to my parole officer.
3. I agree not to leave the State of Oklahoma without prior written permission by my officer and not leave the county without permission of my officer or his/her district office.
4. I agree to report as directed by my officer in person and in writing on the forms provided by my officer. I agree to allow the officer to visit at home, work or other convenient places.
5. I agree to immediately report in person, in writing or by telephone any changes in residence, employment or marital status.
6. I agree not to use or possess drugs other than those legally prescribed by a physician. I agree not to use alcohol nor go onto the premises where alcoholic beverages are served.
7. I agree not to lie or misrepresent the truth to any member of the Pardon and Parole Board, any employee of the Department of Corrections or any official of the government.
8. I agree not to associate with persons on parole or probation or persons with criminal records, communicate with inmates of any penal institution, except members of the immediate family, unless my parole officer gives permission because of work or other good reason.
9. I agree to pay parole fees of $40 per month, payable in cashier's check or money order to the Department of Corrections Restitution and Accounting.
10. I will comply with all lawful directives issued by my supervising officer or any member of the Department of Corrections.
11. I understand that at any time or place, I am subject to search. In addition, my vehicle and any property under my control is subject to search.
12. I agree to submit to urinalysis or any other substance abuse testing procedures as required by my parole officer.
13. I agree to pay, during the term of my parole, all fines and court costs imposed by the court at the time of my conviction.
14. I understand that Oklahoma State Statute 21 § 1283(d) prohibits anyone under the supervision of the Oklahoma Department of Corrections to own or possess a firearm. I agree not to own, possess or travel in a vehicle with a firearm or explosives.
15. Sex offenders will abide by special sex offender rules.
16. I understand that violations may result in the imposition of sanctions including but not limited to:

Financial Planning	Reintegration Training	Electronic Monitoring	Day Reporting
Mental Health Counseling	Intensive Supervision	Community Service	Temporary Placement in
Attend AA	Attend N/A	Victim Impact Panel	a community correctional
Attend MRT	Curfew	Weekend Incarceration	facility or jail for up
GED Courses	Intensive Parole	Nighttime Incarceration	to 30 days

17. I agree to follow the special condition(s) listed below:

     None.

I have read these conditions and understand that I must obey them until the term of my parole expires. I understand that failure to comply with these rules and conditions may result in the imposition of intermediate sanctions or revocation of my parole. I also understand that a finding of guilt, or plea of guilty or nolo contendere will be evidence that I failed to obey the law. I will be arrested and sent back to prison to serve the remainder of my sentence plus any new sentences.

Salt Haywood   *Felix A. McGinnis*
_____   _____
WITNESS SIGNATURE   Felix A. McGinnis   INMATE SIGNATURE
                                                           422797

01/29/03
_____   _____
DATE   INMATE DOC NUMBER

FIGURE 8.8 *Rules and Conditions of Parole.*

Oregon Conditions of Supervision

GENERAL/SPECIAL PAROLE AND POST-PRISON SUPERVISION CONDITIONS

Parole/Post-Prison Supervision is subject to all listed General Conditions and the designated Special Conditions. Prior to release the Board may modify the conditions at any time. After parole/post-prison supervision has commenced, conditions may be added upon your signed consent or after opportunity to be heard, orally or in writing.

Parole or Post-Prison Supervision may be revoked for violation of any of these conditions and/or you may be returned when parole or post-prison supervision is not in your best interest or the best interest of society.

The Board may, at its discretion, sanction violations of Parole or Post-Prison Supervision Conditions; sanctions may include returning you to the Department of Corrections custody.

As used in this exhibit, the following words have the following meanings: "Offender" means persons released to parole or post-prison supervision. "Parole Officer" shall also mean the supervisory authority under the post-prison supervision system.

GENERAL CONDITIONS

1. Pay supervision fees, fines, restitution or other fees ordered by the Board.

2. Not use or possess controlled substances except pursuant to a medical prescription.

3. Submit to testing of breath or urine for controlled substance or alcohol use if the offender has a history of substance abuse or if there is a reasonable suspicion that the offender has illegally used controlled substances.

4. Participate in a substance abuse evaluation as directed by the supervising officer and follow the recommendations of the evaluator if there are reasonable grounds to believe there is a history of substance abuse.

5. Remain in the State of Oregon until written permission to leave is granted by the Department of Corrections or a county community corrections agency. Offender automatically waives extradition if offender absconds supervision out of State.

6. If physically able, find and maintain gainful full-time employment, approved schooling, or a full-time combination of both.

7. Change neither employment nor residence without prior permission from the Department of Corrections or a county community corrections agency.

8. Permit the supervising officer to visit the offender or the offender's residence or work site, and to conduct a walk-through of the common areas and of the rooms in the residence occupied by or under the control of the offender.

9. Consent to the search of person, vehicle or premises upon the request of a representative of the supervising officer if the supervising officer has reasonable grounds to believe that evidence of a violation will be found, and submit to fingerprinting or photographing, or both, when requested by the Department of Corrections or a county community corrections agency for supervision purposes.

10. Obey all laws, municipal, county, state and federal.

11. Promptly and truthfully answer all reasonable inquiries by the Department of Corrections or a county community corrections agency.

12. Not possess weapons, firearms, or dangerous animals.

13. Report as required and abide by the direction of the supervising officer.

SPECIAL CONDITIONS

1. Offender shall be evaluated by a mental health evaluator and follow all treatment recommendations.

FIGURE 8.9 *Conditions of Supervision.*

2. Offender shall continue to take any psychiatric or psychotropic medication that was prescribed prior to or at the time of release from custody until otherwise directed by a physician. At the direction of the parole officer, the offender shall undergo a psychiatric evaluation and take any medications recommended. The offender shall comply with a medication monitoring program at the request of the parole officer.

3. Offender shall have no contact with minor females and shall not frequent any place where minors are likely to congregate (e.g., playgrounds, school grounds, arcades) without prior written approval from their supervising officer.

4. Offender shall have no contact with minor males and shall not frequent any place where minors are likely to congregate (e.g., playgrounds, school grounds, arcades) without prior written approval from their supervising officer.

5. Offender shall submit to random polygraph tests as part of a sex offender surveillance program. Failure to submit to the tests may result in return to custody. Specific responses to the tests shall not be the sole basis for return to custody.

6. Offender shall enter and complete or be successfully discharged from a recognized and approved sex offender treatment program which may include polygraph and/or plethysmograph testing. The offender shall abide by all rules and conditions of the sex offender treatment program. Offender shall abide by a prohibition of sexually deviant materials, activities or behavior that the offender may use for the purpose of deviant sexual arousal, unless otherwise allowed by the Parole Officer in writing.

7. Offender shall pay court ordered restitution to the clerk of the court of the county of sentencing (ORS 137.106, OAR 255-065-0005).

8. If required to report as a sex offender under ORS 181.595, report with the Department of State Police, a Chief of Police, a county Sheriff, or the Supervising Agency when supervision begins, within 10 days of a change in residence and once a year within 10 days of the person's date of birth.

9. Offender shall not possess or use intoxicating beverages.

10. Other: Special conditions may be imposed that are not listed above when the Board of Parole and Post-Prison Supervision determines that such conditions are necessary.

11. Offender shall have no contact direct or indirect with those listed below: (names would be listed).

12. Consent to search of computer or other electronic equipment upon the request of the supervising officer, or their representative, if the supervising officer has reasonable grounds to believe that evidence of a violation will be found.

13. Sex Offender Package:
(a) Agreement to comply with any curfew set by the board, the supervisory authority or the supervising officer.
(b) A prohibition against contacting a person under 18 years of age without the prior written approval of the board, supervisory authority or supervising officer.
(c) A prohibition against frequenting, without the prior written approval of the board, supervisory authority or supervising officer, a place where persons under 18 years of age regularly congregate.
(d) A prohibition against working or volunteering at a school, day care center, park, playground or other place where persons under 18 years of age regularly congregate.
(e) Entry into and completion of or successful discharge from a sex offender treatment program approved by the board, supervisory authority or supervising officer. The offender shall abide by all rules and conditions of the sex offender treatment program. The program may include polygraph and plethysmograph testing. The person is responsible for paying for the treatment program.
(f) A prohibition against any contact with the victim, directly or indirectly, unless approved by the victim, the person's treatment provider and the board, supervisory authority or supervising officer.

FIGURE 8.9 (continued)

(g) Unless otherwise indicated for the treatment required under subparagraph (E) of this paragraph, a prohibition against viewing, listening to, owning or possessing any sexually stimulating visual or auditory materials that are relevant to the person's deviant behavior.

(h) Agreement to consent to a search of the person or the vehicle or residence of the person upon the request of a representative of the board or supervisory authority if the representative has reasonable grounds to believe that evidence of a violation of a condition of post-prison supervision will be found.

(i) Participation in random polygraph examinations to obtain information for risk management and treatment. The person is responsible for paying the expenses of the examinations. The results of a polygraph examination under this subparagraph may not be used in evidence in a hearing to prove a violation of post-prison supervision.

(j) Maintenance of a driving log and a prohibition against driving a motor vehicle alone unless approved by the board, supervisory authority or supervising officer.

(k) A prohibition against using a post-office box unless approved by the board, supervisory authority or supervising officer.

FIGURE 8.9   *(continued)*

performance, a nonlife releasee can be discharged from supervision after 1 year and a lifer after 3 years. In Kentucky, a parolee can request a final discharge from parole after the expiration of 24 months. Those serving a life sentence must wait 5 years. The Hawaii Paroling Authority can issue a discharge whenever "the parolee has demonstrated for a sustained period of time that the parolee is unlikely to commit another crime and the parolee's discharge is compatible with public safety." In any event, parolees under supervision for at least 5 years "shall be brought before the Paroling Authority for purposes of consideration for final discharge." In Alaska, the board may discharge a parolee after he or she has successfully completed 2 years of supervision. In Oklahoma, active supervision of parolees will not normally exceed 3 years. In Alabama, however, "early termination in parole cases may be accomplished only by means of a Pardon, which will be considered after a subject has served five years under supervision." The same board that is responsible for parole in Alabama, the Board of Pardons and Paroles, has the power to grant pardons. In Vermont, "although the Board may terminate parole supervision at any time, it will normally consider termination only after successful completion of one half of the maximum parole term."

Women in Prison and on Parole

Many of the life experiences and needs of female offenders differ from those of male offenders; however, criminal justice institutional practices, services, and facilities have largely been fashioned for men. Today few jails and prisons have separate inmate classification and intake procedures for women, even though women have unique needs and evidence different behavior from men in custody. A large percentage of jails and prisons do not provide for the medical and psychological problems of chemically dependent women. Although most women offenders have children for whom they are or were responsible, few institutions provide facilities and child care services needed to facilitate visits with children. Even though most women offenders are single mothers who obtain little or no financial help from the children's fathers, vocational training within corrections tends to reinforce traditional low-paying occupations for women (Wellisch, Anglin, and Prendergast, 1993: 18).

In New York, relatively few women are sentenced to prison, and they constitute only 6 percent of the parolee caseload; 76 percent of them reside in the New York City area. Women parolees tend to be older than their male counterparts; their education levels are similar, with their unemployment rate slightly higher. Fewer women than men had a history of alcohol abuse, although they were equal with respect to drug abuse problems.

VIOLATION OF PAROLE/CONDITIONAL RELEASE

Probation violation is linked to the judicial system, whereas parole violation is an administrative function typically devoid of court involvement. Although some variation exists with respect to the procedures used, Figure 8.10 presents a general overview of the system and indicates the possibilities available at each stage of the process. Figure 8.11 presents a flowchart of the procedures used in New York.

There are two types of parole violation:

1. **Technical violation.** This occurs when any of the conditions of parole have been violated.
2. **New offense violation.** This involves an arrest and prosecution for the commission of new crime.

In practice, new offense violations often involve technical violations. A new offense violation, for example, an arrest for robbery that involves a firearm, also constitutes a technical violation of the conditions prohibiting possession of firearms.

In either event, the violation process begins when a parole officer (the title varies, for example, probation and parole officer, parole agent, correctional program officer, probation/parole supervisor) becomes aware of a violation. The PO can usually take steps short of a formal violation of parole. The Alaska Division of Community Corrections advises POs that "if the violation is a conditions violation, it does not require any notification to the Parole Board. You, as the Parole Officer, can verbally make the parolee aware of the violation and issue a verbal warning." The Alaska parole officer can also issue a written reprimand and "hold these charges in abeyance should there be any future violations," or the officer can impose more restrictive conditions, but the parolee must agree: "If the parolee does not agree to the new condition, a preliminary hearing must be held within 15 days of the imposition of the condition."

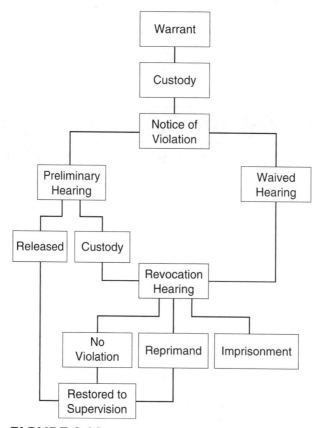

FIGURE 8.10   *Violation of Parole/Probation/Conditional Release Flowchart.*

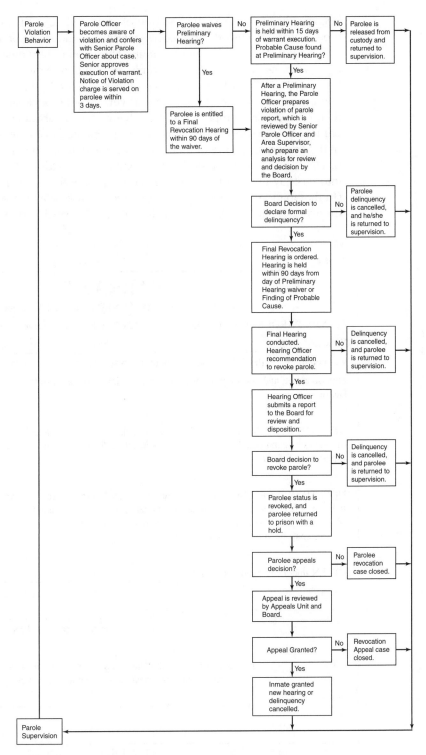

FIGURE 8.11   *Parole Revocation Process.*

(*Source:* New York State Division of Parole.)

In most agencies, after discussing the situation with a supervisor, a decision is made relative to the issuance of a warrant. This stage has the greatest amount of variance between agencies. In Pennsylvania, parole agents can use an "order to detain for 48 hours" in lieu of a warrant when circumstances require it. A similar situation obtains in New York, where field parole officers carry a 24-hour detainer-warrant. Thus, in Pennsylvania and New York, a parole agent/officer who becomes aware of a serious violation of parole while in the field can summarily take the violator into custody and receive telephone authorization for the use of the order to detain or 24-hour detainer-warrant. (These temporary detainers must be replaced by a warrant—in Pennsylvania, within 48 hours; in New York, within 24 hours; see Figure 8.12.) When I was a parole officer in New York, it was not unusual to encounter parolees, unexpectedly, who were in serious violation of the conditions of their release: for example, those heavily involved in abusing heroin (and engaging in criminal acts to support the habit); those prohibited from the use of alcohol (because of the dangerous nature of their behavior while under the influence) and intoxicated; or child sex offenders found in the company of children. I could take such persons into custody immediately and use the telephone for detainer-warrant authorization. (In the opinion of this writer, agencies that do not provide their officers with this authority endanger public safety. This point is discussed further in chapter 10.)

CSN # _____   Warrant # PB _____

WARRANT
FOR RETAKING PRISONER (Technical Violation)

TO ANY PAROLE OFFICER OR ANY OFFICER authorized to serve criminal process in this State:

Whereas, _____ , SS# _____ , ADC # _____

was committed to the Arkansas Department of Correction, to serve a term of _____

imprisonment, and said subject was conditionally released by order of the Arkansas Post-Prison Transfer Board;

AND WHEREAS, having reasonable cause to believe the above-named subject, a prisoner of the State of Arkansas, conditionally released, has violated the release agreement as alleged in a report from his/her supervising officer;

NOW THEREFORE, by virtue of the authority vested in the Board, I declare the release of said subject to be suspended and order that the subject be retaken and held in custody at any suitable detention facility pending disposition of the charges; I hereby authorize and require you to so retake subject; and for doing so, this shall be your sufficient warrant.

GIVEN under my hand and seal this _____ day of _____

_____
for Arkansas Post Prison Transfer Board

I certify that I have this date rendered service of this warrant by delivering a true and exact copy to the above-named subject at

_____

Name	Title	Date

Arkansas Post-Prison Transfer Board

Parole ___ Act 378 ___   FOM Form 32 (Rev 1/7/00) S-5

FIGURE 8.12 *Warrant.*

(*Source:* Arkansas Post-Prison Transfer Board.)

In jurisdictions that are rather conservative about issuing violation warrants, the process may be time consuming and involve a written request to the board of parole. In Oregon, in lieu of a summary arrest, the parole officer may issue a *citation* requiring the parolee/releasee to appear for a violation hearing. This citation is authorized when the person has violated a condition of supervision, but the nature of the violation does not jeopardize the safety of the general public, and the person, if left undetained, is not likely to flee. In Iowa: "A parole officer having probable cause to believe that any person released on parole has violated the conditions of parole may arrest such person, or the parole officer may make a complaint before a magistrate, charging such violation, and if it appears from such complaint . . . that there is probable cause to believe that such person has violated the terms of parole, the magistrate shall issue a warrant for the arrest of such person. In either event, the violator must be taken before a magistrate for consideration of release on bail—'bail is discretionary with the magistrate and is not a matter of right' in Iowa." Most jurisdictions do not permit a parole violator to be released on bail.

In Wisconsin, in lieu of an arrest or warrant issuance, a parole agent's immediate supervisor can order the alleged violator to appear for a *case review*: "The focus of case review is threefold: to determine whether there is probable cause to believe there was a violation of the rules or conditions of probation or parole, to determine whether, if there is probable cause, it makes correctional sense to revoke, and to determine whether the client should remain in custody during revocation proceedings." Although this case review has many of the characteristics of a preliminary hearing, to be discussed shortly, the review is both more broadly focused—can consider issues relating to supervision adjustment—and less formal: "It is hoped by making the proceedings less formal and adversary, the client, the client's attorney, the agent and the agent's supervisor can frankly discuss the issues in an atmosphere that focuses attention on the most important issues."

Parole Violations in Georgia.   When a parolee has reportedly violated a condition of his release, a board warrant may be issued for his or her arrest. If the alleged violation is absconding from parole supervision or if the parolee is otherwise not available to the board for a hearing, a temporary revocation order may be issued. This order suspends the running of the sentence from the date of the order.

Preliminary Hearing.   A parolee arrested on a board warrant for allegedly violating a parole condition is afforded a preliminary hearing within a reasonable time at or near the place of the alleged violation before a board hearing officer not directly involved in the case. The purpose of the preliminary hearing is to determine whether there is probable cause to believe the parolee violated a parole condition and whether he or she should be held under arrest pending the board's decision on revocation.

A preliminary hearing is not required if the parolee is not under arrest on a board warrant, has absconded from supervision, has signed a waiver of preliminary hearing, has admitted any alleged violation to any board representative in the presence of a third party who is not a board employee, or has been convicted of any new crime in a Georgia court, a court of another state, or a federal court.

The parolee is given written notice of the preliminary hearing, allowing reasonable time to prepare his or her case. The parolee may retain counsel to represent him or her at the preliminary hearing. The parolee may present witnesses and documentary evidence in his or her own behalf, and he or she may cross-examine adverse witnesses unless the hearing officer determines that a witness would be subjected to risk of harm if his or her identity were disclosed. The parolee is invited to make statements and answer questions but is not required to do so.

The hearing officer may issue subpoenas to compel the attendance of witnesses resident within the county of the alleged violation. He or she may also issue subpoenas for the production of documents or other written evidence at the hearing. After the preliminary hearing, the hearing officer submits to the board a written report on the testimony, on his or her findings, and on any decision to release the parolee on his or her personal recognizance. The board then ratifies or overrules the hearing officer's findings, including any decision to release, and decides whether to hold a final hearing.

Final Hearing. A parolee charged with violating a parole condition is afforded a final hearing within a reasonable time before the board. The purpose of the final hearing is to determine whether the parolee has violated a parole condition and whether the violation warrants parole revocation. The parolee is given written notice of the final hearing, allowing reasonable time to prepare his or her case. At the final hearing, the parolee has the same rights a parolee has at a preliminary hearing as specified previously. The board may subpoena witnesses from throughout Georgia to appear at the final hearing and may issue subpoenas for the production of documents or other written evidence at the hearing. After the final hearing, the board decides by majority vote whether to continue or revoke parole. A final hearing is not required if the parolee, free on his or her personal recognizance, fails to appear at a final hearing. The board may summarily revoke his or her parole. A final hearing is not required if the parolee has admitted the violation and signed a waiver of final hearing. A final hearing is not permitted and revocation is mandatory by law if the parolee is sentenced by a federal court or a Georgia State or Superior Court to a term of imprisonment, including one reduced to time served, for any felony crime, or for a state misdemeanor involving physical injury to another, which the parolee committed during his or her parole term.

Preliminary Hearing

If a parolee/conditional releasee has been arrested pursuant to a violation warrant, or if the offender is in custody for a new offense and a violation warrant has been filed as a detainer, the PO will provide him or her with a notice of a **preliminary hearing** and a list of the alleged violations. The purpose of the preliminary hearing is to determine if *probable cause* exists to establish that the offender has committed an act(s) that constitutes a violation of the conditions of release.

This hearing is required if the offender is to be detained on a warrant pending a revocation hearing; furthermore, the hearing is required within 15 days of the time the warrant was executed by arrest or filed. If no warrant has been issued—the subject is not being held in custody by parole authorities—but the offender has been summoned to appear for a revocation hearing, a preliminary hearing is not necessary. (About a half-dozen states do not use a preliminary hearing.) The offender may also waive the right to a preliminary hearing.

Probable Cause, Wyoming

The state of facts which would lead a person of ordinary caution or prudence to believe and conscientiously entertain a strong suspicion of an individual's violation of the terms of parole or conditional release. It is a determination that the allegations of the violations are not frivolous, but present a substantial and easily recognizable question which is worthy of consideration by the parole board.

At the preliminary hearing, the parolee/conditional releasee will have an opportunity to challenge the alleged violations and (a limited right) to confront and cross-examine adverse witnesses, including the PO, and to present evidence on his or her own behalf (Figure 8.13). The offender can be represented by legal counsel, although the state is not constitutionally required to provide an attorney (Figure 8.14). As opposed to the rules of evidence in the criminal process, hearsay is admissible at preliminary hearings (although hearsay is not used alone to determine probable cause). The hearing officer who presides is usually an attorney regularly employed for this purpose by the agency. However, any agency employee who is not directly involved in the case may fulfill this role. As a senior (supervisory) parole

NEBRASKA DEPARTMENT OF CORRECTIONAL SERVICES

Parole Violation Advisory of Rights, Waivers & Notification

You are entitled to the following rights and privileges throughout the parole violation-revocation process:

1. You have the right to a preliminary hearing for the purpose of determining if there is probable cause to believe you have committed a violation.
2. You have the right to request your preliminary hearing be held in or reasonably near the county in which the violation occurred, except in the case of abscond.
3. You have the right to appear in person at your hearing.
4. You have the right to present letters, documents and witnesses on your own behalf.
5. You have the right to speak on your own behalf or you may remain silent.
6. You have the right to confront and cross-examine state witnesses as long as it is not determined by the hearing officer that a witness would be subject to risk of harm if his/her identity were disclosed.
7. You may request a continuance of your preliminary hearing, not to exceed 15 days, for just reasons by writing to the hearing officer in a timely manner stating your reasons. See address below.
8. You have the right to a review of parole hearing before the Board of Parole within 30 days after your parole officer's report is forwarded to the Board of Parole (Nebraska Parolees only).
9. You have the right to be represented by an attorney retained at your own expense or you may be entitled to appointed counsel if you satisfy the following conditions: a) you are indigent; b) you have not committed the violation you are charged with or there are substantial reasons which justified or mitigated the violation and make revocation inappropriate; c) the reasons involved are complex or difficult to develop or present thereby preventing you from speaking effectively on your own behalf. If you desire state appointed counsel, write to the hearing officer in a timely manner stating how you qualify under the conditions mentioned in this paragraph.

HEARING OFFICER'S ADDRESS: P. O. Box 94661, Lincoln, Nebraska 68509-4661

NOTICE OF PRELIMINARY HEARING: To: _____ # _____
This is to notify you that a preliminary hearing will be held on _____, 20 __ at ____a.m./p.m. at the _____ in _____, Nebraska.
See PETITION for alleged violation(s).

Initial choices   _____ Request appearance of adverse state's witnesses.
                    _____ Decline appearance of adverse state's witnesses.

_____   _____   _____
PAROLEE   DATE   WITNESS

WAIVER OF PRELIMINARY HEARING: After having been advised of my rights listed above, I hereby voluntarily waive my preliminary hearing with the understanding that I will appear before the Board of Parole on the alleged violation(s). See NOTICE OF REVIEW OF PAROLE HEARING for Date, Time and Location of hearing.

_____   _____   _____
PAROLEE   DATE   WITNESS

REQUEST TO POSTPONE PRELIMINARY HEARING -- CRIMINAL CHARGES PENDING: After having been advised of my rights listed above, I hereby request that my preliminary hearing be postponed pending court action on the charges now pending against me in _____ County, Nebraska. I request this postponement with the understanding that if I am found guilty of, plead guilty or no contest to, any charge, or am bound over to District Court as a result of a preliminary hearing, probable cause will be established and there will be no need for said preliminary hearing and I may be returned for a final hearing before the Board of Parole on this matter. In requesting this postponement, I further agree to waive my right to be heard by the Board of Parole within any required time limits as mandated by law or administrative guideline.

_____   _____   _____
PAROLEE   DATE   WITNESS

FIGURE 8.13   *Parole Violation Advisory.*

(*Source:* Nebraska Department of Correctional Services.)

officer in New York, for example, I served as a hearing officer when personnel normally fulfilling this function were unavailable. Because this hearing is a relatively minimal and informal inquiry, the hearing officer need not hear all the allegations for a finding of probable cause.

If the hearing officer determines that evidence sufficient to make a finding of probable cause has not been presented, the parolee/conditional releasee will be restored to supervision. If probable cause is found, the offender will be held in custody

---

STATE OF NEVADA BOARD OF PAROLE

SUMMARY OF PRELIMINARY INQUIRY HEARING
RE: Blackstone, John L.
    File No. L82-001
    Criminal Case No. 28001

The above-named subject appeared for a Preliminary Inquiry on July 19, 2004, at the hour of 2:20 P.M. at the Carson City Jail.

RIGHTS VERIFIED

Hearing Officer Sally Gomez inquired of defendant Blackstone if he had received copies of the Violation Report dated July 6, 2004, and the "Notice of Preliminary Inquiry Hearing" form listing his rights per the *Morrissey* and *Scarpelli* decisions. Blackstone replied that he had both documents and had read them. He also indicated that he fully understood the charges and his rights during the violation process as explained in the form. It is noted that Blackstone retained as private counsel for this hearing Michael Smith, Esq., of Carson City. Blackstone says he is satisfied with counsel and the time for preparing the defense case. With the indication that Mr. Blackstone fully understands his rights in this matter, we will proceed with the hearing.

VIOLATION CASE

Parole and Probation Officer James Richards read in part the Violation Report dated July 6, 2004, which indicates that Mr. Blackstone is charged with violation of Rule 9 of the Parole Agreement, WEAPONS. It was read that Blackstone was found in possession of a snub-nose .38 pistol by Police Sergeant John Brown in the After Hours Bar, 111 N. Carson Street, City of Carson, Nevada, at about 11:00 P.M. on July 4, 2004. Blackstone had shown the weapon to another customer of the bar, a Mr. William Mundy, allegedly stating to Mundy: "Sucker, I'm going to blow you apart if you keep bugging me tonight." Mundy left the bar and phoned the police to complain of the threat from Blackstone. Sgt. Brown arrived at the bar with several officers and asked Blackstone about the alleged weapon. Blackstone admitted to having an unloaded revolver in his coat pocket, and Sgt. Brown removed same without incident. Blackstone was then placed under arrest for "assault" and an "ex-felon in possession of a firearm." He was transported to the Carson County Jail and booked. Parole Officer Richards placed a Hold for Parole Violation Investigation on Blackstone the following day, July 5, 2004, at about 10:00 A.M.

Officer Richards called William Mundy as his first witness. Mundy told how Blackstone had come into the bar and sat next to him at the counter. Mundy tried to engage Blackstone in some friendly conversation, but Blackstone told him to "shut up and to quit bugging him" or he'd "blow his body apart," showing Mundy a small pistol taken from his coat pocket. Mundy says that he immediately left the bar and called the police, complaining of the incident and asking that the police arrest Blackstone. Mundy identified John L. Blackstone as the person who threatened him in the After Hours Bar on July 4, 2004. Mundy was dismissed after the defense had no questions of him.

Officer Richards called his second witness, Sgt. John Brown of the Carson City Police Department to testify in this case. Brown related that he was dispatched to the After Hours Bar at about 10:55 P.M. on July 4, 2004, to investigate a citizen's complaint of a man with a gun making threats in the bar to shoot him. On arrival, Brown said he was met by Mr. Mundy at the entrance of the bar and that Mundy pointed Mr. Blackstone out for him in the crowded bar. The officer approached Blackstone and asked him if he was carrying a weapon in his coat pocket; Brown said that Blackstone informed him that he had an unloaded pistol in his righthand coat pocket. Sgt. Brown then removed the weapon from Blackstone's right coat pocket and found that it was empty of shells. Sgt. Brown directed Blackstone to step outside the bar with him. Sgt. Brown advised Blackstone that he was being placed under arrest for "simple assault" on the complaint of Mr. William Mundy and that he would

---

FIGURE 8.14 *Summary of a Preliminary/Probable Cause Hearing.*

(*Source:* State of Nevada Board of Parole.)

have to come to the jail for booking but could post bail that evening. Blackstone went along to the jail without incident.

On arrival at the jail, the head jailer told Sgt. Brown that Mr. Blackstone was a parolee and should also be booked for the felony charge of "ex-felon with a firearm." Thus, he was so booked. Sgt. Brown was dismissed after the defense offered no cross-examination.

Officer Richards rested his prosecution case, noting that Blackstone has one felony charge of "Felon in Possession of Firearm" pending in Carson Justice Court. A preliminary hearing has been set for July 30, 2004, on the case. The weapon was not present at this hearing but listed as in the evidence locker of the Carson City Police.

DEFENSE CASE

Attorney for the accused Blackstone stated that he would decline to present any evidence or statements at this time regarding the possession of the weapon as the case was a felony charge awaiting disposition in Justice Court. However, attorney Smith did offer a defense witness, Gary Jones, to tell of the alleged threats in the bar. Jones was called into the hearing room and related he was sitting near the counter at a small table next to John Blackstone and Mundy at about 10:30 on July 4, 2004. Mundy, Jones explained, was "pretty drunk" and kept slapping Blackstone on the back, calling him "pal" and "buddy," and so on. Blackstone told Mundy to leave him alone and Mundy got mad and left the bar in a "huff," Jones testified. A short time later, Jones testified, police officers took Blackstone out of the bar and that is the last time he saw Blackstone until today. Attorney Smith suggested that Blackstone did not threaten Mundy in the manner alleged by Mundy. Hearing Officer Gomez asked Jones if he saw Blackstone take anything out of his coat pocket and show it to Mundy. Jones replied, "no." Richards asked Jones if he could have missed seeing Blackstone show Mundy the gun and say he was going to "blow him apart." Jones was hesitant but said, he was pretty sure; because of the back slapping he was watching the incident pretty closely, wondering what Mundy was going to do next.

Attorney Smith closed the defense, advising Blackstone not to make any statements to the hearing officer until the Justice Court case was held.

FINDINGS

Having considered the evidence presented in this case by both the charging officer and the defendant, this hearing officer finds that probable cause exists to continue detention on the charge of violation of parole rule #9, WEAPONS. The hearing officer has determined that probable cause exists to continue detention pending your formal revocation hearing before the Board of Parole. You are duly notified that at the formal revocation hearing the Board of Parole has the discretion to review and act on all charges that were presented at this preliminary inquiry. With no further evidence to be heard, this hearing will be closed at 3:40 p.m., July 19, 2004.

Respectfully submitted,

Sally Gomez

Hearing Officer

FIGURE 8.14   *(continued)*

pending a revocation hearing. Before the revocation hearing, the PO will prepare a violation of parole report for use at the hearing (Figures 8.15 and 8.16).

Revocation Hearing

A revocation hearing takes place within 90 days of, and is similar to, a preliminary hearing, except that it is comprehensive and the violator is entitled to counsel. In New York, violators have an absolute right to counsel and an attorney will be provided if the parolee cannot afford to hire one. The purpose of the revocation hearing is to determine if the violation of parole/conditional release is serious enough to revoke supervision and return the offender to prison or if some less drastic response is sufficient. In Oregon, certain violators are sent to prison for a time-limited term—6 months—but under rather austere conditions. They are "housed in a medium-security facility and for the first 30 days are allowed out of their individual cells (which have no windows) only three times a week for showers, and for one hour

---

STATE OF NEW YORK - EXECUTIVE DEPARTMENT - DIVISION OF PAROLE

VIOLATION OF RELEASE REPORT
Warrant issued 3-7-2001   *No Warrant Issued*

Name: Hughes, Sam	Date Released: 12-27-2000
NYSID NO: 4172822M	Max. Expiration: 12-27-06
Institution: Woodbourne	Date of Warrant: 3-7-2001
DIN NO: 87-A-5840	Warrant No.: 1234
Date of Birth: 12-23-70	Date Enforced: 3-20-01
Offense: Att. Robb. 1st°/	Location: Brooklyn House of
Att. Robb. 1st°	Detention
Sentence:: 1-6-0/4-6-0/1-6-0/4-6-0	PVU No.: 1234

Delinquency Date: 3-4-01

Since his/her release, the above named individual has violated the Conditions of Release in the following manner:

1. The subject, in violation of rule 2, failed to report to Parole Officer Kaplan at 314 West 40th Street on 3/4/01 as directed on 2/25/01 by P.O. Kaplan.
2. The subject, in violation of rule 4, on or about 3/5/01 admittedly changed his residence of 3140 Atlantic Avenue, Apt. 3B, Brooklyn, NY, without the knowledge or permission of his parole officer.
3. The subject, in violation of rule 13, on 3/5/01 and thereafter admittedly failed to abide by a curfew established on 2/10/01 by being out of his approved residence between the hours of 11:00 P.M. to 6:00 A.M.
4. The subject, in violation of rule 12, on or about 3/5/01 failed to maintain his employment as directed by the Board or Parole by leaving his employment at XYZ Carting and not returning to that employment.
5. The subject, in violation of rule 13, on 3/19/01 used alcoholic beverages after having been specifically directed by his parole officer on 2/10/01 to abstain from such use. The subject was under the influence of alcoholic beverages when apprehended by Sgt. Coors at 6:30 P.M. on that date.
6. The subject, on 3/19/01 in violation of rule 9 at 6:30 P.M. on Flatbush Avenue in Brooklyn possessed a dangerous knife readily capable of causing physical injury without the permission of his parole officer.
7. The subject, in violation of rule 8, on 3/19/01 at 6:30 P.M. on Flatbush Avenue in Brooklyn attempted to take a bank bag from a Susan Anthony without her permission while armed with a knife. Such behavior is a violation of the provisions of the Penal Law and may result in a penalty of imprisonment.

Possible Witnesses:
John Jones
Susan Anthony
Sam Smith
Sgt. Coors, NYPD 84 Precinct

Possible Exhibits:
Arrest Report NYPD
Voluntary Statement
Possible Certificate of Conviction
Special Conditions of Release to Parole Supervision

CRIME OF CONVICTION

The subject is presently serving two consecutive terms of 1-6-0/4-6-0 and 1-6-0/4-6-0 for attempted robbery 1st and attempted robbery 1st. The first conviction indicates that the

---

FIGURE 8.15 *Violation of Release Report.*

(*Source:* State of New York, Executive Department, Division of Parole.)

subject, while acting in concert, on 8/5/97 followed two 10-year-old male children from a store to the lobby of a building. The subject and his codefendants then displayed a knife, twisted one of the victims' arms and demanded money. During the course of the offense they cut one of the victims on the finger. The second offense indicates that the subject followed a pregnant 16-year-old into an elevator, simulated a weapon and took approximately $105 worth of clothing. An underlying charge also included in the plea on this instant offense occurred at the same location approximately two weeks later when the subject took a bag of groceries and $1.75 from another 10-year-old child. The subject was positively identified by all victims in both charges. The parolee met the Board of Parole at Woodbourne Correctional Facility as an initial applicant and was paroled on 12/27/02. He has a projected maximum expiration date of 12/27/06.

PRIOR VIOLATIONS ON THE INSTANT OFFENSE:
This is the subject's first release from this charge.

CRIMINAL HISTORY:

Arrest Date	Charge	Place	Disposition
7-31-88	Sexual Abuse	Kings Crim. Ct.	Prob. 3 yrs. Plea to Public Lewdness
9-9-88	Harassment	Kings Crim. Ct.	Conditional Discharge
3-10-89	Public Lewdness	Kings Crim. Ct.	Dismissed
7-5-89	Public Lewdness	Man. Crim. Ct.	Dismissed
9-20-90	Assault 1st Robbery 2nd	Kings Sup. Ct.	Adjudicated Youthful Off. 1-4-0/4-0-0 yrs.
10-10-91	Att. Sex. Abu.	Kings Crim Ct.	90 days
7-14-93	Dis. Conduct	Bronx Crim. Ct.	Conditional Dischar.
9-22-94	Public Lewd.	Kings Crim. Ct.	Dismissed
10-17-96	Sex. Abuse	Kings Crim. Ct.	Dismissed

The subject has a prior conviction for robbery and assault for which he received youthful offender consideration. It should also be noted that the subject has amassed a number of arrests for sexually oriented types of behavior.

PRIOR PAROLE HISTORY:

The subject was previously on parole as a youthful offender for the act of assault and robbery. The subject was conditionally released and was cited for a violation within a month. The disposition of the Board of Parole at that time was the subject be ordered returned and held to maximum expiration date.

CURRENT VIOLATION BEHAVIOR:

The subject, following only two months in the community, reverted to prior violative behavior in that he immediately became involved in a similar offense to the crime of conviction. The parolee failed to avail himself of parole services in that he stopped reporting. Additionally, referrals made to a mental hygiene unit at Downstate Medical Center were seldom attended by the subject, and he never reinvolved himself in this program.

FIGURE 8.15 *(continued)*

three times a week to exercise in a small concrete structure. After 30 days, they are placed in a two-person cell and given slightly more amenities. After the second 30-day period, they spend the next four months in a dormitory with somewhat increased privileges and amenities" (Parent et al., 1994: 20).

In addition to considering the allegations of parole violation, the revocation hearing will consider information about the offender's adjustment to supervision with respect to making timely reports, maintaining employment/education, supporting dependents, and other critical elements of the supervision process. In most jurisdictions,

GENERAL ADJUSTMENT TO PAROLE SUPERVISION:

The subject initially appeared to be making a good adjustment to parole supervision. He reported regularly and appeared to be functioning as a member in the home. The subject was on intensive supervision and had been directed to report weekly; however, he stopped reporting on 3/4/01. Regular home visits had been made and the wife was very interested in the subject's well being and continued rehabilitation. Present in the home beside the subject's wife, Sylvia Butler, were their three children. Despite his initial satisfactory adjustment, his behavior began to relapse; special conditions were placed upon him and then the home situation improved.

The subject suddenly became antagonistic in the home and refused to participate in the family activities. Because of the wife's fear, she and the three children moved out on 2/27/01.

The subject was released to an employment program at a grocery store in Brooklyn. The job, however, never materialized, but he was able to find employment at XYZ Carting Services also located in Brooklyn. The employer reported that he was an excellent employee and that they would not hesitate to rehire him. Employer indicated that he had a short duration of being tardy, but that situation changed; the employer was disappointed when he left work and did not return; he was therefore discharged. The subject's employer, John Jones, was visited and he appeared very interested in the subject.

The subject was released from the correctional facility with a prescription for hypertension medication. He was referred to Downstate Medical Center, Mental Hygiene Unit to evaluate his mental and physical condition. Additionally, the subject began using and abusing alcohol and was re-referred and directed to attend the program at Downstate Medical Center in an effort to meet all of his needs in one coordinated setting. However, since the subject attended the clinic on an only occasional basis, real change could not occur.

The subject was released from the correctional facility with special conditions of seek, obtain, maintain employment, curfew and support dependents. A Mental Hygiene referral at the discretion of the parole officer was also noted. The subject did abide by the employment condition in that he was employed up until 2/27 with a Carting firm in Brooklyn. He not only complied with this special condition until 2/27, but he appeared to make an excellent adjustment.

A curfew was placed on the subject upon his release; it came to the attention of this writer that he began violating the curfew hours. On 2/10/01 a more strict curfew was established from 11:00 P.M. to 6:00 A.M. A condition of abstention from alcoholic beverages to change his behavior was also mandated. This appeared to work until the end of February when he stopped reporting, quit his job, and his wife left him. The subject had been supporting the home prior thereto. He was referred to Downstate Medical Center for mental hygiene, but his attendance was poor.

PAROLEE STATEMENT:

The parolee was apprehended and a warrant was lodged 3/20/01 at which time he was interviewed at the Brooklyn House of Detention. The subject by his own admission admitted leaving his residence, failing to report, quitting his job and beginning drinking. He stated that everything seemed to be going well and then without notice, everything seemed to start falling apart. He indicated that he couldn't get along at home, people at work didn't like him and people in the community were out to "get him." Subject indicated that he purchased a knife to protect himself. The subject further stated that on 3/19/01 he stopped at the Green Onion Tavern to meet a friend. He indicated that he only had a few drinks, the next thing he knows, he was being booked by NYPD. The subject states that he does not believe he attempted to take anything from anyone, but readily admits that he appears to have blacked out.

PRESENT STATUS:

Time on parole 0 yrs., 2 mos., 7 days
Time owed 5 yrs., 9 mos., 23 days

FIGURE 8.15   *(continued)*

the revocation hearing is presided over by one or more members of the parole board; in other states, it is the responsibility of hearing officers who make recommendations to the parole board for or against revocation. In Iowa, revocation hearings are conducted via two-way fiber optics communications from the board's conference room. If the board votes against revocation, the offender is restored to supervision. In New York, revocation hearings are held before administrative law judges appointed by the parole board, and they have the power to render final decisions.

The subject was afforded a preliminary hearing on 3/30/01 at which time probable cause was found. A final hearing has been scheduled for 5/15/01. The subject was indicted by Kings County Grand Jury on 4/3/01 and is awaiting court action. He is being held at the Brooklyn House of Detention on $30,000 bail and on warrant 1234 is lodged as a detainer; the book and case number is 176-90-14769.

Robert Kaplan

Robert Kaplan

Parole Officer   April 12, 2001

William Haley

William Haley

Senior Parole Officer   April 15, 2001

FIGURE 8.15 *(continued)*

Street Time

If parole/conditional release is revoked, the question arises as to just how much time the parolee must serve in prison. This sentence can vary from jurisdiction to jurisdiction. In California, parolees returned to prison for a technical violation can be confined for only 1 year. In New York, a parolee receives credit for the time spent under supervision ("street time") before the violation. Thus, in New York, an inmate

---

STATE BOARD OF PARDONS AND PAROLES
Montgomery, Alabama

REPORT OF PAROLE VIOLATION

Date: __1/5/02__

Field Office: __Montgomery__

Name of Parolee ____John Doe____   No. __123,456__

Race, Sex, & Age __BM - 30__   County of Conviction __Montgomery__

Offense ____Theft of Property 1st Degree____   Sentence ____2 years penitentiary____

Date Convicted ____4/10/2000____   Date of Parole ____2/17/01____

Date Sentence Expires ____4/10/02____

RESTITUTION

Amount Paid $ __249.00__

Balance $ __101.00__

If declared Delinquent, subject can be located at the following place: __Dan Jones, State Probation Office,__
     Room 334, County Courthouse, Montgomery, Alabama 36104

CHARGE NO. 1

VIOLATION OF CONDITION NO. 7
NEW OFFENSE- BURGLARY III

LEGAL FACTS:

Subject was arrested on 12/24/01, by the Montgomery Police Department for the offense of Burglary 3rd degree, bond was set at $2,000.00. A preliminary hearing was held 1/5/02, and the case was bound to the Grand Jury. Indictment was returned, arraignment held and case set for trial 2/17/02. A Parole Officer's Authorization of Arrest was issued 12/25/01.

Continued:

FIGURE 8.16 *Alabama Parole Violation Report.*

(*Source:* Alabama State Board of Pardons and Paroles.)

DETAILS:

Police reports reflect that at 2 A.M., on 12/24/01, Officer M. D. Jones with the Montgomery Police Department while on routine patrol, observed a black male subject exit Ace Hardware, 4240 Ames Road, Montgomery, Alabama, by way of a back window, in possession of a box. The subject fled on foot but was caught by Officer Jones about three hundred feet from the building. The person was identified as John Doe. He had in his possession property identified as having come from Ace Hardware by the manager, A. L. Pope. It was determined that the hardware store had been entered by forcing open an air conditioning vent at the rear of the store.

CHARGE NO. 2

VIOLATION OF CONDITION NO. 3
FAILURE TO REPORT

LEGAL FACTS:

A Parole Violator's warrant was issued and given to the Sheriff's Office on 12/25, to prevent the subject's release pending Board action.

DETAILS:

According to the records of the supervising officer, on 12/17/01, subject was instructed by Officer Dan Jones regarding parole conditions and specifically that he must report to the Parole Office each month by the 3rd. He stated he understood all parole conditions.

Subject failed to report or have any contact with the parole officer for the months of October, November, and December 2001.

On 9/19/01, he reported for the month of September. He stated he forgot to report by the 3rd. He was reprimanded and encouraged to report in accordance with instructions.

On 10/10/01, I visited his residence. He was not present. His mother, Mae Doe said she had not seen him in three days. I asked that she have him report. On 10/15/01, I wrote subject a letter to report and received no response. On 10/25/01, I visited his home, his mother said he received my letter. He was not present. I requested she attempt to have him report and advised of consequences if he failed.

On 11/5/01, a letter was written to subject reminding and instructing that he make contact with his parole officer. On 11/19/01, I called his residence and spoke with his 17 year old sister, Sue Doe, and requested she tell him to report. On 11/30/01, I visited his father, Joe Doe, at their residence and requested he have subject report.

On 12/6/01, I visited subject's residence and talked with his parents. They stated he had been told to report but he refused. On 12/10/01, I wrote him a letter instructing that he report within 7 days or I would file a Report of Parole Violation, which would likely cause him to be arrested as a parole violator. He failed to contact the Probation Officer thereafter.

RECOMMENDATION:

I recommend revocation.

Signed and dated at Montgomery, Alabama, this 5th day of January, 2002

Dan Jones
Dan Jones
Alabama Probation and Parole Officer

DJ/lm

FIGURE 8.16 *(continued)*

who is paroled after serving 2 years of a 4-year sentence is required to be on parole for 2 years, the remainder of the sentence. If, after 1 year, the parolee violates parole and is returned to prison, he or she will have to serve only the 1 year remaining on the sentence. However, in a state that does not give credit for street time, this same parolee would be required to serve 2 years in prison; the 1 year of satisfactory time on parole would not be credited against the 4-year sentence in the event of a parole violation that results in being returned to prison.

PAROLE SERVICES: EXECUTIVE CLEMENCY

All states and the federal government (Article II, Sec. 2, of the Constitution) have provisions for clemency. In 31 states and the federal government, the chief executive holds the final clemency power, and in most of these states, the parole board or a clemency board appointed by the governor investigates clemency applications at the request of the governor. In some states, clemency authority is vested entirely in a special board, usually a board of pardons and paroles. In North Dakota, there is a pardon advisory board made up of the attorney general, two members of the parole board, and two gubernatorial appointees. Some states conduct formal hearings, and the governor generally must report annually to the legislature on all clemencies granted (National Governors' Association, 1988). Clemency consists of the reprieve, the commutation, and the pardon.

Reprieve

A **reprieve** is a *temporary* suspension of the execution of sentence. As noted in chapter 2, probation developed, in part, out of the judicial reprieve. Its use today is limited and usually concerns cases in which capital punishment has been ordered. In such cases a governor, or the president of the United States, can grant a reprieve—a stay of execution—to provide more time for legal action or other deliberations.

In Georgia, the Board of Pardons and Paroles may grant a reprieve lasting a few hours or a few days to an inmate so he or she may visit a critically ill member of the family or attend the funeral of an immediate member of the family. A reprieve may also be granted in Georgia when it is shown that an inmate is suffering from a definable illness for which necessary treatment is available only outside the state prison system. An inmate granted a reprieve will have the reprieve period credited to the sentence if he or she does not violate any of the conditions of the reprieve.

Commutation

A **commutation** is a modification of sentence to the benefit of an offender. Commutation has been used when an inmate provided some assistance to the prison staff, sometimes during prison riots. Commutation may also be granted to inmates with a severe illness, such as cancer. The laws governing commutation differ from state to state. In New York, an inmate sentenced to more than 1 year who has served at least one-half of the minimum period of imprisonment, and who is not otherwise eligible for release or parole, may have his or her sentence commuted by the governor. In Georgia, the Board of Pardons and Paroles will consider commuting a sentence when it receives substantial evidence that the sentence is either excessive, illegal, unconstitutional, or void; evidence that justice would be served by a commutation; and evidence that commutation would be in the best interests of society and the inmate. The board may also consider commutation of sentences of death after all other legal remedies have been exhausted. A person whose death sentence has been commuted by the board cannot be pardoned or paroled before serving 25 years. In Maryland, correctional personnel identify candidates who meet criteria established by the governor's office for commutation, and their names are submitted to the parole board for a recommendation to the governor.

Pardon

Following the American Revolution, it was necessary to find a new basis for the pardoning power to replace the English theory that it resided in the king as the fountainhead of justice and mercy. This new basis was found in the theory that the power to **pardon** was a sovereign power, inherent in the state, but not necessarily inherent in the executive or in any given branch of government. Rather, because the people were the ultimate sovereign, the power resided in them, and they could provide for its exercise through any agency of government they deemed proper.

Although historically the executive would seem the most natural agency in which to entrust this power, the attitude of the American people after the Revolution was not such as to lead to this conclusion. The struggle with the mother country had left them suspicious of the executive. This conflict was natural enough because the royal governor was not usually sympathetic to the colonists. The champion of the people was usually the lower house of the legislature. Not surprisingly, the early constitutions that replaced the colonial charters tended to place restrictions on the governor's power in many respects, including the power to pardon. Only five states left this power with the governor alone. Six, including the newly admitted state of Vermont, provided that the governor could pardon only with consent of the executive council. Georgia deprived the governor of the pardoning power entirely, giving him only power to reprieve until the meeting of the assembly, which could then make such disposition of the matter as it saw fit. Connecticut and Rhode Island continued to function under their colonial charters, by which the pardoning power was exercised by the general assembly.

By the time the federal Constitution was written, however, opinion had begun to swing back toward placing greater power in the hands of the governor. The framers of the Constitution gave the pardoning power to the president without any limitations as to its exercise or supervision by any other official or agency, and President George Washington was the first to exercise this power in 1795 (when he granted amnesty to participants in the so-called "Whiskey Rebellion"). The executive councils that several states had set up as a means of preventing too much power from being vested in one person began to lose favor about the same time, and several states began abolishing them, giving the power to the governor. Toward the end of the nineteenth century, an overwhelming movement occurred to give the governor some assistance in this task by providing an advisory pardon officer or pardon board. Some states set up pardon boards not merely to advise the governor, but actually to exercise pardoning power, although the governor everywhere was a member, if not the controlling member, of the board (U.S. Attorney General, 1939).

As noted in chapter 7, the pardon has been used historically in the United States as a form of parole. As the indeterminate sentence came into use, pardon boards, originally established to advise the governor with respect to release, began to act independently, developing into parole boards. Despite widespread use of parole, however, the power of pardon has continued. In Utah, for example, the Board of Pardons, an independent state agency, has rather extraordinary powers. This three-member body serves as a board of parole, deciding when and under what conditions persons convicted and serving sentences should be released from imprisonment. In addition, the board can commute sentences of death, reduce terms of imprisonment, and completely terminate an offender's sentence, regardless of whether he or she is an inmate or on parole. The board also has absolute pardoning authority for the state and can forgive the sentence and restore civil rights, although this power is rarely exercised.

The Alabama Board of Pardons and Parole has similar powers (Figure 8.17). Executive clemency is usually limited to deciding on the granting of relief from disabilities, a limited pardon that restores certain civil and political rights, such as the right to apply to vote (the local board of registrars makes final decisions) and hold certain licenses. To be considered for such a pardon, a person discharged from prison without parole must wait 2 years; parolees after 5 years under supervision or 2 years after discharge; and probationers 2 years after discharge from supervision. The pardon report, which is prepared by state probation and parole officers, is exhaustive and allows the board to determine whether the applicant has become a law-abiding person and a useful citizen in the community.

In California, the Board of Prison Terms investigates all pardon petitions from persons who have been free of criminal conduct for 9½ years since discharge from probation, parole, or custody. In Maryland, a pardon requires at least 5 years of exemplary crime-free behavior following release from incarceration and after expiration of any parole supervision. Pardon requests are received by the parole board, which investigates and makes a recommendation to the governor. A governor's pardon restores citizenship rights to the person who has demonstrated a high standard

State Board of Pardons and Paroles
Montgomery, Alabama

CERTIFICATE OF PARDON WITH RESTORATION
OF CIVIL AND POLITICAL RIGHTS

KNOW ALL MEN BY THESE PRESENTS:

It having been made to appear to the Alabama State Board of Pardons and Paroles that

_____

was convicted in _____ County on _____ , 20 _____

of _____ , was sentenced to a term of _____ years;

And it further appearing to the Board from the official report of the Parole Officer which is a part of the record in this case, and with no further information to the contrary, that the above named has so conducted himself as to demonstrate his reformation and to merit pardon with restoration of civil rights;

NOW, In compliance with the authority vested in the State Board of Pardons and Paroles by the Constitution and the Laws of the State of Alabama to grant pardons and to restore civil and political rights, it is

ORDERED that a pardon be granted to the above named as a result of the above stated conviction, and all prior disqualifying convictions, and it is further ordered that all civil and political rights which were forfeited as a result of the conviction be and they are hereby restored.

GIVEN UNDER THE HAND AND SEAL of the State of Pardons and Paroles, this the _____ day of _____ ,20 _____ .

STATE BOARD OF PARDONS AND PAROLES

By _____
Executive Director

FIGURE 8.17 *Certificate of Pardon.*
(*Source:* Alabama State Board of Pardons and Paroles.)

of constructive behavior following conviction for an offense. Pardon applications are considered only after an offender has been discharged from probation or parole for at least 10 years and has not engaged in further criminal conduct. The 10-year rule may be waived in truly exceptional circumstances if the applicant can demonstrate an earlier need for the pardon.

The basis for a pardon may vary in different states, but the pardon is not used extensively anywhere. In New York, the only basis for a pardon is new evidence indicating that the person did not commit the offense for which he or she was convicted. In Florida, a pardon is a declaration of record that a person is relieved from the legal consequences of a particular conviction. As in New York, a pardon will be granted only to a person who proves his or her innocence of the crime for which convicted. Florida also has a *first-offender pardon*, which carries no implication of innocence and may be granted to an actual first offender. This pardon restores civil and political rights and removes legal disabilities resulting from the conviction. A *10-year pardon* works the same way and may be to granted offenders who have had no further convictions for 10 years after completing his or her sentence.

In Georgia, a pardon is a declaration of record by the board that a person is relieved from the legal consequences of a particular conviction; it restores civil and political rights, and removes all legal disabilities resulting from the conviction. A pardon may be granted in two instances. First, a pardon may be granted when a person proves his or her innocence of the crime for which he or she was convicted under Georgia law. Second, a pardon that does not imply innocence may be granted to an applicant who has completed his or her full sentence obligation, including any probated sentence and paying any fine, and who has thereafter completed 5 years without any criminal involvement. The 5-year waiting period may be waived if it is shown to be detrimental to the applicant's livelihood by delaying his or her qualifying for employment in a chosen profession.

The president of the United States typically grants hundreds of pardons: President Gerald Ford pardoned former President Richard Nixon in 1974, Jimmy Carter issued 566 pardons during his 4 years as president, and Ronald Reagan granted 406 during his 8 years as president (Moore, 1989). In 1992, as he was leaving office, President George Bush pardoned six persons alleged to have been involved in the Iran-Contra episode; he granted a total of 71 pardons during his 4 years in office. Bill Clinton pardoned 77 inmates during his 8 years as president, but with only hours before he was to leave office, in a controversial action, he pardoned 140 persons.

Executive Clemency in Texas

Executive clemency is the power of the governor to grant a full or conditional pardon, a full pardon based on innocence, commutation of sentence, remission of a fine or forfeiture resulting from a criminal conviction, emergency medical reprieve, or 30-day reprieve of execution. In accordance with the Texas Constitution, the governor may only grant executive clemency upon the recommendation of the Board of Pardons and Paroles. The board is limited to recommending clemency and to setting minimal eligibility requirements for clemency applicants.

A full pardon restores certain citizenship rights forfeited by law as the result of a criminal conviction, such as the right to vote, the right to serve on a jury, and the right to hold public office. In Texas and many other states, voting rights are automatically restored when one discharges a felony sentence, even without a pardon. A full pardon will remove barriers to some, but not all, types of employment and professional licensing—licenses are granted at the discretion of the state licensing boards of each profession. A pardon will not restore eligibility to become a licensed peace officer in Texas.

A full pardon does not have the legal effect of expunging a criminal record or of exonerating an individual of his or her crime, unless the pardon is based on grounds of innocence. Innocence pardons are extremely unusual and are usually considered only on unanimous recommendation of an applicant's three trial officials (sentencing judge, district attorney, sheriff).

A conditional pardon releases the offender from the conditions of his or her sentence and some disabilities imposed by law, subject to certain conditions. The conditional pardon is often used to release an offender to another country or to immigration officials for deportation. A conditional pardon does not restore civil rights or rights of citizenship.

LEGAL DECISIONS AFFECTING PAROLE

As noted in Part I, legal decisions that affect probation also affect parole. Thus, the decision rendered in *Gagnon v. Scarpelli* (discussed in chapter 2) relating to probation violation used precedents established in the *Morrissey v. Brewer* decision (discussed later in the section on parole revocation), which relates to parole violation. The three theories of parole violation are also similar, if not identical, to the three theories of probation violation.

Parole Release and Parole Hearings

In 1970, the U.S. Court of Appeals for the Second District considered the case of *Menechino v. Oswald* (430 F.2d 403). Joseph Menechino (a "jailhouse lawyer") was serving a 20-year-to-life sentence in New York for murder in the second degree. He was paroled in 1963 and returned to prison as a parole violator 16 months later. Subsequently, he appeared before the board of parole and admitted consorting with persons having criminal records and giving misleading information to his PO.

Two years later, Menechino appeared before the board for a release hearing and parole was denied. He brought a court action claiming that his rights were violated by the absence of legal counsel at both his revocation and parole release hearings. The court held that

- A parole proceeding is nonadversarial in nature because both parties, the board and the inmate, have the same concern—rehabilitation.
- Parole release hearings are not fact-finding determinations because the board makes a determination based on numerous tangible and intangible factors.
- The inmate has "no present private interest" to be protected (**liberty interest**) because he or she is already imprisoned—has nothing to lose—and this "interest" is required before due process is applicable.

The court further stated that "it is questionable whether a board of parole is even required to hold a hearing on the question of whether a prisoner should be released on parole." Relative to the question of parole revocation, however, the court advised that a minimum of procedural due process should be provided because at this stage a parolee has a present private interest in the possible loss of conditional freedom.

Although Menechino's case before the federal court was initiated regarding parole release, it set forth important legal arguments relative to parole revocation. The opinions of the three judges who heard the case clearly indicates that if Menechino had initiated an action concerning his parole revocation, he would have won the case on a 2–1 basis. This fact was duly noted by the New York State Court of Appeals in the second *Menechino* case, discussed later.

In 1979, the U.S. Supreme Court reversed a court of appeals decision in a class action brought by inmates of the Nebraska Penal and Correctional Complex [(*Greenholtz v. Inmates of Nebraska Penal and Correctional Complex* (442 U.S. 1, 1979)]. The inmates claimed that they had been unconstitutionally denied parole release by the board of parole, but the Court established in its decision that

- A convicted inmate has no constitutional right to be released before the expiration of his or her lawful sentence.
- Although a state may establish a parole release system, it has no constitutional obligation to do so.

According to Nebraska law, at least once a year initial parole hearings must be held for every inmate, regardless of parole eligibility. At the initial hearing, the board examines the inmate's total record and provides an informal hearing during which the inmate can present statements and documents in support of a claim for release.

If the board determines from the record and hearing that the inmate is a likely candidate for release, a final hearing is scheduled. However, the Nebraska law provides that the board "shall order an inmate's release unless in the final hearing, the board concludes that inmate's release should be deferred for at least one of four specified reasons." This procedure is a somewhat unusual, peculiar, perhaps, to the state of Nebraska. Rolando del Carmen points out that this amounts to a "state-law created liberty interest," an expectation of being granted parole release (1985: 50). As noted earlier, whenever this "interest" exists, some minimum due process is required.

The board then notifies the inmate of the month in which the final hearing will be held. At the final hearing, the inmate may present evidence, call witnesses, and be represented by private counsel of his or her choice. This hearing is not a traditional adversarial one because the inmate is not permitted to hear adverse testimony or to cross-examine witnesses who present such evidence. If parole is denied, the board furnishes a written statement of the reasons for the denial within 30 days.

In upholding the procedure used by the Nebraska parole board, Chief Justice Warren Burger, speaking for the Court, stated:

> When the Board defers parole after the initial review hearing, it does so because examination of the inmate's file and personal interview satisfied it that the inmate is not ready for conditional release. The parole determination, therefore, must include consideration of what the entire record shows up to the time of the sentence, including the gravity of the offense in the particular case. The behavior record of an inmate during confinement is critical in the sense that it reflects the degree to which the inmate is prepared to adjust to parole release. At the Board's initial interview hearing, the inmate is permitted to appear before the Board and present letters and statements on his own behalf. He is thereby provided with an effective opportunity to insure, first, that the records before the Board are in fact the records relating to his case; and second, to present any special considerations demonstrating why he is an appropriate candidate for parole. Since the decision is one that must be made largely on the basis of an inmate's files, this procedure adequately safeguards against serious risks of error and thus satisfies due process.
>
> Next, we find nothing in the due process concepts as they have thus far evolved that requires the Parole Board to specify the particular "evidence" in the inmate's file or at his interview on which it rests the discretionary determination that an inmate is not ready for conditional release. The Board communicates the reason for its denial as a guide to the inmate for his future behavior. To require the parole authority to provide a summary of the evidence would tend to convert the process into an adversary proceeding and to equate the Board's parole release determination with a guilt determination. . . . [T]he parole decision is . . . essentially an experienced prediction based on a host of variables. The Board's decision is much like a sentencing judge's choice—provided by many states—to grant or deny probation following a judgment of guilt, a choice never thought to require more than what Nebraska now provides for parole release determination.

Del Carmen and Paul Louis conclude that "an inmate does not have a constitutional right to be released on parole, nor does he or she enjoy any constitutional right in the parole release process. In more succinct language, the parole board can do just about anything it pleases [with respect to release], and whatever it says and does prevails because it enjoys immense discretion" (1988: 20). Although parole boards are not constitutionally required to provide reasons for denying release, the use of parole guidelines often provides inmates with such documentation.

Parole Violation and the Three Theories of Parole

Traditionally, a person on parole has not been considered a free person, despite the fact that he or she has been released from imprisonment. The basis for imposing restrictions on a parolee's freedom is contained in three theories:

1. *Grace theory:* Parole is a conditional privilege, a gift from the board of parole. If any of the conditions of this privilege are violated, parole can be revoked.
2. *Contract theory:* Every parolee and (most) conditional releasees are required to agree to certain terms and conditions in return for conditional freedom. A violation of the conditions is a breach of contract, which can result in penalties—a return to prison.
3. *Custody theory:* The parolee is in the legal custody of the prison or parole authorities, and as a result of this quasi-prisoner status, his or her constitutional rights are automatically limited and abridged.

The *Menechino* and *Morrissey* decisions challenged these theories.

Until the 1970s, parole agencies operated without any interference from the judiciary. However, this policy changed when the New York Court of Appeals handed down a decision in *Menechino v. Warden*, which, for the first time, granted parolees the right to counsel and the right to call their own witnesses at parole revocation hearings. Although the decision applied only to New York, it indicated the direction in which the courts would rule in future decisions and provided a precedent for the U.S. Supreme Court.

The 4–3 decision required that an attorney be present at a parole revocation hearing. It also permitted a parolee to call witnesses who would speak on his or her behalf. The New York court recognized that it was entering into an uncharted area of law. The issue the court was called on to resolve was stated succinctly at the beginning of the majority opinion: "whether parolees are constitutionally entitled, under the Federal and State Constitutions, to the assistance of counsel in parole revocation hearings." *Menechino* cited other legal decisions, such as *Mempa v. Rhay* and *In re Gault* (see chapters 2 and 3). Although probationers, juveniles, and welfare recipients had already obtained limited due process protections at hearings that might cause the loss of freedom or financial distress, these protections had not yet been extended to parolees.

Morrissey v. Brewer (408 U.S. 471, 1972) marked the beginning of the U.S. Supreme Court's involvement with parole revocation procedures. Up until June 1972, the Court had not ruled in this area. The issue in this case was whether the due process clause of the Fourteenth Amendment required that a state afford a person the opportunity to be heard before revoking parole.

Morrissey was convicted of the false drawing of checks in 1967 in Iowa. After pleading guilty, he was sentenced to 7 years in prison. Paroled from the Iowa State Penitentiary in June 1968, 7 months later, Morrissey, at the direction of his parole officer, was arrested in his hometown as a parole violator and held in a local jail. One week after review of the parole officer's written report, the Iowa Board of Parole revoked Morrissey's parole, and he was returned to prison. He had received no hearing before the revocation decision.

Morrissey violated the conditions of his parole by buying a car under an assumed name and operating it without the permission of his PO. He also gave false information to the police and an insurance company concerning his address after a minor traffic accident. Besides these violations, Morrissey also obtained credit under an assumed name and failed to report his residence to his PO. According to the parole report, Morrissey could not explain adequately any of these technical violations of parole regulations.

Also considered in the *Morrissey* case was the petition of Booher, a convicted forger who had been returned to prison in Iowa by the Board of Parole without a hearing. Booher had admitted the technical violations of parole charges to his PO when taken into custody.

The Supreme Court considered all arguments that sought to keep the judiciary out of parole matters, and it rejected the "privilege" concept of parole as no longer feasible. The Court pointed out that parole is an established variation of imprisonment of convicted criminals—it occurs with too much regularity to be simply a "privilege." "It is hardly useful any longer to try to deal with this problem in terms of whether the parolee's liberty is a 'right' or a 'privilege.' By whatever name the liberty is valuable and must be seen within the protection of the Fourteenth Amendment. Its termination calls for some orderly process however informal."

The Court pointed out that parole revocation does not occur in just a few isolated cases—it has been estimated that 35 to 40 percent of all parolees are subjected to revocation and return to prison. The Court went on to state that, with the numbers involved, protection of parolees' rights was necessary. The Court did note, however, limitations on a parolee's rights:

> We begin with the proposition that the revocation of parole is not part of the criminal prosecution and thus the full panoply of rights due to the defendant in such a proceeding does not apply to parole revocation. Supervision is not directly by the court but by an administrative agency which sometimes is an arm of the court and sometimes of the executive. Revocation deprives an individual not of absolute liberty to which every citizen is entitled but only the conditional liberty properly dependent on observance of special parole restrictions.

Also found in the decision is the New York State Court of Appeals response to the problem raised by the *Menechino* case. The Supreme Court held: "Society thus has an interest in not having parole revoked because of erroneous information or because of an erroneous evaluation of the need to revoke parole, given the breach of parole regulations. See Parole ex rel *Menechino v. Warden.*"

In *Morrissey,* the Supreme Court viewed parole revocation as a two-stage process: (1) arrest of the parolee and preliminary hearing, and (2) the **revocation hearing.** Because a significant time lapse usually occurred between the arrest and revocation hearing, the Court established an interim process for all parole violators, a hearing before the final or revocation hearing: "Such an inquiry should be seen in the nature of a preliminary hearing to determine whether there is **probable cause** or reasonable grounds to believe that the arrested parolee had committed acts which would constitute a violation of parole conditions."

The Court specified that the hearing officer conducting this preliminary hearing need not be a member of the parole board, only someone who is not involved in the case, that the parolee be given notice of the hearing, and that the purpose be to determine whether there is probable cause to believe that the parolee has violated a condition of parole. On the request of the parolee, persons who have given adverse information on which parole violation is based are to be made available for questioning in the parolee's presence. Based on this information presented before the hearing officer, a determination should be made if a reason exists to warrant the parolee's continued detention (pending a revocation hearing).

The Court stated that "no interest would be served by formalism in this process; informality will not lessen the utility of this inquiry in redressing the risk of error." This author served as an auxiliary hearing officer, conducting preliminary hearings in New York. These were held at local correctional facilities. All persons were placed under oath, and a legal reporter recorded all testimony verbatim. The PO alleging the violation "prosecuted" the case, although in significant cases a legal advocate was provided by the Division of Parole for that purpose. Following all the testimony, I would write down my decision in summary form: The violation of parole charges considered and sustained were listed and a copy given to the parolee.

If none of the charges were sustained, the PO would be directed to arrange for the parolee's release from custody.

In reference to the revocation hearing, the Court stated: "The parolee must have an opportunity to be heard and to show if he can that he did not violate the conditions or if he did, that circumstances in mitigation suggest the violation does not warrant revocation. The revocation hearing must be tendered within a reasonable time after the parolee is taken into custody. A lapse of two months as the state suggests occurs in some cases would not appear to be unreasonable."

The Court also suggested minimum requirements of due process for the revocation hearing:

> Our task is limited to deciding the minimum requirements of due process. They include (1) written notice of the claimed violation of parole; (2) disclosures to the parolee of evidence against him; (3) opportunity to be heard in person and to present witnesses and documentary evidence; (4) the right to confront and cross-examine adverse witnesses (unless the hearing officer specifically finds good cause for not allowing confrontation); (5) "neutral and detached" hearing body such as a traditional parole board, members of which need not be judicial officers or lawyers; and (6) a written statement by the fact finders as to the evidence relied on and reasons for revoking parole.

The Supreme Court left open the question of counsel when it stated: "We do not reach or decide the question whether the parolee is entitled to the assistance of retained or to appointed counsel if he is indigent." In practice, parole boards have permitted parolees to be represented by counsel, although they usually do not provide such assistance.

Parole Board Liability

In a unanimous decision (*Martinez v. California,* 444 U.S. 277, 1980), the Supreme Court affirmed the constitutionality of statutory provisions that provide parole officials with immunity from tort claims. In this instance, Thomas, a parolee convicted of attempted rape, tortured and murdered 15-year-old Mary Martinez 5 months after his parole release from prison. Thomas had been labeled as not amenable to treatment, and the sentencing court recommended that he not be paroled. Nevertheless, after serving 5 years of a 1- to 200-year sentence, Thomas was paroled. The deceased girl's parents argued that in releasing Thomas, parole authorities subjected their daughter to deprivation of her life without due process of law.

Justice Stevens delivered the opinion for the Court:

> Like the California courts, we cannot accept the contention that this statute deprives Thomas' (a paroled offender) victim of her life without due process of law because it condoned a parole decision that led indirectly to her death. The statute neither authorized nor immunized the deliberate killing of any human being. This statute merely provides a defense to potential state tort law liability. At most, the availability of such a defense may have encouraged members of the parole board to take somewhat greater risks of recidivism in exercising their authority to release prisoners than they otherwise might. But the basic risk that repeat offenses may occur is always present in any parole system.

Although parole boards act in a quasijudicial capacity, they do not enjoy the total immunity conferred on judges. Justice Stevens pointed out that in this decision, "We need not and do not decide that a parole official could never be deemed to 'deprive' someone of life by action taken in connection with a prisoner on parole." (See Figure 8.18.)

Now that the examination of the historical, administrative, and legal aspects of probation and parole is complete, chapter 9 turns to rehabilitation theory and practice in probation and parole.

	Absolute[*]	Quasi-judicial[†]	Qualified[§]
Judges	Yes		
Legislators	Yes		
Prosecutors	Yes		
Parole Board Members		Yes, if performing a judgelike function	Yes, if performing other functions
Supervisors			Yes
Probation Officers		Yes, if preparing a presentence report under order of judge	Yes, if performing other functions
Parole Officers			Yes
Police Officers			Yes
Prison Guards			Yes
State Agencies	Yes, unless waived by law or court decision		
Local Agencies	No immunity	No immunity	No immunity

[*]Absolute immunity means that a civil liability suit, if brought, is dismissed by the court without going into the merits of the plaintiff's claim. No liability.

[†]Quasi-judicial immunity means that officers are immune if they are performing judicial-type functions, such as when preparing a presentence report under orders of the judge, and liable if they are performing other functions.

[§]Qualified immunity means that the officer's act is immune from liability if it is discretionary, but not if it is ministerial. Also, an officer may not be liable even if the act is ministerial if it was done in good faith.

FIGURE 8.18   *General Guide to Types of Official Immunity in State Tort Lawsuits.*
(*Source:* del Carmen et al., 2001.)

KEY TERMS

independent model

consolidated model

conditional release

parole board guidelines

technical violation

new offense violation

preliminary hearing

reprieve

commutation

pardon

executive clemency

liberty interest

revocation hearing

probable cause

INTERNET CONNECTIONS

Parole links: crimelynx.com

National Institute of Corrections: nicic.org

American Probation and Parole Association: www.appa-net.org

Parole links: www.talkjustice.com/links.asp?453053932

REVIEW QUESTIONS

1. Distinguish the independent model of parole administration from the consolidated model.
2. What are the advantages and disadvantages of the independent model?
3. What are the advantages and disadvantages of the consolidated model?
4. How does conditional release differ from parole release?

5. Why is the administration of parole less complex than that of probation?
6. What are the three basic services provided by a parole agency?
7. What is conditional release, and how does it differ from parole?
8. Why have parole release hearings been criticized?
9. Why do most parole boards deny inmates the right to legal representation at parole release hearings?
10. What are the two most important factors considered when making a parole release decision?
11. What led to the development of parole release guidelines?
12. How do parole board guidelines take into account both classical and positive school views?
13. How are parole release guidelines used?
14. Why can the parole board be in a better position than the sentencing judge to render a decision based on just deserts?
15. What is the primary responsibility of institutional parole staff? What other services might they provide?
16. What is the purpose of a preliminary parole violation hearing?
17. Provide examples of special rules of parole.
18. How is the length of parole/conditional release supervision determined?
19. How does a technical violation differ from a new offense violation?
20. How does a final or revocation parole hearing differ from a preliminary hearing?
21. What rights does an alleged violator have at violation of parole hearings?
22. With respect to parole release, what has the Supreme Court ruled?
23. What did the Supreme Court rule in the 1972 case of *Morrissey v. Brewer*?
24. What are the different types of executive clemency?
25. What has the Supreme Court ruled with respect to parole board liability?

Rehabilitation and Supervision in Probation and Parole

Rehabilitation: Theory and Practice

Probation and parole (P/P) have traditionally been viewed as having two primary goals: protection of the community and rehabilitation of the offender. Of course, the two are not incompatible: Rehabilitation of the offender improves community safety.

Some modes of rehabilitation[1] are more easily applied than others to P/P practice. Some methods require more training than most P/P officers have received, and their use may require an expenditure of time that is not realistic in most P/P agencies. In practice, P/P officers use a variety of techniques, tailoring them to different clients. They often use techniques without understanding the theoretical base or even recognizing it as part of a particular mode of rehabilitation—"flying by the seat of your pants" is sometimes characteristic of P/P. Nevertheless, most P/P officers, even when they do not provide extensive direct rehabilitative services, refer clients to programs for such problems as substance abuse and pedophilia, unemployment and mental illness. Knowledge of various modalities, therefore, is important in P/P. Therapeutic rehabilitation, however, no matter the discipline, requires a theoretical knowledge and principles applied to specific cases. Being knowledgeable about both theory and therapy enables the P/P officer to make appropriate referrals, understand treatment reports, and better relate to rehabilitation professionals.

THEORY

A **theory** is part of an explanation—a statement about the relationship between two classes of phenomena that permits us to better understand our environment. A theory helps to explain events by organizing them in the world so they can be placed in perspective; a theory also explains the causes of past events and predicts when, where, and how future events will occur. "A theory consists of a set of assumptions; concepts regarding events, situations, individuals, and groups; and propositions that describe the interrelationships among the various assumptions and concepts" (Binder and Geis, 1983: 3).

Theories are abstract, a necessary dimension if they are to be applied to more than one specific set of circumstances, facts, or observations. We cannot determine the cause of particular criminal behavior based on a satisfactory explanation for a

---

[1]Some might object to the use of the term "rehabilitation" because it refers to a restoration of previous functioning. In fact, many P/P clients have never had a satisfactory level of social functioning. "Habilitation," however, has an unfamiliar ring to it, and thus rehabilitation will refer both to a restoration of previous functioning *and* habilitation.

Nature Versus Nurture

Whenever a theory of crime is offered, two essential elements must be considered. Theories of crime can be distinguished by how the authors or supporters conceive of the nature of human behavior. Prominent in any discussion of human behavior is the *nature versus nurture* controversy. Both sides address the same question: What is the dominant force shaping human behavior? Supporters of the *nature* position answer that behavior can be explained primarily by genetic, biological, or other properties inherent in the individual. In short, human behavior is largely inherited. Conversely, proponents of the *nurture* position look to the social environment for the causal factors; that is, human behavior is largely the product of social interaction.

single case. However, if enough individual cases fit into the same explanation, we can develop a theory and test it against future cases of criminal behavior—the ability to predict is a measure of a theory's validity. Validity requires testing, and any theory that cannot be tested—and, therefore, disproved—is not (according to scientific principles) a theory. A purported cause of crime that does not permit testing, therefore, has more in common with theology than criminology—it lacks scientific merit.

There are three basic theoretical models for rehabilitation in P/P:

1. Social casework
2. Reality therapy
3. Behavior/learning theory

To understand social casework, it is necessary to review a theory that also underlies much of clinical psychology and psychiatry.

PSYCHOANALYTIC THEORY

Psychoanalytic theory refers to a body of work fathered by Sigmund Freud (1856–1939). Over the years the theory has undergone change, although Freud's basic contribution, his exposition of the importance of **unconscious** phenomena in human behavior, remains: Personality is strongly influenced by unconscious determinants that develop early in life. Simply put, this concept argues that the most important determinants of our behavior are not available to our conscious thought (Cloninger, 2004). These determinants evolve during the stages of psychological development.

Stages of Psychological Development

Freud postulated unconscious processes in the stages of psychological development that, although not directly observable, were inferred from case studies with patients. He divided mental phenomena into three groups:

1. *Conscious:* what a person is thinking at any given time
2. *Preconscious:* thoughts and memories that can easily be called into conscious awareness
3. *Unconscious:* repressed feelings and experiences that can be made conscious only with great difficulty. "The unconscious is essentially dynamic and capable of profoundly affecting conscious ideational or emotional life without the individual's being aware of this influence" (Healy, Bronner, and Bowers, 1930: 24).

Unconscious feelings and experiences are related to normal stages of psychosexual development through which each person passes on the way to adulthood (psychosexual maturity). Memories of these stages of psychosexual development are repressed and, therefore, unconscious—not part of conscious or preconscious memory—yet they drive behavior and serve as a source of anxiety and guilt, the basis for psychoneurosis and psychosis. The stages overlap, and transition from one to the other is gradual, the time spans being approximate:

1. **Oral stage** (birth to 18 months). The mouth, lips, and tongue are the predominant organs of pleasure for the infant. In the normal infant, the source of pleasure becomes associated with the touch and warmth of the parent, who gratifies oral needs. When this is lacking, deviant behavior, particularly drug and alcohol abuse, is to be expected in the adult. Drugs and alcohol serve as a substitute for maternal attachment, and in adults, drug abuse is seen as a regression back to an unfulfilled oral stage. The infant actually enters the world a "criminal," that is, unsocialized and devoid of self-control.

2. **Anal stage** (18 months to 3 years). The anus becomes the most important site of erotic interest and gratification. Pleasure is closely connected to the retention and expulsion of feces, as well as the bodily processes involved and the feces themselves. During this stage, the only partially socialized child acts out rather destructive urges, breaking toys or even injuring living organisms, such as insects or small animals. A great deal of psychopathology in the adult, including violent behavior and sociopathological personality disorders, is traced to disruptions during this stage.

3. **Genital stage** (3 to 5 years). Erotic interest becomes associated with the genitals, and in normal persons is maintained by them thereafter. During this period of life, the child experiences *Oedipus* (in boys) and *Electra* (in girls) *wishes* in the form of fantasies of incest with the parent of the opposite sex. The healthy child must relinquish the dependent paternal/maternal attachment and deal with the feelings of sadness that result. Sexual problems, such as pedophilia, are linked to this stage when the adult remains fixated on a parent and is not attracted to adults of the opposite sex. Drug and alcohol abuse are also traced to failures during this stage of development (see Abadinsky, 2004).

4. **Latent stage** (5 years to adolescence). A lessening of interest in sexual organs occurs during this period, as well as an expanded relationship with playmates of the same sex and age.

5. **Adolescence-adulthood stage** (13 years to death). A reawakening of genital interest and awareness occurs; the incestuous wish is repressed and emerges in terms of mature (adult) sexuality.

When a person is passing through the first three stages of psychosexual development, the mind simultaneously undergoes the development of three psychic phenomena:

1. **Id.** This mass of powerful drives seeks discharge or gratification—it is asocial, devoid of values and logical processes. Constituting wishes, urges, and psychic tensions, according to Freud (1933: 104), the id is "a cauldron of seething excitement," seeking pleasure and avoiding pain. The id is the driving force of the personality, and from birth until about 7 months of age, it is the total psychic apparatus.

2. **Ego.** Through contact with the reality around them and the influence of training, infants modify their expressions of id drives. This ego development is pragmatic and permits them to obtain maximum gratification with a minimum of difficulty in the form of restrictions that their environment places on them—learning from experience. Without the ego to act as a restraining influence, the id would destroy the person through its blind striving to gratify instincts in complete disregard for reality. As a result of disturbances in psychosexual development, a person may remain at

the ego level of development: "The child remains asocial or behaves as if he had become social without having made actual adjustment to the demands of society" (Aichhorn, 1963: 4). Feelings of rage and aggression associated with the anal stage lurk in the background awaiting an opportunity to break through to satisfaction.

3. **Superego.** Often viewed as a conscience-type mechanism, the superego exercises a criticizing power, a sense of morality over the ego: "It represents the whole demands of morality, and we see all at once that our moral sense of guilt is the expression of tension between the ego [which strives to discharge id drives] and the super-ego" (Freud, 1933: 88). A healthy superego is the result of an identification with a parent(s)—the superego is an internalized parent—that is accomplished during the genital stage of psychosexual development. In other words, "The role which the super-ego undertakes later in life, is at first played by external power, by parental authority" (89). "The super-ego then supports the ego in controlling the instinctive [id] impulses" (Smart, 1970: 45).

A delicate balance is maintained by unconscious forces as a person experiences various sociocultural and biological aspects of existence. When the balance is upset, the psyche passes from the normal to the psychoneurotic or the psychotic (mental illness). The fact that a thin line exists between the normal and the neurotic and between the neurotic and the psychotic is basic to psychoanalytic theory. In fact, only a difference of degree separates the "normal" and the "abnormal." The degree to which there is a malfunctioning in psychic apparatus is the degree to which a person is "abnormal" or "sick," that is, socially dysfunctional.

Crime and the Superego

The "psychoanalytic theory of crime causation does not make the usual distinction between behavior as such and criminal action"; the distinction is a legal one—that is, crime is behavior defined by a society as illegal, an issue discussed in chapter 1 (Falk, 1966: 1). Antisocial behavior is seen as a neurotic manifestation whose origin can be traced back to early stages of development: "There is no fundamental difference between the neurotic criminal and all those socially harmless representatives of the group of neurotic characters; the difference lies merely in the external fact that the neurotic lawbreaker chooses a form of acting out his impulses which is socially harmful or simply illegal" (Alexander and Staub, 1956: 106).

According to August Aichhorn (1963: 221), "the superego takes its form and content from identifications which result from the child's effort to emulate the parent. It is evolved not only because the parent loves the child, but also because the child fears the parent's demands." However, Freud (1933: 92) states that "the superego does not attain to full strength and development if the overcoming of the Oedipus [in males] complex has not been completely successful."

The superego keeps primitive (oral and anal) id impulses from being acted on. Persons with a poorly developed superego, psycho- or sociopaths—**antisocial personality disorder**—are restrained only by the ego, which alone cannot exercise adequate control over id impulses. Such persons suffer little or no guilt as a result of engaging in socially harmful behavior. They are characterized by a combination of antisocial behavior and emotional detachment (Black, 1999).

At the other extreme are persons whose superego (internal parental voice) is destructive. Their superego is overwhelming and cannot distinguish between *thinking* about and *doing* bad deeds. Unresolved conflicts of earlier development and id impulses that are normally repressed or dealt with through other secondary processes (such as reaction formation or sublimation) create a severe sense of (unconscious) guilt. This guilt is experienced (at the unconscious level) as a compulsive need to be punished. To alleviate this (unconscious) guilt, the actor is impelled toward committing acts for which punishment is virtually certain. Delinquents of this

No Willie Sutton!

- Richard G. entered the Bay Bank in Haverhill, Massachusetts, went up to a counter, and wrote on a deposit slip: "This is a holdup. Give me all the money." He left the bank with $5,201. With red dye from an explosive device used to mark stolen bills streaming from his bag, Richard G. mounted an old two-speed bicycle. He was caught within minutes, covered with red dye, sneezing, and coughing. The note he had handed the teller was discovered to contain his name and home address (Associated Press, April 18, 1992).
- Lee W. entered a Connecticut bank and presented a withdrawal slip to the teller on which he had written: "The money." He was quickly arrested by police, who found $3,000 on him—Lee had written his name on the withdrawal slip *twice*.

The FBI catches between 40 and 50 bank robbers per year who write their note demanding money on the back of a deposit slip for their own checking accounts (Martin, 1995).

type are the victims of their own morality (Aichhorn, 1963). Persons employed in the criminal justice system often see cases in which the crime committed was so poorly planned and executed that it would appear that the perpetrator *wished* to be caught.

In sum, criminal behavior is related to the superego function, which is a result of an actor's relationship to parents (or parental figures) during early developmental years. Parental deprivation through absence, lack of affection, or inconsistent discipline stifles the proper development of the superego. Parental influence is thus weakened by deprivation during childhood development, and in adulthood the actor is unable to adequately control aggressive, hostile, or antisocial urges. Overly rigid or punitive parents, conversely, can lead to the creation of a superego that is rigid and punitive, for which the actor seeks punishment as a way of alleviating unconscious "guilt."

A P/P officer must be able to distinguish those offenders with an inadequate superego from those with a punitive one. With the latter, attempts to deter criminal behavior through the application of threats may actually have an opposite effect. With the former, the P/P officer may need to act in a parental role to replace a poorly developed superego.

Psychoanalytic Treatment

Psychic disorders are treated by psychoanalysis or one of its variants, such as psychotherapy. Freud stated that psychoanalysis "aims at inducing the patient to give up the repressions belonging to his early life and to replace them by reactions of a sort that would correspond better to a psychically mature condition." To achieve this goal, a psychoanalyst attempts to get the patient "to recollect certain experiences and the emotions called up by them which he has at the moment forgotten" (Reiff, 1963: 274). To the psychoanalyst, present symptoms are tied to repressed material of early life—the primary stages of psychosexual development. The symptoms will disappear when the repressed material is exposed under psychoanalytic treatment.

Today, most psychoanalytically oriented therapists practice a variety of approaches (such as ego psychology whose focus is more immediate), rather than classical Freudian analysis (Nietzel et al., 2003), and psychoanalysis is not used in P/P—it requires highly trained and thus expensive practitioners, treatment takes many years, and it needs a level of verbal ability in patients beyond that of most persons on P/P. In fact, psychoanalytically oriented therapists may underestimate how difficult it is to verbalize experience, even for otherwise verbal patients (Omer and London, 1988). Instead of psychoanalysis, in P/P, psychoanalytic theory has traditionally been applied through the use of *social casework.*

SOCIAL CASEWORK

Social work has its roots in charity work and **social casework**—the supplying of concrete services to persons in need—solving problems rather than changing personalities. Mary Richmond (1917), whose colleagues included many physicians, presented the practice of social work as including (nonpsychoanalytic) psychological and sociological aspects of a person's behavior. She also set the groundwork for what is sometimes referred to as the **medical model** of therapy, dealing with non-physiological problems through the method of *study, diagnosis,* and *treatment.*

In the years following World War I, social work was characterized by practice based primarily on the psychoanalytic perspective and the medical model (Miley, O'Melia, and DuBois, 2004). During the 1930s, some American physicians began to use psychoanalytic treatment and social workers adopted this "talking cure"—one that did not require medical training—to their own practice (Specht, 1990). Psychoanalytic theory was still central to social work education when this writer received his master's of social work degree in 1970.

Social casework is one of the basic specialties of social work, "an art in which knowledge of the science of human relations and skills in relationship are used to mobilize capacities in the individual and resources in the community appropriate for better adjustment between the client and all or any part of his total environment" (Bowers, 1950: 127). Social casework "can be defined essentially as the development of a relationship between worker and client, within a problem-solving context, and coordinated with the appropriate use of community resources" (Brennan et al., 1986: 342). The purpose of social casework is "the solution of problems that block or minimize the effectiveness of the individual in various roles" (Skidmore, Thackeray, and Farley, 1988: 64).

As Freudian thought had its impact on social work, caseworkers began examining the client's feelings and attitudes to understand and "cope with some of the unreasonable forces that held him in their grip" (Perlman, 1971: 76). The client's behavior was conceived of as purposeful and determined, but some of the determinants are unconscious. Casework was thus expanded to include work with psychological and social or environmental stress. Social casework also adopted the open listening style of relationship, and even the notion of "relationship" is grounded in Freudian thought (Payne, 1997). It is the therapeutic relationship that serves as a medium for facilitating change. The caseworker helps clients to maintain constructive reality-based relationships, solve problems, and achieve adequate and satisfying independent social functioning within the client's existing personality structure (Torgerson, 1962). To accomplish this task, social workers use encouragement and moral support, persuasion and suggestion, training and advice, comfort and reassurance, together with reeducation and some sort of guidance (Kasius, 1950).

Although social casework borrowed much of its theory from Freud, it avoided the psychoanalytical goal of trying to effect personality changes. Instead, a more immediate and pragmatic version of the Freudian model was adopted, helping people "perform in their appropriate social roles by providing information and knowledge, social support, social skills, and opportunity" (Specht, 1990: 354). Twenty-first century social casework, while recognizing the influence of early development, social environments, and traumatic events, generally focuses on immediate concerns and addresses maladaptive behaviors and adverse conditions that perpetuate problems in current functioning (Borden, 2000). Whereas the medical model searches the past to detect problems in the present, contemporary social work—while not discounting the importance of the developmental past—explores the present for client strengths and resources that can promote effective social functioning (Miley et al., 1995).

The importance of social casework in P/P practice goes beyond theory and into the skills and training that schools of social work provide. These include "an extension and refinement of information on how to interview, how to obtain facts about the client's background, how to identify and distinguish surface from underlying problems, what community resources exist, and how to refer" (Wilensky and Lebeaux, 1958: 288–289). "The knowledge base developed for social casework is eclectic, interdisciplinary, tentative at best, complex and often subjective" (Johnson and Yanca, 2004: 42). The newer approaches borrow from ego psychology emphasizing coping and social functioning. Instead of the medical model terms "study," "diagnosis," and "treatment," modern social casework adopted "assessment," "evaluation," and "intervention" (L. Johnson and Yanca, 2004):

1. *Assessment:* collecting and analyzing relevant information upon which to base a plan
2. *Evaluation:* thinking about and organizing facts into a meaningful goal-oriented explanation
3. *Intervention:* implementation of the plan

Assessment

Assessment determines the nature of the client's current situation, resulting in a written report (variously called a psychosocial study, intake report, or social history, among other nomenclature). The assessment involves gathering information from documents and through interviews with persons familiar with the offender and the client him- or herself. It provides the "here and now" and how it got that way. More complex and significant than data collection, assessment incorporates the tasks of deciding which data to seek and how to organize it (Bisman, 2000). Assessment includes identifying strengths and resources that exist within the client and his or her environment (L. Johnson and Yanca, 2004). "When assessment is complete, the social worker should be able to describe the problem or situation accurately and identify what needs to be changed to improve the client's situation" (Sheafor, Horejsi, and Horejsi, 2000: 301).

During this phase, client interviews provide the basis for a relationship. To accomplish this, the worker must be what Gordon Hamilton calls "a person of genuine warmth" (1967: 28). Using face-to-face interviews, the worker conveys acceptance and understanding. Walter Friedlander notes that "caseworkers communicate their respect for and acceptance of the client as a person whose decisions about his own living situation are almost always his own to make" (1958: 22). The caseworker seeks to understand the client's press and stress: "People are affected by *press* from the environment and by *stress* from conflicts within themselves" (Payne, 1997: 80).

Workers know that the way they communicate will have an effect on clients' perceptions of them and the worker–client relationship. Therefore, they must be cognizant of the way they greet clients; their tone of voice, facial expressions, and posture; and the way they express themselves verbally. In P/P practice, workers who exude authority, who are curt, and who emphasize the enforcement aspect of their position will encounter difficulties in establishing a sound casework relationship.

Workers engage clients in the helping process, and they make certain judgments about a client's motivation, how much he or she wants to change, and how willing he or she is to contribute to bringing about change. Workers recognize that a client brings attitudes and preconceptions about being on probation or parole. The P/P client is fearful, or at least realistically on guard, because he or she recognizes the power of the P/P officer.

An anxious client will be resistant to a worker's efforts, and in the mandated setting that is P/P practice, a P/P officer can easily raise a client's anxiety level, thus increasing *resistance*, including "evasive, angry, and uncooperative behaviors"

(Hutchinson, 1987: 591). Psychoanalytic theory also posits resistance that is unconscious. P/P clients frequently have negative impressions of all authority figures. This perception is usually based on experiences with parents, school officials, police officers, court officials, training schools, or prisons. In addition, a client may have a low self-image, a severe superego, or a chronically high anxiety level. The result will be resistance. The worker must not become defensive about client resistance or take negative behavior personally.

To lessen resistance, workers may discuss the client's feelings about being on P/P, allowing him or her to vent some feelings and anxiety. This approach will also enable workers to clarify any misconceptions that clients have about P/P supervision. Elizabeth Hutchinson (1987: 592) suggests "letting it all hang out": "It is essential for the social worker to make early acknowledgement of client reluctance toward the mandated transactions and to validate such reluctance as understandable. This makes the issue explicit rather than latent and assures the client of the acceptability of his or her feelings as well as the genuineness of the social worker."

The client's motivation can also be influenced by (the psychoanalytical concept of) **transference**: He or she may view the worker as a friendly parent or as an authoritarian and demanding mother or father. The worker can be influenced by *countertransference* because he or she may view the client as a childlike figure; if the worker is a great deal younger than the client, the former may view the latter as a parent or older sibling.

The caseworker prepares a psychosocial study of the client. In nonprobation/parole agencies, workers often stress the importance of early childhood development and experiences with a view toward applying a psychoanalytic explanation to the client's behavior. This practice is not usual in P/P settings, where "the unique constellation of social, psychological, and biological determinants of the client's current stressful situation" is more relevant and appropriate to analyze (Friedlander, 1958: 47). In P/P practice, the primary focus of assessment is on the present or the recent past.

The P/P officer seeks information that will provide an indication of the client's view of his or her present situation. He or she is concerned with the client's plans for improving the situation and weighs the sincerity and intensity of the latter's commitment to change. During the assessment phase, "particular attention needs to be given to assessing client strengths"—this "builds hopefulness and uncovers possibilities for dealing with the problem" (Sheafor et al., 2000: 304). When the caseworker interprets the situation as needing to fix something that is wrong, it gives him or her the status of "expert" with the expectation that the worker will bring about change rather than the client: "The real work must be done by the client. Otherwise it either does not get done or the change is temporary" (L. Johnson and Yanca, 2004: 62). The caseworker reviews the client's relationship with his or her family and evaluates the impact of the client's current situation. While engaged in study, the worker must also be aware of the cultural, racial, and ethnic factors that influence a client.

In P/P, material from the unconscious is not sought. However, with clients who are mentally ill, material that in the better-functioning person is normally repressed may be brought to the fore. In such situations, the worker must direct his or her efforts toward keeping the client in touch with reality and should usually avoid exploring the normally repressed material.

Evaluation

The evaluation process converts the assessment content into a goal statement that describes the desired results (L. Johnson and Yanca, 2004). Helen Perlman (1957: 168–169) suggests that this phase of casework involves

- The nature of the problem and the goals sought by the client, in their relationship to

- The nature of the person who bears the problem, his or her social and psychological situation and functioning, and who needs help with his or her problem, in relation to
- The nature and purpose of the agency and the kind of help it can offer or make available.

In discussing the origin of the client's malfunctioning, Perlman refers to "this history of his development as a problem-encountering, problem-solving human being"; she notes that this can provide the worker with an understanding of the client's present difficulties and the probable extent of his or her ability to cope with them (1957: 176). For a plan to be complete, psychological testing or a psychiatric evaluation may be necessary. The results of a clinical examination will indicate if the client is in need of any special therapy—for example, if he or she is psychotic. In many instances a psychological or psychiatric report will not be available, and the P/P worker must make the determination if an evaluation will be of such aid in planning as to justify the expense.

Finally, the evaluation "plan considers both process and outcomes by specifying intermediate objectives as well as end goals" (L. Johnson 1998: 294). Anticipating difficulties that may be encountered, the plan needs to be flexible to be effective. In P/P, the plan provides a basis for holding the offender accountable for his or her efforts toward achieving a productive and law-abiding lifestyle.

Intervention

Intervention involves activity designed to bring about change in a systematic way (L. Johnson and Yanca, 2004). During this stage, the relationship between worker and client enables the P/P officer to use his or her influence. It is a basic concept in social work that the client has a right to **self-determination**: The worker has no right to impose his or her goals. Obviously, the authority inherent in the P/P officer's role necessarily limits self-determination. For example, the P/P officer may be bound by statute or agency regulation to make decisions about the client's living situation. Dale Hardman (1960: 250) states that "authority conflict is a major causative factor in delinquency," a proposition that is widely accepted in correctional social work. Therefore, helping the offender come to grips with the reality of authority is a basic goal of P/P rehabilitation. The client's relationship with a P/P worker is often the only positive experience he or she has ever had in dealing with an authority figure. "Many clients' involvement with the law expresses a need for control they cannot themselves provide. If used with respect and care, the authority of the court can be invoked by the forensic social worker to strengthen the client's weak motive to get treatment and to improve impulse control" (Brennan et al., 1986: 345).

However, social caseworkers in other than correctional settings must also deal with the reality of their authority. They require clients to keep appointments, provide personal information, and pay fees—usually under the threat, implied or expressed, of denying the client the help or service for which the client is asking. Workers in child welfare agencies may even be required to remove children from their parents or guardians in neglect or child abuse cases. In addition, because of the impact of an agency setting, or the phenomenon of transference, the caseworker is always an authority figure. The concept and the use of authority and the limits placed on self-determination by reality are not alien to the practice of social casework. However, "unwilling clients often do not see the need for service, do not believe help is possible, or have difficulty in developing a relationship with the worker" (L. Johnson and Yanca, 2004: 170).

The plan for intervention in social casework will use procedures that, it is hoped, will move the client toward the goal of enhancing the ability to function within the realities placed on him or her by society in general, and the client's present probation/parole status in particular. Three basic techniques are involved.

Changing the Environment.   This approach may involve obtaining needed resources if these are available from the agency or locating other agencies that can provide them. In using this technique, the worker may assume a *mediator* or *advocate* role when the client is unable to secure a service that he or she needs and to which he or she is entitled. In P/P practice, this role is common for the worker. As advocates, they act as intermediaries between clients and agencies, and may function as spokepersons for clients needing to deal with the bureaucratic maze of governmental agencies (Miley et al., 2004). The technique is used by the juvenile P/P officer when seeking placement for a youngster in a foster home, group home, or residential treatment center. The aftercare worker who is trying to place a juvenile back in public school after a stay at a juvenile institution is often a mediator/advocate. The worker may have to intervene on behalf of clients who require financial assistance from the welfare department. P/P workers may help a client to secure a civil service position or a necessary license/certificate to enter a particular trade or profession.

The P/P worker may help his or her client by talking to an employer or school official, at the same time helping the client to modify behavior relative to problems encountered at work or school. Many P/P clients have had few positive work or school experiences, and their difficulty with authority extends to employers and teachers. By using role playing, reflection, and suggestion, the worker tries to modify the client's behavior, at least to the degree required for continued schooling or employment.

While being of direct assistance when necessary, the P/P officer should promote independence on the part of the client. The worker realizes that he or she is not continually available, and treatment is rarely indefinite. *The worker should not do anything for the client that the client is capable of doing for him- or herself.*

Ego Support.   The use of this technique entails attempts by the worker to sustain the client through expressions of interest, sympathy, and confidence. The worker, through the use of his or her relationship with the client, promotes or discourages behavior according to whether the behavior is consistent with the goals of rehabilitation. The worker encourages the client to vent and deals with any anxiety that may inhibit functioning.

Central to the casework process is the relationship between the client and worker. The P/P officer imparts a feeling of confidence in the client's ability to deal with problems. He or she makes suggestions about the client's contemplated actions and indicates approval or suggests alternatives relative to steps that the client has already taken. The officer may, at the very least, provide a willing and sympathetic ear to a troubled and lonely client. It is not unusual for the P/P worker to be the only person available to an offender to whom he or she can relate and talk. When the relationship is a good one, the client cannot help but view the worker as a friend.

The officer is also supportive of the client's family, parents, or spouse. In P/P practice, home visits are a usual part of the worker's responsibilities. During the home visit, the worker has an opportunity to observe the client's environment directly. This firsthand information adds another dimension to the worker's knowledge of the client.

The knowledge that a client lives in substandard housing or in a high-delinquency area is easy for the worker to incorporate into his or her working methodology, but the concept is an intellectual one. A home visit provides direct information about the smell of urine in the hall, roaches, broken fixtures and bathroom facilities, and housing that is hot in the summer and cold in the winter; a home visit also enables the worker to experience the presence of drug addicts huddling in a hallway, waiting for their connection. The worker is able to see, hear, and smell the environment in which a client is forced to live and to understand the hostility and frustration that fill the lives of many P/P clients almost from the time they are born.

By working directly with parents or a spouse, in addition to working with the client, the P/P officer broadens his or her delivery of help to the client. The worker can make referrals for the client's children when special aid is necessary—indeed, he or she can intervene on behalf of the client in the role of *mediator/advocate* to get services for any family member. The P/P officer can assist with marital problems. Marital discord is an acute problem in many parole cases when a client has been incarcerated for many years. The worker may try to deal with the problem directly or may provide a referral to a specialized agency for the client and spouse. For example, it is not unusual for a distraught wife to call the P/P officer to complain about her husband. Sometimes she is merely seeking some way of venting her feelings; at other times, the situation may be more serious—for example, she may have been subjected to physical abuse.

When a client is living with parents, the worker strives to involve them in the rehabilitation effort, which is often difficult. The client may be the perennial black sheep in a large family. He or she may come from a family that also has other members on probation, in prison, or on parole. This may dissipate the family's energy and resources, and directly affect their ability to help the client.

Clarification.   Clarification, states Florence Hollis, is sometimes called counseling because it usually accompanies other forms of rehabilitation in casework practice. Clarification includes providing information that will help a client see what steps he or she should take in various situations. The worker, for example, may help the client weigh the issues and alternatives to provide a better picture on which to base a decision. Hollis notes that the client "may also be helped to become more aware of his own feelings, desires and attitudes" (1950: 418–419).

The client is encouraged to explain what is bothering him or her. If the problem is external, verbalizing it may be relatively easy. If the difficulty is internally caused, however, it may go deep and provoke anxiety. This difficulty will cause resistance, and the P/P officer will need great skill to secure enough information about the problem to be able to be of assistance. In response to the information, the worker may provide a direct interpretation to the client; more often, the P/P officer will ask questions and make suggestions designed to help the client to think out the problem more clearly and to deal with it in a realistic manner.

LEARNING THEORY/BEHAVIOR MODIFICATION

To understand **learning theory/behavior modification**, one may place the various modes of rehabilitation related to P/P practice on a continuum represented by a straight horizontal line. Acceptance of psychoanalytic theory is on the extreme left of this line and rejection on the extreme right. Social casework would be at the left of center; reality therapy (discussed later) is toward the right of center, while behavior modification is firmly on the extreme right of this imaginary line.

```
<Psychoanalytic theory/————————————/————————————Learning theory>
     social casework              Reality therapy        behavior modification
```

Behavior modification, the application of learning theory, which emanated from the science laboratory and experimental psychology, rejects psychoanalytic theory as an unscientific basis for an even more unscientific mode of rehabilitation. B. F. Skinner (1904–1990), America's foremost behaviorist, argued that analytically oriented therapists "rely too much on inferences they make about what is supposedly going on inside their patients, and too little on direct observation of what they do" (Goleman, 1987: 18). "If a client's aggressive behavior has been rewarded, at least part of the time, no further explanation in terms of internal needs is necessary; the client has simply learned to behave aggressively" (Nietzel et al., 2003: 47).

Behaviorists take pride in displaying and subjecting their methods and results to rigorous scientific analysis. Behavior modification proceeds on the theory that all forms of behavior are the result of learning responses to certain stimuli. "Disturbed" behavior, for example, is a matter of learning responses that are inappropriate (London, 1964). The behaviorist contends, and has been able to prove, that animal behavior, human and otherwise, can be modified through the proper application of behaviorist principles.

Behavior is "*strengthened* by its consequences, and for that reason the consequences themselves are called 'reinforcers'" (Skinner, 1972: 40). When some aspect of (animal or human) behavior is followed by a reward, this action is reinforced—more likely to be repeated. "**Reinforcers** are types of consequences that strengthen a behavior" (Baldwin and Baldwin, 1998: 42). The reward is called **positive reinforcement.** If the probability of a behavior goes up after the *removal* of a stimulus, then **negative reinforcement** has occurred: "A negative reinforcer strengthens any behavior that reduces or terminates it" (Skinner, 1972: 47). For example, the negative reinforcement that occurs when a heroin addict fails to ingest enough heroin—withdrawal symptoms—strengthens drug-seeking behavior. As opposed to negative reinforcement, *punishment*—for example, imprisonment—suppresses the frequency of an operant—for example, heroin use. "Punishment either takes away something an organism wants or gives it something it does not want" (Hergenhahn and Olson, 1999: 289). Although punishment is frequently used interchangeably with negative reinforcement, the two are quite different: "Punishment occurs when the introduction of a stimulus decreases the frequency of the behavior" (Oltmanns and Emery, 2004: 35). Thus, according to Skinner (1972), punished behavior such as crime is likely to reappear after the punitive contingencies are withdrawn. These applications form the basis for operant conditioning.

Antisocial behavior is merely the result of learning directly from others—for example, peers—or the failure to learn how to discriminate between competing norms, lawful and unlawful, because of inappropriate reinforcement. When conforming behavior is not adequately reinforced, an actor can more easily be influenced by competing, albeit antisocial, sources of positive reinforcement—for example, money and excitement from criminal behavior. To be effective for learning, however, reinforcement must follow rather closely the behavior that is to be influenced. "Generally, **operant conditioning** is most likely to occur when reinforcers and punishers follow immediately after an operant" (Baldwin and Baldwin, 1998: 89). Offenders have problematic reinforcement contingencies and often engage in behavior that provides an immediate payoff but has negative long-term consequences: If criminal behavior is almost always rewarding, significant but intermittent punishment is unlikely to suppress it.

The behaviorist stresses client analysis to discover the variables that are reinforcing, and then attempts to discover the situational demands and emotions that are related to the patient's behavior. The analysis deals with the day-to-day functioning of the subject in order to discern the cause (independent variables) of the maladaptive behavior (dependent variables). The therapist attempts to elicit specific descriptions of actual events that constitute a problem—functional analysis—so he or she can evaluate which components of the situation are amenable to change by behavioral techniques (Nietzel et al., 2003). The specific description, whenever possible, is based on direct observation or interviews with the client and/or significant others (e.g., parents or spouse), and a review of any relevant records. Maladaptive behavior is analyzed in terms of intensity and frequency, and is often presented in the form of graphs.

The therapist, among other techniques, teaches the client to conduct his or her own functional analysis for subsequent self-produced modification of the environmental contingencies that are reinforcing the maladaptive behavior. The functional analysis can be combined with self-monitoring techniques. Highly motivated clients maintain a daily log of the specific problem—for example, lack of temper control. The client records the number of times that he or she exhibits the specific manifestations of a lack of temper control. Although this technique can be combined with other forms of therapy, alone it seems to have the power to modify behavior because it

> "increases awareness and makes the response sequence less automatic. This may provide the opportunity for the person to suppress the response or engage in some incompatible behavior. In addition, self-monitoring may encourage the person to reward or punish him- or herself, depending on whether appropriate gains have been made. Investigators have shown that self-reinforcing statements, such as "I am doing well," are important in maintaining one's own behavior. A recording system which facilitates this process undoubtedly will be effective in helping people to change their own behavior as well" (Bootzin, 1975: 11).

Cognitive Social Learning.   The need for timely reinforcement makes operant conditioning difficult to apply in P/P practice. For example, stimulants, such as cocaine, and depressants, such as heroin, are powerful reinforcers—they provide instant gratification to those who find their use pleasant; competing with this reality in many cases is difficult and often impossible. Albert Bandura points out, however, that in humans, "outcomes resulting from actions need not necessarily occur instantly," because as opposed to lower animals, people "can cognitively bridge delays between behavior and subsequent reinforcers without impairing the efficacy of incentive operations" (1974: 862).

The cognitive position maintains that it is necessary to look to thoughts, memory, language, and beliefs. The emphasis is on inner rather than environmental determinants of behavior (Hollin, 1990). Bandura (1974) argues that to ignore the influence of covert reinforcement in the regulation of behavior is to deny a uniquely human capacity. Cognitive social learning theory places the stress on cognitive mediational processes. According to this view, humans are active participants in their operant conditioning processes—the individual determines what is and what is not reinforcing. For example, to become a drug abuser, one must *learn* that ingesting certain chemicals is desirable. In other words, human behavior is complex and reinforcement often abstract. Humans have a unique capacity to use abstractions, or symbols, that can serve as important reinforcers, such as the medals and trophies dear to any amateur athlete. Behavior can be learned vicariously through observation without *obvious* reinforcement (Nietzel et al., 2003).

The individual is seen as lacking that level of social competence necessary to cope adequately with a variety of situational demands. The rehabilitation process begins with an assessment of the positive and negative aspects of his or her behavior. The assessment includes a focus on the social, physical, and emotional environments in which the behavior occurs. After the assessment, the role of the therapist is to enable the patient to deal with cues that trigger problem behavior in a manner that avoids resorting to illegal activity, with the patient's own report of the negative aspects—for example, arrest and incarceration—serving as a motivator for adopting more positive coping strategies (Donovan, 1988). Negative reinforcement in the form of avoidance strategies serves to prevent the occurrence of influences that trigger criminal behavior.

Self-reinforcement in humans may take on many tangible or symbolic dimensions. In reality therapy (discussed in a later section in this chapter), praise and encouragement are dispensed by the therapist; in correctional settings, the positive reinforcements are often privileges dispensed through secondary reinforcers or *tokens*.

Token Economy.   Operant conditioning has been used in prisons (and other "total institutions"), where reinforcing variables can be controlled to a degree not possible elsewhere. In the controlled setting of the total institution, the application of behavior modification is often referred to as the *token economy*. The use of tokens has important advantages:

> First, they can be given immediately after a desirable behavior occurs and cashed in at a later time for a backup reinforcer. Thus, they can be used to "bridge" long delays between the target response and the backup reinforcer, which is especially important when delivery of the backup reinforcer immediately after the behavior is impractical or impossible. Second, tokens make it easier to administer consistent and effective reinforcers when dealing with a group of individuals. (Martin and Pear, 1992: 305)

In some correctional programs, inmates are issued punch cards with numbers every morning. As they move through the various prison activities during the day, points are earned and punched out on the cards by correction officers trained in behavior modification techniques. Points can be earned for a variety of "good" behavior—bed making, vocational and educational performance, and so on. The points accumulated on the punch cards are convertible into access to certain privileges, such as the television room, cigarettes, movies, and snacks. Such programs can often reduce the need for standard forms of coercion typically used in correctional institutions. The token economy has limited application:

> One obvious disadvantage related to TE [token economy] is that rather close control over environmental contingencies is required. The status of the S [subject] whose behavior is to be modified is that of a "captive." In the absence of environmental control, it is not possible to introduce critical contingencies. If control is present initially, but is then lost for whatever reason, the removal of the contingencies allows the altered behavior to revert in the direction of its original baseline rate. In an effort to maintain behavior when the subject has lost his status as a captive, operant conditioners have attempted to gradually alter the manipulated contingencies in respect to the behavior being modified so that the changed behavior itself would tend to result in natural intrinsic reinforcement. [The difficulty is that delinquents/criminals] tend to be highly resistant to the usual types of natural or intrinsic reinforcement that appear to function so effectively for other "normal" populations. (Stampfl, 1970: 105)

Other Behavior Modification Systems.   Operant conditioning can also use **aversive therapy.** This approach involves the avoidance of punishment in a controlled situation in which the therapist specifies in advance an unpleasant event that will occur if the subject performs an undesirable behavior. According to a report by the American Psychiatric Association (1974: 25), "the most effective way to eliminate inappropriate behavior appears to be to punish it while at the same time reinforcing the desired behavior." This method of rehabilitation is obviously controversial, and many behaviorists disapprove of the use of punishment on both ethical and treatment grounds—its effects do not seem to last as long as results conditioned by positive reinforcement. According to Skinner, "What's wrong with punishments is that they work immediately, but give no long term results. The responses to punishment are either the urge to escape, to counterattack or a stubborn apathy. These are the bad effects you get in prisons or schools, or wherever punishments are used" (Goleman, 1987: 18).

Some have told "horror stories" about the use of aversive therapy, which was portrayed in the Stanley Kubrick movie *A Clockwork Orange.* In real life, California prisoners were injected with Anectine (succinylcholine), a muscle relaxant that causes brief paralysis but leaves the subject conscious. The prisoners were unable to move or breathe voluntarily, a sensation that simulates the onset of death. At the same time, the therapist would tell the subjects that they must change their behavior. Some observers state that this program was not an example of aversive conditioning but rather merely punishment.

Drug antagonists can serve a similar function by rendering the use of alcohol or other substances ineffective—lacking positive reinforcement—or extremely unpleasant—negative reinforcement or punishment. Disulfiram (Antabuse), metronidazole, or chlorpropamide can serve this purpose for alcohol abusers. Antabuse—the best known of these substances—disrupts the metabolism of alcohol in the liver, producing a severe reaction that includes stomach and head pain, nausea, and vomiting. One substance has the appearance and smell of cocaine and even produces a numbing effect but is not psychoactive. This substance is used in conjunction with an aversive chemical, one that induces vomiting, for example. In voluntary patients, electric shocks may be self-administered whenever a craving for the chemical arises. Alternatively, verbal aversion techniques may be used when a patient is asked to *imagine* strongly aversive stimuli (usually vomiting) in association with imaginal drug-related cues, scenes, or behavior. Similar procedures can be used with sex offenders—for example, pedophiles— by associating erotic feelings toward children with a negative consequence.

Other behavioral therapies use biofeedback and relaxation training, and sometimes assertiveness training, to prepare drug abusers to cope better with stress and anxiety that is believed to be linked to drug use. Researchers have found that certain environmental cues can serve as triggers to activate drug cravings (Dole, 1980). When desensitization is used, "patients are usually first relaxed, then given repeated exposure to a graded hierarchy of anxiety-producing stimuli (real or imaginal)" to provide a form of immunity (Childress, McLellan, and O'Brien, 1985: 957).

Unlike other forms of treatment, to be successful, behavior modification does not require the acquiescence of its subjects. In fact, behavior modification may at times be more successful when used without the knowledge of those whose behaviors are being subjected to it.

As in psychoanalytic theory, learning theory does not distinguish between behavior as such and criminal behavior; both are seen as based on the same principles of learning. In expounding the behaviorist position on crime, C. Ray Jeffrey (1971: 177) states that "there are no criminals, only environmental circumstances which result in criminal behavior. Given the proper environmental structure, anyone will be a criminal or a noncriminal." In both theories—psychoanalytical and learning—the person defined as a criminal is not in control of his or her behavior—a denial of *free will*— that raises serious legal issues with respect to holding persons accountable for their actions. This concept is known in law as *mens rea*.

Behaviorists analyze symptoms in terms of observable behavior components. The therapist keeps a record of "frequency counts" on a particular behavioral component. For example, a parent will be asked to record the number of outbursts exhibited by a youngster within a given period. The therapist then makes a functional analysis designed to determine the circumstances under which the undesirable behavior seems to occur and the elements within the environment that may be supporting (and thus encouraging) the behavior. In this case, the parent may be told to ignore the outbursts, no matter what the intensity, while providing positive reinforcers for positive behavior. The results of this approach will be measured against the original baseline of frequency counts. The empirical nature of the behaviorist approach has significant appeal; however, human behavior is driven by subjective meanings that may be known only to the actor.

Positive reinforcement, the timely application of rewards, is more easily accomplished in an institutional setting, where the environment can be controlled and manipulated to reinforce certain behaviors, than in the community, where most P/P rehabilitation occurs. This accounts for the paucity of articles on the use of behavior modification in P/P in professional journals. In one published report (Thorne, Tharp, and Wetzel, 1967), probation officers were trained in behavior techniques, and they, in turn, gained the cooperation of parents whose youngsters were on probation. The officers explained the behavior techniques to be used and taught the parents how to apply them. Behavior was monitored by the parents, and charts were used to record frequency counts. Positive reinforcers were given for desired behavior, such as attendance at school, scholastic work, and satisfactory behavior, and were withheld when the child misbehaved. The rewards were specific and related directly to the positive behavior. For example, a girl on probation was given telephone privileges and permitted weekend dates, contingent on her attendance at school all day. In this case, the attendance teacher would give a note to the child at the end of the school day attesting to her attendance. When the child gave her mother the note, she earned the privilege of receiving and making calls that day. If she received four notes, she earned a weekend date; five notes earned two weekend dates.

In another case, rewards included both tangible and intangible items. For example, for studying 30 minutes per day, the youngster was both praised and given permission to ride his bicycle. Money, access to television, and other rewards were used as reinforcers for specific behavior on a specified schedule basis. This form of treatment is often referred to as *behavioral contracting*: "an agreement in which the performance of predetermined responsibilities or duties results in receipt of privileges or rewards" (O'Leary and Wilson, 1975: 480). It has been used predominantly with children because (in noninstitutional settings) they can be subjected to greater environmental controls than adults. In another published study on contingency management with adult drug offenders on probation, probation officers used reduction in probation time as a reinforcer (Polakow and Docktor, 1974).

REALITY THERAPY

Reality therapy (RT) was developed as a mode of rehabilitation by William Glasser, a psychiatrist. It is probably the easiest of the three modes of rehabilitation to describe, and simplicity has been a major reason for its popularity in probation and parole practice. Glasser's book *Reality Therapy* (originally published in 1965) contains only 166 pages. Glasser describes RT as a method "that leads all patients toward reality, toward grappling successfully with the tangible aspects of the real world" (1975: 6). As opposed to RT, "conventional therapy goals do not include client responsibility or personal actions as primary" (Bersani, 1989: 177). RT attempts to teach people a better way of fulfilling their needs and taking responsibility for themselves and their behavior—reality therapy stresses accountability.

Although Glasser accepts the developmental theories of psychoanalytic theory, he rejects them as a useful basis for rehabilitation: "It is wishful thinking to believe that a man will give up a phobia once he understands either its origins or the current representation of its origin in the transference relationship" (1975: 53). Glasser believes that conventional treatment depends far too much on the ability of the patient to change his attitude and ultimately his behavior through gaining insight into his unconscious conflicts and inadequacies (51). The reality therapist denies the claims of psychoanalytic theorists that a cure depends on the recovery of traumatic early memories that have been repressed. The ability of psychoanalysis to cure persons, states Melitta Schmideberg (1975), a psychiatrist whose mother (Melanie Klein) was eminent in the field of psychoanalysis, has never been clinically substantiated. "The goal of reality therapy," in contrast to psychoanalytical approaches, "is neither insight about underlying causes of problems nor resolution of unconscious conflicts. Rather, the desired outcome is a change in behavior resulting in need satisfaction and greater happiness" (Wubbolding, 2000: 10).

In a later work, Glasser (1976) reiterates some of his previous positions and elaborates on others. Various mental problems, Glasser argues, are merely symptomatic illnesses that have no presently known medical cause. They act as companions for the lonely people who *choose* them. Glasser states that in cases of so-called mental illness, the behaviors or symptoms are actually chosen by the person from a lifetime of experiences residing in the subconscious. In place of conventional treatment, the reality therapist proposes first substituting the term *irresponsible* for mental health labels (e.g., neurotic, personality disorder, and psychotic). A "healthy" person is called *responsible*, and the task of the therapist is to help an irresponsible person to become responsible.

Furthermore, notes Schmideberg, the psychoanalytic approach of "dwelling on the past encourages the patient to forget his present problems, which is a relief at times, but often—undesirably—the patient feels that after having produced so many interesting memories, he is now entitled to rest on his laurels and make no effort to change his attitude or plans for the future" (1975: 29). This diverts attention from the client's current problem(s), which is a reality that should be dealt with directly.

Glasser argues that conventional treatment does not deal with whether a client's behavior is right or wrong, in terms of morality or law, but "rather, it contends that once the patient is able to resolve his conflicts and get over his mental illness, he will be able to behave correctly" (1975: 56). Societal realities, however, particularly in P/P practice, require direct interventions with a client, with the therapist not accepting "wrong" behavior.

"Reality therapy is based upon the theory that all of us are born with at least two built-in psychological needs: (1) the need to belong and be loved and (2) the need for gaining self-worth and recognition" (Glasser, 1980: 48). According to Glasser, people with serious behavior problems lack the proper involvement with someone, and lacking this involvement, they are unable to satisfy their needs. Therefore, to be a helping person, the therapist must enable the client to gain involvement, first with the worker and then with others. The traditional therapist maintains a professional objectivity or distance, whereas the reality therapist strives for strong feelings between worker and client. This type of relationship is necessary if the worker is to have an impact on the client's behavior. The worker, although always accepting of the client, firmly rejects irresponsible behavior. He or she can then teach the client better ways of behaving.

To accomplish this reeducation, the worker must know about the client's reality—the way he or she lives, and his or her environment, aspirations, and *total reality*. Reality is always influenced by culture, ethnic and racial group, economic class, and intelligence. The worker must be willing to listen open mindedly and learn about the client (Schmideberg, 1975). While observing, the worker develops a relationship with the client, a relationship that can lead to responsible behavior. Alluding to the fact that RT does not always work, Glasser states that the fault is with the therapist who is unable to become involved in a meaningful way with the client. However, mandated correctional clients may avoid counseling because of their difficulties with intimacy (Harris and Watkins, 1987). For many people it feels safer to reject someone trying to help them than to risk accepting that help only to be disappointed. Such clients try to create physical and emotional distance in relationships. Paradoxically, a warm and empathetic counselor often is met with barriers to bonding in the therapeutic relationship, and too much pursuit of the client to bring about intimacy only intensifies the client's anxiety.

Glasser (1976) expresses a great deal of support for the work of P/P officers, although he cautions persons in corrections, as well as other fields, against the use of punishment. "For many delinquents," he notes, "punishment serves as a source of involvement. They receive attention through delinquent behavior, if only that of the police, court, probation counselor, and prison [workers]. . . . A failing person rationalizes the punishment as a reason for the anger that caused him to be hostile" (95).

Like behavior modification, RT is symptom oriented. The P/P client is in treatment because he or she has caused society to take action as a result of his or her behavior. If the worker can remove the symptoms and make the client responsible, that will satisfy society and relieve the client of anxiety caused by fear of being incarcerated. Schmideberg (1975: 24) states that for a delinquent symptom to disappear, it is usually necessary for the person to accomplish three interrelated tasks:

1. Face it full with all its implications and consequences.
2. Decide to stop it and consider the factors that precipitate it.
3. Make a definite effort to stop it.

She maintains that a general and nondirective method is not likely to change symptoms that the client may find satisfying (e.g., drugs to the addict, excitement and money to the robber, or forced sex to the rapist). Reality therapists "ask clients to do more than merely describe their behavior, their wants, their perceptions, their level of commitment, or their plans. They ask clients to make judgments about them," as if they were looking in a mirror (Wubbolding, 2000: 111). RT requires that clients evaluate their actions.

Richard Rachin (1974) states that the reality therapist seeks to help the client act responsibly. As opposed to the more distant approach of social casework, the reality therapist becomes emotionally involved—warm, tough, interested, and a sensitive human being who genuinely gives a damn and demonstrates it. RT is concerned only with behavior that can be tried and tested on a reality basis; only with the problems of the present. The reality therapist is not interested in uncovering underlying motivations or drives; rather, he or she concentrates on helping the person act in a manner that will help him or her meet individual needs responsibly. Although the reality therapist praises responsible behavior and provides recognition for positive accomplishment, he or she offers no crying towel. Sympathy can indicate that the worker lacks confidence in the client's ability to act responsibly.

Glasser developed RT while he was a psychiatrist at the Ventura School, an institution for the treatment of older adolescent girls who had been unsuccessful on probation. Because this technique evolved within the field of corrections and the realities of dealing with delinquent behavior, many have accepted and applied RT to P/P rehabilitation. RT flows easily from the P/P officer's need to hold the offender accountable for his or her behavior. Some maintain that the value emphasis in RT coincides with the paternalistic and perhaps authoritarian attitudes of some P/P officers. Carl Bersani states that "Glasser's writings do not provide a systematic methodology for clearly separating the moral standards of the counselor from that of the client" (1989: 188). Although Glasser does not deal with theory and RT is practice oriented, the theoretical underpinnings are close to those in behavior modification. Instead of manipulating the environment or using tangible reinforcers, the therapist develops a close relationship with the client, and uses praise or concern as positive and negative reinforcers. For this method to be carried out effectively, the worker needs to be a genuinely warm and sympathetic person who can easily relate to persons who have often committed very unpleasant acts and whose personalities may leave a great deal to be desired—no easy task. Thus, although training someone in the use of RT may be relatively easy, success requires qualities of personality that are not part of the basic qualifications for becoming a probation or parole officer.

In more recent books, Glasser (1998, 2000) notes that his earlier work did not present a theoretical foundation for RT, and he offers **choice theory,** replacing "the term responsibility with the more explicit idea that we choose all our behavior because we can't be anything but responsible for all that we choose to do" (Glasser, 2000: 227). He argues that people *choose* problematic behavior as their best effort to deal with a present, unsatisfying relationship, or worse, no relationships at all. According to choice theory, all "significant conscious behaviors that have anything to do directly with satisfying basic needs [love/belonging, freedom, fun, power, and survival] are chosen" (Glasser, 1998: 71). Therefore, "you are either the beneficiary of your own good choices or the victim of your own bad choices" (77). To the person whose behavior is destructive or inimical to his or her interests: "You are choosing what you are doing, but you are capable of choosing something better" (77).

However, RT remains practice-, not theory-based, "to teach clients how to act and think more effectively so they can better satisfy their needs"; guiding people in the direction of actually doing something about their problems (Glasser, 2000: 67).

GROUP WORK

Group work provides a therapeutic milieu wherein individuals agree to help one another; in contrast with the worker in casework, the group is the agency of help. The basic operating premise of social group work is that "groups of people with similar needs can be a source of mutual support, mutual aid and problem solving" (Brown, 1986: 10). In the group, "every member is a potential helper" (11). Helen Northern states that one of the advantages of the use of groups "is that stimulation toward improvement arises from a network of interpersonal influences in which all members participate" (1969: 52). The theory underlying the use of the group is that the impact provided by peer interaction is more powerful than worker–client reactions within the one-to-one situation of social casework. Furthermore, groups "help members realize that they are not alone with their problems" (Toseland and Rivas, 1998: 17). They can instill hope and impart information through a shared interaction. Group members promote the learning of basic social skills. The group serves a cathartic function: Members can experience and express feelings in a safe and confidential environment (Gladding, 1999).

In P/P, groups consist of members who share a common status, in this case legally determined. Groups in P/P may also be organized on the basis of age or around a common problem, such as substance abuse. The group is a mutual aid society in which members are given an opportunity to share experiences and assist each other with problems in a safe, controlled environment. The group helps to confirm for each member the fact that others share similar problems—"are in the same boat"—thus reducing the sense of isolation. With the help of the worker, members are able to share a sense of purpose and develop a commitment to helping each other through patterns of group interaction: "As members offer solutions to common problems, make supportive comments, and share in the skill development of fellow members by participating in group exercises, they become committed to helping each other" (Shaffer and Galinsky, 1987: 26).

The group can reduce the anxiety of having to report alone to a P/P officer; collaboration tends to offset the more direct authority of the one-to-one situation and to lower the impact of sociocultural differences between client and worker. As Gisela Konopka (1983: 93) points out, "In a group members support each other; they are not alone in the face of authority." In a group, she notes, the offender is surrounded by equals; he or she is not a client, but a *member*. This arrangement permits "feelings of identification that are impossible to achieve on an individual basis with even the most accepting social caseworker" (97). Group work also requires a level of skill and training that is not widely available in social work in general and P/P practice in particular. In P/P, the groups are typically open ended because members enter and leave—complete their sentence or violate supervision—at various intervals.

A variety of approaches to group work may be applied in correctional settings, often depending on the theoretical stance of the agency or worker, including gestalt therapy, transactional analysis, and psychoanalytic group therapy, all of which are rooted in psychoanalytic theory; and guided group interaction, which is based on sociological, small group theory and behavior modification.

Cognitive Learning Skills Training.   A popular group approach in probation and parole entails the application of cognitive behavior theory and is known as **cognitive learning skills training** (CST) or *problem-solving therapy* (PST). This approach views criminal behavior not as the symptom of some disease but as the result of a combination of social and economic situations and behavioral factors. For example, a *low social intelligence* involves offenders who have deficits in the ability to envision the consequences of their behavior and are unable to use means-end reasoning to achieve their goals. Operating at the ego level of development, they are unable to place themselves in someone else's position or understand another's behavior. The CST approach is based on a belief that "individuals can be taught to be better problem-solving thinkers" (Husband and Platt, 1993: 34).

CST/PST "emphasizes the importance of problem-solving skills that can be applied to a variety of problem situations. These include skills such as awareness of interpersonal problems, defining problems, causal thinking, consequential or alternative thinking, means-ends thinking, and perspective-taking" (Husband and Platt, 1993: 33).

Moral Reconation Therapy

Used by P/P agencies ranging from Arkansas to the state of Washington, moral reconation therapy (MRT) is a program designed to promote positive lifestyle changes—reconation refers to a redirecting of decision making to higher standards of moral reasoning. This group approach is led by a facilitator trained in the MRT philosophy and method. Participants are chosen based on a perceived willingness to change current lifestyles and typically around a shared problem, such as substance abuse or sex offenses. There are reading and homework assignments. Group members are asked to briefly look at their past to gain insight into choices they have made and the specific motivations behind these choices. Then, they take an in-depth look at what makes up their life situation and how they are spending their time. Participants are encouraged to set goals and break these down in achievable steps.

Training is designed to modify impulsive, egocentric, illogical, and rigid thinking, and to teach offenders to think—consider the consequences—before acting. The sessions can be conducted by P/P officers who receive relevant training. Generally, 40 two-hour sessions with audiovisual presentations, role-playing, behavior rehearsal, and reasoning exercises are offered. With 6 to 10 offenders, the therapist—called a *coach*—leads the group in problem solving, anger management, negotiation skills, value enhancement, critical reasoning, creative thinking, planning, and decision making. A focus is placed on enabling offenders to think in terms of options/alternatives to gain greater control over their own lives. Exercises ask offenders to respond to dilemmas, target skills, apply the skills and techniques, and then return to the group to discuss the experience.

Some problems in implementing CST/PST include that groups require a specific starting and completion date, which is complicated by offenders being placed on supervision and completing supervision at different times. Also, P/P officers may not be comfortable in the role of "coach" and may resist training.

This section has examined psychological theories and methods of rehabilitation; the next one looks at some sociological theories that have application to P/P practice.

SOCIOLOGICAL THEORY

Psychological theory attempts to identify causes of criminal behavior within the individual actor and to treat the causes accordingly. Sociological theory places crime in a social context, adding to our understanding of individual offenders. The following sections briefly review those sociological theories most relevant to P/P practice.

Anomie

The concept of **anomie,** derived from the Greek meaning "lack of law," was developed by the French sociologist Emile Durkheim (1858–1917) to explain variations in suicide rates. In 1938, Robert Merton "Americanized" the concept of anomie, which became part of what are often called **strain theories.** Merton argues that no other society is as close to the United States in considering economic success as an absolute value. Furthermore, he says, in the United States, "the pressure of prestige-bearing success tends to eliminate the effective social constraint over the means employed to this end. The 'end-justifies-the-means' doctrine becomes a guiding tenet for action when the cultural structure unduly exalts the end and the social organization unduly limits possible recourse to approved means" (Merton, 1938: 681):

"The desire to make money without regard to the means in which one sets about doing it, is symptomatic of the malintegration at the heart of American society" (Taylor et al., 1973: 93).

According to Merton, anomie results when people are confronted by the contradiction between goals and means—**strain**—and "become estranged from a society that promises them in principle what they are denied in reality [economic opportunity]" (1964: 218). Despite numerous success stories—the poor boy from humble origins who becomes rich and famous—"we know that in this same society that proclaims the right, and even the duty, of lofty aspirations for all, men do not have equal access to the opportunity structure" (Merton, 1964: 218). This point is particularly true of the most disadvantaged segments of our population who become the clients of our probation, prison, and parole systems.

How do persons respond to the anomic condition? Most simply scale down their aspirations and conform to conventional social norms. Some rebel, rejecting the conventional social structure and seek, instead, to establish a "new social order" through political action or by establishing alternative lifestyles. Two responses, *retreatism* and *innovation*, are of particular interest for P/P practice.

Retreatism means that all attempts to reach conventional social goals are abandoned in favor of a deviant adaptation—a "retreat" to alcohol and drug abuse. Time and energy are now expended to reach an attainable goal: getting "high." **Innovation** is a term used by Merton to describe the adoption of illegitimate means to gain success. Societal goals of success have been incorporated and accepted, but the person finds access to legitimate means for becoming successful limited—and anomie results. Crime is viewed as a basically utilitarian adaptation to the anomic situation. Thus, with the innovation response, "the ends justify the means," whereas with retreatism, the ends ("getting high") are sufficiently reduced as to make the means readily accessible.

Merton assumes a consensus and commitment to "American values"—that is, an attitude fixated on moneymaking pervades our society. This assumption does not account for nonutilitarian deviance or the class-linked dynamics of criminal behavior. More recent versions of strain theory have expanded the goals of American youth to include such short-term variables as popularity with the opposite sex, good school grades, and athletic achievements. This enlargement would explain conditions of strain experienced by middle-class youth because these goals are not necessarily class linked. For adults, the failure to achieve expected goals causes strain that in some persons leads to anger, resentment, and rage—emotional states that can lead to criminal behavior (Agnew, 1992). Robert Agnew (1992) suggests that social justice or equity might be at the root of strain; in this case, a sense of being dealt with unfairly—adversity is blamed on others—and not simply an inability to reach goals, results in strain.

What does the theory of anomie offer the P/P officer and the real problems of his or her practice? One consideration has to do with aspirations. Offenders often have unrealistic goals; their aspirations surpass their ability. In such cases, if anomie is to be avoided, the P/P officer must help the client to make a realistic assessment of the situation, and then to assist him or her with achieving goals that are both constructive and reality based. Each client should be encouraged to achieve to the limits of his or her ability. The officer also has a responsibility to see that the client's goals are not blocked by such barriers as discrimination. In such instances, the P/P officer must make use of the various agencies that are responsible for enforcing equal opportunity laws.

Differential Association

As proposed by Edwin Sutherland (1883–1950), **differential association** explains how criminal behavior is transmitted (not how it originates). According to Sutherland (1973), criminal behavior is learned, and the principal part of learning criminal behavior occurs within intimate personal groups based on the degree of intensity, frequency, and duration of the association. The person learns, in addition to the techniques of committing crime, the drives, attitudes, and rationalizations that add up to a favorable precondition to criminal behavior. Much criminal and noncriminal behavior has the same goal—securing economic and personal status. Differential association accounts for the difference in selecting criminal or noncriminal methods for achieving the goals. The process of learning criminal behavior by association with criminal and anticriminal patterns involves all the mechanisms that are involved in any other learning (Boy Scouts and gangsters learn behavior in the same manner).

In sum, criminal behavior results from the strength or intensity of criminal associations and is the result of an accumulative learning process. A pictorial portrayal of differential association can easily be conceived of in terms of a balanced scale that starts out level. On each side is accumulated the varying weights of criminal and noncriminal associations. At some theoretical point, criminal activity will result with an excess of criminal associations over the noncriminal or prosocial ones.

What import does this theory have for P/P practice? As noted earlier in the discussion of P/P regulations (see chapters 2, 4, and 8), they usually contain prohibitions against certain associations. A person on P/P is usually cautioned against associating with others similarly situated. This recommendation can easily be seen as a practical attempt to respond to the theory of differential association. In addition, the P/P officer can provide exposure to prosocial associations, an exposure and influence that conceivably can help to balance out our theoretical scale. The officer can assist the client with securing and encouraging association with community, charitable, religious, athletic, fraternal, and other such organizations.

Delinquent Subcultures

"**Subcultures** are patterns of values, norms, and behavior which have become traditional among certain groups. These groups may be of many types, including occupational and ethnic groups, social classes, occupants of 'closed institutions' [e.g., prisons, mental hospitals] and various age grades." They are "important frames of reference through which individuals and groups see the world and interpret it" (Short, 1968: 11; emphasis added).

Albert Cohen (1965: 86) argues that certain lower-class subcultures negate middle-class values, and this negation is a severe handicap. Certain cultural characteristics are necessary to achieve success in our society, and the upbringing of a middle-class child is more likely to develop these characteristics—for example, ability to postpone gratification, skills for achievement, industry and thrift, control of physical aggression, and cultivation of manners/politeness. Certainly, most P/P clients lack many of these requisites for adjustment to the wider society.

James Short (1968: 16) concludes that the subcultural delinquent gang discourages expression of conventional values, and "values which are given active support within the context of gang interaction, for example, toughness and sexual prowess, are not conducive to conventional types of achievement." According to Walter Miller (1958), the delinquent is adhering to forms of behavior as they are defined within his or her community. The **delinquent subculture** is different, the focal concern being *trouble*, which often involves fighting or sexual adventures while drinking; troublesome behavior for women frequently means sexual involvement with disadvantageous consequences. Miller contends that any desire to avoid troublesome behavior is based less on a commitment to legal or larger social order norms than on a desire to avoid the possible legal and other undesirable consequences of the action. This position would justify the threat of a P/P violation as a valuable tool for P/P officers. Although trouble-producing behavior is a source of status, nontrouble-producing behavior is required to avoid legal and other complications. This source of conflict for the lower-class youngster may be resolved in a legitimate manner by becoming part of an organization with high levels of discipline, such as the military or the police.

Another focal concern is *toughness*, traced by Miller (1958: 9) to the significant proportion of lower-class boys reared in female-dominated households and the resulting concern over homosexuality, which "runs like a persistent thread through lower-class culture." Miller refers to some of the sentiments commonly expressed in lower-class culture: "No one's going to push me around," and "I'm gonna tell him to take the job and shove it." He states that expressions of autonomy often contrast with actual patterns of behavior and that many lower-class persons actually desire a highly restrictive social environment (ranging from prison to the armed forces) with strong external controls over their behavior. Miller contends that for the lower-class person "being controlled is equated with being cared for" (1958: 13). Thus, the P/P officer will find clients resentful of controls, yet acting in such a manner as to ensure recommitment after a short period of relative freedom. The P/P officer must strive to moderate these extremes for the benefit of the client.

Elijah Anderson (1994: 82) describes a street subculture in African American communities with a "set of informal rules governing interpersonal public behavior, including violence. The rules prescribe both a proper comportment and a proper way to respond if challenged." At the center of this subcultural arrangement is preoccupation with the need for respect, being treated "right," with proper deference. The participant in this street subculture is obsessed with the possibility of being "dissed"—sensitive to slights middle-class persons would regard as petty. Status is associated with showing "nerve," a willingness to "mess" with others' property coupled with a cavalier attitude toward death. Thus, "Generally people outside the ghetto have other ways of gaining status and regard, and thus do not feel so dependent on such physical displays" (89).

The code of the streets is actually a cultural adaptation to a lack of faith in criminal justice and the frustrations of chronic poverty. "The police are most often seen as representing the dominant white society and not caring to protect inner-city residents"—the subcultural adaptation to this dilemma requires "taking care of yourself" (Anderson, 1994: 82). Frustrations associated with chronic poverty create the short-fuse phenomenon; verbal and physical abuse become routine. Children "learn that to solve any kind of interpersonal problem one must quickly resort to hitting or other violent behavior" (83). Furthermore, inner-city children are frequently subjected to neglect and must learn to fend for themselves, further hardening the street code adaptations.

Neutralization

Gresham Sykes and David Matza (1957) refer to a social psychological mechanism—**neutralization**—that permits a delinquent to accept the social norms of the wider society and, at the same time, violate these norms. Sykes and Matza (1957: 664) maintain that the delinquent actually retains his or her belief in the legitimacy of official, middle-class norms: "The juvenile delinquent frequently recognizes both the legitimacy of the dominant social order and its moral rightness." They argue that "if there existed in fact a delinquent subculture such that the delinquent viewed his illegal behavior as morally correct, we could reasonably suppose that he would exhibit no feelings of guilt or shame at detection or confinement. Instead, the major reaction would tend in the direction of indignation or a sense of martyrdom." However, the authors note, many delinquents do, indeed, experience a sense of guilt, "and its outward expression is not to be dismissed as a purely manipulative gesture to appease those in authority" (664–65).

Sykes and Matza (1957) postulate that "the delinquent does not necessarily regard those who abide by the legal rules as wrong or immoral." Furthermore, many delinquents are probably not totally immune from the demands for conformity made by the dominant social order. Therefore, "the juvenile delinquent would appear to be at least partially committed to the dominant social order in that he frequently exhibits guilt or shame when he violates its proscriptions, accords approval to certain conforming figures, and distinguishes between appropriate and inappropriate targets for his deviance" (666). They conclude that "the delinquent represents not a radical opposition to law-abiding society but something like an apologetic failure, often more sinned against than sinning in his own eyes" (667).

By using various *techniques of neutralization*, delinquents are able to avoid guilt feelings for their actions. They contend that rules are merely qualified guidelines limited to time, place, and person conditions. This line of reasoning is in accord with the legal code that requires *mens rea*, criminal intent, to be present for penal sanctions to be imposed. Delinquents justify their actions in a form that, although not valid to the larger society, is valid for them. Sykes and Matza (1957) present five types of neutralization:

1. *Denial of responsibility:* rationalizing that delinquency was not their fault (e.g., they were simply a victim of circumstances)
2. *Denial of injury:* thinking that nobody got hurt (e.g., just a prank was involved, or the insurance company will cover the damage)
3. *Denial of the victim:* believing that the victim deserved to be hurt
4. *Condemnation of the condemners:* dwelling on the weakness and motives of those in authority or judgment (e.g., police, school officials, and judges are corrupt, hate kids, etc.)
5. *Appeal to higher loyalties:* convincing themselves about necessity of action for friends, family, neighborhood, and so on

These sentiments, or variants of them, are often encountered by P/P officers in the course of presentence investigations or P/P supervision. Sykes and Matza (1957) caution against dismissing them as merely postact rationalizations because they indicate a genuine commitment to societal norms and a basis for rehabilitation.

Differential/Limited Opportunity

Richard Cloward and Lloyd Ohlin (1960) attempt to integrate anomie with differential association to explain how delinquent subcultures arise, develop various law-violating ways of life, and persist or change over time. They distinguish among three types of delinquent subculture that are a result of anomie and differential association:

1. *Criminal subculture:* gang activities devoted to utilitarian criminal pursuits (e.g., racketeering)
2. *Conflict subculture:* gang activities devoted to violence and destructive acting out as a way of gaining status
3. *Retreatist subculture:* activities in which drug abuse is the primary focus

Each of these subcultural adaptations arises out of a different set of social circumstances, or *opportunity.* Cloward and Ohlin state that the dilemma of many lower-class people is that they are unable to locate alternative avenues to success or goals (1960: 107): "Delinquent subcultures, we believe, represent specialized modes of adaptation to this problem of adjustment." The criminal and conflict subcultures provide illegal avenues, and the retreatist "anticipates defeat and now seeks to escape from the burden of the future" (1960: 107). Criminal behavior is not viewed as an individual endeavor but as part of a collective adaptation. Cloward and Ohlin note (1960: 106–107) that "many lower-class adolescents experience desperation born of the certainty that their position in the economic structure is relatively fixed and immutable—a desperation made all the more poignant by their exposure to a cultural ideology in which failure to orient oneself upward is regarded as a moral defect and failure to become mobile as proof of it."

The turn toward alternative means of success is to be understood in terms of this social-psychological phenomena. However, Cloward and Ohlin also point out that illegitimate means of success, like legitimate means, are not equally distributed throughout society (1960: 145): "Having decided that he 'can't make it legitimately,' he cannot simply choose among an array of illegitimate means, all equally available to him." Thus, for the average lower-class adolescent, a career in professional or **organized crime** (Abadinsky, 1983, 2003a; Sutherland, 1972) can be as difficult to attain as any lucrative career in the legitimate sphere of society.

This difficulty warns the P/P officer of the need to be able to differentiate persons involved in "professional" and "organized" criminality from the more frequent offender who has only limited skills and contacts. Professional and organized criminals are usually not good candidates for the rehabilitative efforts of P/P agencies. Such persons are not likely to give up criminal skills and status, which were achieved only after a considerable expenditure of time and effort, for a more conventional and law-abiding lifestyle. In these cases, the investigative and control—not the therapeutic—skills of the P/P officer must be used.

Social Control Theory

If as control theorists generally assume, most persons are sufficiently motivated by the potential rewards to commit criminal acts, why do only a few engage in criminal behavior? According to **social control theory,** "delinquent acts result when an individual's bond to society is weak or broken" (Hirschi, 1969: 16). The strength of this bond is determined by internal and external restraints. In other words, internal and external restraints determine if we move in the direction of crime or law-abiding behavior.

Internal restraints include what psychoanalytic theory refers to as the *superego*; they provide a sense of *guilt.* As noted earlier, dysfunction during early stages of childhood development, or parental influences that are not normative, can result in an adult who is devoid of prosocial internal constraints; some refer to this as psychopathology or sociopathology, or apply the diagnostic term antisocial personality disorder[2] (ADR) (Black, 1999). (Some evidence also ties ADR to a central nervous system defect.) Whether they are conceived of in terms of psychology or sociology, internal constraints are linked to the influence of the family (Hirschi, 1969)—an influence that can be supported or weakened by the presence or absence of significant external restraints, such as the P/P officer.

External restraints include social disapproval linked to public shame or social ostracism and fear of punishment. In other words, people are typically deterred from criminal behavior by the possibility of being caught and the punishment that can result, ranging from public shame to imprisonment (and in extreme cases, capital punishment). The strength of official deterrence—force of law—however, is measured according to two dimensions: risk versus reward. Risk involves the ability of the criminal justice system to detect, apprehend, and convict the offender. The amount of risk is weighed against the potential rewards. Both risk and reward, however, are relative to one's socioeconomic situation. In other words, the less one has to lose, the greater is the willingness to engage in risk. The greater the reward, the greater is the willingness to engage in risk. This theory explains why persons in deprived economic circumstances would be more willing to engage in certain criminal behavior. However, the potential rewards and a perception of relatively low risk may also explain why persons in more advantaged economic circumstances would engage in remunerative criminal behavior, such as corporate crime.

Instead of conforming to conventional norms, through differential association, some persons organize their behavior according to the norms of a delinquent or

---

[2]Diagnostic categories are found in the *Diagnostic and Statistical Manual (DSM)* published by the American Psychiatric Association.

criminal group with which they identify or to which they belong. This affiliation is most likely to occur in environments characterized by relative social disorganization, where familial and communal controls are ineffective in exerting a conforming influence. The increasing number of children living below the poverty level intertwined with a collapse of many inner-city families is creating "America's new orphans" (Gross, 1992). Conforming, prosocial behavior may be dependent on the ability of the P/P officer to monitor the client carefully combined with a realistic threat of punishment. From the casework dimension, the P/P officer may offer the client an opportunity to repair weak or broken bonds and thereby move the client in the direction of conventional behavior.

Drift

Does the juvenile delinquent move on to become an adult criminal, or does the youngster mature—and **drift**—into becoming a law-abiding member of society? David Matza (1964: 59) views the delinquent's lifestyle as not fully committed: "He drifts between criminal and conventional action." Matza denies the portrayal of a juvenile delinquent as a person committed to an oppositional culture; instead, the delinquent reveals a basic ambivalence toward his or her behavior. Matza believes that juveniles are less alienated than others in society, and that most of the time the delinquent behaves in a noncriminal manner (1964: 28): "The image of the delinquent I wish to convey is one of drift; an actor neither compelled nor committed to deeds nor freely choosing them; neither different in any single fundamental sense from the law abiding, nor the same; conforming to certain traditions in American life while partially unreceptive to other more conventional traditions."

Although Matza (1964: 158) does not contradict the idea of a delinquent subculture, he finds that the subculture is not a binding force on its members: "Loyalty is a basic issue in the subculture of delinquency partially because its adherents are so regularly disloyal. They regularly abandon the company at the age of remission for more conventional pursuits." The "age of remission" is a time when adolescent antisocial behavior is abandoned in favor of adult prosocial or conventional behavior. The crime-prone years for young men are roughly ages 15 to 25, with remission occurring after age 25. Matza's theory has important policy implications: Justice system intervention can stigmatize—label—a juvenile, thereby blocking entry into a conventional lifestyle as he or she matures into adulthood.

Labeling

A stigma, sometimes referred to in terms of **labeling** or *societal reaction theory*, is the concern of a sociological perspective known as **symbolic interactionism**:

> Symbolic interactionists suggest that categories which individuals use to render the world meaningful, and even the experience of self, are structured by socially acquired definitions. They argue that individuals, in reaction to group rewards and sanctions, gradually internalize group expectations. These internalized social definitions allow people to evaluate their own behavior from the standpoint of the group and in doing so provide a lens through which to view oneself as a social object. (Quadagno and Antonio, 1975: 33)

The focus is not the behavior of any social actor (person), but on how that behavior or actor is viewed by others—society. The societal reaction labels—stigmatizes—the actor, which results in a damaged self-image, deviant identity, and a host of negative social expectations. Think about the societal reaction to the terms *mentally ill, ex-convict,* and *parolee.* Furthermore, some argue, the damaged self-image and its ramifications can result in a "self-fulfilling prophesy." Edwin Schur (1973: 124) notes that "once an individual has been branded as a wrongdoer, it becomes extremely difficult for him to shed that new identity." The ex-convict finds it difficult to secure employment, increasing the attraction of further criminal activity. Furthermore, according to Edwin Lemert, the labeled deviant reorganizes his or her behavior in accordance with the societal reaction and "begins to employ his deviant behavior, or role based on it, as a means of defense, attack, or adjustment to the overt and covert problems created by the consequent societal reaction to him" (1951: 76). Lemert has termed this process *secondary deviation,* which is evidenced by deviants seeking to associate with others like themselves. The negative influence of the delinquent label is viewed as so detrimental to future conduct that Edwin Schur (1973) argues for *radical nonintervention*: The focus should be on avoiding the movement of adolescents into the official agencies of social control.

The P/P officer is constantly faced with the dynamics of labeling as clients encounter difficulty in returning to school, securing employment, obtaining housing, and making friends because of the stigma (label) inherent in the terms *delinquent, criminal, probationer,* and *parolee.* The label results in a negative self-image, whereby the offender's view of him- or herself is that of an inferior and unworthy person. In such a condition, he or she may seek the companionship of others similarly situated and may engage in further antisocial activities in an effort to strike back at the society that is responsible for the labeling.

Conflict Theory

Conflict theory takes its fundamental philosophy primarily from the work of Max Weber and Karl Marx. Conflict theorists are concerned with differences in power relationships. More recent conflict theorists, usually of a Marxist bent, are an outgrowth of the sociopolitical—civil rights, anti–Vietnam War, counterculture—movements of the 1960s and early 1970s. They conceive of society as better characterized by conflict than by consensus; what passes for crime and criminal justice actually represents the interests of powerful classes. Otherwise, they argue, how could a burglary netting a few dollars be classified as a felony, whereas corporate officials who pad defense contracts with millions of dollars in overcharges, or who flagrantly violate safety and restraint of trade laws, avoid incarceration or even the labeling that accompanies the processing of conventional (i.e., poor) delinquents/criminals? As noted in chapter 6, in every generation a specific class of persons always inhabits our prisons—the poor.

The conflict approach eschews theory that treats criminal behavior as a manifestation of individual pathology. Instead, crime is seen as a phenomenon generated by the social arrangements of a capitalist system. Capitalism leads to a class system of severely differentiated wealth and power; inequities in wealth and power—in life

Value of a Bad Reputation

"In fact, far from stigmatizing, prison evidently confers status in some neighborhoods. Jerome Skolnick . . . found that for drug dealers in California, imprisonment confers a certain elevated 'home boy' status, especially for gang members for whom prison and prison gangs can be an alternative site of loyalty. And according to the California Youth Authority, inmates steal state-issued prison clothing for the same reason. Wearing it when they return to the community lets everyone know they have done 'hard time'" (Petersilia, 1995: 23).

chances—causes alienation; an alienated segment of the underclass, those whose interests are not furthered by capitalism, reacts in ways defined as criminal. The legal apparatus, including a monopoly over sanctions and the use of force, serves to control the alienated population and helps to perpetuate domination by the ruling class. The criminal justice system is simply a mechanism through which the self-interests of the ruling classes are protected by functionaries in their employ. Their rule is given legitimacy by an ideology of democracy, free enterprise, and property rights whose benefits accrue primarily to those who already have wealth and power. As Karl Marx pointed out, the ideas of the ruling class are always the ruling ideas.

Within this approach, criminal behavior is sometimes romanticized as "rebellion" and criminals as some type of "primitive rebel," although most conventional crime is committed by the underclass against the underclass. During the 1960s and early 1970s, some offenders on probation or parole or prison inmates espoused conflict theory—a reflection of a politically active era. Conflict theory sensitizes the P/P officer to some of the basic inequities in our society, certainly as they are reflected in criminal justice. Although dealing with system inequities is beyond the role of the P/P officer, he or she does have an advocate role, which is discussed in chapter 10.

KEY TERMS

theory	aversive therapy
psychoanalytic theory	reality therapy
unconscious	choice theory
oral stage	group work
anal stage	cognitive learning skills training
genital stage	anomie
id	strain theories
ego	strain
superego	retreatism
antisocial personality disorder	innovation
social casework	differential association
medical model	delinquent subculture
transference	neutralization
self-determination	organized crime
learning theory/behavior modification	social control theory
reinforcers	drift
positive reinforcement	labeling
negative reinforcement	symbolic interactionism
operant conditioning	conflict theory

INTERNET CONNECTIONS

National Association of Social Workers: naswdc.org

American Psychological Association: apa.org

Glasser Institute on Reality Therapy: wglasser.com

Reality Therapy links: socc.ie/~wgii/address.htm

American Society of Criminology: asc41.com

Academy of Criminal Justice Sciences: acjs.org

REVIEW QUESTIONS

1. What is a theory?
2. What is the importance of psychoanalytic theory in probation and parole?
3. According to psychoanalytic theory, what is the importance of unconscious feelings and experiences?
4. According to psychoanalytic theory, what are the causes of behavior defined as criminal?
5. How can the superego cause criminal behavior?
6. What type of criminal behavior in the adult is related to the anal stage of development?
7. What is the relationship between social casework and the medical model?
8. What should the caseworker accomplish during the study/assessment phase of the rehabilitation process?
9. What is meant by ego support in the social casework process?
10. What is the basis of changing behavior in RT?
11. Why has RT been attractive to probation and parole agencies?
12. According to behavior modification/learning theory, what is the cause of criminal behavior?
13. What are the techniques for changing behavior according to learning theory?
14. Why is it difficult to apply behavior modification techniques to P/P practice?
15. What are the advantages of social group work over the more traditional one-to-one approach to counseling in P/P?
16. What is CST?
17. What is the difference between psychological and sociological explanations of criminal behavior?
18. How does Robert Merton use the concept of anomie to explain certain types of criminal behavior in the United States?
19. How should P/P officers deal with anomie among their clients?
20. What P/P rules are a response to differential association?
21. According to the theory of differential association, what determines if a person becomes a criminal?
22. According to Richard Cloward and Lloyd Ohlin (differential opportunity), what are the three types of delinquent subcultures that are the result of anomie and differential association?
23. According to control theory, what determines if persons engage in criminal behavior?
24. What are the characteristics that Albert Cohen states are necessary to achieve success in our society—characteristics that lower-class youth do not possess?
25. What are "techniques of neutralization"?
26. What are the negative results of labeling?
27. What is the conflict view of criminal behavior?
28. How does labeling impact P/P?

CHAPTER 10

Probation and Parole Officers

This chapter examines P/P officer roles, responsibilities, and qualifications, as well as the use of volunteers. The first section outlines the varied tasks of P/P officers.

THE TASKS OF PROBATION/PAROLE OFFICERS

P/P officers spend their working time writing reports, visiting and interviewing clients, making referrals, and talking to persons in and out of the criminal justice system. These tasks can be divided into 10 parts (based on Strong, 1981):

1. *Information manager.* The primary focus is the collection, classification, and analysis of data about the individual case and the community.

2. *Evaluator.* This involves assessing personal or community problems, weighing alternatives and priorities, and making decisions for action.

3. *Enabler.* The primary objective is to provide support and to facilitate change in the behavior patterns, habits, and perceptions of individual clients. The key assumption is that problems may be alleviated or crises may be prevented by modifying, adding, or extinguishing discrete bits of behavior; increasing insights; or changing values and perceptions.

4. *Educator.* Instruction is used in the sense of an objective rather than a method. The primary objectives are to convey and impart information and knowledge, and to develop various kinds of skills. A great deal of social casework is simple instruction.

5. *Broker.* The primary objective is to steer (refer) clients to existing services that can be of benefit to them. The focus is on enabling or helping people to use the system and to negotiate its pathways. A further objective is to link elements of the service system with one another. The essential benefit of this objective is the physical hookup of the person with the source of help and the physical connection of elements of the service system with one another.

6. *Advocate.* The primary objective is to fight for the rights and dignity of people in need of help. The key assumption is that there will be instances when practices, regulations, and general conditions will prevent individuals from receiving services, using resources, or obtaining help. This position includes the notion of advocating changes in laws, rules, and regulations on behalf of a whole class of persons or segment of society. Advocacy aims at removing obstacles or barriers that prevent people from exercising their rights or receiving benefits and using the resources they need. When I was a parole officer in New York, because of Department of Motor Vehicles

regulations, parolees with legitimate employment needs had a difficult time obtaining a motor vehicle license. Advocacy on the part of the Parole Officers Association was effective in changing these regulations and removing the unnecessary obstacles.

7. *Mediator.* The primary objective is to mediate between people and resource systems and among resource systems. The key assumption is that problems do not exist within people or within resource systems, but rather in the interactions between people and resource systems and between systems. As opposed to the advocate, the mediator stance is one of neutrality.

8. *Community planner.* This involves participating in and assisting neighborhood planning groups, agencies, community agents, or governments in the development of community programs to assure client needs are represented and met to the greatest extent feasible.

9. *Detection.* Detection involves identifying when a client is at risk or when the community is at risk from the client. The first objective for the officer is to identify the individuals who are experiencing difficulty (at crisis) or who are in danger of becoming a risk to the community. A second objective is to identify conditions in the community itself that may be contributing to personal problems of the client and that might raise his or her assigned risk level (such as lack of jobs or job training, or the influx of easily available controlled substances). A third objective is to determine when the community is at risk from the offender and when steps are needed to protect the community.

10. *Enforcer.* This role requires the use of authority to revoke supervision because of changes in the status quo, which involves heightened community or individual risk outside the control of the officer.

The degree to which one task will be favored over another is dependent on the particular model of agency that employs the P/P officer.

PROBATION/PAROLE OFFICER ROLES AND AGENCY MODELS

What role will the P/P officer assume toward the client? The literature (e.g., Allen, Carlson, and Parks, 1979; Klockars, 1972) reveals three basic roles:

1. *Law enforcement:* P/P officer whose primary concern is the protection of the community through control of the P/P client
2. *Rehabilitation:* P/P officer whose primary concern is the improved welfare of the P/P client
3. *Blend:* P/P officer who attempts to effect a combination of law enforcement and treatment

These roles, however, are deficient when discussed outside agency contexts or models:

- **Control model.** Control of the P/P client's activities is the primary focus. Unannounced home and employment visits, checks for drug use, and a close working relationship with law enforcement agencies are the standard practice.
- **Social service model.** The primary focus is on client needs, including employment, housing, and counseling that provide social and psychological support. These agencies often have contracts with private service providers.
- **Combined model.** This model requires P/P officers to provide social services, while attending to control functions.

Control model ⟷ Combined model ⟷ Social service model

Most P/P agencies would be located somewhere in the middle of this continuum, with probation agencies typically found on the right of the combined model and parole agencies on the left. Although it would not be unusual to find many social service model agencies, particularly in probation, the *control* model would not be found anywhere in its pure form, although specific programs—such as electronic monitoring, intensive supervision, or community control (discussed in chapters 12 and 13)—may be based on a control model. The P/P officer with a law enforcement focus is more likely to be found in—indeed, would be appropriate for—the control or combined model agency. The P/P officer with an emphasis on rehabilitation would be most likely found in the social service model agency. The issue, then, is not what role the P/P officer will assume with respect to clients but rather whether the role is compatible with the agency model. In the combined model, some use can be made of P/P officer role variation (I prefer the term *style*). Supervisors can assign cases on the basis of matching the officer's style with the salient characteristics of the offender. For example, an officer with a more authoritarian style would be matched with "heavy" (i.e., professional or career) criminals. An officer with a gentler style would be appropriate for certain situational offenders or perhaps youthful clients.

In a combined model agency, officers should integrate their control or community protection role with their social service role, while maintaining flexibility to stress one over the other in an individualized response to each case. For example, a young offender under supervision for joyriding in a stolen car will receive a different response than an experienced offender who is associated with organized criminal activity. In P/P treatment, officers adapt those methods that are useful to their practice, while sacrificing the rest (sometimes cynically) on the altar of reality. Support for combining the social service with control function comes from Elizabeth Hutchinson (1987), who argues that social workers should avoid sending out other people to carry out coercive actions.

Georgia Parole Officers.   Charged with the task of protecting Georgia's citizens by assisting the reintegration of the inmate back into the community and returning to prison those who fail, they are, on the one hand, a counselor and mentor and, on the other hand, a law enforcement officer and a prosecutor. In the course of 1 day, a parole officer may participate in the arrest of a parole violator, help another get a job, counsel a family dispute, interview an inmate or his family, assist in obtaining treatment for a substance abuser, testify at a parole revocation hearing, and make an assortment of contacts with parolees, their families, and their employers. Every day, parole officers travel Georgia's city streets and rural backroads, in many cases areas that are potentially dangerous, to monitor parolee compliance with the conditions of parole and to help them break with their criminal past. Being a parole officer means being accessible around the clock, with after-hours calls from parolees, anxious families, and law enforcement always a possibility. As certified peace officers, they are frequently called on to assist in emergency situations, such as floods and tornadoes. Still, many parole officers find the time to volunteer for community projects, school programs, church activities, and an assortment of other ways that they know will positively impact the quality of their hometown life. Georgia's parole officers work every day to intervene with and to successfully bring about change in others who had until that point been unable to abide by the rules of society.

Multnomah County (Portland, Oregon) Probation/Parole Officer.   The Multnomah County Department of Community Justice promotes public safety and strives to reduce recidivism among juvenile delinquents and adult offenders through a balance of supervision, services, and sanctions. Officers provide counseling, case management, and supervision of adult clients on formal P/P. They identify individual needs of clients; assess client's immediate functional and dysfunctional patterns;

work with community agencies to develop and implement individual and family treatment plans; and counsel clients on how to comply with their P/P conditions, legal obligations, and other requirements of the court. P/P officers counsel clients on the consequences of noncompliance. They develop time frames to assist clients in meeting goals and court-ordered conditions, and monitor client compliance through provider agency reports and by making unannounced visits to the client's residence or place of employment. They develop individual supervision plans to enhance the client's compliance with P/P conditions and conduct searches and seize evidence as authorized; they may arrest, detain, search, handcuff, and transport clients. They must maintain a chronological record of all contacts and an ongoing evaluation of client's progress. P/P officers also prepare presentence and postsentence investigation reports for the court.

THE PROBATION/PAROLE OFFICER AS AN AGENT OF REHABILITATION

Chapter 9 reviewed a variety of approaches to rehabilitation, the implication being that P/P officers can operationalize these approaches with their clients. However, requirements for P/P officer positions (discussed later in this chapter) are usually a bachelor's degree, which is hardly adequate to provide the background, let alone the skill, for carrying out a sophisticated rehabilitation role. Shelle Dietrich (1979: 15) points out that "the probation officer usually has not received extensive specialized training for the function of change agent; that is, the function of being competent to facilitate another person's changing his behavior, attitude, affect, or personality style." Generally, the P/P officer is not educated or trained to be a treatment agent: "It is an unrealistic expectation of probation [and parole] officers to expect themselves to be competent in an area for which they have not received adequate training" (15).

In a review of the literature purporting to advise P/P officers whose background is otherwise deficient how to become effective change agents, Dietrich (1979: 16–19) found it simplistic and at times potentially harmful to the client. Thus, she argues, professional intrusion is often advocated in areas for which the P/P officer lacks training. Cynically, she proposes, "Why not go ahead and prescribe medications, prepare legal documents, or write an insurance plan for the probationer?" (17). Dietrich cautions: "And what about the probationer? Certainly, his position in relation to the probation officer is a vulnerable one. Shouldn't the probationer be protected from being the involuntary patient of an unlicensed and untrained person, even if the person's intentions are the most purely humanistic?" (18).

Dietrich raises two other related issues:

- Is the therapeutic enterprise possible in a P/P setting?
- Given a positive response to this question, is it realistic to expect the delivery of treatment in P/P, where caseloads usually average between 80 and 100?

She argues that, even if the P/P officer "were optimally skillful in such therapeutic endeavors," without the full promise of confidentiality (impossible in a P/P setting), full and open discussion, the basis for a therapeutic relationship, is not possible (Dietrich, 1979: 18). Dietrich is using a rather narrow definition of *therapy*, however, and within that definition she is correct—therapy is not possible in a P/P setting. This author believes that therapy is more usefully defined here as the purposeful use of self to improve the social and psychological functioning of a client, and thus, therapy is possible within the confidentiality limitations of a P/P agency. Therapy, however, is *not* possible given the lack of adequate education and training and the usual excessive caseloads encountered in P/P practice. Accordingly, some propose that treatment should take the form of the P/P officer acting as broker or advocate.

THE PROBATION/PAROLE OFFICER AS BROKER OR ADVOCATE

The provision of necessary services in P/P practice often requires that the P/P officer act as a **broker** or **advocate.** Private and public agencies may view the P/P client as undesirable or even undeserving. Welfare, mental health, and educational agencies may see the client as threatening. Their responses to a client's needs may lead to frustration and a frustrated client who reacts in a manner that does, indeed, appear threatening—frustration control is often a problem with P/P clientele—a self-fulfilling prophecy.

Eric Carlson and Evalyn Parks see the *brokerage* approach in P/P as almost diametrically opposed to the treatment approach because the P/P officer "is not concerned primarily with understanding or changing the behavior of the probationer, but rather with assessing the concrete needs of the individual and arranging for the probationers to receive services that directly address these needs" (1979: 120). Carlson and Parks point out that in this approach there

> is significantly less emphasis placed on the development of a close, one-to-one relationship between the probation officer and the probationer. The probation officer functions primarily as a manager or broker of resources and social services which are already available from other agencies. It is the task of the probation officer to assess the service needs of the probationer, locate the social service agency which addresses those needs as its primary function, to refer the probationer to the appropriate agency, and to follow up referrals to make sure that the probationer actually received the services. [Thus] under the brokerage approach, it can be said that the probation officer's relationship with community service agencies is more important than his relationship with an individual probationer. The brokerage approach does share with the casework approach the importance of the probationer's participation in developing his own probation plan. (1979: 120–121)

They note that "the essential tasks of the brokerage orientation to probation are the management of available community resources and the use of those services to meet the needs of probation clients" (123).

Accordingly, little emphasis is placed on the quality of the relationship that is developed between probation officers and the probationer; rather, more emphasis is placed on the close working relationship between the probation officer and the staff members of community social service agencies. Counseling and guidance are considered inappropriate activities for the probation officer; no attempt is made to change the behavior of the probationer. The primary function of the probation officer is to assess the concrete needs of each probationer and make appropriate referrals to existing community services. Should the needed service not be available in the community, the probation officer is responsible for encouraging the development of that service.

THE PROBATION/PAROLE OFFICER AS LAW ENFORCEMENT AGENT

The most controversial role of a P/P officer is that of enforcer. The P/P officer as law enforcement agent is related to the *control model* of supervision in much the same way as the rehabilitation or broker-advocate role is related to the *social service model.* For a discussion of the law enforcement role of the P/P officers to be meaningful, one must consider this position within the context of agency model. However, many critics of a law enforcement role for P/P officers render unequivocal statements without any discussion of the model. Thus, without any attention to agency model, the American Correctional Association (1981: 36), in its *Standards for Adult Probation and Parole Field Services,* states: "Probation/parole officers do not routinely carry weapons in the performance of their duties."

A more productive approach is to identify the agency model and then decide if it is compatible with a law enforcement role. Paul Keve (1979: 432) states that agencies "suffer sharp internal problems" when agency policy seems to require surveillance and arrest activities while the agency prohibits officers from carrying firearms. For example, a community corrections (parole) officer in the state of Washington "conducts searches and arrests; detains serious violators after proper approval; serves parole subpoenas; transports arrested offenders to jail"—but can carry a firearm while on duty only if they or their immediate family have been threatened. Montgomery County, Ohio, Community Control (probation) Officers and Solano County, California, probation officers are expected to make arrests and conduct searches and seizures, but are prohibited from carrying firearms or other weapons or chemical agents in the performance of their duties. A more rational approach was taken by the Texas Adult Probation Commission, which voiced its opposition to *both* arrest powers and the carrying of firearms by probation officers (now called community supervision officers).[1] In Virginia, although they are authorized to carry firearms, P/P officers are directed to have law enforcement personnel make arrests and conduct searches.

In 1975, I surveyed 53 adult parole agencies in the United States (the 50 states, the District of Columbia, Puerto Rico, and the U.S. Division of Probation, which also supervised parolees). The survey indicated that parole agencies differ greatly with respect to officers carrying firearms and arresting violators. Several years later, Keve (1979) conducted a similar survey of top administrators in P/P in the United States and found that a little more than half of the jurisdictions prohibited the carrying of a firearm. In 1986, the Oklahoma Department of Corrections surveyed all 50 states with respect to the carrying of firearms by P/P officers: "The study indicated that about 48 percent of all P/P agencies allowed their officers to carry a gun on the job. Only 24 percent of the jurisdictions polled said their officers routinely carried a weapon" (Jones and Robinson, 1989: 90).

In more recent years, as more and more P/P agencies move toward a control model of supervision, arrest powers and the carrying of firearms by P/P officers have become increasingly common—for several compelling reasons. Many agencies are confronted by P/P personnel who feel endangered by having to enter high-crime areas, particularly during evening hours, to visit serious offenders at home. In Winnebago County, Illinois, "the concern of officer safety became apparent because of escalating violence in the community which brought in discretion and common sense in terms of when and when not to accomplish certain field contacts. This also resulted in the development of specific home visit procedural guidelines and availability of pepper spray and a radio." Maryland P/P officers may also opt to carry pepper spray (but not firearms). P/P officers in jurisdictions that require field work but do not permit the carrying of firearms are apparently being exposed to increasing level of danger. A study in Minnesota, for example, found that about

Probation and Parole Models

"There seems little doubt that probation and parole work has moved away from a general embracing of offender assistance [social service] models into a solid marriage with control, compliance, and punishment models of community supervision" (Castellano, 1997: 22).

---

[1]In 1998, Texas P/P officers were given permission to carry concealed firearms, which is the right of any civilian in Texas who has completed the required training.

Hazards of Parole Supervision

The very nature of supervising offenders subjects P/P officers to potentially hazardous events on a routine basis. Fortunately, not every officer has had a bad or harrowing experience, but many have. On one occasion, New York State parole officer Tom Brancato was strangled almost to the point of unconsciousness in a remote wooded area where he stopped to see his parolee at work. This attack occurred by surprise after Officer Brancato had asked the parolee to have a seat in his car. As soon as they were seated the parolee reached over, grabbed Officer Brancato by the throat, and began choking him. Wedged between the bucket seats of his Volkswagen, the officer's right arm and gun were pinned beneath him. After considerable effort he managed to get his gun with his left hand and stick the barrel in the parolee's ear. Case closed.

20 percent of P/P officers had been physically assaulted, 4 percent one or more times in the past year, and 43 percent reported being physically or verbally threatened one or more times during the past year (Arola and Lawrence, 1998). A study in Pennsylvania highlights the danger of P/P work: "Victimization of Pennsylvania probation and parole workers is extensive and pervasive" (Parsonage and Bushey, 1989: 24). William Parsonage (1990) expresses concern over similar findings in other states. In many agencies, officers are demanding protective training and the right to carry firearms, and Parsonage (1990: 35) reports that "during the past few years, an increasing number of agencies have authorized the carrying of firearms under various circumstances." In Minnesota, however, "the majority of probation officers "seem to agree that the authority for carrying firearms and making arrests is best left with police officers" (Arola and Lawrence, 1998: 10). In a dramatic change, in 2003, the New York City Department of Probation began arming its almost 900 officers.

In many jurisdictions, particularly in high-crime urban areas, the police/sheriff are either unwilling or unable to provide sufficient warrant-enforcement services. In 1999, for example, California had 2.5 million unserved warrants (Associated Press, 1999). If the agency does not enforce its own warrants, they often go unattended; the potential danger to the public is obvious as hundreds or, in larger jurisdictions, thousands of P/P warrants go unenforced. Warrants turned over to outside agencies are occasionally used to force P/P violators into becoming informants, and P/P agencies usually have rules against using clients as informants.

Absconders

Absconding from supervision is a perennial problem in P/P: Offenders stop reporting and their whereabouts are unknown. The failure to expeditiously locate and arrest these persons presents a danger to the community and encourages other probationers/parolees to follow their example. The New York State Division of Parole has always placed a high priority on this problem and has a unit in place to track down absconders. Field parole officers have 45 days to follow all readily available leads in locating and arresting their absconders, at which time the case is turned over to the six-person Absconder Search Unit (ASU). Because ASU officers have no caseloads to supervise, they can spend time conducting surveillances of known residences or hangouts, in addition to using other fugitive apprehension techniques.

In practice, P/P agency policy with respect to firearms falls into one of three categories:

1. *Officers are not permitted to carry firearms based either on state law or agency policy.* For example:
   - Arizona. Maricopa County (Phoenix) adult probation officers are peace officers but the agency prohibits the carrying of firearms while on duty.
   - California. Although they are peace officers, probation officers of the Alameda County Probation Department are prohibited from carrying firearms.
   - Hawaii parole officers do not have arrest powers or carry firearms.
   - Illinois. Winnebago County probation officers are not authorized to carry firearms or effect a forcible custodial arrest. (In Illinois, arrest authority and the carrying of firearms by probation officers is at the option of the circuit court of each county.)
   - Indiana probation officers are not considered law enforcement officers and have no powers of arrest. In Marion County, a special unit of probation officers has been certified as special deputies with the county sheriff, and are responsible for serving warrants and conducting high-risk field investigations.
   - In Kansas, although they are authorized to make arrests, probation officers (judicial branch) and parole officers (executive branch) are not permitted to carry firearms while on duty.
   - Minnesota corrections (parole) agents are peace officers, but agency policy prohibits the carrying of firearms.
   - Maryland P/P agents are social workers and have no peace officer responsibilities or powers.
   - Nebraska prohibits parole officers from carrying firearms, although they are authorized to conduct searches and arrest parolees.
   - South Dakota parole agents are not by statute considered law enforcement officers and do not carry weapons.
   - Tennessee parole officers are not permitted to carry firearms on duty.
   - Wyoming P/P agents are not permitted to carry firearms or make arrests.
2. *Officers are by statute peace/law enforcement officers, but the agency either restricts or discourages the carrying of weapons.* For example:
   - California. The San Francisco Adult Probation Department prohibits the routine carrying of firearms, but permits certain officers to carry weapons, for example, those assigned to the gang violence suppression program.
   - Illinois. Cook County adult probation officers are prohibited from carrying firearms, except those assigned to special units such as intensive supervision.
   - Indiana. The Adult Probation Department of Allen County states that, although its personnel are allowed by statute to carry firearms and arrest probationers, the court discourages the carrying of a firearm.
   - Ohio. The Montgomery County Adult Probation Department allows officers to carry firearms *only* on special assignments, such as transportation of a probation violator; or in emergency situations, such as the escape of a dangerous offender or a "highly threatening office disturbance."
   - Pennsylvania. Bucks County probation officers are designated peace officers but prohibited by agency policy from carrying firearms.
   - Washington permits community corrections officers to carry firearms only as a result of a threat while on duty and then only for a maximum of 90 days.
3. *Officers are by statute peace/law enforcement officers and the agency permits or requires all qualified personnel to carry firearms.* For example:
   - Employment as a P/P officer in Alabama and Nevada and a parole officer in New York requires firearms qualification and carrying of weapons while on duty.

- Firearms training is mandatory for Arkansas P/P officers, California (adult and youth) parole agents, Colorado parole officers, North Carolina probation officers, North Dakota field (P/P) officers, Oklahoma P/P officers, and Connecticut correctional rehabilitation services (parole) officers, and they are authorized to carry department-issued weapons.
- Illinois, Kentucky, Massachusetts, Michigan, Missouri, New Jersey, and Pennsylvania parole officers/agents are permitted to carry firearms provided that they have met applicable training and proficiency standards.
- Probation officers in Dauphin County, Pennsylvania; Bibb County, Georgia; Suffolk County, Nassau County, and Onondaga County, New York; Pima County, Arizona; San Bernardino County, California; and Florida correctional probation officers who have qualified in the handling of weapons may carry a firearm.
- Probation officers for the Georgia Department of Corrections who complete firearms training and receive permission from the deputy commissioner may carry firearms on duty.

A gray area on this issue may exist, exemplified by the policy of the Federal Probation and Pretrial Services Division. Although federal probation and pretrial services officers are not permitted to carry firearms routinely, an officer who has presented sufficient reasons why carrying a firearm is necessary in general or for a specific assignment can be granted authority. The actual degree to which firearms authority is granted varies considerably from district to district. In Idaho, although P/P officers are weapons-trained peace officers, they do not routinely carry weapons; however, the district manager can give permission to carry a weapon. In Iowa, each of the state's eight judicial districts is free to decide if its P/P officers will carry firearms.

Should Probation/Parole Officers Make Arrests and Carry Firearms?

In 1975, while still a parole officer, I answered with a resounding "yes." Three decades later, I find myself still in agreement with the legendary parole chief in New York, David Dressler (1951: 152), who wrote: "I am convinced a parole system worth its salt *has* to make its own arrests." Departments that fail to provide the maximum amount of community protection possible within a P/P setting are in danger of having their services shifted or contracted out to public or private social service agencies. The privatization of prisons and, in certain instances, presentence investigation reports, should serve as a warning to the self-interests of P/P personnel.

Although many (typically nonpractitioner) observers bemoan the existence of a role conflict in P/P, or an incompatibility between control and treatment, this author never experienced such conflicts in practice—nor did his colleagues in New York. Indeed, given the nature of P/P clientele, sound treatment demands the use of appropriate methods of control—offenders under supervision often engage in behavior that is self-destructive and dangerous to the community. As a trained social worker,

Soft on Criminals

"Despite its wide usage, probation is often the subject of intense criticism. It suffers from a 'soft on crime' image, and as a result, maintains little public support. Probation is often depicted as permissive, uncaring about crime victims, and blindly advocating a rehabilitative ideal while ignoring the reality of violent, predatory criminals" (Petersilia, 1998a: 30).

I found that the application of casework principles was enhanced by the legal powers inherent in P/P settings. Indeed, if role conflict is inherent in P/P practice, as Todd Clear and Edward Latessa (1989) note, such is the nature of many professional positions. However, "among other professions, role conflict is seldom seen as a justification for eviscerating the profession of a few less salient tasks; rather, it is felt that the 'true' professional finds a way of integrating various role expectations, balancing them and weighing the appropriateness of various expressions of the roles" (2).

Misunderstanding of the control/enforcement role vis-à-vis the social service role is highlighted by Norval Morris and Michael Tonry (1990). They argue, for example, that "there is no way in which effective, regular, but unpredictable urine testing to ensure that the convicted offender is drug free can be made other than as a police-type function" (185). As a social worker, I disagree: Preventing drug abuse—the purpose of drug testing—is to the client's advantage; testing enhances the ego function of the offender, strengthening resolve to avoid harmful substances. Indeed, the client can demur when under pressure from drug-using associates: "Can't man; got to report to my PO and he'll check me out." This approach is sound social work.

As a private citizen with a working knowledge of P/P, I have certain concerns about personal safety—that of my family, friends, and neighbors. From this (I believe typical) layperson's perspective, I evaluate a P/P agency by providing some examples. During the course of an office or home visit, a P/P officer may discover that a client is using heroin or cocaine. If the offender is unemployed, the drug habit is probably financed by criminal activities—the client is a clear and present danger to him- or herself and to the community. A P/P agency whose officers cannot immediately (and safely) arrest such a person is not providing an adequate level of client service or community protection. P/P agencies also supervise offenders who have been involved in sex offenses against children, vehicular homicide as a result of intoxication, burglary, and armed robbery. A P/P agency whose officers have no responsibility to enforce prohibitions, through investigation and arrest, against frequenting play areas, drinking and driving, and carrying tools for forced entry or who cannot investigate money or a lifestyle that cannot be supported by the offender's employment status, is not providing the minimum acceptable level of community safety.

Furthermore, the adult (and, frequently, the juvenile) P/P client is often a serious law violator who has proved to be a potential danger to the community. Many have been involved in crimes of violence, and the public and elected officials expect that probationers and parolees, if they are to remain in the community, will be under the scrutiny of P/P authorities. This scrutiny is why the law of most jurisdictions empowers P/P agencies with law enforcement responsibilities. However, the question is often raised whether the P/P officer should be the law enforcer or merely the treatment agent or broker.

Do arrest powers and the carrying of a firearm interfere with the P/P officer's ability to form a casework relationship with which to provide treatment? I am of the

Parolees, Firearms, and Public Safety

In 1996, parole officers on a routine evening home inspection in Denver found that their client was not at home, but his sister permitted the officers to check the premises. Inside his closet, the officers found a pistol. As they were removing the weapon, the parolee arrived and was met by the officers in front of the house. Informed that he was to be taken into custody, the parolee bolted and ran behind the house with officers in pursuit. Suddenly, he halted, drew a weapon, and aimed at the officers, who fatally shot the parolee.

Firearms and Self-Defense

In 1993, in a change of policy, the Florida legislature authorized correctional probation officers (CPOs) to carry firearms. Subsequently, a CPO made a routine field visit to a client's home. Unknown to the officer, the client had expressed his intention to kill the CPO in retaliation for the arrest of the offender's brother for technical violations—the brother was returned to prison. After the officer completed the visit and was driving from the home, he was shot twice and lost control of his car, which struck a tree. The offender continued to advance toward the car, but the officer was able to draw his weapon and returned fire, striking the offender three times and saving his own life (Papy, 1997).

opinion that they do not. Indeed, because of P/P officers' relationships with their clients, in delinquency situations, they are able to effect an arrest without the tension and hostility that often accompanies arrests made by other law enforcement officers (who have no relationship with the client). In fact, whether the P/P officer actually makes the arrest, the client knows that the P/P officer initiated the warrant action. In Maricopa County, Arizona, probation officers may initiate arrests only when police officers are present. Thus, if an offender who is to be taken into custody reports to the probation office, the probationer must be *deceived* into waiting until the police arrive. This is both poor law enforcement and poor social work.

In my many years of parole work, I often posed the following to clients: "I know that you are determined not to get into trouble, so this is a hypothetical question. If you violate parole, would you prefer the police, or would you rather that I came to arrest you?" Typically, stories about being badly treated by the police ensued before they generally responded, "If I gotta go back, you come, please." In Massachusetts, when it was decided that unarmed probation officers from the Dorchester Division of the District Court would make unannounced home visits at night, they required police escorts—poor social work practice on at least two levels: First, it draws attention to the client, violating confidentiality; and second, it conveys a (perhaps unintended) message that the client is too dangerous to visit without a police escort. This may actually enhance the prestige of gang-involved youth. Nevertheless, the "Massachusetts model" has been extended to Boston and other jurisdictions, such as Alameda County, California, where it is part of a program of "community probation." Although that county's probation officers "shall be active in the enforcement of probation conditions" and wear body armor and are equipped with handcuffs, the department prohibits POs from carrying firearms. ("Project Spotlight," housed at Sam Houston State University in Huntsville, Texas, promotes police officer–probation officer teams to provide intensive supervision and surveillance, including evening, early morning, and weekend visits to the homes and communities

Public Safety

"In managing offenders who are ordered by the court to community supervision or released early from prison with supervision, probation and parole officers need to ensure the safety of victims and the public. Officers should use surveillance to identify offenders who pose a continued threat and improve monitoring efforts such as checking with contacts at the offender's home, employment, and neighbors to ensure that they are meeting the conditions of their probation or parole" (Office for Victims of Crime, 1998: 6).

In the Field

Georgia parole officer Joje Wilson-Gibbs turns into East Lake Meadows, a housing project just inside Atlanta city limits, and notes that the surroundings are particularly lively for so early an hour. Throughout the warren of circling streets sprawl barracklike apartments, several tattooed with graffiti and one encircled by a flower garden. A gray-bearded old man crouches in the corner of his stoop; two carloads of young men pass while slowly inspecting the sedate blue sedan driven by the parole officer.

Wilson-Gibbs is checking on her parolee, but it's not him she fears. Like most parole officers, the unpredictability of the environment most concerns her. Next to her on the seat is a bulky purse, on which is perched a can of pepper gas spray and in which is concealed a .38-caliber revolver. "I don't want to use my gun in a real-life situation," she says. "I don't want to use pepper gas, either, but I feel better knowing I'm trained and can react with these weapons if I'm in a life-threatening situation. All sorts of things add up to a sense of security for me—including having good tires on a reliable car that won't leave you stranded."

of probationers. For more than a decade, I made evening, early morning, and weekend visits to parolees in New York, as did my colleagues, without the need to be escorted by police officers.

In Wyoming, the unarmed P/P agents are encouraged to conduct home visits in teams only after a "pre-plan and prepare" has been developed. Agents conducting solo home visits call or radio their location to a "contact person" who they advise of the estimated length of time to be spent at the residence. "Agents are to make the initial call prior to entering the residence and a second call once exiting the residence." I am refraining from any comment on this approach, but readers can probably guess what it would be.

P/P clients are potentially dangerous and usually reside in high-crime neighborhoods, which is reason enough to be armed. This facet of parole work was dramatically revealed while I was a parole officer in New York. My colleague, 32-year-old Donald Sutherland, attempted to arrest a parole violator on the street and was shot to death. The parolee was subdued at the scene by other parole officers. After being convicted of murder, the parolee escaped from prison and eluded law officers for several weeks (on one occasion after an exchange of gunfire). He was finally killed after refusing to surrender to a combined force of city and state police and parole officers.

Although carrying a firearm does not guarantee safety, a person with a firearm may discourage attacks by carrying him- or herself more confidently than others who might be selected for victimization. Knowing that P/P officers are routinely carrying firearms has a deterrent value. Indeed, many *unarmed* P/P officers (perhaps unknowingly) gain a degree of safety because they are perceived as police officers or otherwise believed to be armed.

Related to this issue is a peculiar prohibition: Some agencies that permit the carrying of firearms on duty forbid P/P officers from carrying a firearm while off duty. In North Dakota, for example, field (title of P/P) officers "will not routinely carry firearms while off duty." In Virginia, P/P officers, although they are authorized to carry weapons on duty, "the weapon will not be carried while in an off duty status." In Cook County, Illinois, probation officers assigned to intensive supervision must be armed while in the field, but the "officer shall not carry a firearm during off-duty hours, except when traveling [not more than 1.5 hours] to and from work." This policy appears to be based on a lack of trust and a fear that weapons would be used off duty in an inappropriate manner by the very officers employed and trained by the agency. The policy is bad for morale and public safety, and unsound P/P practice. If a P/P officer is trained in law enforcement and firearms, he or she should have the same privilege of carrying a weapon off duty as do almost all other peace officers. P/P officers may encounter their clients during off-duty hours, and a hostile (perhaps ex-) client can be dangerous under such circumstances. P/P personnel must not be intimidated, or their effectiveness will be undermined. Yet, the nature of their clientele and the revocation powers of P/P officers make them vulnerable to intimidation. The ability to carry a weapon at all times reduces feelings of vulnerability and, therefore, the potential for intimidation. Furthermore, a community that provides for the salaries of P/P officers is that much safer by having in its midst trained and armed personnel sworn to enforce the law.

Probation and Parole Officers: The Powers of Search and Seizure

"Over the past two decades there has been a dramatic shift in the sympathy displayed by courts regarding the rights of prisoners and those under supervision in the criminal justice system" (Jermstad, 2002: 17). This is highlighted by the interpretation of the Fourth Amendment's protection against unreasonable searches and seizures as applied to probationers and parolees. Persons on probation and parole sign rules of supervision that routinely permit a warrantless search of his or her property and person. In 1987, the Court held (*Griffin v. Wisconsin*, 107 S.Ct. 3164) that the special needs attendant to supervising probationers justified a warrantless search based on "reasonable grounds;" that is, evidence less than the search warrant standard of "probable cause."

In 1998, in another 5–4 decision, the Supreme Court ruled that evidence seized by parole officers without a search warrant, which would be barred at a criminal trial by the exclusionary rule, could be used at a parole violation hearing. In this case (*Pennsylvania Board of Probation and Parole v. Scott*, 524 U.S. 357, 1998) Keith Scott had been serving a 10- to 20-year sentence for third-degree murder when he signed a parole agreement that stipulated: "I expressly consent to the search of my person, property and residence, without a warrant by agents of the Pennsylvania Board of Probation and Parole. Any items in [sic] the possession of which constitutes a violation of parole/reparole shall be subject to seizure, and may be used as evidence in the parole revocation process." After receiving information that Scott had violated his parole by possessing firearms, consuming alcohol, and assaulting a co-worker, parole officers obtained an arrest warrant and arrested him at a diner. Parole officers then went to his residence, where they commenced a search without asking for or receiving permission from Scott's mother, who owned the residence; they found five firearms in Scott's room. The Pennsylvania Supreme Court held that Scott's Fourth Amendment protection was not waived by his signing of the parole agreement. Furthermore, the court ruled that the exclusionary rule applies to parole violation hearings. The U.S. Supreme Court, in overruling the Pennsylvania court, stated:

> In most cases the State is willing to extend parole only because it is able to condition it on compliance with certain requirements. The State thus has an "overwhelming interest" in ensuring that a parolee complies with those requirements and is returned to prison if he fails to do so. The exclusion of evidence establishing a parole violation, hampers the State's ability to ensure compliance with these conditions by permitting the parolee to avoid the consequences of his noncompliance.

The Court noted that the usually adversarial relationship between a criminal suspect and police is not a characteristic of the parole officer/parolee relationship: "Their relationship is more supervisory than adversarial."

In 2001, this time in a unanimous decision (*United States v. Knights*, 122 S.Ct. 587), the Supreme Court expanded the *Scott* decision, ruling that a probationer's residence can be subjected to a warrantless search based on "reasonable suspicion." This does not violate the Fourth Amendment, the Court ruled, even when the search (in this case by sheriff's officers) is for "investigatory" rather than probation purposes. A California court's sentencing order (rules of probation) "included the condition that Knights [the probationer] submit to search at anytime, with or without a search or arrest warrant or reasonable cause, by any probation or law enforcement officer." Knights was "unambiguously informed of the search condition" and, thus, his "reasonable expectation of privacy was significantly diminished." This condition, the Court stated, furthers the two primary goals of probation: rehabilitation and protecting society from future criminal violations. The Court concluded that "the very assumption of probation is that the probationer is more likely than others to violate the law." Thus, the state "may justifiably focus on probationers in a way that it does not on the ordinary citizen." "It is clear from the context and tone of this opinion, that the Supreme Court's overall expectation of probation was to be much more oriented toward law enforcement than serving the needs of probationers" (Jermstad, 2002: 15).

SELECTING PROBATION AND PAROLE OFFICERS

The selection of P/P officers is typically done by a process similar to that used to select most public employees. One of three systems is generally employed: the merit system, the appointment system, or a combined system.

1. **Merit system.** Under the **merit system,** applicants who meet the minimum qualifications for the position are required to pass a competitive written examination. Persons who score at or above the minimum passing grade are placed on a ranked list. From this list, candidates are selected, generally in the order of their rank. In some systems, applicants are graded on the basis of their education and employment background. The merit system was developed to remove public employment from political patronage. Critics argue, however, that a written examination cannot determine who will be a good P/P officer.

2. **Appointment system.** Under the **appointment system,** applicants who meet minimum requirements are hired on the basis of an evaluation by the agency. Applicants do not take a written examination, although they are usually interviewed by an agency representative(s). This system provides agency officials with the greatest amount of flexibility; it also has a history of being used for political purposes.

3. **Combined system.** The **combined system** involves using elements of both the merit and the appointment systems. Applicants are first screened through a qualifying examination. Those who receive a passing grade are placed on a list from which candidates are selected, usually after an interview with an agency representative(s).

Requirements and Training for Georgia Parole Officers

Georgia's parole officers are among the most highly qualified, best-trained community supervision professionals in the country. All are required to have an undergraduate degree and must pass through a complete background check that includes a psychological test to determine their job competency. Some come to the agency directly from college, whereas others come from backgrounds as diverse as law enforcement, social work, education, and private enterprise.

Soon after they are hired, all parole officers attend the agency's Basic Training Program, a 6-week package of instruction at the Georgia Police Training Center in Forsyth. The course of instruction prepares them for the many roles that they will fill as they go about their daily duties. Included are classes and hands-on training in report writing, interpersonal communications, cultural diversity, arrest procedures, lifesaving techniques, and firearms training and certification. On graduation, the new parole officers have the critical knowledge to return to their respective offices and begin their work. Every year parole officers return for more training in the form of 40 hours of agency-mandated in-service training.

New Jersey Parole Officers' Knowledge and Abilities

- Knowledge of the economic, social, emotional, and other problems of paroled persons, and of the reactions to be expected of such persons
- Ability to read, interpret, and apply information on the laws of New Jersey relevant to probation, parole, the operation of law enforcement agencies, and the courts
- Ability to read and interpret information on the theory of modern social casework, penology, sociology, and criminology
- Ability to function as a peace officer for the detection, apprehension, arrest, and conviction of offenders
- Ability to recognize and evaluate potentially dangerous situations involving parolees, and to exercise caution and independent judgment in the handling of these circumstances
- Ability to assist with the work involved in supervising persons on parole who may be of varied ethnic and social backgrounds, who may possess varied levels of intellectual comprehension and English ability, and who may be antagonistic and/or emotionally disturbed
- Ability to visit and speak with businesspersons, employers, judges, clergy, police officers, school officials, and representatives of health, welfare, civic and business organizations to enlist their cooperation in plans for the rehabilitation of parolees and, as required, to collect information for future action
- Ability to conduct interviews and investigations of prospective parolees, and of parole violations
- Ability to set appropriate payments schedules to collect court-imposed revenue obligations concomitant with the capability to pay, to coordinate the efforts necessary to collect payments in default, and to maintain records thereon
- Ability to plan and work constructively with parolees in the areas of improved family life, steady employment, and wholesome personal and neighborhood associates
- Ability to be proficient in the care, use, and security of firearms and other restraint/defense equipment
- Ability to apprehend and arrest parole violators
- Ability to investigate and evaluate the living conditions of parolees
- Ability to prepare correspondence, clear, sound, accurate, and informative case histories, summaries, and other reports concerning parole matters containing findings, conclusions, and recommendations
- Ability to maintain essential records and files

PERSONAL QUALITIES

The characteristics generally considered desirable for P/P officers can be classified into four categories:

1. *Basic knowledge.* A P/P officer should have a working understanding of psychology, sociology, the criminal statutes, police operations, and the court and correctional systems. In some jurisdictions, particularly federal probation, an increase in the number of white-collar offenders referred for a presentence investigation or under supervision requires officers with knowledge of the Internet, securities, accounting, and banking.

2. *Individual characteristics.* A P/P officer needs the ability to relate to all offenders and to deal with their sometimes subtle or overt hostility, to exercise authority in an appropriate manner, to work well with other staff members, and to be able to organize work properly and prepare written reports in a coherent and timely manner.

Qualifications for Probation/Parole Officers

The American Correctional Association sets the following standard for entry-level P/P field positions: "An entry-level probation or parole officer possesses a minimum of a bachelor's degree or has completed a career development program that includes work-related experience, training, or college credits providing a level of achievement equivalent to a bachelor's degree." Virtually all P/P agencies require at least a bachelor's degree, usually in a relevant major: sociology, criminal justice, psychology, or social work. Some require graduate education in a relevant field or counseling experience, and some agencies permit relevant experience to substitute for up to 2 years of the educational requirement.

3. *The agency*. The P/P officer must be willing to accept the responsibilities engendered by working for a public agency that handles offenders, and to enforce rules and adhere to regulations.

4. *Other agencies*. The P/P officer has to be able to deal effectively with many kinds of agencies and persons, usually divided into criminal justice (police, prosecutors, judges, and correctional officials) and social service (treatment, welfare, employment, and educational). These agencies often have varying attitudes toward offenders that must be handled appropriately.

VOLUNTEERS

Probation in the United States originated as a **volunteer** service; in probation, the tradition was reactivated in 1959 by Keith J. Leenhouts, judge of the Royal Oak, Michigan, municipal court. In that city, the municipal (misdemeanor) court probation department was staffed entirely by volunteers. Through the efforts of Judge Leenhouts, a national organization, Volunteers in Prevention, Probation, and Prisons, Inc. (VIP) was formed. VIP merged with the National Council on Crime and Delinquency in 1972; in 1983, it reverted to independent status. Carlson and Parks (1979: 237) present four volunteer service models:

1. *One-to-one model*. On a one-to-one basis, volunteers seek to obtain the trust and confidence of P/P clients and help them to maintain their existence, clarify their role in society, and plan for the future.

2. *Supervision model*. Working as a case aide to a P/P officer, the volunteer provides services to several clients at the direction of the PO.

3. *Professional model*. The volunteer is a professional or semiprofessional in his or her field—teacher or mechanic, for example—who provides specialized services to several clients, for example, help with literacy or skills training. In Florida, for example, the Department of Corrections has volunteer financial planning specialists available to assist probationers with help in maintaining a realistic family budget.

4. *Administrative model*. The volunteer assists with project administrative functions and interacts only indirectly with clients.

The primary approach of Judge Leehouts and VIP is mentoring with the juvenile and misdemeanor court clients. This venue is seen as critical because the "vast majority of all crimes and offenses are tried in these courts . . . [and] it is estimated that as many as 80 percent of all felonies are committed by persons who first are convicted of a misdemeanor or juvenile offense" (Reeves, 2003: v). Therefore, "there is no better place to identify and divert a (usually) young apprehended offender from a life punctuated with habitual criminal activity" (v). Mentors typically work with youths sentenced to probation, spending time that features recreation and education.

Some P/P agencies and staff members are critical of the use of volunteers. They may view the efforts of volunteers as interference with their prerogatives, and they may be concerned about sharing information with volunteers because of the confidential aspect of P/P practice. Chris Eskridge and Eric Carlson (1979) report that in some agencies the regular P/P workers see volunteers as a threat to their jobs. Some P/P officers resent the fact that volunteers are able to play the "good guy," while they have control and enforcement functions. Some complain of volunteers acting as advocates for the offender in opposition to the regular worker.

Because volunteers are not paid, they need to derive some satisfaction from their efforts. Satisfaction results when a level of success exists, and to be successful, volunteers require adequate training and supervision. In other words, the successful use of volunteers is not "cost free"; staff is required for the training, coordination, and supervision of volunteers. If additional staff is not to be employed for these tasks, the agency has to take away from the working time of regular P/P agency personnel. Eskridge and Carlson (1979) report that lack of success in volunteer programs is a function of management operations rather than the volunteer concept. Faulty management includes the inability to assign volunteers expeditiously, inadequate volunteer training, poor supervision or support for volunteers, and a lack of communication between volunteers and officers.

Brockton (MA) Volunteer Probation Officer Program.   For 20 years, the Brockton district court has operated the state's largest continuing volunteer program. With its own director and board of directors—probation officers, past volunteers, and community representatives—the program uses about 600 volunteer probation officers (VPOs) who have completed formal training. The program focuses on repeat offenders ages 17 to 25. Each VPO is matched with three clients to whom they provide a mentoring relationship. The VPO does not substitute for the probation officer, who maintains overall responsibility for supervision, but functions more in the role of older sibling, friend, or even parent surrogate. Several volunteers have been recruited from the ranks of successful probationers. The VPO is in contact with each client at least an hour per week for a year (or less if the client has completed the court's sentence). VPOs report on their activity through weekly contact sheets and attend monthly VPO meetings.

Los Angeles County Reserve Deputy Probation Officer Program.   Reserve deputy probation officers are deputized volunteers who complete a minimum 75-hour training course and a subsequent 6-month on-the-job training period. For specialized assignments, they may be required to complete additional training. The reserve POs work on weekdays, weekends, or evenings for a minimum of 20 hours per month. Under the direct supervision of regular POs, they provide support services and aid in the investigation and supervision of juveniles and adults. Other counties in California, such as San Diego, use reserve deputy probation officers.

New Jersey Volunteers in Parole Program.   As a component of the New Jersey Bureau of Parole, the Volunteers in Parole Program is designed to provide help through a pool of individuals from the community. These individuals are qualified and willing to assist bureau personnel in serving the varied needs of its many diverse clients. The following volunteer categories reflect the service needs of the Bureau of Parole, while showing the scope of ways in which volunteers provide valuable assistance.

- *Parole Officer Aide:* helps the parole officer with various investigations and assists as officer of the day for routine office interviews; however, involvement with law enforcement activities is prohibited

- *Professional Aide:* a member of a profession offering specific services on an as-needed basis
- *Administrative Aide:* works in a district office in an administrative or clerical capacity
- *Student Intern:* assumes the same role as Parole Officer Aide; students from various colleges and universities serve internships within the bureau as part of a cooperative arrangement

Juvenile Court of Jackson County.   In Kansas City, Missouri, the juvenile court of Jackson County has a victim assistance program staffed by volunteers. The program assists victims by empowering them with knowledge of the juvenile court process and being with them at the court hearing. The services provided by the volunteers include

- Visiting victims in cases of delinquency, and preparing an impact statement that informs the court of the victim's losses and attitude toward the offense and the offender
- Providing referrals for those requiring crisis counseling, repair of property, emergency funding, and other vital services
- Informing the victim of the ability to file a civil action to recover losses
- Assisting in the filling out of victim compensation claims
- Assisting victims in recovering their property from police departments where it is being held as evidence
- When necessary, providing transportation to court
- Preparing letters for victims/witnesses for employers relative to any loss of work time
- Meeting with victims/witnesses before their court appearance and staying with them until the hearing is complete
- Providing for mediation of restitution payments if the court decides that the victim should meet with the offender, and the victim agrees
- Providing information to the public on the juvenile court process

Volunteers are used by the *Missouri Board of Probation and Parole* and the *Delaware Department of Correction* on a one-to-one basis. Both agencies use volunteers to increase the services available to P/P clients. In Missouri they are provided with training in reality therapy (discussed in chapter 9) and are expected to influence behavior by setting an example while being patient listeners. The volunteer helps the client to develop and carry out realistic plans, provides advice and encouragement, and may offer concrete assistance by helping the client secure employment.

South Carolina Department of Probation, Parole, and Pardon Services. South Carolina offers a variety of volunteer opportunities:

- *Job Developers* help offenders find employment and learn new job skills. They aid the offender's job search and provide pointers on interviewing, demeanor, and handling job conflicts. They also make referrals to employment agencies and develop a job bank for offenders.
- *Community Sponsors* are matched with offenders to develop a relationship of guidance, support, and motivation. They assist offenders with obtaining support and rehabilitative services. Through recreation, conversation, and other activities, the volunteer provides a positive role model.
- *Court Assistants* aid the department with such tasks as processing offenders placed on probation, investigating and collecting information, reviewing information with offenders, and monitoring other court activity.

- *Agent/Team Assistants* provide P/P agents with assistance in monitoring and meeting the needs of offenders. This includes maintaining contacts with service and referral agencies, law enforcement agencies, court offices, family members, and employers.

Sixth Judicial District (Iowa) Department of Correctional Services.   The department provides opportunities for volunteers and college student interns:

- *Caseworkers* assist offenders who are ordered to provide community service work. They interview and place offenders, communicating with placement agencies, and provide client follow-up.
- *Probation/Parole Trainees* receive a complete and professional hands-on training experience in case management. They monitor offenders for rule compliance, provide service referrals, and complete client reassessments.

Hennepin County (Minnesota) Community Corrections Volunteer Program.
Adult Field Services (Probation) has several volunteer/intern opportunities available. A minimum time commitment of 4 hours per week for 6 to 12 months is required. All positions work directly or indirectly with probation staff. Qualifications range from little work experience plus high school diploma to extensive work experience and college graduate-level work:

- *Probation Officer's Assistant*—Assist Probation staff with caseload ranging from one-on-one work with a high-needs client to handling your own caseload of 30 to 70 clients. All work is done under the direct supervision of a probation officer.
- *Support Staff Assistant*—Assist lead clerical support staff worker with processing P/P paperwork. It may include computer and telephone work.
- *Domestic Special Services*—Monitor defendants who have successfully completed the counseling/therapy component of their probation. Computer skills are very helpful.
- *Case Monitor, Restitution*—Contribute to the restoration of wholeness for crime victims through collection of court-ordered restitution.
- *Drug Court*—Work alongside Drug Court staff. Escort defendants through the court process, prepare and organize documents, and enter and retrieve information on the computer.

Missouri Board of Probation and Parole.   Volunteers may serve as P/P aides who assist officers in the supervision of adults that includes direct offender and collateral contacts. They can opt for serving as reparation board members assisting in the implementation of restorative justice (discussed in chapter 11) programs.
There are also volunteer positions available with juvenile probation:

- *Mentor*—Develop a stable, long-term relationship with a juvenile probationer; 1-year commitment.
- *Probation Officer Assistant*—Work in close cooperation with the assigned probation officer providing supervision, maintaining case records, and being available for court appearances with the juvenile.
- *Sole Sanction Restitution*—Monitor a large number of cases with court-ordered consequences to ensure court orders are followed and restitution payments are made.
- *Victim Services Case Manager*—Contact victims to answer questions regarding victims' rights in the court process and to verify losses.

PROBATION/PAROLE OFFICER LEGAL LIABILITY

P/P officers have generally been successful in avoiding **legal liability** for actions performed in the course of their duties. Although state agencies are generally exempt from liability for their governmental activities unless waived, immunity ordinarily is unavailable to individual state officers who are sued. Therefore, P/P officials may be sued as individuals. Immunity for P/P officers, however, is often dependent on the agencies for which they work and the nature of the functions performed, but in general, as opposed to the absolute immunity enjoyed by judges, they merely have qualified immunity. Probation officers who are employees of the court and work under court supervision do not enjoy the same absolute immunity of judges, but they may be vested with judicial immunity for some acts such as preparing and submitting a presentence report in a criminal case because the probation officer is performing a "quasijudicial" function (del Carmen et al., 2001).

P/P officers may be vulnerable to civil liability for such wrongs as **negligence** and **failure to warn.** Negligence, the most common form of tort action, refers to a failure to exercise that degree of care which a person of ordinary prudence would exercise under similar circumstances or conduct that creates an undue risk of harm to others. There are four elements to a negligence action:

- A legal duty owed to the plaintiff
- A violation of that duty by an act or omission to act, which constitutes a breach of that duty
- Which was the proximate cause of
- The injury or damages suffered by the plaintiff

Although no definitive Supreme Court decision exists concerning the liability of parole officers in the supervision process, state and federal cases have established liability for crimes committed by parolees under their supervision within a narrow set of circumstances. Case law has established a duty to warn third persons when there is a "special relationship" between certain types of professionals and a person under their care. This duty arises because of the professional's training and expertise, which place the professional in a good position to predict that the person presents a reasonably foreseeable risk of harm to a particular third person. This "special relationship" could be seen in the relationship between a P/P officer and an offender under the officer's supervision. The PO, in some situations, could be in a position to predict that the offender presents a reasonably foreseeable risk of harm to a particular third person.

A leading federal case in this area is *Reiser v. District of Columbia* (563 F2d 462, 1977), which found that because of the special relationship between a parole officer and parolee with a history of brutal violence against women, appropriate warnings to employers and other persons foreseeably at risk were required. In this case, the parolee used his position as an apartment building custodian to gain access to a woman's apartment where he murdered her, and the court held the agency liable.

The common element in these circumstances, notes del Carmen and Louis, is the rather unclear concept of a "special duty" on the part of the P/P officer:

> For this "special duty" to be relevant, there must be a *reasonably foreseeable risk* which exists when the circumstances of the relationship between the parolee and a third party suggest that the parolee may engage in criminal or antisocial conduct related to his or her past conduct. This, in turn, results from a combination of three factors: (a) the parolee's job; (b) his or her prior criminal background and conduct; and (c) the type of crime for which he or she was convicted. For example, it is reasonably foreseeable that a parolee convicted of child sexual assault would commit a similar act if employed in a child care center, but not if employed as a janitor on a college campus. (1988: 37, emphasis in original)

Now that we have completed our examination of the tasks and work roles of P/P officers, agency models, and volunteers in P/P, in chapter 11 we review and analyze the supervision process.

KEY TERMS

control model

social service model

combined model

broker

advocate

merit system

appointment system

combined system

volunteer

legal liability

negligence

failure to warn

INTERNET CONNECTIONS

Criminal justice links: faculty.ncwc.edu/toconnor

California Probation, Parole, and Correctional Association: cppca.org

American Probation and Parole Association: www.appa-net.org

Volunteers in Prevention, Probation and Prisons: vipmentoring.org

REVIEW QUESTIONS

1. What are the various tasks of the P/P officer?
2. What are the three basic P/P agency models?
3. What are the three basic roles that may be assumed by P/P officers?
4. What is meant by the broker/advocate role of the P/P officer?
5. What agency model is compatible with a law enforcement role? Why?
6. Why have arrest powers and the carrying of firearms by P/P officers have become increasingly common?
7. What are the arguments for and against a law enforcement role and the carrying of firearms by P/P officers?
8. What are the three basic categories with respect to agency policy regarding P/P officers making arrests and carrying firearms?
9. What are the arguments for and against P/P officers making arrests and carrying firearms?
10. What has the Supreme Court ruled with respect to the search of the residences of probationers and parolees?
11. What are the three systems used to select P/P officers? What are their advantages and disadvantages?
12. What are the various roles that volunteers may play in P/P?
13. What are the advantages and disadvantages of using volunteers in P/P?
14. What have the courts ruled with respect to the liability of P/P officers?

CHAPTER 11

Probation and Parole Supervision

Although P/P supervision across agencies may differ in the details, there are commonly shared concerns: that the offender will recidivate—particularly when the nature of the recidivism generates media coverage—and that personnel resources are insufficient to meet the service needs of clients and the safety concern of the community. In this chapter, we begin our examination of the supervision process with a method for dealing with the problem of insufficient resources—**classification.**

CLASSIFICATION IN PROBATION AND PAROLE

Prisons have traditionally classified inmates on the basis of the security needs of the institution and the physical limitations—handicaps—if any, of the prisoner. With the advent of the corrections model, the classification process was expanded to include items relevant to rehabilitation programs offered by the correctional department in its various facilities. The de-emphasis of the corrections model has, correspondingly, lessened the importance of institutional classification (at least for rehabilitation). However, classification has become widespread in P/P.

During the 1970s, P/P administrators came to the realization that their resources would never be sufficient to even approach the service needs of their clientele. They also realized that the typical P/P officer approximated agency objectives (protection of the community and rehabilitation of the offender) through the use of an unofficial and unarticulated classification system: "Because not all offenders require the same level of supervision or exhibit the same problems, most experienced Probation and Parole agents utilize an intuitive system of classifying offenders into differential treatment or surveillance modes, usually based on their judgments of client needs and their perception of the client's potential for continued unlawful behavior. It seems reasonable to assume that without this type of case load management, successes would diminish and failures increase" (Baird, Heinz, and Bemus, 1982: 36). However, "this untested, highly individualized approach does not provide information necessary to rationally deploy staff and other resources" (36). Enter the *risk/needs assessment.*

Risk/Needs Assessment

During the late 1970s and early 1980s, the use of formal classification in P/P supervision expanded greatly. This movement was led by the state of Wisconsin, which in 1975 received funding from the Law Enforcement Assistance Administration for a

Case Classification/Staff Deployment Project. After 4 years, the **risk/needs assessment** system was designed, implemented, and evaluated statewide.

The risks/needs concept developed in Wisconsin was adopted by the National Institute of Corrections and, subsequently, many other P/P jurisdictions. The basic strength of the risk/needs assessment system is in its completeness and simplicity and its utility to management—indeed, classification for supervision is basically a management tool. Although variations exist between jurisdictions, all risks/needs classification schemes quantify variables along two dimensions:

1. The degree to which the offender presents a *risk* of recidivating (committing new offenses)
2. The degree to which the offender requires assistance, *needs,* from the P/P agency

Taken together, these two dimensions allow for a prognostication that has implications for the level of supervision required and thus for caseload management and deployment of personnel.

The system tested in Wisconsin demonstrated its effectiveness in predicting success or failure in completing P/P terms. In a sample of 8,250 clients, the percentage of individuals rated low risk and later revoked was 3 percent; of the cases rated high risk, 37 percent were revoked. Other jurisdictions have also tested the system. The Los Angeles Probation Department found that the risk scale compared with intuitive judgments by probation officers did well in predicting which cases would be successful and which would not; the needs scale, however, was found to have almost no predictive value (Program Services Office, 1983). In Massachusetts, with a variation of the Wisconsin instrument, half the clients classified as "maximum" risk were subsequently recidivists compared with 36 percent of those classified as "moderate" and 17 percent of those classified as "minimum." It was noted that the predictive ability of the assessment could be improved by using four levels of supervision/risk: intensive, maximum, moderate, and minimum (Brown, 1984). A test of the Wisconsin Juvenile Probation and Aftercare Risk instrument revealed that this basis was not suitable for predicting recidivism (Ashford and LeCroy, 1988).

The instrument used by the Pennsylvania Board of Probation and Parole is typical of most jurisdictions (Figure 11.1). The PO places a number in a box that corresponds with the case record or the officer's assessment for each of the 11 *risk* assessment variables. Then the officer adds up the score and records that in a box labeled "Total." He or she then proceeds to do the same for the 13 *needs* assessment variables. Afterward, the two final scores are compared; whichever is higher (risk or needs) determines the level of supervision—reduced, regular, close, and intensive. (In some jurisdictions, only three levels of supervision exist: minimum, medium, and maximum.) Some flexibility is possible because the procedures provide for an override: "If, after completing the Initial Client Assessment or Client Reassessment, there is a compelling reason to raise or lower the client's grade of supervision, the agent may recommend such a change to his/her supervisor for review and approval/disapproval." Typically, after a case is classified along the risk/needs dimension, it is assigned to a P/P officer according to a predetermined workload distribution.

Texas Classification Levels and Workload Distribution.   Department of Criminal Justice probation guidelines require assignment of cases to POs in "such a manner as to promote public protection through offender supervision and the attainment of a 100 point workload" for each PO using the following weights:

Level I   = 4.00

Level II = 2.50

Level III = 1.33

Level IV = 1.00

COMMONWEALTH OF PENNSYLVANIA
BOARD OF PROBATION AND PAROLE
PBPP-20 (1/85)

INITIAL CLIENT ASSESSMENT

CLIENT NAME (Last, First, Middle Initial)	PAROLE NO.	AGENT NAME	OFFICE	DATE

RISK ASSESSMENT

1. Age at First Conviction: (or juvenile adjudication)
24 or older 0
20-23 2
19 or Younger 4

2. Number of Prior Probation/Parole Revocations: (adult or juvenile)
None 0
One or more 4

3. Number of Prior Felony Convictions: (or juvenile adjudications)
None 0
One 2
Two or more 4

4. Convictions or Juvenile Adjudications for:
(Select applicable and add for score. Do not exceed a total of 5. Include current offense.)
Burglary, theft, auto theft, or robbery 2
Worthless checks or forgery 3

5. Number of Prior Periods of Probation/Parole Supervision:
(Adult or Juvenile)
None 0
One or more 4

6. Conviction or Juvenile Adjudication for Assaultive Offense within Last Five Years: (An offense which involves the use of a weapon, physical force or the threat of force.)
Yes 15
No 0

7. Number of Address Changes in Last 12 Months:
(Prior to incarceration for parolees)
None 0
One 2
Two or more 3

8. Percentage of Time Employed in Last 12 Months:
(Prior to incarceration for parolees)
60% or more 0
40%- 50% 1
Under 40% 2
Not applicable 0

9. Alcohol Usage Problems: (Prior to incarceration for parolees)
No interference with functioning 0
Occasional abuse: some disruption of functioning 2
Frequent abuse; serious disruption; needs treatment 4

10. Other Drug Usage Problems: (Prior to incarceration for parolees)
No interference with functioning 0
Occasional abuse: some disruption of functioning 1
Frequent abuse; serious disruption; needs treatment 2

11. Attitude:
Motivated to change; receptive to assistance 0
Dependent or unwilling to accept responsibility 3
Rationalizes behavior; negative; not motivated to change 5

TOTAL

NEEDS ASSESSMENT

1. Academic/Vocation Skills
High school or above skill level .... −1
Adequate skills; able to handle everyday requirements ... 0
Low skill level causing minor adjustment problems .... +2
Minimal skill level causing serious adjustment problems ...... +4

2. Employment
Satisfactory employment for one year or longer .... −1
Secure employment; no difficulties reported; or homemaker, student or retired 0
Unsatisfactory employment; or unemployed but has adequate job skills .... +3
Unemployed and virtually unemployable; needs training .... +6

3. Financial Management
Long-standing pattern of self-sufficiency; e.g., good credit rating .... −1
No current difficulties 0
Situational or minor difficulties .... +3
Severe difficulties; may include garnishment, bad checks or bankruptcy .... +5

4. Marital/Family Relationships:
Relationships and support exceptionally strong .... −1
Relatively stable relationships 0
Some disorganization or stress but potential for improvement .... +3
Major disorganization or stress .... +5

5. Companions
Good support and influence .... −1
No adverse relationships 0
Associations with occasionally negative results .... +2
Associations almost completely negative .... +4

6. Emotional Stability
Exceptionally well adjusted; accepts responsibility for actions .... −2
No symptoms of emotional instability; appropriate emotional responses 0
Symptoms limit but do not prohibit adequate functioning e.g., excessive anxiety .... +4
Symptoms prohibit adequate functioning; e.g., lashes out or retreats into self .... +7

7. Alcohol Usage
No interference with functioning 0
Occasional abuse; some disruption of functioning ...... +3
Frequent abuse; serious disruption; needs treatment ..... +6

8. Other Drug Usage
No interference with functioning 0
Occasional substance abuse; some disruption of functioning .... +3
Frequent substance abuse; serious disruption; needs treatment .... +5

9. Mental Ability
Able to function independently 0
Some need for assistance; potential for adequate adjustment; mild retardation .... +3
Deficiencies severely limit independent functioning; moderate retardaton .... +6

10. Health
Sound physical health; seldom ill 0
Handicap or illness interferes with functioning on a recurring basis .... +1
Serious handicap or chronic illness; needs frequent medical care. .... +2

11. Sexual Behavior
No apparent dysfunction 0
Real or perceived situational or minor problems .... +3
Real or perceived chronic or severe problems .... +5

12. Recreation/Hobby
Constructive 0
Some constructive activities .... +1
No constructive leisure-time activities or hobbies .... +2

13. Agent's Impression of Client's Needs
Minimum .... −1
Low 0
Medium .... +3
Maximum .... +5

TOTAL

INITIAL ASSESSMENT SCALES

Risk Scale		Needs Scale	
0-5	Reduced Supervision		−8-10
6-18	Regular Supervision		1-10
19-30	Close Supervision		11-25
31 & above	Intensive Supervision		26 & above

SCORING AND OVERRIDE

Score Based/ ... Intensive .... Regular ....
Supervision Level
Close .... Reduced ....

Score Override .... No .... Yes ....

FINAL GRADE .... Intensive .... Regular ....
OF SUPERVISION

Override Explanation: Close .... Reduced ....

FIGURE 11.1 *Initial Client Assessment.*

(*Source:* Commonwealth of Pennsylvania, Board of Probation and Parole.)

Level I. This classification is calculated as 4 workload points and extends the most restrictive nonresidential supervision to offenders who:

1. Have a documented pattern of serious noncompliance while supervised at a less restrictive level
2. Have a motion to revoke filed for a law violation
3. Match the jurisdiction's profile of offenders historically committed to prison/jail
4. Have regressed from a less restrictive level of supervision

Level II. This classification is calculated as 2.5 workload points and extends a heightened level of supervision to offenders who:

1. Are a demonstrable risk based on:
   a. Shock community supervision
   b. In lieu of revocation
   c. Direct sentence
2. Have progressed from a more restrictive level of supervision, including residential supervision
3. Have regressed from a less restrictive level of supervision
4. Have documented special risk or needs that are included in the profile of offenders historically committed to prison/jail

Level III. This classification is calculated as 1.33 workload points and extends a moderate level of supervision to offenders who:

1. Regressed from a less restrictive level of supervision
2. Progressed from a more restrictive level of supervision, including residential supervision
3. Demonstrate a documentable necessity for a moderate level of supervision

Level IV. This classification is calculated as 1 workload point and extends a minimum level of supervision to offenders who:

1. Progressed from a more restrictive level of supervision
2. Present the least risk to the community
3. Are considered to be initial or interim community supervision placements but have not been classified

Supervision Levels in Georgia.   The P/P officer interviews a new client and with the help of the presentence report, institutional reports (for parolees), and other relevant documents, fills out a risk/needs instrument similar to the one used in Pennsylvania (see Figure 11.1). From the scoring of information on the instrument a total is derived, which is plugged into a particular level of supervision; typically, a reassessment is performed every 6 months. Because clients with a higher level of supervision require a greater expenditure of P/P officer time, equity is determined, not simply on the total number of clients supervised (**caseload**), but on the basis of the anticipated amount of time each case will demand (**workload**). This quantification allows for the easy use of computers, which can determine the need for more P/P officers in a particular jurisdiction (or, if additional officers are not economically feasible, a corresponding reduction in the amount of supervisory time devoted to each case). Each case is placed in one of six levels of supervision:

- *Administrative Classification:* Although no standard of supervision is required for this classification, probationers who have absconded, who are serving a prison sentence on a new offense and have not been revoked on the present offense, and who are receiving no direct supervision per court approval should be classified as administrative.
- *Minimum* (Nondirect Supervision): Mail in change of address or employment; monthly payment of fine, restitution, and court costs; and monthly telephone contact with probationer
- *Minimum* (Direct Supervision): Monthly telephone contact and quarterly face-to-face contact
- *Medium:* Monthly telephone contact, quarterly face-to-face contact, and one field contact or collateral contact quarterly.

Nebraska Supervision Levels

Intensive Parole Supervision: Parolees must meet face to face with their POs at least once per week. They must also submit a monthly report and required documentation as directed by their parole agreement once per month. They are required to submit a urine specimen each month.

Maximum: Parolees must meet face to face with their POs at least once per month. They must submit a monthly report and required documentation as directed by their parole agreement.

Medium: Parolees must meet face to face with their POs at least once per month. They must submit a monthly report and required documentation as directed by their parole agreement.

Minimum: Parolees must meet face to face with their POs at least once every 90 days. They must submit a monthly report and required documentation as directed by their parole agreement each month.

Conditional: Parolees must meet face to face with their POs at least twice per year. They must also submit a monthly report (Figure 11.2) and required documentation as directed by their parole agreement.

- *High:* Two monthly face-to-face contacts, monthly field contact, and monthly collateral contact
- *Maximum:* Four monthly face-to-face contacts, two monthly field contacts, and two monthly collateral contacts

The use of the minimum or administrative supervision classification for active cases is troubling because these offenders will not be given an opportunity to develop a personal relationship with a P/P officer: "Clearly, processes of interpersonal change based on offender identification with the change agent and the internalization of new values will not transpire" (Castellano, 1997: 24).

SEND OR DELIVER TO: FILE #: _____ PO: _____
Siskiyou County Probation Department
805 Juvenile Lane
Yreka, CA 96097
Phone: (530) 841-4180 FAX: (530) 841-4188
DATE: _____
NOTE: This form is due on the FIRST day of each month. All lines MUST be filled in completely. Just writing "same" is not acceptable.
Check if this is a new address_____
Name: _____
Address:

_____
Street Number, City, State, Zip Code
Mailing Address:

_____
Street Number, City, State, Zip Code
I live with: _____ Phone No. _____
Employer:

_____

FIGURE 11.2 *Monthly Report Form—Adult.*

(*Source:* Siskiyou County, California, Probation Department.)

Street Number, City, State, Zip Code

Job Title _____ Work Location _____

Take Home Pay/Monthly $_____

Unemployed Since _____ Unemployment/Monthly $ _____

Other Family Income: AFDC, SSI, SSP, Other Amount $ _____

Family Vehicle(s): Year _____ Model _____ Color _____ License No.

_____

Year _____ Model _____ Color _____ License No. _____

Purchases Over $200.00 this Month

_____

NOTE: Fill Out the Following Items If They Are a Term of Your Probation:

Have you been arrested, cited, or contacted by law enforcement since the last report? Yes, No

If yes, please explain _____

I have paid $ _____ on my fine/restitution on _____ (date)

I have paid $ _____ supervision fee on _____ (date)

I have completed _____ hours of community service this month.

I have attended NA/AA _____ times this month on (dates) _____

_____

My counselor is _____

NOTE: Please List Any Changes of Your Probation Status from Last Month:

_____

_____

I have obeyed all the terms of my Probation Yes_____ No_____

I declare that the above information is true to the best of my knowledge.

_____

Signature

FIGURE 11.2 (continued)

PROBATION/PAROLE SUPERVISION

The supervision process in both P/P is similar, if not identical. In fact, P/P are handled by the same agency in many states. However, parolees, by definition, have been imprisoned, and imprisonment generally reflects the severity of the offense and the criminal history of the offender. Therefore, parolees are generally considered a greater danger to the community than are probationers. Furthermore, given the lack of adequate educational and training resources in prison, most parolees leave the institution without the literacy and job skills necessary for employment.

Parolees differ from probationers as a result of their prison experiences. The changeover from prison life to community living requires a major readjustment. In prison, the offenders' lives are rigidly controlled. They are told when to sleep, when to eat, when to work, and when to have recreation. When they are released into the community, they must adjust to managing their own lives. This may be compounded by police harassment, particularly in smaller communities. Social agencies often do not recognize parolees' needs and somehow believe that they should be receiving assistance from the parole agency (Elliot Studt in Law Enforcement Assistance Administration, 1973). Unfortunately, most parole (and probation) agencies are extremely limited in their ability to deliver tangible services. This fact, coupled with the usual lack of employable skills, often makes parolees a burden on their families, worsening what may have been an already difficult family situation.

This is particularly the case with female offenders who are usually poor, lack education and employment skills, and are single mothers of at least two children: "They enter the criminal justice system with a host of unique medical, psychological, and financial problems" (Chesney-Lind, 1997: 170). In Georgia, for example, 99 percent of female parolees are mothers with more than two children. "Women offenders are disproportionately low income women of color who are undereducated and unskilled, with sporadic employment histories" (Bloom,

Owen, and Covington, 2003: 2). Females represent more than 20 percent of the probation population and almost 15 percent of parolees, and "women supervised by justice system agencies were mothers of an estimated 1.3 million minor children" (Greenfeld and Snell, 1999). "The majority of women in the correctional system are mothers, and a major consideration for these women is reunification with their children" (Bloom et al., 2003: 16). Thus, "engaging the family, particularly her children, in the recovery process can promote successful outcomes for a woman" (Bloom and McDiarmid, 2001: 11).

Parolees have told this author that even so minor an experience as taking a bus ride can be traumatic to a newly released offender. Several stated they were not aware of the required fare, and they had a feeling that everyone on the bus, especially the driver, recognized that they had just been released from prison. Being in prison also isolated them from normal social contacts with members of the opposite sex. They were self-conscious and often believed that because of the way they looked at women, everyone would realize that they had been in prison. Parolees must "unlearn" prison habits and acquire new patterns of behavior if readjustment is to be accomplished quickly. Parolees are often subjected to social rejection because of their status, and they usually lack the necessary connections and economic resources that are effective in dealing with crisis situations.

Case Assignment

The supervision process begins when the offender is placed on the caseload/workload of a P/P officer. This aspect of supervision, case assignment, can be accomplished in a variety of ways, depending on the practice used by the particular agency and the scope of its jurisdiction. In agencies that have statewide jurisdiction (such as most parole agencies), district/area offices are located throughout the state and each office covers a specific geographic area. County probation agencies, depending on the size of the county, may also have (sub)offices scattered throughout the jurisdiction. Some P/P agencies are offering services through the use of neighborhood centers, a decentralization that parallels community policing efforts in many communities. Indeed, P/P officers may work out of police substations (Clear and Corbett, 1998). Offenders on P/P are directed to report to the office responsible for the area in which they (intend to) reside. At the P/P office, they will be assigned to a caseload either on a totally random basis or according to the specific area in which they plan to reside. Caseloads incorporating geographic considerations are advantageous insofar as they limit the travel time involved in supervising the offender. Each officer also gains greater familiarity with his or her territory, the social and law enforcement agencies therein (not to mention places to eat and clean washrooms) that can enhance the supervision process. In more rural areas, where travel will be extensive, the caseloads will be smaller than in urban areas, where offenders are usually clustered in certain areas of the city. In the caseload assignment process, the agency typically attempts to achieve parity by keeping the size of caseloads roughly equal. In Beaumont County, Texas, juveniles on probation are placed on caseloads according to their home schools. This allows one officer to see all of his or her clients by making one stop and fosters ongoing relationships with school personnel.

Offenders are assigned to **specialized caseloads** by virtue of a salient characteristic, such as a history of drug abuse or mental illness (discussed in chapter 12). A final model uses classification schemes (discussed previously); quantitative weights are assigned to each case based on the level of supervision prognosticated by case (e.g., risk/needs) classification, and workloads are balanced by maintaining ongoing comparative statistics for P/P officers assigned to field supervision. Although this approach is the most rational one for achieving parity in supervision, it is also the most difficult to operationalize, particularly for an agency that has statewide responsibilities.

Initial Interview

The initial interview in P/P practice is considered a crucial time in the supervision process. The first meeting between the client and the P/P officer usually occurs in the probation or parole office—it is a time of apprehension and anxiety. The officer "represents a power that can, and does, limit his freedom." The offender is in the office *involuntarily* in a situation "where two individuals are joined by legal force in a counseling . . . relationship" (Arcaya, 1973: 58–59). The offender encounters the P/P officer for the first time with a mixture of fear, weariness, and defiance: "Particularly difficult is the nonvoluntary nature of the probationer; this individual places a premium on the skills of the probation officer who must counter resistance with patience, persistence, and good will" (Strong, 1981: 12).

The "sizing up" process at the time of the initial interview works both ways. The P/P officer is meeting a stranger who is usually known only through information in the case record and/or presentence investigation report. Although the record may say a great deal about the offender's background, it may not accurately reflect his or her current attitude toward P/P supervision. How will the client deal with current problems? Will the probationer/parolee follow regulations? Will he or she abscond from supervision if pressured or frustrated? Will the officer be responsible for having a warrant issued and having the offender sent to prison? Will this be, instead, an easy case with a minimum of problems?

The client is asking similar questions. Will the P/P officer give me a difficult time? Will my PO be rigid about every minor rule? Is he or she quick to seek delinquency action? Does the officer have the knowledge and ability to help me secure employment, training, education, and a place to live? During an initial interview, the officer explains the P/P rules, answering questions while attempting to set realistic standards for a client. Several items are usually emphasized:

- The need to make in-person, telephone, or mail reports
- The need to keep the P/P officer informed of his or her place of residence
- The need to seek and maintain lawful employment
- The need to avoid unlawful behavior and report contacts with law enforcement officers

When a particular problem exists, the officer may set special conditions: An offender with a history of sex offenses against children will be required to keep out of areas where children normally congregate, such as playgrounds; an offender with a history of alcoholism may be directed to refrain from using any intoxicating beverages. A young offender may be required to keep a curfew; offenders with chemical abuse problems may be required to attend treatment programs. Some agencies require the PO to negotiate a case plan with the client (Figure 11.3).

Grievance Procedures in Kentucky

The Division of Probation and Parole requires P/P officers to inform all clients at the initial interview of the availability of grievance procedures, which include a written submission with appeals to the district supervisor who will hold a hearing on the matter. A client dissatisfied with the outcome of the hearing can appeal to the director who can opt for a hearing or render a summary judgment.

ATTACHMENT

CASE PLANNING SHEET   PAGE _1_____

NAME: _Jim Doe_____   CASE NO. _35165___   DATE: _July 1, 2003_____

SUPERVISION LEVEL: _Medium_____

NEGOTIATED CASE PLAN

Area of Concern	Objective	Plan of Action	Completion Date - Initial
Criminogenic Needs:			
1) Attitudes	1) Joe will improve his thinking & behavior by participating in & completing the recommended cognitive skills program.	1) Joe will actively participate & complete the cognitive skills program.* PO will refer Joe to the PO currently facilitating the group & will determine when the next opening is available. Once Joe begins group, PO will verify attendance with the PO facilitating group a minimum of one time per month.	1) By 7/04
2) Peer Associations	2) Develop relationships with individuals who have no criminal involvements.	2) Jim will return to his health club & will go 3 times per week: Jim will also begin volunteering at the local YMCA 1 time per week for approximately 4 hours. PO will verify this with the director of the YMCA once per month.	2) By 08/31/03
Court Ordered Conditions:			
3) Employment	3) To improve job skills and obtain employment within 1 month.	3) PO will refer to DVR to address job skills and training. PO will verify Jim's follow though. PO will refer to job services for immediate job search. Jim should have job within 4 weeks or be able to justify failure.	3) By 8/01/03
4) Drug Usage	4) To remain drug free for 3 months.	4) PO will refer Jim to mental health for substance abuse evaluation and to follow their recommendations for treatment. PO will verify with mental health periodically to insure compliance. Jim must arrange first appt. within 1 week. PO will collect random UA's.	4) By 07/04/03

SIGNATURE: _____   AGENT SIGNATURE: _____

FIGURE 11.3 *Negotiated Case Plan.*

(*Source*: State of Wyoming.)

The P/P officer explains that he or she will be visiting the offender's residence periodically. Officers offer clients assistance with employment or other problems. Some clients need financial assistance—one of the immediate problems encountered by a newly released parolee is financial. The money that an inmate receives on release, *gate money*, is usually inadequate for even immediate housing and food needs: This problem continues, despite research (Berk, Lenihan, and Rossi, 1980) indicating that support payments to just-released prisoners reduces recidivism. In Texas, an inmate receives $50 and a bus ticket and an additional $50 upon reporting to the parole office. A parolee may have some funds as a result of prison work, but wages are well below that received on the outside, and some jurisdictions require that any funds possessed by an inmate be used to help pay for his or her incarceration. The P/P officer may refer the client to a public or private agency or a halfway house. An additional issue in placing parolees are statutes requiring notification of local officials and sometimes neighbors when certain offenders plan to live in their community—more than 35 states have such legislation. In some highly publicized cases, officials have been unable to provide housing for sex offenders, particularly when their crimes involved children or violence.

Initial Parole Interview in New York.   As the name implies, this is the first major interview between the PO responsible for the supervision of the case and the newly released parolee. If the arrival report is taken by the PO who will supervise the case, it may be combined with the initial interview. It is at this time that the PO initiates a counseling or casework relationship with the parolee. Because the PO is endeavoring to establish this relationship with individuals whose knowledge of and acceptance of parole varies to a great degree, the interview must be planned and handled with the best casework skills. There are those whose attitudes toward parole are based on prejudices, doubt, and fears brought about by rumors. With this group, only patience and skill will overcome the hostility and resistance to a working relationship.

This is the interview on which the planning for future supervision of the parolee will be based. Therefore, it is important that the PO prepare for it by studying all the pertinent information contained in the case folder. It is also important that this interview be well planned, unhurried, and without interference, if possible. It is the key to the future of the case. The PO undertakes the initial interview with four major objectives in mind:

1. Establish a casework relationship with the parolee.
2. Secure the parolee's participation in an analysis of his or her problems.
3. Make constructive suggestions that will give the parolee "something to do" toward beginning the overall parole program.
4. Leave the parolee with some positive assurance of what there is to look forward to as the parole period progresses.

Suggested Content of Initial Interview. The initial interview will vary with the needs and problems, both immediate and long-range, of the individual case. However, the following items are presented as a general guide to areas that the PO might want to cover in conducting his or her initial interview with the parolee. Several of these areas would have been addressed during the parolee's arrival report, if it was conducted at an earlier time. In that case, these items should now be discussed further to ascertain if there are any continuing or additional problems, and to learn whether the parolee's situation has changed:

1. *Description of the Parolee.* At this time, the parolee's physical appearance should be updated from the time of his arrival report, with any particular changes, such as mode of dress and attitude, noted. It should be borne in mind that an individual's habit of dress and mannerisms often offer nonverbal communication that

can tell us much about how a person regards him- or herself. (From time to time during the parolee's period of supervision, the PO should note whether there are any significant changes in the parolee's mode of dress and mannerisms, as these may signal changes in how the parolee regards him- or herself or the parolee's adjustment pattern.)

2. *Analysis of Problems and Initiating the Casework Process.* In conducting an initial interview, the PO is expected to encourage the parolee's participation in discussion of his problems and goals. This discussion should be based on information contained in the parolee's folder, other knowledge that the PO might have, and the parolee's input.

There should be a discussion of the parole program. Both the residence and employment aspects of the program should be carefully reviewed to ascertain that it is as approved, and the PO should take pains to fill in any information regarding the residence and employment that may otherwise be missing in the reports. Care should be exercised to make sure any questions or concerns the parolee has regarding the program are addressed. The PO should ensure that the parolee understands the employment program, and, if necessary, arrangements should be made for the parolee to report to the employer. The parolee's prompt reporting to a prospective employer or employment program, is, of course, a necessity. The parolee's actual employment or participation in employment program should be verified as soon as possible by the PO.

If the parolee has no specific employment or alternative program, he or she should report promptly to any party or agency that may have offered approved assistance in securing employment. If no such program has been previously established, the PO must assist the parolee during the initial interview to devise a plan for seeking employment. If possible, the PO may provide the parolee with referrals to potential employers or parties who might assist the parolee in securing employment. Information should be provided to the parolee concerning the provisions for discharge after 3 years of successful parole supervision, as well as possible eligibility for a Certificate of Relief from Disabilities or a Certificate of Good Conduct (discussed later).

Before conducting the initial interview, the PO should make every attempt to determine whether the parolee has any questions, reservations, or misconceptions concerning his or her relationship with parole and the conditions of parole. This should be done in such a manner as to ensure him or her that the Parole officer is ready and willing to assist the client in a constructive manner with the problems that might arise during the time on parole.

3. *Reporting Instructions.* Before concluding the initial interview, the parolee should be clearly told why office reports are necessary and helpful. He or she should also understand when, where, and with what frequency to report to his or her PO. If the parolee is to report to the PO at a different location, he or she should be given the address of that location and the time to report. The PO should give the parolee an official business card, writing the parolee's name on the front and reporting instructions on the back. Further, the parolee is to be clearly informed that, should he or she be unable to make a scheduled report, the PO must be contacted in advance for permission to miss a scheduled report and to obtain an alternative appointment.

4. *Attitude Toward the PO and the Interview.* In noting the parolee's attitude toward the PO and the interview, the PO should include a description of the parolee's attitudes, interpretation of these attitudes, and his or her basis for such interpretation.

Recording the Interview. The initial interview is the foundation on which the relationship between the parolee, the PO, and the parole system is established. The way it is conducted and its content are highly important to that relationship. It is also important, from both a casework and a legal perspective, that what transpired during the initial interview be clearly and promptly recorded in the parole case folder. Because much of the information discussed during the initial interview is already recorded in the case folder, it is not necessary to repeat that information, except where it relates directly to the problems that were discussed during the initial interview.

In recording the initial interview, the PO should bear in mind any immediate problems the parolee has and any long-range problems that the PO anticipates. In making this assessment, the PO should also indicate what immediate intervention on the parolee's behalf has been undertaken or is contemplated, what immediate and obtainable goals have been established for, or preferably with, the parolee, and what long-range plans for the parolee are being considered.

The Supervision Planning Process—U.S. Probation.   The supervision planning process is designed to create a strategy-based plan of action to address specific issues (Figure 11.3). This process requires that all supervision activities, including personal contacts, be structured to ensure compliance with the conditions of supervision, protect the community, and provide for correctional treatment. The linking of supervision activities to what is necessary to fulfill relevant statutory responsibilities in each case is intended to provide for efficient and effective use of the officer's time.

This process does not de-emphasize the importance of personal contact with the offender but recognizes that the quality of supervision depends on what is accomplished by a particular activity rather than its frequency. The measure of success of the supervision program is the degree to which the offender conforms to the conditions of supervision, identified supervision issues are resolved, and officer intervention is timely and appropriate.

Supervision planning begins with an initial assessment period during which the officer will obtain and evaluate information regarding the conditions of release, the degree and the kind of risk the offender poses to the community, and the characteristics and conditions of the offender that indicate the need for correctional treatment. Based on the information gathered, the officer will identify as supervision issues those specific conditions of supervision and case problems that require direct action by the officer during the period and then select the supervision strategies necessary to address those issues.

The plan will be reviewed by a supervisor and, when approved, implemented. The officer is responsible for accomplishing those supervision activities selected as being necessary to enforce the conditions, control risk, and provide for correctional treatment for as long as the supervision issue is relevant.

Montgomery County, Ohio, Adult Probation Department Probation Orientation Program.   Each probationer is expected to attend one probation orientation program within the first 30 days of placement under supervision. At least two orientation programs are presented each month. Probationers often have a personal view of what probation is all about as influenced by their own assigned probation officer or fellow probationers. Often they believe there is a difference between probation officers—the way officers handle their cases in terms of service to the client, police tactics, use of special conditions of probation, and so on.

The orientation programs are meant to give each client a clearer understanding of the official probation process and, more important, to introduce them to the services that are available to them through the Community Resource Division of the Adult Probation Department. It is further hoped that the orientation program schedule will allow each client to participate in an orientation session before the formulation of case plans. With the background of the orientation program, the probationer should have more of an opportunity to discuss with the probation officer the types of needs and concerns that he or she personally has that can be addressed by programs within the department, or directly or indirectly supported by it. It is also an opportunity to convey to the new probationers that they can have an active part in the development of programming within the department.

The Initial Interview: Virginia

1. Background material such as the presentence report and the Institutional Progress Report(s) should be reviewed prior to the initial interview. The initial interview is purposeful and includes a thorough review of the conditions of supervision, the home and employment arrangements, and any situation that the offender may view as a problem that would hinder his or her positive adjustment back into the community.

2. This is the first major interview between the officer and the offender. It is at this time that the officer initiates his or her counseling and casework relationship. The supervising officer and the offender should jointly develop objectives and the supervision plan. It is important that the initial interview be well planned, unhurried, and without interruption.

3. The major objectives of the initial interview are
   a. Establish a working relationship with the offender.
   b. Obtain the offender's participation in the analysis of his or her problems, the setting of the objectives, and the establishing of a supervision plan. This should include setting limits and expectations. The supervising officer should make constructive suggestions to assist the offender in making a positive reintegration back into society.
   c. Explain thoroughly the Conditions of Supervision and have the offender sign them.

Pretrial Supervision

Many jurisdictions provide for the supervision of persons on bail or released on their own recognizance, that is, without the need to post bail. Contemporary bail reform efforts can be traced back to a Vera Foundation project in New York City in 1961. In response to a jail overcrowding problem, in a 3-year experiment, the Vera Foundation proved the feasibility and efficacy of a system of bail, based not on personal assets, but on verified social criteria. Programs based on these findings are usually referred to as *pretrial services*. A few years later, the President's Commission on Law Enforcement and Administration of Justice (1972) pointed out that prosecutors often deal with offenders who need treatment or supervision but for whom criminal sanctions would be excessive. Programs implementing this theory are referred to by many names, including *pretrial diversion* and *deferred prosecution*.

These programs use the fact that an arrest has occurred as a means of identifying defendants in need of treatment or, at least, not in need of criminal prosecution. They generally incorporate specific eligibility criteria, a service program, and the opportunity to monitor and control the decision not to prosecute. In eligible cases, the prosecutor agrees not to prosecute for periods ranging from 3 to 12 months, contingent on satisfactory performance during the pretrial period, often under the supervision of a probation officer or similar worker. At the end of a successful pretrial supervision period, the charges are dismissed. This type of diversion helps to remove minimal-risk cases from crowded court calendars while providing services to those who are in need of such help.

Onondaga (Syracuse) County, New York, has had a program in place for more than 30 years whose goal is to ensure no person arrested for a crime remains in jail solely because of an inability to post bail. The unit is staffed by a probation officer and four probation assistants who screen all detained defendants and, when appropriate, recommend persons for pretrial release (PTR) and community supervision. Seven days per week, a probation assistant screens those defendants who have been arrested in the past 24 hours. The defendant's prior record is reviewed, and those individuals who are selected as possible candidates for PTR are then individually interviewed. Typical of all PTR programs, eligibility is determined by using a risk assessment instrument (Figure 11.4). Referral and acceptance of appropriate services is often a condition of these individuals' release. Alcohol and drug abuse are the most frequent problems of defendants being considered for PTR. If it is determined that there is an appropriate community treatment program in which the defendant will not present a threat to the community and will likely reappear in court, the defendant is recommended to the court for PTR.

1. RESIDENCE
   (a) Length at present address
       • 6 months or less; undomiciled......................................2
       • Over 6 months to 1 year...1
       • Over 1 year...0
   (b) Location of residency
       • Out of state or out of country......................................2
       • County resident under 1 year.......................................1
       • County resident over 1 year...0
   (c) Living with at present
       • Nonrelative, friend..2
       • Self..1
       • Relative (including spouse)..0

2. FAMILY IN AREA
       • Family out of state or county.......................................2
       • Family in county...0

3. EMPLOYMENT/SCHOOL
       • Unemployed and/or not attending school...................2
       • Inconsistent, sporadic, or part time
         employment..1
       • Employed at least 20 hours per week or
         relatively stable employment the last year,
         homemaker; attends school regularly;
         disabled..0

4. PRIOR RECORD (past 10 years)
   (a) Felony convictions and delinquent adjudications
       • One or more prior convictions for class X
         or non-probationable class 1 felony............................2
       • One or more prior convictions for a
         probationable offense..1
       • No prior felony convictions...0
   (b) Prior record of misdemeanor, traffic, or local
       ordinance convictions
       • 2 or more misdemeanor convictions............................2
       • 3 or more local ordinance and/or traffic
         convictions or 1 misdemeanor conviction
         (add 1 to score if DUI offense)....................................1
       • No misdemeanor, traffic, or local ordinance
         convictions 0
   (c) Violent/Assaultive convictions
       • One or more prior convictions for violent offenses.....2
       • One or more prior misdemeanor or local ordinance
         convictions for violent offense....................................1
       • No prior record of violence offenses..........................0

FIGURE 11.4 *Illinois Pretrial Services Recommendation Criteria.*

5. PENDING CHARGES
   - Pending felony...2
   - Pending misdemeanor/traffic/ordinance........................1
   - No pending charges..0

6. PREVIOUS FAILURE TO APPEAR (FTA)
   - One or more felony FTA..2
   - One or more misd./traf./ordin. FTA...............................1
   - No prior FTA...0

7. PROBATION/PAROLE STATUS
   - Currently on probation or parole...................................2
   - Prior probation or parole...1
   - No prior probation or parole..0

8. SUBSTANCE USE
   - Regular, active use of drugs/alcohol.............................2
   - Occasional use of drugs/alcohol...................................1
   - No drug/alcohol use reported..0

TOTAL SCORE..._____

RECOMMENDATION
0–9   = Release on recognizance
10–14 = Conditional release
15+   = Cash plus conditional release

FIGURE 11.4 *(continued)*

As with probation cases, PTR clients are required to abide by individual conditions that may include weekly contact with a probation assistant, referrals to community agencies, and continuance in school or employment. The PTR unit also provides a liaison function for the probation department and the courts. PTR staff appear at calendar calls to make PTR recommendations, dispense information on people placed on probation, and gather requests for presentence investigations.

The Florida Department of Corrections operates a pretrial intervention program that diverts from prosecution first-time defendants who are accused of third-degree felonies or misdemeanors; they must volunteer for the program and agree to abide by deferred prosecution conditions of supervision that include restitution and payment of supervision costs. Consent must also be given by the victim, prosecutor, and judge. The subject is placed under the supervision of a correctional probation officer for a period that generally lasts from 90 days to 6 months. Those who complete the program successfully have their charges dismissed; those who fail are subject to prosecution for their original offense(s).

The most extensive program using pretrial supervision is the Pretrial Services of the United States Courts. In 42 districts with large metropolitan areas, pretrial investigation and supervision is provided by pretrial services officers; in the rest, they are provided by U.S. probation officers. The officer submits a Pretrial Services Report, which includes the details of the alleged offense and the history and background of the defendant. Of particular importance is an assessment of the risk the defendant poses for nonappearance and danger to the community. If the investigator determines the defendant poses no risk of nonappearance or danger to the community, he or she recommends release without conditions. If the officer determines the defendant poses some risk of nonappearance or danger to the community, he or she recommends "the least restrictive conditions that would reasonably assure the defendant's appearance and the safety of any other persons and the community." Except that the defendant not commit a crime, there are no general conditions. Instead, they are tailored to the individual appearing before the court (Wolf, 1997: 20). Persons posing a reasonable level of risk are placed under supervision, and the

Typical Day for a Pretrial Services Officer

Routine office activities for a pretrial services officer include meeting with defendants, discussing the release conditions, counseling defendants on drug abuse, encouraging them to maintain or seek employment, monitoring the submission of urine specimens, and reminding defendants of their next court date. Also, officers contact contract agencies to monitor attendance at drug treatment or mental health programs. In addition, officers speak with third-party custodians to assure defendants are abiding by release conditions. Another role of the pretrial services officer is to educate defendants on the court process. Sometimes defendants think every time they appear in court they are going to jail. Pretrial service officers explain the process—which may include a preliminary hearing, grand jury indictment, or arraignment—the role of the probation officer in preparing the presentence report, the sentencing hearing, and the possibility of self-surrender if a prison sentence is imposed. Knowing the process helps defendants alleviate some of their fears.

While completing routine paperwork, meeting with defendants, and handling phone calls, the pretrial services officer may receive a call that a new arrest has been made and the defendant needs to be interviewed in the marshal's cell block. At that time, the officer stops what he or she is doing and proceeds to the cell block to interview the defendant, conduct an investigation, and prepare a report for the defendant's initial appearance (Wolf, 1997: 23).

officer monitors compliance with court-imposed conditions, such as home confinement with electronic monitoring, urinalysis, the surrender of firearms and passports, and any curfew or in-person reports. Home and employment visits are routine and any violations of conditions are reported to the court, which can lead to more restrictive conditions or a revocation of release. The officer may also be called on to conduct diversion investigations for the *U.S.* Attorney when that office is considering pretrial diversion instead of prosecution. If diverted, the officer will provide supervision that includes monitoring the conditions of the diversion agreement.

Ongoing Supervision

Offenders are usually relieved to be out of the office after their first visit. They generally leave with mixed feelings. If the officer has been warm, concerned, and helpful, positive feelings will predominate. If the officer was not sensitive to the attitude conveyed and did not evince a feeling of acceptance, negative feelings will predominate. Claude Mangrum (1972: 48) notes that "there is nothing necessarily incompatible between warmth and acceptance and firm enforcement of the laws of the land. We must take whatever corrective measures are necessary, but these must not permit us to demean the dignity of the individual."

During periodic visits to the client's residence, the P/P officer should try to spend enough time to be able to relate to the client and the client's family. The home visit provides an opportunity to meet family members and interpret the role of the P/P agency to them. The worker should leave a business card and invite inquiries for information or help. The home visit also provides an opportunity to ensure spouse or child abuse is not a problem.

When visiting the home, it is incumbent on the officer to try to protect the confidentiality inherent in each case. Officers do not advertise their business or draw unnecessary attention to the visit to a client's home. Florida advises its correctional probation officers: "In order to help maintain the confidentiality of the Probation and Parole status of offenders under supervision, unmarked vehicles shall be used by

Benefits of Home/Field Visits (Illinois Division of Probation)

1. Probation officer can verify the probationer's address, employment, and so on.
2. Visiting the home helps the probation officer better understand the probationer.
3. Probation officer becomes aware of resources available to help the probationer.
4. Probation officer sees probationer in their natural environment.
5. There is an opportunity to involve other family members in the supervision plan.
6. Home visitation can improve the relationship between the PO and probationer.
7. Surprise visits can catch the probationer off guard and serve as a deterrent to criminal behavior.
8. Probationer sees the probation officer as a human.
9. Field supervision improves the agency's public image.
10. Increased community visibility enhances the relationship with police and other agencies.

officers. Correspondence shall be sent in envelopes which do not contain references to the Department of Corrections or Probation and Parole Services. Notes left at an offender's residence should be done with discretion to avoid broadcasting the status of the offender to others who may have access to the note." In many cases, the client's P/P status is known to neighbors, and the officer may be a familiar figure in the neighborhood. A client or the client's family may escort the officer back to his or her automobile or public transportation as a gesture of concern in high-delinquency areas.

The accompanying excerpt from a case record shows how increased understanding of an offender caused a change in the direction of treatment. It also reveals the value of home visits as a means of gaining new insights into an offender's situation. The second excerpt describes an interview with an offender in jail to indicate how the probation officer approached a hostile and uncooperative offender. The officer guides the interview to avoid futile and repetitious rationalizations and also explores to find some area in which he or she and the offender can work constructively together. The third case (Figure 11.5), shows how probation can impact on a client.

Home Visits by Colorado Parole Officers

Home visits are conducted to

- Confirm parolees' residence locations.
- Identify conditions in which parolees live and potential problems that may exist.
- Acquaint POs with parolees' household relationships.
- Provide POs with opportunities to enforce conditions of supervision, issue lawful directives, advise, and counsel parolees.
- Provide POs with opportunities to scrutinize parolees' residence for contraband.
- Provide POs with opportunities to collect urine specimens from parolees.
- Address any other purpose deemed appropriate for case supervision.

Quarterly Summary

3/9/04	Office report.
3/23/04	Failed to report.
3/30/04	Home visit. Mother and aunt seen.
4/6/04	Failed to report. Notice sent, giving 48 hours to report.
4/9/04	Reported.
4/13/04	Failed to report.
4/20/04	Home visit. Offender and aunt seen.
4/27/04	Reported.
5/1/04	Contact made with Community Settlement.
5/11/04	Reported.
5/25/04	Reported.

During March and April, attempts were made to get the offender to look for work. Early in March, he reported that he had a temporary job as a truck driver and believed that because of this he did not have to report. I corrected this idea and emphasized the importance of keeping his appointments. He had little to say but seemed amenable to conforming. The failure to report in April was excused because of illness.

During home visits, the mother reported that the offender is keeping reasonable hours. She informed me that he spends most of his spare time at the Community Settlement and recently won a trophy for basketball. The aunt, a single woman who lives in the home, takes an active interest in him. She said that the offender is really very shy and needs special attention, which she tries to give him because the mother has little time to spare from the younger children. She has accompanied him to the State Employment Office, where he has been trying to obtain work; however, because he is unskilled, he has few opportunities. Such protectiveness seems inappropriate for a 19-year-old youth.

I called the Community Settlement and talked with the director, Mr. Apt. He is very much interested in the offender, but told me confidentially that he is afraid the subject might be getting into a neighborhood gang that is beginning to form. He has noticed that when the offender leaves the settlement, he often joins other young men, some of whom have been in trouble. The settlement has an employment service for members and will try to help the offender obtain employment. When the offender reported, I suggested that he apply at the settlement employment service. The next day, Mr. Apt telephoned. The offender had been referred to a job in a downtown warehouse. He returned to the settlement in tears. He was so frightened that he had been unable to apply. He does not think he could do such work, although it is simple unskilled labor. Mr. Apt thinks that the offender needs psychiatric attention, but this may be the first time the offender has tried to seek work by himself.

At the time of the last report, the offender discussed some of his fears about work. He speaks warmly of the personnel at the settlement, but somewhat resentfully of his mother and aunt, who "keep nagging" him about work. It is planned to try to encourage this offender by building his self-esteem, giving recognition to his success in settlement activities, and planning visits when he is at home to deal with him directly rather than with relatives. The possibility of psychiatric referral will be explored.

Peter

Peter, age 18, has been on probation for 2 months. He was accorded youthful offender treatment following indictment for an assault during which he threatened to, but did not, use a knife. During the course of our contact, he has been on a weekly reporting schedule. I have concentrated on trying to help him get work. He has conformed in

(continued)

rather surly fashion and has never volunteered to discuss any of his problems. He lives at home with his mother, a divorcee, and an older brother, who is a conforming person who did well in school, has regular employment, and generally does everything he should, thereby winning the mother's approval.

Recently, Peter was arrested for drunk and disorderly conduct. He pleaded guilty and received a 30-day jail sentence, which he is just beginning to serve. The arresting officer's report indicated that he was assaultive and that it required three policemen to get him to the station. I visited him at the jail to obtain information for a violation report to be submitted to the court for action regarding his probation status. When I explained this, Peter went into what threatened to be a long harangue against the police and everyone connected with the current offense. He was in jail, he said, only because his girlfriend's father objected to him and was trying to keep him from dating her. I stated briefly and flatly what I knew about his present situation and noted that his own conduct was the reason for his being here. I asked him to tell me something about his girl, but he cut this off by saying that she and her family had moved to get the girl away from him, and he would not be seeing her any more. I asked what he had been assigned to do in jail. He was just washing dishes and it was a bore, and everyone here was a jerk. Had his family visited him? His mother had, but not his brother. I wondered how he got along with his brother. As if I had turned on a faucet, the story of his resentment toward his brother gushed out. He recalled things that had happened when he was only about 6 years old and revealed that he is conscious of his jealousy over the mother's favoritism.

CASE NOTES

Jones, Herbert L.
CASE # 01-CF-566

10/26/03 Defendant sentenced this date to 3 years' probation; sentenced to credit for time served in jail; fined $300.00 plus costs; ordered to pay $825.00 in restitution to Ace Awning; and ordered to be evaluated by and cooperate with recommended alcohol treatment.

Intake interview conducted by Officer John Miller this date. Conditions read, explained, and signed by defendant in acknowledgment. PSI information reviewed with defendant; no information update. Defendant ordered to contact Sauk River Alcohol Center by 10/30 to obtain an appointment for the evaluation. To report again to this officer at 10:30 A.M., 11/9, to continue intake process.

SUMMARY OF SUBJECT'S BACKGROUND   Herb is 22, a high school graduate, single, and currently unemployed. His last employer, Rydrox Corp., will consider him for rehire, but there were some attendance problems that may keep him from getting a job there at this time.

Herb was previously on probation in this county for misdemeanor theft and supervised by this officer. He reported regularly, paid all his monies, but did not seem motivated to make any change in his life. Besides the prior theft, Herb has also been on unsupervised supervision for DUI, on Conditional Discharge for Illegal Possession of Alcohol, and has had an Illegal Transportation 2, Speeding, and a muffler violation.

Herb has never received any type of counseling. He has no apparent mental health or physical problems. He clearly has a substance abuse problem. He has been drinking since age 14, and using marijuana since 16; he admits to getting drunk twice per week, and going to taverns every Friday and Saturday night. He likes to "party" and does not seem to do much else with his leisure time. Herb's father is a recovering alcoholic and attends Alcoholics Anonymous (AA). Both parents had previously been seen by this officer as enablers of Herb's drinking problems. However, with this last arrest, they decided not to bond him out; this is seen as a realization by them that it was time to stop "taking care of him."

10/27/03 Letter sent to Dennis Goodman, Ace Awning re: court order for restitution. It should be noted that Ace Awning has been paid by the insurance company but because the court order says to pay them, they will have to work out reimbursement with the insurance company (see file).

10/27/03 Referral letter sent to Sauk River Alcohol/Drug Center (see file).

10/28/03 Received statement of costs owed from Circuit Clerk's office: $101.87. Financial sheet updated.

10/29/03 Sauk River Alcohol/Drug Center called. Herb called yesterday for an appointment. He will see Dr. Kim Carter for evaluation on 11/11/01.

11/9/03 Herb failed to keep his appointment as scheduled for this date.

11/10/03 Failure to report letter sent to Herb; rescheduled for 3:30 on 11/16/03.

11/12/03 Herb called to explain that he'd missed his appointment because his grandmother in Oswald, Illinois, fell and broke her hip; he went to visit her at the hospital. Spoke with mother by telephone and she confirmed this.

11/16/03 Herb reported as scheduled. He was advised of the court costs he owed. Herb kept his appointment for alcohol evaluation. Said Dr. Carter was "O.K.," but her tests and questions were "really stupid." He's to see her again on 11/18/03.

Began discussions with Herb about what changes he believes he needs to make in his life to stay out of trouble. The main thing he wants to do is find a job. His parents say he can continue to live with them, but once he goes to work this time he will have to pay them for room and board, plus pay them back for the car payments they have been making for him. Herb says he'll probably look for his own apartment. He will need to learn some better financial habits if he is going to live on his own, pay the court-ordered monies, and pay back his parents. Herb seems to understand that he will have to cooperate with alcohol treatment if recommended. Right now he doesn't believe it is necessary because he does not see his usage as a problem. He does report that he has "only" been out drinking once since his release from jail. He thinks this proves he does not have a drinking problem. Herb is to report again on 11/23/03, after his appointment with Dr. Carter. His case will be assessed by that time, and we will begin the initial case planning.

11/18/03, 7:30 P.M. Unannounced home visit. Herb and both parents were at home. Reminded Herb of his appointment with Dr. Carter and this PO. He has been job hunting, but it doesn't look like Rydrox will rehire him at this time. They flat out asked him if he was still running around with the same people and drinking. He's pretty upset at them for not believing him when he said drinking was not a problem. His parents say it is going better at home. They confirmed that he has been home most nights but were aware of the one night that he did go out drinking. His girlfriend has been coming over to the house frequently and parents feel she's getting on him about his friends, the drinking, and the partying.

11/19/03 Case assessment. Scored "Max" on RISK and a "High Medium" on NEEDS. Identified problem areas are financial management, employment, alcohol usage, drug usage, companions, and attitude toward supervision. Herb will be supervised at the MAXIMUM level.

11/23/03 Phoned Lynnville Police to conduct a record check. They show no police contact; Sgt. Peters said he hasn't seen Herb out and about lately, but his friends are still doing their share of partying.

11/24/03 Herb reported as scheduled. He said that Dr. Carter had recommended he attend alcohol education classes and that he see her for individual counseling every other week. He's not happy about this but decided it would be better than going back to jail. Herb starts class next Monday, and the next appointment with Dr. Carter is 12/2/03. Officer will verify information.

Herb continues to reside with his parents and remains unemployed. He has not gone job hunting since he was turned down at Rydrox. He sees employment as the biggest thing to accomplish, while this office, in addition to the need for seeking employment, stressed the need to comply with alcohol treatment and discontinue usage.

A path to justice. . .

When Cindy came to Arizona in 1989, she arrived with the clothes on her back and a severe heroin addiction. Within a year she was homeless, "strung out," and caught up in the criminal justice system with pending fraud charges. She was sentenced to Intensive Probation Supervision (IPS) and remanded to jail while awaiting placement in residential treatment. She absconded after ten months in residential treatment even though she was near completion of the program. Cindy was arrested and returned to jail two months later; eventually, she was reinstated on IPS with a six-month jail term. She returned to treatment with a renewed desire to succeed and learn from her mistakes; it was this second chance that made the difference.

"I came to the realization that my probation officer, the counselors, and my peers actually cared for me, and that gave me the confidence to make the changes that were necessary," she stated. After months of residential treatment, she enrolled at Pima Community College. She became a volunteer at the treatment center, which eventually led to a part-time staff position. After earning certification, Cindy was promoted to substance abuse counselor. She completed a bachelor's degree, then commenced work on a master's degree in social work through Arizona State University. Today, Cindy is a certified substance abuse counselor, an acupuncturist, a 12-step sponsor, and a genuine role model; she works at a local clinic where she manages an active caseload of 85 clients. "I often tell the clients how fortunate I was to go through probation. It gave me the structure and discipline I never had and so desperately needed. This may sound strange," Cindy concluded, "but I thank God every day for probation helping me get clean and sober."

FIGURE 11.5 *A Path to Justice.*

(*Source:* Pima County, Arizona, Probation Department.)

OFFENDER EMPLOYMENT

Conventional wisdom—often a poor basis for drawing conclusions—argues that unemployment drives criminal behavior, and that unemployment as a negative social experience generates stress-induced aggression against persons and more rational crimes against property. However, research into the connection between unemployment and crime is inconclusive (Carlson and Michalowski, 1997).[1] Definitions of unemployment present further difficulties: Does it include only those who were unemployed and are now looking for full-time or part-time employment? Official unemployment figures cannot include those (usually young inner-city males) not part of labor department statistics because they fail to qualify for unemployment insurance or sign up for help in finding a job. We know many offenders were, in fact, employed at the time of their arrest, but in what is referred to as the secondary labor market—dead-end jobs having no real advancement potential and paying the minimum or near minimum wage. "A growing body of literature, however, suggests that the quality of the work may be more important than the simple existence of a job in the employment–crime relationship" (Henderson, 2004: 84). Under such conditions, explanations of crime may fit the classical model: a rational response to one's financial condition. Or, criminal involvement by persons in the secondary job market could be explained by control theory (discussed in chapter 9): little stake in conforming behavior. In other words, persons who value their employment would be reluctant to engage in behavior that could jeopardize it. "This would suggest that simply forcing former inmates to obtain a job, particularly low paying unskilled employment, upon release may not be enough to prevent them from coming back to prison" (Henderson, 2004: 92).

There are additional problems with the employment–crime hypothesis: "The observed relationship between criminality and unemployment has been explained in different ways. Some researchers have proposed that there is a *causal relationship* between unemployment and crime, while analysts have agreed that unemployment

[1]Indeed, one research effort found that juveniles who were gainfully employed had a *greater* chance of involvement in delinquency (Cullen, Williams, and Wright, 1997).

Employment and Recidivism

"Each year U.S. prisons release more than 400,000 criminal offenders to their communities. Most of those released will not remain crime free, and national statistics show that within 3 years of release, 40 percent will be returned to prison or jail. Experts debate the reasons for such high recidivism rates, but all agree that the lack of adequate job training and work opportunities is a critical factor. Offenders often have few marketable skills and training and, as a result, have a difficult time securing legitimate employment. With no legitimate income, many resort to crime" (Turner and Petersilia, 1996: 1).

and recidivism are highly correlated only because each is associated with another factor (e.g., the influence of family members or a decision to "go straight"), which induced widespread behavioral change. Whatever the explanation, unemployment and recidivism are often closely related" (Toborg et al., 1978: 2). Thus, the variable *employment* may not be the cause of the variable *go straight*, but both variables may actually be dependent on the (independent) variable *motivation*. In other words, whatever it is that motivates an offender to seek and maintain gainful employment (the P/P officer?) also tends to motivate that offender to avoid criminal behavior.

Nevertheless, the securing and maintaining of employment or training for employment have been considered crucial aspects of P/P supervision: "Perhaps the greatest single factor influencing the quality of life of parolees in their communities is the ability to secure and maintain employment" (Davidoff-Kroop, 1983: 1). Many believe that a relationship exists between successful employment and avoidance of further legal difficulties. A study in California revealed that unemployment and underemployment are closely associated with recidivism (Grogger, 1989) and "two parolee follow-up studies in New York showed a high rate of unemployment amongst parolees returned to prison" (Davidoff-Kroop, 1983: 1).

In addition to providing economic rewards, employment also enhances the self-worth and image of the client; however, parolees and probationers "who are often undereducated and with few skills learn that finding work is problematical and frustrating" (Davidoff-Kroop, 1983: 1). The employment problem for parolees is often a great deal more difficult than for probationers. The parolee has been separated

But...

The central assumption in the crime–employment argument is that employment is a resiliency factor that would keep individuals from engaging in criminal conduct because of the economic and affective benefits of employment and high risks of crime and punishment. Some researchers have argued that employment may be, for an undefined percentage of cases, a risk factor—that is, employment increases stress and unhappiness, and leads some to abandon employment for illegal pursuits or add illegal pursuits to legal employment. (Krienert and Fleisher, 2004: 40)

Skills Shop

The Alameda County, California, Probation Department operates a multifaceted approach to aiding client employment efforts. The Probation Center provides computer-based instruction specifically designed so most participants with 10 hours of applied effort per week can learn enough to pass the various GED tests. The computer lab has online programs available to aid with reading, writing, math, and survival skills, such as reading maps, using phone books, and understanding street signs. Individual probation staff are available to assist in meeting client employment and educational goals, such as finding job leads or applying for education and vocational training programs. There are Internet service links for employment and employment workshops.

The first week of the workshop has sessions on topics such as application completion, appropriate attire, interview questions, resume writing, money management, and coping with conflict in the workplace. The second week is devoted to an active job search with participants applying the skills they learned in the workshop. Friday support groups continue after the 2-week program until employment is secured. Newly employed participants are welcome to continue with the support group.

from employment and community contacts, usually for at least 18 months, often longer. The prison environment offers little help. More than two decades ago, the Comptroller General of the United States (1979) reported that federal and state prison systems have been deficient in their approach to training and educating inmates for employment. In view of the punitive shift in corrections, no reason exists to believe that the situation has gotten better since that report was published. In 1999, there were more than 1,231,000 persons in state prisons, but only about 185,000 were receiving job training and job-related education (Shilton, 2000).

In assisting clients with employment, officers make direct referrals to particular employers if they have the necessary contacts, or they may refer clients to other agencies, such as state employment services. Officers may have to provide guidance and counseling concerning some of the basic aspects of securing employment, items that for middle-class persons are taken for granted. For example, officers will emphasize the need to be on time for interviews, in fact, the need to arrive early. They will help to fill out applications or help the client to prepare for this aspect of the job search. Some officers may use role-playing to accustom clients to job interview situations. Officers discuss the importance of good grooming and what type of clothes to wear to an interview.

Mock Job Fair.   In an effort to deal with the chronic problem of offender employment, the state of Texas initiated a prison-based program—Project Re-Enterprise—centering on a mock job fair that enables inmates to hone their job-seeking skills while enabling employers to perform a public service and become familiar with a potential labor pool. The inmates chosen for the program are within 60 days of return to the community, and the program enlists the participation of local business leaders whose firms agree to conduct 30-minute practice job interviews at the institution. Program staff help inmates fill out practice job applications and conduct interview practice sessions. Employers who participate are not pressured to hire inmates they agree to interview, nor are they asked to change company personnel policies or make any commitment beyond participation in the job fair. In practice, "some employers have voluntarily altered their policies and practices" and "placed the corporate community in a position to alter social change" (Moses, 1996: 2). "At the conclusion of the interview, employers complete a short written evaluation of the applicant's performance that is returned to the inmate on the following day in a classroom setting. Evaluations are used as teaching tools" (9).

Job Fair—The Real Thing

Some New Jersey employers are looking to the state prison system to find ways to meet an employee shortfall. They are participating in job fairs sponsored by the Department of Corrections. To qualify, an inmate must be within 18 months of release, write a resume, and undergo educational and vocational training. In 2001, nearly 20 businesses and organizations participated in a job fair at Northern State Prison, where 188 qualified inmates were drawing serious interest. "There's a nationwide shortage of 400,000 drivers. Where are we gonna get them?" asked the owner of a tractor trailer training firm. His company first began interviewing inmates about 3 years ago, and has trained and found jobs for 18 since then, most of whom have done well on the outside. Many have qualities his trucking clients are looking for. "They're highly regimented. They're used to getting up at a certain time each day, doing a job and being done by a certain time. They take direction well" (Parry, 2001).

The Federal Bureau of Prisons (BOP) requires all its facilities to offer release preparation programs "addressing such life skills as parenting, financial management, problem-solving, stress management, avoiding substance abuse, and related free-world survival skills" (McCollum, 2000: 13). Building on the Texas model, the BOP established the Inmate Placement Program Branch, which uses the **mock job fair.** Staff from motor vehicle, social service, and other relevant public and private agencies are invited to send staff who operate information desks during the fair. Participating inmates are required to complete courses whose topics include how to prepare job applications, the importance of good grooming, and proper posture during the job interview. Classes are presented by personnel from local educational and training organizations.

There have been unexpected results, particularly on the cooperating company recruiters: "They left impressed not only with the professionalism of the staff and the orderly appearance of the institution, but also with the skilled labor pool they found among the inmates they interviewed" (McCollum, 2000: 15). Inmates gained interview experience that enhanced their self-confidence. They learned the importance of preparing a resume and having in hand documents such as a birth certificate and Social Security card. The personal contact between employer and inmate has resulted directly in postprison employment.

The Stigma of Conviction

One critical aspect of employment for ex-offenders is the question of revealing their record. I allowed my clients to decide for themselves. However, I did provide guidance by discussing the experiences of other clients relative to this issue. Many clients reported that their candor resulted in not securing employment. Others reported that some employers were interested in providing them with an opportunity "to make it." Unfortunately, many, if not most, employers will not hire an ex-offender if any alternative exists.

Some offenders are required by law or P/P agency policy to reveal their records when applying for certain jobs. For example, most positions with the government require people having a criminal conviction to reveal this fact; they are frequently fingerprinted for this purpose. Banks, hospitals, and other sensitive areas of employment may also require disclosure. Certainly, allowing an offender with a history of drug abuse to work in a hospital or similar situation would not be advisable, especially if the employer did not know of the person's record. Some states (e.g., Illinois) are now making most criminal conviction records available to the public. A growing number of states are offering online databases of inmates and parolees,

The Big Question

An employment-training instructor for ex-inmates in New York City has to deal with *The Big Question*: "You don't check 'yes.' You don't check 'no.' You don't leave it blank. You put down 'Wish to discuss during interview.' Answering 'yes' or leaving it blank almost guarantees rejection. Answering 'no' is lying and grounds for dismissal" (Guggenheim, 1998: Sec. 5: 8).

allowing employers to screen prospective hires. The Kansas Bureau of Investigation, for example, has placed all its criminal history records for the past 65 years on the Internet, which businesses and individuals can access for a fee of $17.50 for each record retrieved. Most of the inquiries come from employers doing background checks. The implications are troubling: Access to such records allows employers to deny employment to otherwise qualified ex-offenders, rendering the probationer/ parolee virtually unemployable. With respect to public employment, 6 states deny the right to public employment to convicted felons, 10 states leave it to the discretion of the employer, 12 apply a "direct relationship test" to determine suitability, and 17 states permit public employment after completion of the sentence (Olivares, Burton, and Cullen, 1996).

An expert in the field of ex-offender employment recommends that "the employer should be made aware of an offender's status only when the pattern of the offender's behavior may result in antisocial behavior," such as a former drug addict working in a medical setting (New York State Employment Services Vocational Rehabilitation Service, 1965: 8). The vocational director of the Osborne Association, a prison reform group, states: "We do not lie about the individual's record but, because of the prejudice that employers may have, we try to postpone complete revelation until the employer has had a chance to try out the offender on the job" (8).

Richard Schwartz and Jerome Skolnick (1962) studied the effects of a criminal record on the employment opportunities of unskilled workers. Four employment folders were prepared, which were the same in all respects except for the criminal record of the applicant, as follows:

1. The first folder indicated that the applicant had been convicted and sentenced for assault.
2. The second noted that he had been tried for assault and acquitted.
3. The third again showed that he was tried for assault and acquitted, but with a letter from the judge certifying the finding of not guilty.
4. The fourth made no mention of any criminal record.

The study involved 100 employers who were divided into units of 25, with each group being shown one of the four folders on the mistaken belief that they were actually considering a real job applicant:

- Of the employers shown the "no record" folder, 36 percent gave positive responses.
- Of the employers shown the "acquitted" folder with the judge's letter, 24 percent expressed an interest in the application.
- Of the employers shown the "acquitted" folder, 12 percent expressed an interest in the applicant.
- Of the employers shown the "convict" folder, only 4 percent expressed interest in the applicant.

Because most persons on P/P are unskilled, the ramifications of these findings are obvious.

A study (Pager, 2003) to test the effect of a "negative credential" impact of a criminal record on employment opportunity, used four 23-year-old college students, two white and two black. They applied for 350 entry-level positions requiring no education greater than high school and no previous experience. The four rotated presenting themselves as having a felony conviction for possession of drugs with intent to sell. The research revealed that race continues to play a dominant role in shaping employment opportunity equal to or greater than the impact of a criminal record: 34 percent of white applicants without a criminal record got callbacks, as opposed to 17 percent of whites with a record; among blacks without a criminal record, only 14 percent received callbacks, compared with 5 percent with a record.

One extensive research effort revealed that "in terms of employer willingness to hire ex-offenders, fewer than 40 percent of all employers claim that they would definitely or probably hire ex-offenders into their most recently filled non-college job. This figure stands in sharp contrast to their general willingness to hire other groups of workers that are commonly stigmatized, such as welfare recipients, applicants with a GED instead of high school diploma, or applicants with spotty work histories" (Holzer, Raphael, and Stoll, 2002: 4).

In an effort to minimize the legal harm caused by a criminal record, some states have removed various statutory restrictions on gaining licenses necessary for employment, and a few have even enacted "fair employment" laws for ex-offenders. New York, for example, prohibits the denial of employment or license because of a conviction unless there is a **direct relationship** between the conviction and the specific employment or license, or unless it involves an "unreasonable risk" to persons or property. A direct relationship requires a showing that the nature of the criminal conduct for which the person was convicted has a direct bearing on the fitness or ability to carry out duties or responsibilities related to the employment or license. The statute requires that a public or private employer provide, on request, a written statement setting forth the reasons for a denial of license or employment and provides for enforcement by the New York State Commission on Human Rights. The Federal Bonding Program, which is administered through state employment services agencies, has a long-standing program that provides bonding for probationers and parolees without any cost to either employee or employer.

States vary in the method and extent to which they provide relief from disabilities incurred by probationers and parolees. Some states have adopted automatic restoration procedures on satisfactory completion of P/P supervision, and many states have statutes designed to restore forfeited rights, although they may be subjected to restrictive interpretation in licensing and occupational areas. In Georgia, the right to vote is automatically restored to offenders who have completed their sentences, and the Board of Pardons and Paroles automatically considers restoring civil and political rights to parolees upon discharge from supervision. Pardon is another method, although its use is generally limited; some states (e.g., Missouri) have limited forms of pardon that restore certain rights (discussed in chapter 8). In New York, the judiciary and parole board have the power to restore certain rights through the granting of a "relief from disabilities."

With respect to voting rights, 48 states deny prisoners the right to vote, whereas 13 states ban some felons either permanently or conditionally from voting. For instance, Arizona and Maryland ban twice-convicted felons from voting permanently, whereas Delaware bans felons from voting until 5 years after they have completed their sentences. Seven states impose lifetime disenfranchisement to anyone convicted of a felony, whereas 22 permit felons on probation to vote ("Court Orders Trial on Ban of Voting by Felons," 2003; Lewin, 1998; Sengupta, 2000; Zielbauer, 2001).

Lifetime disenfranchisement has an ugly history dating back to the years after the Civil War. It was part of a legal strategy to keep the vote from emancipated African Americans in the states of the Confederacy, when the Reconstruction

Congress compelled each confederate state to grant black men the franchise. In 1868, Florida responded by simultaneously disenfranchising many blacks by denying any individual convicted of a felony or larceny the right to vote—such persons were overwhelmingly African American. Throughout the South, poll taxes and literacy tests were also enacted as an attempt to minimize the effect of emancipation. Although the Supreme Court eventually abolished these archaic practices, felon disenfranchisement remains constitutional (Eisenkraft, 2001).

New York State Relief from Civil Disabilities

I. *Certificates of Relief from Disabilities*

    A. *Effect of a Certificate of Relief.* A Certificate of Relief removes any legal bar of disability imposed as a result of conviction of the crime or crimes specified in the certificate, although specific disabilities (such as those relating to weapon possession) may be excepted by the Board of Parole. In addition, by law, the Certificate of Relief may not enable an individual to retain or be eligible for public office. Although removing legal bars does restore to the certificate holder the right to apply, it does compel the granting of employment or license or prevent the potential employer or licensing agency from taking the criminal record into consideration. Possession of a certificate does not authorize an individual to deny that he or she has ever been convicted of a crime.

    B. *Eligibility.* A Certificate of Relief may be issued by the Board of Parole to any eligible offender who has been committed to an institution under the jurisdiction of the New York State Department of Correctional Services. The Board of Parole may also issue a Certificate of Relief to an eligible offender who has been convicted in any other jurisdiction and who now resides in New York State. By law, an eligible offender is defined as one who has not been convicted more than once of a felony. (Two or more felony convictions stemming from the same indictment count as one conviction. Two or more convictions stemming from two or more separate indictments filed in the same court prior to conviction under any of them count as one conviction.) A plea or a verdict of guilty upon which sentence or the execution of sentence has been suspended or upon which a sentence of probation, conditional discharge, or unconditional discharge has been imposed shall be deemed to be a conviction. (It should be noted that juvenile offenders are eligible for Certificates of Relief.)

A Certificate of Relief may be issued upon an eligible individual's release from a correctional facility or at any time thereafter.

II. *Certificates of Good Conduct*

    A. *Effect of a Certificate of Good Conduct.* A Certificate of Good Conduct has the same effect as the Certificate of Relief. In addition, the Certificate of Good Conduct may restore the right of an individual to apply for public office. The certificate may be issued to remove all legal bars or disabilities or to remove only specific bars or disabilities. The board may subsequently issue a supplementary certificate removing those disabilities or bars not previously removed.

    B. *Eligibility.* The Certificate of Good Conduct is available to those individuals convicted of more than one felony. Such individuals, however, do not become eligible for a Certificate of Good Conduct until a minimum period of time has elapsed from the date of conviction, or, if incarcerated, from the date of unrevoked release from custody by parole or termination of sentence. In those cases where the most serious conviction is a misdemeanor, the minimum period of good conduct required is 1 year. In those cases where the most serious conviction is a C, D, or E Felony, the minimum period of good conduct is 3 years. In those cases where the most serious conviction is an A or B Felony, the minimum period is 5 years.

RESTORATIVE AND COMMUNITY JUSTICE

Toward the end of the twentieth century, traditional P/P supervision was being challenged by new paradigms, most notably restorative and community justice.

Restorative Justice

In the current system of criminal justice, "an outgrowth of the historical emergence of the state as the dominant power in modern times, crime is perceived as an act against the state. This approach has led to the gross neglect of individual victims, who have been seen as passive entities, have been almost completely locked out from any decision making in the justice proceedings, and often have not been compensated for the harm that occurred to them" (Niemeyer and Shichor, 1996). Emerging during the 1970s as part of the victim's movement, **restorative justice** (RJ) "views crime as a violation of one person by another, rather than against the state" (Maloney and Umbreit, 1995: 43). This approach has proven so popular in some jurisdictions that entire systems are being redesigned (Levrant et al., 1999). Although restorative justice programs are now quite common at the state and local level in the United States, they handle mostly property offenses and minor assaults by juveniles (Dzur and Wertheimer, 2002).

RJ is the guiding philosophical framework for a new paradigm that seeks to promote maximum involvement of the victim, the offender, and the community (Bazemore and Maloney, 1994). Instead of simply punishing those who commit crimes—*retributive* justice—the focus is on allowing the offender an opportunity to make amends to his or her victim (Crowe, 1998; Wright, 1991; Zehr and Mika, 1998). Restorative justice "views crime as a violation of one person by another, rather than a violation against the state" (Umbreit and Carey, 1995: 47); "the depersonalized mechanisms of corrections fail to deliver the message to the offender that by his/her actions s/he has harmed another human being; and that part of the offender's habilitation or rehabilitation should be geared toward making the victim whole again. The evolution of the criminal justice system in this country has resulted in a deemphasis on the responsibility of the offender toward the victim(s) of his/her wrongful acts. Professionalization and abstract proceduralism . . . hinder the reintegration of offenders into law-abiding society" (Sinclair, 1994: 16).

Punishment—retributive justice—"may have several counterdeterrent effects on offenders, including stigmatization, humiliation, and isolation, that may minimize prospects for regaining self-respect and the respect of the community" (Bazemore and Umbreit, 1995: 300). The treatment response provides little in the way of a message that the offender has harmed someone and should take action to repair damages to the victim. Restorative justice appeals to liberals as an alternative to the punishment-oriented practice that has become so popular, and to conservatives who are attracted to the victim reparation dynamic of RJ (Levrant et al., 1999).

RJ offers a new way to look at the response to crime and criminal behavior beyond the traditional debate over treatment and punishment. Instead of advocating more/better treatment or greater punishment, the new model seeks systemwide change, a new philosophical framework in which the victim is at the center: "While Probation and Parole place a plethora of educational, counseling and social services at the disposal of the offender, little is done to reach out to crime victims with services they may desperately need" (Sinclair, 1994: 15). RJ argues for not only bringing the victim back into the criminal justice system, but also that all parties—victim, offender, and community—should be included in the response to crime. P/P agencies are in a unique position to implement RJ because of their long-term relationships with offenders (Sinclair, 1994).

RJ is accomplished by means of victim–offender mediation through which the parties are given a human face: "Facing the person they violated is not easy for most offenders. While it is often an uncomfortable position for offenders, they are given the equally unusual opportunity to display a more human dimension to their character.

To Crime Victims in Montgomery County, Ohio

As the victim of a crime, you have the unique opportunity, if you choose, to become more involved in the justice process as it involves the crime committed against you. The Montgomery County Common Pleas Court makes it possible for victims and offenders to meet in safe and secure settings for the purpose of resolving issues related to the offense.

What if you could meet and talk to the person who committed the crime? What if a neutral third person—a mediator—was in the room to help you talk freely and safely? What if you tell the offender how the crime affected you and others, and what if you worked out an agreement that seemed fair to you and helped make things right? That is possible when victims and offenders meet.

If property has been lost and restitution is owned, victims have the opportunity to tell the offender how much is owed, and then work out a repayment agreement. Experience has shown that offenders are more likely to complete their obligations when they "put a face on the crime" and are held accountable for their behavior. It is also important to know that offenders who meet with their victims and reach an agreement are less likely to reoffend.

For many, the opportunity to express remorse in a very direct and personal fashion is important. The mediation process allows victims and offenders to deal with each other as people, oftentimes from the same neighborhood, rather than as stereotypes and objects" (Umbreit, 1994: 9).

This is the basis of VORP—the *Victim/Offender Reconciliation Program*—a sentencing alternative popular in a number of communities, including Orange County, California, where it is sponsored by the St. Vincent De Paul Center. VORP handles both juvenile and adult criminal cases often referred by the probation department. Mediators are trained volunteers who receive cases from a case manager, make the initial call to the offender, and meet with that person and his or her parents. If they are willing to participate, the mediator calls the victim and arranges a joint meeting during which each tells his or her story, expresses feelings, and discusses what might be done to make things right. After an agreement is reached, a contract is drafted and the case returned to the VORP office where a staff person follows up on the execution of the agreed-upon conditions.

In meetings that last about an hour, victims typically ask, "Why me?" "Were you watching us?" "Do you have any idea what this has done to me/us/our family?" This process is believed to hold offenders more directly accountable for their actions—they must listen to the human side of the injuries they have caused and must begin to take some responsibility for repairing the damage they caused. In some cases, that might also include offering genuine expressions of remorse (Gehm, 1998).

Participation rates are high. Victims are most likely to participate in cases involving minor personal crimes and least likely to participate when they were victims of serious personal crime. Perpetrators are least likely to agree to participate in minor personal crimes. Noncompliance with contracts is rare (Niemeyer and Shichor, 1996), and probation officers are in a position to insist on participation and compliance with contracts.

In 1994, the Idaho legislature adopted the restorative justice model for its newly created Department of Juvenile Corrections. In Kootenai County, the juvenile probation department uses a trained professional to mediate sessions between victims and offenders. "Through mediation, the victims ask their offenders questions they have struggled to understand, such as: 'Why would you want to harm me or my property? What made you target me over others? How can I be sure that you won't do this again? Should I be afraid of you?'" The department also arranges for restitution and/or community service. "Kids are learning that if caught, they can't just show up at juvenile court, pay a fine and call it a day" (Crowley, 1998: 10).

Vermont's statewide approach to restorative justice requires probationers convicted of minor crimes to meet with the victim and a Reparative Citizen Board made up of volunteers—there are more than 60 of them throughout the state—typically five or six citizens aided by a department of corrections staff person. Together they discuss the offense, its effects on the victim and the community, and the life situations of victim and offender. Participants must agree on a contract to be fulfilled by the probationer that meets the goals of restorative justice (Dzur and Wertheimer, 2002; Kurki, 1999). In Somerset County, Pennsylvania, probationers attend Victim Impact Classes during which, in addition to an academic curriculum, they listen to actual crime victims. Missouri uses volunteer Reparation Boards, which meet probationers and parolees and recommend conditions of supervision along the lines of restorative justice.

In targeting only offenders for intervention, notes Gordon Bazemore (1994: 19), both the surveillance and individual treatment models ignore two primary "clients" or constituents of community corrections—victims and the community—and offer weak choices to criminal justice decision makers. Victim and offender are placed in passive roles: "Holding the offender accountable and responsible—RJ does not simply seek to punish and reintegrate the offender back into the community." Some offenders need incarceration—RJ does not substitute for that need. The offender must take responsibility and perform to restore that which he or she destroyed—damage to the victim and loss of a sense of security to the community. Instead of rehabilitation, RJ seeks competency development—beyond simply trying to get the offender to give up crime—providing life skills so he or she can give back to the victim and community.

Risk management during the time when an offender is under supervision does not enhance community safety in the long range; only offender competence can do this. Providing skills, however, is not enough. The offender must develop empathy for the victim along with skills or else there will be an offender with skills who continues committing crimes (Bazemore and Umbreit, 1994).

Instead of punishment, accountability is the goal. Instead of taking "their punishment," RJ seeks to get offenders to take responsibility for the victim and help repair the loss suffered by the community. According to RJ, the most important aspect of crime is the harm caused the victim, the community, and the offender. RJ says that criminal justice should be about repairing the damage caused by crime—helping communities get offenders to undo the damage their crimes caused. Instead of the

Life Skills

The Delaware Department of Correction has a 4-month Life Skills Program for inmates to deal with handicaps that range far beyond the ability to read and write: job hunting, uncontrolled anger, inability to form healthy personal relationships, and failure to establish realistic—or any—goals. Offenders often lack the ability or willingness to choose ethical behavior over unethical behavior. Meeting in classes of 12 to 15 inmates for 3 hours per day, the curriculum consists of three components: academics, violence reeducation, and applied life skills. The latter includes such practical matters as credit and banking, job search, motor vehicle registration, legal and family responsibilities, health, cultural differences, government, and law. Initially, the program found it difficult to recruit students, but the opportunity to earn additional good time and more favorable consideration at parole hearings provided important incentives that ensure a steady supply of inamtes seeking admission (Finn, 1998).

needs of the offender, the focus is on the needs of the victim. Under RJ, the three clients are the victim, the community (needs to feel safe/secure), and the offender. RJ seeks to make the victim whole by providing for social, psychological, and financial needs (Carlson, 1993).

Although this approach appears appropriate for less serious crimes and offenders, particularly when a prior relationship exists between victim and offender, with more serious crimes and more hardened criminals, RJ appears difficult. When either victim or offender is unwilling to participate, or when the offense is too heinous or the suffering too severe, the offender meets with other victims, often through victim advocate organizations rather than his or her own victim(s) as a step toward assuming responsibility (Zehr, 1990). In some programs, offender–victim discussion occurs through video or written dialogue.

Some observers urge caution in adopting the RJ model. They note that liberals and conservatives also supported determinate sentencing. "The restorative justice movement is reminiscent of the determinate sentencing movement of the 1970s. Both restorative justice and determinate sentencing emerged from contrasting ideologies posited by liberals and conservatives. . . . Liberals sought to limit discretion and create sentencing practices that were more fair while conservatives supported determinate sentencing as a means of controlling crime with harsher sentences that would deter crime and incapacitate criminals. But the conservative view prevailed. RJ, instead of reducing crime through reconciliation, could simply become another variation of the 'get tough on crime' approach. This is particularly troubling because RJ programs typically target low-risk offenders" (Levrant et al., 1999: 7). Crime victim's groups have raised questions about RJ (Smith, 2001: 5):

- "In the hands of community corrections agencies whose habits are offender focused, restorative justice can cast victims as little more than props in a psychodrama focused on the offender to restore him (and thereby render him less likely to offend again)."

- "A victim . . . while engaged in restorative conferencing and feeling genuinely free to speak directly to the offender may press a blaming rather than restorative agenda." Attempts to script victim participation are destructive of the RJ process.

- "Restorative processes depend, case by case, on victims' active participation, in a role more emotionally demanding than that of complaining witness in a conventional prosecution—which is a role avoided by many, perhaps most victims."

Community Justice/"Broken Windows"

According to the American Probation and Parole Association, community justice is a strategic method of crime reduction and prevention that builds or enhances partnerships within communities. Some refer to the approach as "environmental corrections" (e.g., Cullen, Williams, and Wright, 2002), whereas others use the "**broken windows**" metaphor (e.g., Reinventing Probation Council (RPC), 2000; Rhine, 2002) that was first applied to policing (Wilson and Kelling, 1982). Whatever the term, the model stresses that P/P "must move well beyond the management of individual caseloads and engage the community in the business of community supervision" (Rhine, 2002: 39). This neighborhood-based supervision abandons the traditional 9 to 5, Monday through Friday, approach typical of many P/P agency operations. Instead, offenders who are deemed a potential threat to community safety are subject to surveillance and control by officers who have available a continuum of sanctions and a continuum of treatment designed to maintain public safety, and to hold offenders accountable for all violating behaviors (Rhine, 2002; RPC, 2000). There is proactive pursuit of absconders as part of a program of offender accountability.

The focus is on crime fighting policies that "emphasize proactive, problem-solving practices intended to prevent, control, reduce and repair crime's harm" and that "create and contribute to healthy, safe, vibrant and just communities and to improve citizens' quality of life" (RPC, 2000: 16). Regardless of the name, notes Joan Petersilia (2003), the key components of this approach are the same: strengthening linkages with law enforcement and the community. It is a "full service" model that stresses "activist supervision." Officers aggressively "patrol" those neighborhoods of urban America with high concentrations of high-risk offenders. Working out of local offices—community centers, municipal offices, public housing projects, police precincts, mental health centers, and local storefronts—they deliberately maintain a high profile interacting with the police, human service agencies, community groups, and business people. In Bell and Lampasas counties, Texas, high-risk offenders are visited by probation officers wearing official uniform jackets and shirts and driving marked department vehicles (Jermstad, 2002). "By widening the community net, probation officers reduce the anonymity that offenders all too often enjoy while they are under supervision" (RPC, 2000: 21). Supervision officers attend neighborhood meetings and participate in local crime prevention activities. They facilitate the formation of task forces that include, in addition to law enforcement, representatives from human service and the religious community for the purpose of joint staffing and shared accountability for curtailing crime.

The North Carolina Division of Community Corrections has been working to implement the new community probation partnerships in cities across the state. By working side by side at traffic stops, riding together in police squad cars, and sharing desks at community policing substations in high-crime neighborhoods, probation and police officers learn more about each other. In Raleigh, state probation officers have an office in each of the four police substations located in high-crime neighborhoods. On a typical Friday night, six P/P officers don bullet-proof vests and work at the elbows of city police setting up roadblocks in neighborhoods known for drug problems. The police officers pass the drivers' licenses on to the P/P officers who radio back to the P/P office where four officers man computers.

One evening P/P officers intercepted six probationers; three were out past curfew, one was on the run, another was carrying a semiautomatic pistol, and one was driving while intoxicated. Another night, they found a deadbeat dad. In the western North Carolina city of Hendersonville, probation officer David Oates is dressed in black bike shorts and a black shirt, complete with a badge and the words "Probation Officer" emblazoned on the back. Oates is hard to miss as he rides his bicycle along city streets, through neighborhoods and around parks with a Hendersonville police officer. They are part of the Department of Correction's community policing initiative. By leaving behind their offices and the comforts of their cars in favor of policing by bike, the officers have made themselves more visible and accessible to members of the community, resulting in an increased sense of safety.

On a typical 4-hour ride through town, the PO can make 10 to 15 home visits, not to mention the contacts he makes just by running into people on the street or riding through the parks. In fact, Oates said he can make home visits by bike much quicker than he ever could by car, because now he can just ride right up to people's front doors without having to park his car and lock it up. Sometimes he does not even have to get off his bike.

Many of Connecticut's towns and cities have adopted community policing as a law enforcement strategy. Partnerships have been formed with several of Connecticut's largest cities to incorporate POs into their community policing programs. As a result, many parole-related activities are based out of neighborhood substations where caseloads can be assigned geographically to coincide with these local precincts. In addition, POs often team up with local police on routine patrols. These partnerships reaffirm the link between parole and law enforcement and increase the efficiency of parole supervision by enhancing the PO's knowledge of neighborhood crime concerns while enhancing the police officer's knowledge of Connecticut's parole system.

For this approach to be feasible, P/P officers need to be sufficiently trained to offer counseling and/or refer clients to appropriate human service agencies. They must also be trained and equipped in all aspects of personal protection and law enforcement. Supervising high-risk offenders and operating outside normal business hours in high-crime neighborhoods can be intimidating. During his years as a field PO, the writer, at 6'1, 210 pounds, whose recreational activities consisted of weightlifting and boxing, was at times quite uneasy in certain neighborhoods despite carrying a .38 revolver.

Now that the details of P/P supervision have been examined, chapter 12 examines special problems and special supervision units in P/P.

KEY TERMS

classification	mock job fair
risk/needs assessment	direct relationship
caseload	restorative justice
workload	"broken windows"
specialized caseloads	

INTERNET CONNECTIONS

Criminal justice links: faculty.ncwc.edu/toconnor
Center for Community Corrections: communitycorrectionsworks.org
International Community Corrections Association: www.iccaweb.org
Center for Restorative Justice & Peacemaking: 2ssw.che.umn.edu/rjp
Officer.Com Corrections Resources: officer.com/correct.htm
Probation & Parole: talkjustice.com/links.asp?453053932

REVIEW QUESTIONS

1. How did the advent of the corrections model alter the prison classification process?
2. What led to the widespread use of classification in P/P?
3. What are the two dimensions weighed by a risk/needs assessment instrument?
4. What are the purposes of classifying offenders in P/P?
5. Why do parolees often encounter difficulties not experienced by probationers?
6. What are the various methods for assigning cases to P/P officers?
7. What is the purpose of the risk/needs classification system?
8. How does the risk/needs system classify offenders?
9. In assigning cases for supervision, how does caseload differ from workload?
10. What are the advantages of incorporating geographic considerations in assigning caseloads?
11. What items are usually emphasized by the P/P officer during the initial interview with a client?
12. Why is the home visit important in P/P supervision?

13. How can the observed relationship between crime and being employed be explained in different ways?
14. With respect to prohibiting employment discrimination against ex-offenders, what is meant by a "direct relationship"?
15. What are the purposes of the mock job fair?
16. How does restorative justice differ from retributive justice?
17. What is meant by the community justice or "broken windows" model of supervision?

CHAPTER 12

Special Problems and Programs in Probation and Parole

It has long been recognized that offenders with certain salient characteristics could benefit from the services of a specialist—a P/P officer who, as a result of education, training, and experience, is in a better position to provide social services and control functions. Many P/P agencies have specialized units or specialists for particular offenders, for example:

- Substance-abusing offenders
- Sex offenders
- HIV/AIDS offenders
- DWI offenders
- Gang-involved offenders
- Retarded offenders

We examine the problems posed by these special problem offenders and the specialized caseloads organized as a response. Then we review special issues and programs in P/P supervision.

SUBSTANCE-ABUSING CLIENTS

Substance abuse is the single most frequently encountered problem across P/P populations,[1] and P/P officers frequently refer clients to substance abuse treatment programs. Substance abuse treatment typically begins with detoxification with or without the assistance of drugs, for example, the antihypertension drug clonidine, which relieves many of the symptoms of heroin withdrawal. Cocaine detoxification presents serious problems because of the patient's craving for the substance and the extreme depression occurring during the early days of abstinence, which can lead to suicide. Medication, antidepressants, for example, may be needed by those who are suicide risks during the postcocaine "crash," characterized by a lack of energy and an inability to feel pleasure. Those who exhibit transient psychotic or severe delusional states and paranoid reactions from excessive cocaine also require medication. Although withdrawal from heroin and cocaine can be accomplished without using other chemicals—although the patient may feel quite uncomfortable—

---

[1]See, for example, Mumola and Bonczar (1998).

White-Collar Specialists

The U.S. probation system has officers who specialize in supervising white-collar criminals, whose numbers, as a result of new federal legislation, have increased substantially in the past decade. According to the chief federal probation officer in Los Angeles, whose office supervises hundreds of such criminals, "white collar crime covers a lot of ground: setting back odometers and dumping toxic waste; telemarketing fraud and tax evasion. But they all come down to money and they're all more complicated than a stolen wallet or blown-up safe" (Solomon, 1998: 54).

detoxification from sedatives can lead to seizures and cardiac arrest, and therefore, must be accomplished by decreasing dosages.

The use of chemicals to facilitate drug withdrawal can serve to attract drug abusers into treatment and increases the probability that they will complete detoxification. However, at least with respect to heroin abusers, the use of chemical aides has some troubling aspects. Addicts typically enter treatment when their habit is too expensive to support and they have to work quite hard simply to prevent the onset of withdrawal symptoms, while a high level of tolerance to heroin reduces the sought-after high. Under such conditions, addiction is no longer fun: "Then he enters a detoxification ward and is comfortably withdrawn from heroin. Detoxification is made so easy, compared to 'cold turkey,' that addicts are not confronted with negatively reinforcing pharmacological and physiological aspects of addiction" (Bellis, 1981: 139). Detoxification reduces the addict's tolerance so that the high can be enjoyed once again at an affordable price. P/P officers should not be surprised "when addicts leave the detoxification ward and inject heroin within a few minutes or hours" (140).

Some drug programs use chemicals as the primary treatment or as a supplement to, or in conjunction with, some other form of treatment. Scientists have developed a number of heroin **antagonists,** substances that block or counteract the effects of opiates. These substances bind with opiate receptor sites, thereby preventing stimulation, or displace an opiate already at the site (see Abadinsky, 2004, for a discussion). Antagonists, however, often have significant side effects.

Methadone Treatment

Certain synthetic substances—**agonists**—have a chemical makeup similar to that of opioids. The most widely used agonist, **methadone,** a wholly synthetic narcotic, produces virtually the same analgesic and sedative effects as heroin and is no less

Substance-Abusing Inmates

"At least 81 percent of state inmates, 80 percent of federal inmates, and 77 percent of local jail inmates have used an illegal drug regularly (at least weekly for a period of at least one month); have been incarcerated for drug selling or possession, driving under the influence of alcohol (DUI) or another alcohol abuse violation; were under the influence of alcohol or drugs when they committed their crime; committed their offense to get money for drugs; have a history of alcohol abuse, or share some combination of these characteristics" (*Behind Bars*, 1998: 2).

addictive. However, methadone is administered orally, its effects last longer, and as opposed to the shorter-acting opiates such as heroin, the high it produces is less dramatic. Whereas the effects of heroin wear off in 2 to 3 hours, the effects of oral methadone continue for 12 to 24 hours. Methadone can be prepared in a way that makes it difficult to inject, rendering it less likely to be diverted into the black market.

The typical methadone program begins with a period of inpatient care during which low doses of the drug are substituted for heroin (the patient is not informed of the dosage he or she receives). The methadone is usually mixed with orange juice (which helps reduce its bitter taste) and consumed in front of a nurse. Slow increases in dosage reduce the "high," which disappears once significant tolerance develops. Addicts subsequently report daily on an outpatient basis and are given take-home doses for weekends. Patients usually provide a urine specimen before they are given methadone. As they progress, less than daily pickups are permitted. Although methadone impacts on the "high" that usually lasts several hours, it does not affect the euphoric "rush" (which lasts about 10 seconds). Thus, methadone patients, even those at high daily doses, may continue abusing heroin and other drugs. In fact, cocaine is a major drug of abuse among methadone patients.

Behavior Modification

Some treatment programs use behavior modification as the primary treatment method. The strength of psychoactive substances as positive reinforcers and the negative reinforcement associated with abstinence provide conditioned responses that can explain the key difficulty in treating drug abusers—finding reinforcers that can successfully compete with these substances. As noted in chapter 9, according to the principles of operant conditioning, for behavior modification to be effective, reinforcement must follow immediately after the behavior is exhibited; instant gratification is what makes drug use so reinforcing and why it is difficult to use behavior modification techniques with chronic drug users.

Behavior modification can be used with drug antagonists to render opiates or other substances ineffective—lacking positive reinforcement. Disulfiram (Antabuse), metronidazole, or chlorpropamide can serve this purpose for alcohol abusers. Antabuse, the best known of these substances, disrupts the liver's metabolism, producing a severe reaction that includes stomach and head pain, extreme nausea, and vomiting. (Milder reactions can be triggered by any number of products that contain alcohol, such as cough medicine, mouthwash, or even skin creams.) In 1990, a patent was granted for a substance that has the appearance and smell of cocaine, and even produces a numbing effect, but is not psychoactive. The substance is used in conjunction with an aversive chemical.

In voluntary patients, electric shocks may be self-administered whenever a craving for the chemical arises. Some researchers report that the use of chemical or electrical stimuli has not proven effective in producing a conditioned aversion in drug abusers, while success has been reported with verbal aversion techniques in which "a patient is asked to *imagine* strongly aversive stimuli (usually vomiting) in association with imaginal drug-related cues, scenes, and/or behavior" (Childress, McLellan, and O'Brien, 1985: 951). Thus, *imagined* **aversive stimuli** may be superior to *real* aversive stimuli with the drug dependent (although this appears to run contrary to a great deal of research in operant conditioning). In any event, "aversive counterconditioning is not a substitute for support for life-enhancing behavior, rather it suppresses the undesirable behavior while other modalities support positive alternatives" (Frawley and Smith, 1990: 21).

Other behavioral therapies use biofeedback and relaxation training, and sometimes assertiveness training, to prepare drug abusers to better cope with the stress and anxiety believed linked to drug use. Researchers have found that certain environmental cues activate drug cravings. These are countered by desensitization treatment: "Patients are usually first relaxed, then given repeated exposure to a graded hierarchy of anxiety-producing stimuli (real or imaginal)" to provide a form of immunity (Childress et al., 1985: 957).

As noted in chapter 9, *social learning theory*, a variant of behaviorism, views people as active participants in their operant conditioning processes who determine what is and what is not reinforcing. The drug abuser is seen as lacking the level of social competence necessary to cope adequately with a variety of situational demands. In using operant conditioning with drug abusers, social learning stresses patient analysis to discover the variables that are reinforcing. The therapist attempts to discover the situational demands and their related negative emotions that are related to the patient's drug use. Treatment begins with an assessment of the positive and negative aspects of drug use and a self-report on the type, amount, and frequency of drugs used. The assessment includes a focus on the social, physical, and emotional environments in which drug use occurs. After the assessment, the role of the therapist is to enable the patient to deal with triggering behavior so it does not lead to drug use, with the patient's own report of the negative aspects of drug use serving as a motivator for adopting more positive coping strategies (Donovan, 1988).

A cognitive approach developed by Anna Rose Childress (1993) first conducts a study to develop a set of cues that trigger drug cravings. Patients are then taught methods of combating the urges, including a planned delay before acting on a craving, having an alternative behavior planned for this delay period, and systematic relaxation to counter drug arousal. Other techniques include listening to a recording of positive/negative craving consequences that instructs the addict to list the three most negative consequences of relapsing into drugs and the three most positive consequences of not acting on cravings. Negative imagery is used to encourage patients to remember their worst period of addiction—a type of scare tactic.

Therapeutic Community

The **therapeutic community** (TC) is a generic term for residential, self-help, drug-free treatment programs that have some common characteristics, including concepts adopted from Alcoholics Anonymous (DeLong, 1972: 190–191): "There is no such thing as an ex-addict, only an addict who is not using at the moment; the emphasis on mutual support and aid; the distrust of mental-health professionals; and the concept of continual confession and catharsis. However, the TC has extended these notions to include the concept of a live-in community with a rigid structure of day-to-day behavior and a complex system of punishment and rewards."

According to George DeLeon (1994: 19), a considerable number of TC clients "never have acquired conventional lifestyles. Vocational and educational deficits are marked; mainstream values either are missing or unpursued. Most often, these clients emerge from a socially disadvantaged sector where drug abuse is more a social response than a psychological disturbance. Their TC experience can be termed *habilitation*—the development of a socially productive, conventional lifestyle for the first time in their lives."

Therapeutic Communities

"TC programs reflect a view of the drug abuse client as having a social deficit and requiring social treatment. This social treatment may be characterized as an organized effort to resocialize the client, with the community as an agent of personal change" (Tims, Jainchill, and DeLeon, 1994: 2).

The primary aims of a TC are global changes in lifestyle reflecting abstinence from illicit substances, elimination of antisocial activity, increased employability, and prosocial attitudes and values. The therapeutic community becomes a surrogate family and a communal support group for dealing with alienation and drug abuse that derives from it. Its purpose, notes Mitchell Rosenthal (1973), is to strengthen ego functioning. Therapy, except for the time spent asleep, is total. James DeLong (1972) notes that there is a quasievangelistic quality to the "TC movement." The residences are often similar to the communes that were popular during the late 1950s and 1960s counterculture movement, except they generally have a strict hierarchy and insist on rigid adherence to norms even more stringent than those of the proverbial middle class.

A prominent feature of the TC has been the stiff entry requirement: a devastating initial interview that tests an applicant's motivation by focusing on his or her inadequacies and lack of success. Successful applicants must invest completely in the program, which encourages the resident to identify with the former addicts who work in the program and become resocialized into a drug-free existence. The new resident is isolated from all outside contacts, including family and friends. The withdrawal process is accomplished without drugs but with the support of other residents. Once withdrawal has been accomplished, a program of positive and negative reinforcement is implemented. The resident is assigned menial work projects, such as cleaning toilets, but given an opportunity to earn more prestigious assignments and greater freedom through conformity with the program. Transgressions are punished by public humiliation—reprimands, shaved heads, or wearing a sign indicating the nature of the violation. Those who leave and relapse, are required to wear a sign announcing their situation when they return. Shame and guilt are constantly exploited to force the addict to conform and to change his or her view of drugs (Platt and Labate, 1976). There is little privacy. Drug use, physical violence, and sexual activity between residents—who are to relate to one another as family—are punished with expulsion.

Residents are kept busy in a highly structured environment that offers little time for idleness or boredom. They are expected to be active in all aspects of the TC program. Failing to do so becomes the subject of criticism at the encounter session, a central feature of the therapeutic process. The encounter is a relatively unstructured, leaderless group session in which members focus on a particular resident (who occupies the "hot seat") and bombard him or her with criticisms about attitude and behavior. The target is encouraged to fight back—verbally—although the goal of such sessions is to destroy the rationalizations and defenses that help perpetuate irresponsible thought patterns and behavior—a resocialization process. "The style of the encounter, with its abrasive attacks and its permitted verbal violence . . . is designed to encourage the spewing out of pent-up hostility and anger, to force the patient to confront his maladaptive emotional response and behavior patterns" (Rosenthal, 1973: 91).

The TC is an exciting, friendly, and highly moral—almost utopian—environment (Waldorf, 1973). However, it is not for all abusers: "Severe disturbances may be exacerbated by the TC regimen and may have an adverse effect not only on the disturbed client but also on the treatment environment and the progress of others in the treatment population. Also unsuitable for treatment are candidates whose drug involvement is of so limited a nature as to require a less rigorous intervention or who—despite the deleterious effects of drug abuse—are able to function with the help of a positive support network (e.g., family or significant others)" (Rosenthal, 1984: 55).

TCs have been established in prisons in New York, California, and a number of other states. These are called "Stay'N Out" TCs. Inmates selected for the program are recruited at state correctional facilities and housed in units segregated from the general population, although they eat and attend morning activities with other prisoners. The program, which lasts from 6 to 9 months, is staffed by graduates of community TCs and by ex-offenders with prison experience, who act as role models demonstrating successful rehabilitation. Upon release, prison TC graduates are encouraged to become part of the extensive community-based TC network.

Chemical Dependency Programs

During the last several decades, the number of programs to treat substance abusers has increased. Some are profit making and others are nonprofit; many call themselves "therapeutic communities," although they differ dramatically from the TCs already discussed. These programs typically share a number of variables: They do a great deal of outreach—most employ a marketing person—and often advertise for clients likely to have health insurance, such as employed alcohol and cocaine abusers as opposed to heroin addicts, because the costs can run more than $500 per day for inpatient care. Many chemical dependency programs are located in a health care facility, which typically increases the cost of treatment. The treatment approach usually includes individual and group counseling, and the model tends to be eclectic rather than doctrinal. The treatment orientation of these programs is varied, but mainly reflects a mix of traditional mental health and 12-step perspectives (discussed in the next section). They offer a variety of services, including education, nutrition, relaxation training, recreation, counseling-psychotherapy, psychopharmacological adjuncts, and self-help groups.

The typical program is a 3- to 6-week intensive and highly structured inpatient regimen. Patient care begins with a psychiatric and psychosocial evaluation and then follows a general education-oriented program track of daily lectures plus two to three meetings per week in small task-oriented groups. The educational component teaches about the disease concept of dependence, focusing on the harmful medical and psychosocial effects of illicit drugs and excessive alcohol consumption. "There is also an individual prescriptive track for each client, meetings about once per week with a 'focal counselor,' and appointments with other professionals if medical, psychiatric, or family services are needed" (Gerstein and Harwood, 1990: 171). Aftercare services are typically meager and many programs simply refer a patient to an Alcoholics Anonymous or Narcotics Anonymous (NA) group.

Alcoholics and Narcotics Anonymous

AA is a fellowship founded by Robert ("Dr. Bob") Holbrook Smith (1879–1950), a physician and alcoholic, and William ("Bill W.") Wilson (1895–1971), a financial investigator and alcoholic. Bill W. helped Dr. Bob become abstinent, and the two recognized that success in helping alcoholics was not to be found in preaching abstinence, but rather in a fellowship where each alcoholic simply relates his or her story of drunkenness and conversion to a nonalcoholic lifestyle. The "listening" was as important as the "telling." The group became known as Alcoholics Anonymous after the title of Wilson's 1939 book, which AA members often refer to as "The Big Book" (it was quite bulky when originally published). Wilson, who died in 1971, was supported by the substantial royalties the book eventually generated. His wife, who was a nonalcoholic, established Al-Anon, patterned on the AA model, for the family members of alcoholics (Pace, 1988). There are now similar groups for the family and friends of cocaine users—Co-Anon.

AA is the original **12-step program** and requires an act of surrender—an acknowledgment of being an alcoholic and of the destructiveness that results—a bearing of witness, and an acknowledgment of a higher power. Although AA is nondenominational, there is a strong repent-of-your-sins revivalism—groups begin or end their meetings holding hands in a circle and reciting the Lord's Prayer (Robertson, 1988b) or the Serenity Prayer: "God grant me the serenity to accept the things I cannot change; courage to change the things I can; and wisdom to know the difference" (DuPont and McGovern, 1994: 27). As in Protestant revival meetings, the alcoholic/sinner seeks salvation through personal testimony, public contrition, and submission to a higher authority (Delbanco and Delbanco, 1995; Peele, 1985). AA also provides "an important social network through which members learn appropriate behavior and coping skills in drinking situations and become involved in various (nondrinking) leisure activities with other recovering alcoholics" (McElrath, 1995: 314).

AA Alternatives

The "spiritual" dimension of AA and its insistence on a disease model of alcoholism—alcoholics cannot help themselves—have encountered opposition and led to the establishment of alternative groups, such as Rational Recovery (RR) and Secular Organization for Sobriety. Although it is a voluntary self-help group in the AA mode, RR rejects the 12-step approach as fostering dependency and instead argues that alcoholic participants are not powerless but fully capable of overcoming their addiction (Hall, 1990). According to RR, alcoholism is not a disease but an individual shortcoming. Their approach emphasizes taking personal responsibility for behavior ("Clean and Sober—And Agnostic," 1991).

RR uses "The Big Plan," a commitment never to drink again. It focuses on planning to prevent relapses and attempting to gain insight into how self-defeating beliefs encourage drinking behavior. Various strategies are discussed to deal with "high-risk" situations where temptations may run high (Galaif and Sussman, 1995). There are also groups that reject the total abstinence proviso of AA and, instead, emphasize sobriety—drinking in moderation—such as Moderation Management (MM) (Marriott, 1995). MM is designed for persons who want to limit, rather than eliminate, their drinking (Foderaro, 1995).

AA recognizes the potency of shared honesty and mutual vulnerability openly acknowledged, and the AA group supports each member in his or her effort to remain alcohol free. "Maintenance of sobriety depends on our sharing of our experiences, strength and hope with each other, thus helping to identify and understand the nature of our disease" (AA literature). The AA conceptual model is that alcoholism is a disease, a controllable disability that cannot be cured—thus, there are no ex-alcoholics, merely recovering alcoholics. AA members are encouraged to accept the belief that they are powerless over alcohol, that they cannot control their intake, and that total abstinence is required. New members are advised to obtain a sponsor who has remained abstinent and who will help the initiate work through the 12 steps that are the essence of the AA program. Those who are successful, "twelfth steppers," carry the AA message and program to other alcoholics—they become "missionaries" for AA.

AA and groups based on the AA approach "attempt to instill the substitution of more adaptive attitudes to replace habitual dysfunctional ones. The extreme use of denial and projection of responsibility for chemical dependency onto other people, circumstances, or conditions outside oneself is an example of a target behavior strongly challenged in the substance abuse self-help group. The familiar opening statement of 'I'm an alcoholic and/or drug addict' epitomizes the concrete representation that defense mechanisms of projection and denial run counter to the group culture and norms" (Spitz, 1987: 160).

The basic AA unit is the local group, which is autonomous except in matters affecting other AA groups or the fellowship as a whole: "No group has powers over its members and instead of officers with authority, groups rotate leadership" (AA literature). A secretary chosen by the members plans the meetings and sets the agenda. In most local groups, the position is rotated every 6 months. There are no entry requirements or dues—"the hat is passed" at most meetings to defray costs. Because of their fear of losing employment, recovering alcoholics were often unwilling to admit their problem in front of others—hence, strict anonymity became part of the AA approach.

Because many AA groups are less than accepting of persons addicted to substances other than alcohol—Bill Wilson was opposed to allowing heroin addicts to become part of AA—there are separate groups for drug abusers based on the 12-step approach, such as NA and Cocaine Anonymous (CA).

The AA approach has been criticized because of its emphasis on total abstinence and its lack of research support: "The erstwhile abstainer who, for whatever reason, takes a drink may in effect be induced to go on a spree by the belief that this is inevitable. Spree drinking could also be induced by the fact that status in A.A. is correlated with length of sobriety. Years of sobriety with their attendant symbols and status can be obliterated by one slip, so the social cost of a single drink is as great as the cost of an all-out binge" (Ogborne and Glaser, 1985: 176). Some 12-step groups "do not consider members 'clean and sober' when they are using any psychoactive medication. Cases of adverse treatment consequences, even suicide, have resulted from well-meaning 12-step members dissuading individuals from taking prescribed medications" (DuPont and McGovern, 1994: 56).

Drug Testing

Drug testing can only determine that the subject has used a drug recently; it cannot determine when or how much. Primarily because of its low cost, about $5 per test, the enzyme-multiplied immune test (EMIT) is the most frequently used urinalysis (Wish, n.d.: 2): "These tests depend on a chemical reaction between the specimen and an antibody designed to react to a specific drug. The chemical reaction causes a change in the specimen's transmission of light, which is measured by a machine. If the reading is higher than a given standard, the specimen is positive for the drug." There have been relatively high rates of false-positives using this test, sometimes as a result of commonly used licit drugs cross-reacting with the test's antibody. "Sloppy recording procedures by laboratory staff and failure to maintain careful controls over the chain of custody of the specimen can also produce serious test errors" (Wish, n.d.: 2).

The most accurate test, gas chromatography/mass spectroscopy, is relatively expensive, about $100 per specimen for screening and confirmation. Drug-testing programs often use EMIT for an initial screening and then submit positives for gas chromatography/mass spectroscopy. Because of the legal implications of a false-positive, new controls have been added, resulting in significant improvements over testing methods used during the 1980s (Wish, n.d.). The National Institute of Drug Abuse certifies drug-testing firms, a necessity for securing federal contracts.

Additional problems involve the timing and method of collecting urine samples. Detecting cocaine and opiates by urinalysis requires securing a sample within 48 to 72 hours of drug use, after which the sample must be refrigerated. To maintain test integrity, the subject must be closely monitored during urination to ensure a negative sample has not been switched for a positive one. This is particularly problematic with female offenders who have been known to secrete false samples in their vaginas. As a result of these problems, new methods for detecting drug use have been emerging, particularly hair assays. The complications inherent in collecting, storing, and shipping urine samples is revealed by the regulations for testing parolees in Nebraska (Figure 12.1).

Collecting hair samples is easy and is not subject to evasive actions designed to produce false-negatives—shampooing, for example, can reduce the concentration but not the presence of drugs of abuse that become trapped in the cortex of the hair follicle. Hair analysis has been used for some time to detect exposure to such toxic metals as mercury and lead. In a process similar to urinalysis, dissolved hair shafts reveal whether drugs are in the blood. Because of the unique qualities of hair growth—about one-half inch per month—it may be possible to determine the amount of drug use over a period of several months and whether it is increasing or decreasing. There are complications, however: The test can also be positive for those who come into contact with drugs via touching the skin or sweat of a user or through exposure to air where the substance has been smoked (Baumgartner, Hill, and Blahd, 1989). Hair analysis has been suggested as an initial screening method for drug use, positives to be corroborated by urinalysis (Magura, Kang, and Shapiro, 1995; Mieczkowski, 1995).

DEPARTMENT OF CORRECTIONAL SERVICES STATE OF NEBRASKA

III. DRUG/ALCOHOL TESTING PROCEDURES

    A. Testing procedures shall be conducted in private areas/enclosures. Same gender staff will observe parolee's urine samples.

    B. The parolee shall be asked if he/she has been taking any medications recently, and the parolee's response shall be noted on the appropriate attachment.

    C. The parolee will be pat searched prior to submitting a urine sample and all objects which may adulterate the sample will be removed from his/her person.

    D. Staff shall wear protective gloves when collecting and testing urine samples and performing breath tests. Staff will instruct parolees to wash their hands thoroughly and will issue and ensure that protective gloves are worn by the parolee being tested. Urine samples will be collected in on-site drug testing device or regular specimen cups. After on-site testing is complete on negative samples staff shall dispose of urine samples in a toilet and place cups and protective gloves in a biohazard disposal container.

    E. To the extent possible, staff shall witness the parolee's urine flow from the parolee's body to the container. Staff shall maintain observation, watching for attempts to adulterate the urine sample. A minimum of 30 ml (approximately the width of two fingers) of the specimen is required by the lab. Staff shall immediately obtain the specimen cup upon completion denying the parolee the opportunity to adulterate the specimen with water or other substance.

    F. If the parolee cannot provide a urine sample immediately, he/she will be allowed two (2) hours to comply.

        1. The parolee may consume up to eight (8) ounces of water every two (2) hours, to assist in giving a urine sample.

        2. Staff may delegate collection of a urine sample to law enforcement or other DCS personnel during the two (2) hour waiting period as long as Parole Administration procedures or approved law enforcement procedures are followed.

        3. If a parolee cannot provide a urine specimen immediately under observation in the presence of the parole officer and a dry room with staff in the area are available, the officer will escort the parolee to that dry room. All procedures of the facility where the dry room is located regarding the taking of urine specimens will be followed.

        4. At the end of two (2) hours, if a urine sample is not obtained, the parolee will be charged with failure to submit to test.

    G. If a parolee fails to submit an adequate urine sample or breath test, adulterates a urine specimen or fails to follow staff or law enforcement instructions for collecting a urine specimen he/she will be charged with failure to submit a valid test. Additionally, if a parolee avoids submitting a urine sample or breath test by failing to report in as directed, his/her case will be treated as a failure to submit to test.

    H. Drug testing will be accomplished in one of the following manners:

        1. Lab testing—Staff (or law enforcement if necessary) will use a regular specimen cup to collect the urine sample from the parolee according to established procedures, and will complete Attachment A entitled, "Statement of Testing Urine for Drugs/Alcohol." After collection, the sample will be forwarded to the appropriate facility for laboratory testing.

        2. On-site Drug Testing—Staff (or law enforcement, if necessary) will use an appropriate on-site drug testing device to collect the urine sample from the parolee according to established procedures and will complete Attachment A. Staff will then test the urine for the presence of drugs as outlined in that attachment. All positive samples will be forwarded to a DCS designated lab for further testing.

        3. Alcohol testing will be conducted via portable breath testing device and in accordance to the checklist technique prescribed by 177NAC 1 of the Department of Health and Human Services Division of Regulation. Parole Officers conducting tests with the ALCO-SENSOR III will use HHSR&L Attachment 4, (see Attachment B) and tests with the LION ALCOMETER S-D2, will be done according to HHSR&L Attachment 18, (see Attachment C).

    I. Processing the Urine Specimen:

        1. A specimen cup will be labeled with parolee's name, number, date and time taken. An "evidence" seal will be placed over the joint of the cup and its lid and placed in an evidence bag. An evidence tag, Attachment D, will be properly filled out and attached to the evidence bag.

        2. All specimens shall be refrigerated after collection. The limit on refrigeration is TWO days. After that time, the specimens must be frozen. All specimens will be locked in a refrigerator or freezer with limited access until being transported to the appropriate laboratory or storage site.

FIGURE 12.1 *Drug/Alcohol Testing Procedures.*

(*Source:* Nebraska Department of Correctional Services.)

Pennsylvania.   The Pennsylvania Board of Probation and Parole operates a drug unit in Philadelphia that uses extensive urinalysis. Caseloads are limited to 50, and all offenders referred for supervision must have been using drugs for at least 3 years. Parole agents assigned to the unit have undergone specialized training and are rotated every 2 to 3 years to regular units "to avoid burnout." All clients assigned to the unit are tested for drug use every 90 days, unless circumstances demand more frequent testing. Offenders who remain drug free for 9 months are reviewed for transfer to general supervision units. Immediately before such a transfer, however, there is a final urinalysis.

Clients whose test results are positive are tested weekly; two positive opiate urinalyses within a 4-month period require that the client be placed in a withdrawal treatment program. If the parole agent believes that a client's pattern of drug abuse is disruptive to the reintegration and treatment process, or if the client's behavior constitutes a threat to the community or the client, the agent may place the offender in "protective custody" for 48 hours. If the agent believes that the client should be subjected to violation-of-parole procedures, the detention continues until the hearing is conducted.

The board also has programs for parolees whose technical violations involve substance abuse. Nonviolent offenders are diverted to an inpatient drug and alcohol treatment facility for 90 days, where they receive drug and alcohol education, emotion management, relapse prevention, leisure time management, vocational and educational assessment, and reintegration planning. Released back into the community, the offender will be subjected to electronic monitoring, curfews, and intensive outpatient therapy for 90 days, after which the supervision and therapy levels are reduced. The complete program takes 1 year, after which the offender is placed on regular supervision with frequent urinalysis.

Another program is designed as an alternative to long-term incarceration for technical violations by those with a history of substance abuse. Phase I consists of 6 months in a therapeutic community housed in a correctional facility. Active participation and the development of an approved aftercare plan leads to phase II, a 6-month placement in a community corrections center and intensive outpatient treatment. The offender needs to obtain a sponsor and attends group meetings; vocational and employment training are provided. Success in phase II results in reparole and intensive supervision—weekly contact with parole agent and frequent urinalysis.

HIV/AIDS

As noted in chapter 6, HIV/AIDS is a significant problem in America's prisons. Although some P/P officers may have personal concerns, the manner in which the disease is transmitted places them at low risk. (The primary risk occurs during a search of clients who could have a contaminated hypodermic needle on their person.) Difficult questions concern enforcement of rules and confidentiality. Offenders who are sexually active place their partners in jeopardy. Can the client be required to refrain from unprotected sexual activity? How would this rule be enforced? Should the spouse or sex partner(s) be informed of the client's condition? If so, how is this to be accomplished? These are serious public safety and liability issues with which P/P agencies are struggling.

Probation officers in Kansas are advised that "when staff become aware a specific offender is HIV-positive, disclosure without the subject's informed consent may be a violation of the offender's right to privacy. In special cases where there is evidence suggesting ongoing high risk behavior that might result in the infection of a third party, the right to privacy may be outweighed by a duty to warn possible victims. In such cases, staff should be encouraged to seek supervisory and legal assistance on a case by case basis." Parole agents in California are warned that willful or negligent disclosure of HIV information by a peace officer is a misdemeanor.

"If it becomes known to a parole agent that a parolee who has tested positive for HIV or AIDS has not informed his or her spouse, the agent *may* request that only the chief medical officer of the parolee's releasing institution, or the physician treating the spouse or parolee, inform the spouse. The parole agent *shall* seek to ensure that counseling is provided to the spouse by the person providing the information to the spouse."

In New York, medical information, including HIV/AIDS, "will not be disclosed within or outside the Division of Parole without written consent of the protected individual." In Multnomah County, Oregon, confidentiality rules determine how client information is to be recorded. Offenders who refuse to sign releases will have their HIV-related issues, such as an inability to work, recorded in a manner that does not disclose their status, for example, "This offender is unable to meet the probation condition of obtaining employment for he is under doctor's orders to not work until further notice." And "HIV infected clients who are known to be engaging in activities that put others at risk of HIV infection will be counseled to stop those activities. If such activities continue, the client may be reported to the County Health Officer." The Alabama Board of Pardons and Paroles requires infected inmates to sign a statement of "commitment to a course of personal conduct which maximizes his/her efforts to prevent any risk of transmission of the infection to others." If the board believes the inmate is not prepared to live up to these conditions, it will deny parole. The board also imposes special conditions to protect the parolee's family or co-residents. A failure to abide by these conditions can result in parole being revoked. Some agencies have formed special units or designated officers as HIV/AIDS specialists.

Federal HIV/AIDS Specialists

In the federal system, some districts, such as the Southern District of New York, have officers in specialist positions who handle an HIV/AIDS caseload. "The officers who supervise this special population frequently excuse offenders who are not able to report to the office for various health-related reasons. Contact is maintained through frequent telephone calls and field visits. And officers often find that their field visits are to the hospital. Sometimes family and friends of these offenders shun them, and the probation officer is the only visitor they receive. Once a hospital called an officer here to inform her of an offender's death—the offender had named the officer as his next of kin." Officers who supervise these offenders also serve as HIV/AIDS resources: "They keep abreast of new findings and developments and pass the information along to offenders to help them choose the course of treatment that suits them best. They share their knowledge with their colleagues, presenting training programs to educate their coworkers about HIV and AIDS" (Holmes, 1997: 28).

New York State Division of Parole AIDS Caseloads

The Division of Parole established two specialized AIDS caseloads to develop a working model for providing special assistance to HIV/AIDS parolees; POs are volunteers. The need for specialized assistance was increased by a law passed in 1992 that permits the parole board to release certain terminally ill inmates before their parole eligibility date—many of these candidates have AIDS. Parolees often experience difficulties with the community reintegration process, and AIDS is an additional complicating factor. The specialist POs participate in ongoing training regarding the illness and its management, and each supervises no more than 20 clients, permitting time to visit clients and arrange contracts with service providers or negotiate with service agencies. About 20 percent of the clients are hospitalized during some point each month, and many others are on nonreport status because of their physical condition; caseload attrition through death is extraordinarily high, which can have a serious impact on officer morale.

PO activities resemble those typically provided by medical social workers, including aid with securing social security, public assistance, and Medicaid. The PO works with the client's family providing support and information under trying circumstances. In many cases, the PO must arrange for housing for clients who lack family resources. Parolees are not required to disclose their condition. With respect to disclosure of the client's HIV/AIDS:

> From a legal perspective, disclosure of anyone's HIV-status without consent is against the law. In keeping with this, the Division of Parole's policy is that education, rather than disclosure, is key. While the Division may have knowledge that certain parolees are HIV-positive, there are others that the Division is not aware of. Therefore, even if disclosure were permitted, it would only be marginally effective at reducing transmission. The most effective course of action for the Division to take in response to the risk of transmission is to educate all parolees' families regarding HIV, and appropriate measures to take to reduce potential risks.

Home visits are often accomplished in teams that facilitate working with families and parolees. The visits are considerably longer than those with routine caseloads. Some POs use group methods (discussed in chapter 9) with their clients. Despite their medical condition, some HIV clients manage to get involved with serious criminal activity and are returned to prison. Because of the problem of HIV-infected clients who also suffer from tuberculosis, POs take special precautions to reduce the possibility of infection.

SEX OFFENDERS

The category "sex offender" represents a number of different types of offender, ranging from a 19-year-old who had consensual sex with a 16-year-old, to the sexual predator who stalks children in parks and playgrounds (Jenuwine, Simmons, and Swies, 2003). Although child sexual abuse is a serious and widespread problem in the United States, P/P agencies have been slow to respond adequately to this type of offender when he (they are overwhelmingly male) is on a supervision caseload. Indeed, child sexual offenders often end up on probation because of the extreme level of prison overcrowding (Lurigio, Jones, and Smith, 1995).[2] Relatively few probation agencies have specialized units to monitor these offenders—units with intensively trained officers and reduced caseloads.

Sex offenders, particularly those who prey on children, present significant risk factors to the community and supervision problems for the P/P agency. Trauma inflicted on young victims and resulting community outrage pose problems not typically encountered with other types of offenders. This has been highlighted by the passage of registration statutes in virtually every state, a requirement of the federal 1994 Violent Crime Control and Law Enforcement Act. Registration is designed to deter potential offenders while providing law enforcement agencies with a registry to aid in their investigations. In addition, most states have enacted notification statutes that either make information about sex offenders available on request to individuals and organizations, or that authorize or require P/P agencies, law enforcement agencies, or prosecutor offices to disseminate information to the community at large. These laws pose problems for P/P officers who must help offenders deal with potential vigilantism, as well as the stigma that presents a significant barrier to housing

[2]Statutes allowing violent sex offenders to be kept in custody beyond their sentence have encountered severe financing problems associated with the cost of providing medical and legal professionals required in such cases (Parsons, 1998), although the U.S. Supreme Court has ruled the practice constitutional in an 8–1 decision (*Seling v. Young*, 531 U.S. 250, 2001).

Sex Offender Recidivism

Sex offenders are not a homogeneous group, and their rates of reoffending differ. They have a wide variety of racial, ethnic, and socioeconomic backgrounds, and the majority of them do not have extensive criminal histories or "traditional" criminal lifestyles, and differ significantly in age (Gilligan and Talbot, 2000). Studies indicate that for child molesters, the recidivism rate is between 13 and 20 percent, and for rapists, 19 percent. Individual characteristics further distinguish rates of sexual reoffending. One study found that offenders whose female victims were not relatives had a recidivism rate of 18 percent, whereas for male victims the rate was 35 percent. Of course, these statistics can only account for offenders that were convicted—many sex offenses are never even reported (CSOM, 2001a). An Oregon study also confirmed that, unlike other offenders who tend to "age out" of their criminal behavior as they grow older, many sex offenders continue to abuse throughout their lifetimes. Finally, the study revealed that sex offenders frequently score in the low range on traditional correctional risk assessment instruments because these instruments do not address many of the areas that are indicators of risk for sex offenders (Gilligan and Talbot, 2000). A study of sex offenders released in 1994 revealed that 3.5 percent were reconvicted of a sex crime within 3 years. Within the first 3 years following release from prison, 3.3 percent of the released child molesters were rearrested for another sex crime against a child (Langan and Durose, 2003).

and employment. Because sex offenders must be prevented from employment where they would have access to potential victims, unnecessary impediments present frustrations that can impact the offender's behavior. In jurisdictions where community notification is discretionary with the P/P agency, it is sometimes used to motivate offenders to comply with conditions of supervision and treatment efforts (Finn, 1997).

Sexual assault that is most profound in its traumatic implications involves a violation of trust that occurs when, as in most sexual assault victimizations, offenders are known to victims. "Trauma and length and level of recovery seem linked to trust violation more than to many other factors. Thus, what might be regarded by some as a relatively minor type of sexual assault (e.g., 'just fondling') can be extremely traumatic to a victim who trusted the perpetrator" (English, Pullen, and Jones, 1997: 1). Approximately 60 percent of boys and 80 percent of girls who are sexually victimized are abused by someone known to the child or the child's family—relatives, babysitters, persons in authority over the child, or persons who supervise children (Center for Sex Offender Management [CSOM], 2001a).

There is general agreement in the P/P field that sex offenders need to be treated and supervised differently from other criminals. They typically share certain characteristics (English et al., 1997: 2):

- Sex offenders have secretive and manipulative lifestyles, and many of their sexual assaults are so well planned that they appear to occur without forethought. The skills used to manipulate victims have also been employed to manipulate criminal justice officials.
- Many sex offenders are otherwise highly functioning people who use their social skills to commit their crimes.
- Sex offenders typically have developed complicated and persistent psychological and social systems constructed to assist them in denying or minimizing the harm they inflict on others, and often they are very accomplished at presenting to others a facade designed to hide the truth about themselves.
- Many sex offenders commit a wide range and large number of sexually deviant acts during their lives and show a continued propensity to reoffend.

Because of these characteristics, in the supervision of sex offenders, the focus is usually on *containment:* Preventing recidivism is the singular goal, and the client is the community. As part of this approach, sex offenders may be subjected to periodic polygraph, examinations, and the rules of supervision are quite restrictive (Figure 12.2). For example, avoiding places where children can be expected to congregate,

---

SEX OFFENDER SUPERVISION AGREEMENT

NAME _____   DOC NUMBER _____

In accordance with the authority granted the Missouri Department of Corrections, Board of Probation and Parole or any Circuit Court by the laws of the State of Missouri, you have been ordered to participate in the Sex Offender Supervision Program and are subject to the following conditions:

1. I will comply with all registration requirements that apply to me. I understand that failure to comply with the registration requirements will subject me to be charged with new criminal charges.

2. Any employment or residence must be approved by my supervising officer. Prior approval from my supervising officer is needed for any changes.

3. I will advise my supervising officer of the names, dates of birth and gender of all persons residing at my residence. I will advise all adult members in the household of my criminal convictions.

4. I will participate in a sex offender treatment program approved by my supervising officer, at my own expense. My participation will continue as long as deemed necessary by the supervising officer with consultation from treatment staff.

5. I will submit, at my own expense, to assessment and treatment procedures required by my therapist or supervising officer, which may include, but is not limited to a polygraph or penile plethysmograph.

6. I will not have any contact with the victim, or the victim's family, directly, indirectly, or through a third party unless otherwise specified by the Court or Parole Board.

7. I will have no unsupervised contact with any person age 16 or under, or any incapacitated person without the prior approval of my supervising officer.

8. If my illegal conduct involved a person 16 years of age or under, I will avoid parks, schools, daycare centers, toy stores, pools, carnivals, or other places where children are known to frequent, unless prior approval is given to me by supervising officer.

9. I will not possess or access pornographic material which may include, but not limited to: pornography on any electronic media, adult bookstores, and adult theaters.

10. I understand that additional special conditions may be added to address specific needs. (For example: cannot hold a membership in organizations or groups for the purpose of child victimization; cannot order sexual paraphernalia by mail; cannot volunteer in civic or religious organizations where possible victims can be identified; cannot access electronic media/INTERNET/WEB TV.)

I have read or have had read to me the Sex Offender Supervision Agreement, and agree to abide by the conditions set forth in this document.

_____   _____
Offender's Signature   Date

_____   _____
Witness   Date

FIGURE 12.2 *Sex Offender Supervision Agreement.*

(*Source:* Missouri Department of Corrections.)

not having contact with persons younger than 18, maintaining a driving log containing mileage, time of departure, arrival, return, routes traveled and with whom, and not possessing or viewing any sexually oriented media—printed, video, audio, telephonic, and electronic—relevant to the deviant behavior pattern. The rules are enforced by unannounced home visits and surveillance activities (Figure 12.3). In Cook County, Illinois, probation officers in their Adult Sex Offender Program report that many offenders "have expressed the view that their probation officers serve as an external conscience," and the intensive supervision program "serves to constantly remind each probationer of the consequences for re-offense" (Jenuwine et al., 2003: 22).

Research (Gilligan and Talbot, 2000) indicates that clear advantages of specialized sex offender caseloads. Specialized caseloads allow supervision staff to

- Gain expertise and training related to sex offender management.
- Ensure sex offenders, who might have become "lost" on nonspecialized caseloads because of their seemingly compliant nature, are supervised intensively.
- Establish rapport with sex offenders in order to encourage them to talk openly about their thoughts and activities.
- Promote feelings of camaraderie and support among officers who maintain these caseloads in order to reduce secondary trauma.
- Increase agencywide consistency in sex offender supervision practices.

Texas Sex Offender Caseload

In Texas, each district office of the Pardons and Paroles Division has at least one designated sex offender officer. Such officers receive specialized training, and attend ongoing seminars to stay current with treatment and supervision issues concerning this special category of client. Offenders classified as exhibitionists, pedophiles, and rapists are referred to the special sex offender officer whose caseload does not exceed 45. Specialized treatment is provided through contractual arrangement with public and private resources. Place of residence is closely monitored, and a sex offender is not permitted to reside with a past victim or potential victims. Pedophiles are prohibited from any contact with children younger than age 17, unless specific arrangements have been made and permission has been granted by the PO after consultation with the therapist; an adult must be present during such contacts. POs also ensure compliance with the state's Sex Offender Registration Program. With the endorsement of his or her therapist, a parolee may be transferred from the Sex Offender Caseload to regular supervision.

Hunt County Sex Offender Unit

The Hunt County, Texas, Probation Department's Sex Offender Accountability Program (SOAP) is a specialized caseload monitoring sexual abusers' compliance with conditions of supervision. SOAP uses a team comprised of a probation officer, sex offender therapist, and polygraph examiner. The PO, accompanied by a peace officer for security reasons, makes random checks of offenders' home environments to discuss special issues and monitor their surroundings for warning signs of risk.

Sex offenders must adhere to the 18 standard conditions of supervision common to all felony offenders. These conditions include refraining from criminal conduct, drug/alcohol use, and association with felons; reporting to the probation officer as directed; and submitting to drug testing. In addition, sex offenders are required to attend and participate in sex offender treatment with a registered treatment provider. These treatment groups typically meet once per week.

The offender must submit to and pay for polygraph testing. These examinations may be required every 6 to 12 months. Assistance is available for indigent

Bucks County Adult Probation and Parole Department

SPECIAL OFFENDER CASE PLAN

PROGRAMMING / TREATMENT

___ You must successfully enroll, participate in, and complete a program for sex offenders approved by the Court.

    Program _____
    Telephone Number _____
    Contact by _____

___ You must maintain use of prescribed medications.

___ Other _____

ALCOHOL AND DRUGS

___ You may not use alcohol.

___ You may not frequent bars, taverns, and businesses whose primary function is to serve alcoholic beverages.

___ You may not associate with alcohol and drug abusers.

___ You will attend and successfully complete an alcohol and/or drug treatment program.

___ Other _____

SOCIAL

___ You may not associate with ex-felons unless they are in treatment with you and your therapist and PO approve of the association.

___ You must inform all persons with whom you have a significant relationship or close affiliation of your sexual offending history. Therapist and/or PO will determine who shall be informed.

___ You may not participate in friendships or relationships with women/men who have children.

___ You may not socialize with individuals under the age of 16 in work or social situations unless accompanied by a responsible adult (approved by your therapist and/or PO) who is aware of your sexual abusive pattern.

___ You may not engage in activities that will bring you in close contact with children.

___ Other _____

MONITORING

___ You are required to meet with your probation/parole officer at least three (3) times per month.

___ You are required to give your PO search and seizure privileges to confiscate drugs, erotica, and pornography.

___ You must maintain a daily journal (including such items as daily activities, fantasies, etc.).

___ You must participate in a plethysmographic examination to determine your sexual arousal to abusive themes. These examinations will be periodic upon the therapist's request.

___ Other _____

DRIVING

___ You must maintain a driving log (mileage; time of departure, arrival & return; destination; routes traveled; with whom, etc.).

___ You may not pick up hitchhikers.

___ You must comply with specified limitations on driving, i.e., not driving at night, not driving alone, not driving at key times, not driving with female passengers, etc., depending upon your individual criminal history and offense patterns.

___ You may not drive with a female unless there is a specific reason, for example a prearranged date whose name, address, and phone number you have reported to your PO and/or therapist.

___ Other _____

VICTIM CONTACT

___ You may not have any contact with the victim(s) (including letters, phone calls, tapes, videos, visits, or any form of contact through a third party) until approved by your Judge, therapist, the victim (and the victim's parents if the victim is a child), and the victim's therapist.

___ You (as an incest offender) may not have visitation with the victim unless approved by your Judge, therapist, the victim, the victim's therapist, and the Children and Youth Services agency.

___ Other _____

OFFENSE-SPECIFIC CONDITIONS

___ You may not view videotapes, films, or television shows that are geared towards your modus operandi, act as a stimulus for your abusive cycle, or act as a stimulus to arouse you in an abusive fashion, i.e., pedophiles may not view shows whose primary character is a child.

___ You may not use pornography, erotica; you may not frequent adult book stores, sex shops, topless bars, massage parlors, etc.

___ You may not frequent places where children congregate, i.e., parks, playgrounds, schools, etc.

___ Since you have photographed your victims in the past, you may not possess a camera or video recorder.

___ Other _____

DAILY LIVING

___ You must reside in a residence approved by your PO.

___ You must maintain full-time school and/or employment.

___ Your employer must be approved by your PO and therapist.

___ Other _____

GENERAL

___ You must observe curfew restrictions.

___ Other _____

_____   Date _____
Client

_____   Date _____
Probation/Parole Officer

_____   Date _____
Probation/Parole Supervisor
☐ Copy to therapist

spciotf2.frm/041394

PROBATION / PAROLE DEPARTMENT FILE

FIGURE 12.3 *Special Offender Case Plan.*

(*Source:* Bucks County, Pennsylvania, Probation and Parole Department.)

offenders. There is some variation in probation conditions regarding contact with children. Most offenders are initially prohibited from any contact with children. Some offenders are permitted to have supervised contact with their biological children. As an offender participates and progresses in sex offender treatment, his conditions may be modified gradually to allow more supervised contact with children. An offender cannot reside near a school or daycare center and cannot go to places where children are known to congregate.

SOAP offenders are prohibited from viewing or purchasing pornography or going to sexually oriented businesses. They are typically restricted from accessing the Internet. Texas law allows the judge placing an offender on probation to order him to serve time in the local jail (up to 180 days) as a condition of supervision. This is an option often used by the Hunt County Courts. Electronic monitoring and home curfews are also an option the court may use.

Sex offenders in the program are ordered by the court to submit a blood sample. This sample is sent to the crime lab in Austin, and a DNA record is made. The DNA database is used to assist in the investigation of unsolved crimes.

Maricopa County Sex Offender Program

In 1987, the Arizona legislature passed a law mandating lifetime probation for sex offenders convicted of crimes against children. The Maricopa County Adult Probation Department's response includes intensive supervision, subsidized treatment and assessment, and services for victims and their families. Maricopa County is a mostly urban jurisdiction, with more than 2.5 million people living in a metropolitan area that includes Phoenix and Scottsdale. Approximately two-thirds of the state's population resides within the county.

Assessment involves the use of psychological testing and plethysmographies that electronically measure an offender's penile arousal to various audiovisual stimuli. The instrument, similar to a blood pressure gauge, is attached to the offender's penis and measures the arousal, recording changes in penile tumescence, when different types of deviant and nondeviant stimuli are presented. Along with the **plethysmograph,** a polygraph is used to secure a complete sexual history and to periodically monitor compliance with probation regulations.

Offenders begin their probation terms by participating in 45 classroom hours on sexuality and sexual deviation. They are placed in treatment groups that usually use a cognitive-behavioral approach and that can last from 18 months to 2 years or, in some cases, longer. Those with the means are expected to pay for the therapy. Offenders are subject to a curfew and may not operate a motor vehicle without the consent of their probation officer.

The supervision units consist of 21 specialized probation officers and 10 surveillance officers. The average caseload size for probation officers is 53 offenders. Surveillance officers work with two probation officers, averaging about 100 offenders each. Probation officers supervise progress in dealing with behavioral and life issues, and compliance with program conditions. Surveillance officers make random field visits, particularly evening and weekend visits, and work closely with the other officers.

Jefferson County Juvenile Sex Offender Unit

Jefferson County is a suburban county west of Denver, Colorado, with a growing population of more than a half-million persons. County juvenile officers began to apply the models of specialized treatment and supervision that were being used with adults to the young offenders on their caseloads, and developed the first specialized juvenile sex offender unit in the state. There are an average of 160 juveniles on probation in Jefferson County for sexual offenses. About 75 percent of these offenders were adjudicated for felonies, while the remainder were adjudicated for misdemeanors. Most were charged with assaulting younger people; about 10 percent of the juvenile offenders are girls. Two probation officers provide supervision to all juvenile sex offenders in the county. The juvenile unit is coordinated by a unit supervisor. One officer is responsible for preparing presentence investigations for juvenile sex offenders. Each officer carries approximately 80 cases.

About 98 percent of all juvenile sex offenders in Jefferson County receive a probation sentence. Maximum probation sentences are statutorily limited to 2 years. Juveniles start supervision at the highest level of supervision. They are classified within 2 months, based on their scores on the Colorado Young Offender Level of Services Inventory (general risk assessment tool) and the Protective Factor Scale (to determine the offender's treatment needs). The unit's probation officers meet up to three times each month to review an offender's supervision plan (Figure 12.4.)

Juveniles attend weekly group therapy sessions that are cognitive based and focused on learning about their offending behaviors, the abuse cycle, relapse prevention, and victim empathy. Individual and family sessions are held at a minimum of once per month. Probation officers meet frequently with treatment providers and attend treatment sessions and case staffings about once per month. Juveniles are also administered polygraph exams and plethysmographs when therapists and officers agree they are needed. Polygraphs are administered to juveniles as young as 12 years old, depending on their level of functioning and the seriousness of their offending behavior. Plethysmographs are used less frequently and are generally administered on older juveniles when there are concerns about deviant arousal patterns.

Juvenile sex offenders are subject to expulsion from the public school system, but in most cases expulsion is counterproductive to the youth's treatment plan. Rather, careful supervision and collaboration between the schools and criminal justice have resulted in the return of the majority of sex offenders to the classroom. Staff are careful not to return offenders to school who clearly pose a threat to school personnel or other children. Probation staff work closely with school principals to establish structured schedules for offenders. Other school personnel are notified of the offenders' circumstances only on a need-to-know basis.

New Haven Sex Offender Intensive Supervision Unit

The city of New Haven, Connecticut, has a population of about 150,000. It is a diverse urban area and the home of Yale University, but it is one of the poorest cities in the nation. The Sex Offender Intensive Supervision Unit is a cooperative effort of the Office of Adult Probation (OAP), a statewide agency housed within the judicial branch, and the Center for the Treatment of Problem Sexual Behavior (CTPSB), a private nonprofit community-based treatment program that operates statewide. The unit supervises high-risk adult sex offenders (age 16 and older) identified through risk assessment by probation and treatment staff. All offenders on the caseload have been convicted of a sex offense and are under the legal supervision of the OAP.

The team consists of a lead probation officer, four probation officers, three treatment providers from CTPSB, and a victim advocate from Connecticut Sexual Assault Crisis Services, whose position is funded by OAP and housed primarily within the New Haven Probation office. Three probation officers supervise a maximum of 25 high-risk offenders each. These officers are responsible for 24-hour supervision, 7 days per week. They are highly mobile and very proactive. They are in contact with the offenders on their caseload nearly every day. The officers routinely make unannounced home visits (including evenings, weekends, and holidays); maintain communication with family members, friends, and employers; assess the appropriateness of offenders' residence and employment; search for at-risk behaviors (including evidence of contact or potential contact with children, pornography, illegal substances or alcohol, and Internet checks); and collaborate with local law enforcement.

The fourth probation officer is a Relapse Prevention Specialist and has a maximum caseload of 50 offenders. As offenders progress in treatment, they transition from specialized Intensive Supervision to the Relapse Prevention caseload. This transition is based on time in treatment, stable behavior, and active engagement in the treatment

Part I – General Information

Offender Name: _____

Date of Assessment: _____

Number: _____   Date of Birth: _____

Date of Offense: _____

Current Sex Offense: _____

Penal Code Citation: _____

Evaluator's Name: _____

Title: _____

Location: _____

Anticipated Date of Release: _____

Part II – Variables

Score

1. CURRENT SEX OFFENSE:
A. Seriousness of Sex Offense
      Felony 1
      Misdemeanor 0
B. Use of Weapon in the Sex Offense
      Firearm/Cutting Instrument..2
      Other Weapon 1
      None...0

2. AGE AT FIRST REFERRAL
      10 Years of Age..2
      11–14 Years of Age..1
      15–16 Years of Age..0

3. PRIOR ADJUDICATIONS FOR SEX OFFENSES
      2 or more prior adjudications for sex offenses....................2
      1 prior adjudication for sex offense(s)..................................1
      No prior adjudications for sex offense..................................0

4. PRIOR REFERRALS FOR SEX OFFENSES
      2 or more prior referrals for sex offenses............................2
      1 referral for a sex offense..1
      No referrals 0

5. PRIOR ADJUDICATIONS FOR FELONY OFFENSES
      2 or more prior adjudications for felony offenses...............2
      1 prior adjudication for a felony offense(s)..........................1
      No prior adjudications for felony offense.............................0

6. PRIOR FELONY REFERRALS
      2 or more prior felony referrals...2
      1 felony referral 1
      No felony referrals...0

SCORE RANGE		RISK LEVEL	TOTAL SCORE_____
0 – 5	Moderate Range	2	
6 – 13	High Range	1	RISK LEVEL _____

FIGURE 12.4 *Texas Juvenile Sex Offender Risk Assessment Instrument.*

(Source: State of Texas.)

process. The Relapse Prevention caseload provides heightened but less intense monitoring. Offenders move toward incorporation in nonspecialized "regular" high-risk supervision (maximum caseload of 75). The Relapse Prevention officer receives specialized training, collaborates with treatment providers, and co-facilitates groups.

The CTPSB treatment staff provide assessment and treatment, and often accompany probation officers on home visits. Treatment staff use a psychopathy checklist, psychological survey, and a risk assessment instrument based on current research. Offenders are accepted for treatment if the nature of their offense and their history indicate they would benefit from treatment. Offenders who are assessed as having psychopathic personalities (this is very uncommon) are often rejected from treatment because such offenders may pose greater risks with treatment. Generally, an offender's evaluation determines the type of treatment received.

Treatment staff are responsible for group therapy provided to offenders. Most offenders begin with an introductory group (the "cognitive lab"), which provides treatment orientation and expectations and lasts about 14 weeks. Treatment draws on cognitive-behavioral approaches, and includes cognitive restructuring, victim empathy training, sexual education, and relapse prevention training. CTPSB offers special bilingual groups and groups for people with developmental disabilities. They also offer a "family seminar" before family reunification. Whenever possible, rapists, child molesters, and exhibitionists/voyeurs are assigned to separate, specialized groups. A portion of the offenders also receive specialized medication to control their impulses and behavior.

Treatment proceeds toward realization of 14 goals, categorized as immediate, intermediate, and extended. The first immediate goal is acceptance of responsibility for the sexual offense. The final goal is to "learn about, and utilize, a Relapse Prevention Strategy and an Offense Prevention Plan." Length of time in treatment depends on the individual's progress because treatment is considered open ended. It ranges from 1 to 7 years.

A victim advocate supports supervision activities by accompanying probation officers on home and field visits, attending case review meetings, and leading the victim empathy component of treatment groups. She initiates contact with the victim and/or victim's family and maintains that contact as long as necessary. The advocate provides information and raises concerns to probation officers and treatment staff throughout the supervision process. She provides referrals for counseling and other services. She obtains background information from all probation files on each individual supervised by the unit. She also gathers information from victims or significant others and family members about an offender's behavior as part of supervision.

Notification is provided to victims, victims' parents or guardians (as appropriate), the police, the offender's immediate family members, other occupants of the offender's residence, and treatment providers. For the highest risk cases, including most unit cases, the team may decide to include notification to other neighbors, local schools, employers, and organizations with which the offender is involved. Notification is a probation responsibility, but often involves both the probation officer and the victim advocate. Notification is also regarded as an important opportunity for public education about sex offenders. The advocate and/or the officers hold public meetings in advance of notification when possible.

Orange County Probation Department Adult Sex Offender Unit

California's Orange County, with a population of nearly 3 million, is located south of Los Angeles. The Adult Sex Offender Unit (ASOU) has a staff of 11 officers: one supervisor, eight deputy probation officers who supervise approximately 40 high-risk cases each, and two deputy probation officers who conduct assessments of incoming cases classifying each into low-, medium-, and high-risk levels. Risk is reassessed every 6 months, and low-risk cases can be transitioned to regular supervision caseloads. Officers have received specialized training.

Supervision includes at least three in-person contacts per month, plus evening and weekend surveillance activities. All information provided by offenders is verified, and there is ongoing contact with victims to ensure no-contact orders are being obeyed. Specialized sex offender treatment is mandatory, and there is ongoing coordination with treatment providers.

Probationers must provide restitution for victim medical and/or psychological treatment and reimbursement for the cost incurred by police in gathering forensic evidence. They can be required to submit to AIDS and DNA testing, and undergo periodic polygraph examinations. They are prohibited from viewing or possessing sexually explicit materials or any other exposures that act as a stimulus for their crimes, or being in contact with children or frequenting places where children congregate. Their residence, vehicle, and personal effects are subject to search (Center for Sex Offender Management, 2001b).

INTOXICATED DRIVERS

Increasing public concern, if not outrage, over the fatalities resulting from driving while intoxicated, has led to increased penalties for those convicted of DWI. However, this response has affected correctional officials attempting to deal with jail and prison overcrowding, hence, the logic for community-based responses that protect the public without contributing to the jail/prison crisis. As a result, about a half-million DWI offenders are on probation, and many states have established diversion programs for DWI cases.

Nassau County DWI Unit

In Nassau County (Long Island), New York, the DWI unit is provided with a list of DWI defendants for whom PSI reports have been requested by the court. Each case is computer-checked for prior criminal record, outstanding warrants, and motor vehicle record. Cases with multiple DWI arrests are flagged, and their names entered into a prescreening log. This log is used by the unit supervisor to monitor DWI court activity in anticipation of future screening and assignment to probation supervision. This information is then sent to the PO assigned to conduct the PSI.

When the case is flagged by the DWI unit, the PSI officer sends it to the mental health unit, where a consultant determines if the defendant is a candidate for the county's drug and alcohol abuse agency. The consultant also makes a recommendation regarding therapy that will accompany the final PSI report sent to the sentencing judge. The judge revokes the defendant's motor vehicle license at this time (6 months for misdemeanors and 1 year for felonies), and the case is submitted for DWI unit screening. Eligible defendants who

- Have a blood/alcohol level of 0.15 or above at the time of arrest or who refuse to submit to a chemical test
- Have two or more DWI arrests (including the instant offense)
- Are not on parole or a defendant in another case
- Use alcohol as their primary drug of abuse
- Have no extensive psychiatric history
- Are suitable for therapy based on their evaluation
- Are available for evening therapy sessions
- Are required to participate because of a concerned family member

Each unit PO maintains a caseload of no more than 30 DWI probationers in a designated area of the county (which is updated periodically in order to conform better to the distribution of DWI clientele). DWI supervision requires the offender to report weekly to a designated agency where he or she completes a 10-week alcohol education program and a 24-week closed group therapy session program. The group sessions are co-led by a probation officer and alcohol counselor. Individual counseling is made available on an as-needed basis. Clients are subjected to random alcohol testing, and a positive reading can result in a variety of sanctions. On completion of the agency program, the client is encouraged to participate in an AA program. The client is required to report in person to the PO, and the officer makes periodic home visits. On successful completion of the program, a letter is sent to the Department of Motor Vehicles, indicating that the subject is no longer prohibited from obtaining a driver's license.

OFFENDERS WHO ARE MENTALLY RETARDED

The offender who is developmentally challenged presents supervision problems not typically found with other types of cases. Without specific training and given the myriad of problems experienced by rather large caseloads, P/P officers are often unable to meet the needs of these clients; hence, the logic of specialized caseloads.

Cuyahoga County (Cleveland), Ohio, Mentally Retarded Offender Unit

Compared with the size of regular caseloads, usually more than 200, the mentally retarded offender unit averages between 55 and 65 probationers. Clients have a tested IQ of 75 or less, and the level of supervision for each offender is determined by a risk/needs classification: extended (mail contact only), low, medium, high, and superhigh. The unit has a clinical director who is a licensed psychologist. Each case is evaluated by the PO and clinical director, and probationers are then referred for appropriate services. An interdisciplinary team—representatives from public and private service and advocacy groups specializing in mental retardation, and public welfare agencies—aids in case planning for each probationer.

The rules and regulations of probation have been drafted in a form more easily understood by this population, and probation violation hearings are conducted in a manner more likely to be understood by the offender who is mentally retarded. For purposes of evaluation, the unit receives cases the court believes are mentally retarded. Probation officers spend a great deal of time securing services for their clients. Many social service agencies are reluctant to aid retarded offenders, both out of fear and due to the difficulties such clients present due to their disability.

Erie County Special Probation Services

Erie County, Pennsylvania, Adult Probation/Parole and Mental Health/Mental Retardation Offices jointly fund Special Probation Services that provide County Court of Common Pleas judges with alternatives to incarceration for offenders who are mentally retarded—persons with a full scale IQ score of 74 and below. Special Probation Services is designed to provide individualized and specialized services to persons who are developmentally disabled and receive an Erie County sentence. The program offers the structure and the support of the criminal justice system simultaneously with the expertise of the mental retardation system. The P/P officer is responsible for monitoring and enforcing the P/P conditions. The case manager is responsible for coordinating community services to meet the individual's needs.

In addition, Special Probation Services monitors inmates released under pretrial conditions. The case manager participates on an interdisciplinary evaluation committee, which screens pretrial inmates for program eligibility. A judge can elect to release the qualified offender into the community under the supervision of the Special Probation Services pending disposition. The unit participates on an interdisciplinary team to screen and review case histories of newly incarcerated inmates in the Erie County Prison. Persons suspected of being mentally impaired are further evaluated to determine if they are mentally retarded and eligible for services. In addition, referrals are taken from Adult Probation and other agencies. The unit coordinates services with drug and alcohol, mental health, and mental retardation programs.

GANG INTERVENTION UNIT

The Tulare County, California, Probation Department has a unit that targets individuals throughout the county who are involved with gangs at a variety of levels. The goal is to deter youths from gang affiliation and to disengage youths and adults from the gangs once they have become affiliated. Three probation officers are assigned to monitor 300 minors in 10 community schools; two POs provide aftercare services to minors released from the Probation Youth Facility; and two supervise 100 gang-involved, high-risk minors. One probation officer is assigned to the sheriff's Gang Violence Suppression Unit and another to the Interagency Narcotics Enforcement Team. In a

---

THE SUPERIOR COURT PROBATION DEPARTMENT OF PIMA COUNTY
SPECIAL CONDITIONS OF PROBATION FOR GANG MEMBERS

Defendant _____

CR#_____

1. You shall have on your person, at all times, photo ID approved by your Probation Officer.
2. You shall provide your photo ID, true name, date of birth, address and name of your Probation Officer if contacted by law enforcement. Further, you shall report said contact or arrest to your Probation Officer immediately.
3. You shall not associate with any gang members.
4. You shall not recruit or coerce others to become involved in gang activity.
5. You shall not associate with juveniles without prior approval of your Probation Officer.
6. You shall not frequent any school grounds without prior approval of your Probation Officer unless you are a student registered at that school.
7. You shall not frequent _____.
8. You shall not wear, display, use or possess any insignias, emblems, badges, buttons, caps, hats, jackets, shoes, flags, scarves, bandannas, shirts, or other articles of clothing, which are evidence of gang affiliation.
9. You shall not display any gang signs or gestures.
10. You shall not appear in Court or at the Courthouse unless you are a party in the proceedings or reporting to your Probation Officer.
11. You shall not associate with any person who has firearms, weapons, or replicas in their possession.
12. You shall not frequent places where firearms or weapons are used either illegally or legally.
13. You shall not possess countersurveillance devices, beepers or pagers except in the course of lawful employment.
14. You shall not be an occupant in any stolen vehicle or vehicle that you should have known was stolen.
15. You shall not drive any vehicle without a valid driver's license, registration and proof of insurance.
16. You shall enroll in educational or vocational programs or maintain full time employment. If not in school or employed, you will participate in a day reporting program.
17. You shall participate in alcohol and substance abuse monitoring, screening and counseling as directed by your Probation Officer.
18. You shall complete _____ hours of community service at a rate of _____ hours per month in the Graffiti Abatement Program or other approved program.
19. You shall abide by a _____ curfew and approved weekly schedule.
20. _____
    _____
21. _____
    _____

Date _____   JUDGE OF THE SUPERIOR COURT

Date _____   PROBATIONER

FIGURE 12.5 *Special Conditions for Gang Members.*

(*Source:* Pima County, Arizona, Superior Court Probation Department.)

cooperative effort with the district attorney's office, the sheriff's office, and other law enforcement gang units, the unit develops intelligence sources to identify gang members and suppress their ability to engage in further violence and criminal activity.

Unit POs actively enforce the terms of probation (Figure 12.5) by making personal contacts and conducting random searches for weapons and tests for drugs. Probationers who fail to fully comply with their terms of probation are taken into custody. Probation officers, along with other county and state law enforcement agencies, also provide counseling to gang members through the Alternative Youth Support Group (AYSG). Participation in the AYSG is mandated by the court and is designed to provide alternatives to the gang lifestyle.

RESTITUTION AND COMMUNITY SERVICE

Restitution—an act of restoring, or a condition of being restored, or a making good or giving an equivalent for some injury—has become a popular condition of P/P. In addition to paying for court costs, fines, and fees, a probationer may be required to make restitution; paying a percentage of his or her income, as determined by the court or parole board, to the victim of the offense for any property damage or medical expenses sustained as a direct result of the commission of the offense. This concept has an ancient history: The Bible (Exodus 21, 22; Leviticus 5) orders restitution for theft, burglary, or robbery, and a form of "community service"—indentured servitude—in the event the criminal has no means of providing restitution. Restitution fell out of favor when monarchs, seeking to centralize power, made crime a public (state) matter and directed payments (fines) away from the victim or his or her kin, in favor of the crown. (Personal claims had to be brought in civil court.) Community service emerged as a modern sentencing option in Alameda County, California, in 1966, and the Minnesota Restitution Program was established in 1972. Persons convicted of property offenses were given the opportunity to reduce their jail sentence or avoid incarceration altogether if they secured employment and provided restitution to their victims. The idea soon spread to other states.

Douglas McDonald (1988: 2) notes that, in addition to aiding victims, restitution and community service are animated by the belief that they may contribute to the rehabilitation of offenders:

> Disciplined work has long been considered reformative. In addition, offenders performing community service may acquire some employable skills, improved work habits, and a record of quasi-employment that may be longer than any job they've held before. Victim restitution, when it brings offenders and victims face to face, also forces offenders to see firsthand the consequences of their deeds and thus may encourage the development of greater social responsibility and maturity.

Texas is so committed to the concept of restitution that since 1983, based on models established in Georgia and Mississippi, it has operated "restitution centers" throughout the state. As a condition of probation, nonviolent, employable felony offenders who would have otherwise been imprisoned can be sent to a restitution center for between 6 and 12 months, during which time the restitution center director attempts to secure employment for each resident. The director also attempts to place each probationer as a worker in a community service project either during off-work hours if the probationer is employed, or full-time if the probationer is unable to find employment. The restitution facility, which is operated by probation staff, accommodates between 30 to 60 persons and is usually located in light industrial areas for access to employment.

The probationer's salary is submitted by the employer directly to the director of the restitution center. The director deducts the cost of food, housing, and supervision, support for the probationer's dependents, and restitution to the victim(s)—the remainder, if any, going to the probationer upon release from the center. If a restitution center director determines that the probationer is knowingly or intentionally failing to seek employment, the director requests that the court having jurisdiction over the case revoke probation and transfer the probationer to the custody of the Texas Department of Corrections. If the judge determines that a resident has demonstrated an acceptance of responsibility, the court may order the resident released from the center. The first 2 months following release, the former resident is on intensive supervision before being transferred to a regular probation caseload.

Community Service

Because relatively few offenders coming into the criminal justice system are in a position to provide meaningful financial restitution, the alternative of **community service** has gained in popularity. In New Jersey, offenders sentenced to community service work without monetary compensation at public or private nonprofit agencies in the community. They usually perform their community service during the evenings and on weekends to complete their sentences: "The punitive aspect of a community service order is reflected in the imposition upon the time and freedom of offenders. While functioning in the traditional role as punishment, a community service order also directly benefits the public through the performance of services that may otherwise not be available" (Administrative Office of the Court, n.d.: 11).

Community service in Georgia is seen as "an alternative sentencing option which is definitely punitive, yet is not perceived as being as harsh as incarceration, nor as lenient as regular probation." In the state of Washington, compulsory service without compensation performed for the benefit of the community is available as an alternative to incarceration for certain nonviolent crimes. The Department of Corrections Division of Community Services solicits requests for personnel services from nonprofit or governmental agencies. Community service has included chore service, work in food banks, park and street cleanup, industrial oil removal, and recycling. The requesting agency is expected to

1. Refrain from displacing a paid worker with an offender.
2. Supply a description of the work site and tasks.
3. Assign a supervisor for training and supervision of the offender.
4. Provide working conditions for the offender equal to that of paid staff.
5. Provide written verification of offender performance.

Similar programs exist in several states, including Georgia, Indiana, Kansas, Louisiana, Maryland, Minnesota, Ohio, Oregon, and Virginia. In Illinois and New Jersey, community service is used as an alternative for persons convicted of driving while intoxicated. In New Jersey, the community service program is the responsibility of the county probation department. Although no offender is automatically disqualified for the community service alternative in New Jersey, the Administrative Office of the Courts recommends that persons suffering from chronic alcohol or drug abuse problems, persons convicted of arson or assaultive offenses, and those with previous convictions for certain sex offenses be excluded. In Georgia, community service is recommended for, but not limited to, persons convicted of traffic and ordinance violations, and nonviolent, nondestructive misdemeanors and felonies. In other cases, "The judge may confer with the prosecutor, defense attorney, probation supervisor, community service officer, or other interested persons to determine if the community service program is appropriate for an offender." Typical placements in Georgia have included hospitals, Red Cross, parks and recreation systems, senior citizen centers, associations for the blind and deaf, and humane societies (Figure 12.6).

AGREEMENT BETWEEN PLACEMENT AGENCY AND PROGRAM

A. PURPOSE:

The purpose of this agreement is to formalize and enhance the working relationship between participating placement agencies and the Bucks County, Pennsylvania, Community Service Program.

B. DEFINITIONS:

"Community Service" shall be defined as uncompensated labor for an agency whose purpose is to enhance physical or mental stability, environmental quality or the social welfare.

"Agency" means a non-profit organization or public body agreeing to accept community service from offenders and to report on the progress of ordered community service to the court or its delegate.

C. PROGRAM DESCRIPTIONS:

Program staff interview and screen convicted offenders who have been sentenced by judges to perform a specific number of hours of community service work. In cooperation with participating placement agencies, program liaisons assign community service clients to placement agencies to perform the required community service work by a specific deadline. These liaisons monitor the progress of the client and assist placement agencies in working with the clients. Based on information supplied by placement agencies, program staff make periodic reports to judges, probation officers, and other members of the justice system.

D. AGENCY RESPONSIBILITIES:

1. The placement agency will designate a specific agency staff person who will act as the agency contact. The agency contact will be responsible for accepting or rejecting potential community service volunteers and will provide necessary information to the program liaisons.
2. The placement agency will not discriminate in serving or in selecting clients on the basis of race, sex, age, marital status, religion, handicap, color, political affiliations, national origin, or any other nonmerit factors.
3. The placement agency contact will interview the potential community service volunteer.
a. If the potential client is accepted by the placement agency, the interviewer and client will establish work schedules and work assignments. The placement agency will provide reasonable training necessary for the successful completion of the work assigned to the client.
b. If the potential client is not accepted by the placement agency, the agency will notify the liaison, and will explain why the client was rejected by the agency.
4. The placement agency will document the hours worked by the client and will record that information on the log sheets. The placement agency will report the hours worked upon the liaison's request. The agency will also notify the liaison upon the completion of hours.
5. The placement agency will report any supervision problems and physical injuries received by the client. When an injury occurs, the placement agency will insure that proper medical care is provided and will notify the Community Service Program liaison within one working day.
6. The placement agency will advise the liaison of any changes in the agency that would affect future use of the agency as a community service placement site.

E. PROGRAM RESPONSIBILITIES:

1. The Program Coordinator will assign a staff liaison to each placement agency. Each agency will be visited at least three times a year by the liaison. The liaison will describe the program to the agency contact and will gather necessary information about the agency.
2. Whenever needed, the program staff will provide assistance to the placement agencies to improve the agencies' use of clients and maintenance of information.
3. The Program will provide resource information about working with the offenders in a community setting.
4. The Liaison will advise agency contacts of any changes in the program that impact placement agencies.
5. Program staff will assist placement agency personnel in resolving specific problems with individual clients.
6. Based on information provided by clients and placement agencies, program staff will assign appropriate clients to the placement agencies.

FIGURE 12.6 *Agreement Between Placement Agency and Program.*
(*Source:* Dauphin County, Pennsylvania, Adult Probation/Parole Department.)

FIGURE 12.7 *Offender Community Service Agreement.*

(*Source:* Arkansas Department of Community Punishment.)

The Dauphin County, Pennsylvania, Adult Probation/Parole Department has a Community Resource Program in conjunction with the Harrisburg chapter of the American Red Cross. Clients placed at the Red Cross are regarded as volunteers (even though participation is a mandatory condition of the sentence of probation or county parole) and are provided with the same training, expectations, and benefits that any Red Cross volunteer receives. The Red Cross provides monthly evaluation reports. If work is satisfactory, a completion letter is given to the client and a copy to the P/P officer; unsatisfactory work results in a termination letter. Clients have served as first aid providers and assistants to an instructor of first aid courses, and have conducted their own courses in first aid using multimedia systems; others serve in clerical, public relations, custodial, and research positions. Although no restrictions are placed on who may enter the program, clients have been nonviolent offenders (Figure 12.7).

PROBATION/PAROLE FEES

The imposition of "user" fees—as distinct from "service" fees, such as for electronic monitoring and drug testing—has grown in popularity, and most P/P agencies impose them. These fees frequently account for a significant portion of the agency budget. In Texas, there is considerable pressure on probation officers for successful collection of fees, and there has been a great deal of success in collecting fees, although a few states scrapped their collection programs because they did not generate enough money to make the effort worthwhile (Finn and Parent, 1992; Mills, 1992). Illinois requires the imposition of a fee of $25 for each month of probation supervision ordered by the court. Instead of collecting monthly fees, Kansas imposes a one-time probation fee: $50 for felonies and $25 for misdemeanors. Alabama charges probationers and parolees a $20 per month supervision fee. Kentucky charges not less than $10 per month with the maximum for a felony set at $2,500, and for a misdemeanor, $500. New York state law permits a 5 to 10 percent fee on restitution cases, the higher amount when actual collection costs exceed 5 percent. The Onondaga (Syracuse), New York, Probation Department imposes a variety of fees for different services (e.g., $200 for a custody/visitation investigation and $150 to $500 for an adoption investigation), depending on adjusted gross income. The department charges $50 for alcohol/drug testing, while probationers under supervision for driving while intoxicated pay $30 per month. In Suffolk County, New York, probationers must pay a **supervision fee** of $30 per month; they are charged an additional $10 for each month they are tested for drug use. In Iowa, the Sixth District Department of Correctional Services requires those on probation or parole to pay a one-time fee of $150 if they were convicted of a felony, $125 for an aggravated misdemeanor, and $100 for a simple misdemeanor. The state of Washington charges parolees $20 to $40 per year, depending on the nature of their classification level and supervision status. In Arkansas, offenders on intensive supervision pay $10 per month above the basic assessment for regular probation or parole supervision. Those electronically monitored pay $20 above the basic P/P fee. In Marion County, Indiana, felony probationers pay an intake fee of $100 and a monthly supervision fee of $15; misdemeanants pay $50 and $10.

The use of probation violation as a fee-compliance mechanism has been rare, and prison overcrowding makes judges reluctant to revoke probation even for willful failure to pay. Instead, intermediate punishments, such as a short jail stay or several weeks of community service, may be imposed. In 1992, New York enacted legislation requiring parolees to pay a supervision fee of $30 per month. Failure to comply does not result in a violation of parole; instead, interest and late payment fees are assessed through (civil) court action that can lead to garnishment of wages or attachment of income tax refunds. Parolees falling below economic standards set by the Division of Parole can be given a temporary waiver. Those who are disabled or suffering from a terminal medical condition can be given a permanent waiver. A study found that fees and restitution, "if used appropriately and judiciously, can be an effective criminal sanction," although there is a bias by probation officers against collections efforts: POs viewing themselves more as *helpers* than *collectors* (Allen and Treger, 1994: 39).

Discussion

Steven L. Chesney (n.d.: 158) studied the use of restitution in Minnesota and reports that "it is clear that the most important determinant of whether an otherwise eligible defendant was to be ordered to make restitution was his supposed 'ability to pay.'" As evident both from interviews with judges and from the cases themselves, this criterion was generally operationalized by choosing offenders who were white, well-educated, and from the working and middle classes. This contrasted markedly with what is known about the criminal justice system in general. Those caught up in the system are overwhelmingly the poor, the lower class, and members of minority groups. He raises some issues with respect to the use of restitution:

- Perhaps the relatively well-educated and well-employed group of offenders that is able to pay restitution is the group of offenders for whom restitution has the least meaning.
- Restitution may be one way that members of the more affluent social classes can avoid incarceration.

Chesney (n.d.: 169) concludes that

> restitution is not addressed to a rehabilitative or a victim compensatory need; instead, it answers a moral need. It reflects the way we feel that people should treat other people. As such, the evaluations of the effects of restitution may need to show only that it is no worse than other rehabilitative alternatives and that it does compensate some victims. Any effects beyond these are serendipitous because the primary goal of restitution is the elimination of the contradictions between our systems of morality and our criminal justice system.

Although restitution would appear to be a win–win practice, the use of supervision fees raises serious questions:

- Will persons who can pay fees be more likely to be granted P/P?
- Will the need to collect fees change the focus of P/P supervision away from providing services?
- Will the failure to pay fees result in P/P revocation?
- Will persons be kept under supervision longer because of their ability to pay fees or a need to collect unpaid fees? Will a person who can pay fees be less likely to be cited for a P/P violation?
- Will the imposition of fees cause an increase in absconding from supervision?
- Will fee collection responsibilities detract from the work of already overburdened P/P officers?

Answers to these questions are part of the continuing debate over supervision fees.

In 1983, the Supreme Court (*Beardon v. Georgia*, 461 U.S. 660) ruled that probation cannot be revoked because of an inability to pay a fine and restitution as a condition of probation that is a result of indigence and not a refusal to pay. This point would appear to apply to supervision fees. Fahy Mullaney found that failure to pay restitution or fees often results in an extension of time an offender is under supervision: "In fact, some offenders are kept on intensive supervision although they completed all their probation conditions except final payment on a fee" (1988: 15). Furthermore, collection-related tasks require 10 percent additional staff time, whereas extending supervision further increases the demands on staff. There are also "subtle value shifts in community corrections agencies, raising the priority of fiscal matters rather than of community safety, community justice, or human restoration" (15). She cautions: "In the early history of incarceration, offenders were required to pay for admission to jail, to pay the jailer for food and bedding while there, and finally to pay upon release. Today we are aghast that such counterproductive, unjust practices could ever exist" (15). Nevertheless, "across this country, we are swiftly adopting new sanctions, especially fees and special assessments, that have a dramatic financial impact on those who go through our criminal justice system. Without thoughtful development of policy and practice to guide and limit this movement, we may well repeat history rather than learn from it" (21). In Texas, defenders of the system, where about three-fourths of the state's counties collect fees equal to one-half or more of their total expenses, state that rather than detracting from casework, aggressive fee collection actually furthers the goal of helping probationers avoid relapsing into criminal behavior. "They argue that the regularity of fee payments is a good barometer of a probationer's overall adjustment to supervision. . . . Some probation staff believe that the emphasis on fee collections provides an opportunity to help teach offenders how to budget and meet ongoing financial obligations on time" (Finn and Parent, 1992: 11–12).

WORK RELEASE

Many states have prison work release programs, and in some instances these programs involve P/P staff. **Work release** allows people serving sentences to work in the community, returning each evening to the institution. They are still subject to institutional controls (and absconding is considered an escape from confinement), and additional regulations apply to their extrainstitutional status. Under this system, inmates are able to earn a salary and pay taxes, contribute to their families' income, repay debts, make restitution, and even contribute to their keep at the institution. In addition, work release enhances an inmate's self-image.

Legislation authorizing work release programs was enacted in Wisconsin in 1913, but it took more than 40 years before it spread to other states: California and North Carolina enacted work release legislation in 1957. By 1965, 24 states had such legislation, and by 1975, all 50 states and the federal government had legislation authorizing some form of community work and educational release (Rosenblum and Whitcomb, 1978). More recently, however, work release programs have declined and only about one-third of U.S. prisons report operating such programs with fewer than 3 percent of total inmates participating in them: "As the rehabilitation ideal—of which work release was very much a part—started to fade, the public embraced imprisonment as the only sure way to forestall crime" (Turner and Petersilia, 1996: 2).

States vary with respect to the criteria used in selecting inmates for work release programs; some automatically excuse those serving life sentences or inmates who have detainers filed against them. In some states, the court must authorize work release; in others, the parole board has this responsibility. The final responsibility for selecting candidates, however, is usually under the aegis of the correctional authorities who administer the program. States may have specific restrictions governing who may participate in work release, but more often they use such general expressions as "not a high-security risk" or "not likely to commit a crime of violence." States vary in the number of inmates involved in work release, and in some, the program is combined with furloughs enabling eligible inmates to leave the institution for specific periods of time to seek employment or educational opportunities.

Unfortunately, many, if not most, correctional institutions are isolated from urban areas where employment opportunities are more readily available. Responding to this deficiency, some states operate a variety of facilities for housing work release participants in proximity to areas of employment. These facilities include minimum-security prisons or work release centers, halfway houses, or rented quarters in hotels or Young Men's Christian Associations. Idaho, for example, operates community work release centers that provide 4- to 6-month prerelease programming for inmates within 10 months of their release date. Violent offenders and sex offenders are ineligible. Basic restrictions are typically placed on the employment situation available to inmates:

- Inmates cannot work in a skilled area where a surplus labor force already exists.
- Conditions of employment must be commensurate with nonoffenders.
- If a union is involved, it must be consulted, and no work releasee can work while a labor dispute is in progress.

The state of Washington has had a work release program in place since 1970. The Department of Corrections (DOC) has contracts with 15 residential work-release facilities that house more than 350 mostly male offenders on any single day. According to the 1991 Sentencing Reform Act, eligible inmates must be within 6 months of their release date, have minimum security status, and not been convicted of first-degree rape or murder. Those meeting basic criteria will be denied work release if they exhibited assaultive behavior in prison, the offender's victim lives in the area, the offender has made threats against the victim, or the offender has had two or more prior work-release failures during the current commitment: "Once DOC judges an offender eligible for work release, the work release facilities' Community Screening Board, consisting of work release staff and local citizens, must agree to accept the inmate for admission" (Turner and Petersilia, 1996: 4).

Offenders are responsible for finding their own employment or employment training, although they receive assistance from facility staff. The residents pay $10 per day for room and board, and must support their dependents and make any court-ordered restitution. Community correction officers are assigned to the facilities to monitor resident behavior and can order them returned to prison for rule violations. A study of the program concluded: "The program achieved its most important goal: preparing inmates for final release and facilitating their adjustment to the community. The program did not cost the State more than it would have if the releasees had remained in prison. The public safety risks were nearly nonexistent because almost no work releasee committed new crimes [some minor property crime], and when they committed rule violations they were quickly returned to prison" (Turner and Pertersilia, 1996: 2).

HALFWAY HOUSES

"The concept of **halfway houses** was introduced in 1817 by the Massachusetts Prison Commission. This group recommended the establishment of temporary homes for destitute released offenders as a measure to reduce recidivism" (Rosenblum and Whitcomb, 1978: 9; emphasis added). "It is intended to afford a temporary shelter in this building, if they choose to accept it, to such discharged convicts as may have conducted themselves well in prison at a cheap rate, and have a chance to occupy themselves in their trade, until some opportunity offers a placing of themselves where they can gain an honest livelihood in society. A refuge of this kind, to this destitute class, would be found perhaps humane and politic" (Commonwealth of Massachusetts Legislative Document, Senate No. 2, 1830).

The name *halfway house* itself

> suggests its position in the corrections world: halfway-in, a more structured environment than probation and parole; halfway-out, a less structured environment than institutions. As halfway-in houses they represent a last step before incarceration for probationers and parolees facing or having faced revocation; as halfway-out houses, they provide services to prereleasees and parolees leaving institutions. Halfway houses also provide a residential alternative to jail or outright release for accused offenders awaiting trial or convicted offenders awaiting sentencing. (Thalheimer, 1975: 1)

Victor Goetting notes that "it is accepted that these facilities are based on sound correctional theory; in order to ultimately place a person in society successfully that person should not be any further removed from that society than is necessary" (1974: 27). When used in conjunction with prison or training school release programs, the halfway house provides (1) assistance with obtaining employment, (2) an increased ability to use community resources, and (3) needed support during the difficult initial release period (Griggs and McCune, 1972). The various types of halfway houses operated by public and private agencies and groups can be divided basically into those that provide bed, board, and some help with employment, and those that provide a full range of services, including treatment. The latter includes a variety of methods, from guided group interaction, to psychotherapy, reality therapy, or behavior modification. A halfway house may be primarily for released inmates, for parolees, or for probationers as an alternative to imprisonment. Halfway houses may also be used for probationers or parolees who violate their conditions of supervision but not seriously enough to cause them to be imprisoned.

The Texas Adult Probation Commission has funded a series of halfway houses (called residential treatment facilities) throughout the state. These facilities house felony offenders in need of a brief residency in a structured environment that offers treatment services, rather than placing them in prison or on regular probation. These offenders often need treatment for drug or alcohol abuse, job skills training, and basic education. The facilities offer a homelike atmosphere with a minimum of security measures. Residents are classified according to their individual needs and assigned to a treatment regimen that usually includes counseling, educational classes, and vocational training; they also share in the housekeeping responsibilities. As residents advance in the program, they are allowed to check in and out of the facility to go to work or training in the community. If unemployed, they may be assigned to do community service work. When residents have advanced to an acceptable level in their treatment plan, they are released from the center and placed under regular probation supervision.

The Georgia Department of Offender Rehabilitation has established more than a dozen halfway houses (called residential diversion centers) to provide judges with an option for sentencing "marginal cases"—an alternative between imprisonment and regular probation. Two centers for female offenders are available. The program requires residents to work, pay for their room and board, and provide restitution to their victims. To qualify for the program, a defendant must:

1. Be one who would otherwise be incarcerated
2. Be a nonviolent property offender
3. Not be regarded as a habitual criminal
4. Be capable of maintaining employment

Each center has the capacity for between 40 and 50 residents who serve an average of 4 to 5 months before being released to regular probation supervision. The centers provide counseling, basic education, high school equivalency examination preparation, and recreation. Release is based on a satisfactory completion of the treatment contract that the offender needs to qualify for the program. The centers serve three daily meals, and takeout lunches are furnished to residents who are out to work. Residents are responsible for maintaining the facility and are allowed visitors on the weekends during specified hours. After the fourth week, residents may earn weekend passes. Failure to comply with rules and regulations, or absconding from the facility, means imprisonment.

The major difficulty with opening and maintaining a halfway house is community reaction. A Lou Harris poll, for example, found that 77 percent of the representative U.S. sample favored the halfway-house concept, whereas 50 percent would not want one in *their* neighborhood, and only 22 percent believed that people in *their* neighborhood would favor a halfway house being located there. Experts stress the importance of getting community support for the project before opening a halfway house. Among some of the strategies used in gaining support is the formation of an advisory board made up of influential community people. Community residents may be placed on the board of directors and hired as staff for the facility. Local citizenry often fear that unwanted criminal elements will come into the area, and he suggests two ways of dealing with such fears. First, the facility can be restricted to serve people who would ordinarily reside in the community; second, if outside persons are to be brought in, a screening panel can be formed to alleviate some of the fear. The committee can be made up of community persons who work for the police, sheriff, courts, or P/P agencies (Victor Goetting in Bakal, 1974).

Massachusetts Halfway Houses, Inc.

Massachusetts Halfway Houses, Inc. (MHHI) is a private nonprofit corporation that began its operations in 1965, serving 31 parolees in a 15-bed facility. The corporation now operates halfway house programs in eight locations providing residential services to more than 1,300 juvenile and adult offenders each year. In addition to its extensive residential program, MHHI also offers nonresidential vocational and employment placement services. Most clients are from the greater Boston area, although MHHI now has contracts with the sheriffs of Suffolk and Norfolk Counties to provide services to prerelease residents as a result of overcrowding at county jails. A preparole residential program also exists for state prison inmates who have been granted parole and a residential program for parole violators whose parole adjustment might be enhanced by a structured community environment as an alternative to reimprisonment in an overcrowded and costly state or county institution.

The basic residential program lasts from 60 to 90 days, and each resident is assigned a counselor. The program uses a mutual agreement contract to set specific goals to be achieved within that time frame. These include full-time vocational activity; money management; steps to overcome any specialized problem, such as substance abuse or family difficulties; and the development of a network of community resources, for example, new peer associates and new recreational activities. Once developed, reintegration plans are formalized into a written mutual agreement program contract. This document spells out the mutual responsibilities of residents and staff in each of the primary areas as well as time frames for achievement of specific objectives. The counseling process follows the tenets of reality therapy (discussed in chapter 9). The counselor initially acts as the resident's advocate in dealing with community agencies.

St. Leonard's House

St. Leonard's House, on Chicago's West Side, was established in 1956 by, and continues to be operated under the auspices of, the Episcopal Church. The facility provides residential and rehabilitative services for 42 men recently released from prison who are under parole supervision; a close working relationship exists between parole agents and house staff. Each resident stays between 30 and 90 days, and others make many more requests for services than the facility can handle. St. Leonard's enforces a curfew and residents are permitted to have visitors and weekend passes. Drugs, alcohol, sex, threats, violence, stealing, gambling, or lending money results in immediate expulsion.

Staff members include job counselors, addiction counselors, mental health counselors, former residents, and numerous volunteers. From 6:30 A.M. to 9 P.M., the counseling staff staggers hours to be available to clients, especially in the early hours before school and job training and before the search for employment begins. They are on duty again late in the day when the men return for supper and evening meetings at the house. Education leading to a GED is available at St. Leonard's.

No fees are charged, although residents are expected to complete various housekeeping chores. A personal program for each resident begins at intake, during which he spends several hours per day, over a period of 3 to 5 days, being interviewed. As his needs are assessed, he begins to feel his way into the program and with the help of counselors sets personal goals. There is a program of personal and group counseling, peer meetings, opportunities to meet with the chaplain and the employment counselor—all designed to assure each resident gets as much help as possible in reestablishing and reordering his life. In 1998, St. Leonard's opened a three-story housing facility for graduates of its program.

Hopper Home

Operated by the Women's Prison Association in New York City, the Hopper Home houses 30 women who face P/P revocation or lengthy imprisonment under mandatory sentencing laws. Most have histories of substance abuse, and they are referred by P/P officers or district attorney's staff. Residents remain at the home for approximately 8 months moving through four program phases; at the end of each, they must assess their own progress and make formal presentations to the case management team outlining the reasons they are entitled to additional privileges such as weekend passes. Rule violations result in a loss of privileges; serious violations—bringing drugs or alcohol into or having sexual activity in the home—result in an immediate termination. Those with substance abuse problems are enrolled in day treatment programs in the community. All residents participate in a regimen of group counseling, life-skills workshops, and household work assignments. Cultural events are scheduled once a month and include trips to museums, plays, musical performances, and other events in the community.

Before being discharged from the Hopper Home—phase four—residents must show proof of stable housing and other prosocial community ties, including membership in a relevant substance abuse program. Afterward, for 6 months they return to the residence 3 times per week for drug screening, meetings with their case manager, and group meetings (Conly, 1998).

INTERSTATE ADULT AND JUVENILE COMPACTS

In the Crime Control Consent Act of 1934, Congress authorized two or more states to enter into agreements or **interstate compacts** for cooperative efforts and mutual assistance in the prevention of crime. Pursuant to this legislation, in 1937, a group of states signed the *Interstate Compact for the Supervision of Probationers and Parolees*, which enabled them to serve as each other's agents in the supervision of persons on P/P. By 1951, all 48 (and now all 50) states and the District of Columbia, Puerto Rico, and the Virgin Islands were signatories of the compact. In 1998, a revised Interstate Compact for Adult Offender Supervision was developed, and by 2002, 35 states had become members.

The compact provides a system whereby a person under supervision can leave the state of conviction—the **sending state**—and proceed to another state for employment, family, or health reasons, and at the same time guarantees that the **receiving state** will provide supervision of the offender. The state of original jurisdiction (where the offender was convicted) retains authority over the probationer/parolee and is kept advised of his or her whereabouts and activities by the receiving state. The compact also provides for P/P violators to be returned without the need to resort to time-consuming extradition procedures. Because it is based on a federal statute and governed by the substantive law of contracts, the interstate compact supersedes state law. (The U.S. Supreme Court has never ruled on the constitutionality of the compact, having denied certiorari whenever the issue has been raised.) About 115,000 probationers and parolees are supervised through the compact.

Before the establishment of the compact, thousands of convicted felons were permitted to leave the state of conviction with no verified or approved plan of residence and employment in the receiving state. On occasion, dangerous criminals were released by states and permitted (sometimes forced into "internal exile" or "sundown probation/parole") to enter other states without any provision for supervision or even the knowledge of any official body in the receiving state. The compact provides a systematic method for supervision purposes for the receiving state to verify and approve a plan of residence and employment or education before a probationer or parolee is permitted to enter the state (Figures 12.8 and 12.9).

VIRGINIA DEPARTMENT OF CORRECTIONS
Parole and Probation Form III
Application for Compact Services and Agreement to Return

Sending State: ___Virginia_____ Receiving State: _____

RE: _____

I, _____ , hereby apply for supervision as a Probation/Parolee
pursuant to the Interstate Compact for the Supervision of Probationers/Parolees. I understand
that the very fact that supervision will be in another state makes it likely that there will be
certain different applications between the supervision I would receive in Virginia and the
supervision which I will receive in any state to which I am asking to go. However, I urge the
authorities to whom this application is made, and all other judicial and administrative authorities,
to recognize that supervision in another state, if granted as requested in this application, will be
a benefit to me and will improve my opportunities to make a good adjustment. In order to get
the advantages of supervision under the Interstate Compact for the Supervision of Probationers/
Parolees, I do hereby accept such differences in the course and character of supervision as may
be provided, and I do state that I consider the benefits of supervision under the Compact to be
worth any adjustments in my situation which may be occasioned.

I also consent to the release of any drug, alcohol treatment information by the State of
___Virginia_____ to any authorized agent of the State of _____
for the purpose of transferring supervision. This consent remains in effect from _____
to _____ and becomes revocable upon _____.

1. That I will make my home with (name) _____
   (address) _____
   until a change of residence is duly authorized by the proper authorities of
   (receiving state) _____.

2. That I will comply with the conditions of probation/parole as fixed by both the State of
   Virginia and _____.

3. That I will, when duly instructed by Virginia, return at any time to the said state.

4. That I hereby do waive extradition to the State of Virginia from any jurisdiction in or outside
   the United States where I may be found and also agree that I will not contest any effort by
   any jurisdiction to return me to the State of Virginia.

5. Failure to comply with the above will be deemed to be a violation of the terms and
   conditions of probation/parole for which I may be returned to the State of Virginia.

I (have read the above)(have had the above read) and explained to me and I understand its
meaning and agree thereto.

Date: _____ Signed: _____
                                                             Probationer/Parolee

Witnesses:_____

          _____

On the _____ day of _____ , 20__ , permission was granted to the above probationer/parolee
to reside in the State of _____ and be supervised by _____.

                                   Signed _____
                                   For the Compact Administrator

DISTRIBUTION:

FIGURE 12.8 *Application for Compact Services and Agreement to Return.*

(*Source:* Virginia Department of Corrections.)

COLORADO DEPARTMENT OF CORRECTIONS
DIVISION OF ADULT PAROLE SUPERVISION
COOPERATIVE CASE REPORT.

To: Texas Interstate   Date: 12-5-03
      P. O. Box 13401
      Capitol Station   Name: Smith, Robert
      Austin, TX 78711   TX # 574,566
                                                                DOC#   CO # X94-1200

SUBJECT MATTER: REPORT OF INVESTIGATION/ACCEPTANCE

The proposed residence at 433 Briar Drive, Woodland Park, Colorado, 80863, is verified.
This is the residence of Mr. Richard Smith, the parolee's father. The father is a willing sponsor, and
the residence is certainly adequate to house the addition of the parolee in the home. The Woodland
Park Police Department was also contacted on December 1, 2003 and they are aware of Mr. Richard
Smith's hunting business called the Ace Sports Club and note that the parolee's father has a good
reputation in the community.

Regarding employment the placement request from the State of Texas notes that the father has offered employment with his business known as the Ace Sports Club, 1400 W. Hwy 24, Woodland
Park, Colorado 80866. However, it should be noted that this is a seasonal business and that Richard
Smith would not be able to offer his son employment until the hunting season started next year.
Therefore, the parolee would, in effect, have to secure his own employment for approximately the
next six months until the Colorado hunting season started for the 2004 calendar year. Of primary
concern to Colorado authorities is the offense for which the parolee was most recently incarcerated, that being Aggravated Robbery With A Deadly Weapon. For this reason, the Texas Department of
Criminal Justice has listed the parolee's supervision level as "L"—highest level. For this reason, Colorado will accept the parolee's supervision with the understanding that he will be on ISP supervision with electronic monitoring for 180 days. The potential sponsors have already agreed to this
type of supervision in their home. Also, the parolee will be expected to submit to drug and other
substance abuse counseling through our TASC Office and will be held financially responsible for
any treatment expenses.

If the parolee is willing to agree to these conditions, please have him report to Parole Officer Tom
Peterson immediately upon arrival in the Colorado Springs area at the address listed below.

TOP/js

Direct Correspondence to: *Tom Peterson*
                                                   _____
                                                   Tom Peterson
                                                   Parole Officer

Office: Colorado Springs Parole Office   *Larry C Stuart*
          25 N. Spruce Street, Suite 300   _____
          Colorado Springs, CO 80905   Larry C. Stuart
          (719) 635-0800 Fax (719) 473-5152   Reviewing Officer

FIGURE 12.9 *Cooperative Case Report.*

(*Source:* Colorado Department of Corrections, Division of Adult Parole Supervision.)

After a probationer or parolee is accepted for supervision by the receiving
state, the latter sends quarterly "progress and conduct" reports to the sending state
(Figure 12.10). The compact also regulates interstate travel by probationers and
parolees; each state issues a travel pass, a copy of which is sent to the interstate administrator, who notifies the receiving state of the impending visit (Figure 12.11).

STATE OF WASHINGTON
DEPARTMENT OF CORRECTIONS

COMPACT-PROGRESS REPORT

REPORT TO: Compact Administrator   **DATE:** 12-22-03
State of Oklahoma

NAME: Sue Fields   **DOC NUMBER:** 10158736

DOB: 07-11-80
11375   **SENTENCE:** Ten years suspended (2 years supervised probation)

CRIME: Manufacture C/S, Unlawful   **TERMINATION DATE:** 10-01-03 (end of supervised 2 years)
use of Police radio,
Possession of a firearm
during felony, Possession
of a C/S, Possess/Furnish
Precursor Substance, Poss
Drug Paraphernalia

DATE OF SENTENCE: 10-01-03   **STATUS:** Active
                                             CLASSIFICATION: RMC

Sue Fields began reporting to the Washington Department of Corrections in December 2001. She has been very diligent in reporting as directed and following instructions. She obtained a substance abuse assessment as part of her conditions of supervision in December 2002 and was placed in Intensive Outpatient Treatment. She successfully completed that phase of counseling on 02-25-03. She entered into weekly aftercare on March 5th, 2003. Progress notes received from Lourdes Counseling Center show that she attended aftercare through September 2003 and there were no indications of problems.

In addition, subject has submitted to drug testing with the Department of Corrections. All results have been negative for illegal substances.

She is employed with a local Grocery store, "Winco", and has been there for well over a year. I have personally seen and talked with her there on many occasions and it appears she is a reliable employee. Fields has also been attending college classes and has plans on receiving an associates degree as a paralegal or related field. In addition to these activities, Fields cares for her 3 young children as a single mother. She remains at the same address that she released to, and all appears quite stable for her at this time.

Because her conditions from Oklahoma are for a 10 year sentence with 2 years being supervised, I am requesting that Oklahoma confirm that her active supervision has expired. According to our records, Ms. Fields period of active supervision would have expired on 10-01-03. Unless we are directed to continue supervising her, the Department of Corrections will be forwarding a notice of interest being closed in the next month. Please advise on this matter.

12-22-03

I certify or declare under penalty of perjury of the laws of the State of Washington that the foregoing statements are true and correct to the best of my knowledge and belief.

Submitted By:

Erika L. Foster   12-22-03

_____   _____
Erika Foster   DATE
Community Corrections Officer III
Department of Corrections
500 N. Morain #1101
Kennewick, Wa. 99336
Telephone (509) 734 - 5615

FIGURE 12.10 *Compact—Progress Report.*

(*Source:* State of Washington, Department of Corrections.)

Court of Common Pleas
GENERAL DIVISION
MONTGOMERY COUNTY
ADULT PROBATION DEPARTMENT

TRAVEL PERMIT

COURTS BUILDING
ROOM 107
41 NORTH PERRY STREET
P.O. BOX 972
DAYTON, OHIO 45422-2001
(937) 225-4264
Fax (937) 225-4360

TO WHOM IT MAY CONCERN:			
Probationer's Name			Case Number
Address		Race	Date of Birth
DESTINATION	City and State		
VISITING	Name, Address, and Telephone of Persons To Be Visited and Relationship		
REASON FOR TRIP	Specify:		
STARTING DATE:		**RETURNING DATE:**	
METHOD OF TRAVEL	Specify: If auto, give license plate and name of owner		
COMPANIONS	List Name(s) and Relationship(s)		
REPORT IN PERSON TO	Name and Address of Officer, Agent, or Out-of-State Parole Officer		

I SHALL HAVE THE ORIGINAL COPY OF THIS PERMIT COUNTERSIGNED IN THE SPACE PROVIDED BELOW.

SPECIAL INSTRUCTIONS:

I have been given this permission with the explicit understanding I am to continue to follow the rules and regulations of my Probation that I am to cooperate with my Probation Officer or any authorized agent of Probation while on this trip. If I should be arrested in any State during the period of visit granted to me, I will waive extradition and will not resist being returned to the State of Ohio.

Probationer's Signature

ISSUING OFFICER:	Name, Address, and Telephone Number	
Issuing Officer's Signature:		

THIS IS TO CERTIFY THAT THE ABOVE NAMED PROBATIONER HAS REPORTED AS DIRECTED ABOVE

Date	Time	Place
Countersigning Officer's Signature		
Countersigning Officer's Remarks		

Probationer: Is to return his/her copy of this permit to the issuing officer within forty-eight (48) hours following his/her return from this trip.

PERMIT RETURNED: Date	Issuing Officer's Signature:

FIGURE 12.11 *Travel Permit.*

(*Source:* Montgomery County, Ohio, Adult Probation Department.)

The Association of Administrators of the Interstate formed in 1946, now known as the Interstate Commission for Adult Offender Supervision, has a designated commissioner from each state who is that state's compact administrator, and meets at least once per year, prepares uniform reports and procedures, and attempts to reconcile any difficulties that have arisen with respect to the compact.

Some problems remain.[3] One is the difference in P/P administration. In all states, parole is an executive function with statewide procedures; interstate activities

---

[3]See Clem, Krauth, and Linke (1998) for an evaluation of the interstate compact.

are centralized through a compact administrator in each state. Probation, however, can be administered on a county basis, and it may lack statewide coordination. The local autonomy that often exists in the judicial branch can cause difficulties in using and administering the pact in probation cases. In such cases, the probation officer of the sending state may need to make direct contact and arrangements with the court of the receiving jurisdiction.

Another problem results from different approaches to supervision in various states. One state may exercise close control and require strict enforcement of the conditions of P/P. Another state may be more flexible, or it may simply be incapable of close supervision and control because of the size of caseloads. When a "strict" state notifies a "permissive" sending state that one of its probationers or parolees is in violation, the sending state may not consider it serious and may leave the offender in the receiving state with a request that it continue supervision. In some cases, the sending state may not want to incur the expense of transporting the violator back to one of its state prisons, which are probably overcrowded anyway (Figure 12.12). The receiving state has two options: Continue to supervise an offender it considers in violation, or discontinue supervision and leave the offender without any controls at all. Problems are also associated with the collection of restitution and supervision fees. These types of situations may make a receiving state reluctant to accept future cases from a particular sending state, a situation that needs to be reconciled at the compact administrator's meeting.

States sometimes allow probationers or parolees to go to a receiving state under the guise of a visit when the offender's intentions are to stay permanently. The receiving state is then contacted by the sending state to investigate "with a view toward accepting supervision." The receiving state is faced with a *fait accompli*.

The *Interstate Compact on Juveniles* governs the movement of juvenile cases interstate. In the early 1950s, legal and financial problems involving the supervision, transportation, and control of juvenile cases among states reached the point where most of those involved acknowledged the need for some form of interstate compact patterned on the one used for adult cases. In 1954, the National Council on Juvenile Court Judges drafted a preliminary compact on juveniles. Later that year, several groups, under the coordination of the Council on State Governments, drafted the Interstate Compact on Juveniles. In 1955, 10 states adopted the compact, and currently all states and the District of Columbia are signatories. In addition to providing for cooperative supervision, the compact provides for the return of juvenile P/P absconders and escapees and the return of nondelinquent runaways (Figure 12.13). The Association of Juvenile Compact Administrators is responsible for developing rules and regulations that govern the administration of the compact.

In contrast to the compact for adults, the juvenile compact has mandatory and discretionary cases. Thus, the receiving state must accept supervision whenever a juvenile will be returning to or has already been placed in the home of his or her legal parents or guardians, and each state must accept its own residents. Other cases are discretionary. When supervision has been arranged, the sending state retains jurisdiction and the receiving state becomes the agent of the sending state. Because of variations in state laws regarding juveniles, a person who is a juvenile in one state may be considered an adult in another. The compact overcomes this problem by applying the law of the state from which the juvenile has run away or from which he or she was sent for supervision: If a person is a juvenile under law in his or her home state, he or she is a juvenile to all member states. Although the compact does not deal with child custody cases, it can provide for the return of a child to wherever a court has determined legal custody is maintained.

In chapter 13, we examine the intermediate punishment response to the problem of prison overcrowding.

STATE OF IOWA

THOMAS J. VILSACK, GOVERNOR   DEPARTMENT OF CORRECTIONS
SALLY J. PEDERSON, LT. GOVERNOR   GARY D. MAYNARD, DIRECTOR

VIOLATION REPORT FORM
Parole and Probation Form VIIA

Date: _November 19, 2003_

To: _COMPACT ADMINISTRATOR_
Name: _Earl King_   State: _Oklahoma_   Number: _831567_
Supervision Status: _Probation_   SSN: _105-53-0132_   County/Cause #: _Tulsa/_

Type of Report
☒ Delinquency w/o Arrest   ☐ Arrest   ☐ Conviction   ☐ Follow-up

Recommendations
☒ Warrant Requested ☐ Remain under Supervision ☒ Return for suspension/revocation hearing

Arrest Data
Date: _NA_   City: _NS_   County: _NA_   Agency: _NA_
Specific Charge or Technical Violation   Date Offense or Violation Occurred
(If technical list rules violated and document under additional comments section)

Rule #2: *I will not use or be in possession of intoxicants or illicit drugs of any kind, or visit places where illicit drugs are unlawfully sold, dispensed or used. I understand that I am not allowed to enter or loiter around beer taverns or clubs.*

Rule #6: *I will carry out all instructions the supervising authority may give me, including but not limited to, urinalysis, curfew, and treatment*

Additional comments: *Earl King did violate Rule #2 of the Probation Agreement as follows: On 10/7/03, King provided a urinalysis specimen, which tested positive for the presence of Methamphetamine. On 10/27/03, he provided a urinalysis specimen, which tested positive for Methamphetamine. He denied the above violations and was given the opportunity to have the specimens sent for confirmation. On each occasion, he failed to provide the $35.00 needed to send the specimens to the lab.*

King did violate Rule #6 of the Probation Agreement as follows: On 11/03/03, he failed to report to this office for urinalysis testing.

This is the second Report of Violation in this case. The first Report of Violation was dated January 22, 2003. After the first report was filed, he did participate in recommended treatment through the Area Substance Abuse Council (ASAC). He did comply with the terms of his probation up until his recent relapse.

As evidenced by this Report of Violation, King has violated the terms and conditions of his probation and should be held accountable. He has participated in recommended treatment and has successfully completed the same. Earl King continues to use illegal substances and has failed to internalize the treatment that has been provided.

Court Data
Date of sentence: _November 5, 2001_   Offense: _Possession of a Controlled Drug_
Name and Location of Court: _State of Oklahoma-Tulsa_
Date of Conviction: _November 5, 2001_
Specific Sentence: _4 years suspended, probation_

Submitted By: _____*Kevin Weideman*_____   Approved By: _____*Larry A. Bergrud*_____
              Kevin Weideman, Probation/   Larry A. Bergrud, Probation/
              Parole Officer II   Parole Supervisor II

FIGURE 12.12 *Violation Report Form.*

(Source: State of Iowa, Department of Corrections.)

STATE OF MISSOURI

INTERSTATE COMPACT ON JUVENILES

REQUISITION FOR RUNAWAY JUVENILE

TO: _____ DATE: _____

FROM: _____

RE: _____

This court requisitions the return of _____

in accordance to the Interstate Compact on Juveniles, Article IV, Return of Runaway.

Said juvenile is believed to be in your jurisdiction. (Additional information attached, if

available).

On the basis of the evidence before it, this court finds said juvenile was born on _____

Juvenile's physical description: Height _____ , Weight _____ , Eyes _____ ,

Hair _____ . Identifying marks or scars: _____

_____

This court further finds that said juvenile should rightfully be in the custody of _____

_____ who is the _____ and who is located at

              (Relationship to juvenile)

_____ , within the territorial jurisdiction of this court; that said juvenile

     (Address)

has run away without permission and that said juvenile's continued absence from rightful

custody and control is detrimental to the best interest of said juvenile and the public.

  If requisition is honored, please notify _____

                (Name, title, address and telephone)

_____ by collect telephone call or wire when _____

minor will be available for release to our agent.

Attached are: Petition for Requisition to Return a Runaway Juvenile verified by Affidavit,

and certified documents verifying petitioner's entitlement to the juvenile's custody.

Signed _____

                           Judge

FIGURE 12.13 *Requisition for Runaway Juvenile.*

(*Source:* State of Missouri.)

KEY TERMS

antagonists

agonists

methadone

aversive stimuli

therapeutic community

12-step program

plethysmograph

restitution

community service

supervision fee

work release

halfway houses

interstate compacts

sending state

receiving state

INTERNET CONNECTIONS

Addictions page: www.well.com/user/woa

National Institute on Drug Abuse: www.nida.nih.gov

Alcoholics Anonymous: alcoholics-anonymous.org

American Probation and Parole Association: www.appa-net.org

National Institute of Corrections: nicic.org

Smart Recovery: smartrecovery.org

International Community Corrections Association: iccaweb.org

Center for Community Corrections: communitycorrectionsworks.org

Center for Sex Offender Management: csom.org

Parole and Probation Compact Administrators' Association: doc.state.ok.us./PPCAA/index.htm

Interstate Compact handbook: www.ppcaa.net/pubs/Handbook/PPCAA%20Handbook.pdf

Interstate Compact guide: www.nicic.org/resources/topics/InterstateCompact.aspx

REVIEW QUESTIONS

1. What are the types of specialized units in P/P?
2. How are various chemicals used in substance abuse treatment?
3. Why is behavior modification difficult to use in treating drug-abusing offenders?
4. What is the TC?
5. What is the AA approach to substance abuse?
6. How have P/P agencies responded to the problem of HIV/AIDS?
7. How have P/P agencies responded to the problem of sex offenders?
8. What is controversial about requiring offenders to provide restitution?
9. What are the arguments for and against supervision fees?
10. What has the Supreme Court ruled (*Beardon v. Georgia*) with respect to requiring probationers to pay a fine and/or restitution as a condition of probation?
11. What are the problems encountered in work release programs?
12. What is the major difficulty with opening and maintaining a halfway house?
13. What is the purpose of the interstate compact?
14. What are the problems of the interstate compact?

CHAPTER 13

Intermediate Punishments

The stated explanation for **intermediate punishments** is a classical emphasis matching the sanction to the offense, while the actual purpose is to reduce incarceration. The trend in favor of classicalism—just deserts and determinate sentencing—has been intertwined with the reality of jail and prison overcrowding. Widespread support for punishment and deterrence through greater use of incarceration—for example, truth in sentencing and three strikes and you're out—has encountered serious financial limitations. Judges have been unwilling to permit conditions of incarceration that violate the Eighth Amendment's prohibition against cruel and unusual punishment, thereby increasing the cost of a punishment-by-way-of-incarceration policy. In response, officials have scrambled to create alternative systems that satisfy a public/political appetite for punishment, while limiting the financial costs involved (Figure 13.1).

Intermediate punishments "can be understood in terms of risk management rather than rehabilitative or correctional aspirations. Rather than instruments of reintegrating offenders into the community, they function as mechanisms to maintain control, often through frequent drug testing, over low-risk offenders for whom the more secure form of custody are judged too expensive or unnecessary" (Feeley and Simon, 1992: 461). Intermediate punishments are also used to expand the response to probation and parole violators: "In the past, officials had two sanctions for violators—either to continue supervision (perhaps with modest changes in conditions) or to revoke and imprison the violator. Often the choice of options was either too lenient or too harsh for the circumstances of the violation" (Parent et al., 1994: 13).

Iowa Violation Program

The Iowa Violation Program (IVP) provides an intermediate sanction for P/P violators who would otherwise be admitted to the prison system. They are assigned to the program at revocation hearings on the recommendation of the P/P officer. Those who successfully complete the 60-day residential program are returned to community supervision to complete their probation or parole term. IVP has 60 beds at the Women's Reformatory and 100 at the Release Center. At each facility, participants are segregated from the general population and have treatment staff assigned solely to the program.

IVP employs a cognitive approach aimed at changing thinking styles. The major underlying assumption is that offenders typically exhibit cognitive deficiencies such as lack of self-control and lack of problem-solving skills. Upon admission to the program, participants have a 1- to 5-day orientation period, during which administrative paperwork and some diagnostic procedures are completed. Orientation time varies because inmates are assigned to a group of 3 to 12 who go through the program together—the administration will wait for all members of a new group to arrive and be oriented together. Participants are acquainted with the general rules of the program and the institution. Following orientation, participants settle into a routine of attending classes from 7:30 A.M. to approximately 4:30 P.M. Classes are organized into different modules representing various facets of the program: drug abuse, reasoning, problem solving, values, and group therapy. Each class lasts about 2 hours and employs a variety of techniques, including various exercises and role-playing. Physical fitness activities and homework must be completed during free hours.

Basic Probation

Basic Probation

Probationers are assessed as to risk and need. The level of supervision afforded the offender is based on the resulting score. Additional special conditions such as fines, restitution, community service, etc., may be included.

Community Service

Community Service

As a special condition of probation, the offender may be ordered to perform uncompensated work for the community under the supervision of the Community Service Program. Primary consideration should be given to traffic or ordinance violations and noninjurious, nondestructive, nonviolent misdemeanors and felonies.

Intensive Probation

Intensive Probation Supervision

The IPS program provides more structured supervision than can be afforded under basic probation supervision for felony offenders who pose a manageable risk to the community. Requirements include one to four contacts per week, as well as home, employment, night, and weekend checks.

Probation Diversion Center

Diversion Center

As a condition of probation, a judge may require that a probationer be assigned to a Diversion Center. The probationer lives at the center, works at a regular job in the community, performs community service, and may participate in a variety of educational and counseling programs. The probationer's paycheck is turned in to the Center, and room, board, fines, restitution and family support are deducted.

Probation Detention Center

Detention Center

The Detention Center is a community-based, residential facility housing nonviolent offenders in a secure, restrictive environment. Offenders work on unpaid community work details supervised by correctional officers. No age restrictions apply, but the probationer must be physically able to comply with program requirements.

Probation Boot Camp

Probation Boot Camp

The 90-day Probation Boot Camp offers felony offenders ages 17 to 30 an alternative to long-term incarceration. The program combines military-style basic training and programs to address substance abuse and other offender problems. A supervised period of community adjustment on probation follows release.

Prison

State Prison

Imprisonment is a last resort—either for a clearly dangerous violent offender who can be housed nowhere else, or for a nonviolent offender who has exhausted all alternative forms of punishment.

FIGURE 13.1 *Continuum of Sentencing Options for Georgia's Judiciary.*

(*Source:* State of Georgia.)

INTENSIVE PROBATION/PAROLE SUPERVISION

If one can judge by the amount of agency literature and research efforts, **intensive supervision** (IPS) has become the most popular program in P/P. Early versions of intensive supervision were based on the premise that increased client contact would enhance rehabilitation while affording greater client control. Current programs are simply a means of easing the burden of prison overcrowding. Thus, the Colorado Department of Corrections notes that its intensive supervision program "expands prison capacity by requiring participation of selected offenders who would otherwise be incarcerated in departmental facilities." In any event, by 1990, jurisdictions in all 50 states had instituted a community-based sanction called *intensive probation supervision* (Petersilia and Turner, 1991).

In probation, intensive supervision is usually viewed as an alternative to incarceration. In other words, persons who are placed on IPS are supposed to be those offenders who, in the absence of intensive supervision, would have been sentenced to imprisonment. In parole, intensive supervision is viewed as risk management—allowing for a high-risk inmate to be paroled but under the most restrictive of circumstances. In either case, intensive supervision is a response to prison overcrowding. Thus, although intensive supervision is invariably more costly than regular supervision, the costs "are compared not with the costs of normal supervision but rather with the costs of incarceration" (Bennett, 1988: 298).

IPS can be classified into those types that stress **diversion** and those that stress enhancement:

- *Diversion* is commonly referred to as a "front door" program because its goal is to limit the number of offenders entering prison. Prison diversion programs generally identify lower-risk, incoming inmates to participate in IPS as a substitute for a prison term.
- *Enhancement* programs generally select already sentenced probationers and parolees and subject them to closer supervision in the community than regular P/P. People placed on IPS-enhanced P/P show evidence of failure under routine supervision or have committed offenses deemed to be too serious for supervision on routine caseloads (Petersilia and Turner, 1993).

Intensive supervision actually takes many shapes. In Texas, for example, intensive probation supervision involves an experienced probation officer whose maximum caseload does not exceed 40. In Suffolk County, New York, IPS clients are required to attend a day reporting center where they pass through four program phases until placed on regular supervision.

Florida Community Control

According to the Florida Department of Corrections, its program of community control "is not intensive probation," but "a distinctively different type of program that is punishment oriented and allows selected offenders to serve their sentences confined to their homes under 'house arrest' instead of prison." That is, offenders must remain home when not at, or traveling to and from, their place of employment or mandated public service job. They are supervised by special (community control) correctional probation officers who have a maximum caseload of 20. In addition to being armed, the officers are equipped with portable radios for quick access to law enforcement assistance: "Florida's community control initiative represents the single largest intensive supervision prison diversion program in the Nation" (Wagner and Baird, 1993: 1).

Persons may be placed on community control by the sentencing judge if found guilty of a noncapital felony but are considered unsuitable for regular probation, or they may be probation or parole violators. The target population, however, is offenders who have committed nonviolent crimes and would not otherwise be placed on regular probation because of the seriousness of their criminal history (Baird and Wagner, 1990). A correctional probation officer conducting a PSI who plans to recommend that a particular offender be sent to prison because of his or her criminal background or the seriousness of the crime may recommend community control as an alternative.

With community control cases, correctional probation officers are required to make a minimum of seven contacts per week with the offender and others in the community, for example, employers and law enforcement agencies. Two of these visits must be in person, including at least one in the field. The offender is required to make weekly office visits during which he or she can be subjected to urinalysis. The officer also makes at least 16 personal telephone contacts to ensure the offender is at home as required by curfew restrictions.

Georgia Intensive Probation Supervision

In 1982, faced with the reality of prison overcrowding, the Department of Offender Rehabilitation inaugurated IPS. Although this plan began as a pilot program, IPS has now become a routine method of keeping down prison commitments. In addition to seeking to divert offenders from prison, the program attempts to accomplish the goal of punishment. IPS provides close community supervision to selected offenders who normally would have entered prison if it were not for the existence of the program: "The IPS team, composed of an experienced Probation Officer and a Surveillance Officer, supervise a maximum caseload of twenty-five (25) offenders [or two surveillance officers and 40 cases] who present no unacceptable risk to the community in which they are supervised. The caseload consists primarily of nonviolent felony offenders who have been convicted of property offenses."

Program standards include

- Five face-to-face contacts per week
- A total of 132 hours of mandatory community service
- Mandatory curfew
- Mandatory employment
- Weekly check of local arrest records
- Automatic notification of arrest elsewhere via the state crime information system
- Routine and unannounced alcohol and drug testing

Georgia IPS skims off low-risk offenders for the program—persons who are nonviolent property offenders and drug- and alcohol-related offenders—although most have been sentenced to imprisonment. An analysis of the program revealed that as a result of IPS, the percentage of offenders sentenced to prison decreased and the number of probationers increased. Furthermore, the "kinds of offenders diverted were more similar to prison inmates than to regular probationers, suggesting that the program selected the most suitable offenders" (Erwin and Bennett, 1987: 2). However, Georgia incarcerates many offenders for nonviolent offenses, including driving with a suspended driver's license, punishable in Georgia by up to 5 years in prison. Thus, the IPS program may indeed be diverting offenders from prison, but there is a serious question of why such persons are being sentenced to imprisonment in the first place. Georgia is in the "top 10" when it comes to rates of incarceration.

Cook County (Chicago, Illinois) Juvenile Intensive Probation Supervision

In operation since 1984, Cook County IPS is funded by the Illinois Supreme Court as a way to decrease juvenile facility overcrowding; whereas it costs about $35,000 per year to keep a juvenile institutionalized, the cost of IPS is $3,000. The program was originally intended for nonviolent offenders, but as the number of violent offenders grew, IPS was expanded to include them. Of the county's 300 juvenile probation officers, 18 are assigned to IPS; whereas regular caseloads average 42, each team of 3 IPS officers has a maximum of 45 cases. "IPS officers [who are unarmed but wear bulletproof vests] can drop in on their kids whenever they want, and they shift their schedules from days to nights to weekends to make it harder to predict when they'll come. They also occasionally do 'double backs,' dropping by and then returning later to see if the kids have taken off [in violation of their curfew]" (Krause, 1997: 14).

IPS clients, usually ranging from 13 to 17, are received directly from juvenile court or are releasees from residential care, remain on home confinement for the first 30 days, permitted to leave only to go to school, work, or other approved destinations. They do a minimum of 60 hours of community service and must avoid any gang involvement—most of the youngsters are gang members—including wearing gang clothing. The probation officers must be familiar with gang territoriality—some youngsters cannot be sent to certain neighborhoods for employment or social services because of gang rivalries. Periodically, there are "roundups" during which the youngsters and their guardians (mostly mothers) are to appear at the juvenile court building auditorium where they are given information about meetings, camp opportunities, and training programs; many do not show up. The youngsters then break up into small groups for sessions with probation officers while the parents stay behind to ask questions. When the youngsters return from their group sessions, each meets with the three members of their IPS team.

"Robert" is a typical case: At age 16, he was on IPS for armed robbery and firearms possession. He has not completed high school and lives at home with his mother who is unemployed; he rarely sees his father. His girlfriend has a baby and is pregnant again. Many of the youngsters' parents are drug abusers, and many of the youngsters have been selling drugs for older gang members.

If a youngster violates the conditions of supervision in a serious manner, a juvenile warrant is issued and sent to the police for enforcement—juvenile probation officers do not have arrest authority.

New York and Colorado

Demonstrating through empirical evidence that 80 percent of the parolees who violate their parole conditions do so during their first 15 months under supervision, the critical determinant of *differential supervision* is time under supervision. In both New York and Colorado, those parolees within their first 15 months on the street are designated "intensives." In New York, after 15 months, the offender is placed on "regular" supervision with less stringent contact standards. Although regular caseloads average 97 parolees, POs with intensive cases supervise 38 parolees. In areas where density of parolees is sparse and traveling time between clients poses an obstacle to efficient supervision, POs have mixed—intensive and regular—with each intensive case counted as 2.55 regular cases.

Colorado also has a time-limited intensive supervision program for parolees, but the time ranges from a minimum of 90 days to a maximum of 180 days, at which the time parolee is transferred to regular supervision. ISP caseloads do not exceed 20, and the focus is clearly on control: weekly face-to-face meetings, daily telephone contact, electronically monitored curfew, and weekly alcohol and drug testing.

Somerset County (Pennsylvania) Day Report Intensive Probation Program

With caseloads that do not exceed 18, probation officers supervise offenders who would have been considered for a term of incarceration and are nonviolent or technical probation violators. They are required to pay a supervision fee and report to the probation office or alternative site Monday through Friday. If unemployed, they must attend job readiness classes in addition to any counseling for drugs, alcohol, family, mental, financial, or employment problems. Offenders must provide a daily schedule of planned activities and are subject to random telephone checks as part of curfew enforcement. They are subject to this program from 1 to 5 months.

Lucas County (Toledo, Ohio) Juvenile Intensive Probation Supervision

To reduce institutional commitments, the Lucas County Juvenile IPS selection is limited to those juveniles already sentenced to incarceration. For youngsters meeting program requirements, the judge is petitioned for a change in the commitment order. Supervision is indeed intensive: IPS probation counselor caseloads are no more than 15; they see the youth a minimum of twice per week during the first 4 to 5 months, and surveillance staff see the youth at least twice each day 7 days per week for the first several months. Individual and group counseling is mandatory, and clients are subject to urinalysis, house arrest, or hourly monitoring of school attendance and behavior. On Saturdays, youngsters spend 6 to 8 hours for about 2 months engaged in work activities. There are also bimonthly family conferences and the use of tokens for positive reinforcement, in this case, coupons that can be redeemed for prizes and privileges, such as concert tickets and relaxed curfew (Wiebush and Hamparian, 1991).

Dauphin County (Pennsylvania) Intensive Juvenile Probation

The Dauphin County Probation Department has a juvenile intensive probation supervision program geared to reduce the level of institutional commitments. Each youngster is placed on a suspended commitment to an appropriate juvenile institution with the understanding that he or she would have been committed to this institution if intensive supervision did not exist. Each case is screened to ensure the youngster is not a distinct serious threat to either him- or herself or the community. In addition, sufficient family stability must exist so the probation officer can work with the family as a unit. The family has to be willing to cooperate with the program. If the screening PO determines that the case is appropriate for intensive supervision, the youngster is scheduled for a juvenile court hearing, and the PO recommends that the respondent be sentenced to a suspended commitment to an appropriate institution and placed in the intensive supervision program.

Each caseload with a maximum of 18 cases is supervised by one probation officer and one part-time PO; the term of IPS supervision is 6 to 9 months. Each juvenile must follow regulations that include a curfew and mandatory school or work attendance. A treatment plan is based on the needs and interests of the client. Each youngster is seen three to five times weekly, which includes counseling sessions in the office and at home, in both individual and family sessions. The IPS officer maintains a high level of visibility with both the client and the community.

Texas Intensive Supervision Program

Created in 1981 to deal with a prison crisis, the Texas Intensive Supervision Program (ISP) attempts to divert selected felony offenders by offering an alternative to incarceration. For these offenders, intensive supervision is a condition of probation. In most Texas probation departments, ISP caseloads do not exceed 40, and the probation officers are specially selected and trained for the assignment. In some Texas jurisdictions, however, probation officers supervise a mixed ISP and regular caseload. Whenever this occurs, the mixed caseloads may comprise no more than 125 regular probationers before officers receive the first ISP case, and then they must be reduced by five regular cases each time a new ISP case is assigned to the caseload. Either cases are received directly from the court after sentencing, or they involve persons facing probation revocation and shock probationers (discussed later in this chapter). To qualify, offenders must meet one or more of the program's criteria:

- One or more prior jail or prison commitments
- One or more convictions

Documentable
- Chronic unemployment
- Alcohol dependency
- Drug dependency
- Mental retardation or psychological problem
- Seriousness of current offense

Using a risk/needs assessment classification (discussed in chapter 11), the IPS officer develops a supervision plan that outlines behavioral objectives to be met by the offender within specific time frames. By contracting with various community resources, the IPS officer negotiates for the exact type of services needed for each client. A formal reassessment occurs every 90 days. Typically, an IPS client remains under intensive supervision for 1 year or less and is then transferred to regular supervision. However, the court may amend the terms of probation to continue the offender under intensive supervision for an additional year. In rare and exceptional cases, the period may last beyond 2 years.

Texas also has a *superintensive supervision* program called "surveillance probation." It is reserved for cases whose regular probation has been revoked, those sentenced to shock probation, or as a special judicially imposed condition pursuant to a grant of probation. Each offender remains in the program for 90 days, although an extension can be granted, during which time two probation officers (who supervise no more than 20 cases) maintain a minimum of five contacts per week, three of which are in person. A mandatory curfew exists, and frequent drug and alcohol testing is required.

North Carolina Probation/Parole Surveillance Officer

This position partners with a P/P (intensive case) officer in the supervision and surveillance of high-risk felon and misdemeanor offenders placed under community-intensive supervision in lieu of incarceration. The officer prepares investigative and other reports for, and testifies in court and before the parole commission; supervises absconder caseload of probationers/parolees; conducts in-home visits, drug screening, employment verifications, and criminal record checks; transports offenders, and deals with crisis intervention, arrest, and search and seizures. This position requires the employee to work various shifts during each 28-day period. May serve on the electronic house arrest team, which includes on-call status and respond to electronic house arrest violations. The employee must qualify with Department of Correction, Division of Community Corrections-issued firearm.

INTENSIVE SUPERVISION: RESEARCH FINDINGS

Before we begin our examination of the effectiveness of intensive supervision, we should note that the establishment of IPS programming was not based on careful research and evaluation but is simply a response—perhaps ill conceived—to jail and prison overcrowding (Clear, Flynn, and Shapiro, 1987). Indeed, policy implications of evaluative research into IPS may be irrelevant: "If the results are negative . . . then these findings will be viewed as support for both the continued use of incapacitation and the development of even more intrusive, surveillance-oriented community control programs" (Byrne, 1990: 8). In fact, although evidence of the effectiveness of IPS is wanting, the program has been a public relations success (Clear and Hardyman, 1990).

Intensive supervision is usually accomplished by severely reducing caseload size per P/P officer based on the assumption that it will lead to increased contact between the officer and the client or their significant others (such as spouse or parents), and that this increased contact will improve service delivery and control and thus reduce recidivism. Some programs, however, have had difficulty achieving *intensity:* "While it may be inconceivable for intensive supervision to occur in caseloads that exceed some finite number, such as fifty persons, it is certainly conceivable that much smaller caseloads might not result in significant levels of intensity" (Clear and Hardyman, 1990: 44). Two researchers claim that intensive supervision does indeed increase case contacts, often by 50 percent or more, and the amount of time spent in contact also increases significantly. However, "the difference between spending one-half hour per month with a client and spending an hour per month is, relatively speaking, an extremely small difference considering the magnitude of the treatment and service provision task which the probation officer is trying to accomplish" (Carlson and Parks, 1979: 72).

In one Tennessee county, a comparison between a sample of regular and intensively supervised probationers over a 3-year period revealed significant differences in recidivism: 25.8 percent of the regular probationers had new felony arrests, whereas the rate for the ISP sample was 8 percent. The results for technical violations were the reverse: 60 percent of the ISP and 34 percent of the regular probationers (Burrow, Joseph, and Whitehead, 2001). Perhaps ISP was successful in screening out—by way of technical violations—those probationers most likely to reoffend. Intensive supervision for drug offenders on probation in seven cities (Seattle, Washington; Des Moines, Iowa; Santa Fe, New Mexico; Atlanta, Georgia; Macon, Georgia; Waycross, Georgia; Winchester, Virginia) did not appear to impact recidivism. Research revealed no significant differences between the arrest rates for ISP participants and a control group receiving regular supervision during a 12-month period (Petersilia, Turner, and Deschenes, 1992). Similar findings were reported in a study of IPS programs in 14 other cities (Petersilia and Turner, 1993). As noted by the researchers, however, drawing conclusions from recidivism statistics can be misleading because recidivism could be a feature of the intensity of the supervision—IPS could increase the probability of new criminal activity being *discovered* (this issue is discussed in chapter 14).

Research into the effectiveness of intensive supervision dates back to 1953, when California conducted "probably the most extensively controlled experiment in American correctional history" (Glaser, 1969: 311).

California

The California Special Intensive Parole Unit experiment ran from 1953 until 1964, during which time caseload sizes were varied from 15 to 35. In addition, research was conducted into the impact of increased supervision on particular risk classes of offender. A positive outcome occurred only with those parolees classified as "lower-middle risk"—they had significantly fewer violations. In a review of this research, however, Robert Martinson (1974) found that the successful cases were concentrated in northern California, where agents were more apt than agents in southern California to cite both the experimentals and the controls for violating parole. The limited success, Martinson argues, was not due to the intensive nature of supervision, but was the result of a realistic threat of reimprisonment. A problem also exists with using parole violation as a criterion for success because of what researchers refer to as the "halo effect," a tendency on the part of P/P officers to tolerate greater levels of misbehavior than is usual to prove the experiment successful.

More recent research into California IPS was conducted in three counties. Cases were randomly assigned from a pool of high-risk offenders on probation to IPS caseloads of 40 (Contra Costa), 19 (Ventura), and 33 (Los Angeles), or control caseloads that averaged 150 to 300 offenders. After 6 months, IPS clients received more intensive supervision: two to three times the usual number of contacts. About 30 percent of the IPS cases had a technical violation, a much higher rate than the control caseloads; however, no statistically significant difference existed between new arrest rates for IPS or control cases. The research revealed that intensive supervision in these counties did not affect the rate of new arrests: IPS failed to enhance the rehabilitative or control function of supervision (Petersilia and Turner, 1990). The researchers conclude: "When compared with routine probationers, the ISP participants, with few exceptions, had similar rates of technical violations and new arrests" (Petersilia and Turner, 1991: 9).

Research on a Los Angeles Probation Department IPS program involving gang-member drug offenders also had disappointing results. Although caseloads were small—33 as opposed to 300—the supervision that resulted was hardly intensive, and home visits were infrequent (Agopian, 1990). Reducing caseload size and *calling* a program "intensive" is obviously not the same as *providing* intensive supervision.

Georgia

Research in Georgia has produced mixed results for the concept of intensive supervision. As noted earlier, IPS probationers are under the joint supervision of a probation officer and a surveillance officer in caseloads that do not exceed 25. One comparison of outcomes for 542 IPS probationers and a matched sample of 752 regular probationers revealed that 13.7 percent of the IPS group had their probation revoked for new crimes (none for violent crimes), whereas 10.2 percent was the figure for the control sample. The IPS group had a higher rate of technical violations (11.8 percent) than the control sample (6.5 percent)—which the researchers argue is to be expected considering the intensive supervision—and there was little difference in the absconder rate: 2.2 percent for the IPS, and 2.4 percent for the control sample. A second study of the program revealed that 18.5 percent of the IPS probationers and 24.0 percent of the regular probationers were convicted of new crimes. However, 42.3 percent of prison releasees during the same period were convicted of new offenses, and "59.4 percent of the IPS cases were more similar to those incarcerated than to those placed on probation" (Erwin, 1984; Erwin and Bennett, 1987: 4).

According to Joan Petersilia (1988a), any number of states have adopted IPS programming based on the apparent success of the Georgia program. However, she cautions, judges in Georgia, like those in many southern states, tend toward the punitive, imposing more sentences of imprisonment and for longer terms than elsewhere. Thus, there is a greater pool of IPS prospects—nonviolent offenders—than would be expected outside of the South, in general, and Georgia, in particular. In fact, when it comes to the risk of new criminal behavior, IPS clients are not markedly different from the regular probation population in Georgia. The basic claims of IPS in Georgia with respect to cost effectiveness, diversion of offenders, and improved public safety "are not supported by the available research evidence"

(Clear et al., 1987: 35). In fact, "a convincing argument can be presented that the Georgia evaluation actually demonstrates the opposite" (Byrne, Lurigio, and Baird, 1989: 27).

According to the plan, the IPS probation officer is supposed to provide typical professional casework services, whereas the probation surveillance officer (with less education, training, and salary) provides "24 hour surveillance capability through day, night, and weekend visits and telephone contacts." Surveillance officers, however, developed greater rapport with clients and their families than did probation officers. The surveillance officer had more direct contact with, and was more easily accessible to, the client and his or her family:

> One of the most interesting findings of the IPS evaluation is the near impossibility of separating treatment from enforcement. The Georgia design places the Probation Officer in charge of case management, treatment and counseling services, and court-related activities. Surveillance Officers, who usually have law enforcement or correctional backgrounds, have primary responsibility for frequently visiting the home unannounced, checking curfews, performing drug and alcohol tests using portable equipment, and checking arrest records weekly. The Surveillance Officer becomes well acquainted with the family and is often present in critical situations. Both the Probation and Surveillance Officers report a great deal of overlap of functions and even a reversal of their roles. (Erwin and Bennett, 1987: 6)

In practice, the surveillance officer was doing the work of a professional PO, while the latter's role was either redundant or reduced to that of a paper-pushing case analyst.

Louisiana

A study of shock incarceration ("boot camp" to be discussed later) found that positive results were a function of the intensive supervision offenders received after being paroled: "the more intense the supervision, the better these offenders adjusted during community supervision." In addition, "parolees' performance declined over 6 months of community supervision as the intensity of supervision was reduced." The study concludes: "In general, the more intense the supervision the better the offenders performed, probably because this was required of them. There was a threat of revocation if they did not comply" (MacKenzie, Shaw, and Souryal, 1992: 450). Another study of shock incarceration in Louisiana found that boot camp graduates were subjected to more technical violations than regular supervisees; regular P/P supervisees, however, were convicted at higher rates for new crimes. The differences were ascribed to the impact of the intensive supervision given to boot camp graduates (MacKenzie and Shaw, 1993).

Minnesota

Intensive supervision has centered mostly on probation: "Relatively few jurisdictions have implemented prison-diversion ISP programs—programs that divert offenders from prison sentences to terms of supervision in the community" (Deschenes, Turner, and Petersilia, 1995: 331). Intensive supervision was tested in Minnesota as a cost-saving device using 300 cases. Experimental and control groups were randomly assigned from a cohort of recently convicted inmates with sentences of 27 months or less and probation violators committed to prison. None had a record of victim harm or weapons use, and they were employable with a suitable residence—a "boy scout" population. A second set of experimental and control groups consisted of good-time releasees who had served two-thirds of their sentence.

Parole agents in the intensive units supervised caseloads of 12 to 15 offenders (size of control units not indicated). Intensive cases spent the first 6 months on home confinement, during which time they could leave their residence only for employment or with specific permission. Results: There were no statistically significant outcome differences between the experimental and control caseloads, but savings were realized—$5,000 per offender per year—from the early release of inmates (although these persons apparently could have been placed on regular supervision).

New Jersey

Limited to 500 highly select offenders diverted from prison after several months of incarceration, IPS cases were compared with a sample of offenders eligible for the program but who were, instead, incarcerated, and released on parole. The IPS participants' new conviction rate averaged roughly 10 percentage points lower than that of the comparison group, leading one researcher to conclude that in New Jersey IPS works fairly well with felons who are neither dangerous nor habitual criminals: "The program saves a modest amount of prison space without increasing recidivism; it has been cost-effective compared to ordinary terms of imprisonment and parole; it has been monetarily beneficial (in terms of earnings, taxes, payments to a fund for victims, and so on); and it does provide a level of punishment between probation on the one hand and ordinary imprisonment on the other" (Pearson, 1988: 447).

The "New Jersey program evaluation—by design—should make the IPS program look quite good because it compares IPS cases with a group of class 3 and class 4 felons who represent the poorest risks and who receive the harshest treatment by the New Jersey corrections system" (Byrne et al., 1989: 30). Other researchers find it ironic that the relatively low-risk offenders in the New Jersey program are receiving intensive supervision, whereas the far higher-risk parolee joins a caseload in excess of 100 (Clear et al., 1987).

New York

Research conducted by the New York State Division of Parole (Collier, 1980) indicates that intensive supervision can have a modest effect on violent felony offenders. In 1978, the legislature provided funding for the supervision of violent felony offenders. In 1979, all released inmates who had been convicted of a violent felony (crimes ranging from robbery to arson—most were imprisoned for robbery) were placed in intensive units whose POs supervised no more than 35 cases: 97 percent were male; the median age was 27.3; blacks constituted 57.5 percent, whites 23 percent, and Hispanics 19.5 percent; 62 percent completed less than the twelfth grade; and 80 percent were unskilled laborers. Interestingly, two-thirds of this group had little or no prior criminal history.

After 1 year, the 1,905 violent felony offenders released in 1979 and placed under intensive supervision were compared with 1,732 of the same population released in 1978 to regular supervision. The results:

- 12.6 percent of the (1978) controls and 1.8 percent of the (1979) intensives were returned to prison for a new offense.
- 3.3 percent of the controls and 4.0 percent of the intensives were returned to prison for technical violations of parole.
- 5.0 percent of the controls and 3.4 percent of the intensives absconded from supervision.
- As of the end of the 1-year research period (3/31/80), 6.5 percent of the controls and 3.9 percent of the intensives had parole violation or court hearings pending.

Ohio

Funded by a state probation subsidy program, the Lucas County Incarceration Diversion Unit (IDU) consists of four probation officers, each with a caseload maximum of 25, with the exception of the supervisor, who is assigned 15. The IDU probationers were compared with a group of shock probationers under regular supervision. (The study did not indicate the size of regular shock probation caseloads.) The researchers found that the IDU officers recorded almost four times as many client contacts, and more social services were provided to their clients. However, no statistically significant differences with respect to recidivism occurred; the IDU group did have significantly fewer technical violations, which the researchers conclude was the result of a realistic fear of being sent to prison because of the nature of IDU supervision and strict violation practices. (An alternative hypothesis would raise questions about the quality of the supervision.) The researchers (Latessa and Vito, 1988: 327) conclude that their study "should provide a word of caution to officials seeking ways to limit incarceration rates" by using intensive supervision.

The Lucus County Intensive Supervision Unit (ISU) was designed to divert nonviolent felony offenders who had already been committed to a Department of Youth Services (DYS) facility; DYS facilities were under pressure from overcrowding. The program excluded youth whose instant offense involved drugs, use of a weapon, or victim injury. Research compared ISU youngsters with similar youth committed to a DYS facility and paroled. The supervision provided by ISU was indeed intensive, with respect to both control and rehabilitative services, but no significant difference in recidivism occurred. It was rather high for both—almost 50 percent of both groups were reinstitutionalized within the 18-month period of the research. However, there was a potential savings—the annual per client cost of ISU was more than $6,000, as contrasted with more than $32,000 for incarceration (Wiebush, 1993).

A study in Montgomery County (Dayton), Ohio, compared matched samples from IPS units, with 25 cases per officer, and regular units (caseload size not indicated). The research revealed that 11.7 percent of the intensive supervision cases ended with a felony conviction, against 3.8 percent for regular supervision; 1.2 percent of the intensive cases were incarcerated for misdemeanors as opposed to 6.2 percent of the regular cases. Interestingly, the IPS officers, on average, made fewer than one face-to-face contact per month with their clients in the client's home—hardly an *intensive* level of supervision (Noonan and Latessa, 1987).

A study of IPS in the rural Ohio county of Clermont noted that implementing a special supervision program in rural areas is difficult because of long travel times to reach clients, making unannounced visits problematic. The researchers found that persons assigned to IPS were clearly higher risk than those on regular caseloads, but they were unable to determine if these were prison-bound cases. As might be expected, if supervision is indeed intensive, the IPS clients had a higher rate of technical violations: 39 percent IPS; 24 percent regular; however, "there were no significant differences in the number of felony arrests, convictions, or completion rates of probation. A high percentage of both groups were classified as successful" (Haas and Latessa, 1995: 168).

Washington State

The stated objective of the Washington State Adult Corrections Division was to save tax dollars by removing *low-risk offenders* from the state's prisons. Persons released into the program had on average served less than 3 months in prison. They (289) were placed under the intensive supervision of a PO whose caseload did not exceed 20. At the end of 1 year, it was determined whether the individual's behavior warranted a conditional discharge from supervision or supervision by a regular PO.

To evaluate the program a matched historical sample (102) was selected as the control group. Random assignment was ruled out because of "equal treatment under the law considerations." The control group was made up of inmates who were paroled at the same time as those selected for early release and intensive supervision. However, the control group subjects were released after having served normal sentences to a PO who supervised an average caseload of 73. A person in the control group was selected on the basis of the same criteria as for those in the test group, with the following results (Fallen et al., 1981):

1. After 1 year of supervision, 19 percent of the test (IPS) group had been arrested or convicted for new (nontraffic) offenses, whereas the figure for control cases was 40 percent.
2. The IPS POs showed a strong tendency to invoke delinquency action. After 1 year, 42 percent of the test group had been cited for technical parole violations as opposed to 24 percent for the control group.
3. The 1-year revocation rate for the IPS group was 17 percent; for the control group, it was 6.1 percent (the average for general supervision in Washington is 15 percent).

The researchers speculate on explanations for their findings:

- Intensive parolees were less likely to commit new offenses because of a fear of detection produced by increased supervision.
- By brief incarceration, intensive parolees received the initial "shock value" of prison but were not in long enough to learn the "skills" or adopt the values of the incarcerated criminal population.
- Because many intensive parolees received formal technical violations, these served as effective warnings that undesirable behavior would not be tolerated.
- Because many intensive parolees were revoked for technical violations only, this occurrence may have screened out those disposed to commit new offenses.

Wisconsin

In 1984, the Wisconsin Division of Corrections established an experimental IPS program for high-risk offenders. Thirty offenders (later increased to 40) were supervised by two-agent teams in two locations. The research did not indicate the caseload for non-IPS parole agents. Experienced agents screened all new cases in their areas and selected only high-risk offenders (HROs) as clients. To qualify as an HRO, the client requires a history of assaultive behavior; other distinguishing characteristics include a lengthy criminal record, poor prison adjustment record, and poor attitude toward community supervision, as well as an unwillingness to participate in drug, alcohol abuse, or mental health programs.

As part of intensive supervision, specialized rules were tailored for each offender; these restricted certain associations, use of motor vehicles, and evening hours: "The general tactic is to establish rules which restrict behavior(s) associated with a past criminal pattern" (Wagner, 1989: 23). Offenders were required to provide a weekly schedule indicating where they will be at any given time. Each client registered with the local police, submitting a photograph, fingerprints, handwriting sample, past offense history, and current address. The police were expected to assist in the offender-monitoring process. Parole agents made at least four in-person contacts each month, including two visits, scheduled and unscheduled, to the offender's residence. Frequent collateral visits with police, employers, landlords, and associates occurred. In at least one case, school officials and parent association members were informed of the release of a child sex offender so they could aid in the surveillance process.

The HRO group under IPS was compared with a matched sample that received regular supervision. The results were dramatic. After 1 year, only 3 percent of the IPS parolees had been convicted of a felony; it was 27 percent for the control group. The statistics for parole violation provide at least a partial explanation for these differences. Only 12 percent of the control group were returned to prison for parole violations, whereas the number was 40 percent for the IPS group. A researcher for the state of Wisconsin concludes that "the IPS program suppresses criminal behavior by preempting it" (Wagner, 1989: 26). The research does not indicate how many of the remaining IPS clients successfully completed their entire supervision period.

Discussion

Despite the modest, at best, results of intensive supervision, the programs remain popular while there has been a dramatic absence of continuing research into IPS. To evaluate IPS, we need to examine the two premises on which it is based.

Premise One: Intensive probation supervision will divert offenders who would otherwise be incarcerated. In any number of jurisdictions, this goal is not being accomplished. A study in Tennessee, for example, revealed that even though some offenders were being diverted away from prison, many more IPS clients would have normally been sentenced to regular probation (Whitehead, Miller, and Myers, 1995). Judges continued to send probation-eligible offenders to prison, while using IPS for those who would be sentenced to probation in any event. The Florida IPS (Community Control) Program received offenders who were often more serious than those on probation or in jail, but less serious than those sentenced to prison. An undetermined number of these borderline cases, however, perhaps more than one-half, would have been sent to prison in the absence of IPS (Baird and Wagner, 1990). A study of ISP in Colorado found no significant differences between cases recommended for ISP and those not recommended, leading the researchers to conclude that this program "may not be one of prison-diversion as the state guidelines proclaim" (Reichel and Sudbrack, 1994: 57). Needless to say, this will affect the results of any research on an IPS program.

For the diversion goal to be accomplished, cases need to be assigned to IPS *after* a sentence of imprisonment. Only after conviction, sentence, and remand to jail pending transportation to prison should the IPS screening officer review the case and, if appropriate, submit a recommendation for resentencing. Cases not intercepted should proceed to state prison. With respect to parole, parole boards often assign cases to intensive supervision that would have been granted parole even in the absence of an intensive program. If intensive supervision is to serve the goal of reducing the prison population, it should be reserved for cases that have been denied parole. A screening officer (institutional PO) should review the case *after* parole has been denied and, if appropriate, submit a recommendation for reconsideration of parole with intensive supervision.

In sum, many, if not most, intensive supervision programs are not actually diverting offenders—they are simply providing judges and parole boards with an additional supervision option that is not being used in lieu of prison (although this may not have the effect of lowering prison commitments, it certainly has merits of its own). Many IPS programs appear to be accepting those offenders who are not at high risk, who probably should have been on regular probation in the first instance. In some counties, the probation department routinely recommends inappropriate cases for IPS. This serves two intertwined purposes: First, it ensures the IPS program will deliver "good stats"; and second, it helps keep down regular caseloads by shifting some cases to probation officers funded by special allocations (and the continuation of these allocations is dependent on "good stats").

However, intensive supervision for inappropriate cases unnecessarily increases the cost of probation and may be harmful to the client: "Behavioral scientists have long speculated that the addition of strains and controls to a human system can, at some time, result in a reaction that is contrary to the direction of the controls" (Clear and Hardyman, 1990: 55). According to the labeling perspective (discussed in chapter 9), an offender inappropriately identified as "high risk" by virtue of IPS status may indeed assume that role and organize his or her behavior accordingly—subjecting low-risk offenders to intensive supervision may lead to more, not less, trouble with the law (Altschuler and Armstrong, 1994).

An additional problem involves offenders who believe intensive supervision is as punitive as imprisonment: "In many states, given the option of serving prison terms or participating in IPS, many offenders have chosen prison" (Petersilia, 1990: 23; emphasis deleted). Petersilia points out that for many/most serious offenders, imprisonment and the stigma that can result are not the frightening phenomena that they are for the community at large: "For many offenders, it may seem preferable to get that short stay in prison over rather than spend five times as long in an IPS" (25; see also 1994). Under these conditions, for intensive supervision to work, it may be necessary to offer it as an option for much more serious offenders than are now being subjected to IPS.

In sum, large amounts of scarce resources are being allocated to less serious offenders, whereas more dangerous offenders are released to the community under parole supervision that is often inadequate because of lack of funding (Clear et al., 1987) or is simply nonexistent in those states that have discontinued postprison community supervision. It is the worst "Alice in Wonderland" situation when armed robbers and other dangerous offenders are released from prison with inadequate or no supervision, and property offenders are placed on IPS. In Florida, for example, lesser offenders are placed on intensive community control, whereas the more serious offenders released from prison are not supervised (Wagner and Baird, 1993).

This irrational approach to crime and justice is exemplified by a 1988 Texas Adult Probation Commission Study. IPS cases were compared with cases eligible for probation but sentenced to imprisonment and cases not eligible for probation and sentenced to imprisonment, using the "risk" part of the Texas Risk/Needs Assessment form. The mean scores were

Intensive probation supervision	20.10
Eligible for probation but incarcerated	18.93
Ineligible for a sentence of probation	26.26

In other words, although the IPS program was apparently diverting offenders from prison (a risk mean of 20.10), there were less serious risks (risk mean of 18.93) who were, nevertheless, imprisoned; and the high-risk offenders (risk mean 26.26) who were imprisoned will be released to parole supervision that is not intensive. A similar situation exists in Illinois, where the state has been funding extensive IPS programs while 60 percent of the state's parole agents were laid off.

Alan Schuman (1989: 29) argues that "the new IPS concept actually depicts local communities' original image of how probation services should operate. IPS provides the type of comprehensive surveillance services, restitution payments, drug testing and treatment, employment verification, and networking with other community services that should be expected of all probation agencies that are adequately funded." Gerald Buck (1989: 66) argues that intensive supervision "*is* probation practiced as it was originally intended to be. Other probation programs are a sham that ought not be called probation supervision" (emphasis in original).

Premise Two: More of whatever it is that the P/P agency does with routine cases will have a salutary effect on cases at greater risk. Although several research studies have challenged this premise, a strong, if unproven, belief in P/P is that *more is better.* I want to dwell on the question, *"More of what?"* The implication of intensive supervision—the bait that hooks funding from elected officials—is that offenders will be closely monitored, under surveillance, and made to fear detection for any violations they might be inclined to commit. Thus, note Arthur Lurigio and Joan Petersilia (1992: 9), "an important assumption of IPS programs is that close supervision should increase the probability of detecting and arresting offenders who are not deterred by the program and who continue to commit crimes. Speedy revocation to custody results in incapacitation, and, because IPS participants are encouraged to be employed and to attend counseling sessions, rehabilitation *may* occur. However, newer IPS programs are designed to boost offenders' perceptions of the effectiveness of the system in detecting and punishing their criminal behavior."

P/P officers are portrayed as making unannounced contacts with offenders, whom they are monitoring around the clock, ready to take immediate action to prevent any danger to the community. For agencies whose officers are armed and trained in law enforcement, this approach is a natural extension of the services they are already providing. Agencies in which officers do not have adequate law enforcement training or authority, however, cannot live up to the image of *intensive*. Indeed, agencies that adopt a meaningful form of intensive supervision—one that does indeed increase unannounced face-to-face in-field contacts—but fail to equip and train their officers accordingly, place these officers in danger. In Vermont, for example, officers expressed a great deal of concern for their safety because intensive supervision meant frequent unannounced visits by unarmed officers. When I worked as a PO in New York, unannounced visits found parolees with firearms left on the dresser, large amounts of heroin and drug paraphernalia on the kitchen table, and other potentially dangerous situations. The neighborhoods in which most clients live are high-crime areas, which can be particularly hazardous at night. Minnesota parole agents providing intensive supervision, for example, "are required to make visits to clientele at all hours in a variety of situations and neighborhoods." However, they carry no firearms, although they are authorized to carry chemical substances to aid in a "safe retreat."

ISPs are typically set up outside the traditional supervision structure. Clients and officers are hand picked; the latter receive special training, sometimes salary increases, and report to their own supervisory chain of command. This hierarchy can affect general agency morale because the IPS unit receives a disproportionate share of resources and attention. In some agencies, such as the Cook County (Chicago, Illinois) Adult Probation Department, only IPS officers are authorized to carry firearms, and they are viewed as "elite." These special units experience strong pressure to demonstrate results:

> This is one reason why these programs often seem to be encased in an atmosphere of caution—they are very vulnerable to errors. Based on a rationale of effective offender control, and in contrast to seemingly more lenient traditional probation methods, the idea of intensive probation can be seriously damaged by even one publicized incident of serious client failure, such as a violent crime. Therefore, despite the control rhetoric, program officials seem to bend over backward to avoid the riskiest clients and to resist giving accepted clients many chances to violate probation. (Clear et al., 1987: 42)

This accounts for the relatively high rate of probation violations in most IPS programs.

In New York, when I was a PO, each caseload had some cases designated "intensive" by the parole board, and they required at least one face-to-face unannounced home visit and four in-person office visits each month. Cases were subjected to more supervisory review and there was less latitude—in the event of a technical violation of the rules, such offenders were more likely to be taken into custody and returned to prison. New York State POs are required to carry firearms while on duty. This system avoided the elitism that has apparently reared its head in at least some P/P agencies with IPS programs.

There is also a problem inherent in evaluating IPS effectiveness. Random assignment of high-risk cases between the IPS and routine caseloads fails to account for the classification and unofficial intensive supervision typically carried out by P/P officers. When confronted with unmanageable caseloads, POs identify those cases with greatest risk/needs and devote most of their quality working time with these clients (at the expense of most other cases that receive little but "paper" attention).

Thus, experimental model research is often comparing IPS with quasi-IPS. Recidivism rates may vary according to the ability of the police, the skill of perpetrators, and cooperation between P/P agencies and law enforcement agencies.

ELECTRONIC MONITORING

Electronic monitoring (EM) is used in conjunction with a variety of programs, in particular, home detention instead of jail for defendants awaiting trial and intensive community supervision. Home confinement with EM has proven appealing because it has the potential to satisfy the goals of imprisonment without the social and financial costs normally associated with imprisonment:

- To satisfy the demand for punishment
- To provide a deterrent effect
- To provide for community protection

EM can serve to enforce curfews, usually restricting the offender from leaving home at night; for detention—a stricter curfew—requiring the offender to remain at home at all times except for employment, education, or other specified activities; or incarceration, whereby the offender is required to be at home at all times except for very limited activities, such as medical treatment (U.S. Bureau of Justice Assistance, 1989).

The first system of EM monitored the location of parolees, mental patients, and volunteers in Massachusetts from 1964 through 1970. Although interest in EM of offenders always existed, until the crisis in prison overcrowding "market conditions were never attractive enough to make the technology commercially available" (Przybylski, 1988: 1). Reputedly inspired by a "Spiderman" comic strip, Albuquerque District Court Judge Jack Love asked Michael Goss to develop a device suitable to monitor probation curfews. The "Gosslink" was first attached to the ankle of a 30-year-old probation violator for a 1-month period starting in 1983. Judge Love subsequently sentenced four other offenders to monitored home confinement.

Meanwhile, a Monroe County, Florida, judge tried a new EM system with 12 offenders over a 6-month period; they served house-confinement sentences ranging from 2 days to 4 months. As a result, the state of Florida incorporated electronic home confinement in the Correctional Reform Act of 1983, and the following year a pilot program was initiated in Palm Beach County for misdemeanants, mostly drunken drivers. By 1988, EM was being used in 33 states for 2,277 offenders: "Most of those monitored were sentenced offenders on probation or parole, participating in a program of intensive supervision in the community" (Schmidt, 1989: 2). That number has now grown to about 75,000.

EM has been associated primarily with probation, and there is little literature on its use in a parole setting. Parole officers in Utah have used continuously signaling EM on a limited scale to supplement curfew restrictions. The New York Division of Parole uses EM for several hundred offenders as an alternative to incarceration for parole violation, for special high-risk cases, and for those who pose a potential danger to spouse or family.

Several different types of systems are used for EM, but they can be divided into two basic categories (Przybylski, 1988):

1. Active/continuously signaling
2. Passive/programmed contact

Continuously Signaling Systems.   Two primary types of **continuously signaling** systems are available: those that use telephone lines, and those that use a radiolike transmitter and receiver. One system that uses the telephone lines (or cellular

FIGURE 13.2 *Continuously Signaling—BI HomeGuard ® 200.*

(*Source:* BI Incorporated, Boulder, CO.)

wireless communication) involves the offender wearing a battery-powered moisture-, water-, and shock-proof transmitter that is about the size of a pack of cigarettes and weighs about 6 ounces (Figures 13.2 and 13.3). The device is securely fastened by riveted plastic straps just above the ankle or on the wrist. Once strapped on, it can only be removed by stretching or cutting the straps in a manner easily detected by visual inspection. More modern versions provide an immediate electronic alert if the band is subjected to tampering. A circuit board contained in the transmitter has an individually calibrated and unique identification code. The transmitter emits a signal at regular intervals with a range of about 100 to 150 feet. The signal is monitored by a receiver connected to a 110-volt outlet and a standard telephone jack installed in the residence. The receiver automatically dials a central computer describing the time the person goes beyond the range of the signal or returns within range and automatically dials the computer when it has been subjected to tampering. If the dialer is disconnected or loses its source of power (by a power outage, for example), the message is stored until such time as power is restored; at that time, a delayed message describing the time of each activity is sent to the computer.

Simpler continuously signaling systems that do not use a telephone consist of only two basic components: a transmitter and a portable receiver. The transmitter,

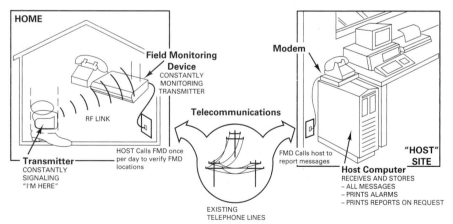

FIGURE 13.3 *Continuously Signaling System—BI Sobrietor ®.*

(*Source:* BI Incorporated, Boulder, CO.)

FIGURE 13.4 *Drive-BI* ®.
(*Source:* BI Incorporated, Boulder, CO.)

which is strapped to the offender's ankle or wrist or worn around the neck, emits a radio signal that travels about one city block. By driving past the offender's residence, place of employment, or treatment center, with the handheld portable receiver (Figure 13.4), the officer can verify his or her presence. This system was used in a pilot program by the New York State Division of Parole to provide enhanced monitoring of parolees whose behavior indicated they were reverting to criminal behavior or otherwise in violation of parole rules. They were confined to their homes for not less than 60 nor more than 120 days. Few hardware failures occurred, and the PO was able to repair them on site. The agency concluded that EM offered a feasible community supervision alternative to incarceration, allowing certain parolees the opportunity to seek treatment while remaining in the community.

A consent form for participation in a home confinement program appears in Figure 13.5.

VIRGINIA DEPARTMENT OF CORRECTIONS
Home Electronic Monitoring Program Rules

NAME: _____   INMATE #/SSN: _____

ADDRESS: _____   TELEPHONE #: _____

You are eligible/ordered to serve on the Home Electronic Monitoring Program (HEM). Any violation of the program rules or regulations may terminate this contract. If this contract is terminated, this will result in a probation/parole violation.

1. The client shall reside at the above address, unless given permission <u>in advance</u>, to be anywhere else. The client will not leave that residence at any other time unless authorized by his probation/parole officer, except in a life-threatening emergency.

FIGURE 13.5 *Home Electronic Monitoring Program Rules.*
(*Source:* Virginia Department of Corrections.)

2. The client authorizes the Home Electronic Monitoring Staff, to enter his residence to monitor the system at any time, and will make himself available at any time.

3. The client shall maintain an operable telephone at his residence. The telephone service must be basic, no call forwarding or call waiting or any additional phones or answering machines. Any change in your telephone service without prior approval from our staff, could result in termination.

4. All clients must agree that they will not tamper with the Home Electronic Monitoring Anklet or Box while on the program. Any attempt to do so may result in your immediate termination from the program.

5. The client shall maintain operable electricity to ensure that the system will work properly. Failure to do so will result in termination.

6. The client shall provide the Staff with any other telephone number that exists within the household.

7. Any changes in the client's HEM schedule must be reported to the staff. Clients may be required to submit pay stubs, time sheets, or other documentation signed by an authorized individual to verify a need to change the HEM schedule.

8. A fee of $30, due by the end of the HEM supervision, will be required from all clients placed on HEM supervision. Failure to pay the fee will be considered a violation of the program's rules and regulations.

I certify that I have read or have had read to me the above conditions and I agree to abide by them.

_____   _____
(CLIENT'S SIGNATURE)   (DATE)

_____   _____
(PROBATION & PAROLE OFFICER)   (DATE)

FIGURE 13.5 (continued)

Programmed Contact Systems.   One **programmed contact** system relies on the telephone and computerized voice identification. The computer records the offender's voice and is then programmed to call him or her at random times and request that a series of words or phrases be repeated. They are then matched with the earlier recording to verify presence. In the event of a failure to answer the telephone or a voice verification failure, the computer reports a monitoring infraction. Another system requires the offender to wear a pager that is beeped on a random basis, after which he or she is required to call a toll-free number. The caller's voice is verified against an original voice print and the telephone number from which the call is being placed is captured. If the voice does not match or the offender is not where he or she should be, the PO is notified by page within 3 minutes. One programmed contact system uses visual verification through telephone units that transmit black-and-white still pictures of the callers on a 3-inch screen. Another program uses an encoder device attached to a wrist band; the band cannot be removed without breaking it. The encoder must be inserted into a verifier box attached to the telephone whenever a computer-generated call is received. Taking advantage of satellite-based technology, some P/P agencies are using *global positioning systems* (GPSs) that can pinpoint the exact location of a probationer or parolee who is required to carry a GPS receiver. Issues of cost and the bulkiness of the GPS receiver are limiting factors of the use of this technology.

In an effort to address the problem of the repeat drunk driving offender, Kent County and the Maryland Division of Parole and Probation began a home detention project alternative to incarceration for second- and third-time offenders. These persons, who would normally be incarcerated, are allowed to remain in the community under probation supervision but are restricted to their homes during the evening hours. This latter aspect of supervision is accomplished via a computer that dials the client's home telephone number on random days and times during evening hours. The client answers, and by placing an electronic bracelet attached to his or her wrist to the telephone, sends a code to the computer. The computer then asks several questions of the client. After the call has been processed, a report is sent to the office that confirms that the client's phone number was dialed and verified, and gives the date and time. The report is reviewed by the P/P agent the following morning.

Three upstate New York counties, Monroe, Niagara, and Onondaga, used EM with adjudicated juvenile delinquents as a local alternative to out-of-home placement. Participants had been recommended for institutional placement and were instead supervised by a probation officer with a caseload of eight; they were monitored from 3 to 6 months. EM was used primarily to monitor curfew compliance and was supplemented with drug and alcohol tests. Because of caseload size, there was nearly daily contact between the youngster and PO at home, school, or elsewhere. An evaluation of the program was generally positive but noted a threat to public safety by not having the ability to expeditiously take EM violators into custody—probation officers were not authorized to make arrests.

Discussion

The appeal of EM is easy to understand when we consider that the cost of imprisonment can be in excess of $20,000 per year, and the cost of building a new prison can be in excess of $100,000 per bed. Unfortunately, accurate estimates of the cost of imprisonment and the cost of community supervision, intensive or otherwise, do not exist. However, startup costs for EM are high—Albuquerque paid $100,000 for its first 25 devices. To offset these costs, offenders can be required to pay supervision fees or pay for the cost of installing the monitoring telephone, a practice that raises important ethical and legal issues. Should an offender who is otherwise qualified for home confinement be denied access to the program—and thereby face imprisonment—because he or she lacks the ability to pay fees or does not have a residence? If the answer is "no," how far should the county or state go in providing a residence and, in some systems, a telephone? The answers will impact the cost effectiveness of any electronic home-confinement program. Some firms rent and monitor the equipment, but this can be costly, about $25 a day per offender, which does not include personnel costs involved in responding to signal disruptions or checking to see that the equipment has not been tampered with.

Candidates for electronic home confinement are typically low-risk offenders who, in most jurisdictions, would be candidates for probation. Thus, the program may actually be adding to the cost of supervision without affecting the problem of jail/prison overcrowding. Conversely, the system is typically used for drunk drivers, and some object that home confinement does not serve as a significant deterrent for a crime that is potentially life threatening, while leaving the offender in a position to repeat his or her criminal act. Home confinement is devoid of any rehabilitative dimension, provides no services to persons who often have extensive social service needs. Researchers found that the electronic surveillance programs they examined have not affected jail or prison commitments in any noticeable manner. Persons selected for EM are typically from social and economic circumstances that, in any event, would predict a positive outcome. There is also concern over the impact of such programming on P/P officers: "Are these professionals going to see their relationships to offenders change from helping agents to surveillance agents?" (Ball, Huff, and Lilly, 1988: 97). EM has the potential to downgrade the role of P/P officers, and what about the impact of home confinement on the offender's family?

During 1992, as the popularity of EM grew, news stories began to appear with some frequency detailing the inadequacies of controlling offender behavior through electronic means. The articles highlighted several problems:

- Offenders committing crimes after taking off the device—some while still wearing them
- Failure to replace older devices with more advanced technology, resulting in a failure to monitor offenders adequately
- Lack of personnel available to respond quickly to tampering or other violations of the conditions of EM

Many agencies using EM fail to recognize that EM does not prevent crime; it is designed simply to assist in curfew management. Curfew enforcement is dependent on having sufficient personnel monitoring the equipment and personnel to dispatch to check into reported violations.

In addition to community-based intermediate punishments are those using short-term incarceration that "shock" the miscreant while saving prison space.

SHOCK PROBATION/PAROLE

Shock probation/parole was pioneered by the state of Ohio, which enacted legislation in 1965 permitting the early release from prison of convicted felons either on probation (within 30 to 120 days of imprisonment) or parole (within 6 months of imprisonment). Since that time, other states (such as Idaho, Indiana, Kentucky, Maine, North Carolina, and Texas) have adopted similar statutes. To be eligible for shock probation in Ohio, the offender must be otherwise eligible for a sentence of probation and must file a petition with the court. Those not eligible for probation may file a request with the parole board for shock parole (which excludes those convicted of such crimes as rape, armed robbery, kidnapping, major drug violations, and some burglaries).

Shock probation was authorized by the Texas legislature in 1977 as a rehabilitation technique in which an offender is given a sample of jail/prison and then placed on probation for the remainder of the sentence. Data from Texas indicate that the typical shock probationer is a white, single male in his early twenties, a laborer with a tenth- or eleventh-grade education; he was convicted of burglary as a first offense, and the crime is usually drug or alcohol related.

SHOCK INCARCERATION/BOOT CAMP

In 1983, the states of Georgia and Oklahoma, in an effort to deal with their problems of prison overcrowding, devised **shock incarceration/boot camp** (SI). Georgia has community-based probation boot camps (Figure 13.6) that receive offenders directly from the sentencing court, as well as inmate boot camps whose candidates are selected by the Board of Pardons and Paroles.

By the end of 1988, 11 states had initiated similar programs; except for New York and Michigan, they are all in the South. By 1992, SI state-operated programs for adult offenders were available in 25 states (MacKenzie and Souryal, 1994). The boot camp resembles its military counterpart—a spartan regimen of rigorous discipline and exercise. (It is of historical interest to note that the use of military discipline was standard in New York's Elmira Reformatory well into the twentieth century— "reinventing the wheel" is symptomatic of American penology.)

An SI program requires short stays of imprisonment—3 to 6 months—combined with shaved heads, marching, close order drills, exercise, and harassment by correction officer/drill instructors during 12-hour days. No television, radio, or telephone privileges are available. According to Doris MacKenzie et al. (1995: 327), "most are designed for

Hours	Activity
0500	Count
0530	Wake up
0530–0600	Building and quarters cleanup, standby inspection, outside-of-quarters cleanup, sick call, count
0600–0700	Physical training
0700–0800	Breakfast, quarters inspection, laundry turn-in, mail pick-up
0800	Work call
1130	Return to quarters, prepare for lunch
1200	Count
1215–1300	Lunch
1300–1640	Work call/program call
(1400–1500)	Commissary call (Friday only)
1640–1700	Return to quarters, police grounds, mail call, building and quarters cleanup
1700	Count
1715–1800	Dinner, police grounds
1820–2130	Program call, privileged telephone use, religious services, counseling, life skills groups, programs
2130–2200	Return to quarters
2200	Lights out
2400	Count

FIGURE 13.6 *Typical Weekday Schedule of Activities for a Boot Camp in Georgia.*

young offenders convicted of nonviolent crimes who do not have a prior history of imprisonment." They point out that although "all boot camp prisons use military basic training as a model, they differ considerably in other aspects. For example, some programs select participants from a pool of prisoners sentenced to a traditional sentence of incarceration. Other programs receive inmates directly from the sentencing court" (328).

Boot Camp for Young Offenders—Historical Antecedent

"As part of the institutional regime, they [inmates] are advisedly ordered for supreme military test as to all-around steadiness, which embraces everything a soldier should do, or leave undone; everything from the strictest of undivided attention under command, to execution that exemplifies the highest order of muscular reaction to command, of which constantly improving stature is a component exaction" (Col. Vincent M. Masten, Military Instructor, Elmira Reformatory, 1896–1924, in Allen, 1926: 378).

Women in Shock Incarceration

Rita finishes 50 situps and springs to her feet. At 6 A.M., her platoon begins a 5-mile run, the last portion of the morning's physical training. After 5 months in New York's Lakeview Shock Incarceration Correctional Facility, the morning workout is easy. Rita even enjoys it, taking pride in her physical conditioning.

When Rita graduates and returns to New York City, she will face 6 months of intensive supervision before moving to regular parole. More than two-fifths of Rita's platoon did not make it this far; some withdrew voluntarily, and the rest were removed for misconduct or failure to participate satisfactorily. By completing shock incarceration, she will enter parole 11 months before her minimum release date.

The requirements for completing shock incarceration are the same for male and female inmates. The women live in a separate housing area of the Lakeview facility. Otherwise, men and women participate in the same education, physical training, drill and ceremony, drug education, and counseling programs. Men and women are assigned to separate work details and attend Network group meetings held in inmates' living units (Clark, Aziz, and MacKenzie, 1994).

One program operates in the medium-security prison near Baton Rouge, Louisiana. At dawn there is reveille, and inmates quickly dress in fatigue uniforms, make tight beds, and 1 hour later have formed into four platoons marching to breakfast in step and cadence (Spencer, 1987):

Warden, warden can't you see
What this program's done for me.
Sat me down in a barber chair
Turned around and had no hair.
Took away my faded jeans
Now I'm wearing army greens

They also spend a considerable portion of their day in counseling and treatment before release to intensive supervision (MacKenzie et al., 1992). At a prison facility in Beaver Dams (in Schuyler County), New York: A bugle blares at precisely 5:30 A.M., and 32 inmates leap from their bunks:

"Good morning, Sir!" they scream to the scowling corrections officer/drill instructor.

"Are you motivated?" he barks.

"Motivated! Motivated! Motivated! Sir," the young inmates shout.

In a fury they are dressed, beds made tight, and roaring in unison they are out the door single file. The last man out, a drug dealer from the Bronx, grabs the platoon flag as he runs by (Martin, 1988: 15). This regimen lasts 6 months, and on successful completion, the inmates are released to parole supervision. The program is limited to persons younger than 26 who have been convicted of nonviolent crimes and are serving their first prison sentence (Bohlen, 1989). Because of the physical nature of the program, candidates have typically been required to be in good health. In 1998, the Supreme Court ruled that an otherwise eligible candidate could not be denied the boot camp alternative because of a history of hypertension; his rejection was ruled a violation of the 1990 Americans with Disabilities Act (*Pennsylvania Department of Corrections et al. v. Yeskey*, No. 97-634).

Boot Camp

"Perhaps no other intermediate sanction or prison alternative has captured more attention from the public or policy makers than the boot camp prison. Its combination of punitiveness, visual appeal, and, in the view of some, rehabilitative value seems to offer everything to everyone frustrated with crime committed by young adults, especially males. The idea underlying boot camps is based on simple common sense: give a young rebel a sound three or four month-long thrashing and some firm discipline and that youth will see the evil of his/her way, become an adult, and sin no more" (Jones and Ross, 1997: 147).

The New York program (Figure 13.7) was authorized by the legislature in 1987 as a way of easing overcrowding—it is the only way inmates (male and female) can be released before reaching their parole eligibility date. Inmates up to the age of 39 participate if they are within 3 years of release and have not been convicted of a violent felony offense, a sex offense, an escape, or an absconding offense.

Successful SI graduates are typically released 9 months before their eligibility date. The parole division's "Aftershock" program in New York City provides comprehensive services for the parolee's first 6 months on the street. These services are designed to maintain the motivation and discipline with which the parolees are released. Shock parolees are supervised at a ratio of 25:1.

By 1991, New York had the largest SI program in the country and estimated that, for every 100 SI inmates released, the state saved $1.94 million that would otherwise be expended for care and custody, plus capital costs associated with the need for greater institutional space. The daily per-inmate expense for SI, however,

A.M.	
5:30	Wake up and standing count
5:45–6:30	Calisthenics and drill
6:30–7:00	Run
7:00–8:00	Mandatory breakfast/cleanup
8:15	Standing count and company formation
8:30–11:55	Work/school schedules
P.M.	
12:00–12:30	Mandatory lunch and standing count
12:30–3:30	Afternoon work/school schedule
3:30–4:00	Shower
4:00–4:45	Network community meeting
4:45–5:45	Mandatory dinner, prepare for evening
6:00–9:00	School, group counseling, drug counseling, prerelease counseling, decision-making classes
8:00	Count while in programs
9:15–9:30	Squad bay, prepare for bed
9:30	Standing count, lights out

FIGURE 13.7 *Daily Schedule for Offenders in New York Shock Incarceration Facilities.*

Boot Camp, Illinois Style

In Greene County, the Illinois Department of Corrections operates a 200-bed facility where inmates rise at 5:30 A.M. and retire at 9:30 P.M. During that time, they perform 6 hours of manual labor, run two 1.5-mile jogs, and end the day with about 2 hours of basic education and drug treatment. The shaven-headed inmates move double-time everywhere, while correction officers shout orders and refer to them as "knotheads," "vermin," and "maggots." They are constantly quizzed on the camp's general rules that include always asking for permission to speak; not "gaping" at visitors; and taking one step back, turning, and waiting for permission to leave after receiving an order. The boot camp term lasts 4 months (Marx, 1994a).

exceeds that of medium-security facilities or camps. The relatively high cost may be linked to the services provided at the New York SI camps—the state rejects the "boot camp" label because that term belies the therapeutic environment that the program strives to achieve. Although the New York program is considered one of the best, it has a dropout rate of about 25 percent.

The idea behind shock incarceration "is to break the prisoners down, strip them of their street identity, and then systematically build them up by providing discipline and self-control" (Spencer, 1987: Sec. 3: 1). Offenders must be young, usually 17 to 25 years old, and in good health; they must volunteer for the program—dropouts return to complete their sentences of imprisonment, and many drop out (Parent, 1988). New York SI uses a recycling program for inmates removed for disciplinary reasons and for those who are in danger of being removed for unsatisfactory adjustment. It consists of being sent back for refresher training, during which behavior is closely monitored. Success in recycling leads to being integrated into an existing platoon that will graduate at a date closest to the time owed by the inmate. Inmates who do not perform well after 2 weeks in recycling are removed from the program and returned to prison.

New York, which runs the nation's largest SI program, has a focus on treatment that is absent from most boot camp programs. More than 40 percent of inmate time is spent on treatment and education: 12 hours of academic education, drug and alcohol treatment, prerelease counseling, and decision-making classes (Clark et al., 1994; *Seventh Annual Shock Legislative Report*, 1995). The Willard Drug Treatment Campus is staffed by corrections and parole personnel, and features a quasi-boot camp environment in which residents participate in daily physical fitness regimens and abide by military standards of bearing, behavior, and dress. Willard is licensed by the Office of Alcoholism and Substance Abuse and must meet standards regarding the number of hours spent in therapy, educational and vocational development, and individual growth activities. The residents are parole violators involved in substance abuse and offenders judicially sanctioned—sent directly to parole supervision by the court for a drug conviction and required to complete the 90-day Willard program. Aftercare includes continuing substance abuse treatment for 6 months through contract agencies.

Discussion

Critics of the "shock" approach argue that it has not proven to have any salutary effect on postincarceration behavior, and (even) short-term imprisonment exposes the offender to the destructive effects of institutionalization, disrupts his or her life in the community, and further stigmatizes the offender for having been imprisoned (National Advisory Commission on Criminal Justice Standards and Goals, 1975).

Tough Love

At age 14, Gina was in boot camp for a series of petty thefts. The overweight youngster was with 15 other girls on a mandatory 2.6-mile jog at about 6:30 A.M. when she began to lag behind. Two counselors shouted for her to catch up. About 500 feet from the finish, Gina collapsed. Counselors called to her to stop faking. After being examined by a staff nurse, Gina struggled to her feet and began walking to the air-conditioned cottage when she collapsed again. Believing she was faking "again," the staff did nothing. By the time she was transported to a hospital, Gina was dead from heatstroke (Selcraig, 2000).

Furthermore, many/most SI inmates are released without receiving education or having developed any additional employment skills. No doubt exists that these programs do release strong, healthy, unemployed young men into the community after only a brief term of incarceration. However, in an Oklahoma study, SI graduates returned to prison at a higher rate than did other inmates; in Alabama, boot camp residents, who were first-time, nonviolent offenders, had a recidivism rate slightly worse than that of a comparative group of regular inmates (Burns and Vito, 1995). A Georgia study found no difference in return rates between SI and regular inmates (Parent, 1989). In Texas, SI appears to do more harm than good because within 4 years of release almost 62 percent of boot camp graduates are serving a traditional prison sentence (Anderson, Dyson, and Lee, 1997). MacKenzie and her colleagues (2001: 2) conclude that "in general, no significant differences have been found for either adults or juveniles when recidivism rates of boot camp participants have been compared with others receiving more traditional correctional options."

A study of the program in Louisiana found no evidence that SI reduces recidivism. There were no significant differences in recidivism between SI inmates and either parolees from traditional prisons or probationers. All had recidivism rates of approximately 30 percent during their first year of community supervision (MacKenzie et al., 1992). A New York in-house research effort revealed that 23 percent of shock parolees were returned to prison within 1 year of their release compared with 28 percent of a comparison group (Office of Policy Analysis and Information, 1989). In a later effort (1992), SI graduates in New York were compared with parolees who matched the SI criteria but who were committed to prison before the establishment of the program (pre-SI), as well as to parolees who had been removed from the program (removals), and, finally, to a group who met the SI criteria but did not enter the program (considered). SI graduates were more likely than the comparison groups to be drug offenders with longer maximum sentences. (Those with shorter sentences were less likely to volunteer for SI and more likely to drop out.) After all subjects were out at least 1 year, the following rates of return to prison for violations were recorded:

	Total	**Percentage**	
		Violation—Technical	**Violation—Criminal**
SI	1641	7	7
Pre-SI	1418	11	8
Removals	1662	11	9
Considered	366	11	11

After 24 months, SI parolees continued to have lower rates of return to prison for technical and new arrest violations than those of any of the comparison groups (although many of the comparison group members had already been discharged

Boot Camp Tough

Seven guards from Maryland's boot camps for juvenile offenders were fired for assaulting delinquents in their care. The guards were among 14 from three camps placed on administrative duty because of accusations they assaulted teens for more than 3 years. Youths assigned to the camps told state officials they were routinely kicked, punched, and slammed to the ground for little or no reason. Some juveniles had their teeth knocked out and, in one case, a juvenile's wrist was broken on his first day (Associated Press, 2000).

from parole supervision). The New York researchers conclude that SI parolees are more likely to be successful than are comparison group parolees after the completion of 12, 18, and 24 months' time, despite having spent considerably less time in a state prison. A subsequent in-house study (*Seventh Annual Shock Legislative Report*, 1995) revealed that shock parolees are generally more likely, or just as likely, to be successful than a similar comparison group. Shock incarceration was found particularly effective for young drug offenders.

Boot camp (IMPACT) was created in North Carolina in 1989. To be eligible, offenders must be ages 16 to 25, physically fit, not previously served over 120 days in an adult correctional facility, who have been convicted of misdemeanors and nonserious felonies. Participants stay for 90 days of drilling, marching, and exercise, which can be extended to 120 days in the event of disciplinary problems, after which they are released to probation supervision. Those without high school diplomas receive educational services, and 70 percent who take the equivalency test receive their GED.

Researchers compared IMPACT graduates with a similar group on probation who had not gone through boot camp. They found that while other similar studies reported little or no differences, in North Carolina, *boot camp participation was significantly associated with rearrest.* They note that while shock incarceration aims to instill pride and responsibility, the boot camp graduates must now bear the stigma of being an "ex-con," a significant barrier to gainful employment (Jones and Ross, 1997). Similar results were found in a Cleveland, Ohio, boot camp program where 72 percent of the graduates recidivated, as opposed to 50 percent of a control group released from Ohio Department of Youth Services facilities (Peters, Thomas, and Zamberlan, 1997).

Boot camp programs are in place to save prison or juvenile institutional resources; an offender sent to a shock program avoids long-term incarceration. This point assumes that in the absence of such programming, the offender would have been incarcerated and not placed on probation. In Florida, for example, candidates for SI are selected from among those sentenced to traditional incarceration, although one study found that they tended to be those who were less serious offenders (Sechcrest, 1989). In Georgia, however, SI is used by judges as part of probation sentences. In Alabama, boot camp is part of the discretionary sentencing power of a judge and is sometimes the result of a plea bargain agreement (Burns, 1993). In Arizona, which established its program in 1988, research found that only some of the inmates in boot camp were diverted from prison—"the rest would have been placed on regular probation or intensive probation" (Palumbo and Peterson, 1994: 8).

Although SI might not meet the needs of rehabilitation and community safety, it appears to meet the short-term needs of political officials who can boast of "doing something" about crime and criminals. Dale Parent found that SI was given to "the very offenders who would likely have been given nonconfinement sentences if SI were not available—thus using more, not less, prison space"—referred to as "net widening" (1989: 12). This is not the case in New York, where Department of Corrections (DOC) personnel, not judges, have charge of the program: "New York law

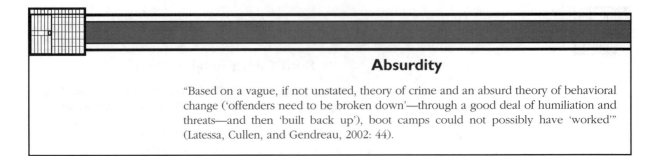

Absurdity

"Based on a vague, if not unstated, theory of crime and an absurd theory of behavioral change ('offenders need to be broken down'—through a good deal of humiliation and threats—and then 'built back up'), boot camps could not possibly have 'worked'" (Latessa, Cullen, and Gendreau, 2002: 44).

defines SI eligibility criteria. The New York DOC screens prison admissions to identify cases that meet these criteria. If inmates pass their physical examinations, they may volunteer to participate. Judges have no veto power. When inmates complete the program, they are released by the parole board, not by judges. By consulting New York's parole guidelines, the DOC estimates that the average inmate who completes SI will shorten his or her prison term by 12 to 18 months" (15).

An element of absurdity exists in the prison-as-boot camp approach, particularly in light of the fact that the military has drastically changed the way it trains recruits, away from abusive or degrading methods: "While the military has reduced the harshness of its training, boot-camp prisons have embraced an outdated version of military basic training" (Jacoby et al., 1994: 32). "The very idea of using physically and verbally aggressive tactics in an effort to 'train' people to act in a prosocial manner is fraught with contradiction" (Morash and Rucker, 1990: 214). Such programs run the risk of turning out young men who are more aggressive and hostile than they would have been under routine imprisonment: "The irony in emphasizing an aggressive model of masculinity in a correctional setting is that these very characteristics may explain criminality" (216). A cynic might argue that the boot camp approach is simply a scam for gaining public acquiescence to the (otherwise politically unacceptable) early discharge of inmates. Two researchers posit a grim possibility—that "the effect of boot camp is that it will be effective for those who will subsequently put their lessons of discipline and organization to use in street gangs and drug distribution networks" (Feeley and Simon, 1992: 464).

Others note that after boot camp, military personnel enter a structured, stable environment that provides for their basic needs, food, shelter, clothing, employment, and health care; very different from the environment to which most shock incarceration subjects will return (Mathias and Mathews, 1991). MacKenzie (1994: 65) concludes: "If the core components of boot camps (military atmosphere, drill, hard labor, physical training) reduced recidivism, we would have expected that the boot camp releasees in all states would do better than the offenders in the comparison groups. This did not happen. The military atmosphere does not appear to reduce recidivism." The military atmosphere, she notes, did not increase recidivism among boot camp graduates, whereas postrelease intensive supervision was associated with better adjustment for both boot camp and comparison groups (Cronin with Han, 1994; MacKenzie and Souryal, 1994).

In 1994, Connecticut closed the nation's first boot camp for juveniles run by the National Guard after an investigation revealed gang activity, drug use, and violence (Johnson, 1994). Other states, faced with scandals—beatings of young inmates—and poor result statistics have done the same (Blair, 2000).

In Conclusion. Based on 10 years of data, while boot camp participants reported positive short-term changes in attitudes and behaviors and they also had better problem-solving and coping skills, with few exceptions, these positive changes did not lead to reduced recidivism. Those boot camps that produced lower recidivism rates offered more treatment services, had longer sessions, and included more intensive postrelease supervision. However, not all programs with these features had successful results. The length of stay in boot camps—usually from 90 to 120 days—is too brief to realistically affect recidivism, and there is typically insufficient preparation for reentry into the community. Many boot camps provide little or no postrelease programming to prepare graduates to lead productive lives (Parent, 2003).

DAY REPORTING CENTERS

The concept of the **day reporting center** originated in Great Britain as a response to less serious but chronic offenders who lacked basic skills and were often dependent on drugs or alcohol. The British experience led Connecticut and Massachusetts to set up day reporting centers (DRCs) in 1986. The purposes of a DRC are "to heighten control and surveillance of offenders placed on community supervision, to increase offender access to treatment programs and services, to give officials more proportional and certain sanctions to be used for less serious probation or parole violations, or to reduce prison or jail crowding" (Parent, 1990: 9). "Offenders report to the centers frequently (usually once or even twice a day), and treatment services are usually provided on-site either by the [public or private] agency running the program or by other human services agencies whose staff work at the site" (Parent, 1996: 51).

Typically, offenders must be on the DRC premises 18 hours per week during the program's most intensive phase. An offender usually checks in at the DRC early each morning, and briefly talks with a counselor before going to work. After work, offenders often return to the DRC for an evening group counseling session. When not in the DRC, they are monitored by telephone calls to offenders' job sites, homes, or other locations where they are supposed to be. Each offender fills out a daily itinerary, which helps to keep track of their whereabouts in the community: "Itineraries teach offenders the importance of scheduling and planning and of managing one's time to avoid situations that may lead to drug use relapse, to new crimes, or to violations of the conditions of supervision" (Parent, 1996: 52). Most DRCs provide job training and placement services, counseling, and education. They also require offenders to provide restitution and perform community service.

In 1990, the Social Services Department of the District of Columbia Superior Court, which administers probation services, established the *Probation and Parole Resource Center* (PPRC) to provide a structured nonresidential program for high-risk offenders with a history of drug abuse. This DRC is located in an independent site, separate from routine P/P operations, northeast of the nation's capitol. The PPRC has P/P officers who are certified addiction counselors (CACs) as full-time staff members. Professional staff include employees from appropriate DC government agencies assigned to provide on-site direct services or referrals. Staff work on varying shifts to provide comprehensive monitoring of PPRC clients and maintenance of center operations. The project also contracts for additional services from the private sector.

The PPRC program consists of three distinct phases: assessment, treatment, and continuing care. A caseload management approach is employed and coordinated with staff from other participating agencies. The P/P officers/CACs monitor and supervise program participants throughout the treatment and continuing care phases. The assessment phase begins with a series of diagnostic services: intake interviews and medical and psychiatric or psychological screening. In the second phase, drug treatment strategies, education, counseling, support services delivery, and various supervision activities are tailored to meet the identified needs of each client. This includes a range of community sanctions such as curfew, home detention, and electronic surveillance. The continuing care phase carries over into existing P/P supervision programs, where participants are assigned to other P/P officers who are CACs. These officers provide long-term treatment and supervision through the remainder of the court-imposed sentence.

The Adult Probation Department of Maricopa County, Arizona, has 3 DRCs for nonviolent offenders during the final 60 days of their jail sentence. The participant follows an hour-by-hour schedule of courses offered at the DRC and other community-based agencies and/or participates in a job search program until employed. Participants with employment follow daily schedules and when not participating in work or programs, participants are required to remain at home where they are monitored by probation and surveillance officers. After completing the program, participants continue under standard or IPS. A failure to complete the program results in reinarceration.

Now that we have examined intermediate punishments, in chapter 14 we review research and issues related to the effectiveness of P/P.

KEY TERMS

intermediate punishments

intensive supervision

diversion

electronic monitoring

continuously signaling

programmed contact

shock probation/parole

shock incarceration/boot camp

day reporting center

INTERNET CONNECTIONS

American Probation and Parole Association: www.appa-net.org

National Institute of Corrections: nicic.org

American Correctional Association: corrections.com/aca/index

International Community Corrections Association: iccaweb.org

The Center for Community Corrections: communitycorrectionsworks.org

REVIEW QUESTIONS

1. What is the real goal of intermediate punishments?
2. What are the different types of programs that come under intermediate punishments?
3. What are the two premises on which intensive supervision is based?
4. Why haven't these two premises been realized?
5. What has research into intensive supervision revealed?
6. What led to the use of EM in P/P?
7. How is EM accomplished?
8. What are the advantages of shock P/P?
9. What are the shortcomings of shock P/P?
10. What are the shortcomings of SI/boot camp?
11. What has research into the effectiveness of SI found?
12. What are the purposes of a DRC?

Probation and Parole in the Twenty-First Century

This concluding chapter examines the question of "success" and the interrelated issue of recidivism, followed by an exploration of the direction of P/P in the twenty-first century.

PROBATION AND PAROLE: SUCCESS OR FAILURE?

In examining the degree to which P/P are "successful," the results are often contradictory. The methodology of some research efforts is simply unsound; however, even methodologically sound research has not allowed us to answer the question: *probation and parole: success or failure?* For example, a study (Lerner, 1977) found that parole supervision in New York reduced the postrelease criminal activity of a group of (conditional) releasees compared with a group of dischargees released from the same institution without supervision. A similar study (Sachs and Logan, 1979) found that in Connecticut parole supervision resulted in only a modest reduction in recidivism. In California, however, no significant difference was found in the recidivism rates of persons released with or without parole supervision (Jackson, 1983; Star, 1979). A New Orleans study (Geerken and Hayes, 1993) found that 8 percent of adult arrests for burglary or armed robbery from 1974 to 1986 involved offenders who were on probation; the figure for parolees was less than 2 percent. A study in New York of 22,941 conditional releasees (15 percent) and parolees (85 percent) released in 1991 and supervised by POs were tracked for 2 years: fewer than 13 percent were returned to prison for new felony convictions (New York State Division of Parole, 1994). A 1994 to 1995 study of more than 2,000 felons placed on probation in Arizona in 1989 and 1990 revealed that 61 percent had completed their term of supervision and 25 percent were convicted of new crimes and sentenced to prison; 4 percent absconded (Administrative Office of the Courts, 1996). The figures for probation in Marion County, Indiana, in 2002 was 63 percent successfully completing supervision, 13.2 percent revoked for a new offense, and 23.9 percent revoked for a technical violation. A study of parolees in Hawaii (Kassebaum et al., 1999) who were tracked for 3 years found that 70.7 percent had no criminal convictions; 11 percent had one or more felony convictions; and approximately one-half had their parole revoked, mostly for technical violations. Do these studies indicate success or failure?

A major part of the problem is the word **success.** For example, a researcher for the California Youth Authority candidly portrays his own findings, noting that "success" depends on which statistics one decides to emphasize. Thus,

Parole behavior in the sample can be made to look quite good, especially considering the high levels of pre–Youth Authority crime, or quite bad. For example, only 13 percent were sent to state prison for parole-period offenses during the 24 months of followup, resulting in an 87 percent "success rate" by this criterion. Some correctional jurisdictions who report spectacularly high success rates, in fact use such a restricted measure. Alternatively, regarding the same sample we could accurately report that 77 percent of the sample had been arrested or temporarily detained during the 24 months leaving a "success rate" by this criterion of only 23 percent. (Wiederanders, 1983: 4)

According to the Bureau of Justice Statistics (2001), success rates of those under parole supervision have remained relatively stable for more than a decade. About 4 in every 10 persons discharged from parole successfully complete their term of supervision in the community. As might be expected, the success rates for those released by a parole board are higher (54 percent) than for those who were released under good time provisions/mandatory release (33 percent).

The "success" of a probation or parole system is usually conceived of in terms of **recidivism** (Maltz, 1984: 54). However, "when recidivism is discussed in a correctional context, its meaning seems fairly clear. The word is derived from the Latin *recidere*, to fall back. A recidivist is one who, after release from custody for having committed a crime, is not rehabilitated. Instead, he or she falls back, relapses, into former behavior patterns and commits more crimes. This conceptual definition of recidivism may seem quite straightforward; however, an operational definition, one that permits measurement, is not so simple."

The 1976 edition of the *Dictionary of Criminal Justice Data Terminology* defines recidivism as "the repetition of criminal behavior; habitual criminality." However, the 1981 edition avoids providing a definition and, instead, notes: "Efforts to arrive at a single standard statistical definition of recidivism have been hampered by the fact that the correct referent of the term is the actual repeated criminal or delinquent behavior of a given person or group, yet the only available statistical indicators of that behavior are records of such system events as rearrests, reconvictions, and probation or parole violations or revocations. It is recognized that these data reflect agency decisions about events and do not closely correspond with actual criminal behavior."

Jay Albanese and his colleagues (1981: 51) point out that

- A wide disparity exists in the definition of revocation and recidivism.
- Revocation/recidivism rates without a standardized definition have little comparative value.
- A criterion (or criteria) of "effectiveness" is not well defined.

Gordon Waldo and David Griswold (1979: 230) note that being arrested and convicted for any crime is not sufficient as an operational definition of recidivism. They quote Charles Tittle: "Being arrested for gambling cannot be accepted as evidence of recidivism for a burglar." In addition, the extensive use of plea bargaining means that merely looking at the crime for which a person is convicted does not allow for a determination of whether the person has committed the same crime again, or a less serious or more serious crime. Similarly, with respect to probation recidivism rates, it is necessary to distinguish between those under supervision for misdemeanors and those convicted of felonies because felony probationers have significantly higher rates of recidivism than misdemeanants (Petersilia, 1998b). Then there is the problem of technical violations—do we rate them as "recidivism"? No consistent definition of recidivism exists, and "one cannot state with any degree of assurance whether a given recidivism rate is high or low; there is no 'normal' recidivism rate as there is a normal body temperature" (Maltz, 1984: 23).

Further complicating efforts to determine success is the issue of *selection*: P/P agencies receiving (via judges and parole boards) a greater amount of low-risk offenders are more likely to have higher rates of success. A conservative judge/parole board, or perhaps one fearful of an adverse public reaction, will release fewer offenders to supervision. Those who are placed on P/P will tend to be the "boy scouts"—lower-risk offenders who will probably *produce* impressive (statistical) measurements of success for the agency. Is it relevant to compare the "success" rates of AIDS doctors with those treating less catastrophic ailments?

Research has identified a number of variables that correlate well with success or failure on probation: age (younger offenders have greater difficulty adhering to probation conditions), employment (those who are employed and financially stable do better), marital status (those who are married are less likely to violate probation), and offense (those on probation for drug- and theft-related crimes have higher recidivism rates) (Liberton, Silverman, and Blount, 1990). The reverse is also true: High-risk offenders lessen the chances of success. This is not only so in P/P, but also in education and medicine. Inner-city schools with high rates of disorganization and families living in poverty, or hospitals serving these same populations, will have less successful outcomes than their counterparts in middle-class environs. Is crime a symptom, a result, or a causal factor of these conditions? If crime is a dependent variable, what can reasonably be expected of P/P?

Alvin Cohen (2002: 7) points to a policy problem with respect to "success" research in P/P: If an intensive supervision program costs $1,000 a year per offender and has a 55 percent "success" rate, is it worth spending $1,500 to achieve a 60 percent success rate—assuming that is possible? Suppose it costs $2,000 or $3,000. Is the cost–benefit outcome worthwhile? Research cannot answer such questions.

The basic mechanism of P/P supervision is client contact. Thus, as noted in chapter 13, issues of caseload size and increased contacts have been something of a preoccupation in this field.

Contacts are easily quantifiable and little has been sought beyond a "numbers game." Faye Taxman (2002) notes that the endeavor is essentially atheoretical because other than it being some type of control, there has been an absence of interest in the quality of the contact, be it for control or rehabilitation. This issue is of great import because studies of reduced caseload size reveal that "unless the contacts are more than 'check-ins,' it is unlikely that they will impact on offender outcomes" (17). This is critical because there is research indicating that providing therapy predicts better outcomes. Such provision should follow social service protocols that stress **continuity of care**: "Interventions offered in prison, the community, or community-based facilities should be built on each other." Because it is likely that clientele will be involved in various interventions during the various phases of the justice process, "it is important for the approaches to be compatible" (20).

Parole Success

According to the U.S. Bureau of Justice Statistics, parole success rates have remained relatively stable since 1990. About 4 in every 10 persons discharged from parole in 1999 had successfully completed their term of supervision in the community. The success rate was higher among parolees who had been released from a state prison by a parole board (54 percent) than for parolees whose release was required by law (33 percent).

FELONY PROBATION

Joan Petersilia and her colleagues (1985: v), researchers for the Rand Corporation, noted that "over one-third of California's probation population consists of felons convicted in Superior Court—persons who are often quite different from the less serious offenders probation was originally conceived and structured to handle." They found that 51 percent of a sample of California offenders on **felony probation** who were sentenced in 1980 and tracked for 40 months were reconvicted, 18 percent for violent crime. They conclude (vi) that "felons granted probation present a serious threat to public safety," and this threat is not being adequately managed by probation agencies in California and probably elsewhere. In Massachusetts, for example, the number of persons sentenced to probation for crimes against persons increased between 1982 and 1993 by more than 250 percent. As noted in chapter 1, dramatic increases in probation are often linked to prison overcrowding, sometimes, as in Virginia, exacerbated by abolishing parole.

Research into felony probation in Missouri and Kentucky revealed a different outcome. Both studies were designed to replicate that of Petersilia and her colleagues in California. That is, to determine whether felony offenders placed on probation in Missouri and Kentucky presented risks similar to those in California. Significant differences were found (McGaha, Fichter, and Hirschburg, 1987):

	California (%)	Missouri (%)	Kentucky (%)
Rearrests	65.0	22.3	22.1
Reconvictions	51.0	12.0	17.7
Violent felony	18.0	7.1	4.1

The results of research into felony probation in New Jersey fell about midway between the findings in California and those in Kentucky and Missouri. Four years after they were sentenced to probation, 40 percent had been rearrested, and 35 percent were reconvicted (Whitehead, 1989).

Based on their research, Petersilia et al. (1985: 64) argue that "routine probation, by definition, is *inappropriate for most felons.*" What, other than imprisonment, *is appropriate* for most felons? "We believe that the criminal justice system needs an alternative, indeterminate form of punishment for those offenders who are too antisocial for the relative freedom that probation now offers, but not so seriously criminal as to require imprisonment. A sanction is needed that would impose intensive surveillance, coupled with substantial community service and restitution. It should be structured to satisfy public demands that the punishment fit the crime, to show criminals that crime really does not pay, and to control potential recidivists" (ix).

The Rand Corporation researchers (Petersilia et al., 1985: xiii) recommend a different form of probation supervision:

> In response to changes in the probation population, the system should redefine the role and powers of probation officers. Probation officers cannot deal with felony probationers in the same ways they have dealt with misdemeanants. We certainly do not recommend that they abandon their counseling or rehabilitative roles; however, because the probation population includes a large number of active criminals, we support the growing legal and policy trend toward quasi-policing roles for probation officers, whenever the situation warrants it. Attention should be paid to the recruitment and training of probation officers. Different skills may be required of officers whose primary responsibility is surveillance rather than rehabilitation.

This is the **combined**—control/social service—**model** discussed in chapter 10—unannounced home and employment visits, checks for drug use, and a close working relationship with law enforcement agencies; and attention to client needs, including employment, housing, and counseling that provides social and psychological support.

GOALS OF PROBATION AND PAROLE

What are the goals of P/P? Success can be measured only against anticipated outcome. If a P/P agency is based on a **social service model,** success is measured by the delivery of, or by referral to, services, such as education, training, employment, and counseling, and client–consumer satisfaction with the level of service. This type of agency will often be affected by variables beyond its control, for example, variations in the unemployment rate particularly for low-skilled workers. Indeed, a relatively low rate of unemployment has apparently made it easier for ex-offenders to secure employment (Meredith, 2000). A jurisdiction with readily available employment will presumably do better at job placement than the same agency in a jurisdiction that has a relatively high rate of unemployment. Similarly, an agency located in a community with a variety of available social services will be more likely to show a greater level of success than will one in a community with a paucity of such agencies. The interrelated problems of poverty and the collapse of inner-city families are important problems with which P/P agencies have to contend but are helpless to affect.

If a P/P agency is based on a **control model,** success is measured according to the agency's ability to hold the offender accountable for his or her behavior. The discovery of supervision violations and/or new crimes by close P/P monitoring, however, could statistically increase recidivism rates by uncovering behavior that might not otherwise be discovered. Recidivism may also be related to unemployment—and to the extent that it is, the success of this type of agency will depend in part on the state of the economy. Recidivism is also related to other practical issues. First, one cannot account for undetected criminality; second, arrest and prosecution are often a measure of the law enforcement activity in a given community. Thus, different levels of law enforcement will produce different levels of official (statistical) recidivism, regardless of P/P agency effectiveness. Indeed, a more effective control model agency may enhance the law enforcement function (e.g., through close cooperation with the police) and will thus help to (statistically) *produce* more recidivism—arrests and convictions of agency clientele. David Stanley points out that if we use recidivism as a measure, "An offender can be unemployed, ignorant, promiscuous, and drunk but still a success as far as the criminal justice system is concerned if he commits no crime" (1976: 173). Indeed, a cynic (realist?) might suggest encouraging drug abusers to become alcoholics instead.

Further, how are technical violations of P/P rules to be treated (statistically) with respect to agency goals? More vigorous (i.e., intensive) supervision may *produce* more technical violations (although the research is still not clear on this issue), whereas an agency that provides little or no supervision will have few (detected) technical violations—hence, fewer revocations of P/P. The level of individual and agency tolerance for technical violations will also affect the revocation rate, and a higher revocation rate of technical violations may result in a lower number of new convictions—offenders screened out of supervision before they can be arrested for new crimes.

Because neither the social service nor the control model agency need make any claim about rehabilitation, the question of postsupervision arrests and convictions need not be raised. In agencies that include rehabilitation as a (or perhaps *the*) goal, this issue needs to be considered. How long does the agency retain (statistical) responsibility for success or failure of a client who has completed supervision— 6 months, a year, or life? The implication is that such an agency will succeed in producing a lasting change in client behavior. Is it reasonable to expect a P/P agency—or any other brief intervention—to "correct" a lifetime of problems and problematic behavior? An additional question is how to weigh recidivism when the instant offense is a great deal less serious than the original crime. For example, is an armed robber convicted of shoplifting considered a success or failure?

"We promised far too much, and created unrealistic expectations among politicians and public."

—Barry J. Nidorf, Chief Probation Officer, Los Angeles County, 1995

Perhaps the most difficult agency to evaluate in terms success or failure is one based on a combined model. Most P/P agencies in the United States fall into this category. In this type of agency, an explicit or implicit claim is usually related to service, rehabilitation, *and* control. An agency with such broad purposes—a plethora of complicated goals—cannot *fail*, nor can it *succeed*—it presents no clear-cut basis for measuring anticipated outcome. The claims are too broad, too many, and too dependent on variables beyond agency control (such as the economy, level of law enforcement in the community, screening of offenders by judges/parole boards, availability of resources in the community, and so on) for a research effort to analyze in any relevant manner. As a result, this type of agency has been subjected to criticism on the basis of research that "microscopes" one goal and finds it wanting. The goals are literally picked apart, leaving the agency vulnerable to those who would discredit P/P.

Petersilia (1993: 69) argues that P/P agencies need to "customize their mission statement, methods, and performance indicators so that they reflect local resources and priorities." The mission should be one that can reasonably be expected to be fulfilled, clearly related to the unique services provided by the agency, and performance indicators should be specified: "When public agencies fail to define their mission internally, political influences are more apt to define it for them. And when they fail to articulate how they should be evaluated, outcome measurements such as recidivism rates will likely be imposed upon them" (76). Petersilia (1998a, 1998b) notes that responsibilities of P/P agencies include functions that cannot be measured by recidivism rates. This would include presentence and executive clemency investigations; collecting fines and fees; monitoring community service, work release, and furloughs; and providing victim services.

One should consider the very reason that P/P exist. As penological history in the United States indicates—discussed in chapters 1, 6, and 7—stripped of the humanistic dynamic, P/P exist for *economic reasons*. If P/P were as costly (in terms of budgetary considerations) as, or even equal in cost to, imprisonment, it would be so severely restricted as to no longer constitute an important issue in criminal justice.

Tough Talk, Weak Policy

"By exercising discretion, parole boards can single out the more violent and dangerous offenders for longer incarceration. When States abolish parole or reduce the discretion of parole authorities, they replace a rational, controlled system of 'earned' release for selected inmates with 'automatic' release for nearly all inmates.

No-parole systems sound tough but remove a gatekeeping role that can protect victims and communities. Parole boards can demand that released inmates receive drug treatment, and research shows that coerced treatment is as successful as voluntary participation. If parole boards also require a plan for the released offender to secure a job and a place to live in the community, the added benefit is to refocus prison staff and corrections budgets on transition planning" (Petersilia, 2000b: 5).

With Cash Tight, States Reassess Long Jail Terms: Strict Laws Loosened

"After two decades of passing ever tougher sentencing laws promoting a prison build-ing boom, state legislatures facing budget crises are beginning to rethink their costly ap-proaches to crime," Fox Butterfield, *New York Times* (November 10, 2003a: 1).

As noted in chapter 1, most serious crimes do not result in an arrest. Of those arrested for felonies, well in excess of 50 percent are not prosecuted for felony crimes. Most of those prosecuted for felonies plead guilty, usually the result of negotiations—plea bargaining. Thus, when discussing issues of punishment, *residuals* are involved—but these are sufficiently large so common sense indicates they cannot all be incarcerated. Even if that were a proper response, enough prison space could not be created expeditiously, nor would taxpayers be willing to pay the required taxes and/or shifting of public resources—California is spending more money on prisons than on public colleges and universities, and other states are fol-lowing California's lead (Butterfield, 1995a). What options remain viable in the wake of a downturn in the economy and revenue shortfalls in many states?

Probation offers the first line of defense against prison overcrowding. If no parole system is in operation, probation becomes *the* method by which prison populations are controlled. As a result, serious felony offenders, for whom probation has historically not been intended, become probation clients. At the other end, mandatory prison releasees typically receive inadequate, if any, supervision, because little incentive exists for politicians to expend tax dollars on programs for nondiscretionary-released offenders—absence of a public official on whom to lay blame in the event a releasee generates negative publicity. In any event, relatively few offenders will remain in prison their entire lives—more than 97 percent of all state prison inmates will even-tually be released (Schriro, 2000).

In the year 2000, more than half a million persons were released from prison. By way of comparison, in 1980, fewer than 170,000 were released (Travis, 2000). The issue remains: Who will make the release decision: judges, prison officials, or parole boards? Will these decisions involve a careful analysis of the case, comparing it to similar cases—issues of equity—and reasonable predictions of future behavior, or risk control? Petersilia (2000a) notes that when states abolish parole or reduce the amount of parole board discretion, they effectively replace a rational controlled sys-tem of "earned" release for selected inmates with automatic release for nearly all in-mates. And what happens after they are released? "Underfunded parole agencies in many jurisdictions have made parole more a legal status than a systematic process of reintegrating returning prisoners" (Travis, 2000: 1).

In Alabama

The Alabama Board of Pardons and Paroles believes that its primary business is com-munity protection. "With or without parole, approximately 95 percent of incarcerated offenders will walk the streets again. The real question then is not whether offenders should be released, but rather when should offenders be released and what are the best circumstances for their release?"

WHERE HAVE WE BEEN, WHERE ARE WE NOW, AND WHERE ARE WE GOING?

When the first edition of this book was published in 1977, the indeterminate sentence and parole were under great scrutiny and pressure, the result of Robert Martinson's "What Works?" (1974) and publication of the full study (Lipton, Martinson, and Wilks, 1975) the following year (discussed in chapter 7). In the years that followed, about a dozen states adopted determinate sentencing and abolished parole release. By the twenty-first century, most states had either abolished the indeterminate sentence or severely restricted the categories of offenders eligible for parole release—a turn toward **classicalism.** Although failing to accomplish equal punishment for crimes of equal severity, as per classicalism, determinate sentencing removed a rational vehicle for responding to prison overcrowding. Policy makers and public officials failed to learn the lessons of penal history reviewed in chapter 6. The establishment of parole with the onset of the Great Depression was a means of alleviating prison overcrowding—rehabilitation was not a motivating factor.

The rightward movement of politics in the United States swept the criminal justice system into overdrive; "law and order" rhetoric beget a policy leading to more arrests and more convictions, particularly for drug offenses. States began abolishing the **indeterminate sentence** and parole or severely restricting its use. In Georgia, for example, all violent offenders and residential burglars serve a minimum of 90 percent of their sentence. Offenders convicted of murder, various sex offenses, and armed robbery serve 100 percent of their prison sentence. In New York, violent offenders are not eligible for parole.

These policies were the driving force behind the corrections overload as prison populations reached record levels and the courts began to intervene. Overcrowding and court intervention led to forced releases, and some states passed "one-in/one-out" legislation. This proved insufficient. As pressure built, criminal justice systems increased their use of probation, particularly in those states without parole release. Offenders who would otherwise have been incarcerated, serious felons who were not candidates for traditional probation, burdened ill-equipped probation agencies.

In 1994, Congress enacted the Violent Crime Control and Law Enforcement Act providing incentive grants to states that adopted truth-in-sentencing (TIS) laws. TIS requires an offender to serve a fixed portion of his or her sentence before being eligible for release. States that require offenders convicted of a federal-defined Part 1 violent crime (see chapter 1) to serve at least 85 percent of their sentences are eligible for federal TIS grants. The funds awarded can be used to build or expand prisons to

Déja Vu

The Manhattan grand jury was led to believe that the murders of several policemen were due to an "alleged laxity in the state parole system. The grand jurors started under the impression, assiduously fostered by J. Edgar Hoover and reactionary policemen, that parole is crooked and incompetent and habitually frees dangerous criminals. They were surprised to discover the murders in question were not to be blamed on parole, and that the parole system was a valuable agency of public protection. In most states, parole continues to be merely a disguise for executive clemency, a means of emptying the prisons and keeping their budgets down. In other states, notably New York, the majority of prisoners continue to be released after a certain time, to live under rigid supervision and to be sent summarily back to prison if they don't behave." Parole judgments are "necessarily fallible, and when the inevitable mistakes are made, the propagandists shout about the inequities of parole" (Crime reporter Hickman Powell [2000: 38fn] in 1939).

house violent offenders or to construct or enhance correctional facilities for nonviolent offenders in order to free up bed space for violent criminals. The TIS money covers bricks and mortar, but not the staggering operating costs associated with prisons. As noted in chapter 6, prison systems throughout the United States are struggling with the problem of recruiting and maintaining an adequate number of correction officers.

A hurried scramble for ways to deal with opposing pressures—arrest and incarcerate/decrease prison populations—ensued. New terminology resulted: **Corrections** was displaced by the buzzwords of a new era—**intermediate sanctions.** Under this rubric were regurgitated models from the late nineteenth century—boot camps—the old Elmira System reinvented for the 1990s; the California Special Intensive Parole Unit of the early 1950s was reinvented as IPS; fondness for technology led penology to adopt electronic surveillance.

New "What Works?" research was critical of these schemes because they failed to control recidivism while having little impact on the central problem of prison overcrowding. Despite decreases in the crime rate, prison overcrowding continued with the enactment of more "get tough" legislation. For example, Arizona, in 1994, when the state ranked sixth in rates of incarceration, enacted a TIS law eliminating parole and reducing good time to no more than 15 percent of the sentence. "Three strikes and you're out" became a popular metaphor—life without parole on the third (sometimes the second) felony conviction. As a crime policy, it raises important questions, not the least of which is the cost of turning prisons into expensive geriatric facilities for elderly offenders often convicted of nonviolent crimes. In 2003, for example, California imprisoned more 300 men whose "third strike" was for petty theft (Greenhouse, 2003). Even the terminology began to change. In 1999, Florida, for example, turned back the clock, renaming prison superintendents as "wardens", and Arkansas has a Department of Community Punishment.

As the trend toward narrowing or eliminating the discretionary release of prison inmates continues, correction departments are frequently able to use "special good time" provisions—TIS not withstanding—while new schemes have been implemented. For example, some jurisdictions are empowering judges to either place offenders directly on parole (New York) or to use split sentences. Thus, Connecticut judges are authorized to impose special parole terms on any prison sentence in excess of 2 years; the length of special parole is at the court's discretion but may not exceed 10 years, and in combination with the prison term, may not exceed the maximum sentence allowable for the crime of conviction. For certain sex offenses special parole is required. It is easy to see why a governor would find this approach attractive: It accomplishes the early release and supervision of offenders without the need for action by a politically vulnerable parole board. These schemes fail to promote equity and are devoid of accountability. They abandon both classical and positive approaches in favor of the gross politicization of our system of justice.

What is the public safety cost of this approach? "No one is more dangerous than a criminal who has no incentive to straighten himself out while in prison and who returns to society without a structured and supervised release plan" (Petersilia, 2003: 18). Petersilia notes, "discretionary parole systems provided a means by which inmates who represent continuing public safety risks can be kept in prison" while focusing "prison staff and corrections budgets on planning for release, not just opening the door at release" (18).

Traditional P/P still bear the major burden, and some states that had gone over to **determinate sentencing**, reintroduced parole release. At the same time, the law enforcement role and training of P/P officers increased dramatically as the control model became predominant, while some states with determinate sentencing, such as Illinois and Virginia, in an effort to save money, have gone to the opposite extreme—virtually ending supervision of offenders released from prison. Some states, such as Oregon and Washington, no longer allow parolees to be returned to prison for technical violations (Petersilia, 2000b). Illinois, which does not have a parole board, paid a price for its approach. In 1994, after serving 5 years of a 14-year sentence for torture and rape—the prison system was overcrowded—Paul Runge was released with a recommendation that he be monitored closely in the community. However, there were not enough POs to provide monitoring, and Runge, who had refused to undergo sex offender treatment while in prison, went on a rape and murder spree that did not end until he was arrested in 2001.

In California and other states, there has been a dramatic increase in the number of persons returned to prison for violating the conditions of their release—the result of a form of supervision dominated by control devoid of the social service concerns of an earlier era (Beck, 2000b; Butterfield, 2000b). In the fourth edition of this book (Abadinsky, 1991: 386), I expressed concern over the movement toward a control model: "This direction brings with it the danger that probation and parole will become simply offender-monitoring activities devoid of any rehabilitative components." In 1991 (386), I advocated a balanced approach and continue to do so: "A balanced approach to probation and parole requires that the goal remain protection of the community, but with recognition that this is best accomplished by rehabilitating offenders." I believe that sometime during this new century, a sense of equilibrium, if not a sense of history, will result in a balanced response that combines the needs of offenders and victims with the community's reasonable expectation of safety.

KEY TERMS

success	control model
recidivism	classicalism
continuity of care	indeterminate sentence
felony probation	corrections
combined model	intermediate sanctions
social service model	determinate sentencing

INTERNET CONNECTIONS

Corrections Connection: corrections.com
Center for Community Corrections: communitycorrectionsworks.org
American Probation and Parole Association: www.appa-net.org

REVIEW QUESTIONS

1. What has research found with respect to success in P/P?
2. Why is it difficult to provide a definition of recidivism for statistical purposes?
3. What is the "selection" problem with respect to determining success in P/P?
4. What are the variables over which a P/P agency has no control and that can affect case outcome?
5. What did the "felony probation" research by Joan Petersilia and her colleagues reveal about probation in California?
6. What did Petersilia and her colleagues recommend in response to their findings?
7. How should the success of a P/P agency based on a *service model* be measured?
8. How should the success of a P/P agency based on a *control model* be measured?
9. What actions of a control model agency could increase the measured rate of recidivism?
10. Why has the movement in P/P been toward a control model?
11. Why would the abolition of parole lead to greater use of probation?

Glossary

abandonment: The most common legal grounds for termination of parental rights, also a form of child abuse in most states. Sporadic visits, a few phone calls, or birthday cards are not sufficient to maintain parental rights. Fathers who manifest indifference toward a pregnant mother are also viewed as abandoning the child when it is born.

absconders: An offender who is no longer residing at his or her approved residence and whose whereabouts are unknown.

abuse: Term for acts or omissions by a legal caregiver. Encompasses a broad range of acts and usually requires proof of intent.

acquittal: When a defendant is found not guilty.

addiction: A preoccupation with the use of psychoactive substances characterized by neurochemical and molecular changes in the brain.

adjournment: A delay in trial ordered by the judge, usually at the request of one of the lawyers.

adjudication: A judgment or decision.

adjudicatory hearing: Trial in juvenile court.

administrative law: Body of law created by administrative and regulatory bodies such as a parole board.

adversarial method: System of fact finding used in American trials in which each side is represented by an attorney who acts as an advocate.

affidavit: A sworn, written statement of facts.

affirm: Uphold the decision of a lower court.

aftercare: Outpatient support after the intensive phase of drug or alcohol treatment is concluded; parole for juveniles.

aggravating factors: Elements present in a crime that the judge can take into account at the time of sentencing.

anal stage: According to psychoanalytic theory, the second stage of psychosexual development.

anomie: A condition characterized by estrangement from society; the result of being unable to achieve financial success through legitimate avenues.

antisocial personality disorder: Exhibits psycho- or sociopathic behavior.

appeal: Legal challenge to a decision by a lower court.

appellate jurisdiction: A court having authority to review and modify the decision of a lower court.

appellate review: The consideration of a case by a court of appeals.

arbitration: The submission of a dispute to a nonjudicial third party for binding judgment.

arraignment: Early stage in the judicial process when the defendant is informed of the charges and enters a plea of guilty, *nolo contendere*, or not guilty.

arrest: The physical taking into custody of a suspected law violator or juvenile.

arrest warrant: A document issued by a judicial or administrative officer authorizing the arrest of a specific person.

Ashurst–Sumners Act: A 1939 federal statute that effectively ended the prison contract system.

Auburn system: Fortress-style prisons characterized by a factory system exploiting inmate labor.

attorney of record: The attorney whose name appears on the permanent case files.

bail: Money or other security placed in custody of the court in order to ensure the return of a defendant to stand trial.

behavior modification: Psychological approach that emphasizes positive and negative reinforcement.

best interests of the child: Legal doctrine establishing court as determiner of best environment for raising children.

Big House: Auburn-style prison devoid of a factory system.

blended sentence: A combination of juvenile and criminal sanctions given to young offenders.

blood-alcohol level (BAL): Amount of alcohol in the blood: .08 or .10 is legal standard for determining intoxication usually measured by a breathalyzer test.

bond: Personal recognizance/release on recognizance (ROR). Document signed by a defendant in which he or she agrees to return to court at a subsequent date to stand trial.

bond hearing: An appearance before a judicial officer who determines the conditions of release–bail–pending trial.

booking: The process of photographing, fingerprinting, and recording of identifying data subsequent to a suspect's arrest.

boot camp: A form of special probation/split sentence that requires offenders, usually between the ages of 16 and 30, to reside in a quasimilitary residential program for 90 to 120 days.

brief: Report prepared by an attorney and filed in court that sets forth facts and applicable law in support of a case.

"broken windows" supervision: Approach that emphasizes strengthening linkages with law enforcement and the community.

burden of proof: The need to establish a claim or allegation; in a criminal case, the state has the burden of proof.

calendar: A list of cases to be heard in a trial court on a specific date, containing the title of the case, the lawyers involved, and the case number.

case law: Previous decisions of appellate courts, particularly the Supreme Court.

casework: System of counseling.

cause: Any question/action subject to litigation before court.

cause of action: Facts that give rise to a matter before the court.

change of venue: Moving a trial to a county where the crime did not occur in order to avoid an unfair trial due to pretrial publicity.

charge: Accusation against the accused that he or she violated a specific criminal law(s).

chief judge: Judge who has primary responsibility for court administration.

child in need of supervision (CHINS): Status offender.

child-saving movement: Activities of middle- and upper-class women of the late nineteenth century to establish the juvenile court.

circumstantial evidence: Indirect evidence, such as fingerprints, from which an inference can be drawn.

civil protection order: Court order according to which an adult suspected of abuse must leave and remain away from the home.

classical conditioning: Learning in which a primary stimulus that naturally produces a specific response is repeatedly paired with a neutral stimulus. With repeated pairing, the neutral stimulus becomes a conditioned stimulus that can evoke a response similar to that of the primary stimulus.

classification: Procedure in which information is gathered about an offender for law enforcement, correctional, or court agencies, including an offender's behavior patterns, needs, skills, and aptitude, as well as factors related to criminal conduct.

clear and convincing evidence: Standard of evidence for certain civil cases that exceeds preponderance of evidence but is lower than beyond a reasonable doubt.

clemency: A grant of mercy, such as a pardon, by a chief executive.

clerk of the court: Official responsible for managing the flow of cases and maintaining court records.

classicalism: An outgrowth of Enlightenment philosophy that stresses free will and equality before law—"all men are created equal"—and provides a basis for determinate sentencing.

cognitive behavior therapy: form of treatment that focuses on helping the client learn and use new thinking skills to modify negative behaviors.

cognitive learning skills training: Rehabilitation approach that emphasizes the importance of problem-solving skills that can be applied to a variety of problem situations.

commit: Court order sending a person to an institution such as a prison, a hospital, or reformatory.

community corrections: In addition to traditional probation and parole, a variety of local, state, or federal activities involving punishment and management of offenders within their local communities through such programs as community service, restitution, day reporting centers, drug and alcohol treatment, and electronic monitoring.

community courts: Pioneered in New York City, these courts provide speedy adjudication of minor offenses and misdemeanors, as well as restitution and supervision of offenders.

community service: Sentence requiring an offender to work a certain number of hours as reparation to the community.

commutation: A shortening of sentence provided by a governor or president as part of the powers of executive clemency.

concurrent jurisdiction: That shared by different courts.

concurrent sentence: Sentences for more than one crime that are served simultaneously.

conditional release: Release from prison based on the accumulation of time off for good behavior and requiring the releasee to abide by certain regulations.

conflict theory: A view of society as characterized by a struggle for power that disadvantages those without financial resources.

consolidated model: Parole incorporated into a corrections department.

continuance: A delay in trial granted by the judge at the request of either attorney in a case; an adjournment.

contract system: A method for exploiting inmate labor during the Auburn era.

control model: Probation/parole supervision that emphasizes law enforcement.

corroboration: Supplementary evidence that tends to strengthen or confirm other evidence previously introduced.

court of general jurisdiction: Trial court that can adjudicate any type of case.

court of last resort: Highest appellate court in a jurisdiction.

court of limited jurisdiction: Court that can only adjudicate certain minor cases.

court reporter: Skilled stenographer who makes a word-by-word record of what is said in court.

cross-examination: The questioning of a witness by the attorney who did not call the witness; questions aimed at discrediting the courtroom testimony of an opposition witness.

custody theory: Obsolete legal view that probationers and parolees are in custody of the courts/prisons and therefore not entitled to due process.

day reporting center: An intermediate punishment requiring attendance at a facility on a daily or otherwise regular basis at specified times for a specific length of time in order to participate in activities such as substance abuse counseling, social skills training, or employment training.

defendant: Person accused of a crime or against whom the plaintiff brings suit.

deferred sentencing: After a plea of guilty, the defendant is placed under supervision, the successful completion of which can wipe out the conviction.

definite sentence: *See* determinate sentence.

delinquent: A person found to have violated the law, but whose age prevents defining him or her as a criminal.

delinquent subculture: Milieu in which antisocial activity is given high status.

dependant: Anyone under the care of someone else. A child ceases to be a dependent when they reach the age of emancipation, which varies by state law, and even then, some states allow for continued treatment as a dependent.

determinate sentence: That having a specific number of years and no provision for discretionary release (parole).

differential association: View of criminal behavior as being the result of associating with those involved in crime.

direct evidence: That which stands on its own to prove an allegation; usually eyewitness testimony.

direct examination: Questions asked of a friendly witness by counsel at trial.

disposition: Phase of delinquency proceeding similar to "sentencing" phase of adult trial.

diversion: An alternative to trial decided on at intake to refer a child or adult to counseling or other social services, permitting a person charged with an offense to avoid prosecution in exchange for participation in a rehabilitative or restitution program.

docket: Log containing the complete history of each case in the form of a brief chronology.

double jeopardy: Trying a defendant a second time for the same offense after he or she has already been found not guilty.

drift: View that most juvenile delinquents "drift" out of their antisocial behavior.

drug court: Court in which the judge, the district attorney, and defense attorney work together in a nonadversarial fashion to help chemically dependent offenders obtain needed treatment and rehabilitation in the hopes of breaking the cycle of crime and addiction.

due process: Those procedural guarantees to which every criminal defendant is entitled under the Constitution and its interpretation by the Supreme Court (e.g., the right to remain silent, to a trial by jury).

due process clause: Fifth and Fourteenth amendments, which prohibit government from taking life, liberty, or property without due process of law.

ego: The psyche's contact with reality that maximizes gratification with a minimum of difficulties.

electronic monitoring: Surveillance technology, usually by means of a wrist or ankle bracelet, to monitor an offender's movements from a central location on a 24-hour basis.

emancipation: Independence of a minor from his or her parents before reaching age of majority.

EMIT: Commonly used drug test.

entrapment: The behavior of an agent of government that encourages the committing of a criminal act by a person who was not predisposed to do so. Constitutes an affirmative defense.

equal protection: Fourteenth Amendment clause requiring government to treat similarly situated people the same or have good reason for treating them differently.

evidence, circumstantial: That from which something can be inferred (e.g., fingerprints).

evidence, direct: Eyewitness testimony.

exclusionary rule: A legal doctrine prohibiting evidence secured in an improper manner from being used at a trial.

executive clemency: A pardon, reprieve, or commutation.

family court: Court having jurisdiction over juvenile cases, as well as issues such as divorce and custody.

felony: The more serious of the two basic types of criminal behavior, usually bearing a possible penalty in excess of 1 year in prison.

finding: The verdict in a juvenile court.

flat sentence: *See* determinate sentence.

foster care: Temporary care funded by government and arranged by a child welfare agency.

free will: According to classical theory, each person has the opportunity to be law abiding or criminal (*mens rea*), and therefore, the person who opts to commit a crime is deserving of punishment commensurate with the offense.

full faith and credit: The constitutional requirement that the official judicial acts of one state will be respected by every other state.

general jurisdiction: The ability of a trial court to hear any type of case.

genital stage: According to psychoanalytic theory, third stage of psychosexual development.

good faith exception: Exception to the exclusionary rule that allows the admission of evidence based on the officer's reasonable, but mistaken, belief that his or her action was proper.

good time: A reduction of the time served in prison as a reward for not violating prison rules; usually one-third to one-half off the maximum sentence.

grand jury: A group of citizens, usually numbering 23, who are assembled in secret to hear or investigate allegations of criminal behavior.

guardian ad litem: "For the Proceeding" referring to adults, often volunteers, appointed by a court to look after the interests of a minor during the course of a judicial proceeding.

guilty but insane: A legal concept according to which a person who is suffering from a mental illness is not relieved of criminal responsibility.

habeas corpus: A legal document challenging custody and designed to force authorities holding a prisoner to produce him or her and justify the custody. Often used as an alternate method of appealing a conviction.

halfway house: Place where offenders work and pay rent while undergoing counseling and job training.

hearsay: Statement by a witness who did not hear or see the incident but heard about it from someone else; a statement whose veracity cannot be subjected to cross-examination and is therefore generally not admissible (although there are many exceptions).

high risk: Supervision level for offenders with high risk/high need. Close supervision with at least two personal contacts per month.

house arrest: An intermediate punishment that requires an offender to be confined to his or her residence for a period of time unless authorized to leave by the court, parole commission, or supervising officer. House arrest may or may not be accompanied by electronic monitoring.

House of Refuge: Prejuvenile court facility for children without adult guardians.

id: According to psychoanalytic theory, a primitive human drive.

immunity: Exemption from a civil or criminal action.

independent model: Parole board responsible for release decisions and supervision of those released.

indigent: Unable to afford counsel.

infancy: A legal age at which a person cannot be held criminally responsible.

innovation: Sophisticated criminal behavior.

intake: Procedure prior to preliminary hearing in which a probation officer interviews the police officer or other official, parent, and child, in order to determine if the matter is to be handled formally or informally.

intensive supervision: That which focuses on control characterized by a high amount of contacts and unannounced home visits.

intermediate punishments: Also known as intermediate sanctions, these punishments are more severe than traditional probation, but less severe than prison. They encompass community corrections measures such as day reporting centers and electronic monitoring.

Interstate Compact: Agreement between the states that allows travel by probationers and parolees from one state to another, and permits them to reside and be supervised in another state.

jail: A local, municipal, or county institution used to house those awaiting trial, those convicted of a misdemeanor, and those convicted of a felony and awaiting transfer to a prison.

judicial conference: A body of judges established to provide uniformity of policy and to consider matters of judicial discipline.

judicial review: The power of the judicial branch to declare acts of the executive and legislative branches unconstitutional.

jurisdiction: The authority to adjudicate a case based on a variety of factors, such as geography, seriousness of the crime, or the value of the amount in dispute.

just deserts: View that punishment should be based exclusively on the seriousness of the offense.

justice model: An argument in favor of determinate sentencing devoid of any concern for rehabilitation.

juvenile: Person who has not achieved an age set by law.

labeling: View that a negative identification, a stigma such as "ex-convict", can cause a societal reaction that permanently disadvantages the individual and can cause him or her to act in a manner referred to as a "self-fulfilling prophesy."

learning theory: Basis for the psychological view (behaviorism) of behavior as explained by its consequences.

lease system: Used to exploit inmate labor by "renting" it out to private entrepreneurs.

least restrictive alternative: Juvenile court concept for sentencing youngsters to that which restricts liberty the least while meeting the needs of the youngster.

legal aid: Legal services provided by an agency to indigent persons.

liberty interest: Concept that requires due process procedures whenever any type of freedom is at risk from government action.

limited jurisdiction: Refers to a trial court that can only hear certain types of cases.

magistrate: Judicial officer in a court of limited jurisdiction.

mandatory release: The release of an inmate at the end of his or her sentence minus any good time.

mandatory sentences: Sentences required by law to be imposed for certain crimes.

maximum: Level of offender supervision or the the highest range of an indeterminate sentence.

mediation: Submitting a dispute to a nonjudicial third party who attempts to get the parties to agree on an outcome.

medical model: Metaphor for providing rehabilitative services that parallel the way physicians treat patients.

***mens rea*:** The "guilty mind"—intent—necessary to establish criminal responsibility.

merit system: Method for appointing and promoting public employees that avoids political influence.

methadone: An artificial opiate used to treat heroin addicts.

minimum: Supervision level for low-risk/low-need offenders. Can be a beginning level or usually as a step down from maximum. Lowest of the range in an indeterminate sentence.

misdemeanor: An offense less severe than a felony, that is normally punished by a fine, a community sanction, or time in county jail.

mitigating factors: Elements present in the commission of a crime that may be taken into account by the judge to lower a sentence to prison or jail, or to select a more appropriate sentence than incarceration.

mock job fair: Method for preparing offenders for seeking employment.

negative reinforcement: Behaviorist concept that occurs when probability of a behavior goes up after the removal of a stimulus.

neglect: Parental failure to provide a child with basic necessities when able to do so. Encompasses a variety of forms of abuse that do not require the element of intent.

neoclassicalism: Classical approach that encompasses such mitigating factors as age and prior record.

neutralization: Sociological concept that explains how a person can support conventional values while violating the law.

new offense violation: Probation/parole violation that involves an arrest for a new offense.

***nolle prosequi*:** A decision by the prosecutor declining to prosecute a particular defendant.

***nolo contendere*:** A plea of "no contest" to criminal charges. Has the same effect as a plea of guilty, but cannot be used as evidence of a criminal conviction at any subsequent civil trial related to the criminal act.

no true bill: Grand jury decision not to indict.

operant conditioning: Application of positive and negative reinforcement.

oral stage: Earliest stage in psychosexual development.

ordinance: A statute enacted by a municipality or county.

organized crime: Refers to persons involved in ongoing criminal conspiracies whose goals are personal gain and who may persist indefinitely.

overcharging: A practice of alleging an excessive number of criminal violations when charging a suspect.

pardon: An act of executive clemency that has the effect of releasing an inmate from prison and/or removing certain legal disabilities from persons convicted of crimes.

***parens patriae*:** Legal doctrine that refers to the obligation of the state toward persons who are unable to care for themselves, such as children or the mentally ill.

parole: The release of a prison inmate prior to the expiration of sentence by a board authorized to make such a decision, followed by a period of supervision by a parole officer.

parole board: An administrative body whose members are chosen to review the cases of prisoners eligible for release on parole. The board has the authority to release such persons and to return them to prison for violating the conditions of parole.

pat-down: Refers to frisking, placing the hands about the body of a suspect in order to detect any weapons that he or she may be carrying.

Pennsylvania system: Nineteenth-century prisons characterized by solitary confinement.

person in need of supervision (PINS): Status offender.

petit jury: Trial jury composed of 6 or 12 persons.

petition: Formal written request or "prayer" for action; form of complaint used in juvenile proceedings.

plaintiff: Person initiating an action in a civil case or on appeal.

plea: Criminal defendant's response to the charges.

plea bargain: A legal transaction in which a defendant pleads guilty in exchange for some form of leniency.

pleading: Written statements of contentions submitted by parties in a legal action, each responding to the other, until the points at issue are sufficiently narrowed to proceed to trial.

plethysmography: Method of testing erectile response to erotic stimuli usually involving children.

positivism: Use of the scientific method to study crime and criminals; denies that crime is simply the result of free will and provides the basis for the indeterminate sentence.

positive reinforcement: Behavior shaped by rewarding consequences.

predisposition report: Comprehensive report on a juvenile subsequent to a finding of delinquency or status offense.

preliminary hearing: The bringing of a juvenile before a magistrate or judge in which charges are formally presented. Similar to an arraignment in adult court, and also called "advisory hearings" or "initial appearances" in some state juvenile justice systems.

preponderance of the evidence: Standard used to determine the outcome of a noncriminal action and probation and parole revocation.

presentence investigation report: A document submitted by a probation department to a judge containing information about the offender on which the judge can base his or her sentencing decision.

presumptive sentence: Has decreased use of judicial discretion in individual sentencing cases in an effort to make sentencing more equitable overall.

presumptive waiver: Provisions according to which certain juvenile offenders must be waived to criminal court unless they can prove they are amenable to rehabilitation, shifting the burden from the prosecutor to the juvenile.

pretrial release: Setting free a defendant without requiring bail; ROR (release on recognizance).

preventive detention: Holding a defendant in custody pending trial on the belief that he or she is likely to commit further criminal acts.

probable cause: The minimum level of evidence needed to make a lawful arrest or secure certain warrants; a level of information that would lead a prudent person to believe that a crime was being, or had been, committed by a specific perpetrator.

probable cause hearing: A court hearing to determine if an arrest was justified—did the officer have probable cause?

probation: A community punishment that requires the offender to comply with certain court-ordered conditions, such as curfew or attendance at a day reporting center, and may subject him or her to various levels of supervision based on public safety and rehabilitative needs.

probation officer: Public official authorized to accomplish presentence reports and supervise probationers.

probation subsidy: State grant to encourage the granting of probation.

procedural law: Specific instructions for invoking substantive law.

psychoanalytic theory: Belief that unconscious material controls conscious behavior.

public defender: An attorney employed by government to represent indigent defendants.

public safety exception: An exception to the exclusionary rule on the grounds that the action that resulted in securing evidence that would normally be suppressed was necessary to protect the public from some immediate danger.

pretrial services: System of screening services and investigation that may lead to community supervision, including electronic monitoring, for selected individuals who otherwise would be in jail while awaiting trial.

prison: A state-run facility where a person convicted of one or more felonies serves the sentence behind bars. Prisons can vary in security, from maximum to medium, to minimum, to prerelease.

reality therapy: Treatment method whose focus is the present and stresses the need to adopt conventional behavior.

reasonable doubt: Standard of evidence; doubt that a reasonable person could have with respect to the evidence.

recidivism: The term used to express the return to criminal activity of persons previously convicted of crimes. Recidivism rate refers to the percentage of those who return to crime once sentence has been served.

recognizance: Obligation to perform some act, usually returning to court to stand trial.

reformatory: Penal institution for younger offenders.

reinforcement: Consequence of a behavior that increases the likelihood that it will reoccur.

released on own recognizance: Releasing a defendant without the need to post bail; referred to as ROR.

remand: To send back, usually for a new trial or sentencing.

reprieve: A temporary stay of the execution of a sentence to allow more time for judicial review.

residential treatment center: Private facility for juveniles.

restitution: Act of giving money or services to the victim by the offender, often imposed as a condition of probation.

restorative justice: Approach to criminal justice in which the victim is at the center; emphasizes the way in which crimes hurt relationships between people who live in a community.

retainer: An advance paid by a client to an attorney in order to engage the attorney's services.

retreatism: Response to anomie that refers to substance abuse.

reverse: Act of an appellate court setting aside the decision of a trial court.

revocation: The administrative or court action that removes a person from either probation or parole status in response to his or her violation of the conditions of probation or parole, and results in imprisonment.

risk/needs assessment: Classification system that uses the degree to which an offender is likely to recidivate and the amount of help required.

rules of evidence: Standards governing the admission of evidence.

self-incrimination: Forcing a suspect to provide evidence against him- or herself; prohibited by the Fifth Amendment.

sentencing guidelines: System that directs or guides a sentencing judge.

shelter: Temporary residential facility for children in need of emergency care.

shock incarceration: "Boot camp," a facility that duplicates the military environment.

shock probation/parole: A brief incarceration followed by community supervision.

social casework: System for providing assistance based on social work concepts.

social contract: Belief that society is tied together by general agreements to conform to law.

social control theory: A person's ties to conventional society determines behavior.

social investigation: A study prepared by a probation officer in juvenile court to provide the judge with information on which to base a disposition.

state use system: Prison labor that produces products for government.

status offense: Actions that would not constitute a crime if the actor were an adult (e.g., truancy) but, in accord with *parens patriae*, can subject the youngster to the juvenile court process.

street time: Amount of time spent under supervision prior to a finding of violation.

superego: Conscious-like mechanism that exerts a sense of morality.

supermax prison: High-security facility that features solitary confinement.

subpoena *ad testificandum*: A court order requiring a witness to appear and testify.

subpoena *duces tecum*: "Bring with you"; a court order requiring a witness to bring all relevant documents that might affect the outcome of legal proceedings.

superior court: Court that can hold felony trials.

technical violation: Probation/parole violation of rules that does not involve a new crime.

termination hearing: Process for legally severing the parent–child relationship. Initiated by the filing of a petition in family court, and almost always brought forth by a child welfare agency. Requires a finding of "unfitness" and a determination of the best interests of the child.

theory: Building block for scientific knowledge that organizes events, explains past events, and predicts future ones.

therapeutic community: Residential drug treatment program based on Alcoholics Anonymous, emphasizing addicts helping one another to become socially conforming persons.

"three strikes and you're out": Metaphor for life imprisonment upon conviction for a third felony.

token economy: Method for employment of positive reinforcement.

training school: State facility that houses young offenders.

"truth in sentencing": System that excludes discretionary release and severely limits time off for good behavior.

twelve-step programs: Method for treating substance abuse; Alcoholics Anonymous.

unconscious: "Hidden" psychic phenomenon that drives conscious.

victim impact statement: That part of a presentence report that addresses harm to the victim.

victim services: A range of activities, which attend to the needs of victims and witnesses, coordinate their testimony, and support them until their case is resolved in the criminal justice system.

waiver of jurisdiction: A court action "certifying" the youth as eligible for trial as an adult because it appears rehabilitation is unlikely or the crime was particularly atrocious.

work release: Program that permits select inmates to leave incarceration during the day for employment.

youth authority: State agency responsible for the incarceration and supervision of young offenders.

References

Abadinsky, Howard
    1983   *The Criminal Elite: Professional and Organized Crime.* Westport, CT: Green-
                wood.
    2003a   *Organized Crime,* 7th ed. Belmont, CA: Wadsworth.
    2003b   *Law and Justice,* 5th ed. Upper Saddle River, NJ: Prentice Hall.
    2004   *Drugs: An Introduction,* 5th ed. Belmont, CA: Wadsworth.

Abruzzese, George
    1999   "Idaho Youth Ranch: A Seamless Continuum of Care for Today's Youth."
                Juvenile Justice Magazine (January/February): Internet.

Adair, David N. and Toby D. Slawsky
    1991   "Looking at the Law: Fact-Finding in Sentencing." *Federal Probation* 55
                (December): 58–72.

Administrative Office of the Courts n.d. *Community Service.* Trenton, NJ: AOC.
    1996   *Overview and Summary of the Arizona Probation Outcome Study.* Phoenix:
                Arizona Supreme Court.

Agnew, Robert
    1992   "Foundation for a General Strain Theory of Crime and Delinquency." *Crimi-
                nology* 30 (February): 47–87.

Agopian, Michael W.
    1990   "The Impact of Intensive Supervision Probation on Gang-Drug Offenders."
                Criminal Justice Policy 4 (3): 214–22.

Aichhorn, August
    1963   *Wayward Youth.* New York: Viking Press.

Albanese, Jay S., Bernadette A. Fiore, Jerie H. Powell, and Janet R. Storti
    1981   *Is Probation Working?* Washington, DC: University Press of America.

Alexander, Franz and Hugo Staub
    1956   *The Criminal, the Judge, and the Public.* Glencoe, IL: Free Press.

Allen, Fred C., ed.
    1926   *Extracts from Penological Reports and Lectures Written by Members of the
                Management and Staff of the New York State Reformatory, Elmira, N.Y.*
                Elmira, NY: Summary Press.

Allen, G. Frederick and Harvey Treger
   1994   "Fines and Restitution Orders: Probationers' Perceptions." *Federal Probation* 58 (June): 34–40.

Allen, Harry, Eric Carlson, and Evalyn Parks
   1979   *Critical Issues in Probation.* Washington, DC: U.S. Government Printing Office.

Altschuler, David M. and Troy L. Armstrong
   1994   *Intensive Aftercare for High-Risk Juveniles.* Washington, DC: Office of Juvenile Justice and Delinquency Prevention.

American Bar Association (ABA)
   1970   *Standards Relating to Probation.* Chicago: ABA.

American Correctional Association (ACA)
   1981   *Standards for Adult Probation and Parole Field Services.* Rockville, MD: ACA.

American Friends Service Committee (AFSC)
   1971   *Struggle for Justice.* New York: Hill and Wang.

American Justice Institute
   1981   *Presentence Investigation Report Program.* Sacramento, CA: American Justice Institute.

American Probation and Parole Association (APPA)
   1995   *Abolishing Parole: Why the Emperor Has No Clothes.* Lexington, KY: APPA.

Anderson, Elijah
   1994   "The Code of the Streets." *Atlantic Monthly* (May): 80–94.

Anderson, James F., Laronistine Dyson, and Tazinski Lee
   1997   "A Four Year Tracking Investigation on Boot Camp Participants: A Study of Recidivism Outcome." *Justice Professional* 10 (September): 199–213.

Anderson, Lisa
   1998   "Is 'Supermax' Too Much?" *Chicago Tribune* (August 2): 1, 15.

Andreski, Stanislav, ed.
   1971   *Herbert Spencer: Structure, Function and Evolution.* New York: Scribners.

Andrews, D. A., Ivan Zinger, Robert D. Hoge, James Bonta, Paul Gendreau, and Francis T. Cullen
   1990   "Does Correctional Treatment Work? Clinically Relevant and Psychologically Informed Mcta-Analysis." *Criminology* 28 (August): 369–404.
   1991   *Annual Report of the San Francisco Adult Probation Department.* San Francisco, CA.

Andrews, Edmund L.
   2003   "Economic Inequality Grew in 90's Boom, Fed Reports." *New York Times* (January 23): C1, 7.

Anspach, Donald F. and S. Henry Monsen
   1989   "Indeterminate Sentencing, Formal Rationality, and Khadi Justice in Maine: An Application of Weber's Typology." *Journal of Criminal Justice* 17: 471–85.

APPA. *See* American Probation and Parole Association.

Arcaya, Jose
   1973   "The Multiple Realities Inherent in Probation Counseling." *Federal Probation* 37 (December).

"Arkansas: Early Release for 680 Inmates."
   2003   *New York Times* (June 2): 14.

Arola, Terryl and Richard Lawrence

    1998   "Assaults and Threats Against Probation Officers and Some Responses to Officers' Safety Concerns." Paper presented at the annual meeting of the Academy of Criminal Justice Sciences, March 12.

Ashford, Jose B. and Craig Winston LeCroy

    1988   "Predicting Recidivism: An Evaluation of the Wisconsin Juvenile Probation and Aftercare Risk Instrument." *Criminal Justice and Behavior* 15 (June): 141–49.

Associated Press

    1995   "Sweep of State Prison for Drugs Termed Largest Such Raid Ever." *New York Times* (October 24): 12.

    1998   "12 Convicted in Prison Plot to Control Drug Gangs." *New York Times* (May 31): 8.

    1999   "California Has 2.5 Million Unserved Warrants" (June 23): Internet.

    2000   "Guards Fired Over Camp Activities" (January 11): Internet.

    2001   "Arkansas Corrections Board Agrees to Release Prisoners Early to Ease Overcrowding." *New Jersey Online* (November 27): Internet.

Atherton, Alexine L.

    1987   "Journal Retrospective, 1845–1986: 200 Years of Prison Society History as Reflected in the *Prison Journal.*" *Prison Journal* (Spring-Summer): 1–37.

Attica Commission. *See* New York State Special Commission on Attica.

"Auburn Correctional Facility"

    1998   *Department of Correctional Services Today* (April): Internet.

Auerbach, Barbara J., George E. Sexton, Franklin C. Farrow, and Robert H. Lawson

    1988   *Work in American Prisons: The Private Sector Gets Involved.* Washington, DC: U.S. Government Printing Office.

Augustus, John

    1972   *John Augustus, First Probation Officer.* Montclair, NJ: Patterson Smith.

Austin, James and Garry Coventry

    2001   *Emerging Issues on Privatized Prisons.* Washington, DC: Bureau of Justice Assistance.

    2003   "A Second Look at the Private Prison Debate." *The Criminologist* 28 (September/October): 1, 3–9.

Austin, James and John Irwin

    2001   *It's About Time: America's Imprisonment Binge,* 3rd ed. Belmont, CA: Wadsworth.

Baird, S. Christopher, Richard C. Heinz, and Brian J. Bemus

    1982   "The Wisconsin Case Classification/Staff Development Project: A Two-Year Follow-Up Report," in *Classification: American Correctional Association Monographs.* College Park, MD: American Correctional Association.

Baird, S. Christopher and Dennis Wagner

    1990   "Measuring Diversion: The Florida Community Control Program." *Crime and Delinquency* 36 (January): 112–25.

Bakal, Yitzhak

    1974   *Closing Correctional Institutions.* Lexington, MA: D.C. Heath.

Baldwin, John D. and Janice I.

    1998   *Behavior Principles in Everyday Life,* 3rd ed. Upper Saddle River, NJ: Prentice Hall.

Bales, William D. and Linda G. Dees

    1992   "Mandatory Minimum Sentences in Florida: Past Trends and Future Implications." *Crime and Delinquency* 38 (July): 309–29.

Ball, Richard A., C. Ronald Huff, and J. Robert Lilly

    1988   *House Arrest and Correctional Policy: Doing Time at Home.* Beverly Hills, CA: Sage.

Bandura, Albert

    1974   "Behavior Theory and the Models of Man." *American Psychologist* 29 (December): 859–69.

Barnes, Carole Wolff and Randal S. Franz

    1989   "Questionably Adult: Determinants and Effects of the Juvenile Waiver Decision." *Justice Quarterly* 6 (March): 117–35.

Baumgartner, Werner A., Virginia Hill, and William H. Blahd

    1989   "Hair Analysis for Drugs of Abuse." *Journal of Forensic Sciences* 34 (November): 1433–53.

Bazemore, Gordon

    1994   "Developing a Victim Orientation for Community Corrections: A Restorative Justice Paradigm and a Balanced Mission." *Perspectives* (special issue): 19–24.

Bazemore, Gordon and Dennis Maloney

    1994   "Rehabilitating Community Service: Toward Restorative Service Sanctions in a Balanced Justice System." *Federal Probation* 58 (March): 24–35.

Bazemore, Gordon and Mark S. Umbreit

    1994   *Balanced and Restorative Justice: Program Summary.* Washington, DC: Office of Juvenile Justice and Delinquency Prevention.

    1995   "Rethinking the Sanctioning Function in Juvenile Court: Retributive or Restorative Responses to Youth Crime." *Crime and Delinquency* 41 (July): 296–316.

Beaumont, Gustave de and Alexis de Tocqueville

    1964   *On the Penitentiary System in the United States and Its Application in France.* Carbondale, IL: Southern Illinois University Press. (Originally published in 1833.)

Beck, Allen J.

    2000a   *Prison and Jail Inmates at Midyear 1999.* Washington, DC: Office of Justice Programs.

    2000b   *Prisoners in 1999.* Washington, DC: Office of Justice Programs.

Beck, Allen J. and Jennifer C. Karberg

    2001   *Prison and Jail Inmates at Midyear 2000.* Washington, DC: Office of Justice Programs.

Becker, Gary S.

    1968   *The Economic Approach to Human Behavior.* Chicago: University of Chicago Press.

Behind Bars

    1998   Washington, DC: National Institute of Justice.

Bellis, David J.

    1981   *Heroin and Politicians: The Failure of Public Policy to Control Addiction in America.* Westport, CT: Greenwood.

Belluck, Pam

    2001   "Desperate for Prison Guards, Some States Even Rob the Cradle." *New York Times* (April 21): 1, 10.

Bennett, Lawrence A.

    1988   "Practice in Search of a Theory: The Case of Intensive Supervision—An Extension of an Old Practice." *American Journal of Criminal Justice* 12: 293–310.

Berg, Michael H.

1997   "United States Probation Officers: The Court's Financial Investigators." *Federal Probation* 61 (March): 28–30.

Bersani, Carl A.

1989   "Reality Therapy: Issues and a Review of Research." In *Correctional Counseling and Treatment*, edited by Peter C. Kratcoski, 2: 177–95. Prospect Heights, IL: Waveland Press.

Binder, Arnold and Gilbert Geis

1983   *Methods of Research in Criminology and Criminal Justice.* New York: McGraw-Hill.

Bishop, Donna M., Charles F. Frazier, and John C. Henretta

1989   "Prosecutorial Waiver: Case Study of a Questionable Reform." *Crime and Delinquency* 35 (April): 179–201.

Bisman, Cynthia D.

2000   "Social Work Assessment: Case Theory Construction." *Families in Society: The Journal of Contemporary Human Services* 80 (May–June): 240–47

Black, Donald W. with C. Lindon Larson

1999   *Confronting Antisocial Personality Disorder.* New York: Oxford University Press.

Blair, Jayson

2000   "Boot Camps: An Idea Whose Time Came and Went." *New York Times* (January 2): WK 3.

Bloom, Barbara and Anne McDiarmid

2001   "Gender-Responsive Supervision and Programming for Women Offenders in the Community." Pages 11–18 in *Responding to Women Offenders in the Community.* Washington, DC: National Institute of Corrections.

Bloom, Barbara, Barbara Owen, and Stephanie Covington

2003   *Gender-Responsive Strategies Research, Practice, and Guiding Principles for Women Offenders.* Washington, DC: National Institute of Corrections.

Blumberg, Abraham

1970   *Criminal Justice.* Chicago: Quadrangle Books.

Blumenstein, Alfred

1984   "Sentencing Reforms: Impacts and Implications." *Judicature* 68 (October-November).

Bodapati, Madhava R., James W. Marquardt, and Steven J. Cuvelier

1993   "Influence of Race and Gender in Parole Decision Making in Texas: 1980–1991." Paper presented at the annual meeting of the Academy of Criminal Justice Sciences, Kansas City, MO, March 16–20.

Bohlen, Celestine

1989   "Expansion Sought for 'Shock' Prison." *New York Times* (June 8): 14.

Boldt, Richard C.

1998   "Rehabilitative Punishment and the Drug Treatment Court Movement." *Washington University Law Quarterly* 76: 1205–1306.

Bootzin, Richard R.

1975   *Behavior Modification and Therapy: An Introduction.* Cambridge, MA: Winthrop.

Borden, William

2000   "The Relational Paradigm in Contemporary Psychoanalysis: Toward a Psychodynamically Informed Social Work Perspective." *Social Service Review* 74 (September): 352–79.

Boswell, John
 1989 *The Kindness of Strangers: The Abandonment of Children in Western Europe from Antiquity to the Renaissance.* New York: Pantheon.

Bowers, Swithun
 1950 "The Nature and Definition of Social Casework." In *Principles and Techniques in Social Casework: Selected Articles, 1940–1950,* edited by Cora Kasius, 97–27. New York: Family Service Association of America.

Bradsher, Keith
 1995a "Gap in Wealth in U.S. Called Widest in West." *New York Times* (April 17): 1, C4.
 1995b "Low Ranking for Poor American Children." *New York Times* (August 14): 7.

Breed, Allen F.
 1998 "Corrections: A Victim of Situational Ethics." *Crime and Delinquency* 44 (January): 9–18.

Brennan, Thomas P., Amy E. Gedrich, Susan E. Jacoby, Michael J. Tardy, and Katherine B. Tyson
 1986 "Forensic Social Work: Practice and Vision." *Social Casework* 67: 340–50.

Brockway, Z. R.
 1926 "Character of Reformatory Prisoners." In *Extracts from Penological Reports and Lectures Written by Members of the Management and Staff of the New York State Reformatory, Elmira, N.Y.,* edited by Fred C. Allen, 110–18. Elmira, NY: Summary Press.

Broder, John M.
 2004 "Dismal California Prisons Hold Juvenile Offenders." *New York Times* (February 15): 18.

Brooke, James
 1997 "Prisons: A Growth Industry for Some." *New York Times* (November 2): 14.

Brown, Allan G.
 1986 *Group Work,* 2nd ed. Brookfield, VT: Gower.

Brown, Marjorie
 1984 *Executive Summary of Research Findings from the Massachusetts Risk/Need Classification System, Report 5.* Boston: Office of the Commissioner of Probation.

Brown, Waln K., Timothy Miller, Richard L. Jenkins, and Warren A. Rhodes
 1991 "The Human Costs of 'Giving the Kid Another Chance.'" *International Journal of Offender Therapy and Comparative Criminology* 35: 296–302.

Bureau of Justice Statistics
 2001 "Forty-Two Percent of State Parole Discharges Were Successful." Press release (October 3).

Burns, Jerald C.
 1993 "Rediscovering That Rehabilitation Works: The Alabama Boot Camp Experience." Paper presented at the annual meeting of the Academy of Criminal Justice Sciences, Kansas City, MO, March 16–20.

Burns, Jerald C. and Gennaro F. Vito
 1995 "An Impact Analysis of the Alabama Boot Camp Program." *Federal Probation* 59 (March): 63–67.

Burrow, Linda, Jennifer Joseph, and John Whitehead
 2001 "A Comparison of Recidivism in Intensive Supervision and Regular Probation: Results from a Southern Jurisdiction." Paper presented at the annual meeting of the Academy of Criminal Justice Sciences, Washington, DC, April 3–7.

Butterfield, Fox

> 1995a   "Prison-Building Binge in California Casts Shadow on Higher Education." *New York Times* (April 12): 11.
>
> 1998b   "Prisons Replace Hospitals for the Nation's Mentally Ill." *New York Times* (March 5): 1, 18.
>
> 1998c   "U.S. and Georgia in Deal to Improve Juvenile Prisons." *New York Times* (March 22): 16.
>
> 1998d   "Profits at Juvenile Prisons Earned at a Chilling Cost." *New York Times* (July 15): 1, 14.
>
> 1998e   "U.S. Suing Louisiana on Prison Ills." *New York Times* (November 6): 14.
>
> 2000a   "Louisiana Settles Suite, Abandoning Private Youth Prisons." *New York Times* (September 8): 12.
>
> 2000b   "Often, Parole is One Stop on the Way Back to Prison." *New York Times* (November 29): 1, 28.
>
> 2003a   "Inmates Go Free to Reduce Deficits." *New York Times* (December 19): 1, 20
>
> 2003b   "Infections in Newly Released Inmates Are Rising Concern." *New York Times* (January 28): 14.
>
> 2004a   "Study Tracks Boom in Prisons and Notes Impact on Counties." *New York Times* (April 30): 19.
>
> 2004b   "Almost 10% of All Prisoners Are Now Serving Life Terms." *New York Times* (May 12): 17.

Butts, Jeffrey A., Howard W. Snyder, Terrence A. Finnegan, Anne L. Aughenbaugh, and Rowen S. Poole

> 1996   *Juvenile Court Statistics 1994.* Washington, DC: Office of Juvenile Justice and Delinquency Prevention.

Byrne, James M.

> 1990   "The Future of Intensive Probation Supervision and the New Intermediate Sanction." *Crime and Delinquency* 36 (January): 6–41.

Byrne, James M., Arthur J. Lurigio, and S. Christopher Baird

> 1989   "The Effectiveness of New Intensive Probation Supervision Programs." *Research in Corrections* 2 (September): 1–48.

Cahalan, Margaret Werner

> 1986   *Historical Corrections Statistics in the United States, 1850–1984.* Washington, DC: U.S. Government Printing Office.

Campbell, Curtis, Candace McCoy, and Chimezie A. B. Osigweh

> 1990   "The Influence of Probation Recommendations on Sentencing Decisions and Their Predictive Accuracy." *Federal Probation* 54 (December): 13–21.

Carlson, Eric and Evalyn Parks

> 1979   *Critical Issues in Adult Probation: Issues in Probation Management.* Washington, DC: U.S. Government Printing Office.

Carlson, Jill M.

> 1993   "Restorative Justice: Beyond Crime and Punishment." Master of Science Thesis, Mankato State University, Minnesota.

Carlson, Susan M. and Michael Michalowski

> 1997   "Crime, Unemployment, and Social Structures of Accumulation: An Inquiry Into Historical Contingency." *Justice Quarterly* 14 (June): 209–41.

Carter, Robert M.

> 1966   "It Is Respectfully Recommended . . ." *Federal Probation* (June).

Castellano, Thomas C.

> 1997   *Illinois' PreStart Program Revisited: A Further Look at Its Impact on Staff, the Prison System, and Offender Rehabilitation.* Chicago: Illinois Criminal Justice Information Authority.

Center for Sex Offender Management (CSOM)

2001a   "Myths and Facts About Sex Offenders." *Perspectives* 25 (Summer): 34–39.
2001b   Case Studies on the Center for Sex Offender Management's National Resource Sites, 2nd ed. Silver Spring, MD: CSOM.

Champion, Dean J.

1988a   "Felony Plea Bargaining and Probation: A Growing Judicial and Prosecutorial Dilemma." *Journal of Criminal Justice* 16: 291–301.
1988b   *Felony Probation: Problems and Prospects*. New York: Praeger.

Chapin, Bradley

1983   *Criminal Justice in Colonial America: 1600–1660*. Athens: University of Georgia Press.

Chen, David W.

2000   "Compensation Set on Attica Uprising." *New York Times* (August 29): 1, 25.

Chesney, Steven L.

n.d.   "The Assessment of Restitution in the Minnesota Probation Services." In *Restitution in Criminal Justice*, edited by Joe Hudson. St. Paul: Minnesota Department of Corrections.

Chesney-Lind, Meda

1997   *The Female Offender: Girls, Women, and Crime*. Thousand Oaks, CA: Sage.

Childress, Anna Rose

1993   "Medications in Drug Abuse Treatment." Pages 73–75 in *Second Annual Conference on Drug Abuse Research and Practice: An Alliance for the 21st Century*. Rockville, MD: National Institute on Drug Abuse.

Childress, Anna Rose, A. Thomas McLellan, and Charles P. O'Brien

1985   "Behavioral Therapies for Substance Abuse." *International Journal of the Addictions* 20: 947–69.

Chira, Susan

1994   "Study Confirms Worst Fears on U.S. Children." *New York Times* (April 12): 1, 11.

Clark, Cherie L., David W. Aziz, and Doris L. MacKenzie

1994   *Shock Incarceration in New York: Focus on Treatment*. Washington, DC: National Institute of Justice.

"Clean and Sober—And Agnostic"

1991   *Newsweek* (July 8): 62–63.

Clear, Todd and Ronald P. Corbett

1998   "Community Corrections of Place." *Perspectives* 23 (Winter): 24–32.

Clear, Todd R., Suzanne Flynn, and Carol Shapiro

1987   "Intensive Supervision in Probation: A Comparison of Three Projects." In *Intermediate Punishments: Intensive Supervision, Home Confinement and Electronic Surveillance*, edited by Belinda R. McCarthy, 31–50. Monsey, NY: Criminal Justice Press.

Clear, Todd R. and Patricia R. Hardyman

1990   "The New Intensive Supervision Movement." *Crime and Delinquency* 36 (January): 42–60.

Clear, Todd R. and Edward J. Latessa

1989   "Intensive Supervision: Surveillance vs. Treatment." Paper presented at the annual meeting of the Academy of Criminal Justice Sciences, Washington, DC, March 30.

Clem, Constance, Barbara Krauth, and Larry Linke

1998   *A Field Evaluation of the Interstate Compact for Probation and Parole: Findings from an NIC Survey*. Washington, DC: National Institute of Corrections.

Clemmer, Donald
      1958   *The Prison Community*. New York: Holt, Rinehart and Winston.

Cloninger, Susan C.
      2004   *Theories of Personality: Understanding Persons*, 4th ed. Upper Saddle River, NJ: Prentice Hall.

Cloward, Richard A., and Lloyd E. Ohlin
      1960   *Delinquency and Opportunity*. New York: Free Press.

Cohen, Albert K.
      1965   *Delinquent Boys*. New York: Free Press.

Cohen, Lawrence E.
      1975   *New Directions in Processing of Juvenile Offenders: The Denver Model*. Washington, DC: U.S. Government Printing Office.

Cohen, Noam S.
      1992   "20 Years After Siege Ended in Blood, Attica Is New Prison but Wary Town." *New York Times* (September 1): 15.

Cohn, Alvin W.
      2002   "Managing the Correctional Enterprise—The Quest for 'What Works.'" *Federal Probation* 66 (September): 4–9.

Collier, Walter V.
      1980   *Summary of First Year Evaluation of the Special Parole Supervision for Violent Felony Offenders*. Albany: New York State Division of Parole.

Comptroller General of the United States
      1979   *Correctional Institutions Can Do More to Improve the Employability of Offenders*. Washington, DC: U.S. Government Printing Office.

Cooper, Irving Ben
      1977   "*United States v. Unterman:* The Role of Counsel at Sentencing." *Criminal Law Bulletin* 13.

"Court Orders Trial on Ban of Voting By Felons."
      2003   *New York Times* (December 20): 15.

Crawford, Cheryl A.
      1994   "Health Care Needs in Corrections: NIJ Responds." *National Institute of Justice Journal* (November): 31–8.

Crawford, William B., Jr.
      1988   "Inmates Suing Over Gangs Lose Case." *Chicago Tribune* (March 8): Sec. 2: 3.

Cromwell, Paul F., Jr.
      1978   "The Halfway House and Offender Reintegration." In *Corrections in the Community*, 2nd ed., edited by George C. Killinger, and Paul F. Cromwell, Jr. St. Paul, MN: West.

Cronin, Roberta C. with Mei Han
      1994   *Boot Camp for Adult and Juvenile Offenders: Overview and Update*. Washington, DC: National Institute of Justice.

Crowe, Ann H.
      1998   "Restorative Justice and Offender Rehabilitation: A Meeting of the Minds." *Perspectives* 22 (Summer): 28–40.

Crowley, Jim
      1998   "Victim-Offender Mediation: Paradigm Shift or Old Fashioned Accountability?" *Community Links* (Spring): 10.

Cullen, Francis T. and Karen E. Gilbert
      1982   *Reaffirming Rehabilitation*. Cincinnati: Anderson.

Cullen, Francis T., Nicholas Williams, and John Paul Wright

    1997   "Work Conditions and Juvenile Delinquency: Is Youth Employment Criminogenic?" *Criminal Justice Policy Review* 8 (2–3): 119–43.

    2002   "Environmental Corrections—A New Paradigm for Effective Probation and Parole Supervision." Federal *Probation* 66 (September): 28–37.

Curran, Daniel J.

    1988   "Destructuring Privatization and the Promise of Juvenile Diversion: Compromising Community-Based Corrections." *Crime and Delinquency* 34 (October): 363–78.

Czajkoski, Eugene H.

    1973   "Exposing the Quasi-Judicial Role of the Probation Officer." *Federal Probation* 37 (September): 9–13.

Darrow, Clarence

    1975   *Address to the Prisoners in the Cook County Jail, 1902.* Chicago: Charles H. Kerr.

Davidoff-Kroop, Joy

    1983   *An Initial Assessment of the Division of Parole's Employment Services.* Albany: New York State Division of Parole.

Degler, Carl N.

    1991   *In Search of Human Nature: The Decline and Revival of Darwinism in American Social Thought.* New York: Oxford University Press.

Delbanco, Andrew and Thomas Delbanco

    1995   "At the Crossroads." *New Yorker* (March 20): 50–63.

del Carmen, Rolando V.

    1985   "Legal Issues and Liabilities in Community Corrections." In *Probation, Parole, and Community Corrections: A Reader*, edited by Lawrence F. Travis III, 47–70. Prospect Heights, IL: Waveland Press.

del Carmen, Rolando V., Maldine Beth Barnhill, Gene Bonham, Jr., Lance Hignite, and Todd Jermstad

    2001   *Civil Liabilities and Other Legal Issues for Probation/Parole Officers and Supervisors.* Washington, DC: National Institute of Corrections.

del Carmen, Rolando V. and Paul T. Louis

    1988   *Civil Liabilities of Parole Personnel for Release, Non-Release, Supervision, and Revocation.* Washington, DC: National Institute of Corrections.

De Leon, George

    1994   "The Therapeutic Community: Toward a General Theory and Model." Pages 16–53 in *Therapeutic Community: Advances in Research and Application.* Rockville, MD: National Institute on Drug Abuse.

DeLong, James V.

    1972   "Treatment and Rehabilitation." Pages 173–254 in *Dealing With Drug Abuse: A Report to the Ford Foundation.* New York: Praeger.

Denzlinger, Jerry D. and David E. Miller

    1991   "The Federal Probation Officer: Life Before and After Guideline Sentencing." *Federal Probation* 55 (December): 49–63.

Deschenes, Elizabeth Piper, Susan Turner, and Joan Petersilia

    1995   "A Dual Experiment in Intensive Community Supervision: Minnesota's Prison Diversion and Enhanced Supervised Release Programs." *The Prison Journal* 75 (September): 330–56.

Dickey, Walter

    1979   "The Lawyer and the Accuracy of the Presentence Report." *Federal Probation* 43 (June): 29–39.

Dietrich, Shelle
>   1979   "The Probation Officer as Therapist: Examination of Three Major Problem Areas." *Federal Probation* 43 (June).

Dighton, Daniel
>   1997   "States Broaden Scope of Transfer Laws." *The Compiler* 17 (Fall): 11–15.

DiIulio, John J., Jr.
>   1993   "Rethinking the Criminal Justice System: Toward a New Paradigm." In *Performance Measures for the Criminal Justice System,* 1–16. Washington, DC: Bureau of Justice Statistics.

Division of Probation
>   1974   "The Selective Presentence Investigation." *Federal Probation* 38 (December).

Dobrzynski, Judith H.
>   1997   "For a Summer Getaway, a Model Prison." *New York Times* (July 11): B1.

Dolan, Edward J., Richard Lunden, and Rosemary Barberet
>   1987   "Prison Behavior and Parole Outcome in Massachusetts." Paper presented at the annual meeting of the American Society of Criminology, Montreal, November 11–14.

Dole, Vincent
>   1980   "Addictive Behavior." *Scientific American* 243: 138–54.

Donovan, Dennis M.
>   1988   "Assessment of Addictive Behaviors: Implications for an Emerging Bio-psychosocial Model." Pages 3–48 in *Assessment of Addictive Behaviors,* edited by Dennis M. Donovan and G. Alan Marrlatt. New York: Guilford.

Dressler, David
>   1951   *Parole Chief.* New York: Viking.

Drug Court Movement
>   1995   Washington, DC: National Institute of Justice.

Dumm, Thomas L.
>   1987   *Democracy and Punishment: Disciplinary Origins of the United States.* Madison: University of Wisconsin Press.

Dunn, Ashley
>   1995   "U.S. Inquiry Finds Detention Center Was Poorly Run." *New York Times* (July 22): 1, 8.

DuPont, Robert L. and John P. McGovern
>   1994   *A Bridge to Recovery: An Introduction to 12-Step Programs.* Washington, DC: American Psychiatric Press.

Durham, Alexis M., III
>   1989a   "Origins of Interest in the Privatization of Punishment: The Nineteenth and Twentieth Century American Experience." *Criminology* 27 (February): 107–39.
>   1989c   "Newgate of Connecticut: Origins and Early Days of an Early American Prison." *Justice Quarterly* 6 (March): 89–116.

Dzur, Albert W. and Alan Wertheimer
>   2002   "Forgiveness and Public Deliberation: The Practice of Restorative Justice." *Criminal Justice Ethics* 21 (Winter/Spring): 3–21.

Eig, Jonathan
>   1998   "Deep Hole." *Chicago* (July): 60–4, 87–9.

Eisenkraft, Noah
>   2001   "Taxation Without Representation." *Harvard Political Review* (Winter): Internet.

"Elmira"

    1998   *DOC Today* (October): Internet.

Empey, LaMar T., ed.

    1979   *Juvenile Justice: The Progressive Legacy and Current Reforms.* Charlottesville: University Press of Virginia.

English, Kim, Suzanne Pullen, and Linda Jones

    1997   *Managing Adult Sex Offenders in the Community—A Containment Approach.* Washington, DC: National Institute of Justice.

Erikkson, Torsten

    1976   *The Reformers: An Historical Survey of Pioneer Experiments in the Treatment of Criminals.* New York: Elsevier.

Erwin, Billie S.

    1984   *Evaluation of Intensive Supervision in Georgia.* Atlanta: Georgia Department of Offender Rehabilitation.

Erwin, Billie S. and Lawrence A. Bennett

    1987   *New Dimensions in Probation: Georgia's Experience with Intensive Probation Supervision.* Washington, DC: National Institute of Justice.

Eskridge, Chris W. and Eric W. Carlson

    1979   "The Use of Volunteers in Probation: A National Synthesis." *Journal of Offender Counseling Services and Rehabilitation* 4 (Winter).

Fabricant, Michael

    1983   *Juveniles in the Family Courts.* Lexington, MA: D. C. Heath.

Falk, Gerhard

    1966   "The Psychoanalytic Theories of Crime Causation." *Criminologica* 4 (May).

Fallen, David L., Craig D. Apperson, Joan Hall-Milligan, and Steven Aos

    1981   *Intensive Parole Supervision.* Olympia: Washington Department of Social and Health Services.

Feeley, Malcolm M.

    1979   *The Process Is Punishment: Handling Cases in a Lower Court.* New York: Russell Sage Foundation.

Feeley, Malcolm M. and Jonathan Simon

    1992   "The New Penology: Note on the Emerging Strategy of Corrections and Its Implications." *Criminology* 30 (November): 449–74.

Feld, Barry C.

    1988   "In Re Gault Revisited: A Cross-State Comparison of the Right to Counsel in Juvenile Court." *Crime and Delinquency* 34 (October): 393–424.

    1992   "Criminalizing the Juvenile Court: A Research Agenda for the 1990s." In *Juvenile Justice and Public Policy: Toward a National Agenda,* edited by Ira M. Schwartz, 59–88. Lexington, MA: Lexington Books.

    2003   "The Politics of Race and Juvenile Justice: The 'Due Process Revolution' and the Conservative Reaction." *Justice Quarterly* 20 (December): 765–800.

Female Offender Resource Center

    1979   *Little Sisters and the Law.* Washington, DC: U.S. Government Printing Office.

Finckenauer, James O.

    1984   *Juvenile Delinquency and Corrections: The Gap Between Theory and Practice.* New York: Academic Press.

Finder, Alan

    1997   "New York's Chief Judge Moves to Assure Family Courts are Open to Public." *New York Times* (June 19): 18.

Finn, Peter

    1997   *Sex Offender Community Notification.* Washington, DC: National Institute of Justice.

    1998   *The Delaware Department of Corrections Life Skills Program.* Washington, DC: National Institute of Justice.

Finn, Peter and Dale Parent

    1992   *Making the Offender Foot the Bill: A Texas Program.* Washington, DC: National Institute of Justice.

Foderaro, Lisa W.

    1995   "Can Problem Drinkers Really Just Cut Back?" *New York Times* (May 28): 15.

Fogel, David

    1975   *We Are the Living Proof.* Cincinnati, OH: Anderson.

Fox, Vernon

    1977   *Community-Based Corrections.* Upper Saddle River, NJ: Prentice Hall.

France, Anatole

    1927   *The Red Lily,* translated by Winifred Stephens. New York: Dodd, Mead.

Frawley, P. Joseph and James W. Smith

    1990   "Chemical Aversion Therapy in the Treatment of Cocaine Dependence as Part of a Mulitmodal Treatment Program." *Journal of Substance Abuse Treatment* 7: 21–9.

Freud, Sigmund

    1933   *New Introductory Lectures on Psychoanalysis.* New York: W. W. Norton.

Friedlander, Walter A.

    1958   *Concepts and Methods of Social Work.* Upper Saddle River, NJ: Prentice Hall.

Friedman, Lawrence M.

    1973   *A History of American Law.* New York: Simon and Schuster.

"Full-Employment Prisons"

    2001   *New York Times* editorial (August 23): 20.

Galaif, Elisha and Steve Sussman

    1995   "For Whom Does Alcoholics Anonymous Work?" *International Journal of the Addictions* 30 (No. 2): 161–84.

Gaylin, Willard

    1974   *Partial Justice: A Study of Bias in Sentencing.* New York: Alfred A. Knopf.

Gebelein, Richard S.

    2000   *The Rebirth of Rehabilitation: Promise and Perils of Drug Courts.* Washington, DC: Office of Justice Programs.

Geerken, Michael R. and Hennessey D. Hayes

    1993   "Probation and Parole: Public Risk and the Future of Incarceration Alternatives." *Criminology* 31 (November): 549–64.

Gehm, John R.

    1998   "Victim-Offender Mediation Programs: An Exploration of Practice and Theoretical Frameworks." *Western Criminology Review* 1 (1): Internet.

Gendreau, Paul and Robert R. Ross

    1987   "Revivification of Rehabilitation: Evidence from the 1980s." *Justice Quarterly* 4 (September): 350–407.

Gerstein, Dean R. and Henrick J. Harwood, eds.

    1990   *Treating Drug Problems, Vol. I: A Study of the Evolution, Effectiveness, and Financing of Public and Private Drug Treatment Systems.* Washington, DC: National Academy Press.

Gilligan, Leilah and Tom Talbot

    2000   *Community Supervision of the Sex Offender: An Overview of Current and Promising Practices.* Silver Spring, MD: Center for Sex Offender Management.

Gillin, John T.

    1931   *Taming the Criminal.* New York: Macmillan.

Gladding, Samuel T.

    1999   *Group Work: A Counseling Specialty.* Upper Saddle River, NJ: Prentice Hall.

Glaser, Daniel

    1969   *The Effectiveness of a Prison and Parole System.* Indianapolis, IN: Bobbs-Merrill.

Glasser, William

    1975   *Reality Therapy.* New York: Harper and Row. (Originally published in 1965.)
    1976   *The Identity Society.* New York: Harper and Row.
    1980   "Reality Therapy: An Explanation of the Steps of Reality Therapy." In *What Are You Doing? How People Are Helped Through Reality Therapy*, edited by Naomi Glasser. New York: Harper and Row.
    1998   *Choice Theory: A New Psychology of Personal Freedom.* New York: HarperCollins.
    2000   *Reality Therapy in Action.* New York: HarperCollins.

Glaze, Lauren E.

    2003   *Probation and Parole in the United States, 2002.* Washington, DC: Bureau of Justice Statistics.

Glueck, Sheldon, ed.

    1933   *Probation and Criminal Justice.* New York: Macmillan.

Goetting, Victor L.

    1974   "Some Pragmatic Aspects of Opening a Halfway House." *Federal Probation* 38 (December).

Goffman, Erving

    1961   *Asylums: Essays on the Social Situation of Mental Patients and Other Inmates.* Garden City, NY: Doubleday.

Goleman, Daniel

    1987   "Embattled Giant of Psychology Speaks His Mind." *New York Times* (August 25): 17, 18.

Goodstein, Lynne and John Hepburn

    1985   *Determinate Sentencing and Imprisonment: A Failure of Reform.* Cincinnati, OH: Anderson.

Graham, Judith

    2001a   "Low-Paying But Crucial Jobs Go Unfilled by the Thousands." *Chicago Tribune* (March 11): 1, 16.
    2001b   "Report Says Guard Shortages Threaten Texas Prison Safety." *Chicago Tribune* (February 24): 11.

Grann, David

    2004   "The Brand." *ss* (February 16 & 23): 157–71.

Greenberg, David F.

    1975   "Problems in Community Corrections." *Issues in Criminology* 10 (Spring).

Greenberg, David F. and Drew Humphries

    1980   "The Cooptation of Fixed Sentencing Reform." *Crime and Delinquency* 26 (April).

Greenfeld, Lawrence A. and Tracy L. Snell

    1999   *Women Offenders.* Washington, DC: Office of Justice Programs.

Greenhouse, Linda

 1997 "Immunity from Suits Is Withheld for Guards in Privately Run Jails." *New York Times* (June 24): 12.

 2003 "Justices Uphold Long Prison Terms in Repeat Crimes." *New York Times* (March 6): 1, 26.

Griggs, Bertram S. and Gary R. McCune

 1972 "Community-Based Correctional Programs: A Survey and Analysis." *Federal Probation* 36 (June).

Grissom, Grant R. and William L. Dubnov

 1989 *Without Locks and Bars: Reforming Our Reform Schools.* New York: Praeger.

Grogger, Jeffrey

 1989 *Employment and Crime.* Sacramento: Bureau of Criminal Statistics and Special Services.

Gross, Jane

 1992 "Collapse of Inner-City Families Creates America's New Orphans." *New York Times* (March 29): 1, 15.

Haas, Stephen and Edward J. Latessa

 1995 "Intensive Supervision in a Rural County: Diversion and Outcome." Pages 153-69 in *Intermediate Sanctions: Sentencing in the 1990s*, edited by John Ortiz Smykla and William Selke. Cincinnati: Anderson.

Haberman, Clyde

 2000 "In Turbulent Times, a Prison Boiled Over." *New York Times* (January 5): 23.

Hagerty, J. E.

 1934 *Twentieth Century Crime, Eighteenth Century Methods of Control.* Boston: Stratford.

Hahn, Paul H.

 1976 *Community Based Corrections and the Criminal Justice System.* Santa Cruz, CA: Davis.

Hall, Jerome

 1952 *Theft, Law and Society.* Indianapolis, IN: Bobbs-Merrill.

Hall, Trish

 1990 "New Way to Treat Alcoholism Discards Spiritualism of A.A." *New York Times* (December 24): 1, 10.

Hallet, Michael

 2004 "An Introduction to Prison Privatization." Pages 528–52 in *Visions for Change: Crime and Justice in the Twenty-First Century*, edited by Roslyn Ruskin and Albert R. Roberts. Upper Saddle River, NJ: Prentice-Hall.

Hammett, Theodore M., Lynne Harrold, and Joel Epstein

 1994 *Tuberculosis in Correctional Facilities.* Washington, DC: U.S. Government Printing Office.

Hardman, Dale G.

 1960 "Constructive Use of Authority." *Crime and Delinquency* 6 (July).

Harper, Robert Francis

 1904 *The Code of Hammurabi.* Chicago: University of Chicago Press.

Harris, George A. and David Watkins

 1987 *Counseling the Involuntary and Resistant Client.* College Park, MD: American Correctional Association.

Harris, Patricia M. and Lisa Graff

 1988 "A Critique of Juvenile Sentence Reform." *Federal Probation* 52 (September): 66–71.

Harrison, Paige M. and Allen J. Beck

    2003   *Prisoners in 2002.* Washington, DC: U.S. Bureau of Justice Statistics.

Hartman, Todd

    1994   "Suit Targets Neighbors Who Oppose Group Home." *Miami Herald* (November 11): B1, 3.

Healy, William, Augusta F. Bronner, and Anna Mae Bowers

    1930   *The Structure and Meaning of Psychoanalysis.* New York: Knopf.

Hemmens, Craig and Rolando del Carmen

    1997   "The Exclusionary Rule in Probation and Parole Revocation Proceedings: Does It Apply?" *Federal Probation* 61 (September): 32–9.

Henderson, Marta L.

    2004   "Employment and Crime from the Inmate's Perspective." Pages 84–94 in *Crime and Employment: Critical Issues in Crime Reduction for Corrections.* Edited by Jessie L. Krienert and Mark S. Fisher. Walnut Creek, CA: AltaMira Press.

Hergenhahn, B. R. and Matthew H. Olson

    1999   *An Introduction to Theories of Personality,* 5th ed. Upper Saddle River, NJ: Prentice Hall.

Herman, Ellen

    1995   *The Romance of American Psychology: Political Culture in the Age of Experts, 1940–1970.* Berkeley: University of California Press.

Hibbert, Christopher

    1968   *The Roots of Evil: A Social History of Crime and Punishment.* Boston: Little, Brown.

Hirsch, Adam Jay

    1992   *The Rise of the Penitentiary: Prisons and Punishment in Early America.* New Haven, CT: Yale University Press.

Hirschi, Travis

    1969   *Causes of Delinquency.* Berkeley: University of California Press.

Hollin, Clive R.

    1990   *Cognitive-Behavioral Interventions with Young Offenders.* New York: Pergamon Press.

Hollis, Florence

    1950   "The Techniques of Casework." In *Principles and Techniques of Social Casework: Selected Articles, 1940–1950,* edited by Cora Kasius, 412–26. New York: Family Service Association of America.

Holloway, Lynette

    1995   "Home for Handicapped Still Faces Rough Path." *New York Times* (July 18): 13.

Holmes, Cheryl L.

    1997   "AIDS and Supervision." *Federal Probation* 61 (March): 28.

Holzer, Harry J., Steven Raphael, and Michael A. Stoll

    2002   *Prisoner Reentry and the Institutions of Civil Society: Bridges and Barriers to Successful Reintegration.* Washington, DC: The Urban Institute.

Hoover, Kent

    2001   "Prison Program May Lose Contracting Monopoly." *BizJournals.com* (June 18): Internet.

Hughes, Robert

    1987   *The Fatal Shore: The Epic of Australia's Founding.* New York: Knopf.

Hurl, Lorna F. and David J. Tucker

1997   "The Michigan County Agents and the Development of Juvenile Probation." *Journal of Social History* (Summer): 905–35.

Hurst, Hunter IV and Patricia McFall Torbet

1993   *Organization and Administration of Juvenile Services: Probation, Aftercare, and State Institutions for Delinquent Youth.* Pittsburgh, PA: National Center for Juvenile Justice.

Hurst, James W.

1950   *The Growth of American Law: The Law Makers.* Boston: Little, Brown.

Husband, Stephen D. and Jerome J. Platt

1993   "The Cognitive Skills Component in Substance Abuse Treatment in Correctional Settings: A Brief Review." *Journal of Drug Issues* 23 (Winter): 31–42.

Hutchinson, Elizabeth D.

1987   "Use of Authority in Direct Social Work Practice with Mandated Clients." *Social Service Review* 61 (December): 581–98.

Ignatieff, Michael

1978   *A Just Measure of Pain: The Penitentiary in the Industrial Revolution.* New York: Pantheon.

Illinois Criminal Justice Authority

1999   "Drug Court Provides Treatment Alternative to Incarceration." *On Good Authority* 2 (April): 1–4.

Irwin, John

1980   *Prisons in Turmoil.* Boston: Little, Brown.

Irwin, John and James Austin

1994   *It's About Time: America's Imprisonment Binge.* Belmont, CA: Wadsworth.

Jackson, David and Cornelia Grumman

1999   "State Puts Kids' Lives on the Block." *Chicago Tribune* (September 26): 1, 18, 19.

Jackson, Patrick G.

1983   "Some Effects of Parole Supervision on Recidivism." *British Journal of Criminology* 23 (January): 17–34.

Jacobs, James B.

1980   "The Prisoners' Rights Movement and Its Impacts, 1960–80." Pages 429–70 in *Crime and Justice*, Volume 2, edited by Norval Morris and Michael Tonry. Chicago: University of Chicago Press.

Jeffrey, C. Ray

1971   *Crime Prevention Through Environmental Design.* Beverly Hills, CA: Sage.

Jenuwine, Michael J., Ronald Simmons, and Edward Swies

2003   "Community Supervision of Sex Offenders—Integrating Probation and Clinical Treatment." *Federal Probation* 67 (December): 20–7.

Jermstad, Todd

2002   "*United States v. Knights* and the Diminished Liberty Interests of Probationers." *Executive Exchange* (Spring): 13–7.

Johnson, Kirk

1989a   "U.S. Sues Town over Rights of Retarded." *New York Times* (June 27): 7.
1994   "Connecticut Closes Boot Camp Built to Assist Troubled Youths." *New York Times* (June 11): 8.

Johnson, Louise C.

1998   *Social Work Practice: A Generalist Approach.* Boston: Allyn and Bacon.

Jones, Justin and Carol Robinson

1989   "Keeping the Piece: Probation and Parole Officers' Right to Bear Arms." *Corrections Today* (February): 88, 90.

Jones, Mark and Darrell L. Ross

1997   "Is Less Better? Boot Camp, Regular Probation and Rearrest in North Carolina." *American Journal of Criminal Justice* 21 (Spring): 147–61.

Kassebaum, Gene, Mel Silverio, Nancy Marker, Paul Perrone, Joseph Allen, and James Richmond

1999   *Survival on Parole: A Study of Post-Prison Adjustment and the Risk of Returning to Prison in the State of Hawaii.* Honolulu: Hawaii Attorney General.

Kelly, William R. and Sheldon Ekland-Olson

1991   "The Response of the Criminal Justice System to Prison Overcrowding: Recidivism Patterns Among Four Successive Parolee Cohorts." *Law and Society Review* 25 (3): 601–20.

Kelman, Mark

1987   *A Guide to Critical Legal Studies.* Cambridge, MA: Harvard University Press.

Keve, Paul

1979   "No Farewell to Arms." *Crime and Delinquency* 25 (October).

Kiernan, Louise

1997   "Trial: At Juvenile Court, an Ongoing Struggle to Mend Broken Lives." *Chicago Tribune Magazine* (January 19): 11–8.

Kilborn, Peter T.

2001   "Rural Towns Turn to Prisons to Reignite Their Economies." *New York Times* (August 1): Internet.

King, Ryan Scott, Marc Mauer, Tracy Huling

2004   "An Analysis of the Economics of Prison Siting in Rural Communities." *Criminology and Public Policy* 3 (July): 453–80.

Kingsnorth, Rodney and Louis Rizzo

1979   "Decision-Making in the Criminal Court: Continuities and Discontinuities." *Criminology* 17 (May).

Klein, Eric C.

1998   "Dennis the Menace or Billy the Kid: An Analysis of the Role of Transfer to Criminal Court in Juvenile Justice." *American Criminal Law Review* 35 (Winter): 371–401.

Kolbert, Elizabeth

1989   "Court Awards $1.3 Million to Inmates Injured at Attica." *New York Times* (October 26): 14.

Konopka, Gisela

1983   *Social Group Work: A Helping Process*, 3rd ed. Upper Saddle River, NJ: Prentice Hall.

Krajick, Kevin

1978   "Parole: Discretion is Out, Guidelines Are In." *Corrections Magazine* 4 (December).

Krause, Kitry

1997   "Borrowed Time: Intensive Probation Offers Kids in Trouble One Last Chance to Stay Out of Jail." *Reader* (January 17): 1, 14, 16, 18–25.

Krauth, Barbara

1987   "Parole: Controversial Component of the Criminal Justice System." Pages 51–7 in *Observations on Parole: A Collection of Readings from Western Europe, Canada and the United States,* edited by Edward E. Rhine and Ronald W. Jackson. Washington, DC: U.S. Government Printing Office.

Krienert, Jessie L. and Mark S. Fleisher, eds.

2004   *Crime and Employment: Critical Issues in Crime Reduction for Corrections.* Walnut Creek, CA: AltaMira Press.

Krisberg, Barry

1988   *The Juvenile Court: Reclaiming the Vision.* San Francisco: National Council on Crime and Delinquency.

Kurki, Leena

1999   *Incorporating Restorative and Community Justice into American Sentencing and Corrections.* Washington, DC: National Institute of Justice.

Kurlychek, Megan C. and Brian D. Johnson

2004   "The Juvenile Penalty: A Comparison of Juvenile and Young Adult Sentencing Outcomes in Criminal Court." *Criminology* 42 (May): 485–517.

Lab, Steven P. and John T. Cullen

1990   "From 'Nothing Works' to 'The Appropriate Works': The Latest Stop on the Search for the Secular Grail." *Criminology* 28 (August): 405–17.

Latessa, Edward J., Frank T. Cullen, and Paul Gendreau

2002   "Beyond Correctional Quakery—Professionalism and the Possibility of Effective Treatment." *Federal Probation* 66 (September): 40–43.

Latessa, Edward J. and Gennaro F. Vito

1988   "The Effects of Intensive Supervision on Shock Probationers." *Journal of Criminal Justice* 16: 319–30.

Lemert, Edwin M.

1951   *Social Pathology.* New York: McGraw-Hill.

Lenroot, Katherine F. and Emma O. Lundberg

1925   *Juvenile Courts at Work.* Washington, DC: U.S. Government Printing Office.

Leonhardt, David

2000   "As Prison Labor Grows, So Does the Debate." *New York Times* (March 19): 1, 22.

Lerner, Mark Jay

1977   "The Effectiveness of a Definite Sentence Parole Program." *Criminology* 15 (August).

Levrant, Sharon, Francis T. Cullen, Betsy Fulton, and John F. Wozniak

1999   "Reconsidering Restorative Justice: The Corruption of Benevolence Revisited?" *Crime and Delinquency* 45 (January): 3–27.

Lewin, Tamar

1998   "Crime Costs Many Black Men the Vote, Study Says." *New York Times* (October 23): 12.

2001a   "Little Sympathy or Remedy for Inmates Who Are Raped." *New York Times* (April 15): 1, 14.

Lewis, W. David

1965   *From Newgate to Dannemora.* Ithaca, NY: Cornell University Press.

Liberton, Michael, Mitchell Silverman, and William R. Blount

1990   "An Analysis Used to Predict Success of First-Time Offenders While Under Probation Supervision." Paper presented at the annual meeting of the Academy of Criminal Justice Sciences, April, Denver, CO. Published in 1992 in the *International Journal of Offender Therapy and Comparative Criminology* 36 (4): 335–47.

Lilly, J. Robert and Richard A. Ball

 1987 "A Brief History of House Arrest and Electronic Monitoring." *Northern Kentucky Law Review* 13: 343–74.

Lindner, Charles and Margaret R. Savarese

 1984 "The Evolution of Probation." *Federal Probation* 48 (December).

Liptak, Adam

 2004 "Sentencing Decision's Reach Is Far and Wide." *New York Times* (June 27): 16.

Lipton, Douglas, Robert Martinson, and Judith Wilks

 1975 *The Effectiveness of Correctional Treatment: A Survey of Treatment Evaluation Studies*. New York: Praeger.

Logan, Charles H.

 1990 *Private Prisons: Cons and Pros*. New York: Oxford University Press.

Lombroso, Cesare

 1968 *Crime: Its Causes and Remedies*. Montclair, NJ: Patterson Smith. (Originally published in 1911.)

London, Perry

 1964 *The Modes and Morals of Psychotherapy*. New York: Holt, Rinehart and Winston.

Lou, Herbert H.

 1972 *Juvenile Courts in the United States*. New York: Arno Press. (Originally published in 1927.)

Lurigio, Arthur J., Marylouise Jones, and Barbara E. Smith

 1995 "Child Sexual Abuse: Its Causes, Consequences, and Implications for Probation Practice." *Federal Probation* 69 (September): 69–76.

Lurigio, Arthur J. and Joan Petersilia

 1992 "The Emergence of Intensive Probation Supervision Programs in the United States." Pages 3–17 in *Smart Sentencing: The Emergence of Intermediate Sanctions*. Edited by James M. Byrne, Arthur J. Lurigio, and Joan Petersilia, Newbury Park, CA: Sage.

Luther, Betty

 1995 "The Politics of Criminal Justice: A Study of the Impact of Executive Influence on Massachusetts Parole Decisions Between 1985 and 1992." Paper presented at the annual meeting of the Academy of Criminal Justice Sciences, Boston, March 7–11.

MacKenzie, Doris Layton

 1994 "Results of a Multistate Study of Boot Camp Prisons." *Federal Probation* 58 (June): 60–6.

MacKenzie, Doris Layton, Robert Brame, David McDowall, and Claire Souryal

 1995 "Boot Camp Prisons in Eight States." *Criminology* 33 (August): 327–57.

MacKenzie, Doris Layton, Angela R. Grover, Gaylene Stywe Armstrong, and Ojmarrh Mitchell

 2001 *A National Study Comparing the Environments of Boot Camps with Traditional Facilities for Juvenile Offenders*. Washington, DC: National Institute of Justice.

MacKenzie, Doris Layton and James W. Shaw

 1993 "The Impact of Shock Incarceration on Technical Violations and New Criminal Activities." *Justice Quarterly* 10 (September): 463–87.

MacKenzie, Doris Layton, James W. Shaw, and Claire Souryal

 1992 "Characteristics Associated with Successful Adjustment to Supervision: A Comparison of Parolees, Probationers, Shock Participants, and Shock Dropouts." *Criminal Justice and Behavior* 19 (December): 437–54.

MacKenzie, Doris Layton and Claire Souryal
    1994   *Multisite Evaluation of Shock Incarceration.* Washington, DC: National Institute of Justice.

MacNamara, Donal E. J.
    1977   "The Medical Model in Corrections: Requiescat in Pace." *Criminology* 14 (February): 439–48.

Maestro, Marcello
    1973   *Cesare Beccaria and the Origins of Penal Reform.* Philadelphia: Temple University Press.

Magura, Stephen, Sung-Yeon Kang, and Janet L. Shapiro
    1995   "Measuring Cocaine Use by Hair Analysis Among Criminally-Involved Youth." *Journal of Drug Issues* 25 (Fall): 683–701.

Malcolm, Andrew H.
    1989a   "Florida's Jammed Prisons: More in Means More Out." *New York Times* (July 3): 1, 7.
    1989b   "More and More, Prison Is America's Answer to Crime." *New York Times* (November 26): E1, 4.
    1989c   "Explosive Drug Use in Prisons Is Creating a New Underworld." *New York Times* (December 30): 1, 10.

Maloney, Dennis M. and Mark S. Umbreit
    1995   "Managing Change: Toward a Balanced and Restorative Justice Model." *Perspectives* 19 (Spring): 43–6.

Maltz, Michael D.
    1984   *Recidivism.* Orlando, FL: Academic Press.

Mander, Anthony M., Martin E. Atrops, Allan R. Barnes, and Roseanne Munafo
    1996   *Sex Offender Treatment Program: Initial Recidivism Study.* Executive Summary. Anchorage: Alaska Department of Corrections.

Mangrum, Claude
    1972   "The Humanity of Probation Officers." *Federal Probation* 36 (June).

Mann, Dale
    1976   *Intervening with Convicted Serious Juvenile Offenders.* Washington, DC: U.S. Government Printing Office.

"Manufacturers Complain of Prison Work Programs"
    1997   *Chicago Tribune* (November 28): 8.

Marriott, Michael
    1995   "Half Steps vs. 12 Steps." *Newsweek* (March 27): 62.

Marshall, Franklin H.
    1989   "Diversion and Probation Under the New Sentencing Guidelines: One Officer's Observations." Paper presented at the annual meeting of the Academy of Criminal Justice Sciences, Washington, DC, March 30.

Martin, Andrew
    1995   "Few Brains Behind Bank Heists." *Chicago Tribune* (June 28): Sec. 2: 1, 4.

Martin, Douglas
    1988   "New York Tests Inmates' Boot Camp." *New York Times* (March 4): 15.

Martin, Garry and Joseph Pear
    1992   *Behavior Modification: What It Is and How to Do It,* 4th ed. Upper Saddle River, NJ: Prentice Hall.

Martinson, Robert
    1974   "What Works? Questions and Answers about Prison Reform." *The Public Interest* 35 (Spring): 22–54.

Maruschak, Laura M.

2001   *HIV in Prisons and Jails, 1999*. Washington, DC: Office of Justice Programs.

Marx, Gary

1994a   "Hard Time." *Chicago Tribune* (October 24): Sec. 5: 1, 6.
1998   "Panel Uncovers Security Leaks at Juvenile Jail." *Chicago Tribune* (March 2): 1, 12.

Mathias, Rudolf E. S. and James W. Mathews

1991   "The Boot Camp Program for Offenders: Does the Shoe Fit." *International Journal of Offender Therapy and Comparative Criminology* 35: 322–7.

Matza, David

1964   *Delinquency and Drift*. New York: Wiley.

McCarthy, Belinda Rogers, and Bernard J. McCarthy

1984   *Community-Based Corrections*. Monterey, CA: Brooks/Cole.

McCollum, Sylvia G.

2000   "Mock Job Fairs in Prison: Tracking Participants." *Federal Probation* (June): 13–8.

McDonald, Douglas C.

1988   *Restitution and Community Service*. Washington, DC: National Institute of Justice.

McElrath, Karen

1995   "Alcoholics Anonymous." Pages 314–37 in the *American Drug Scene: An Anthology*, edited by James A. Inciardi and Karen McElrath. Los Angeles: Roxbury.

McFadden, Robert D.

1997   "Ex-Attica Inmate Wins $4 Million in Suit Over Reprisals After 1971 Uprising." *New York Times* (June 6): 20.

McGaha, Johnny, Michael Fichter, and Peter Hirschburg

1987   "Felony Probation: A Re-Examination of Public Risk." *American Journal of Criminal Justice* 11: 1–9.

McKelvey, Blake

1972   *American Prisons: A Study in American Social History Prior to 1815*. Montclair, NJ: Patterson Smith.
1977   *American Prisons: A History of Good Intentions*. Montclair, NJ: Patterson Smith.

McShane, Marilyn D. and Frank P. Williams III

1989   "The Prison Adjustment of Juvenile Offenders." *Crime and Delinquency* 35 (April): 254–69.

Melossi, Dario and Massimo Pavarini

1981   *The Prison and the Factory: Origins of the Penitentiary System*. Totowa, NJ: Barnes and Noble.

Mennel, Robert M.

1973   *Thorns and Thistles: Juvenile Delinquents in the United States, 1825–1940*. Hanover, NH: University Press of New England.

Meredith, Robyn

2000   "Road From Prison to Jobs Gets Smoother." *New York Times* (April 3): 12.

Merlo, Alida V., Peter J. Benekos, and William J. Cook

1997   "Waiver and Juvenile Justice Reform: Widening the Punitive Net." *Criminal Justice Policy Review* 8 (2–3): 145–68.

Merton, Robert K.

    1938   "Social Structure and Anomie." *American Sociological Review* 3: 672–82.

    1964   "Anomie, Anomia, and Social Interaction." In *Anomie and Deviant Behavior*, edited by Marshall B. Clinard, 213–42. New York: Free Press.

Mieczkowski, Thomas

    1995   *Hair Analysis as a Drug Detector.* Washington, DC: National Institute of Justice.

Miley, Karla Krogsrud, Michael O'Melia, and Brenda L. DuBois

    2004   *Generalist Social Work Practice: An Empowering Approach.* Boston: Allyn and Bacon.

Miller, Jerome

    1992   *Last One Over the Wall: The Massachusetts Experiment in Closing Reform Schools.* Columbus: Ohio State University.

Miller, Walter B.

    1958   "Lower Class Culture as a Generating Milieu of Gang Delinquency." *Journal of Social Issues* 14: 5–19.

Mills, Jim

    1992   "Supervision Fees." *Perspectives* (Fall): 10–2.

Mohler, Henry Calvin

    1925   "Convict Labor Policies." *Journal of Criminal Law, Criminology and Police Science* 15: 530–97.

Monti, Crostin

    1997   "Prison Treatment Program Seeks to Change Sex Offender Behavior." *The Compiler* 17 (Summer): 4–6.

Moore, Kathleen Dean

    1989   *Pardons: Justice, Mercy, and the Public Interest.* New York: Oxford University Press.

Morash, Merry and Lila Rucker

    1990   "A Critical Look at the Idea of Boot Camp as a Correctional Reform." *Crime and Delinquency* 36 (April): 204–22.

Moritz, John

    2001   "Prison Population in Texas Declines." *Fort Worth Star Telegram* (July 3): Internet.

Morris, Norval and Michael Tonry

    1990   *Between Prison and Probation: Intermediate Punishments in a Rational Sentencing System.* New York: Oxford University Press.

Moses, Marilyn C.

    1996   *Project Re-Enterprise: A Texas Program.* Washington, DC: Office of Justice Programs.

Mullaney, Fahy G.

    1988   *Economic Sanctions in Community Corrections.* Washington, DC: National Institute of Corrections.

Mullen, Joan

    1985   "Corrections and the Private Sector." *NIJ Reports* (May).

Mumola, Christopher J. and Thomas P. Bonczar

    1998   *Substance Abuse and Treatment of Adults on Probation, 1995.* Washington, DC: Bureau of Justice Statistics.

Murphy, Cait

    2001   "Crime and Punishment." *Fortune* 143 (April 30): 126–35.

Mydans, Seth
 1995 "Racial Tensions on the Rise in Los Angeles Jail System," *New York Times* (February 6): 8.

Myers, Linnet
 1995 "Cultural Divide Over Crime and Punishment." *Chicago Tribune* (October 13): 1, 8.

National Advisory Commission on Criminal Justice Standards and Goals
 1973 *Corrections.* Washington, DC: U.S. Government Printing Office.
 1975 *A National Strategy to Reduce Crime.* New York: Avon.

National Governors' Association
 1988 *Guide to Executive Clemency Among the American States.* Washington, DC: National Institute of Corrections.

Nelson, E. Kim, Howard Ohmart, and Nora Harlow
 1978 *Promising Strategies in Probation and Parole.* Washington, DC: U.S. Government Printing Office.

"Newgate"
 1998 *DOC Today* (February): Internet.

New York State Division of Parole
 1953 *Parole Officer's Manual.* Albany: Division of Parole.
 1984 *1982–83 Annual Report.* Albany: Division of Parole.
 1994 *1993–1994 Report.* Albany: Division of Parole.

New York State Employment Services Vocational Rehabilitation Service
 1965 "Vocational Counseling with the Offender" (mimeo). Albany: Vocational Rehabilitation Service.

New York State Special Commission on Attica (Attica Commission)
 1972 *Attica.* New York: Praeger.

New York Times Editorial, "Dark Side of America," May 17, 2004: 20.

Niemeyer, Mike and David Shichor
 1996 "A Preliminary Study of a Large Victim/Offender Reconciliation Program." *Federal Probation* 60 (September): 30–4.

Nietzel, Michael T., Douglas A. Bernstein, Geoffrey P. Kramer, Richard Milich
 2003 *Introduction to Clinical Psychology,* 6th ed. Upper Saddle River, NJ: Prentice Hall.

Noonan, Susan B. and Edward J. Latessa
 1987 "Intensive Probation: An Examination of Recidivism and Social Adjustment." *American Journal of Criminal Justice* 11: 45–61.

Norman, Michael D. and Robert C. Wadman
 2000 "Probation Department Sentencing Recommendations in Two Utah Counties." *Federal Probation* (December): 47–51.

Northern, Helen
 1969 *Social Work with Groups.* New York: Columbia University Press.

Office for Victims of Crime
 1998 *New Directions From the Field: Victims' Rights and Services for the 21st Century.* Washington, DC: U.S. Department of Justice.

Office of Policy Analysis and Information
 1989 *Shock Incarceration: One Year Out.* Albany: New York State Division of Parole.

Ogborne, Alan C. and Frederick B. Glaser
 1985 "Evaluating Alcoholics Anonymous." Pages 176–92 in *Alcoholism and Substance Abuse,* edited by Thomas E. Bratter and Gary G. Forrest. New York: Free Press.

OJJDP Research 2000
    2001   Washington, DC: Office of Juvenile Justice and Delinquency Prevention.

O'Leary, K. Daniel and G. Terrance Wilson
    1975   *Behavior Therapy: Application and Outcome.* Upper Saddle River, NJ: Prentice Hall.

Olivares, Kathleen M., Velmer S. Burton, Frances T. Cullen, Debra Oldenettel, and Madeline Wordes
    1996   "The Collateral Consequences of a Felony Conviction: A National Study of State Legal Codes 10 Years Later." *Federal Probation* 60 (September): 10–7.
    2000   *The Community Assessment Center Concept.* Washington, DC: Office of Juvenile Justice and Delinquency Prevention.

Oltmanns, Thomas F. and Robert E. Emery
    2004   *Abnormal Psychology,* 4th ed. Upper Saddle River, NJ: Prentice Hall.

Omer, Haim and Perry London
    1988   "Metamorphosis in Psychotherapy: End of the Systems Era." *Psychotherapy* 25 (Summer): 171–80.

Pace, Eric
    1988   "Lois Burnham Wilson, a Founder of Al-Anon Groups, Is Dead at 97." *New York Times* (October 4): 15.

Pager, Devah
    2003   "The Mark of a Criminal Record." *American Journal Sociology* 108 (March): 937–75.

Palumbo, Dennis J. and Rebecca D. Peterson
    1994   "Shock Incarceration and Intermediate Punishments: Reform or Recycled 'Get Tough' Policy?" Paper presented at the annual meeting of the American Society of Criminology, Miami, Florida, November.

Papy, Joseph E.
    1997   "Florida's Approach to Probation and Parole Staff Safety." Pages 23–5 in *Topics in Community Corrections.* Washington, DC: National Institute of Corrections.

Parent, Dale G
    1988   "Overview: Shock-Incarceration Programs." *Perspectives* 12 (July): 9–15.
    1989   *Shock Incarceration: An Overview of Existing Programs.* Washington, DC: U.S. Government Printing Office.
    1990   *Day Reporting Centers for Criminal Offenders—A Descriptive Analysis of Existing Programs.* Washington, DC: Office of Justice Programs.
    1996   "Day Reporting Centers: An Evolving Intermediate Sanction." *Federal Probation* 60 (December): 51–4.
    2003   *Correctional Boot Camps: Lessons from a Decade of Research.* Washington, DC: National Institute of Justice.

Parent, Dale G., Dan Wentworth, Peggy Burke, and Becky Ney
    1994   *Responding to Probation and Parole Violations.* Washington, DC: National Institute of Justice.

Parker, William
    1975   *Parole.* College Park, MD: American Correctional Association.

Parry, Wayne
    2001   "Employers Seeking Workers from Newark Prison Ranks." Associated Press (May 17): Internet.

Parsonage, William H.
    1990   *Worker Safety in Probation and Parole.* Longmont, CO: National Institute of Corrections.

Parsonage, William H. and W. Conway Bushey

1989   "The Victimization of Probation and Parole Workers in the Line of Duty: An Exploratory Study." Paper presented at the annual meeting of the Academy of Criminal Justice Sciences, Washington, DC, March.

Parsons, Christi

1998   "Jury Out on Sex-Offender Law." *Chicago Tribune* (June 28): 1, 12.

Payne, Malcolm

1997   *Modern Social Work Theory*, 2nd ed. Chicago: Lyceum.

Pearson, Frank S.

1988   "Evaluation of New Jersey's Intensive Supervision Program." *Crime and Delinquency* 34 (October): 437–48.

Peele, Stanton

1985   *The Meaning of Addiction: Compulsive Experience and Its Interpretation.* Lexington, MA: D.C. Heath.

Peréz-Peña, Richard

1997   "New York's Income Gap Largest in the Nation." *New York Times* (December 17): 14.

1998   "Pataki Plan to End Parole Is Tougher Than Others." *New York Times* (January 26): 18.

Perlman, Helen Harris

1957   *Perspectives on Social Casework.* Philadelphia: Temple University Press.

1971   *Perspectives on Social Casework: A Problem Solving Process.* Chicago: University of Chicago Press.

Peters, Michael, David Thomas, and Christopher Zamberlan

1997   *Boot Camp for Juvenile Offenders: Program Summary.* Washington, DC: Office of Juvenile Justice and Delinquency Prevention.

Petersilia, Joan M.

1988a   "Georgia's Intensive Probation: Will the Model Work Elsewhere?" Pages 15–30 in *Intermediate Punishments: Intensive Supervision, Home Confinement and Electronic Surveillance*, edited by Belinda R. McCarthy. Monsey, NY: Criminal Justice Press.

1990   "When Probation Becomes More Dreaded Than Prison." *Federal Probation* 54 (March): 23–7.

1993   "Measuring the Performance of Community Corrections." In *Performance Measures for the Criminal Justice System*, 61–85. Washington, DC: Bureau of Justice Statistics.

1995   "A Crime Control Rationale for Reinvesting in Community Corrections." *Spectrum* (Summer): 16–27.

1998a   "Probation in the United States, Part I." *Perspectives* 22 (Spring): 30–41.

1998b   "Probation in the United States, Part II." *Perspectives* 22 (Summer): 42–9.

2000a   "Parole and Prison Reentry in the United States." *Perspectives* 24 (Fall): 38–47.

2000b   *When Prisoners Return to the Community: Political, Economic, and Social Consequences.* Washington, DC: Office of Justice Programs.

Petersilia, Joan

2003   *When Prisoners Come Home: Parole and Prisoner Re-Entry.* New York: Oxford University Press.

Petersilia, Joan and Susan Turner

1990   "Comparing Intensive and Regular Supervision for High-Risk Probationers: Early Results from an Experiment in California." *Crime and Delinquency* 36 (January): 87–111.

1991   "Is ISP a Viable Sanction for High Risk Probationers?" *Perspectives* 15 (Summer): 8–11.

1993   *Evaluating Intensive Supervision Probation/Parole: Results of a Nationwide Experiment.* Washington, DC: National Institute of Justice.

Petersilia, Joan, Susan Turner, and Elizabeth Piper Deschenes

    1992   "Intensive Supervision Programs for Drug Offenders." Pages 18–37 in *Smart Sentencing: The Emergence of Intermediate Sanctions*, edited by James M. Byrne, Arthur J. Lurigio, and Joan Petersilia. Newbury Park, CA: Sage.

Petersilia, Joan, Susan Turner, James Kahan, and Joyce Peterson

    1985   *Granting Felons Probation: Public Risks and Alternatives.* Santa Monica, CA: Rand.

Pisciotta, Alexander W.

    1992   "Doing Parole: The Promise and Practice of the Minnesota and Illinois Reformatories, 1889–1990." Paper presented at the annual meeting of the American Society of Criminology, New Orleans, LA, November.

    1994   *Benevolent Repression: Social Control and the American Reformatory-Prison Movement.* New York: New York University Press.

Platt, Anthony M.

    1974   *The Childsavers: The Invention of Delinquency.* Chicago: University of Chicago Press.

Platt, Jerome J. and Christina Labate

    1976   *Heroin Addiction: Research and Treatment.* New York: Wiley.

Polakow, Robert L. and Ronald M. Docktor

    1974   "A Behavioral Modification Program for Adult Drug Offenders." *Journal of Research in Crime and Delinquency* 11 (January): 63–9.

Porter, Bruce

    1995   "Terror on an Eight-Hour Shift." *New York Times Magazine* (November 26): 42–7, 56, 59, 72, 76, 80, 82.

Powell, Hickman

    2000   *Lucky Luciano: The Man Who Organized Crime in America.* New York: Barricade Books. (Originally published in 1939.)

President's Commission on Law Enforcement and Administration of Justice

    1972   *The Challenge of Crime in a Free Society.* New York: Avon.

President's Commission on Organized Crime (PCOC)

    1986   *The Impact: Organized Crime Today.* Washington, DC: U.S. Government Printing Office.

Prison Association of New York

    1936   *The Ninety-First Annual Report.* Albany, NY: J. B. Lyon.

Privacy and Juvenile Justice Records: A Mid-Decade Status Report

    1997   Washington, DC: Office of Justice Programs.

Program Services Office

    1983   *Probation Classification and Service Delivery Approach.* Los Angeles: County Probation Department.

Przybylski, Roger

    1988   *Electronically Monitored Home Confinement in Illinois.* Chicago: Illinois Criminal Justice Information Authority.

Purdy, Matthew

    1995   "Bars Don't Stop Flow of Drugs Into the Prisons." *New York Times* (July 2): 1, 12, 13.

    1997   "As AIDS Increases Behind Bars, Costs Dim Promise of New Drugs." *New York Times* (May 26): 1, 12.

Puritz, Patricia and Mary Ann Scali

    1998   *Beyond the Walls: Improving Conditions of Confinement for Youth in Custody.* Washington, DC: Office of Juvenile Justice and Delinquency Prevention.

Puzzanchera, Charles M.

    2001   *Delinquency Cases Waived to Criminal Court, 1989–1998.* Washington, DC: Office of Justice Programs.

Quadagno, Jill S. and Robert J. Antonio

    1975   "Labeling Theory as an Oversocialized Conception of Man: The Case of Mental Illness." *Sociology and Social Research* 60 (October): 33–45.

Rachin, Richard

    1974   "Reality Therapy: Helping People Help Themselves." *Crime and Delinquency* 20 (January).

"Rape Crisis in U.S. Prisons"

    2001   *Human Rights Watch* (April 19): Internet.

Reichel, Phillip L. and Billie D. Sudbrack

    1994   "Differences Among Eligibles: Who Gets an ISP Sentence?" *Federal Probation* (58): 51–62.

Reiff, Phillip, ed.

    1963   *Freud, Therapy and Techniques.* New York: Crowell-Collier.

Reiman, Jeffrey

    1998   *The Rich Get Richer and the Poor Get Prison*, 5th ed. New York: Macmillan.

Reinventing Probation Council (RPC)

    2000   *Transforming Probation Through Leadership: The "Broken Windows" Model.* New York: Center for Civic Innovation at the Manhattan Institute.

Rhine, Edward E.

    2002   "Why 'What Works' Matters Under the 'Broken Windows' Model of Supervision." *Federal Probation* 66 (September): 38–42.

Rhode, David

    2001   "A Health Danger From a Needle Becomes a Scourge Behind Bars." *New York Times* (August 6): 1, 14.

Richmond, Mary

    1917   *Social Diagnosis.* New York: Russell Sage.

Rimer, Sara

    2001   "States Adjust Their Adult Prisons to the Needs of Youth Inmates." *New York Times* (July 25): 1, 13.

Robbins, Ira P.

    1988   *The Legal Dimensions of Private Incarceration.* Washington, DC: American Bar Association.

Robertson, John A.

    1974   *Rough Justice: Perspectives on Lower Courts.* Boston: Little, Brown.

Robertson, Nan

    1988b   *Getting Better: Inside Alcoholics Anonymous.* New York: William Morrow.

Robitscher, Jonas

    1980   *The Power of Psychiatry.* Boston: Houghton Mifflin.

Rosenblum, Robert and Debra Whitcomb

    1978   *Montgomery County Work Release/Pre-Release Program.* Washington, DC: U.S. Government Printing Office.

Rosenthal, Mitchell S.

    1984   "Therapeutic Communities: A Treatment Alternative for Many but Not All." *Journal of Substance Abuse Treatment* 1: 55–8.

    1973   "New York City Phoenix House: A Therapeutic Community for the Treatment of Drug Abusers and Drug Addicts." Pages 83–102 in *Yearbook of Drug Abuse*, edited by Leon Brill and Earnest Harms. New York: Behavioral Publications.

Roshier, Bob

    1989   *Controlling Crime: The Classical Perspective in Criminology*. Chicago: Lyceum.

Rothman, David

    1971   *The Discovery of the Asylum*. Boston: Little, Brown.

Rottman, David B., Carol R. Flango, Melissa T. Cantrell, Randall Hansen, and Neil LaFountain

    2000   *State Court Organization 1998*. Washington, DC: National Institute of Justice.

Rousseau, Jean Jacques

    1954   *The Social Contract*. Chicago: Henry Regnery. (Originally published in 1762.)

Rubin, H. Ted

    1980   "The Emerging Prosecutor Dominance of the Juvenile Court Intake Process." *Crime and Delinquency* 26 (July).

Sachs, Howard and Charles Logan

    1979   *Does Parole Make a Difference?* West Hartford: University of Connecticut Law School.

Sagatun, Inger, Loretta McCollum, and Michael Edwards

    1985   "The Effect of Transfers from Juvenile to Criminal Court: A Loglinear Analysis." *Journal of Crime and Justice* 8: 65–92.

Sanborn, Joseph B., Jr.

    1992   "Pleading Guilty in Juvenile Court: Minimal Ado About Something Very Important to Young Defendants." *Justice Quarterly* 9 (March): 127–50.

Schlosser, Eric

    1998   "The Prison-Industrial Complex." *Atlantic Monthly* (December): 51–77.

Schlossman, Steven L.

    1977   *Love and the American Delinquent: The Theory and Practice of "Progressive" Juvenile Justice, 1825–1920*. Chicago: University of Chicago Press.

Schmideberg, Melitta

    1975   "Some Basic Principles of Offender Therapy: Part II." *International Journal of Offender Therapy and Comparative Criminology* 1.

Schram, Donna D., Jill G. McKelvy, Anne L. Schneider, and David B. Griswold

    1981   *Preliminary Findings: Assessment of the Juvenile Code* (mimeo). State of Washington.

Schriro, Dora

    2000   *Correcting Corrections: Missouri's Parallel Universe*. Washington, DC: National Institute of Justice.

Schultz, J. Lawrence

    1973   "The Cycle of Juvenile Court History." *Crime and Delinquency* 19 (October).

Schur, Edwin M.

    1973   *Radical Non-Intervention: Rethinking the Delinquency Problem*. Englewood Cliffs, NJ: Prentice Hall.

Schwartz, Richard and Jerome H. Skolnick

    1962   "Two Studies in Legal Stigma." *Social Problems* 10: 133–42.

Scull, Andrew T.
    1977   *Decarceration.* Englewood Cliffs, NJ: Prentice Hall.

Sechcrest, Dale K.
    1989   "Prison 'Boot Camps' Do Not Measure Up." *Federal Probation* 53 (September): 15–20.

Sechrest, Lee, Susan O. White, and Elizabeth D. Brown
    1979   *The Rehabilitation of Criminal Offenders: Problems and Prospects.* Washington, DC: National Academy of Sciences.

Selcraig, Bruce
    2000   "Camp Fear." *Mother Jones* (December): 64–71.

Sellin, Thorston
    1967   "A Look at Prison History." *Federal Probation* 31 (September): 18.

Sengupta, Somini
    2000   "Felony Costs Voting Rights for a Lifetime in 9 States." *New York Times* (November 3): 18.

Seventh Annual Shock Legislative Report
    1995   Albany: State of New York Department of Correctional Services and Division of Parole.

Sever, Brian
    2000   "County Sales Tax, Crime Rate, and Prison Bed Use in Florida: Implications for the Misuse of Prison Space." *Criminal Justice Policy Review* 11 (June): 91–112.

Sexton, Joe
    1997   "Opening the Doors on Family Court's Secrets." *New York Times* (September 13): 1, 10.

Shaffer, John and M. David Galinsky
    1987   *Models of Group Therapy*, 2nd ed. Upper Saddle River, NJ: Prentice Hall.

Sheafor, Bradford W., Charles R. Horejsi, and Gloria A. Horejsi
    2000   *Techniques and Guidelines for Social Work Practice*, 5th ed. Boston: Allyn and Bacon.

Sheldon, Randall G., John A. Horvath, and Sharon Tracy
    1989   "Do Status Offenders Get Worse? Some Clarifications on the Question of Escalation." *Crime and Delinquency* 35 (April): 202–16.

Shichor, David and Clemens Bartollas
    1990   "Private and Public Juvenile Placements: Is There a Difference?" *Crime and Delinquency* 36 (April): 286–99.

Shilton, Mary K.
    2000   *Increasing Offender Employment in the Community.* Washington, DC: Center for Community Corrections.

Short, James R., Jr.
    1968   *Gang Delinquency and Delinquent Subcultures.* New York: Harper and Row.

Sickmund, Melissa, Howard Snyder, and Eileen Poe-Yamagata
    1997   *Juvenile Offenders and Victims: 1997 Update on Violence.* Washington, DC: Office of Juvenile Justice and Delinquency Prevention.

Silverman, Ira J.
    2001   *Corrections: Comprehensive View*, 2nd ed. Belmont, CA: Wadsworth.

Silverman, Mitchell
    1994   "Ethical Issues in the Field of Probation." *International Journal of Offender Therapy and Comparative Criminology* 37 (1): 85–94.

Sinclair, Jim
    1994   "APPA's Public Hearings Explore Probation and Parole's Response to Victim's of Crime: Speakers Call for a New Approach to Victim Issues." *Perspectives* (Special issue): 15–7.

Skidmore, Rex A., Milton G. Thackeray, and O. William Farley
    1988   *Introduction to Social Work,* 4th ed. Upper Saddle River, NJ: Prentice Hall.

Skinner, B. F.
    1972   *Beyond Freedom and Dignity.* New York: Knopf.

Smart, Frances
    1970   *Neuroses and Crime.* New York: Barnes and Noble.

Smith, Michael E.
    2001   *What Future for "Public Safety" and "Restorative Justice" in Community Corrections?* Washington, DC: National Institute of Justice.

Solomon, Jolie
    1998   "Watching Mike." *Newsweek* (March 2): 54–5.

Specht, Harry
    1990   "Social Work and the Popular Psychotherapies." *Social Service Review* 64 (September): 345–57.

Spencer, Herbert
    1961   *The Study of Sociology.* Ann Arbor: University of Michigan Press. (Originally published in 1871.)

Spencer, Jim
    1987   "'Knock 'em Out, Trainee.'" *Chicago Tribune* (July 26): Sec. 3: 1, 2.

Spitz, Henry I.
    1987   "Cocaine Abuse: Therapeutic Group Approaches." Pages 156–201 in *Cocaine Abuse: New Directions in Treatment and Research,* edited by Henry I. Spitz and Jeffrey S. Rosecan. New York: Brunner/Mazel.

Stampfl, Thomas G.
    1970   "Comment" [on token economies]. In *Learning Approaches to Therapeutic Behavior Change,* edited by Donald H. Levis. Chicago: Aldine.

Stanley, David T.
    1976   *Prisoners Among Us: The Problem of Parole.* Washington, DC: Brookings Institution.

Star, Deborah
    1979   *Summary Parole: A Six and Twelve Month Follow-Up Evaluation.* Sacramento, CA: California Department of Corrections.

Stephen, James J.
    2004   *State Prison Expenditures, 2001.* Washington, DC: Bureau of Justice Statistics.

Stevenson, Carol S., Carol S. Larson, Lucy S. Carter, Deanna S. Gomby, Donna L. Terman, and Richard E. Behrman
    1996   "The Juvenile Court: Analysis and Recommendations." *The Future of Children* 6 (Winter): 4–28.

Stille, Alexander
    2001   "Grounded by an Income Gap." *New York Times* (December 15): 15, 17.

Stolberg, Sheryl Gay
    2001   "Behind Bars, New Effort to Care for the Dying." *New York Times* (April 1): 1, 20.

Storm, John P.
    1997   "What United States Probation Officers Do." *Federal Probation* 61 (March): 13–8.

Strong, Ann
   1981   *Case Classification Manual, Module One: Technical Aspects of Interviewing.* Austin: Texas Adult Probation Commission.

Sullivan, John and Matthew Purdy
   1995   "In Corrections Business, Shrewdness Pays." *New York Times* (July 23): 1, 13.

Sutherland, Edwin H.
   1972   *The Professional Thief.* Chicago: University of Chicago Press.
   1973   *Edwin Sutherland: On Analyzing Crime*, edited by Karl Schuessler. Chicago: University of Chicago Press.

Sutton, John R.
   1988   *Stubborn Children: Controlling Delinquency in the United States, 1649–1981.* Berkeley: University of California Press.

Swanger, Harry F.
   1988   "*Hendrickson v. Griggs*: A Review of the Legal and Policy Implications for Juvenile Justice Policymakers." *Crime and Delinquency* 34 (April): 209–27.

Sykes, Gresham M. and David Matza
   1957   "Techniques of Neutralization: A Theory of Delinquency." *American Sociological Review* 22 (December): 664–70.

Takagi, Paul
   1975   "The Walnut Street Jail: A Penal Reform to Centralize the Powers of the State." *Federal Probation* 39 (December): 18–26.

Task Force on Corrections
   1966   *Task Force Report: Corrections.* Washington, DC: U.S. Government Printing Office.

Taxman, Faye S.
   2002   "Supervision—Exploring the Dimensions of Effectiveness." Federal *Probation* 66 (September): 14–27.

Taylor, Ian, Paul Walton, and Jock Young
   1973   *The New Criminology.* New York: Harper and Row.

Teeters, Negley K.
   1970   "The Passing of Cherry Hill: Most Famous Prison in the World." *Prison Journal* 50 (Spring-Summer): 1–12.
   1993   "Town Builds a Prison and Stores Its Hopes There." *New York Times* (January 3): 9. Texas Adult Probation Commission

Thalheimer, Donald J.
   1975   *Halfway Houses*, Vol. 2. Washington, DC: U.S. Government Printing Office.

Thorne, Gaylord L., Roland G. Tharp, and Ralph J. Wetzel
   1967   "Behavior Modification Techniques: New Tools for Probation Officers." *Federal Probation* 31 (June): 21–7.

Tims, Frank M., Nancy Jainchill, and George DeLeon
   1994   "Therapeutic Communities and Treatment Research." Pages 1–15 in *Therapeutic Community: Advances in Research and Application.* Rockville, MD: National Institute on Drug Abuse.

Toborg, Mary A., Lawrence J. Carter, Raymond H. Milkman, and Dennis W. Davis
   1978   *The Transition from Prison to Employment: An Assessment of Community-Based Programs.* Washington, DC: U.S. Government Printing Office.

Torbet, Patricia, Richard Gable, Hunter Hurst IV, Imogene Montgomery, Linda Szymanski, and Douglas Thomas
   1996   *State Responses to Serious and Violent Juvenile Crime.* Washington, DC: Office of Juvenile Justice and Delinquency Prevention.

Torbet, Patricia, Patrick Griffen, Hunter Hurst, Jr., and Lynn Ryan MacKenzie
 2000 *Juveniles Facing Criminal Sanctions: Three States that Changed the Rules.* Washington, DC: Office of Juvenile Justice and Delinquency Prevention.

Torgerson, Fernando G.
 1962 "Differentiating and Defining Casework and Psychotherapy." *Social Casework* 43 (April).

Torres, Sam
 1999 "Early Termination: Outdated Concept in an Era of Punitiveness." *Federal Probation* 63 (June): 35–41.

Toseland, Robert W., and Robert F. Rivas
 1998 *An Introduction to Group Work Practice,* 4 ed. Boston: Allyn & Bacon.

Travis, Jeremy
 2000 *But They All Come Back: Rethinking Prisoner Reentry.* Washington, DC: National Institute of Justice.

Treaster, Joseph B.
 1994 "Beyond Probation: Breaking the Cycle of Juvenile Arrests." *New York Times* (December 29): 1, 11.

Turner, Susan and Joan Petersilia
 1996 *Work Release: Recidivism and Corrections Costs in Washington State.* Washington, DC: Office of Justice Programs.

Twentieth Century Fund Task Force on Sentencing
 1976 *Fair and Certain Punishment.* New York: McGraw-Hill.

Umbreit, Mark S.
 1994 *Victim Meets Offender: The Impact of Restorative Justice and Mediation.* Monsey, NY: Willow Tree Press.

Umbreit, Mark S. and Mark Carey
 1995 "Restorative Justice: Implications for Organizational Change." *Federal Probation* 59 (March): 47–54.

Urbina, Ian
 2003 "New York's Federal Judges Protest Sentencing Procedures." *New York Times* (December 8): B1, 4.

U.S. Attorney General
 1939 *Attorney General's Survey of Release Procedures: Pardon.* Washington, DC: U.S. Government Printing Office.

U.S. Bureau of Justice Assistance
 1989 *Electronic Monitoring in Intensive Probation and Parole Programs.* Washington, DC: U.S. Government Printing Office.

Vold, George B. and Thomas J. Bernard
 1986 *Theoretical Criminology,* 3rd ed. New York: Oxford University Press.

von Hirsch, Andrew
 1976 *Doing Justice: The Choice of Punishments.* New York: Hill and Wang.

von Hirsch, Andrew and Kathleen J. Hanrahan
 1978 *Abolish Parole?* Washington, DC: U.S. Government Printing Office.

Wagner, Dennis
 1989 "An Evaluation of the High Risk Offender Intensive Supervision Project." *Perspectives* 13 (Summer): 22–7.

Wagner, Dennis and Christopher Baird
 1993 *Evaluation of the Florida Community Control Program.* Washington, DC: National Institute of Justice.

Waldo, Gordon, and David Griswold

    1979   "Issues in the Measurement of Recidivism." In *The Rehabilitation of Criminal Offenders: Problems and Prospects*, edited by Lee Sechrest, Susan O. White, and Elizabeth D. Brown. Washington, DC: National Academy of Sciences.

Waldorf, Dan

    1973   *Careers in Dope.* Englewood Cliffs, NJ: Prentice Hall.

Walker, Samuel

    1980   *Popular Justice: A History of American Criminal Justice.* New York: Oxford University Press.

Weber, Max

    1958   *Protestant Ethic and the Spirit of Capitalism.* New York: Scribner's.

Weed, William Speed

    2001   "Incubating Disease." *Mother Jones* (July 10): Internet.

Weisheit, Ralph H. and Diane M. Alexander

    1988   "Juvenile Justice and the Demise of Parens Patriae." *Federal Probation* 52 (December): 56–63.

Weiss, Robert P.

    2001   "'Repatriating' Low-Wage Work: The Political Economy of Prison Labor Reprivatization in the Postindustrial United States." *Criminology* 39 (May): 253–91.

Wellisch, Jean, M. Douglas Anglin, and Michael L. Prendergast

    1993   "Numbers and Characteristics of Drug-Using Women in the Criminal Justice System: Implications for Treatment." *Journal of Drug Issues* 23 (Winter): 7–30.

Whitehead, John T.

    1989   "The Effectiveness of Felony Probation: A Replication and Extension of Three Studies." Paper presented at the annual meeting of the American Society of Criminology, Reno, NV, November; *Justice Quarterly* 4 (December 1991): 525–43.

Whitehead, John T., Larry T. Miler, and Laura B. Myers

    1995   "The Diversionary Effectiveness of Intensive Supervision and Community Corrections Programs." Pages 135–51 in *Intermediate Sanctions: Sentencing in the 1990s*, edited by John Ortiz Smykla and William Selke. Cincinnati: Anderson.

Wicker, Tom

    1975   *A Time to Die.* New York: Quadrangle.

Widom, Cathy S. and Michael G. Maxfield

    2001   *An Update on the "Cycle of Violence."* Washington, DC: National Institute of Justice.

Wiebush, Richard G.

    1993   "Juvenile Intensive Supervision: The Impact on Felony Offenders Diverted from Institutional Placement." *Crime and Delinquency* 39 (January): 68–89.

Wiebush, Richard G. and Donna M. Hamparian

    1991   "Variations in 'Doing' Juvenile Intensive Supervision: Programmatic Issues in Four Ohio Jurisdictions." Pages 153–88 in *Intensive Interventions with High-Risk Youths in Juvenile Probation and Parole*, edited by Troy L. Armstrong, 153–88. Monsey, NY: Criminal Justice Press.

Wiederanders, Mark R.

    1983   *Success on Parole.* Sacramento: California Department of Corrections.

Wilcock, Katherine, Theodore M. Hammett, and Dale G. Parent

    1995   *Controlling Tuberculosis in Community Corrections.* Washington, DC: National Institute of Justice.

Wilensky, Harold L. and Charles N. Lebeaux
    1958   *Industrial Society and Social Welfare*. New York: Russell Sage Foundation.

Wilson, James Q. and George Kelling
    1982   "Broken Windows: The Police and Neighborhood Safety." *Atlantic Monthly* (March): 29–38.

Wines, Frederick Howard
    1975   *Punishment and Reformation: A Study of the Penitentiary System*. New York: Thomas Y. Crowell.

Wolf, Thomas J.
    1997   "What United States Pretrial Officers Do." *Federal Probation* 61 (March): 19–24.

Wright, Martin
    1991   *Justice for Victims and Offenders: A Restorative Response to Crime*. Philadelphia: Open University.

Wright, Ronald F.
    1998   *Managing Prison Growth in North Carolina Through Structured Sentencing*. Washington, DC: National Institute of Justice.

Wubbolding, Robert E.
    2000   *Reality Therapy for the 21st Century*. Philadelphia: Taylor and Francis.

Yeoman, Barry
    2000   "Steeltown." *Mother Jones* (May/June): 38–47.

"Youth Justice, Separate and Unequal"
    2000   *Chicago Tribune* editorial (November 21): 22.

Zawitz, Marianne W., ed.
    1988   *Report to the Nation on Crime and Justice*. Washington, DC: U.S. Government Printing Office.

Zehr, Howard
    1990   *Changing Lenses: A New Focus for Crime and Justice*. Schottdale, PA: Herald Press.

Zehr, Howard and Harry Mika
    1998   "Fundamental Concepts of Restorative Justice." *Contemporary Justice Review* 1 (1): 47–55.

Zevitz, Richard G., and Susan R. Takata
    1988   "Paroling Prisoners Sentenced to County Jail: An Analysis of 75 Years of Misdemeanor Parole Legislation." *Journal of Criminal Justice* 11: 61–86.

Zielbauer, Paul
    2001   "Felons Gain Voting Rights In Connecticut." *New York Times* (May 15): Internet.

Zimring, Franklin E., and Gordon Hawkins
    1995   *Incapacitation: Penal Confinement and the Restraint of Crime*. New York: Oxford University Press.

Indexes

Name Index

Subject Index